50% OFF

Online GED Prep Course!

By Mometrix

Dear Customer,

We consider it an honor and a privilege that you chose our GED Study Guide. As a way of showing our appreciation and to help us better serve you, we are offering **50% off our online GED Prep Course.** Many GED courses cost hundreds of dollars and don't deliver enough value. With our course, you get access to the best GED prep material, and **you only pay half price**.

We have structured our online course to perfectly complement your printed study guide. Our GED Prep Course contains **in-depth lessons** that cover all the most important topics, **340+ video reviews** that explain difficult concepts, over **1,250 practice questions** to ensure you feel prepared, and more than **300 digital flashcards**, so you can fit in some studying while you're on the go.

Online GED Prep Course

Topics Covered:

- Reasoning Through Language Arts
    - Reading Comprehension
    - Critical Thinking
    - Writing
- Mathematical Reasoning
    - Number Operations
    - Algebra, Functions, and Patterns
    - Measurement and Geometry
- Science
    - Physical Science
    - Earth and Space Science
- Social Studies
    - History and Government
    - Economics

Course Features:

- GED Study Guide
    - Get content that complements our best-selling study guide.
- 6 Full-Length Practice Tests
    - With over 1,250 practice questions, you can test yourself again and again.
- Mobile Friendly
    - If you need to study on the go, the course is easily accessible from your mobile device.
- GED Flashcards
    - Our course includes a flashcard mode consisting of over 300 content cards to help you study.

To receive this discount, visit our website at mometrix.com/university/ged/ or simply scan this QR code with your smartphone. Enter code **ged50off** at checkout.

If you have any questions or concerns, please contact us at support@mometrix.com.

FREE Study Skills Videos/DVD Offer

Dear Customer,

Thank you for your purchase from Mometrix! We consider it an honor and a privilege that you have purchased our product and we want to ensure your satisfaction.

As part of our ongoing effort to meet the needs of test takers, we have developed a set of Study Skills Videos that we would like to give you for FREE. These videos cover our *best practices* for getting ready for your exam, from how to use our study materials to how to best prepare for the day of the test.

All that we ask is that you email us with feedback that would describe your experience so far with our product. Good, bad, or indifferent, we want to know what you think!

To get your FREE Study Skills Videos, you can use the **QR code** below, or send us an **email** at studyvideos@mometrix.com with *FREE VIDEOS* in the subject line and the following information in the body of the email:

- The name of the product you purchased.
- Your product rating on a scale of 1-5, with 5 being the highest rating.
- Your feedback. It can be long, short, or anything in between. We just want to know your impressions and experience so far with our product. (Good feedback might include how our study material met your needs and ways we might be able to make it even better. You could highlight features that you found helpful or features that you think we should add.)

If you have any questions or concerns, please don't hesitate to contact me directly.

Thanks again!

Sincerely,

Jay Willis
Vice President
jay.willis@mometrix.com
1-800-673-8175

Mometrix
TEST PREPARATION

GED®

Study Guide
2024-2025 All Subjects
GED Prep Book Secrets

3 Full-Length Practice Tests

300+ Online Video Tutorials

Certified Content Alignment

Written and edited by the Mometrix High School Equivalency Test Team

Printed in the United States of America

This paper meets the requirements of ANSI/NISO Z39.48-1992 (Permanence of Paper).

Paperback
ISBN 13: 978-1-5167-2688-2
ISBN 10: 1-5167-2688-X

DEAR FUTURE EXAM SUCCESS STORY

First of all, **THANK YOU** for purchasing Mometrix study materials!

Second, congratulations! You are one of the few determined test-takers who are committed to doing whatever it takes to excel on your exam. **You have come to the right place.** We developed these study materials with one goal in mind: to deliver you the information you need in a format that's concise and easy to use.

In addition to optimizing your guide for the content of the test, we've outlined our recommended steps for breaking down the preparation process into small, attainable goals so you can make sure you stay on track.

We've also analyzed the entire test-taking process, identifying the most common pitfalls and showing how you can overcome them and be ready for any curveball the test throws you.

Standardized testing is one of the biggest obstacles on your road to success, which only increases the importance of doing well in the high-pressure, high-stakes environment of test day. Your results on this test could have a significant impact on your future, and this guide provides the information and practical advice to help you achieve your full potential on test day.

Your success is our success

We would love to hear from you! If you would like to share the story of your exam success or if you have any questions or comments in regard to our products, please contact us at **800-673-8175** or **support@mometrix.com**.

Thanks again for your business and we wish you continued success!

Sincerely,
The Mometrix Test Preparation Team

TABLE OF CONTENTS

INTRODUCTION 1

SECRET KEY #1 – PLAN BIG, STUDY SMALL 2

SECRET KEY #2 – MAKE YOUR STUDYING COUNT 3

SECRET KEY #3 – PRACTICE THE RIGHT WAY 4

SECRET KEY #4 – PACE YOURSELF 6

SECRET KEY #5 – HAVE A PLAN FOR GUESSING 7

TEST-TAKING STRATEGIES 10

GED STUDY PLAN 15

- WEEK 1: MATHEMATICAL REASONING 16
- WEEK 2: REASONING THROUGH LANGUAGE ARTS 17
- WEEK 3: SCIENCE 18
- WEEK 4: SOCIAL STUDIES 20

MATHEMATICAL REASONING 21

- BASIC MATH 21
- GEOMETRY 43
- BASIC ALGEBRA 63
- GRAPHS AND FUNCTIONS 83

REASONING THROUGH LANGUAGE ARTS 97

- READING FOR MEANING 97
- IDENTIFYING AND CREATING ARGUMENTS 139
- GRAMMAR AND LANGUAGE 149
- WRITING 183
- CHAPTER QUIZ 185

SOCIAL STUDIES 186

- READING FOR MEANING IN SOCIAL STUDIES 186
- ANALYZING HISTORICAL EVENTS AND ARGUMENTS IN SOCIAL STUDIES 188
- USING NUMBERS AND GRAPHICS IN SOCIAL STUDIES 194
- US HISTORY 200
- WORLD HISTORY 209
- US GOVERNMENT AND CITIZENSHIP 213
- UNITED STATES POLITICAL SYSTEMS 218
- ECONOMICS 223
- GEOGRAPHY 225
- CULTURAL STUDIES 233
- CHAPTER QUIZ 236

SCIENCE 237

- READING FOR MEANING IN SCIENCE 237
- DESIGNING AND INTERPRETING SCIENCE EXPERIMENTS 239
- USING NUMBERS AND GRAPHICS IN SCIENCE 246

Scientific Inquiry and Reasoning 252
Physics 256
Chemistry 263
Biology 271
Ecology 280
Geology 282
Earth Science and Weather 288
Space Science 292
Chapter Quiz 294
GED Practice Test #1 295
Reasoning Through Language Arts—Reading 295
Reasoning Through Language Arts—Writing 307
Reasoning Through Language Arts—Extended Response 319
Mathematics—No Calculator 320
Mathematics—Calculator 321
Science 331
Social Studies 347
Answer Key and Explanations #1 369
Reasoning Through Language Arts—Reading 369
Reasoning Through Language Arts—Writing 373
Reasoning Through Language Arts—Extended Response 377
Mathematics—No Calculator 378
Mathematics—Calculator 379
Science 389
Social Studies 394
GED Practice Tests #2 and #3 400
How to Overcome Test Anxiety 401
Tell Us Your Story 407
Additional Bonus Material 408

Introduction

Thank you for purchasing this resource! You have made the choice to prepare yourself for a test that could have a huge impact on your future, and this guide is designed to help you be fully ready for test day. Obviously, it's important to have a solid understanding of the test material, but you also need to be prepared for the unique environment and stressors of the test, so that you can perform to the best of your abilities.

For this purpose, the first section that appears in this guide is the **Secret Keys**. We've devoted countless hours to meticulously researching what works and what doesn't, and we've boiled down our findings to the five most impactful steps you can take to improve your performance on the test. We start at the beginning with study planning and move through the preparation process, all the way to the testing strategies that will help you get the most out of what you know when you're finally sitting in front of the test.

We recommend that you start preparing for your test as far in advance as possible. However, if you've bought this guide as a last-minute study resource and only have a few days before your test, we recommend that you skip over the first two Secret Keys since they address a long-term study plan.

If you struggle with **test anxiety**, we strongly encourage you to check out our recommendations for how you can overcome it. Test anxiety is a formidable foe, but it can be beaten, and we want to make sure you have the tools you need to defeat it.

Secret Key #1 – Plan Big, Study Small

There's a lot riding on your performance. If you want to ace this test, you're going to need to keep your skills sharp and the material fresh in your mind. You need a plan that lets you review everything you need to know while still fitting in your schedule. We'll break this strategy down into three categories.

Information Organization

Start with the information you already have: the official test outline. From this, you can make a complete list of all the concepts you need to cover before the test. Organize these concepts into groups that can be studied together, and create a list of any related vocabulary you need to learn so you can brush up on any difficult terms. You'll want to keep this vocabulary list handy once you actually start studying since you may need to add to it along the way.

Time Management

Once you have your set of study concepts, decide how to spread them out over the time you have left before the test. Break your study plan into small, clear goals so you have a manageable task for each day and know exactly what you're doing. Then just focus on one small step at a time. When you manage your time this way, you don't need to spend hours at a time studying. Studying a small block of content for a short period each day helps you retain information better and avoid stressing over how much you have left to do. You can relax knowing that you have a plan to cover everything in time. In order for this strategy to be effective though, you have to start studying early and stick to your schedule. Avoid the exhaustion and futility that comes from last-minute cramming!

Study Environment

The environment you study in has a big impact on your learning. Studying in a coffee shop, while probably more enjoyable, is not likely to be as fruitful as studying in a quiet room. It's important to keep distractions to a minimum. You're only planning to study for a short block of time, so make the most of it. Don't pause to check your phone or get up to find a snack. It's also important to **avoid multitasking**. Research has consistently shown that multitasking will make your studying dramatically less effective. Your study area should also be comfortable and well-lit so you don't have the distraction of straining your eyes or sitting on an uncomfortable chair.

The time of day you study is also important. You want to be rested and alert. Don't wait until just before bedtime. Study when you'll be most likely to comprehend and remember. Even better, if you know what time of day your test will be, set that time aside for study. That way your brain will be used to working on that subject at that specific time and you'll have a better chance of recalling information.

Finally, it can be helpful to team up with others who are studying for the same test. Your actual studying should be done in as isolated an environment as possible, but the work of organizing the information and setting up the study plan can be divided up. In between study sessions, you can discuss with your teammates the concepts that you're all studying and quiz each other on the details. Just be sure that your teammates are as serious about the test as you are. If you find that your study time is being replaced with social time, you might need to find a new team.

Secret Key #2 – Make Your Studying Count

You're devoting a lot of time and effort to preparing for this test, so you want to be absolutely certain it will pay off. This means doing more than just reading the content and hoping you can remember it on test day. It's important to make every minute of study count. There are two main areas you can focus on to make your studying count.

Retention

It doesn't matter how much time you study if you can't remember the material. You need to make sure you are retaining the concepts. To check your retention of the information you're learning, try recalling it at later times with minimal prompting. Try carrying around flashcards and glance at one or two from time to time or ask a friend who's also studying for the test to quiz you.

To enhance your retention, look for ways to put the information into practice so that you can apply it rather than simply recalling it. If you're using the information in practical ways, it will be much easier to remember. Similarly, it helps to solidify a concept in your mind if you're not only reading it to yourself but also explaining it to someone else. Ask a friend to let you teach them about a concept you're a little shaky on (or speak aloud to an imaginary audience if necessary). As you try to summarize, define, give examples, and answer your friend's questions, you'll understand the concepts better and they will stay with you longer. Finally, step back for a big picture view and ask yourself how each piece of information fits with the whole subject. When you link the different concepts together and see them working together as a whole, it's easier to remember the individual components.

Finally, practice showing your work on any multi-step problems, even if you're just studying. Writing out each step you take to solve a problem will help solidify the process in your mind, and you'll be more likely to remember it during the test.

Modality

Modality simply refers to the means or method by which you study. Choosing a study modality that fits your own individual learning style is crucial. No two people learn best in exactly the same way, so it's important to know your strengths and use them to your advantage.

For example, if you learn best by visualization, focus on visualizing a concept in your mind and draw an image or a diagram. Try color-coding your notes, illustrating them, or creating symbols that will trigger your mind to recall a learned concept. If you learn best by hearing or discussing information, find a study partner who learns the same way or read aloud to yourself. Think about how to put the information in your own words. Imagine that you are giving a lecture on the topic and record yourself so you can listen to it later.

For any learning style, flashcards can be helpful. Organize the information so you can take advantage of spare moments to review. Underline key words or phrases. Use different colors for different categories. Mnemonic devices (such as creating a short list in which every item starts with the same letter) can also help with retention. Find what works best for you and use it to store the information in your mind most effectively and easily.

Secret Key #3 – Practice the Right Way

Your success on test day depends not only on how many hours you put into preparing, but also on whether you prepared the right way. It's good to check along the way to see if your studying is paying off. One of the most effective ways to do this is by taking practice tests to evaluate your progress. Practice tests are useful because they show exactly where you need to improve. Every time you take a practice test, pay special attention to these three groups of questions:

- The questions you got wrong
- The questions you had to guess on, even if you guessed right
- The questions you found difficult or slow to work through

This will show you exactly what your weak areas are, and where you need to devote more study time. Ask yourself why each of these questions gave you trouble. Was it because you didn't understand the material? Was it because you didn't remember the vocabulary? Do you need more repetitions on this type of question to build speed and confidence? Dig into those questions and figure out how you can strengthen your weak areas as you go back to review the material.

Additionally, many practice tests have a section explaining the answer choices. It can be tempting to read the explanation and think that you now have a good understanding of the concept. However, an explanation likely only covers part of the question's broader context. Even if the explanation makes perfect sense, **go back and investigate** every concept related to the question until you're positive you have a thorough understanding.

As you go along, keep in mind that the practice test is just that: practice. Memorizing these questions and answers will not be very helpful on the actual test because it is unlikely to have any of the same exact questions. If you only know the right answers to the sample questions, you won't be prepared for the real thing. **Study the concepts** until you understand them fully, and then you'll be able to answer any question that shows up on the test.

It's important to wait on the practice tests until you're ready. If you take a test on your first day of study, you may be overwhelmed by the amount of material covered and how much you need to learn. Work up to it gradually.

On test day, you'll need to be prepared for answering questions, managing your time, and using the test-taking strategies you've learned. It's a lot to balance, like a mental marathon that will have a big impact on your future. Like training for a marathon, you'll need to start slowly and work your way up. When test day arrives, you'll be ready.

Start with the strategies you've read in the first two Secret Keys—plan your course and study in the way that works best for you. If you have time, consider using multiple study resources to get different approaches to the same concepts. It can be helpful to see difficult concepts from more than one angle. Then find a good source for practice tests. Many times, the test website will suggest potential study resources or provide sample tests.

Practice Test Strategy

If you're able to find at least three practice tests, we recommend this strategy:

UNTIMED AND OPEN-BOOK PRACTICE

Take the first test with no time constraints and with your notes and study guide handy. Take your time and focus on applying the strategies you've learned.

TIMED AND OPEN-BOOK PRACTICE

Take the second practice test open-book as well, but set a timer and practice pacing yourself to finish in time.

TIMED AND CLOSED-BOOK PRACTICE

Take any other practice tests as if it were test day. Set a timer and put away your study materials. Sit at a table or desk in a quiet room, imagine yourself at the testing center, and answer questions as quickly and accurately as possible.

Keep repeating timed and closed-book tests on a regular basis until you run out of practice tests or it's time for the actual test. Your mind will be ready for the schedule and stress of test day, and you'll be able to focus on recalling the material you've learned.

Secret Key #4 – Pace Yourself

Once you're fully prepared for the material on the test, your biggest challenge on test day will be managing your time. Just knowing that the clock is ticking can make you panic even if you have plenty of time left. Work on pacing yourself so you can build confidence against the time constraints of the exam. Pacing is a difficult skill to master, especially in a high-pressure environment, so **practice is vital**.

Set time expectations for your pace based on how much time is available. For example, if a section has 60 questions and the time limit is 30 minutes, you know you have to average 30 seconds or less per question in order to answer them all. Although 30 seconds is the hard limit, set 25 seconds per question as your goal, so you reserve extra time to spend on harder questions. When you budget extra time for the harder questions, you no longer have any reason to stress when those questions take longer to answer.

Don't let this time expectation distract you from working through the test at a calm, steady pace, but keep it in mind so you don't spend too much time on any one question. Recognize that taking extra time on one question you don't understand may keep you from answering two that you do understand later in the test. If your time limit for a question is up and you're still not sure of the answer, mark it and move on, and come back to it later if the time and the test format allow. If the testing format doesn't allow you to return to earlier questions, just make an educated guess; then put it out of your mind and move on.

On the easier questions, be careful not to rush. It may seem wise to hurry through them so you have more time for the challenging ones, but it's not worth missing one if you know the concept and just didn't take the time to read the question fully. Work efficiently but make sure you understand the question and have looked at all of the answer choices, since more than one may seem right at first.

Even if you're paying attention to the time, you may find yourself a little behind at some point. You should speed up to get back on track, but do so wisely. Don't panic; just take a few seconds less on each question until you're caught up. Don't guess without thinking, but do look through the answer choices and eliminate any you know are wrong. If you can get down to two choices, it is often worthwhile to guess from those. Once you've chosen an answer, move on and don't dwell on any that you skipped or had to hurry through. If a question was taking too long, chances are it was one of the harder ones, so you weren't as likely to get it right anyway.

On the other hand, if you find yourself getting ahead of schedule, it may be beneficial to slow down a little. The more quickly you work, the more likely you are to make a careless mistake that will affect your score. You've budgeted time for each question, so don't be afraid to spend that time. Practice an efficient but careful pace to get the most out of the time you have.

Secret Key #5 – Have a Plan for Guessing

When you're taking the test, you may find yourself stuck on a question. Some of the answer choices seem better than others, but you don't see the one answer choice that is obviously correct. What do you do?

The scenario described above is very common, yet most test takers have not effectively prepared for it. Developing and practicing a plan for guessing may be one of the single most effective uses of your time as you get ready for the exam.

In developing your plan for guessing, there are three questions to address:

- When should you start the guessing process?
- How should you narrow down the choices?
- Which answer should you choose?

When to Start the Guessing Process

Unless your plan for guessing is to select C every time (which, despite its merits, is not what we recommend), you need to leave yourself enough time to apply your answer elimination strategies. Since you have a limited amount of time for each question, that means that if you're going to give yourself the best shot at guessing correctly, you have to decide quickly whether or not you will guess.

Of course, the best-case scenario is that you don't have to guess at all, so first, see if you can answer the question based on your knowledge of the subject and basic reasoning skills. Focus on the key words in the question and try to jog your memory of related topics. Give yourself a chance to bring the knowledge to mind, but once you realize that you don't have (or you can't access) the knowledge you need to answer the question, it's time to start the guessing process.

It's almost always better to start the guessing process too early than too late. It only takes a few seconds to remember something and answer the question from knowledge. Carefully eliminating wrong answer choices takes longer. Plus, going through the process of eliminating answer choices can actually help jog your memory.

Summary: Start the guessing process as soon as you decide that you can't answer the question based on your knowledge.

How to Narrow Down the Choices

The next chapter in this book (**Test-Taking Strategies**) includes a wide range of strategies for how to approach questions and how to look for answer choices to eliminate. You will definitely want to read those carefully, practice them, and figure out which ones work best for you. Here though, we're going to address a mindset rather than a particular strategy.

Your odds of guessing an answer correctly depend on how many options you are choosing from.

Number of options left	5	4	3	2	1
Odds of guessing correctly	20%	25%	33%	50%	100%

You can see from this chart just how valuable it is to be able to eliminate incorrect answers and make an educated guess, but there are two things that many test takers do that cause them to miss out on the benefits of guessing:

- Accidentally eliminating the correct answer
- Selecting an answer based on an impression

We'll look at the first one here, and the second one in the next section.

To avoid accidentally eliminating the correct answer, we recommend a thought exercise called **the $5 challenge**. In this challenge, you only eliminate an answer choice from contention if you are willing to bet $5 on it being wrong. Why $5? Five dollars is a small but not insignificant amount of money. It's an amount you could afford to lose but wouldn't want to throw away. And while losing $5 once might not hurt too much, doing it twenty times will set you back $100. In the same way, each small decision you make—eliminating a choice here, guessing on a question there—won't by itself impact your score very much, but when you put them all together, they can make a big difference. By holding each answer choice elimination decision to a higher standard, you can reduce the risk of accidentally eliminating the correct answer.

The $5 challenge can also be applied in a positive sense: If you are willing to bet $5 that an answer choice *is* correct, go ahead and mark it as correct.

Summary: Only eliminate an answer choice if you are willing to bet $5 that it is wrong.

Which Answer to Choose

You're taking the test. You've run into a hard question and decided you'll have to guess. You've eliminated all the answer choices you're willing to bet $5 on. Now you have to pick an answer. Why do we even need to talk about this? Why can't you just pick whichever one you feel like when the time comes?

The answer to these questions is that if you don't come into the test with a plan, you'll rely on your impression to select an answer choice, and if you do that, you risk falling into a trap. The test writers know that everyone who takes their test will be guessing on some of the questions, so they intentionally write wrong answer choices to seem plausible. You still have to pick an answer though, and if the wrong answer choices are designed to look right, how can you ever be sure that you're not falling for their trap? The best solution we've found to this dilemma is to take the decision out of your hands entirely. Here is the process we recommend:

Once you've eliminated any choices that you are confident (willing to bet $5) are wrong, select the first remaining choice as your answer.

Whether you choose to select the first remaining choice, the second, or the last, the important thing is that you use some preselected standard. Using this approach guarantees that you will not be enticed into selecting an answer choice that looks right, because you are not basing your decision on how the answer choices look.

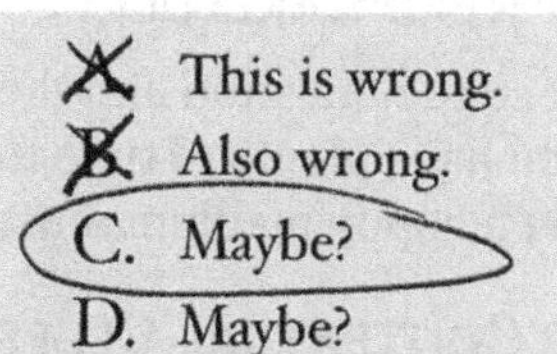

This is not meant to make you question your knowledge. Instead, it is to help you recognize the difference between your knowledge and your impressions. There's a huge difference between thinking an answer is right because of what you know, and thinking an answer is right because it looks or sounds like it should be right.

Summary: To ensure that your selection is appropriately random, make a predetermined selection from among all answer choices you have not eliminated.

Test-Taking Strategies

This section contains a list of test-taking strategies that you may find helpful as you work through the test. By taking what you know and applying logical thought, you can maximize your chances of answering any question correctly!

It is very important to realize that every question is different and every person is different: no single strategy will work on every question, and no single strategy will work for every person. That's why we've included all of them here, so you can try them out and determine which ones work best for different types of questions and which ones work best for you.

Question Strategies

✓ Read Carefully

Read the question and the answer choices carefully. Don't miss the question because you misread the terms. You have plenty of time to read each question thoroughly and make sure you understand what is being asked. Yet a happy medium must be attained, so don't waste too much time. You must read carefully and efficiently.

✓ Contextual Clues

Look for contextual clues. If the question includes a word you are not familiar with, look at the immediate context for some indication of what the word might mean. Contextual clues can often give you all the information you need to decipher the meaning of an unfamiliar word. Even if you can't determine the meaning, you may be able to narrow down the possibilities enough to make a solid guess at the answer to the question.

✓ Prefixes

If you're having trouble with a word in the question or answer choices, try dissecting it. Take advantage of every clue that the word might include. Prefixes can be a huge help. Usually, they allow you to determine a basic meaning. *Pre-* means before, *post-* means after, *pro-* is positive, *de-* is negative. From prefixes, you can get an idea of the general meaning of the word and try to put it into context.

✓ Hedge Words

Watch out for critical hedge words, such as *likely, may, can, sometimes, often, almost, mostly, usually, generally, rarely*, and *sometimes*. Question writers insert these hedge phrases to cover every possibility. Often an answer choice will be wrong simply because it leaves no room for exception. Be on guard for answer choices that have definitive words such as *exactly* and *always*.

✓ Switchback Words

Stay alert for *switchbacks*. These are the words and phrases frequently used to alert you to shifts in thought. The most common switchback words are *but, although*, and *however*. Others include *nevertheless, on the other hand, even though, while, in spite of, despite*, and *regardless of*. Switchback words are important to catch because they can change the direction of the question or an answer choice.

✓ Face Value

When in doubt, use common sense. Accept the situation in the problem at face value. Don't read too much into it. These problems will not require you to make wild assumptions. If you have to go beyond creativity and warp time or space in order to have an answer choice fit the question, then you should move on and consider the other answer choices. These are normal problems rooted in reality. The applicable relationship or explanation may not be readily apparent, but it is there for you to figure out. Use your common sense to interpret anything that isn't clear.

Answer Choice Strategies

⊘ Answer Selection

The most thorough way to pick an answer choice is to identify and eliminate wrong answers until only one is left, then confirm it is the correct answer. Sometimes an answer choice may immediately seem right, but be careful. The test writers will usually put more than one reasonable answer choice on each question, so take a second to read all of them and make sure that the other choices are not equally obvious. As long as you have time left, it is better to read every answer choice than to pick the first one that looks right without checking the others.

⊘ Answer Choice Families

An answer choice family consists of two (in rare cases, three) answer choices that are very similar in construction and cannot all be true at the same time. If you see two answer choices that are direct opposites or parallels, one of them is usually the correct answer. For instance, if one answer choice says that quantity x increases and another either says that quantity x decreases (opposite) or says that quantity y increases (parallel), then those answer choices would fall into the same family. An answer choice that doesn't match the construction of the answer choice family is more likely to be incorrect. Most questions will not have answer choice families, but when they do appear, you should be prepared to recognize them.

⊘ Eliminate Answers

Eliminate answer choices as soon as you realize they are wrong, but make sure you consider all possibilities. If you are eliminating answer choices and realize that the last one you are left with is also wrong, don't panic. Start over and consider each choice again. There may be something you missed the first time that you will realize on the second pass.

⊘ Avoid Fact Traps

Don't be distracted by an answer choice that is factually true but doesn't answer the question. You are looking for the choice that answers the question. Stay focused on what the question is asking for so you don't accidentally pick an answer that is true but incorrect. Always go back to the question and make sure the answer choice you've selected actually answers the question and is not merely a true statement.

⊘ Extreme Statements

In general, you should avoid answers that put forth extreme actions as standard practice or proclaim controversial ideas as established fact. An answer choice that states the "process should be used in certain situations, if..." is much more likely to be correct than one that states the "process should be discontinued completely." The first is a calm rational statement and doesn't even make a definitive, uncompromising stance, using a hedge word *if* to provide wiggle room, whereas the second choice is far more extreme.

⊘ Benchmark

As you read through the answer choices and you come across one that seems to answer the question well, mentally select that answer choice. This is not your final answer, but it's the one that will help you evaluate the other answer choices. The one that you selected is your benchmark or standard for judging each of the other answer choices. Every other answer choice must be compared to your benchmark. That choice is correct until proven otherwise by another answer choice beating it. If you find a better answer, then that one becomes your new benchmark. Once you've decided that no other choice answers the question as well as your benchmark, you have your final answer.

✓ Predict the Answer

Before you even start looking at the answer choices, it is often best to try to predict the answer. When you come up with the answer on your own, it is easier to avoid distractions and traps because you will know exactly what to look for. The right answer choice is unlikely to be word-for-word what you came up with, but it should be a close match. Even if you are confident that you have the right answer, you should still take the time to read each option before moving on.

General Strategies

✓ Tough Questions

If you are stumped on a problem or it appears too hard or too difficult, don't waste time. Move on! Remember though, if you can quickly check for obviously incorrect answer choices, your chances of guessing correctly are greatly improved. Before you completely give up, at least try to knock out a couple of possible answers. Eliminate what you can and then guess at the remaining answer choices before moving on.

✓ Check Your Work

Since you will probably not know every term listed and the answer to every question, it is important that you get credit for the ones that you do know. Don't miss any questions through careless mistakes. If at all possible, try to take a second to look back over your answer selection and make sure you've selected the correct answer choice and haven't made a costly careless mistake (such as marking an answer choice that you didn't mean to mark). This quick double check should more than pay for itself in caught mistakes for the time it costs.

✓ Pace Yourself

It's easy to be overwhelmed when you're looking at a page full of questions; your mind is confused and full of random thoughts, and the clock is ticking down faster than you would like. Calm down and maintain the pace that you have set for yourself. Especially as you get down to the last few minutes of the test, don't let the small numbers on the clock make you panic. As long as you are on track by monitoring your pace, you are guaranteed to have time for each question.

✓ Don't Rush

It is very easy to make errors when you are in a hurry. Maintaining a fast pace in answering questions is pointless if it makes you miss questions that you would have gotten right otherwise. Test writers like to include distracting information and wrong answers that seem right. Taking a little extra time to avoid careless mistakes can make all the difference in your test score. Find a pace that allows you to be confident in the answers that you select.

✓ Keep Moving

Panicking will not help you pass the test, so do your best to stay calm and keep moving. Taking deep breaths and going through the answer elimination steps you practiced can help to break through a stress barrier and keep your pace.

Final Notes

The combination of a solid foundation of content knowledge and the confidence that comes from practicing your plan for applying that knowledge is the key to maximizing your performance on test day. As your foundation of content knowledge is built up and strengthened, you'll find that the strategies included in this chapter become more and more effective in helping you quickly sift through the distractions and traps of the test to isolate the correct answer.

Now that you're preparing to move forward into the test content chapters of this book, be sure to keep your goal in mind. As you read, think about how you will be able to apply this information on the test. If you've already seen sample questions for the test and you have an idea of the question format and style, try to come up with questions of your own that you can answer based on what you're reading. This will give you valuable practice applying your knowledge in the same ways you can expect to on test day.

Good luck and good studying!

GED Study Plan

On the next few pages, we've provided an optional study plan to help you use this study guide to its fullest potential over the course of four weeks. If you only have two weeks to study before your exam, you can double up this four-week timeline, completing two weeks' worth of studying each week. If you have eight weeks available and want to spread it out more, spend two weeks on each section of the plan.

Below is a quick summary of the subjects covered in each week of the plan.

- Week 1: Mathematical Reasoning
- Week 2: Reasoning Through Language Arts
- Week 3: Science
- Week 4: Social Studies

Please note that not all subjects will take the same amount of time to work through.

Three full-length practice tests are included with this study guide. We recommend saving the third practice test for after you've completed the study plan. Take this practice test timed and without any reference materials a day or two before the real thing as one last practice run to get you in the mode of answering questions at a good pace.

Week 1: Mathematical Reasoning

Instructional Content

First, read carefully through the Mathematical Reasoning chapter in this book, checking off your progress as you go:

- ❏ Basic Math
- ❏ Geometry
- ❏ Statistics and Probability
- ❏ Algebra

As you read, do the following:

- Highlight any areas you think are important
- Draw an asterisk (*) next to any areas you are struggling with
- Watch the review videos to gain more understanding of a particular topic
- Take notes in your notebook or in the margins of this book

After you've read through everything, go back and review any sections that you highlighted or that you drew an asterisk next to, referencing your notes along the way.

Practice Test #1

Now that you've read over the instructional content, it's time to take a practice test. Complete the Mathematical Reasoning section of Practice Test #1. Take this test with **no time constraints**, and feel free to reference the applicable sections of this guide as you go. Once you've finished, check your answers against the provided answer key. For any questions you answered incorrectly, review the answer rationale, and then **go back and review** the applicable sections of the book. The goal in this stage is to understand why you answered the question incorrectly, and make sure that the next time you see a similar question, you will get it right.

Practice Test #2

Next, take the Mathematical Reasoning section of Practice Test #2. This time, give yourself **115 minutes** (the amount of time you will have on the real GED) to complete all of the questions. You should again feel free to reference the guide and your notes, but be mindful of the clock. If you run out of time before you finish all of the questions, mark where you were when time expired, but go ahead and finish taking the practice test—note that the real test will have approximately 49 questions. Once you've finished, check your answers against the provided answer key and as before, review the answer rationale for any that you answered incorrectly and go back and review the associated instructional content. Your goal is still to increase understanding of the content but also to get used to the time constraints you will face on the test.

Week 2: Reasoning Through Language Arts

Instructional Content

First, read carefully through the Reasoning Through Language Arts chapter in this book, checking off your progress as you go:

- ❏ Reading for Meaning
- ❏ Identifying and Creating Arguments
- ❏ Foundations of Grammar
- ❏ Agreement and Sentence Structure
- ❏ Usage Errors
- ❏ Punctuation
- ❏ Strategy for the Extended Response Section

As you read, do the following:

- Highlight any sections, tables, formulas, etc. you think are important
- Draw an asterisk (*) next to any areas you are struggling with
- Watch the review videos to gain more understanding of a particular topic
- Take notes in your notebook or in the margins of this book

After you've read through everything, go back and review any sections that you highlighted or that you drew an asterisk next to, referencing your notes along the way.

Practice Test #1

Now that you've read over the instructional content, it's time to take a practice test. Complete the Reasoning Through Language Arts section of Practice Test #1. Take this test with **no time constraints**, and feel free to reference the applicable sections of this guide as you go. Once you've finished, check your answers against the provided answer key. For any questions you answered incorrectly, review the answer rationale, and then **go back and review** the applicable sections of the book. The goal in this stage is to understand why you answered the question incorrectly, and make sure that the next time you see a similar question, you will get it right.

Practice Test #2

Next, take the Reasoning Through Language Arts section of Practice Test #2. This time, give yourself **150 minutes** (the amount of time you will have on the real GED) to complete all of the questions. This time includes **35 minutes** for Section 1, **45 minutes** for Section 2 (written essay) a **10-minute** break between Sections 2 and 3, and **60 minutes** for Section 3 itself. You should again feel free to reference the guide and your notes, but be mindful of the clock. If you run out of time before you finish all of the questions, mark where you were when time expired, but go ahead and finish taking the practice test. Once you've finished, check your answers against the provided answer key, and as before, review the answer rationale for any that you answered incorrectly and then go back and review the associated instructional content. Your goal is still to increase understanding of the content but also to get used to the time constraints you will face on the test.

Week 3: Science

Instructional Content

First, read carefully through the Science chapter in this book, checking off your progress as you go:

- ❑ Reading for Meaning in Science
- ❑ Designing and Interpreting Science Experiments
- ❑ Using Numbers and Graphics in Science
- ❑ Chemical Properties
- ❑ Physical Science
- ❑ Motion, Force, and Work
- ❑ Human Body and Health
- ❑ Functions for Life and Energy
- ❑ Organization of Life
- ❑ Genetics
- ❑ Evolution
- ❑ Ecosystems
- ❑ Earth's Structure and Systems
- ❑ Organization of Outer Space

As you read, do the following:

- Highlight any sections, diagrams, terms, etc. you think are important
- Draw an asterisk (*) next to any areas you are struggling with
- Watch the review videos to gain more understanding of a particular topic
- Take notes in your notebook or in the margins of this book

After you've read through everything, go back and review any sections that you highlighted or that you drew an asterisk next to, referencing your notes along the way.

PRACTICE TEST #1

Now that you've read over the instructional content, it's time to take a practice test. Complete the Science section of Practice Test #1. Take this test with **no time constraints**, and feel free to reference the applicable sections of this guide as you go. Once you've finished, check your answers against the provided answer key. For any questions you answered incorrectly, review the answer rationale, and then **go back and review** the applicable sections of the book. The goal in this stage is to understand why you answered the question incorrectly, and make sure that the next time you see a similar question, you will get it right.

PRACTICE TEST #2

Next, take the Science section of Practice Test #2. This time, give yourself **90 minutes** (the amount of time you will have on the real GED) to complete all of the questions. You should again feel free to reference the guide and your notes, but be mindful of the clock. If you run out of time before you finish all of the questions, mark where you were when time expired, but go ahead and finish taking the practice test—note that the real test will have approximately 40 questions. Once you've finished, check your answers against the provided answer key, and as before, review the answer rationale for any that you answered incorrectly and then go back and review the associated instructional content. Your goal is still to increase understanding of the content but also to get used to the time constraints you will face on the test.

Week 4: Social Studies

Instructional Content

First, read carefully through the Social Studies chapter in this book, checking off your progress as you go:

- ❏ Reading for Meaning in Social Studies
- ❏ Analyzing Historical Events and Arguments in Social Studies
- ❏ Using Numbers and Graphics in Social Studies
- ❏ Civics and Government
- ❏ United States History
- ❏ Economics
- ❏ Ancient World History
- ❏ Geography

As you read, do the following:

- Highlight any sections, tables, vocabulary words, etc. you think are important
- Draw an asterisk (*) next to any areas you are struggling with
- Watch the review videos to gain more understanding of a particular topic
- Take notes in your notebook or in the margins of this book

After you've read through everything, go back and review any sections that you highlighted or that you drew an asterisk next to, referencing your notes along the way.

Practice Test #1

Now that you've read over the instructional content, it's time to take a practice test. Complete the Social Studies section of Practice Test #1. Take this test with **no time constraints**, and feel free to reference the applicable sections of this guide as you go. Once you've finished, check your answers against the provided answer key. For any questions you answered incorrectly, review the answer rationale, and then **go back and review** the applicable sections of the book. The goal in this stage is to understand why you answered the question incorrectly, and make sure that the next time you see a similar question, you will get it right.

Practice Test #2

Next, take the Social Studies section of Practice Test #2. This time, give yourself **70 minutes** (the amount of time you will have on the real GED) to complete all of the questions. You should again feel free to reference the guide and your notes, but be mindful of the clock. If you run out of time before you finish all of the questions, mark where you were when time expired, but go ahead and finish taking the practice test—note that the real test will have approximately 44 questions. Once you've finished, check your answers against the provided answer key, and as before, review the answer rationale for any that you answered incorrectly and then go back and review the associated instructional content. Your goal is still to increase understanding of the content but also to get used to the time constraints you will face on the test.

Mathematical Reasoning

Basic Math

Number Basics

Classifications of Numbers

Numbers are the basic building blocks of mathematics. Specific features of numbers are identified by the following terms:

Integer – any positive or negative whole number, including zero. Integers do not include fractions $\left(\frac{1}{3}\right)$, decimals (0.56), or mixed numbers $\left(7\frac{3}{4}\right)$.

Prime number – any whole number greater than 1 that has only two factors, itself and 1; that is, a number that can be divided evenly only by 1 and itself.

Composite number – any whole number greater than 1 that has more than two different factors; in other words, any whole number that is not a prime number. For example: The composite number 8 has the factors of 1, 2, 4, and 8.

Even number – any integer that can be divided by 2 without leaving a remainder. For example: 2, 4, 6, 8, and so on.

Odd number – any integer that cannot be divided evenly by 2. For example: 3, 5, 7, 9, and so on.

Decimal number – any number that uses a decimal point to show the part of the number that is less than one. Example: 1.234.

Decimal point – a symbol used to separate the ones place from the tenths place in decimals or dollars from cents in currency.

Decimal place – the position of a number to the right of the decimal point. In the decimal 0.123, the 1 is in the first place to the right of the decimal point, indicating tenths; the 2 is in the second place, indicating hundredths; and the 3 is in the third place, indicating thousandths.

The **decimal**, or base 10, system is a number system that uses ten different digits (0, 1, 2, 3, 4, 5, 6, 7, 8, 9). An example of a number system that uses something other than ten digits is the **binary**, or base 2, number system, used by computers, which uses only the numbers 0 and 1. It is thought that the decimal system originated because people had only their 10 fingers for counting.

Rational numbers include all integers, decimals, and fractions. Any terminating or repeating decimal number is a rational number.

Irrational numbers cannot be written as fractions or decimals because the number of decimal places is infinite and there is no recurring pattern of digits within the number. For example, pi (π) begins with 3.141592 and continues without terminating or repeating, so pi is an irrational number.

Real numbers are the set of all rational and irrational numbers.

> **Review Video: Classification of Numbers**
> Visit mometrix.com/academy and enter code: 461071
>
> **Review Video: Prime and Composite Numbers**
> Visit mometrix.com/academy and enter code: 565581

NUMBERS IN WORD FORM AND PLACE VALUE

When writing numbers out in word form or translating word form to numbers, it is essential to understand how a place value system works. In the decimal or base-10 system, each digit of a number represents how many of the corresponding place value—a specific factor of 10—are contained in the number being represented. To make reading numbers easier, every three digits to the left of the decimal place is preceded by a comma. The following table demonstrates some of the place values:

Power of 10	10^3	10^2	10^1	10^0	10^{-1}	10^{-2}	10^{-3}
Value	1,000	100	10	1	0.1	0.01	0.001
Place	thousands	hundreds	tens	ones	tenths	hundredths	thousandths

For example, consider the number 4,546.09, which can be separated into each place value like this:

4: thousands
5: hundreds
4: tens
6: ones
0: tenths
9: hundredths

This number in word form would be *four thousand five hundred forty-six and nine hundredths.*

> **Review Video: Place Value**
> Visit mometrix.com/academy and enter code: 205433

RATIONAL NUMBERS

The term **rational** means that the number can be expressed as a ratio or fraction. That is, a number, r, is rational if and only if it can be represented by a fraction $\frac{a}{b}$ where a and b are integers and b does not equal 0. The set of rational numbers includes integers and decimals. If there is no finite way to represent a value with a fraction of integers, then the number is **irrational**. Common examples of irrational numbers include: $\sqrt{5}$, $(1+\sqrt{2})$, and π.

> **Review Video: Rational and Irrational Numbers**
> Visit mometrix.com/academy and enter code: 280645
>
> **Review Video: Ordering Rational Numbers**
> Visit mometrix.com/academy and enter code: 419578

NUMBER LINES

A number line is a graph to see the distance between numbers. Basically, this graph shows the relationship between numbers. So a number line may have a point for zero and may show negative numbers on the left side of the line. Any positive numbers are placed on the right side of the line. For example, consider the points labeled on the following number line:

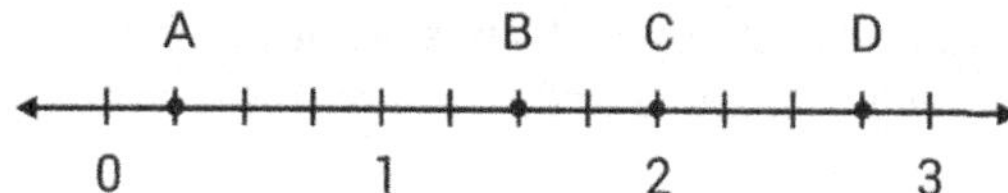

We can use the dashed lines on the number line to identify each point. Each dashed line between two whole numbers is $\frac{1}{4}$. The line halfway between two numbers is $\frac{1}{2}$.

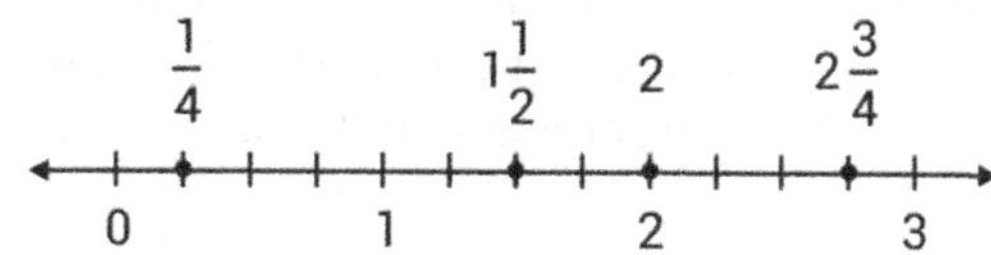

Review Video: The Number Line
Visit mometrix.com/academy and enter code: 816439

Rounding and Estimation

Rounding is reducing the digits in a number while still trying to keep the value similar. The result will be less accurate but in a simpler form and easier to use. Whole numbers can be rounded to the nearest ten, hundred, or thousand.

When you are asked to estimate the solution to a problem, you will need to provide only an approximate figure or **estimation** for your answer. In this situation, you will need to round each number in the calculation to the level indicated (nearest hundred, nearest thousand, etc.) or to a level that makes sense for the numbers involved. When estimating a sum **all numbers must be rounded to the same level**. You cannot round one number to the nearest thousand while rounding another to the nearest hundred.

Review Video: Rounding and Estimation
Visit mometrix.com/academy and enter code: 126243

Absolute Value

A precursor to working with negative numbers is understanding what **absolute values** are. A number's absolute value is simply the distance away from zero a number is on the number line. The absolute value of a number is always positive and is written $|x|$. For example, the absolute value of 3, written as $|3|$, is 3 because the distance between 0 and 3 on a number line is three units. Likewise, the absolute value of −3, written as $|-3|$, is 3 because the distance between 0 and −3 on a number line is three units. So $|3| = |-3|$.

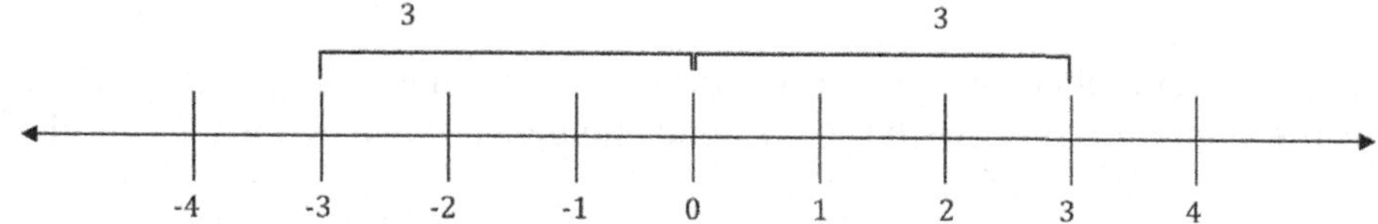

Review Video: Absolute Value
Visit mometrix.com/academy and enter code: 314669

Mathematical Reasoning

Operations

An **operation** is simply a mathematical process that takes some value(s) as input(s) and produces an output. Elementary operations are often written in the following form: *value operation value*. For instance, in the expression $1 + 2$ the values are 1 and 2 and the operation is addition. Performing the operation gives the output of 3. In this way we can say that $1 + 2$ and 3 are equal, or $1 + 2 = 3$.

Addition

Addition increases the value of one quantity by the value of another quantity (both called **addends**). Example: $2 + 4 = 6$ or $8 + 9 = 17$. The result is called the **sum**. With addition, the order does not matter, $4 + 2 = 2 + 4$.

When adding signed numbers, if the signs are the same simply add the absolute values of the addends and apply the original sign to the sum. For example, $(+4) + (+8) = +12$ and $(-4) + (-8) = -12$. When the original signs are different, take the absolute values of the addends and subtract the smaller value from the larger value, then apply the original sign of the larger value to the difference. Example: $(+4) + (-8) = -4$ and $(-4) + (+8) = +4$.

Subtraction

Subtraction is the opposite operation to addition; it decreases the value of one quantity (the **minuend**) by the value of another quantity (the **subtrahend**). For example, $6 - 4 = 2$ or $17 - 8 = 9$. The result is called the **difference**. Note that with subtraction, the order does matter, $6 - 4 \neq 4 - 6$.

For subtracting signed numbers, change the sign of the subtrahend and then follow the same rules used for addition. Example: $(+4) - (+8) = (+4) + (-8) = -4$

Multiplication

Multiplication can be thought of as repeated addition. One number (the **multiplier**) indicates how many times to add the other number (the **multiplicand**) to itself. Example: $3 \times 2 = 2 + 2 + 2 = 6$. With multiplication, the order does not matter, $2 \times 3 = 3 \times 2$ or $3 + 3 = 2 + 2 + 2$, either way the result (the **product**) is the same.

If the signs are the same, the product is positive when multiplying signed numbers. Example: $(+4) \times (+8) = +32$ and $(-4) \times (-8) = +32$. If the signs are opposite, the product is negative. Example: $(+4) \times (-8) = -32$ and $(-4) \times (+8) = -32$. When more than two factors are multiplied together, the sign of the product is determined by how many negative factors are present. If there are an odd number of negative factors then the product is negative, whereas an even number of negative factors indicates a positive product. Example: $(+4) \times (-8) \times (-2) = +64$ and $(-4) \times (-8) \times (-2) = -64$.

Division

Division is the opposite operation to multiplication; one number (the **divisor**) tells us how many parts to divide the other number (the **dividend**) into. The result of division is called the **quotient**. Example: $20 \div 4 = 5$. If 20 is split into 4 equal parts, each part is 5. With division, the order of the numbers does matter, $20 \div 4 \neq 4 \div 20$.

The rules for dividing signed numbers are similar to multiplying signed numbers. If the dividend and divisor have the same sign, the quotient is positive. If the dividend and divisor have opposite signs, the quotient is negative. Example: $(-4) \div (+8) = -0.5$.

Review Video: Mathematical Operations
Visit mometrix.com/academy and enter code: 208095

PARENTHESES

Parentheses are used to designate which operations should be done first when there are multiple operations. Example: $4 - (2 + 1) = 1$; the parentheses tell us that we must add 2 and 1, and then subtract the sum from 4, rather than subtracting 2 from 4 and then adding 1 (this would give us an answer of 3).

> **Review Video: Mathematical Parentheses**
> Visit mometrix.com/academy and enter code: 978600

EXPONENTS

An **exponent** is a superscript number placed next to another number at the top right. It indicates how many times the base number is to be multiplied by itself. Exponents provide a shorthand way to write what would be a longer mathematical expression, Example: $2^4 = 2 \times 2 \times 2 \times 2$. A number with an exponent of 2 is said to be "squared," while a number with an exponent of 3 is said to be "cubed." The value of a number raised to an exponent is called its power. So 8^4 is read as "8 to the 4th power," or "8 raised to the power of 4."

> **Review Video: Exponents**
> Visit mometrix.com/academy and enter code: 600998

ROOTS

A **root**, such as a square root, is another way of writing a fractional exponent. Instead of using a superscript, roots use the radical symbol ($\sqrt{\square}$) to indicate the operation. A radical will have a number underneath the bar, and may sometimes have a number in the upper left: $\sqrt[n]{a}$, read as "the nth root of a." The relationship between radical notation and exponent notation can be described by this equation:

$$\sqrt[n]{a} = a^{\frac{1}{n}}$$

The two special cases of $n = 2$ and $n = 3$ are called square roots and cube roots. If there is no number to the upper left, the radical is understood to be a square root ($n = 2$). Nearly all of the roots you encounter will be square roots. A square root is the same as a number raised to the one-half power. When we say that a is the square root of b ($a = \sqrt{b}$), we mean that a multiplied by itself equals b: ($a \times a = b$).

A **perfect square** is a number that has an integer for its square root. There are 10 perfect squares from 1 to 100: 1, 4, 9, 16, 25, 36, 49, 64, 81, 100 (the squares of integers 1 through 10).

> **Review Video: Roots**
> Visit mometrix.com/academy and enter code: 795655
>
> **Review Video: Perfect Squares and Square Roots**
> Visit mometrix.com/academy and enter code: 648063

WORD PROBLEMS AND MATHEMATICAL SYMBOLS

When working on word problems, you must be able to translate verbal expressions or "math words" into math symbols. This chart contains several "math words" and their appropriate symbols:

Phrase	Symbol
equal, is, was, will be, has, costs, gets to, is the same as, becomes	$=$
times, of, multiplied by, product of, twice, doubles, halves, triples	$\times$
divided by, per, ratio of/to, out of	$\div$
plus, added to, sum, combined, and, more than, totals of	$+$
subtracted from, less than, decreased by, minus, difference between	$-$
what, how much, original value, how many, a number, a variable	x, n, etc.

EXAMPLES OF TRANSLATED MATHEMATICAL PHRASES

- The phrase four more than twice a number can be written algebraically as $2x + 4$.
- The phrase half a number decreased by six can be written algebraically as $\frac{1}{2}x - 6$.
- The phrase the sum of a number and the product of five and that number can be written algebraically as $x + 5x$.
- You may see a test question that says, "Olivia is constructing a bookcase from seven boards. Two of them are for vertical supports and five are for shelves. The height of the bookcase is twice the width of the bookcase. If the seven boards total 36 feet in length, what will be the height of Olivia's bookcase?" You would need to make a sketch and then create the equation to determine the width of the shelves. The height can be represented as double the width. (If x represents the width of the shelves in feet, then the height of the bookcase is $2x$. Since the seven boards total 36 feet, $2x + 2x + x + x + x + x + x = 36$ or $9x = 36$; $x = 4$. The height is twice the width, or 8 feet.)

SUBTRACTION WITH REGROUPING

A great way to make use of some of the features built into the decimal system would be regrouping when attempting longform subtraction operations. When subtracting within a place value, sometimes the minuend is smaller than the subtrahend, **regrouping** enables you to 'borrow' a unit from a place value to the left in order to get a positive difference. For example, consider subtracting 189 from 525 with regrouping.

First, set up the subtraction problem in vertical form:

$$\begin{array}{r} 525 \\ -\ 189 \\ \hline \end{array}$$

Notice that the numbers in the ones and tens columns of 525 are smaller than the numbers in the ones and tens columns of 189. This means you will need to use regrouping to perform subtraction:

$$\begin{array}{rrrr} & 5 & 2 & 5 \\ - & 1 & 8 & 9 \\ \hline \end{array}$$

To subtract 9 from 5 in the ones column you will need to borrow from the 2 in the tens columns:

$$\begin{array}{rrrr} & 5 & 1 & 15 \\ - & 1 & 8 & 9 \\ \hline & & & 6 \end{array}$$

Next, to subtract 8 from 1 in the tens column you will need to borrow from the 5 in the hundreds column:

$$\begin{array}{rrrr} & 4 & 11 & 15 \\ - & 1 & 8 & 9 \\ \hline & & 3 & 6 \end{array}$$

Last, subtract the 1 from the 4 in the hundreds column:

$$\begin{array}{rrrr} & 4 & 11 & 15 \\ - & 1 & 8 & 9 \\ \hline & 3 & 3 & 6 \end{array}$$

Review Video: Subtracting Large Numbers
Visit mometrix.com/academy and enter code: 603350

Order of Operations

The **order of operations** is a set of rules that dictates the order in which we must perform each operation in an expression so that we will evaluate it accurately. If we have an expression that includes multiple different operations, the order of operations tells us which operations to do first. The most common mnemonic for the order of operations is **PEMDAS**, or "Please Excuse My Dear Aunt Sally." PEMDAS stands for parentheses, exponents, multiplication, division, addition, and subtraction. It is important to understand that multiplication and division have equal precedence, as do addition and subtraction, so those pairs of operations are simply worked from left to right in order.

For example, evaluating the expression $5 + 20 \div 4 \times (2 + 3)^2 - 6$ using the correct order of operations would be done like this:

- **P:** Perform the operations inside the parentheses: $(2 + 3) = 5$
- **E:** Simplify the exponents: $(5)^2 = 5 \times 5 = 25$
    - The expression now looks like this: $5 + 20 \div 4 \times 25 - 6$
- **MD:** Perform multiplication and division from left to right: $20 \div 4 = 5$; then $5 \times 25 = 125$
    - The expression now looks like this: $5 + 125 - 6$
- **AS:** Perform addition and subtraction from left to right: $5 + 125 = 130$; then $130 - 6 = 124$

Review Video: Order of Operations
Visit mometrix.com/academy and enter code: 259675

Properties of Exponents

The properties of exponents are as follows:

Property	Description
$a^1 = a$	Any number to the power of 1 is equal to itself
$1^n = 1$	The number 1 raised to any power is equal to 1
$a^0 = 1$	Any number raised to the power of 0 is equal to 1
$a^n \times a^m = a^{n+m}$	Add exponents to multiply powers of the same base number
$a^n \div a^m = a^{n-m}$	Subtract exponents to divide powers of the same base number
$(a^n)^m = a^{n \times m}$	When a power is raised to a power, the exponents are multiplied
$(a \times b)^n = a^n \times b^n$ $(a \div b)^n = a^n \div b^n$	Multiplication and division operations inside parentheses can be raised to a power. This is the same as each term being raised to that power.
$a^{-n} = \frac{1}{a^n}$	A negative exponent is the same as the reciprocal of a positive exponent

Note that exponents do not have to be integers. Fractional or decimal exponents follow all the rules above as well. Example: $5^{\frac{1}{4}} \times 5^{\frac{3}{4}} = 5^{\frac{1}{4}+\frac{3}{4}} = 5^1 = 5$.

Review Video: Properties of Exponents
Visit mometrix.com/academy and enter code: 532558

Scientific Notation

Scientific notation is a way of writing large numbers in a shorter form. The form $a \times 10^n$ is used in scientific notation, where a is greater than or equal to 1 but less than 10, and n is the number of places the decimal must move to get from the original number to a. Example: The number 230,400,000 is cumbersome to write. To write the value in scientific notation, place a decimal point between the first and second numbers, and include all digits through the last non-zero digit ($a = 2.304$). To find the appropriate power of 10, count the number of places the decimal point had to move ($n = 8$). The number is positive if the decimal moved to the left, and negative if it moved to the right. We can then write 230,400,000 as 2.304×10^8. If we look instead at the number 0.00002304, we have the same value for a, but this time the decimal moved 5 places to the right ($n = -5$). Thus, 0.00002304 can be written as 2.304×10^{-5}. Using this notation makes it simple to compare very large or very small numbers. By comparing exponents, it is easy to see that 3.28×10^4 is smaller than 1.51×10^5, because 4 is less than 5.

Review Video: Scientific Notation
Visit mometrix.com/academy and enter code: 976454

Factors and Multiples

Factors and Greatest Common Factor

Factors are numbers that are multiplied together to obtain a **product**. For example, in the equation $2 \times 3 = 6$, the numbers 2 and 3 are factors. A **prime number** has only two factors (1 and itself), but other numbers can have many factors.

A **common factor** is a number that divides exactly into two or more other numbers. For example, the factors of 12 are 1, 2, 3, 4, 6, and 12, while the factors of 15 are 1, 3, 5, and 15. The common factors of 12 and 15 are 1 and 3.

A **prime factor** is also a prime number. Therefore, the prime factors of 12 are 2 and 3. For 15, the prime factors are 3 and 5.

The **greatest common factor** (**GCF**) is the largest number that is a factor of two or more numbers. For example, the factors of 15 are 1, 3, 5, and 15; the factors of 35 are 1, 5, 7, and 35. Therefore, the greatest common factor of 15 and 35 is 5.

Review Video: Factors
Visit mometrix.com/academy and enter code: 920086

Review Video: Prime Numbers and Factorization
Visit mometrix.com/academy and enter code: 760669

Review Video: Greatest Common Factor and Least Common Multiple
Visit mometrix.com/academy and enter code: 838699

Multiples and Least Common Multiple

Often listed out in multiplication tables, **multiples** are integer increments of a given factor. In other words, dividing a multiple by the factor will result in an integer. For example, the multiples of 7 include: $1 \times 7 = 7$, $2 \times 7 = 14$, $3 \times 7 = 21$, $4 \times 7 = 28$, $5 \times 7 = 35$. Dividing 7, 14, 21, 28, or 35 by 7 will result in the integers 1, 2, 3, 4, and 5, respectively.

The least common multiple (**LCM**) is the smallest number that is a multiple of two or more numbers. For example, the multiples of 3 include 3, 6, 9, 12, 15, etc.; the multiples of 5 include 5, 10, 15, 20, etc. Therefore, the least common multiple of 3 and 5 is 15.

Review Video: Multiples
Visit mometrix.com/academy and enter code: 626738

Fractions, Decimals, and Percentages

Fractions

A **fraction** is a number that is expressed as one integer written above another integer, with a dividing line between them $\left(\frac{x}{y}\right)$. It represents the **quotient** of the two numbers "x divided by y." It can also be thought of as x out of y equal parts.

The top number of a fraction is called the **numerator**, and it represents the number of parts under consideration. The 1 in $\frac{1}{4}$ means that 1 part out of the whole is being considered in the calculation. The bottom number of a fraction is called the **denominator**, and it represents the total number of equal parts. The 4 in $\frac{1}{4}$ means that the whole consists of 4 equal parts. A fraction cannot have a denominator of zero; this is referred to as "*undefined*."

Fractions can be manipulated, without changing the value of the fraction, by multiplying or dividing (but not adding or subtracting) both the numerator and denominator by the same number. If you divide both numbers by a common factor, you are **reducing** or simplifying the fraction. Two fractions that have the same value but are expressed differently are known as **equivalent fractions**. For example, $\frac{2}{10}, \frac{3}{15}, \frac{4}{20}$, and $\frac{5}{25}$ are all equivalent fractions. They can also all be reduced or simplified to $\frac{1}{5}$.

When two fractions are manipulated so that they have the same denominator, this is known as finding a **common denominator**. The number chosen to be that common denominator should be the least common multiple of the two original denominators. Example: $\frac{3}{4}$ and $\frac{5}{6}$; the least common multiple of 4 and 6 is 12. Manipulating to achieve the common denominator: $\frac{3}{4} = \frac{9}{12}; \frac{5}{6} = \frac{10}{12}$.

Review Video: Overview of Fractions
Visit mometrix.com/academy and enter code: 262335

Proper Fractions and Mixed Numbers

A fraction whose denominator is greater than its numerator is known as a **proper fraction**, while a fraction whose numerator is greater than its denominator is known as an **improper fraction**. Proper fractions have values *less than one* and improper fractions have values *greater than one.*

A **mixed number** is a number that contains both an integer and a fraction. Any improper fraction can be rewritten as a mixed number. Example: $\frac{8}{3} = \frac{6}{3} + \frac{2}{3} = 2 + \frac{2}{3} = 2\frac{2}{3}$. Similarly, any mixed number can be rewritten as an improper fraction. Example: $1\frac{3}{5} = 1 + \frac{3}{5} = \frac{5}{5} + \frac{3}{5} = \frac{8}{5}$.

Review Video: Proper and Improper Fractions and Mixed Numbers
Visit mometrix.com/academy and enter code: 211077

Adding and Subtracting Fractions

If two fractions have a common denominator, they can be added or subtracted simply by adding or subtracting the two numerators and retaining the same denominator. If the two fractions do not already have the same denominator, one or both of them must be manipulated to achieve a common denominator before they can be added or subtracted. Example: $\frac{1}{2}+\frac{1}{4}=\frac{2}{4}+\frac{1}{4}=\frac{3}{4}$.

Review Video: Adding and Subtracting Fractions
Visit mometrix.com/academy and enter code: 378080

Multiplying Fractions

Two fractions can be multiplied by multiplying the two numerators to find the new numerator and the two denominators to find the new denominator. Example: $\frac{1}{3}\times\frac{2}{3}=\frac{1\times2}{3\times3}=\frac{2}{9}$.

Dividing Fractions

Two fractions can be divided by flipping the numerator and denominator of the second fraction and then proceeding as though it were a multiplication problem. Example: $\frac{2}{3}\div\frac{3}{4}=\frac{2}{3}\times\frac{4}{3}=\frac{8}{9}$.

Review Video: Multiplying and Dividing Fractions
Visit mometrix.com/academy and enter code: 473632

Multiplying a Mixed Number by a Whole Number or a Decimal

When multiplying a mixed number by something, it is usually best to convert it to an improper fraction first. Additionally, if the multiplicand is a decimal, it is most often simplest to convert it to a fraction. For instance, to multiply $4\frac{3}{8}$ by 3.5, begin by rewriting each quantity as a whole number plus a proper fraction. Remember, a mixed number is a fraction added to a whole number and a decimal is a representation of the sum of fractions, specifically tenths, hundredths, thousandths, and so on:

$$4\frac{3}{8}\times 3.5=\left(4+\frac{3}{8}\right)\times\left(3+\frac{1}{2}\right)$$

Next, the quantities being added need to be expressed with the same denominator. This is achieved by multiplying and dividing the whole number by the denominator of the fraction. Recall that a whole number is equivalent to that number divided by 1:

$$=\left(\frac{4}{1}\times\frac{8}{8}+\frac{3}{8}\right)\times\left(\frac{3}{1}\times\frac{2}{2}+\frac{1}{2}\right)$$

When multiplying fractions, remember to multiply the numerators and denominators separately:

$$=\left(\frac{4\times 8}{1\times 8}+\frac{3}{8}\right)\times\left(\frac{3\times 2}{1\times 2}+\frac{1}{2}\right)$$
$$=\left(\frac{32}{8}+\frac{3}{8}\right)\times\left(\frac{6}{2}+\frac{1}{2}\right)$$

Now that the fractions have the same denominators, they can be added:

$$=\frac{35}{8}\times\frac{7}{2}$$

Finally, perform the last multiplication and then simplify:

$$=\frac{35\times 7}{8\times 2}=\frac{245}{16}=\frac{240}{16}+\frac{5}{16}=15\frac{5}{16}$$

Comparing Fractions

It is important to master the ability to compare and order fractions. This skill is relevant to many real-world scenarios. For example, carpenters often compare fractional construction nail lengths when preparing for a project, and bakers often compare fractional measurements to have the correct ratio of ingredients. There are three commonly used strategies when comparing fractions. These strategies are referred to as the common denominator approach, the decimal approach, and the cross-multiplication approach.

Using a Common Denominator to Compare Fractions

The fractions $\frac{2}{3}$ and $\frac{4}{7}$ have different denominators. $\frac{2}{3}$ has a denominator of 3, and $\frac{4}{7}$ has a denominator of 7. In order to precisely compare these two fractions, it is necessary to use a common denominator. A common denominator is a common multiple that is shared by both denominators. In this case, the denominators 3 and 7 share a multiple of 21. In general, it is most efficient to select the least common multiple for the two denominators.

Rewrite each fraction with the common denominator of 21. Then, calculate the new numerators as illustrated below.

$$\frac{2}{3} \overset{\times 7}{=} \frac{14}{21} \qquad \frac{4}{7} \overset{\times 3}{=} \frac{12}{21}$$

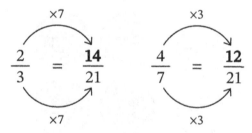

For $\frac{2}{3}$, multiply the numerator and denominator by 7. The result is $\frac{14}{21}$.

For $\frac{4}{7}$, multiply the numerator and denominator by 3. The result is $\frac{12}{21}$.

Now that both fractions have a denominator of 21, the fractions can accurately be compared by comparing the numerators. Since 14 is greater than 12, the fraction $\frac{14}{21}$ is greater than $\frac{12}{21}$. This means that $\frac{2}{3}$ is greater than $\frac{4}{7}$.

Using Decimals to Compare Fractions

Sometimes decimal values are easier to compare than fraction values. For example, $\frac{5}{8}$ is equivalent to 0.625 and $\frac{3}{5}$ is equivalent to 0.6. This means that the comparison of $\frac{5}{8}$ and $\frac{3}{5}$ can be determined by comparing the decimals 0.625 and 0.6. When both decimal values are extended to the thousandths place, they become 0.625 and 0.600, respectively. It becomes clear that 0.625 is greater than 0.600 because 625 thousandths is greater than 600 thousandths. In other words, $\frac{5}{8}$ is greater than $\frac{3}{5}$ because 0.625 is greater than 0.6.

Using Cross-Multiplication to Compare Fractions

Cross-multiplication is an efficient strategy for comparing fractions. This is a shortcut for the common denominator strategy. Start by writing each fraction next to one another. Multiply the numerator of the fraction on the left by the denominator of the fraction on the right. Write down the result next to the fraction on the left. Now multiply the numerator of the fraction on the right by the denominator of the fraction on the left. Write down the result next to the fraction on the right. Compare both products. The fraction with the larger result is the larger fraction.

Consider the fractions $\frac{4}{7}$ and $\frac{5}{9}$.

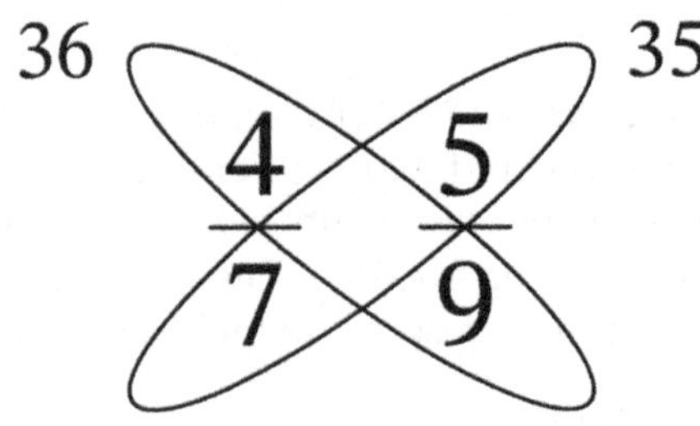

36 is greater than 35. Therefore, $\frac{4}{7}$ is greater than $\frac{5}{9}$.

Decimals

Decimals are one way to represent parts of a whole. Using the place value system, each digit to the right of a decimal point denotes the number of units of a corresponding *negative* power of ten. For example, consider the decimal 0.24. We can use a model to represent the decimal. Since a dime is worth one-tenth of a dollar and a penny is worth one-hundredth of a dollar, one possible model to represent this fraction is to have 2 dimes representing the 2 in the tenths place and 4 pennies representing the 4 in the hundredths place:

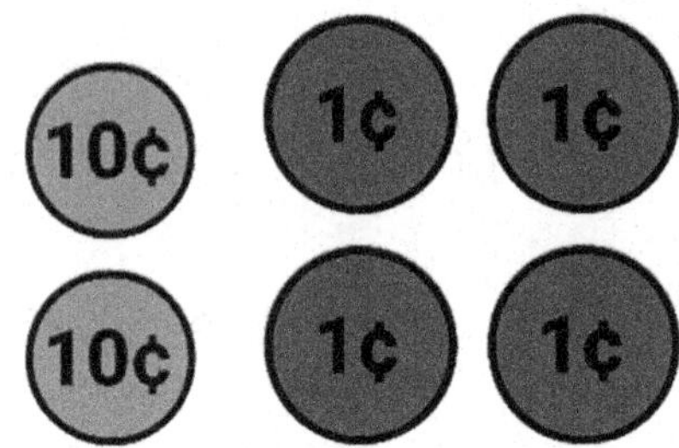

To write the decimal as a fraction, put the decimal in the numerator with 1 in the denominator. Multiply the numerator and denominator by tens until there are no more decimal places. Then simplify the fraction to lowest terms. For example, converting 0.24 to a fraction:

$$0.24 = \frac{0.24}{1} = \frac{0.24 \times 100}{1 \times 100} = \frac{24}{100} = \frac{6}{25}$$

Review Video: Decimals
Visit mometrix.com/academy and enter code: 837268

Operations with Decimals

Adding and Subtracting Decimals

When adding and subtracting decimals, the decimal points must always be aligned. Adding decimals is just like adding regular whole numbers. Example: $4.5 + 2.0 = 6.5$.

If the problem-solver does not properly align the decimal points, an incorrect answer of 4.7 may result. An easy way to add decimals is to align all of the decimal points in a vertical column visually. This will allow you to see exactly where the decimal should be placed in the final answer. Begin adding from right to left. Add each column in turn, making sure to carry the number to the left if a column adds up to more than 9. The same rules apply to the subtraction of decimals.

Review Video: Adding and Subtracting Decimals
Visit mometrix.com/academy and enter code: 381101

Multiplying Decimals

A simple multiplication problem has two components: a **multiplicand** and a **multiplier**. When multiplying decimals, work as though the numbers were whole rather than decimals. Once the final product is calculated, count the number of places to the right of the decimal in both the multiplicand and the multiplier. Then, count that number of places from the right of the product and place the decimal in that position.

For example, 12.3×2.56 has a total of three places to the right of the respective decimals. Multiply 123×256 to get 31,488. Now, beginning on the right, count three places to the left and insert the decimal. The final product will be 31.488.

> **Review Video: How to Multiply Decimals**
> Visit mometrix.com/academy and enter code: 731574

Dividing Decimals

Every division problem has a **divisor** and a **dividend**. The dividend is the number that is being divided. In the problem $14 \div 7$, 14 is the dividend and 7 is the divisor. In a division problem with decimals, the divisor must be converted into a whole number. Begin by moving the decimal in the divisor to the right until a whole number is created. Next, move the decimal in the dividend the same number of spaces to the right. For example, 4.9 into 24.5 would become 49 into 245. The decimal was moved one space to the right to create a whole number in the divisor, and then the same was done for the dividend. Once the whole numbers are created, the problem is carried out normally: $245 \div 49 = 5$.

> **Review Video: Dividing Decimals**
> Visit mometrix.com/academy and enter code: 560690
>
> **Review Video: Dividing Decimals by Whole Numbers**
> Visit mometrix.com/academy and enter code: 535669

Percentages

Percentages can be thought of as fractions that are based on a whole of 100; that is, one whole is equal to 100%. The word **percent** means "per hundred." Percentage problems are often presented in three main ways:

- Find what percentage of some number another number is.
  - Example: What percentage of 40 is 8?
- Find what number is some percentage of a given number.
  - Example: What number is 20% of 40?
- Find what number another number is a given percentage of.
  - Example: What number is 8 20% of?

There are three components in each of these cases: a **whole** (W), a **part** (P), and a **percentage** (%). These are related by the equation: $P = W \times \%$. This can easily be rearranged into other forms that may suit different questions better: $\% = \frac{P}{W}$ and $W = \frac{P}{\%}$. Percentage problems are often also word problems. As such, a large part of solving them is figuring out which quantities are what. For example, consider the following word problem:

In a school cafeteria, 7 students choose pizza, 9 choose hamburgers, and 4 choose tacos. What percentage of student choose tacos?

To find the whole, you must first add all of the parts: $7 + 9 + 4 = 20$. The percentage can then be found by dividing the part by the whole $\left(\% = \frac{P}{W}\right)$: $\frac{4}{20} = \frac{20}{100} = 20\%$.

> **Review Video: Computation with Percentages**
> Visit mometrix.com/academy and enter code: 693099

Converting Between Percentages, Fractions, and Decimals

Converting decimals to percentages and percentages to decimals is as simple as moving the decimal point. To *convert from a decimal to a percentage,* move the decimal point **two places to the right**. To *convert from a percentage to a decimal,* move it **two places to the left**. It may be helpful to remember that the percentage number will always be larger than the equivalent decimal number. Example:

$$0.23 = 23\% \quad 5.34 = 534\% \quad 0.007 = 0.7\%$$
$$700\% = 7.00 \quad 86\% = 0.86 \quad 0.15\% = 0.0015$$

To convert a fraction to a decimal, simply divide the numerator by the denominator in the fraction. To convert a decimal to a fraction, put the decimal in the numerator with 1 in the denominator. Multiply the numerator and denominator by tens until there are no more decimal places. Then simplify the fraction to lowest terms. For example, converting 0.24 to a fraction:

$$0.24 = \frac{0.24}{1} = \frac{0.24 \times 100}{1 \times 100} = \frac{24}{100} = \frac{6}{25}$$

Fractions can be converted to a percentage by finding equivalent fractions with a denominator of 100. Example:

$$\frac{7}{10} = \frac{70}{100} = 70\% \quad \frac{1}{4} = \frac{25}{100} = 25\%$$

To convert a percentage to a fraction, divide the percentage number by 100 and reduce the fraction to its simplest possible terms. Example:

$$60\% = \frac{60}{100} = \frac{3}{5} \quad 96\% = \frac{96}{100} = \frac{24}{25}$$

Review Video: Converting Fractions to Percentages and Decimals
Visit mometrix.com/academy and enter code: 306233

Review Video: Converting Percentages to Decimals and Fractions
Visit mometrix.com/academy and enter code: 287297

Review Video: Converting Decimals to Fractions and Percentages
Visit mometrix.com/academy and enter code: 986765

Review Video: Converting Decimals, Improper Fractions, and Mixed Numbers
Visit mometrix.com/academy and enter code: 696924

Proportions and Ratios

Proportions

A proportion is a relationship between two quantities that dictates how one changes when the other changes. A **direct proportion** describes a relationship in which a quantity increases by a set amount for every increase in the other quantity, or decreases by that same amount for every decrease in the other quantity. Example:

Assuming a constant driving speed, the time required for a car trip increases as the distance of the trip increases. The distance to be traveled and the time required to travel are directly proportional.

An **inverse proportion** is a relationship in which an increase in one quantity is accompanied by a decrease in the other, or vice versa. Example: the time required for a car trip decreases as the speed increases and increases as the speed decreases, so the time required is inversely proportional to the speed of the car.

> **Review Video: Proportions**
> Visit mometrix.com/academy and enter code: 505355

Ratios

A **ratio** is a comparison of two quantities in a particular order. Example: If there are 14 computers in a lab, and the class has 20 students, there is a student to computer ratio of 20 to 14, commonly written as 20: 14. Ratios are normally reduced to their smallest whole number representation, so 20: 14 would be reduced to 10: 7 by dividing both sides by 2.

> **Review Video: Ratios**
> Visit mometrix.com/academy and enter code: 996914

Constant of Proportionality

When two quantities have a proportional relationship, there exists a **constant of proportionality** between the quantities. The product of this constant and one of the quantities is equal to the other quantity. For example, if one lemon costs $0.25, two lemons cost $0.50, and three lemons cost $0.75, there is a proportional relationship between the total cost of lemons and the number of lemons purchased. The constant of proportionality is the **unit price**, namely $0.25/lemon. Notice that the total price of lemons, t, can be found by multiplying the unit price of lemons, p, and the number of lemons, n: $t = pn$.

Work/Unit Rate

Unit rate expresses a quantity of one thing in terms of one unit of another. For example, if you travel 30 miles every two hours, a unit rate expresses this comparison in terms of one hour: in one hour you travel 15 miles, so your unit rate is 15 miles per hour. Other examples are how much one ounce of food costs (price per ounce) or figuring out how much one egg costs out of the dozen (price per 1 egg, instead of price per 12 eggs). The denominator of a unit rate is always 1. Unit rates are used to compare different situations to solve problems. For example, to make sure you get the best deal when deciding which kind of soda to buy, you can find the unit rate of each. If soda #1 costs $1.50 for a 1-liter bottle, and soda #2 costs $2.75 for a 2-liter bottle, it would be a better deal to buy soda #2, because its unit rate is only $1.375 per 1-liter, which is cheaper than soda #1. Unit rates can also help determine the length of time a given event will take. For example, if you can paint 2 rooms in 4.5 hours, you can determine how long it will take you to paint 5 rooms by solving for the unit rate per room and then multiplying that by 5.

> **Review Video: Rates and Unit Rates**
> Visit mometrix.com/academy and enter code: 185363

METRIC AND CUSTOMARY MEASUREMENTS

METRIC MEASUREMENT PREFIXES

Giga-	One billion	1 *giga*watt is one billion watts
Mega-	One million	1 *mega*hertz is one million hertz
Kilo-	One thousand	1 *kilo*gram is one thousand grams
Deci-	One-tenth	1 *deci*meter is one-tenth of a meter
Centi-	One-hundredth	1 *centi*meter is one-hundredth of a meter
Milli-	One-thousandth	1 *milli*liter is one-thousandth of a liter
Micro-	One-millionth	1 *micro*gram is one-millionth of a gram

Review Video: How the Metric System Works
Visit mometrix.com/academy and enter code: 163709

MEASUREMENT CONVERSION

When converting between units, the goal is to maintain the same meaning but change the way it is displayed. In order to go from a larger unit to a smaller unit, multiply the number of the known amount by the equivalent amount. When going from a smaller unit to a larger unit, divide the number of the known amount by the equivalent amount.

For complicated conversions, it may be helpful to set up conversion fractions. In these fractions, one fraction is the **conversion factor**. The other fraction has the unknown amount in the numerator. So, the known value is placed in the denominator. Sometimes, the second fraction has the known value from the problem in the numerator and the unknown in the denominator. Multiply the two fractions to get the converted measurement. Note that since the numerator and the denominator of the factor are equivalent, the value of the fraction is 1. That is why we can say that the result in the new units is equal to the result in the old units even though they have different numbers.

It can often be necessary to chain known conversion factors together. As an example, consider converting 512 square inches to square meters. We know that there are 2.54 centimeters in an inch and 100 centimeters in a meter, and we know we will need to square each of these factors to achieve the conversion we are looking for.

$$\frac{512\text{ in}^2}{1} \times \left(\frac{2.54\text{ cm}}{1\text{ in}}\right)^2 \times \left(\frac{1\text{ m}}{100\text{ cm}}\right)^2 = \frac{512\;\cancel{\text{in}^2}}{1} \times \left(\frac{6.4516\;\cancel{\text{cm}^2}}{1\;\cancel{\text{in}^2}}\right) \times \left(\frac{1\text{ m}^2}{10{,}000\;\cancel{\text{cm}^2}}\right) = 0.330\text{ m}^2$$

Review Video: Measurement Conversions
Visit mometrix.com/academy and enter code: 316703

Common Units and Equivalents

Metric Equivalents

1000 μg (microgram)	1 mg
1000 mg (milligram)	1 g
1000 g (gram)	1 kg
1000 kg (kilogram)	1 metric ton
1000 mL (milliliter)	1 L
1000 μm (micrometer)	1 mm
1000 mm (millimeter)	1 m
100 cm (centimeter)	1 m
1000 m (meter)	1 km

Distance and Area Measurement

Unit	Abbreviation	US equivalent	Metric equivalent
Inch	in	1 inch	2.54 centimeters
Foot	ft	12 inches	0.305 meters
Yard	yd	3 feet	0.914 meters
Mile	mi	5280 feet	1.609 kilometers
Acre	ac	4840 square yards	0.405 hectares
Square Mile	sq. mi. or $mi.^2$	640 acres	2.590 square kilometers

Capacity Measurements

Unit	Abbreviation	US equivalent	Metric equivalent
Fluid Ounce	fl oz	8 fluid drams	29.573 milliliters
Cup	c	8 fluid ounces	0.237 liter
Pint	pt.	16 fluid ounces	0.473 liter
Quart	qt.	2 pints	0.946 liter
Gallon	gal.	4 quarts	3.785 liters
Teaspoon	t or tsp.	1 fluid dram	5 milliliters
Tablespoon	T or tbsp.	4 fluid drams	15 or 16 milliliters
Cubic Centimeter	cc or cm^3	0.271 drams	1 milliliter

Weight Measurements

Unit	Abbreviation	US equivalent	Metric equivalent
Ounce	oz	16 drams	28.35 grams
Pound	lb	16 ounces	453.6 grams
Ton	tn.	2,000 pounds	907.2 kilograms

Volume and Weight Measurement Clarifications

Always be careful when using ounces and fluid ounces. They are not equivalent.

1 pint = 16 fluid ounces	1 fluid ounce ≠ 1 ounce
1 pound = 16 ounces	1 pint ≠ 1 pound

Having one pint of something does not mean you have one pound of it. In the same way, just because something weighs one pound does not mean that its volume is one pint.

In the United States, the word "ton" by itself refers to a short ton or a net ton. Do not confuse this with a long ton (also called a gross ton) or a metric ton (also spelled *tonne*), which have different measurement equivalents.

$$1 \text{ US ton} = 2000 \text{ pounds} \quad \neq \quad 1 \text{ metric ton} = 1000 \text{ kilograms}$$

Mathematical Reasoning

PROBABILITY

Probability is the likelihood of a certain outcome occurring for a given event. An **event** is any situation that produces a result. It could be something as simple as flipping a coin or as complex as launching a rocket. Determining the probability of an outcome for an event can be equally simple or complex. As such, there are specific terms used in the study of probability that need to be understood:

- **Compound event**—an event that involves two or more independent events (rolling a pair of dice and taking the sum)
- **Desired outcome** (or success)—an outcome that meets a particular set of criteria (a roll of 1 or 2 if we are looking for numbers less than 3)
- **Independent events**—two or more events whose outcomes do not affect one another (two coins tossed at the same time)
- **Dependent events**—two or more events whose outcomes affect one another (two cards drawn consecutively from the same deck)
- **Certain outcome**—probability of outcome is 100% or 1
- **Impossible outcome**—probability of outcome is 0% or 0
- **Mutually exclusive outcomes**—two or more outcomes whose criteria cannot all be satisfied in a single event (a coin coming up heads and tails on the same toss)
- **Random variable**—refers to all possible outcomes of a single event which may be discrete or continuous.

Review Video: Intro to Probability
Visit mometrix.com/academy and enter code: 212374

SAMPLE SPACE

The total set of all possible results of a test or experiment is called a **sample space**, or sometimes a universal sample space. The sample space, represented by one of the variables S, Ω, or U (for universal sample space) has individual elements called outcomes. Other terms for outcome that may be used interchangeably include elementary outcome, simple event, or sample point. The number of outcomes in a given sample space could be infinite or finite, and some tests may yield multiple unique sample sets. For example, tests conducted by drawing playing cards from a standard deck would have one sample space of the card values, another sample space of the card suits, and a third sample space of suit-denomination combinations. For most tests, the sample spaces considered will be finite.

An **event**, represented by the variable E, is a portion of a sample space. It may be one outcome or a group of outcomes from the same sample space. If an event occurs, then the test or experiment will generate an outcome that satisfies the requirement of that event. For example, given a standard deck of 52 playing cards as the sample space, and defining the event as the collection of face cards, then the event will occur if the card drawn is a J, Q, or K. If any other card is drawn, the event is said to have not occurred.

For every sample space, each possible outcome has a specific likelihood, or probability, that it will occur. The probability measure, also called the **distribution**, is a function that assigns a real number probability, from zero to one, to each outcome. For a probability measure to be accurate, every outcome must have a real number probability measure that is greater than or equal to zero and less than or equal to one. Also, the probability measure of the sample space must equal one, and the probability measure of the union of multiple outcomes must equal the sum of the individual probability measures.

Probabilities of events are expressed as real numbers from zero to one. They give a numerical value to the chance that a particular event will occur. The probability of an event occurring is the sum of the probabilities of the individual elements of that event. For example, in a standard deck of 52 playing cards as the sample space and the collection of face cards as the event, the probability of drawing a specific face card is $\frac{1}{52} = 0.019$, but the probability of drawing any one of the twelve face cards is $12(0.019) = 0.228$. Note that rounding of numbers can generate different results. If you multiplied 12 by the fraction $\frac{1}{52}$ before converting to a decimal, you would get the answer $\frac{12}{52} = 0.231$.

THEORETICAL AND EXPERIMENTAL PROBABILITY

Theoretical probability can usually be determined without actually performing the event. The likelihood of an outcome occurring, or the probability of an outcome occurring, is given by the formula:

$$P(A) = \frac{\text{Number of acceptable outcomes}}{\text{Number of possible outcomes}}$$

Note that $P(A)$ is the probability of an outcome A occurring, and each outcome is just as likely to occur as any other outcome. If each outcome has the same probability of occurring as every other possible outcome, the outcomes are said to be equally likely to occur. The total number of acceptable outcomes must be less than or equal to the total number of possible outcomes. If the two are equal, then the outcome is certain to occur and the probability is 1. If the number of acceptable outcomes is zero, then the outcome is impossible and the probability is 0. For example, if there are 20 marbles in a bag and 5 are red, then the theoretical probability of randomly selecting a red marble is 5 out of 20, $\left(\frac{5}{20} = \frac{1}{4}, 0.25, \text{or } 25\%\right)$.

If the theoretical probability is unknown or too complicated to calculate, it can be estimated by an experimental probability. **Experimental probability**, also called empirical probability, is an estimate of the likelihood of a certain outcome based on repeated experiments or collected data. In other words, while theoretical probability is based on what *should* happen, experimental probability is based on what *has* happened. Experimental probability is calculated in the same way as theoretical probability, except that actual outcomes are used instead of possible outcomes. The more experiments performed or datapoints gathered, the better the estimate should be.

Theoretical and experimental probability do not always line up with one another. Theoretical probability says that out of 20 coin-tosses, 10 should be heads. However, if we were actually to toss 20 coins, we might record just 5 heads. This doesn't mean that our theoretical probability is incorrect; it just means that this particular experiment had results that were different from what was predicted. A practical application of empirical probability is the insurance industry. There are no set functions that define lifespan, health, or safety. Insurance companies look at factors from hundreds of thousands of individuals to find patterns that they then use to set the formulas for insurance premiums.

Review Video: Empirical Probability
Visit mometrix.com/academy and enter code: 513468

OBJECTIVE AND SUBJECTIVE PROBABILITY

Objective probability is based on mathematical formulas and documented evidence. Examples of objective probability include raffles or lottery drawings where there is a pre-determined number of possible outcomes and a predetermined number of outcomes that correspond to an event. Other cases of objective probability include probabilities of rolling dice, flipping coins, or drawing cards. Most gambling games are based on objective probability.

In contrast, **subjective probability** is based on personal or professional feelings and judgments. Often, there is a lot of guesswork following extensive research. Areas where subjective probability is applicable include sales trends and business expenses. Attractions set admission prices based on subjective probabilities of attendance based on varying admission rates in an effort to maximize their profit.

Complement of an Event

Sometimes it may be easier to calculate the possibility of something not happening, or the **complement of an event**. Represented by the symbol $\bar{A}$, the complement of A is the probability that event A does not happen. When you know the probability of event A occurring, you can use the formula $P(\bar{A}) = 1 - P(A)$, where $P(\bar{A})$ is the probability of event A not occurring, and $P(A)$ is the probability of event A occurring.

Addition Rule

The **addition rule** for probability is used for finding the probability of a compound event. Use the formula $P(A \cup B) = P(A) + P(B) - P(A \cap B)$, where $P(A \cap B)$ is the probability of both events occurring to find the probability of a compound event. The probability of both events occurring at the same time must be subtracted to eliminate any overlap in the first two probabilities.

Conditional Probability

Given two events A and B, the **conditional probability** $P(A|B)$ is the probability that event A will occur, given that event B has occurred. The conditional probability cannot be calculated simply from $P(A)$ and $P(B)$; these probabilities alone do not give sufficient information to determine the conditional probability. It can, however, be determined if you are also given the probability of the intersection of events A and B, $P(A \cap B)$, the probability that events A and B both occur. Specifically, $P(A|B) = \frac{P(A \cap B)}{P(B)}$. For instance, suppose you have a jar containing two red marbles and two blue marbles, and you draw two marbles at random. Consider event A being the event that the first marble drawn is red, and event B being the event that the second marble drawn is blue. If we want to find the probability that B occurs given that A occurred, $P(B|A)$, then we can compute it using the fact that $P(A)$ is $\frac{1}{2}$, and $P(A \cap B)$ is $\frac{1}{3}$. (The latter may not be obvious, but may be determined by finding the product of $\frac{1}{2}$ and $\frac{2}{3}$). Therefore $P(B|A) = \frac{P(A \cap B)}{P(A)} = \frac{1/3}{1/2} = \frac{2}{3}$.

Conditional Probability in Everyday Situations

Conditional probability often arises in everyday situations in, for example, estimating the risk or benefit of certain activities. The conditional probability of having a heart attack given that you exercise daily may be smaller than the overall probability of having a heart attack. The conditional probability of having lung cancer given that you are a smoker is larger than the overall probability of having lung cancer. Note that changing the order of the conditional probability changes the meaning: the conditional probability of having lung cancer given that you are a smoker is a very different thing from the probability of being a smoker given that you have lung cancer. In an extreme case, suppose that a certain rare disease is caused only by eating a certain food, but even then, it is unlikely. Then the conditional probability of having that disease given that you eat the dangerous food is nonzero but low, but the conditional probability of having eaten that food given that you have the disease is 100%!

Review Video: Conditional Probability
Visit mometrix.com/academy and enter code: 397924

Independence

The conditional probability $P(A|B)$ is the probability that event A will occur given that event B occurs. If the two events are independent, we do not expect that whether or not event B occurs should have any effect on whether or not event A occurs. In other words, we expect $P(A|B) = P(A)$.

This can be proven using the usual equations for conditional probability and the joint probability of independent events. The conditional probability $P(A|B) = \frac{P(A \cap B)}{P(B)}$. If A and B are independent, then $P(A \cap B) = P(A)P(B)$. So $P(A|B) = \frac{P(A)P(B)}{P(B)} = P(A)$. By similar reasoning, if A and B are independent then $P(B|A) = P(B)$.

Multiplication Rule

The **multiplication rule** can be used to find the probability of two independent events occurring using the formula $P(A \cap B) = P(A) \times P(B)$, where $P(A \cap B)$ is the probability of two independent events occurring, $P(A)$ is the probability of the first event occurring, and $P(B)$ is the probability of the second event occurring.

The multiplication rule can also be used to find the probability of two dependent events occurring using the formula $P(A \cap B) = P(A) \times P(B|A)$, where $P(A \cap B)$ is the probability of two dependent events occurring and $P(B|A)$ is the probability of the second event occurring after the first event has already occurred.

Use a **combination of the multiplication** rule and the rule of complements to find the probability that at least one outcome of the element will occur. This is given by the general formula $P(\text{at least one event occurring}) = 1 - P(\text{no outcomes occurring})$. For example, to find the probability that at least one even number will show when a pair of dice is rolled, find the probability that two odd numbers will be rolled (no even numbers) and subtract from one. You can always use a tree diagram or make a chart to list the possible outcomes when the sample space is small, such as in the dice-rolling example, but in most cases it will be much faster to use the multiplication and complement formulas.

Review Video: Multiplication Rule
Visit mometrix.com/academy and enter code: 782598

Union and Intersection of Two Sets of Outcomes

If A and B are each a set of elements or outcomes from an experiment, then the **union** (symbol ∪) of the two sets is the set of elements found in set A or set B. For example, if $A = \{2, 3, 4\}$ and $B = \{3, 4, 5\}$, $A \cup B = \{2, 3, 4, 5\}$. Note that the outcomes 3 and 4 appear only once in the union. For statistical events, the union is equivalent to "or"; $P(A \cup B)$ is the same thing as $P(A \text{ or } B)$. The **intersection** (symbol ∩) of two sets is the set of outcomes common to both sets. For the above sets A and B, $A \cap B = \{3, 4\}$. For statistical events, the intersection is equivalent to "and"; $P(A \cap B)$ is the same thing as $P(A \text{ and } B)$. It is important to note that union and intersection operations commute. That is:

$$A \cup B = B \cup A \text{ and } A \cap B = B \cap A$$

Permutations and Combinations in Probability

When trying to calculate the probability of an event using the $\frac{\text{desired outcomes}}{\text{total outcomes}}$ formula, you may frequently find that there are too many outcomes to individually count them. **Permutation** and **combination formulas** offer a shortcut to counting outcomes. A permutation is an arrangement of a specific number of a set of objects in a specific order. The number of **permutations** of r items given a set of n items can be calculated as ${}_nP_r = \frac{n!}{(n-r)!}$. Combinations are similar to permutations, except there are no restrictions regarding the order of the elements. While ABC is considered a different permutation than BCA, ABC and BCA are considered the same combination. The number of **combinations** of r items given a set of n items can be calculated as ${}_nC_r = \frac{n!}{r!(n-r)!}$ or ${}_nC_r = \frac{{}_nP_r}{r!}$.

Suppose you want to calculate how many different 5-card hands can be drawn from a deck of 52 cards. This is a combination since the order of the cards in a hand does not matter. There are 52 cards available, and 5 to be selected. Thus, the number of different hands is ${}_{52}C_5 = \frac{52!}{5! \times 47!} = 2{,}598{,}960$.

Review Video: Probability - Permutation and Combination
Visit mometrix.com/academy and enter code: 907664

Measures of Central Tendency

A **measure of central tendency** is a statistical value that gives a reasonable estimate for the center of a group of data. There are several different ways of describing the measure of central tendency. Each one has a unique way it is calculated, and each one gives a slightly different perspective on the data set. Whenever you give a measure of central tendency, always make sure the units are the same. If the data has different units, such as hours, minutes, and seconds, convert all the data to the same unit, and use the same unit in the measure of central tendency. If no units are given in the data, do not give units for the measure of central tendency.

Mean

The **statistical mean** of a group of data is the same as the arithmetic average of that group. To find the mean of a set of data, first convert each value to the same units, if necessary. Then find the sum of all the values, and count the total number of data values, making sure you take into consideration each individual value. If a value appears more than once, count it more than once. Divide the sum of the values by the total number of values and apply the units, if any. Note that the mean does not have to be one of the data values in the set, and may not divide evenly.

$$\text{mean} = \frac{\text{sum of the data values}}{\text{quantity of data values}}$$

For instance, the mean of the data set {88, 72, 61, 90, 97, 68, 88, 79, 86, 93, 97, 71, 80, 84, 89} would be the sum of the fifteen numbers divided by 15:

$$\frac{88 + 72 + 61 + 90 + 97 + 68 + 88 + 79 + 86 + 93 + 97 + 71 + 80 + 84 + 89}{15} = \frac{1242}{15} = 82.8$$

While the mean is relatively easy to calculate and averages are understood by most people, the mean can be very misleading if it is used as the sole measure of central tendency. If the data set has outliers (data values that are unusually high or unusually low compared to the rest of the data values), the mean can be very distorted, especially if the data set has a small number of values. If unusually high values are countered with unusually low values, the mean is not affected as much. For example, if five of twenty students in a class get a 100 on a test, but the other 15 students have an average of 60 on the same test, the class average would appear as 70. Whenever the mean is skewed by outliers, it is always a good idea to include the median as an alternate measure of central tendency.

A **weighted mean**, or weighted average, is a mean that uses "weighted" values. The formula is weighted mean $= \frac{w_1x_1 + w_2x_2 + w_3x_3 \ldots + w_nx_n}{w_1 + w_2 + w_3 + \cdots + w_n}$. Weighted values, such as $w_1, w_2, w_3, \ldots w_n$ are assigned to each member of the set $x_1, x_2, x_3, \ldots x_n$. When calculating the weighted mean, make sure a weight value for each member of the set is used.

Review Video: All About Averages
Visit mometrix.com/academy and enter code: 176521

Median

The **statistical median** is the value in the middle of the set of data. To find the median, list all data values in order from smallest to largest or from largest to smallest. Any value that is repeated in the set must be listed the number of times it appears. If there are an odd number of data values, the median is the value in the middle of the list. If there is an even number of data values, the median is the arithmetic mean of the two middle values.

For example, the median of the data set {88, 72, 61, 90, 97, 68, 88, 79, 86, 93, 97, 71, 80, 84, 88} is 86 since the ordered set is {61, 68, 71, 72, 79, 80, 84, **86**, 88, 88, 88, 90, 93, 97, 97}.

The big disadvantage of using the median as a measure of central tendency is that is relies solely on a value's relative size as compared to the other values in the set. When the individual values in a set of data are evenly dispersed, the median can be an accurate tool. However, if there is a group of rather large values or a group of rather small values that are not offset by a different group of values, the information that can be inferred from the median may not be accurate because the distribution of values is skewed.

Mode

The **statistical mode** is the data value that occurs the greatest number of times in the data set. It is possible to have exactly one mode, more than one mode, or no mode. To find the mode of a set of data, arrange the data like you do to find the median (all values in order, listing all multiples of data values). Count the number of times each value appears in the data set. If all values appear an equal number of times, there is no mode. If one value appears more than any other value, that value is the mode. If two or more values appear the same number of times, but there are other values that appear fewer times and no values that appear more times, all of those values are the modes.

For example, the mode of the data set {**88**, 72, 61, 90, 97, 68, **88**, 79, 86, 93, 97, 71, 80, 84, **88**} is 88.

The main disadvantage of the mode is that the values of the other data in the set have no bearing on the mode. The mode may be the largest value, the smallest value, or a value anywhere in between in the set. The mode only tells which value or values, if any, occurred the greatest number of times. It does not give any suggestions about the remaining values in the set.

Review Video: Mean, Median, and Mode
Visit mometrix.com/academy and enter code: 286207

Geometry

Points, Lines, and Planes

Points and Lines

A **point** is a fixed location in space, has no size or dimensions, and is commonly represented by a dot. A **line** is a set of points that extends infinitely in two opposite directions. It has length, but no width or depth. A line can be defined by any two distinct points that it contains. A **line segment** is a portion of a line that has definite endpoints. A **ray** is a portion of a line that extends from a single point on that line in one direction along the line. It has a definite beginning, but no ending.

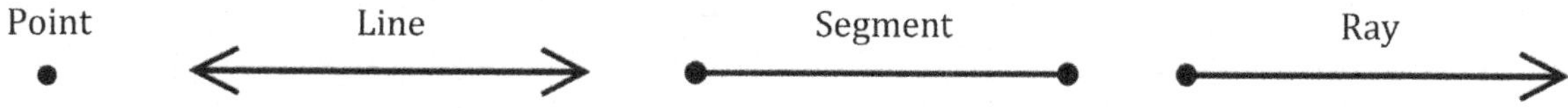

Interactions Between Lines

Intersecting lines are lines that have exactly one point in common. **Concurrent lines** are multiple lines that intersect at a single point. **Perpendicular lines** are lines that intersect at right angles. They are represented by the symbol ⊥. The shortest distance from a line to a point not on the line is a perpendicular segment from the point to the line. **Parallel lines** are lines in the same plane that have no points in common and never meet. It is possible for lines to be in different planes, have no points in common, and never meet, but they are not parallel because they are in different planes.

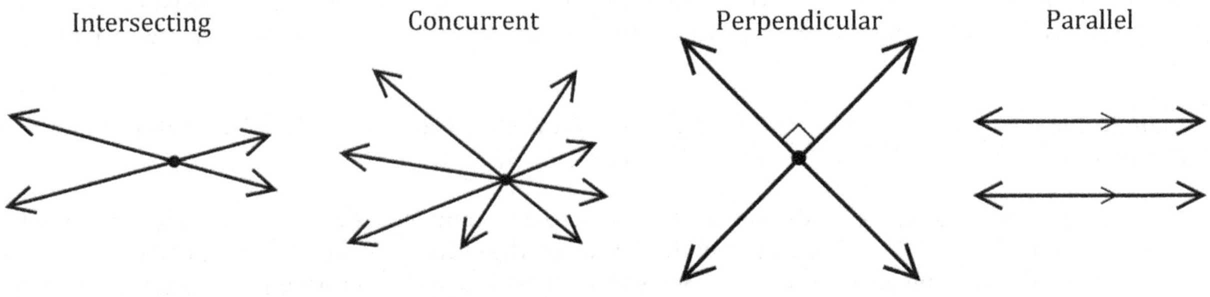

Review Video: Parallel and Perpendicular Lines
Visit mometrix.com/academy and enter code: 815923

A **transversal** is a line that intersects at least two other lines, which may or may not be parallel to one another. A transversal that intersects parallel lines is a common occurrence in geometry. A **bisector** is a line or line segment that divides another line segment into two equal lengths. A **perpendicular bisector** of a line segment is composed of points that are equidistant from the endpoints of the segment it is dividing.

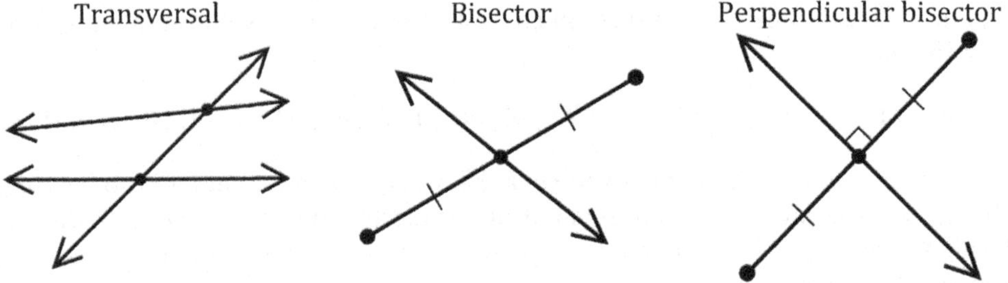

The **projection of a point on a line** is the point at which a perpendicular line drawn from the given point to the given line intersects the line. This is also the shortest distance from the given point to the line. The **projection of a segment on a line** is a segment whose endpoints are the points formed when perpendicular lines are drawn from the endpoints of the given segment to the given line. This is similar to the length a diagonal line appears to be when viewed from above.

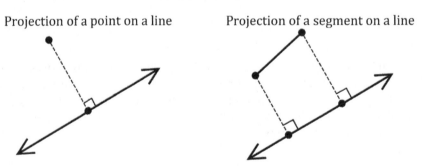

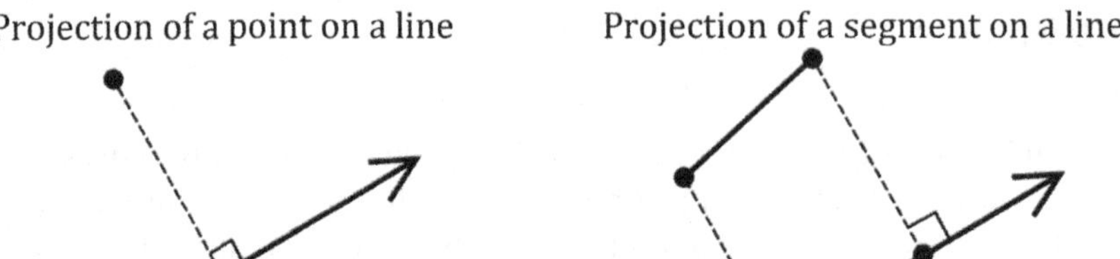

PLANES

A **plane** is a two-dimensional flat surface defined by three non-collinear points. A plane extends an infinite distance in all directions in those two dimensions. It contains an infinite number of points, parallel lines and segments, intersecting lines and segments, as well as parallel or intersecting rays. A plane will never contain a three-dimensional figure or skew lines, which are lines that don't intersect and are not parallel. Two given planes are either parallel or they intersect at a line. A plane may intersect a circular conic surface to form **conic sections**, such as a parabola, hyperbola, circle or ellipse.

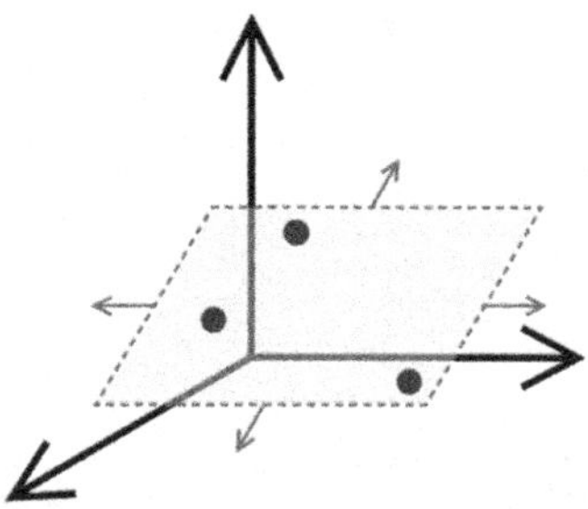

Review Video: Lines and Planes
Visit mometrix.com/academy and enter code: 554267

ANGLES

ANGLES AND VERTICES

An **angle** is formed when two lines or line segments meet at a common point. It may be a common starting point for a pair of segments or rays, or it may be the intersection of lines. Angles are represented by the symbol ∠.

The **vertex** is the point at which two segments or rays meet to form an angle. If the angle is formed by intersecting rays, lines, and/or line segments, the vertex is the point at which four angles are formed. The pairs of angles opposite one another are called vertical angles, and their measures are equal.

- An **acute** angle is an angle with a degree measure less than 90°.
- A **right** angle is an angle with a degree measure of exactly 90°.
- An **obtuse** angle is an angle with a degree measure greater than 90° but less than 180°.
- A **straight angle** is an angle with a degree measure of exactly 180°. This is also a semicircle.
- A **reflex angle** is an angle with a degree measure greater than 180° but less than 360°.
- A **full angle** is an angle with a degree measure of exactly 360°. This is also a circle.

Review Video: Angles
Visit mometrix.com/academy and enter code: 264624

RELATIONSHIPS BETWEEN ANGLES

Two angles whose sum is exactly 90° are said to be **complementary**. The two angles may or may not be adjacent. In a right triangle, the two acute angles are complementary.

Two angles whose sum is exactly 180° are said to be **supplementary**. The two angles may or may not be adjacent. Two intersecting lines always form two pairs of supplementary angles. Adjacent supplementary angles will always form a straight line.

Two angles that have the same vertex and share a side are said to be **adjacent**. Vertical angles are not adjacent because they share a vertex but no common side.

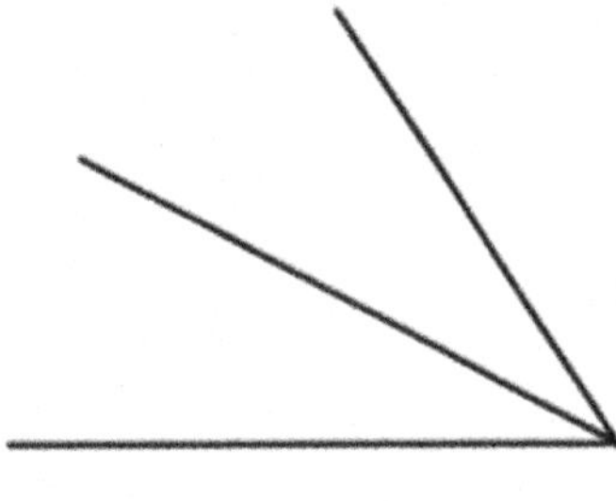

Adjacent
Share vertex and side

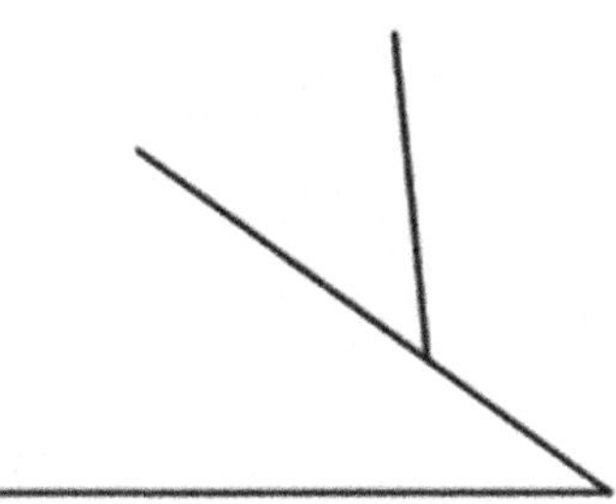

Not adjacent
Share part of a side, but not vertex

When two parallel lines are cut by a transversal, the angles that are between the two parallel lines are **interior angles**. In the diagram below, angles 3, 4, 5, and 6 are interior angles.

When two parallel lines are cut by a transversal, the angles that are outside the parallel lines are **exterior angles**. In the diagram below, angles 1, 2, 7, and 8 are exterior angles.

When two parallel lines are cut by a transversal, the angles that are in the same position relative to the transversal and a parallel line are **corresponding angles**. The diagram below has four pairs of corresponding angles: angles 1 and 5, angles 2 and 6, angles 3 and 7, and angles 4 and 8. Corresponding angles formed by parallel lines are congruent.

When two parallel lines are cut by a transversal, the two interior angles that are on opposite sides of the transversal are called **alternate interior angles**. In the diagram below, there are two pairs of alternate interior angles: angles 3 and 6, and angles 4 and 5. Alternate interior angles formed by parallel lines are congruent.

When two parallel lines are cut by a transversal, the two exterior angles that are on opposite sides of the transversal are called **alternate exterior angles**.

In the diagram below, there are two pairs of alternate exterior angles: angles 1 and 8, and angles 2 and 7. Alternate exterior angles formed by parallel lines are congruent.

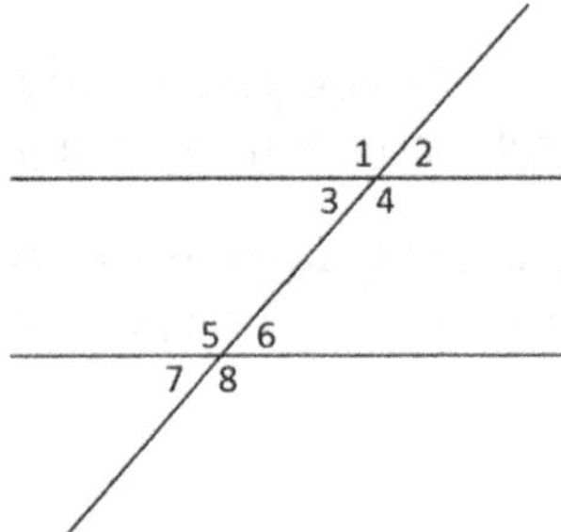

When two lines intersect, four angles are formed. The non-adjacent angles at this vertex are called vertical angles. Vertical angles are congruent. In the diagram, $\angle ABD \cong \angle CBE$ and $\angle ABC \cong \angle DBE$. The other pairs of angles, $(\angle ABC, \angle CBE)$ and $(\angle ABD, \angle DBE)$, are supplementary, meaning the pairs sum to 180°.

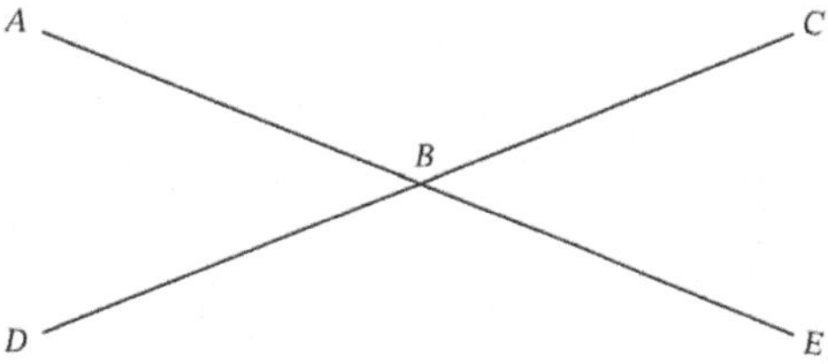

POLYGONS

A **polygon** is a closed, two-dimensional figure with three or more straight line segments called **sides**. The point at which two sides of a polygon intersect is called the **vertex**. In a polygon, the number of sides is always equal to the number of vertices. A polygon with all sides congruent and all angles equal is called a **regular polygon**. Common polygons are:

$$\begin{aligned} \text{Triangle} &= 3 \text{ sides} \\ \text{Quadrilateral} &= 4 \text{ sides} \\ \text{Pentagon} &= 5 \text{ sides} \\ \text{Hexagon} &= 6 \text{ sides} \\ \text{Heptagon} &= 7 \text{ sides} \\ \text{Octagon} &= 8 \text{ sides} \\ \text{Nonagon} &= 9 \text{ sides} \\ \text{Decagon} &= 10 \text{ sides} \\ \text{Dodecagon} &= 12 \text{ sides} \end{aligned}$$

More generally, an n-gon is a polygon that has n angles and n sides.

Review Video: Intro to Polygons
Visit mometrix.com/academy and enter code: 271869

The sum of the interior angles of an n-sided polygon is $(n - 2) \times 180°$. For example, in a triangle $n = 3$. So the sum of the interior angles is $(3 - 2) \times 180° = 180°$. In a quadrilateral, $n = 4$, and the sum of the angles is $(4 - 2) \times 180° = 360°$.

Review Video: Sum of Interior Angles
Visit mometrix.com/academy and enter code: 984991

CONVEX AND CONCAVE POLYGONS

A **convex polygon** is a polygon whose diagonals all lie within the interior of the polygon. A **concave polygon** is a polygon with a least one diagonal that is outside the polygon. In the diagram below, quadrilateral $ABCD$ is concave because diagonal $\overline{AC}$ lies outside the polygon and quadrilateral $EFGH$ is convex because both diagonals lie inside the polygon.

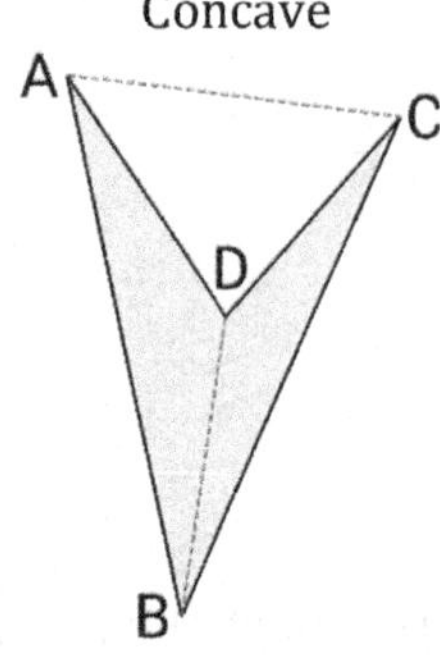

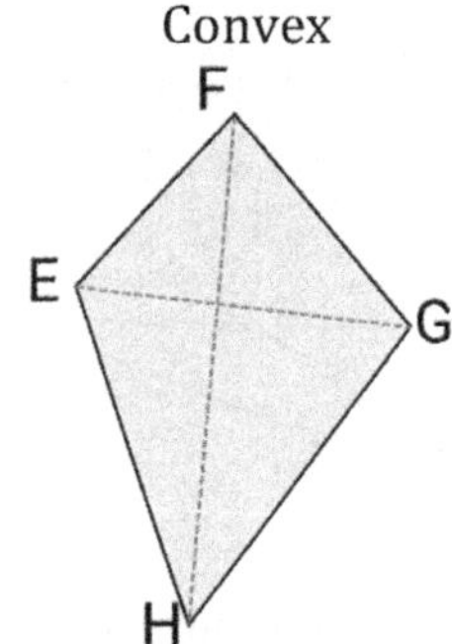

Congruence and Similarity

Congruent figures are geometric figures that have the same size and shape. All corresponding angles are equal, and all corresponding sides are equal. Congruence is indicated by the symbol $\cong$.

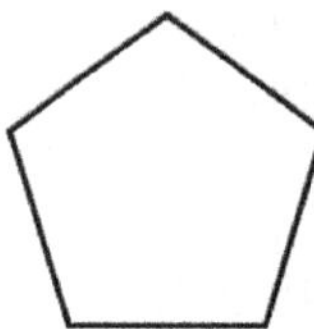

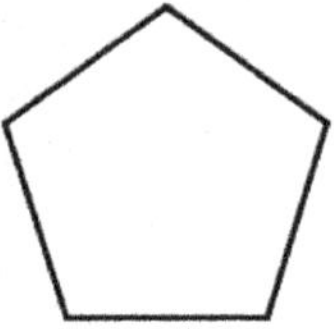

Congruent polygons

Similar figures are geometric figures that have the same shape, but do not necessarily have the same size. All corresponding angles are equal, and all corresponding sides are proportional, but they do not have to be equal. It is indicated by the symbol $\sim$.

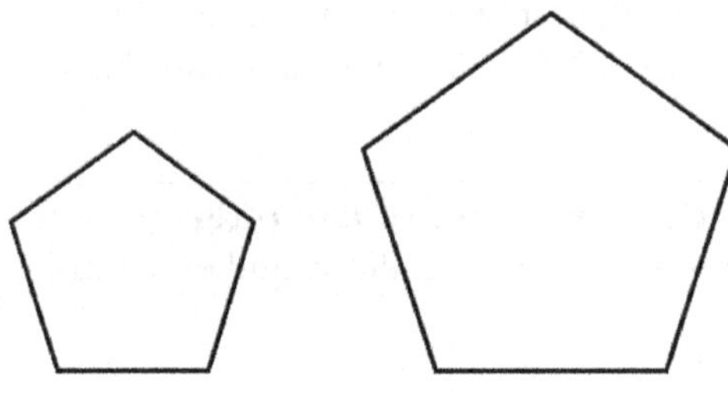

Similar polygons

Note that all congruent figures are also similar, but not all similar figures are congruent.

Review Video: Congruent Shapes
Visit mometrix.com/academy and enter code: 492281

LINE OF SYMMETRY

A line that divides a figure or object into congruent parts is called a **line of symmetry**. An object may have no lines of symmetry, one line of symmetry, or multiple (i.e., more than one) lines of symmetry.

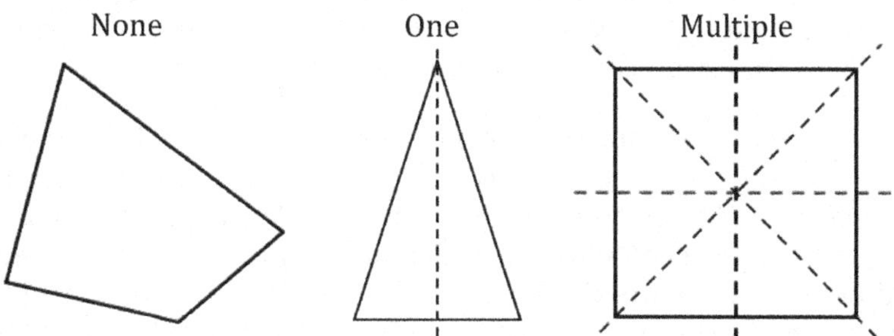

Review Video: Symmetry
Visit mometrix.com/academy and enter code: 528106

TRIANGLES

A triangle is a three-sided figure with the sum of its interior angles being 180°. The **perimeter of any triangle** is found by summing the three side lengths; $P = a + b + c$. For an equilateral triangle, this is the same as $P = 3a$, where a is any side length, since all three sides are the same length.

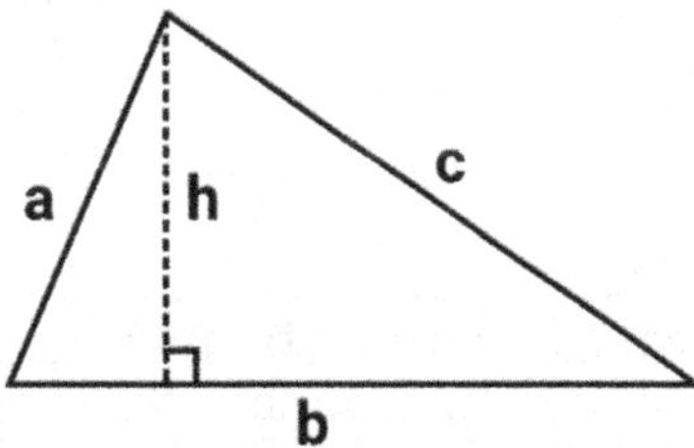

Review Video: Proof that a Triangle is 180 Degrees
Visit mometrix.com/academy and enter code: 687591

Review Video: Area and Perimeter of a Triangle
Visit mometrix.com/academy and enter code: 853779

The **area of any triangle** can be found by taking half the product of one side length referred to as the base, often given the variable b and the perpendicular distance from that side to the opposite vertex called the altitude or height and given the variable h. In equation form that is $A = \frac{1}{2}bh$. Another formula that works for any triangle is $A = \sqrt{s(s-a)(s-b)(s-c)}$, where s is the semiperimeter: $\frac{a+b+c}{2}$, and a, b, and c are the lengths of the three sides. Special cases include isosceles triangles, $A = \frac{1}{2}b\sqrt{a^2 - \frac{b^2}{4}}$, where b is the unique side and a is the length of one of the two congruent sides, and equilateral triangles, $A = \frac{\sqrt{3}}{4}a^2$, where a is the length of a side.

Review Video: Area of Any Triangle
Visit mometrix.com/academy and enter code: 138510

Parts of a Triangle

An **altitude** of a triangle is a line segment drawn from one vertex perpendicular to the opposite side. In the diagram that follows, $\overline{BE}$, $\overline{AD}$, and $\overline{CF}$ are altitudes. The length of an altitude is also called the height of the triangle. The three altitudes in a triangle are always concurrent. The point of concurrency of the altitudes of a triangle, O, is called the **orthocenter**. Note that in an obtuse triangle, the orthocenter will be outside the triangle, and in a right triangle, the orthocenter is the vertex of the right angle.

A **median** of a triangle is a line segment drawn from one vertex to the midpoint of the opposite side. In the diagram that follows, $\overline{BH}$, $\overline{AG}$, and $\overline{CI}$ are medians. This is not the same as the altitude, except the altitude to the base of an isosceles triangle and all three altitudes of an equilateral triangle. The point of concurrency of the medians of a triangle, T, is called the **centroid**. This is the same point as the orthocenter only in an equilateral triangle. Unlike the orthocenter, the centroid is always inside the triangle. The centroid can also be considered the exact center of the triangle. Any shape triangle can be perfectly balanced on a tip placed at the centroid. The centroid is also the point that is two-thirds the distance from the vertex to the opposite side.

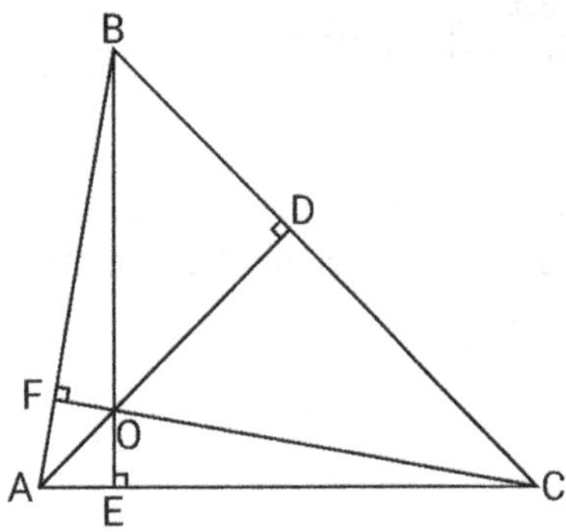

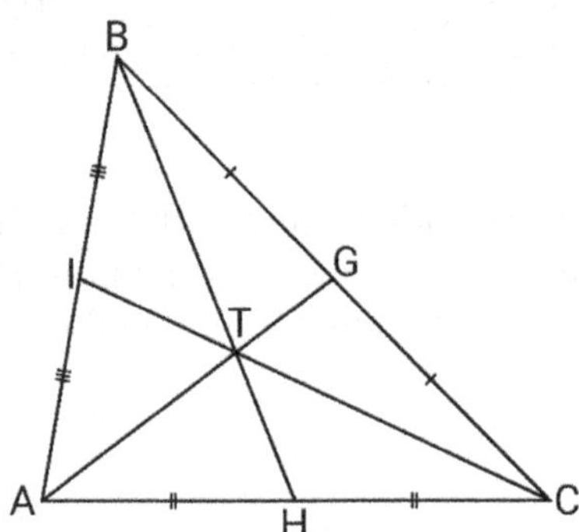

Review Video: Centroid, Incenter, Circumcenter, and Orthocenter
Visit mometrix.com/academy and enter code: 598260

Triangle Properties

Classifications of Triangles

A **scalene triangle** is a triangle with no congruent sides. A scalene triangle will also have three angles of different measures. The angle with the largest measure is opposite the longest side, and the angle with the smallest measure is opposite the shortest side. An **acute triangle** is a triangle whose three angles are all less than 90°. If two of the angles are equal, the acute triangle is also an **isosceles triangle**. An isosceles triangle will also have two congruent angles opposite the two congruent sides. If the three angles are all equal, the acute triangle is also an **equilateral triangle**. An equilateral triangle will also have three congruent angles, each 60°. All equilateral triangles are also acute triangles. An **obtuse triangle** is a triangle with exactly one angle greater than 90°. The other two angles may or may not be equal. If the two remaining angles are equal, the obtuse triangle is also an isosceles triangle. A **right triangle** is a triangle with exactly one angle equal to 90°. All right triangles follow the Pythagorean theorem. A right triangle can never be acute or obtuse.

The table below illustrates how each descriptor places a different restriction on the triangle:

Angles / Sides	Acute: All angles < 90°	Obtuse: One angle > 90°	Right: One angle = 90°
Scalene: No equal side lengths	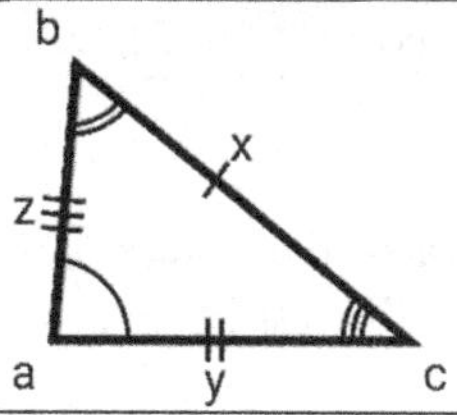 $90° > \angle a > \angle b > \angle c$ $x > y > z$	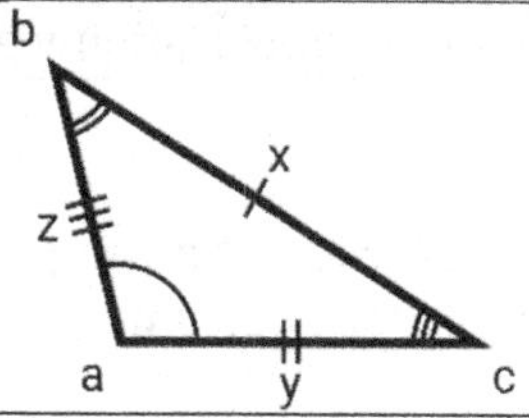 $\angle a > 90° > \angle b > \angle c$ $x > y > z$	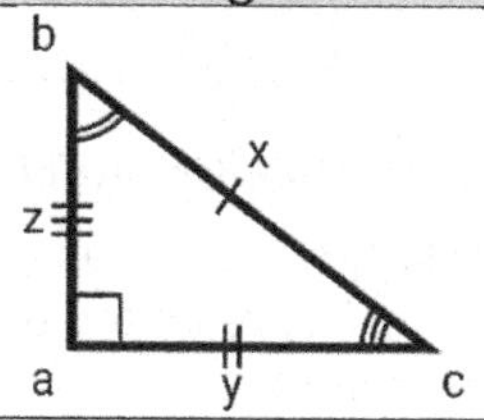 $90° = \angle a > \angle b > \angle c$ $x > y > z$
Isosceles: Two equal side lengths	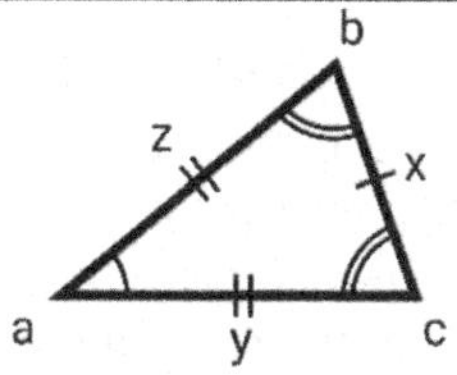 $90° > \angle a, \angle b, or\ \angle c$ $\angle b = \angle c, \quad y = z$	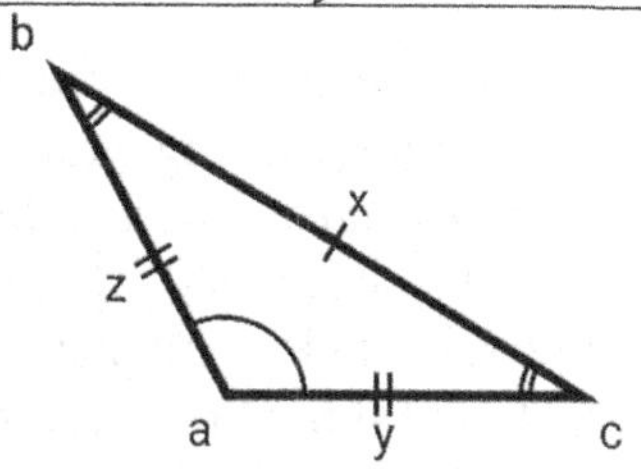 $\angle a > 90° > \angle b = \angle c$ $x > y = z$	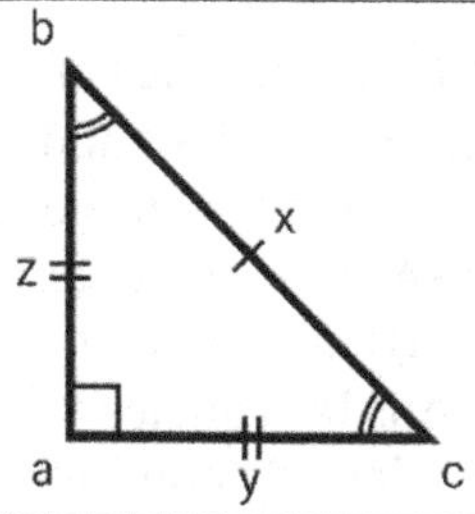 $\angle a = 90°$ $\angle b = \angle c = 45°$ $x > y = z$
Equilateral: Three equal side lengths	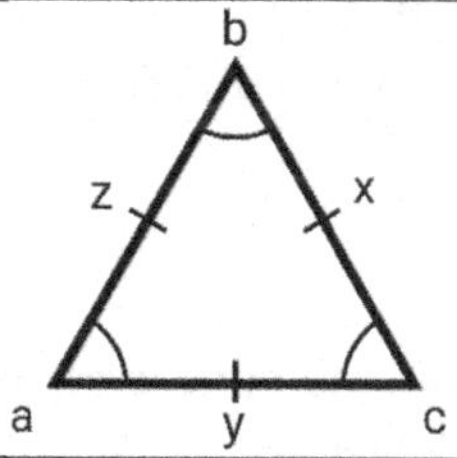 $60° = \angle a = \angle b = \angle c$ $x = y = z$		

Review Video: Introduction to Types of Triangles
Visit mometrix.com/academy and enter code: 511711

General Rules for Triangles

The **triangle inequality theorem** states that the sum of the measures of any two sides of a triangle is always greater than the measure of the third side. If the sum of the measures of two sides were equal to the third side, a triangle would be impossible because the two sides would lie flat across the third side and there would be no vertex. If the sum of the measures of two of the sides was less than the third side, a closed figure would be impossible because the two shortest sides would never meet. In other words, for a triangle with sides lengths A, B, and C: $A + B > C, B + C > A$, and $A + C > B$.

The sum of the measures of the interior angles of a triangle is always 180°. Therefore, a triangle can never have more than one angle greater than or equal to 90°.

In any triangle, the angles opposite congruent sides are congruent, and the sides opposite congruent angles are congruent. The largest angle is always opposite the longest side, and the smallest angle is always opposite the shortest side.

The line segment that joins the midpoints of any two sides of a triangle is always parallel to the third side and exactly half the length of the third side.

> **Review Video: General Rules (Triangle Inequality Theorem)**
> Visit mometrix.com/academy and enter code: 166488

Similarity and Congruence Rules

Similar triangles are triangles whose corresponding angles are equal and whose corresponding sides are proportional. Represented by AAA. Similar triangles whose corresponding sides are congruent are also congruent triangles.

Triangles can be shown to be **congruent** in 5 ways:

- **SSS**: Three sides of one triangle are congruent to the three corresponding sides of the second triangle.
- **SAS**: Two sides and the included angle (the angle formed by those two sides) of one triangle are congruent to the corresponding two sides and included angle of the second triangle.
- **ASA**: Two angles and the included side (the side that joins the two angles) of one triangle are congruent to the corresponding two angles and included side of the second triangle.
- **AAS**: Two angles and a non-included side of one triangle are congruent to the corresponding two angles and non-included side of the second triangle.
- **HL**: The hypotenuse and leg of one right triangle are congruent to the corresponding hypotenuse and leg of the second right triangle.

> **Review Video: Similar Triangles**
> Visit mometrix.com/academy and enter code: 398538

Transformations

Rotation

A **rotation** is a transformation that turns a figure around a point called the **center of rotation**, which can lie anywhere in the plane. If a line is drawn from a point on a figure to the center of rotation, and another line is drawn from the center to the rotated image of that point, the angle between the two lines is the **angle of rotation**. The vertex of the angle of rotation is the center of rotation.

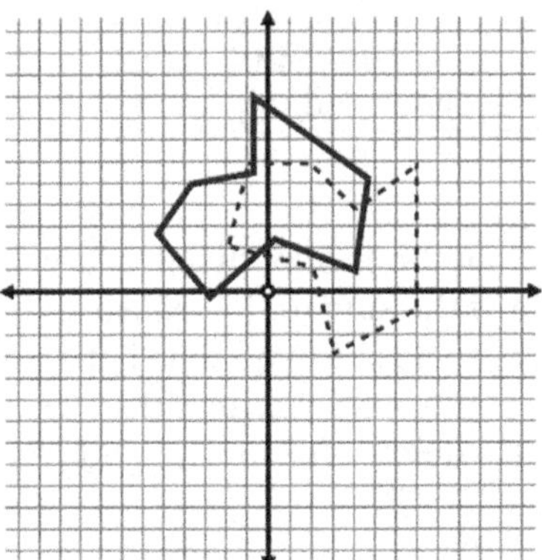

> **Review Video: Rotation**
> Visit mometrix.com/academy and enter code: 602600

Translation and Dilation

A **translation** is a transformation which slides a figure from one position in the plane to another position in the plane. The original figure and the translated figure have the same size, shape, and orientation. A **dilation** is a transformation which proportionally stretches or shrinks a figure by a **scale factor**. The dilated image is the same shape and orientation as the original image but a different size. A polygon and its dilated image are similar.

Translation

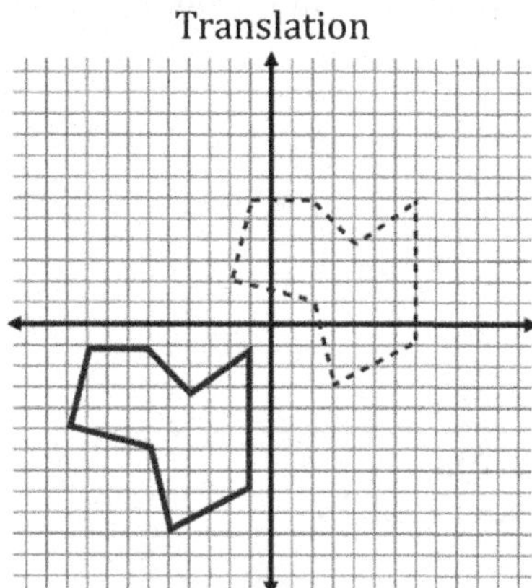

Dilation

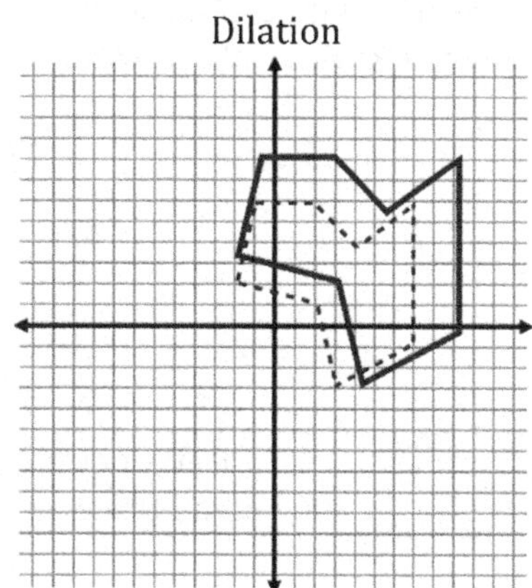

Review Video: Translation
Visit mometrix.com/academy and enter code: 718628

Review Video: Dilation
Visit mometrix.com/academy and enter code: 471630

A **reflection of a figure over a line** (a "flip") creates a congruent image that is the same distance from the line as the original figure but on the opposite side. The **line of reflection** is the perpendicular bisector of any line segment drawn from a point on the original figure to its reflected image (unless the point and its reflected image happen to be the same point, which happens when a figure is reflected over one of its own sides). A **reflection of a figure over a point** (an inversion) in two dimensions is the same as the rotation of the figure 180° about that point. The image of the figure is congruent to the original figure. The **point of reflection** is the midpoint of a line segment which connects a point in the figure to its image (unless the point and its reflected image happen to be the same point, which happens when a figure is reflected in one of its own points).

Reflection of a figure over a line

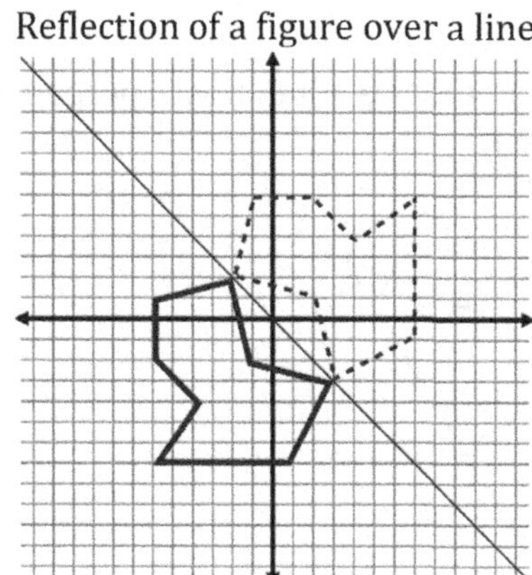

Reflection of a figure over a point

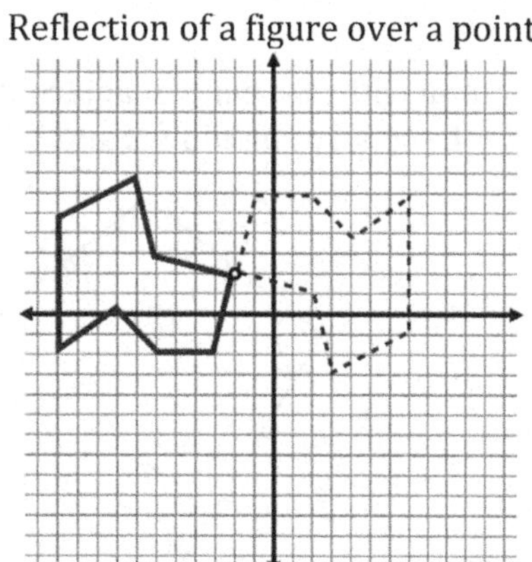

Review Video: Reflection
Visit mometrix.com/academy and enter code: 955068

Pythagorean Theorem

The side of a triangle opposite the right angle is called the **hypotenuse**. The other two sides are called the legs. The Pythagorean theorem states a relationship among the legs and hypotenuse of a right triangle: ($a^2 + b^2 = c^2$), where a and b are the lengths of the legs of a right triangle, and c is the length of the hypotenuse. Note that this formula will only work with right triangles.

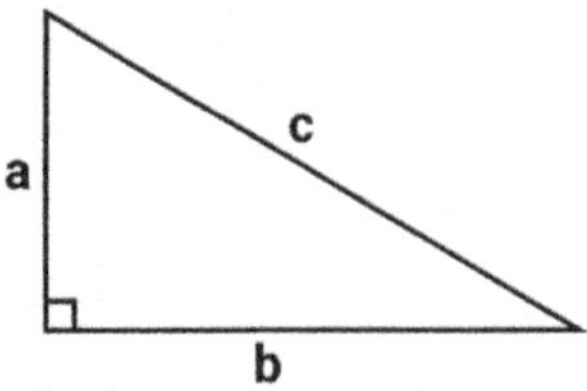

Review Video: Pythagorean Theorem
Visit mometrix.com/academy and enter code: 906576

Quadrilaterals

A **quadrilateral** is a closed two-dimensional geometric figure that has four straight sides. The sum of the interior angles of any quadrilateral is 360°.

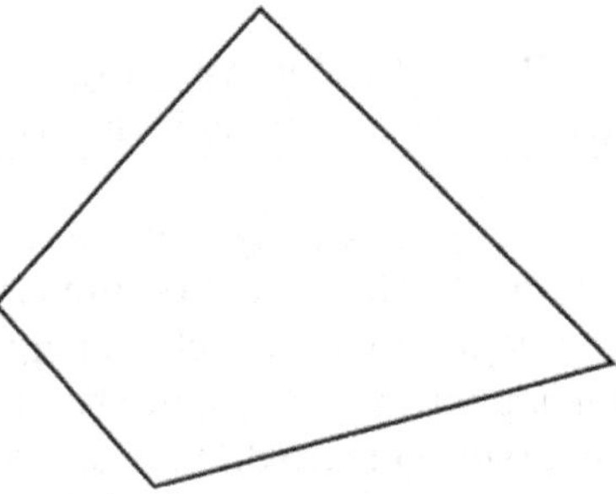

Review Video: Diagonals of Parallelograms, Rectangles, and Rhombi
Visit mometrix.com/academy and enter code: 320040

Kite

A **kite** is a quadrilateral with two pairs of adjacent sides that are congruent. A result of this is perpendicular diagonals. A kite can be concave or convex and has one line of symmetry.

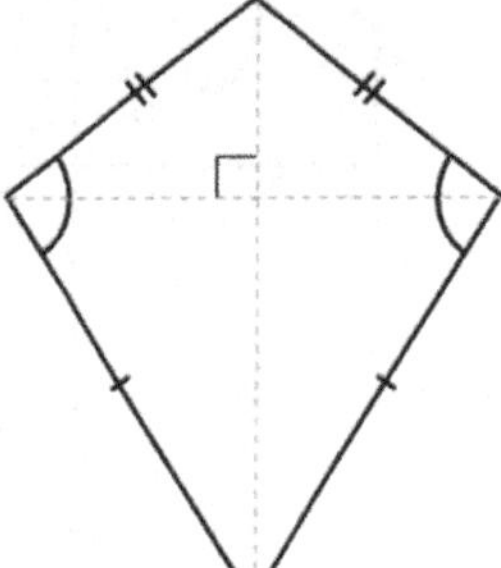

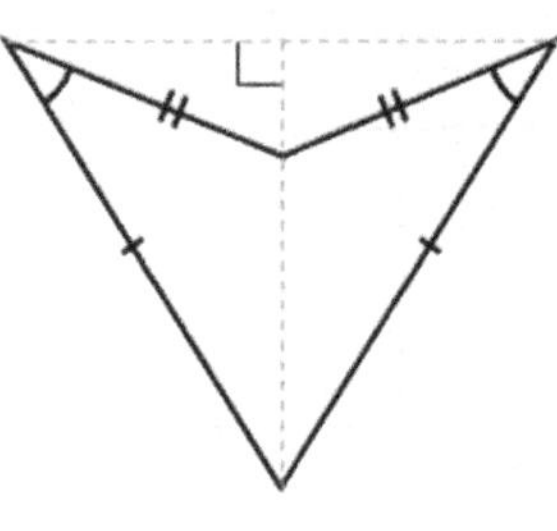

TRAPEZOID

Trapezoid: A trapezoid is defined as a quadrilateral that has at least one pair of parallel sides. There are no rules for the second pair of sides. So, there are no rules for the diagonals and no lines of symmetry for a trapezoid.

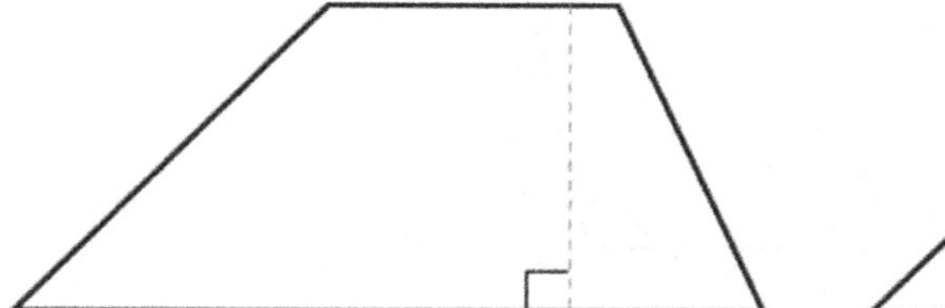
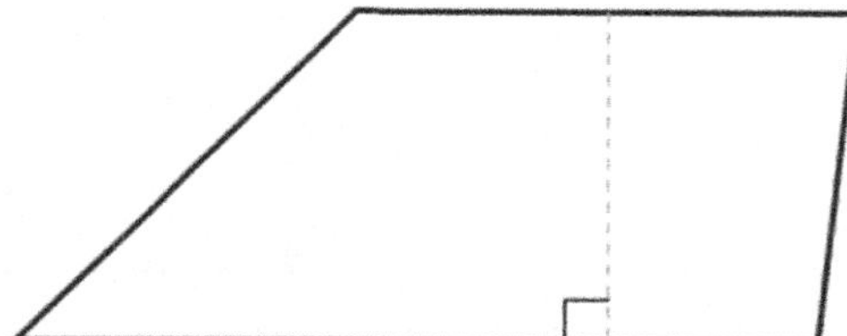

The **area of a trapezoid** is found by the formula $A = \frac{1}{2}h(b_1 + b_2)$, where h is the height (segment joining and perpendicular to the parallel bases), and b_1 and b_2 are the two parallel sides (bases). Do not use one of the other two sides as the height unless that side is also perpendicular to the parallel bases.

The **perimeter of a trapezoid** is found by the formula $P = a + b_1 + c + b_2$, where a, b_1, c, and b_2 are the four sides of the trapezoid.

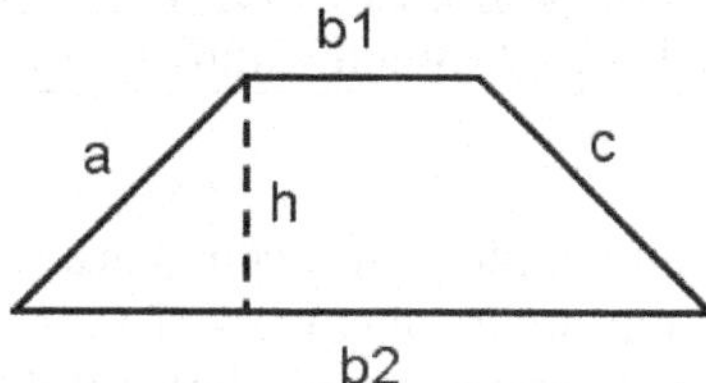

Review Video: Area and Perimeter of a Trapezoid
Visit mometrix.com/academy and enter code: 587523

Isosceles trapezoid: A trapezoid with equal base angles. This gives rise to other properties including: the two nonparallel sides have the same length, the two non-base angles are also equal, and there is one line of symmetry through the midpoints of the parallel sides.

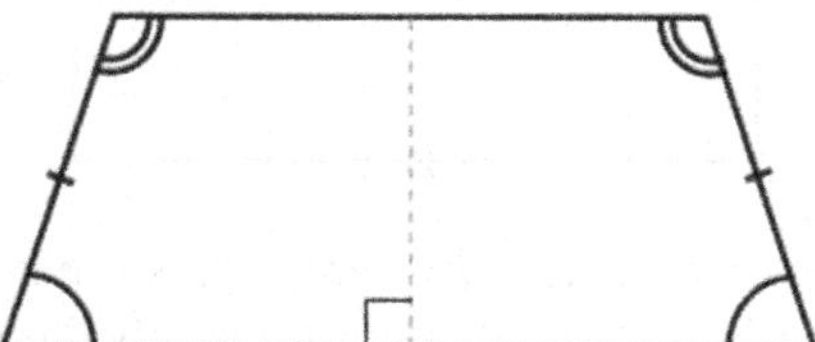

PARALLELOGRAM

A **parallelogram** is a quadrilateral that has two pairs of opposite parallel sides. As such it is a special type of trapezoid. The sides that are parallel are also congruent. The opposite interior angles are always congruent, and the consecutive interior angles are supplementary. The diagonals of a parallelogram divide each other.

Each diagonal divides the parallelogram into two congruent triangles. A parallelogram has no line of symmetry, but does have 180-degree rotational symmetry about the midpoint.

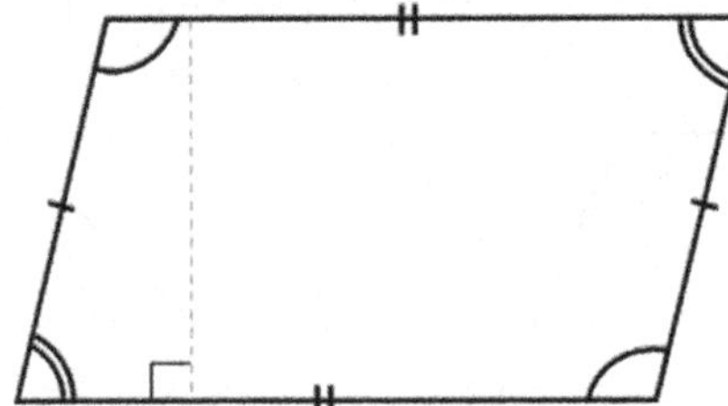

The **area of a parallelogram** is found by the formula $A = bh$, where b is the length of the base, and h is the height. Note that the base and height correspond to the length and width in a rectangle, so this formula would apply to rectangles as well. Do not confuse the height of a parallelogram with the length of the second side. The two are only the same measure in the case of a rectangle.

The **perimeter of a parallelogram** is found by the formula $P = 2a + 2b$ or $P = 2(a + b)$, where a and b are the lengths of the two sides.

Review Video: Area and Perimeter of a Parallelogram
Visit mometrix.com/academy and enter code: 718313

RECTANGLE

A **rectangle** is a quadrilateral with four right angles. All rectangles are parallelograms and trapezoids, but not all parallelograms or trapezoids are rectangles. The diagonals of a rectangle are congruent. Rectangles have two lines of symmetry (through each pair of opposing midpoints) and 180-degree rotational symmetry about the midpoint.

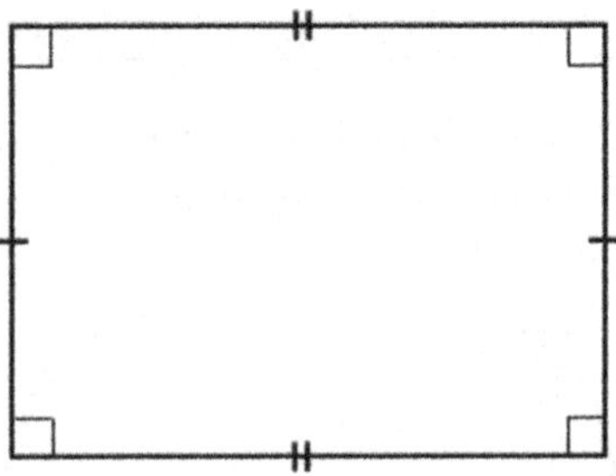

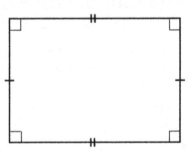

The **area of a rectangle** is found by the formula $A = lw$, where A is the area of the rectangle, l is the length (usually considered to be the longer side) and w is the width (usually considered to be the shorter side). The numbers for l and w are interchangeable.

The **perimeter of a rectangle** is found by the formula $P = 2l + 2w$ or $P = 2(l + w)$, where l is the length, and w is the width. It may be easier to add the length and width first and then double the result, as in the second formula.

RHOMBUS

A **rhombus** is a quadrilateral with four congruent sides. All rhombuses are parallelograms and kites; thus, they inherit all the properties of both types of quadrilaterals. The diagonals of a rhombus are perpendicular to each other. Rhombi have two lines of symmetry (along each of the diagonals) and 180° rotational symmetry. The

area of a rhombus is half the product of the diagonals: $A = \frac{d_1 d_2}{2}$ and the perimeter of a rhombus is: $P = 2\sqrt{(d_1)^2 + (d_2)^2}$.

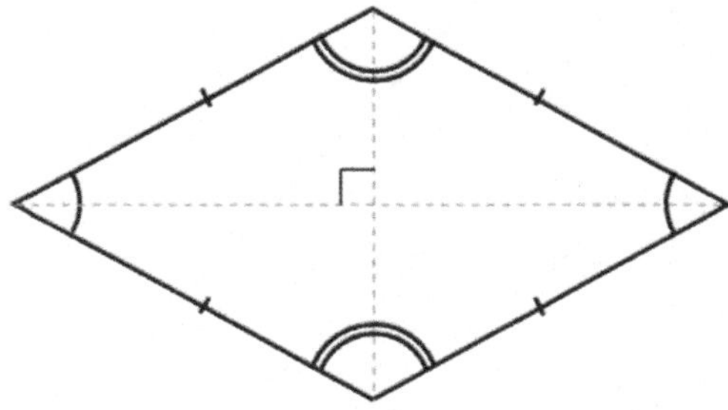

SQUARE

A **square** is a quadrilateral with four right angles and four congruent sides. Squares satisfy the criteria of all other types of quadrilaterals. The diagonals of a square are congruent and perpendicular to each other. Squares have four lines of symmetry (through each pair of opposing midpoints and along each of the diagonals) as well as 90° rotational symmetry about the midpoint.

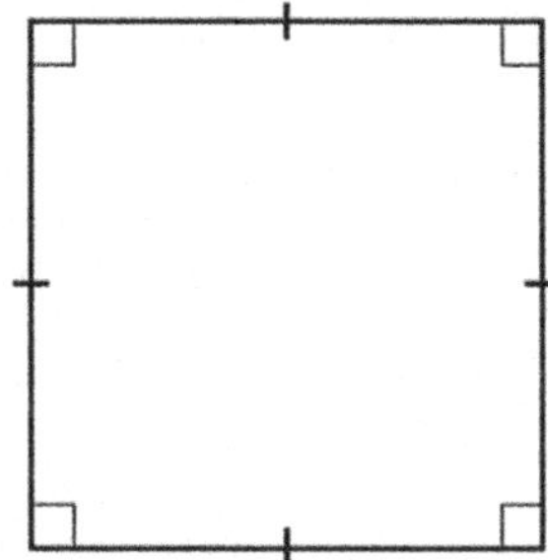

The **area of a square** is found by using the formula $A = s^2$, where s is the length of one side. The **perimeter of a square** is found by using the formula $P = 4s$, where s is the length of one side. Because all four sides are equal in a square, it is faster to multiply the length of one side by 4 than to add the same number four times. You could use the formulas for rectangles and get the same answer.

Review Video: Area and Perimeter of Rectangles and Squares
Visit mometrix.com/academy and enter code: 428109

Hierarchy of Quadrilaterals

The hierarchy of quadrilaterals is as follows:

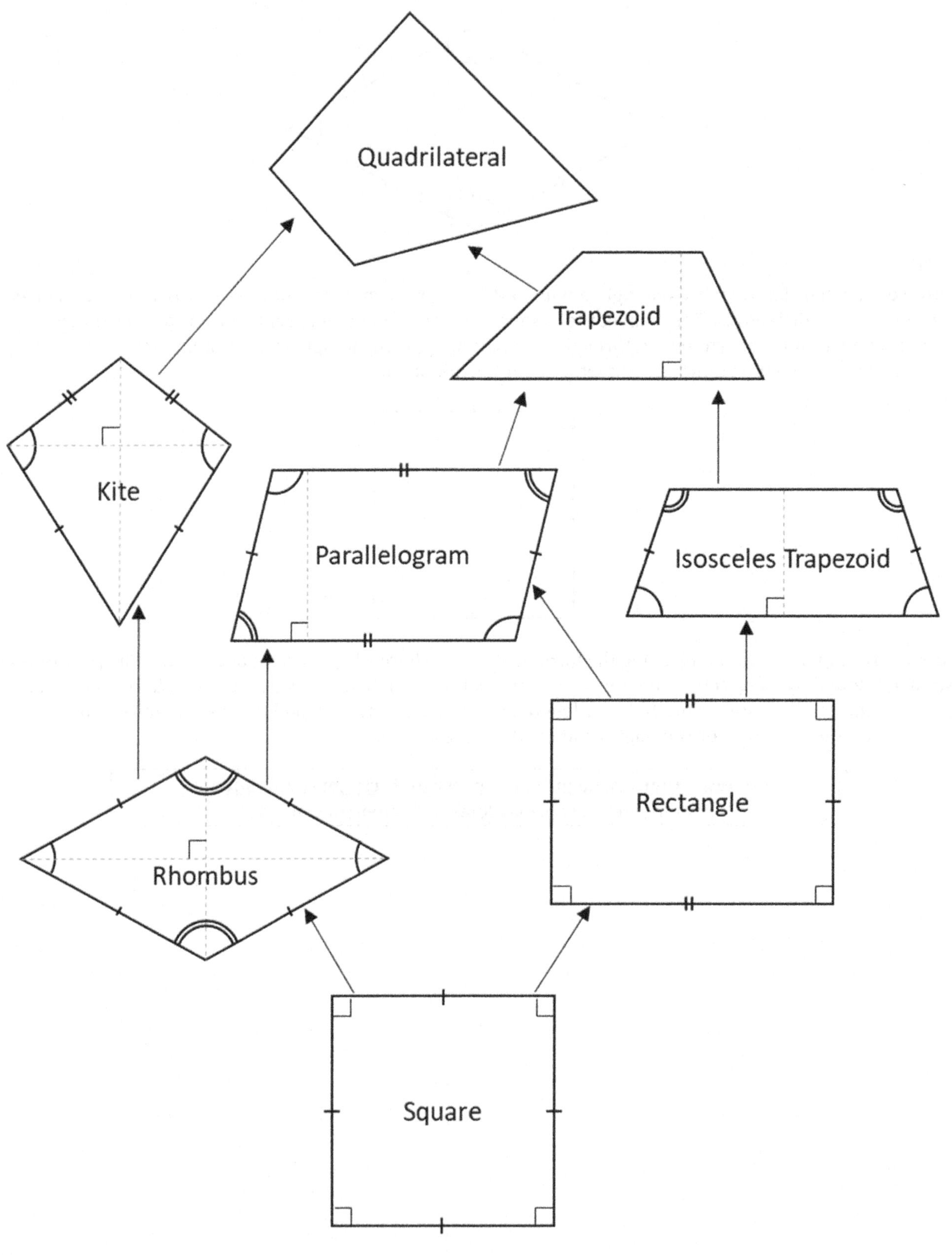

CIRCLES

The **center** of a circle is the single point from which every point on the circle is **equidistant**. The **radius** is a line segment that joins the center of the circle and any one point on the circle. All radii of a circle are equal. Circles that have the same center but not the same length of radii are **concentric**. The **diameter** is a line segment that passes through the center of the circle and has both endpoints on the circle. The length of the diameter is exactly twice the length of the radius. Point O in the diagram below is the center of the circle, segments $\overline{OX}$, $\overline{OY}$, and $\overline{OZ}$ are radii; and segment $\overline{XZ}$ is a diameter.

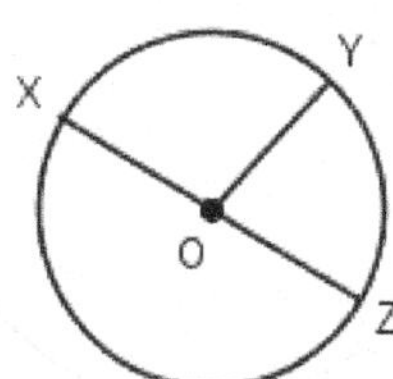

> **Review Video: Points of a Circle**
> Visit mometrix.com/academy and enter code: 420746
>
> **Review Video: Diameter, Radius, and Circumference**
> Visit mometrix.com/academy and enter code: 448988

The **area of a circle** is found by the formula $A = \pi r^2$, where r is the length of the radius. If the diameter of the circle is given, remember to divide it in half to get the length of the radius before proceeding.

The **circumference** of a circle is found by the formula $C = 2\pi r$, where r is the radius. Again, remember to convert the diameter if you are given that measure rather than the radius.

> **Review Video: Area and Circumference of a Circle**
> Visit mometrix.com/academy and enter code: 243015

INSCRIBED AND CIRCUMSCRIBED FIGURES

These terms can both be used to describe a given arrangement of figures, depending on perspective. If each of the vertices of figure A lie on figure B, then it can be said that figure A is **inscribed** in figure B, but it can also be said that figure B is **circumscribed** about figure A. The following table and examples help to illustrate the concept. Note that the figures cannot both be circles, as they would be completely overlapping and neither would be inscribed or circumscribed.

Given	Description	Equivalent Description	Figures
Each of the sides of a pentagon is tangent to a circle	The circle is inscribed in the pentagon	The pentagon is circumscribed about the circle	
Each of the vertices of a pentagon lie on a circle	The pentagon is inscribed in the circle	The circle is circumscribed about the pentagon	

3D SHAPES

SOLIDS

The **surface area of a solid object** is the area of all sides or exterior surfaces. For objects such as prisms and pyramids, a further distinction is made between base surface area (B) and lateral surface area (LA). For a prism, the total surface area (SA) is $SA = LA + 2B$. For a pyramid or cone, the total surface area is $SA = LA + B$.

The **surface area of a sphere** can be found by the formula $A = 4\pi r^2$, where r is the radius. The volume is given by the formula $V = \frac{4}{3}\pi r^3$, where r is the radius. Both quantities are generally given in terms of π.

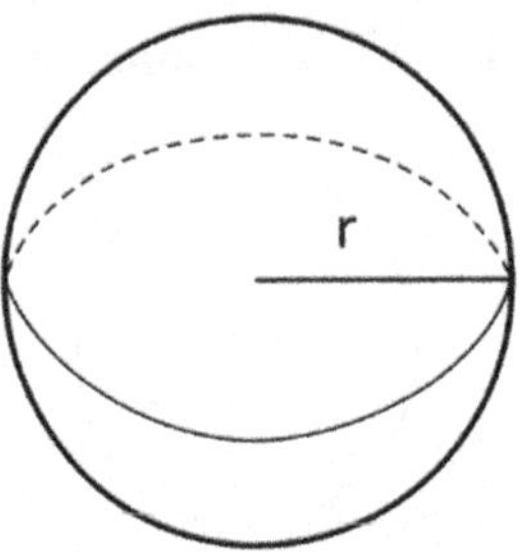

Review Video: Volume and Surface Area of a Sphere
Visit mometrix.com/academy and enter code: 786928

Review Video: How to Calculate the Volume of 3D Objects
Visit mometrix.com/academy and enter code: 163343

The **volume of any prism** is found by the formula $V = Bh$, where B is the area of the base, and h is the height (perpendicular distance between the bases). The surface area of any prism is the sum of the areas of both bases and all sides. It can be calculated as $SA = 2B + Ph$, where P is the perimeter of the base.

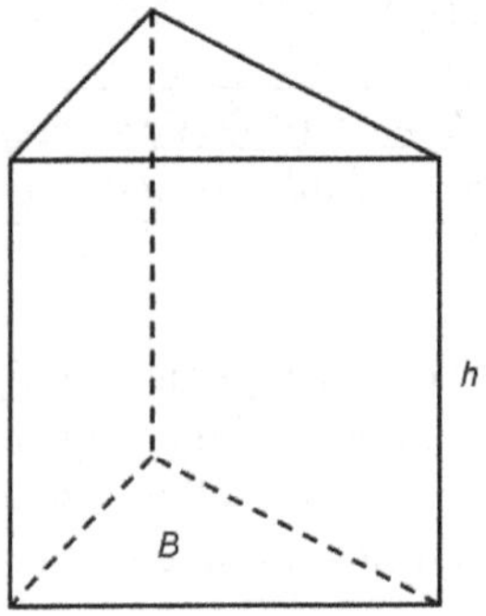

Review Video: Volume and Surface Area of a Prism
Visit mometrix.com/academy and enter code: 420158

For a **rectangular prism**, the volume can be found by the formula $V = lwh$, where V is the volume, l is the length, w is the width, and h is the height. The surface area can be calculated as $SA = 2lw + 2hl + 2wh$ or $SA = 2(lw + hl + wh)$.

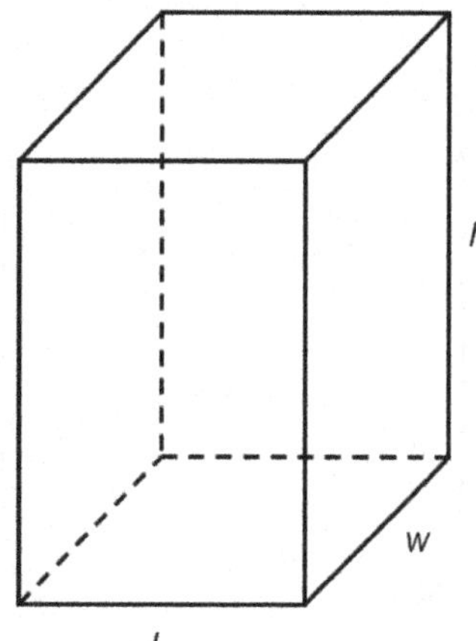

Review Video: Volume and Surface Area of a Rectangular Prism
Visit mometrix.com/academy and enter code: 282814

The **volume of a cube** can be found by the formula $V = s^3$, where s is the length of a side. The surface area of a cube is calculated as $SA = 6s^2$, where SA is the total surface area and s is the length of a side. These formulas are the same as the ones used for the volume and surface area of a rectangular prism, but simplified since all three quantities (length, width, and height) are the same.

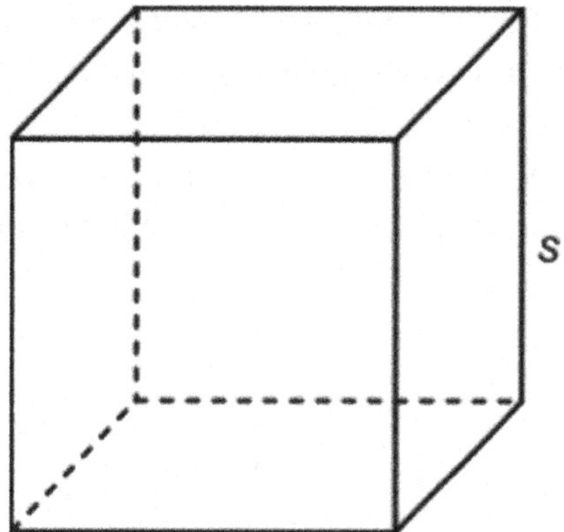

Review Video: Volume and Surface Area of a Cube
Visit mometrix.com/academy and enter code: 664455

The **volume of a cylinder** can be calculated by the formula $V = \pi r^2 h$, where r is the radius, and h is the height. The surface area of a cylinder can be found by the formula $SA = 2\pi r^2 + 2\pi rh$. The first term is the base area multiplied by two, and the second term is the perimeter of the base multiplied by the height.

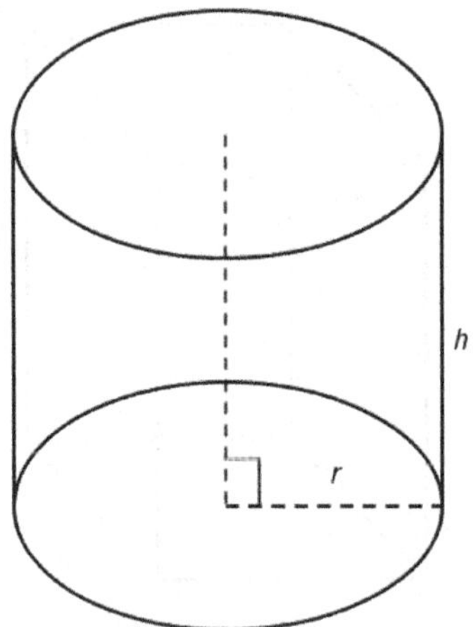

Review Video: Volume and Surface Area of a Right Circular Cylinder
Visit mometrix.com/academy and enter code: 226463

The **volume of a pyramid** is found by the formula $V = \frac{1}{3}Bh$, where B is the area of the base, and h is the height (perpendicular distance from the vertex to the base). Notice this formula is the same as $\frac{1}{3}$ times the volume of a prism. Like a prism, the base of a pyramid can be any shape.

Finding the **surface area of a pyramid** is not as simple as the other shapes we've looked at thus far. If the pyramid is a right pyramid, meaning the base is a regular polygon and the vertex is directly over the center of that polygon, the surface area can be calculated as $SA = B + \frac{1}{2}Ph_s$, where P is the perimeter of the base, and h_s is the slant height (distance from the vertex to the midpoint of one side of the base). If the pyramid is irregular, the area of each triangle side must be calculated individually and then summed, along with the base.

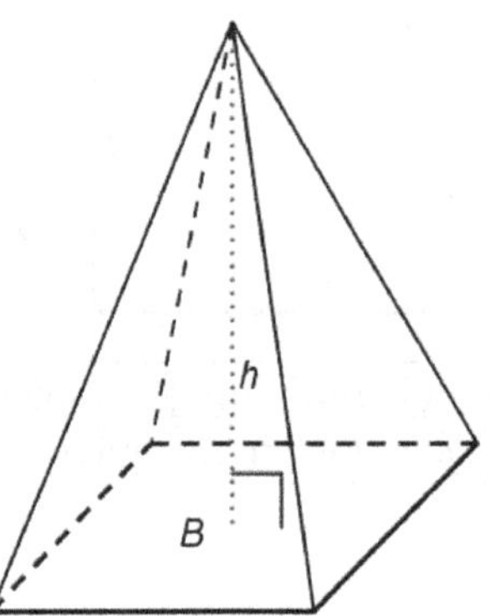

Review Video: Volume and Surface Area of a Pyramid
Visit mometrix.com/academy and enter code: 621932

The **volume of a cone** is found by the formula $V = \frac{1}{3}\pi r^2 h$, where r is the radius, and h is the height. Notice this is the same as $\frac{1}{3}$ times the volume of a cylinder. The surface area can be calculated as $SA = \pi r^2 + \pi rs$, where s

is the slant height. The slant height can be calculated using the Pythagorean theorem to be $\sqrt{r^2 + h^2}$, so the surface area formula can also be written as $SA = \pi r^2 + \pi r\sqrt{r^2 + h^2}$.

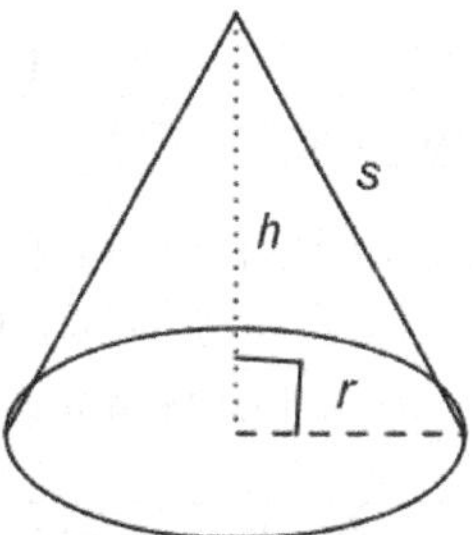

Review Video: Volume and Surface Area of a Right Circular Cone
Visit mometrix.com/academy and enter code: 573574

Basic Algebra

Linear Expressions

Terms and Coefficients

Mathematical expressions consist of a combination of one or more values arranged in terms that are added together. As such, an expression could be just a single number, including zero. A **variable term** is the product of a real number, also called a **coefficient**, and one or more variables, each of which may be raised to an exponent. Expressions may also include numbers without a variable, called **constants** or **constant terms**. The expression $6s^2$, for example, is a single term where the coefficient is the real number 6 and the variable term is s^2. Note that if a term is written as simply a variable to some exponent, like t^2, then the coefficient is 1, because $t^2 = 1t^2$.

Linear Expressions

A **single variable linear expression** is the sum of a single variable term, where the variable has no exponent, and a constant, which may be zero. For instance, the expression $2w + 7$ has $2w$ as the variable term and 7 as the constant term. It is important to realize that terms are separated by addition or subtraction. Since an expression is a sum of terms, expressions such as $5x - 3$ can be written as $5x + (-3)$ to emphasize that the constant term is negative. A real-world example of a single variable linear expression is the perimeter of a square, four times the side length, often expressed: $4s$.

In general, a **linear expression** is the sum of any number of variable terms so long as none of the variables have an exponent. For example, $3m + 8n - \frac{1}{4}p + 5.5q - 1$ is a linear expression, but $3y^3$ is not. In the same way, the expression for the perimeter of a general triangle, the sum of the side lengths $(a + b + c)$ is considered to be linear, but the expression for the area of a square, the side length squared (s^2) is not.

Slope

On a graph with two points, (x_1, y_1) and (x_2, y_2), the **slope** is found with the formula $m = \frac{y_2 - y_1}{x_2 - x_1}$; where $x_1 \neq x_2$ and m stands for slope. If the value of the slope is **positive**, the line has an *upward direction* from left to right. If the value of the slope is **negative**, the line has a *downward direction* from left to right. Consider the following example:

A new book goes on sale in bookstores and online stores. In the first month, 5,000 copies of the book are sold. Over time, the book continues to grow in popularity. The data for the number of copies sold is in the table below.

# of Months on Sale	1	2	3	4	5
# of Copies Sold (In Thousands)	5	10	15	20	25

So, the number of copies that are sold and the time that the book is on sale is a proportional relationship. In this example, an equation can be used to show the data: $y = 5x$, where x is the number of months that the book is on sale. Also, y is the number of copies sold. So, the slope of the corresponding line is $\frac{\text{rise}}{\text{run}} = \frac{5}{1} = 5$.

Review Video: Finding the Slope of a Line
Visit mometrix.com/academy and enter code: 766664

Linear Equations

Equations that can be written as $ax + b = 0$, where $a \neq 0$, are referred to as **one variable linear equations**. A solution to such an equation is called a **root**. In the case where we have the equation $5x + 10 = 0$, if we solve for x we get a solution of $x = -2$. In other words, the root of the equation is -2. This is found by first subtracting 10 from both sides, which gives $5x = -10$. Next, simply divide both sides by the coefficient of the variable, in this case 5, to get $x = -2$. This can be checked by plugging -2 back into the original equation $(5)(-2) + 10 = -10 + 10 = 0$.

The **solution set** is the set of all solutions of an equation. In our example, the solution set would simply be -2. If there were more solutions (there usually are in multivariable equations) then they would also be included in the solution set. When an equation has no true solutions, it is referred to as an **empty set**. Equations with identical solution sets are **equivalent equations**. An **identity** is a term whose value or determinant is equal to 1.

Linear equations can be written many ways. Below is a list of some forms linear equations can take:

- **Standard Form**: $Ax + By = C$; the slope is $\frac{-A}{B}$ and the y-intercept is $\frac{C}{B}$
- **Slope Intercept Form**: $y = mx + b$, where m is the slope and b is the y-intercept
- **Point-Slope Form**: $y - y_1 = m(x - x_1)$, where m is the slope and (x_1, y_1) is a point on the line
- **Two-Point Form**: $\frac{y-y_1}{x-x_1} = \frac{y_2-y_1}{x_2-x_1}$, where (x_1, y_1) and (x_2, y_2) are two points on the given line
- **Intercept Form**: $\frac{x}{x_1} + \frac{y}{y_1} = 1$, where $(x_1, 0)$ is the point at which a line intersects the x-axis, and $(0, y_1)$ is the point at which the same line intersects the y-axis

Review Video: Slope-Intercept and Point-Slope Forms
Visit mometrix.com/academy and enter code: 113216

Review Video: Linear Equations Basics
Visit mometrix.com/academy and enter code: 793005

Solving Equations

Solving One-Variable Linear Equations

Multiply all terms by the lowest common denominator to eliminate any fractions. Look for addition or subtraction to undo so you can isolate the variable on one side of the equal sign. Divide both sides by the coefficient of the variable. When you have a value for the variable, substitute this value into the original equation to make sure you have a true equation. Consider the following example:

Kim's savings are represented by the table below. Represent her savings, using an equation.

X (Months)	Y (Total Savings)
2	$1,300
5	$2,050
9	$3,050
11	$3,550
16	$4,800

The table shows a function with a constant rate of change, or slope, of 250. Given the points on the table, the slopes can be calculated as $\frac{(2{,}050-1300)}{(5-2)}$, $\frac{(3{,}050-2{,}050)}{(9-5)}$, $\frac{(3{,}550-3{,}050)}{(11-9)}$, and $\frac{(4{,}800-3{,}550)}{(16-11)}$, each of which equals 250. Thus, the table shows a constant rate of change, indicating a linear function. The slope-intercept form of a linear equation is written as $y = mx + b$, where m represents the slope and b represents the y-intercept. Substituting the slope into this form gives $y = 250x + b$. Substituting corresponding x- and y-values from any point into this equation will give the y-intercept, or b. Using the point, (2, 1,300), gives $1{,}300 = 250(2) + b$, which simplifies as $b = 800$. Thus, her savings may be represented by the equation, $y = 250x + 800$.

RULES FOR MANIPULATING EQUATIONS

LIKE TERMS

Like terms are terms in an equation that have the same variable, regardless of whether or not they also have the same coefficient. This includes terms that *lack* a variable; all constants (i.e., numbers without variables) are considered like terms. If the equation involves terms with a variable raised to different powers, the like terms are those that have the variable raised to the same power.

For example, consider the equation $x^2 + 3x + 2 = 2x^2 + x - 7 + 2x$. In this equation, 2 and -7 are like terms; they are both constants. $3x$, x, and $2x$ are like terms, they all include the variable x raised to the first power. x^2 and $2x^2$ are like terms, they both include the variable x, raised to the second power. $2x$ and $2x^2$ are not like terms; although they both involve the variable x, the variable is not raised to the same power in both terms. The fact that they have the same coefficient, 2, is not relevant.

Review Video: Rules for Manipulating Equations
Visit mometrix.com/academy and enter code: 838871

CARRYING OUT THE SAME OPERATION ON BOTH SIDES OF AN EQUATION

When solving an equation, the general procedure is to carry out a series of operations on both sides of an equation, choosing operations that will tend to simplify the equation when doing so. The reason why the same operation must be carried out on both sides of the equation is because that leaves the meaning of the equation unchanged, and yields a result that is equivalent to the original equation. This would not be the case if we carried out an operation on one side of an equation and not the other. Consider what an equation means: it is a statement that two values or expressions are equal. If we carry out the same operation on both sides of the equation—add 3 to both sides, for example—then the two sides of the equation are changed in the same way, and so remain equal. If we do that to only one side of the equation—add 3 to one side but not the other—then that wouldn't be true; if we change one side of the equation but not the other then the two sides are no longer equal.

Advantage of Combining Like Terms

Combining like terms refers to adding or subtracting like terms—terms with the same variable—and therefore reducing sets of like terms to a single term. The main advantage of doing this is that it simplifies the equation. Often, combining like terms can be done as the first step in solving an equation, though it can also be done later, such as after distributing terms in a product.

For example, consider the equation $2(x + 3) + 3(2 + x + 3) = -4$. The 2 and the 3 in the second set of parentheses are like terms, and we can combine them, yielding $2(x + 3) + 3(x + 5) = -4$. Now we can carry out the multiplications implied by the parentheses, distributing the outer 2 and 3 accordingly: $2x + 6 + 3x + 15 = -4$. The $2x$ and the $3x$ are like terms, and we can add them together: $5x + 6 + 15 = -4$. Now, the constants 6, 15, and -4 are also like terms, and we can combine them as well: subtracting 6 and 15 from both sides of the equation, we get $5x = -4 - 6 - 15$, or $5x = -25$, which simplifies further to $x = -5$.

> **Review Video: Solving Equations by Combining Like Terms**
> Visit mometrix.com/academy and enter code: 668506

Canceling Terms on Opposite Sides of an Equation

Two terms on opposite sides of an equation can be canceled if and only if they *exactly* match each other. They must have the same variable raised to the same power and the same coefficient. For example, in the equation $3x + 2x^2 + 6 = 2x^2 - 6$, $2x^2$ appears on both sides of the equation and can be canceled, leaving $3x + 6 = -6$. The 6 on each side of the equation *cannot* be canceled, because it is added on one side of the equation and subtracted on the other. While they cannot be canceled, however, the 6 and -6 are like terms and can be combined, yielding $3x = -12$, which simplifies further to $x = -4$.

It's also important to note that the terms to be canceled must be independent terms and cannot be part of a larger term. For example, consider the equation $2(x + 6) = 3(x + 4) + 1$. We cannot cancel the x's, because even though they match each other they are part of the larger terms $2(x + 6)$ and $3(x + 4)$. We must first distribute the 2 and 3, yielding $2x + 12 = 3x + 12 + 1$. Now we see that the terms with the x's do not match, but the 12s do, and can be canceled, leaving $2x = 3x + 1$, which simplifies to $x = -1$.

Process for Manipulating Equations

Isolating Variables

To **isolate a variable** means to manipulate the equation so that the variable appears by itself on one side of the equation, and does not appear at all on the other side. Generally, an equation or inequality is considered to be solved once the variable is isolated and the other side of the equation or inequality is simplified as much as possible. In the case of a two-variable equation or inequality, only one variable needs to be isolated; it will not usually be possible to simultaneously isolate both variables.

For a linear equation—an equation in which the variable only appears raised to the first power—isolating a variable can be done by first moving all the terms with the variable to one side of the equation and all other terms to the other side. (*Moving* a term really means adding the inverse of the term to both sides; when a term is *moved* to the other side of the equation its sign is flipped.) Then combine like terms on each side. Finally, divide both sides by the coefficient of the variable, if applicable. The steps need not necessarily be done in this order, but this order will always work.

> **Review Video: Solving One-Step Equations**
> Visit mometrix.com/academy and enter code: 777004

Equations with More Than One Solution

Some types of non-linear equations, such as equations involving squares of variables, may have more than one solution. For example, the equation $x^2 = 4$ has two solutions: 2 and -2. Equations with absolute values can also have multiple solutions: $|x| = 1$ has the solutions $x = 1$ and $x = -1$.

It is also possible for a linear equation to have more than one solution, but only if the equation is true regardless of the value of the variable. In this case, the equation is considered to have infinitely many solutions, because any possible value of the variable is a solution. We know a linear equation has infinitely many solutions if when we combine like terms the variables cancel, leaving a true statement. For example, consider the equation $2(3x + 5) = x + 5(x + 2)$. Distributing, we get $6x + 10 = x + 5x + 10$; combining like terms gives $6x + 10 = 6x + 10$, and the $6x$-terms cancel to leave $10 = 10$. This is clearly true, so the original equation is true for any value of x. We could also have canceled the 10s leaving $0 = 0$, but again this is clearly true—in general if both sides of the equation match exactly, it has infinitely many solutions.

Equations with No Solution

Some types of non-linear equations, such as equations involving squares of variables, may have no solution. For example, the equation $x^2 = -2$ has no solutions in the real numbers, because the square of any real number must be positive. Similarly, $|x| = -1$ has no solution, because the absolute value of a number is always positive.

It is also possible for an equation to have no solution even if does not involve any powers greater than one, absolute values, or other special functions. For example, the equation $2(x + 3) + x = 3x$ has no solution. We can see that if we try to solve it: first we distribute, leaving $2x + 6 + x = 3x$. But now if we try to combine all the terms with the variable, we find that they cancel: we have $3x$ on the left and $3x$ on the right, canceling to leave us with $6 = 0$. This is clearly false. In general, whenever the variable terms in an equation cancel leaving different constants on both sides, it means that the equation has no solution. (If we are left with the *same* constant on both sides, the equation has infinitely many solutions instead.)

Mathematical Reasoning

Features of Equations That Require Special Treatment

Linear Equations

A linear equation is an equation in which variables only appear by themselves: not multiplied together, not with exponents other than one, and not inside absolute value signs or any other functions. For example, the equation $x + 1 - 3x = 5 - x$ is a linear equation; while x appears multiple times, it never appears with an exponent other than one, or inside any function. The two-variable equation $2x - 3y = 5 + 2x$ is also a linear equation. In contrast, the equation $x^2 - 5 = 3x$ is *not* a linear equation, because it involves the term x^2. $\sqrt{x} = 5$ is not a linear equation, because it involves a square root. $(x - 1)^2 = 4$ is not a linear equation because even though there's no exponent on the x directly, it appears as part of an expression that is squared. The two-variable equation $x + xy - y = 5$ is not a linear equation because it includes the term xy, where two variables are multiplied together.

Linear equations can always be solved (or shown to have no solution) by combining like terms and performing simple operations on both sides of the equation. Some non-linear equations can be solved by similar methods, but others may require more advanced methods of solution, if they can be solved analytically at all.

Solving Equations Involving Roots

In an equation involving roots, the first step is to isolate the term with the root, if possible, and then raise both sides of the equation to the appropriate power to eliminate it. Consider an example equation, $2\sqrt{x + 1} - 1 = 3$. In this case, begin by adding 1 to both sides, yielding $2\sqrt{x + 1} = 4$, and then dividing both sides by 2, yielding $\sqrt{x + 1} = 2$. Now square both sides, yielding $x + 1 = 4$. Finally, subtracting 1 from both sides yields $x = 3$.

Squaring both sides of an equation may, however, yield a spurious solution—a solution to the squared equation that is *not* a solution of the original equation. It's therefore necessary to plug the solution back into the original equation to make sure it works. In this case, it does: $2\sqrt{3 + 1} - 1 = 2\sqrt{4} - 1 = 2(2) - 1 = 4 - 1 = 3$.

The same procedure applies for other roots as well. For example, given the equation $3 + \sqrt[3]{2x} = 5$, we can first subtract 3 from both sides, yielding $\sqrt[3]{2x} = 2$ and isolating the root. Raising both sides to the third power yields $2x = 2^3$; i.e., $2x = 8$. We can now divide both sides by 2 to get $x = 4$.

Review Video: Solving Equations Involving Roots
Visit mometrix.com/academy and enter code: 297670

Solving Equations with Exponents

To solve an equation involving an exponent, the first step is to isolate the variable with the exponent. We can then take the appropriate root of both sides to eliminate the exponent. For instance, for the equation $2x^3 + 17 = 5x^3 - 7$, we can subtract $5x^3$ from both sides to get $-3x^3 + 17 = -7$, and then subtract 17 from both sides to get $-3x^3 = -24$. Finally, we can divide both sides by -3 to get $x^3 = 8$. Finally, we can take the cube root of both sides to get $x = \sqrt[3]{8} = 2$.

One important but often overlooked point is that equations with an exponent greater than 1 may have more than one answer. The solution to $x^2 = 9$ isn't simply $x = 3$; it's $x = \pm 3$ (that is, $x = 3$ or $x = -3$). For a slightly more complicated example, consider the equation $(x-1)^2 - 1 = 3$. Adding 1 to both sides yields $(x-1)^2 = 4$; taking the square root of both sides yields $x - 1 = 2$. We can then add 1 to both sides to get $x = 3$. However, there's a second solution. We also have the possibility that $x - 1 = -2$, in which case $x = -1$. Both $x = 3$ and $x = -1$ are valid solutions, as can be verified by substituting them both into the original equation.

Review Video: Solving Equations with Exponents
Visit mometrix.com/academy and enter code: 514557

Solving Equations with Absolute Values

When solving an equation with an absolute value, the first step is to isolate the absolute value term. We then consider two possibilities: when the expression inside the absolute value is positive or when it is negative. In the former case, the expression in the absolute value equals the expression on the other side of the equation; in the latter, it equals the additive inverse of that expression—the expression times negative one. We consider each case separately and finally check for spurious solutions.

For instance, consider solving $|2x - 1| + x = 5$ for x. We can first isolate the absolute value by moving the x to the other side: $|2x - 1| = -x + 5$. Now, we have two possibilities. First, that $2x - 1$ is positive, and hence $2x - 1 = -x + 5$. Rearranging and combining like terms yields $3x = 6$, and hence $x = 2$. The other possibility is that $2x - 1$ is negative, and hence $2x - 1 = -(-x + 5) = x - 5$. In this case, rearranging and combining like terms yields $x = -4$. Substituting $x = 2$ and $x = -4$ back into the original equation, we see that they are both valid solutions.

Note that the absolute value of a sum or difference applies to the sum or difference as a whole, not to the individual terms; in general, $|2x - 1|$ is not equal to $|2x + 1|$ or to $|2x| - 1$.

Spurious Solutions

A **spurious solution** may arise when we square both sides of an equation as a step in solving it or under certain other operations on the equation. It is a solution to the squared or otherwise modified equation that is *not* a solution of the original equation. To identify a spurious solution, it's useful when you solve an equation involving roots or absolute values to plug the solution back into the original equation to make sure it's valid.

Choosing Which Variable to Isolate in Two-Variable Equations

Similar to methods for a one-variable equation, solving a two-variable equation involves isolating a variable: manipulating the equation so that a variable appears by itself on one side of the equation, and not at all on the other side. However, in a two-variable equation, you will usually only be able to isolate one of the variables; the other variable may appear on the other side along with constant terms, or with exponents or other functions.

Often one variable will be much more easily isolated than the other, and therefore that's the variable you should choose. If one variable appears with various exponents, and the other is only raised to the first power, the latter variable is the one to isolate: given the equation $a^2 + 2b = a^3 + b + 3$, the b only appears to the first power, whereas a appears squared and cubed, so b is the variable that can be solved for: combining like terms and isolating the b on the left side of the equation, we get $b = a^3 - a^2 + 3$. If both variables are equally easy to isolate, then it's best to isolate the dependent variable, if one is defined; if the two variables are x and y, the convention is that y is the dependent variable.

> **Review Video: Solving Equations with Variables on Both Sides**
> Visit mometrix.com/academy and enter code: 402497

Cross Multiplication

Finding an Unknown in Equivalent Expressions

It is often necessary to apply information given about a rate or proportion to a new scenario. For example, if you know that Jedha can run a marathon (26.2 miles) in 3 hours, how long would it take her to run 10 miles at the same pace? Start by setting up equivalent expressions:

$$\frac{26.2 \text{ mi}}{3 \text{ hr}} = \frac{10 \text{ mi}}{x \text{ hr}}$$

Now, cross multiply and solve for x:

$$\begin{aligned} 26.2x &= 30 \\ x &= \frac{30}{26.2} = \frac{15}{13.1} \\ x &\approx 1.15 \text{ hrs } or \text{ 1 hr 9 min} \end{aligned}$$

So, at this pace, Jedha could run 10 miles in about 1.15 hours or about 1 hour and 9 minutes.

> **Review Video: Cross Multiplying Fractions**
> Visit mometrix.com/academy and enter code: 893904

Graphing Equations

Graphical Solutions to Equations

When equations are shown graphically, they are usually shown on a **Cartesian coordinate plane**. The Cartesian coordinate plane consists of two number lines placed perpendicular to each other and intersecting at the zero point, also known as the origin. The horizontal number line is known as the x-axis, with positive values to the right of the origin, and negative values to the left of the origin. The vertical number line is known as the y-axis, with positive values above the origin, and negative values below the origin. Any point on the plane can be identified by an ordered pair in the form (x, y), called coordinates. The x-value of the coordinate is called the abscissa, and the y-value of the coordinate is called the ordinate. The two number lines divide the plane into **four quadrants**: I, II, III, and IV.

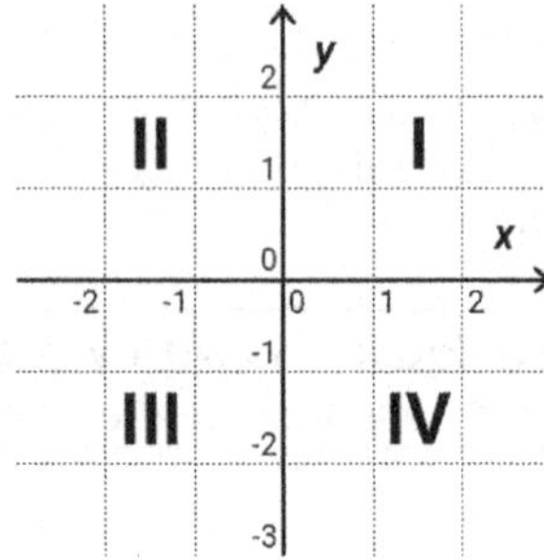

Note that in quadrant I $x > 0$ and $y > 0$, in quadrant II $x < 0$ and $y > 0$, in quadrant III $x < 0$ and $y < 0$, and in quadrant IV $x > 0$ and $y < 0$.

Recall that if the value of the slope of a line is positive, the line slopes upward from left to right. If the value of the slope is negative, the line slopes downward from left to right. If the y-coordinates are the same for two points on a line, the slope is 0 and the line is a **horizontal line**. If the x-coordinates are the same for two points on a line, there is no slope and the line is a **vertical line**. Two or more lines that have equivalent slopes are **parallel lines**. **Perpendicular lines** have slopes that are negative reciprocals of each other, such as $\frac{a}{b}$ and $\frac{-b}{a}$.

Review Video: Cartesian Coordinate Plane and Graphing
Visit mometrix.com/academy and enter code: 115173

Graphing Equations in Two Variables

One way of graphing an equation in two variables is to plot enough points to get an idea for its shape and then draw the appropriate curve through those points. A point can be plotted by substituting in a value for one variable and solving for the other. If the equation is linear, we only need two points and can then draw a straight line between them.

For example, consider the equation $y = 2x - 1$. This is a linear equation—both variables only appear raised to the first power—so we only need two points. When $x = 0, y = 2(0) - 1 = -1$. When $x = 2, y = 2(2) - 1 = 3$. We can therefore choose the points $(0, -1)$ and $(2, 3)$, and draw a line between them:

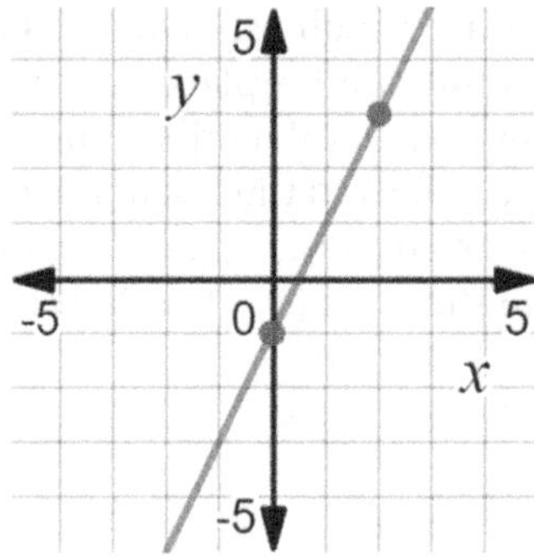

Inequalities

Working with Inequalities

Commonly in algebra and other upper-level fields of math you find yourself working with mathematical expressions that do not equal each other. The statement comparing such expressions with symbols such as < (less than) or > (greater than) is called an *inequality*. An example of an inequality is $7x > 5$. To solve for x, simply divide both sides by 7 and the solution is shown to be $x > \frac{5}{7}$. Graphs of the solution set of inequalities are represented on a number line. Open circles are used to show that an expression approaches a number but is never quite equal to that number.

Review Video: Solving Multi-Step Inequalities
Visit mometrix.com/academy and enter code: 347842

Review Video: Solving Inequalities Using All 4 Basic Operations
Visit mometrix.com/academy and enter code: 401111

Conditional inequalities are those with certain values for the variable that will make the condition true and other values for the variable where the condition will be false. **Absolute inequalities** can have any real number as the value for the variable to make the condition true, while there is no real number value for the variable that will make the condition false. Solving inequalities is done by following the same rules for solving equations with the exception that when multiplying or dividing by a negative number the direction of the inequality sign must be flipped or reversed. **Double inequalities** are situations where two inequality statements apply to the same variable expression. Example: $-c < ax + b < c$.

Review Video: Conditional and Absolute Inequalities
Visit mometrix.com/academy and enter code: 980164

Determining Solutions to Inequalities

To determine whether a coordinate is a solution of an inequality, you can substitute the values of the coordinate into the inequality, simplify, and check whether the resulting statement holds true. For instance, to determine whether $(-2,4)$ is a solution of the inequality $y \geq -2x + 3$, substitute the values into the inequality, $4 \geq -2(-2) + 3$. Simplify the right side of the inequality and the result is $4 \geq 7$, which is a false statement. Therefore, the coordinate is not a solution of the inequality. You can also use this method to determine which part of the graph of an inequality is shaded. The graph of $y \geq -2x + 3$ includes the solid line $y = -2x + 3$ and, since it excludes the point $(-2,4)$ to the left of the line, it is shaded to the right of the line.

Review Video: Graphing Linear Inequalities
Visit mometrix.com/academy and enter code: 439421

Flipping Inequality Signs

When given an inequality, we can always turn the entire inequality around, swapping the two sides of the inequality and changing the inequality sign. For instance, $x + 2 > 2x - 3$ is equivalent to $2x - 3 < x + 2$. Aside from that, normally the inequality does not change if we carry out the same operation on both sides of the inequality. There is, however, one principal exception: if we *multiply* or *divide* both sides of the inequality by a *negative number*, the inequality is flipped. For example, if we take the inequality $-2x < 6$ and divide both sides by -2, the inequality flips and we are left with $x > -3$. This *only* applies to multiplication and division, and only with negative numbers. Multiplying or dividing both sides by a positive number, or adding or subtracting any number regardless of sign, does not flip the inequality. Another special case that flips the inequality sign is when reciprocals are used. For instance, $3 > 2$ but the relation of the reciprocals is $\frac{1}{2} < \frac{1}{3}$.

Compound Inequalities

A **compound inequality** is an equality that consists of two inequalities combined with *and* or *or*. The two components of a proper compound inequality must be of opposite type: that is, one must be greater than (or greater than or equal to), the other less than (or less than or equal to). For instance, "$x + 1 < 2$ or $x + 1 > 3$" is a compound inequality, as is "$2x \geq 4$ and $2x \leq 6$." An *and* inequality can be written more compactly by having one inequality on each side of the common part: "$2x \geq 1$ and $2x \leq 6$," can also be written as $1 \leq 2x \leq 6$.

In order for the compound inequality to be meaningful, the two parts of an *and* inequality must overlap; otherwise, no numbers satisfy the inequality. On the other hand, if the two parts of an *or* inequality overlap, then *all* numbers satisfy the inequality and as such the inequality is usually not meaningful.

Solving a compound inequality requires solving each part separately. For example, given the compound inequality "$x + 1 < 2$ or $x + 1 > 3$," the first inequality, $x + 1 < 2$, reduces to $x < 1$, and the second part, $x + 1 > 3$, reduces to $x > 2$, so the whole compound inequality can be written as "$x < 1$ or $x > 2$." Similarly, $1 \leq 2x \leq 6$ can be solved by dividing each term by 2, yielding $\frac{1}{2} \leq x \leq 3$.

Review Video: Compound Inequalities
Visit mometrix.com/academy and enter code: 786318

Solving Inequalities Involving Absolute Values

To solve an inequality involving an absolute value, first isolate the term with the absolute value. Then proceed to treat the two cases separately as with an absolute value equation, but flipping the inequality in the case where the expression in the absolute value is negative (since that essentially involves multiplying both sides by −1.) The two cases are then combined into a compound inequality; if the absolute value is on the greater side of the inequality, then it is an *or* compound inequality, if on the lesser side, then it's an *and*.

Consider the inequality $2 + |x - 1| \geq 3$. We can isolate the absolute value term by subtracting 2 from both sides: $|x - 1| \geq 1$. Now, we're left with the two cases $x - 1 \geq 1$ or $x - 1 \leq -1$: note that in the latter, negative case, the inequality is flipped. $x - 1 \geq 1$ reduces to $x \geq 2$, and $x - 1 \leq -1$ reduces to $x \leq 0$. Since in the inequality $|x - 1| \geq 1$ the absolute value is on the greater side, the two cases combine into an *or* compound inequality, so the final, solved inequality is "$x \leq 0$ or $x \geq 2$."

Review Video: Solving Absolute Value Inequalities
Visit mometrix.com/academy and enter code: 997008

Solving Inequalities Involving Square Roots

Solving an inequality with a square root involves two parts. First, we solve the inequality as if it were an equation, isolating the square root and then squaring both sides of the equation. Second, we restrict the solution to the set of values of x for which the value inside the square root sign is non-negative.

For example, in the inequality, $\sqrt{x - 2} + 1 < 5$, we can isolate the square root by subtracting 1 from both sides, yielding $\sqrt{x - 2} < 4$. Squaring both sides of the inequality yields $x - 2 < 16$, so $x < 18$. Since we can't take the square root of a negative number, we also require the part inside the square root to be non-negative. In this case, that means $x - 2 \geq 0$. Adding 2 to both sides of the inequality yields $x \geq 2$. Our final answer is a compound inequality combining the two simple inequalities: $x \geq 2$ and $x < 18$, or $2 \leq x < 18$.

Note that we only get a compound inequality if the two simple inequalities are in opposite directions; otherwise, we take the one that is more restrictive.

The same technique can be used for other even roots, such as fourth roots. It is *not*, however, used for cube roots or other odd roots—negative numbers *do* have cube roots, so the condition that the quantity inside the root sign cannot be negative does not apply.

Review Video: Solving Inequalities Involving Square Roots
Visit mometrix.com/academy and enter code: 800288

Special Circumstances

Sometimes an inequality involving an absolute value or an even exponent is true for all values of x, and we don't need to do any further work to solve it. This is true if the inequality, once the absolute value or exponent term is isolated, says that term is greater than a negative number (or greater than or equal to zero). Since an absolute value or a number raised to an even exponent is *always* non-negative, this inequality is always true.

Graphical Solutions to Inequalities

Graphing Simple Inequalities

To graph a simple inequality, we first mark on the number line the value that signifies the end point of the inequality. If the inequality is strict (involves a less than or greater than), we use a hollow circle; if it is not strict (less than or equal to or greater than or equal to), we use a solid circle. We then fill in the part of the number line that satisfies the inequality: to the left of the marked point for less than (or less than or equal to), to the right for greater than (or greater than or equal to).

For example, we would graph the inequality $x < 5$ by putting a hollow circle at 5 and filling in the part of the line to the left:

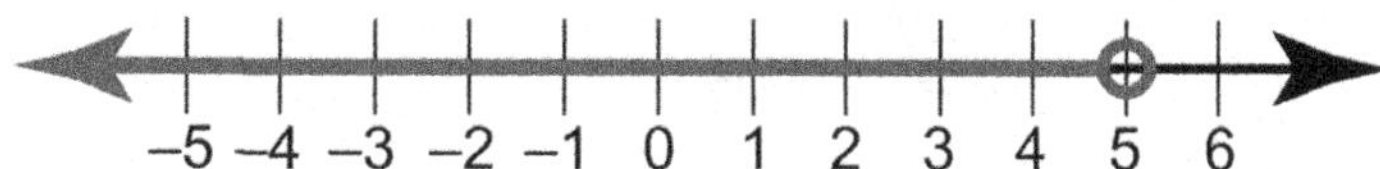

Graphing Compound Inequalities

To graph a compound inequality, we fill in both parts of the inequality for an *or* inequality, or the overlap between them for an *and* inequality. More specifically, we start by plotting the endpoints of each inequality on the number line. For an *or* inequality, we then fill in the appropriate side of the line for each inequality. Typically, the two component inequalities do not overlap, which means the shaded part is *outside* the two points. For an *and* inequality, we instead fill in the part of the line that meets both inequalities.

For the inequality "$x \leq -3$ or $x > 4$," we first put a solid circle at -3 and a hollow circle at 4. We then fill the parts of the line *outside* these circles:

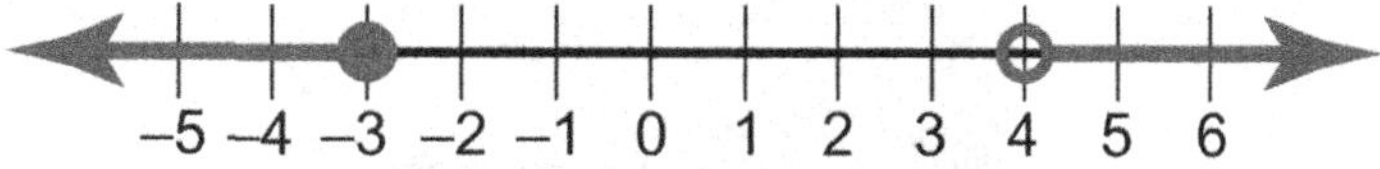

Graphing Inequalities Including Absolute Values

An inequality with an absolute value can be converted to a compound inequality. To graph the inequality, first convert it to a compound inequality, and then graph that normally. If the absolute value is on the greater side of the inequality, we end up with an *or* inequality; we plot the endpoints of the inequality on the number line and fill in the part of the line *outside* those points. If the absolute value is on the smaller side of the inequality, we end up with an *and* inequality; we plot the endpoints of the inequality on the number line and fill in the part of the line *between* those points.

For example, the inequality $|x + 1| \geq 4$ can be rewritten as $x \geq 3$ or $x \leq -5$. We place solid circles at the points 3 and -5 and fill in the part of the line *outside* them:

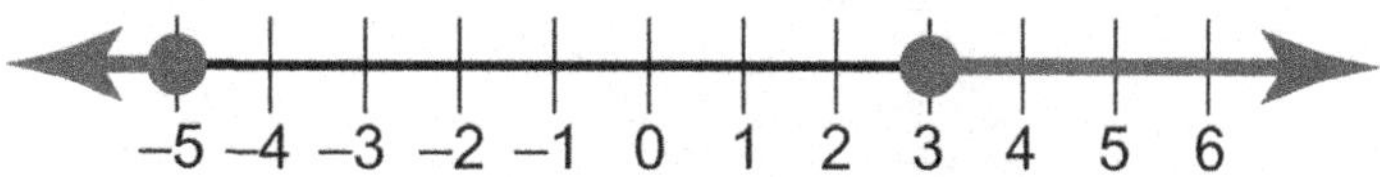

Graphing Inequalities in Two Variables

To graph an inequality in two variables, we first graph the border of the inequality. This means graphing the equation that we get if we replace the inequality sign with an equals sign. If the inequality is strict ($>$ or $<$), we graph the border with a dashed or dotted line; if it is not strict ($\geq$ or $\leq$), we use a solid line. We can then test any point not on the border to see if it satisfies the inequality. If it does, we shade in that side of the border; if not, we shade in the other side. As an example, consider $y > 2x + 2$. To graph this inequality, we first graph the border, $y = 2x + 2$. Since it is a strict inequality, we use a dashed line. Then, we choose a test point. This can be any point not on the border; in this case, we will choose the origin, (0,0). (This makes the calculation easy and is generally a good choice unless the border passes through the origin.) Putting this into the original inequality, we get $0 > 2(0) + 2$, i.e., $0 > 2$. This is *not* true, so we shade in the side of the border that does *not* include the point (0,0):

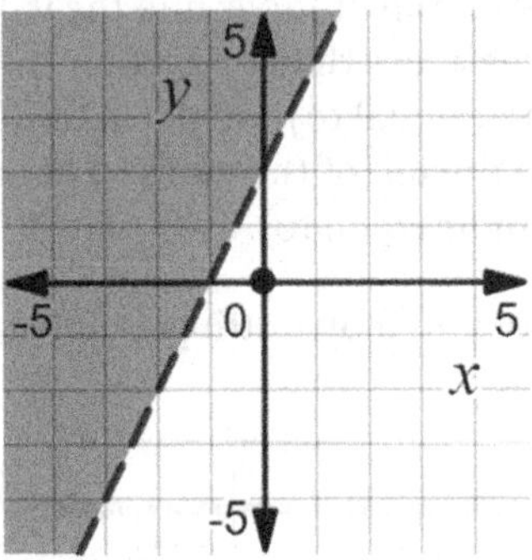

Graphing Compound Inequalities in Two Variables

One way to graph a compound inequality in two variables is to first graph each of the component inequalities. For an *and* inequality, we then shade in only the parts where the two graphs overlap; for an *or* inequality, we shade in any region that pertains to either of the individual inequalities.

Consider the graph of "$y \geq x - 1$ and $y \leq -x$":

We first shade in the individual inequalities:

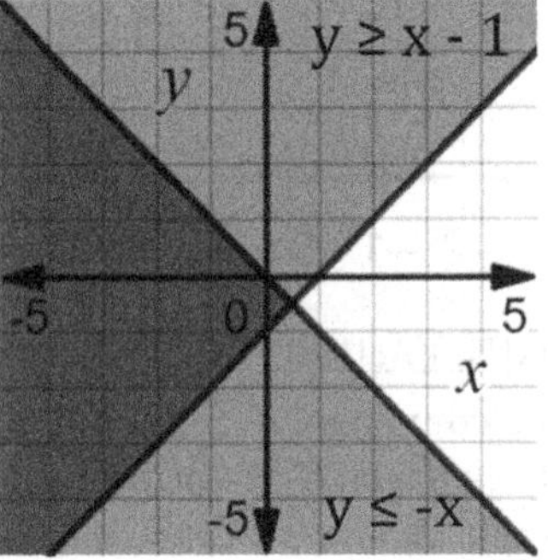

Now, since the compound inequality has an *and*, we only leave shaded the overlap—the part that pertains to *both* inequalities:

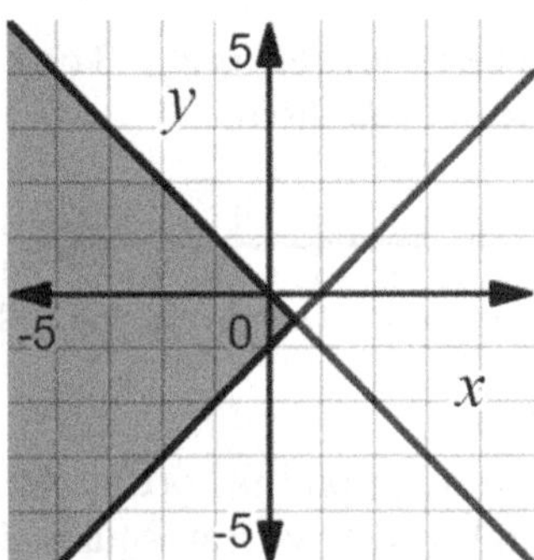

If instead the inequality had been "$y \geq x - 1$ or $y \leq -x$," our final graph would involve the *total* shaded area:

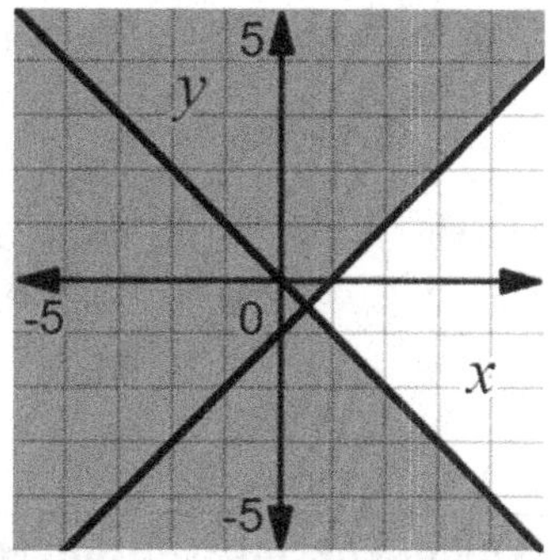

Review Video: Graphing Solutions to Inequalities
Visit mometrix.com/academy and enter code: 391281

SYSTEMS OF EQUATIONS

SOLVING SYSTEMS OF EQUATIONS

A **system of equations** is a set of simultaneous equations that all use the same variables. A solution to a system of equations must be true for each equation in the system. **Consistent systems** are those with at least one solution. **Inconsistent systems** are systems of equations that have no solution.

Review Video: Solving Systems of Linear Equations
Visit mometrix.com/academy and enter code: 746745

SUBSTITUTION

To solve a system of linear equations by **substitution**, start with the easier equation and solve for one of the variables. Express this variable in terms of the other variable. Substitute this expression in the other equation and solve for the other variable. The solution should be expressed in the form (x, y). Substitute the values into both of the original equations to check your answer. Consider the following system of equations:

$$x + 6y = 15$$
$$3x - 12y = 18$$

Solving the first equation for x: $x = 15 - 6y$

Substitute this value in place of x in the second equation, and solve for y:

$$\begin{aligned} 3(15 - 6y) - 12y &= 18 \\ 45 - 18y - 12y &= 18 \\ 30y &= 27 \\ y &= \frac{27}{30} = \frac{9}{10} = 0.9 \end{aligned}$$

Plug this value for y back into the first equation to solve for x:

$$x = 15 - 6(0.9) = 15 - 5.4 = 9.6$$

Check both equations if you have time:

$$\begin{aligned} 9.6 + 6(0.9) &= 15 \\ 9.6 + 5.4 &= 15 \\ 15 &= 15 \end{aligned} \qquad \begin{aligned} 3(9.6) - 12(0.9) &= 18 \\ 28.8 - 10.8 &= 18 \\ 18 &= 18 \end{aligned}$$

Therefore, the solution is (9.6,0.9).

Review Video: The Substitution Method
Visit mometrix.com/academy and enter code: 565151

Review Video: Substitution and Elimination
Visit mometrix.com/academy and enter code: 958611

ELIMINATION

To solve a system of equations using **elimination**, begin by rewriting both equations in standard form $Ax + By = C$. Check to see if the coefficients of one pair of like variables add to zero. If not, multiply one or both of the equations by a non-zero number to make one set of like variables add to zero. Add the two equations to solve for one of the variables. Substitute this value into one of the original equations to solve for the other variable. Check your work by substituting into the other equation. Now, let's look at solving the following system using the elimination method:

$$\begin{aligned} 5x + 6y &= 4 \\ x + 2y &= 4 \end{aligned}$$

If we multiply the second equation by -3, we can eliminate the y-terms:

$$\begin{aligned} 5x + 6y &= 4 \\ -3x - 6y &= -12 \end{aligned}$$

Add the equations together and solve for x:

$$\begin{aligned} 2x &= -8 \\ x &= \frac{-8}{2} = -4 \end{aligned}$$

Plug the value for x back in to either of the original equations and solve for y:

$$\begin{aligned} -4 + 2y &= 4 \\ y &= \frac{4 + 4}{2} = 4 \end{aligned}$$

Check both equations if you have time:

$$\begin{aligned} 5(-4) + 6(4) &= 4 \\ -20 + 24 &= 4 \\ 4 &= 4 \end{aligned} \qquad \begin{aligned} -4 + 2(4) &= 4 \\ -4 + 8 &= 4 \\ 4 &= 4 \end{aligned}$$

Therefore, the solution is $(-4,4)$.

Review Video: The Elimination Method
Visit mometrix.com/academy and enter code: 449121

GRAPHICALLY

To solve a system of linear equations **graphically**, plot both equations on the same graph. The solution of the equations is the point where both lines cross. If the lines do not cross (are parallel), then there is **no solution**.

For example, consider the following system of equations:

$$y = 2x + 7$$
$$y = -x + 1$$

Since these equations are given in slope-intercept form, they are easy to graph; the y-intercepts of the lines are $(0,7)$ and $(0,1)$. The respective slopes are 2 and –1, thus the graphs look like this:

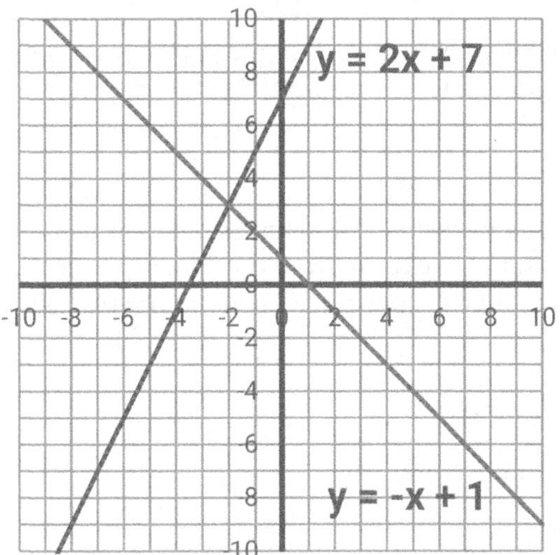

The two lines intersect at the point $(-2,3)$, thus this is the solution to the system of equations.

Solving a system graphically is generally only practical if both coordinates of the solution are integers; otherwise the intersection will lie between gridlines on the graph and the coordinates will be difficult or impossible to determine exactly. It also helps if, as in this example, the equations are in slope-intercept form or some other form that makes them easy to graph. Otherwise, another method of solution (by substitution or elimination) is likely to be more useful.

Review Video: Solving Systems by Graphing
Visit mometrix.com/academy and enter code: 634812

SOLVING SYSTEMS OF EQUATIONS USING THE TRACE FEATURE

Using the trace feature on a calculator requires that you rewrite each equation, isolating the y-variable on one side of the equal sign. Enter both equations in the graphing calculator and plot the graphs simultaneously. Use the trace cursor to find where the two lines cross. Use the zoom feature if necessary to obtain more accurate results. Always check your answer by substituting into the original equations. The trace method is likely to be less accurate than other methods due to the resolution of graphing calculators but is a useful tool to provide an approximate answer.

Mathematical Reasoning

POLYNOMIALS

MONOMIALS AND POLYNOMIALS

A **monomial** is a single constant, variable, or product of constants and variables, such as 7, x, $2x$, or x^3y. There will never be addition or subtraction symbols in a monomial. Like monomials have like variables, but they may have different coefficients. **Polynomials** are algebraic expressions that use addition and subtraction to combine two or more monomials. Two terms make a **binomial**, three terms make a **trinomial**, etc. The **degree of a monomial** is the sum of the exponents of the variables. The **degree of a polynomial** is the highest degree of any individual term.

Review Video: Polynomials
Visit mometrix.com/academy and enter code: 305005

SIMPLIFYING POLYNOMIALS

Simplifying polynomials requires combining like terms. The like terms in a polynomial expression are those that have the same variable raised to the same power. It is often helpful to connect the like terms with arrows or lines in order to separate them from the other monomials. Once you have determined the like terms, you can rearrange the polynomial by placing them together. Remember to include the sign that is in front of each term. Once the like terms are placed together, you can apply each operation and simplify. When adding and subtracting polynomials, only add and subtract the **coefficient**, or the number part; the variable and exponent stay the same.

ADD POLYNOMIALS

To add polynomials, you need to add like terms. These terms have the same variable part. An example is $4x^2$ and $3x^2$ have x^2 terms. To find the sum of like terms, find the sum of the coefficients. Then, keep the same variable part. You can use the distributive property to distribute the plus sign to each term of the polynomial. For example:

$$(4x^2 - 5x + 7) + (3x^2 + 2x + 1) =$$
$$(4x^2 - 5x + 7) + 3x^2 + 2x + 1 =$$
$$(4x^2 + 3x^2) + (-5x + 2x) + (7 + 1) =$$
$$7x^2 - 3x + 8$$

SUBTRACT POLYNOMIALS

To subtract polynomials, you need to subtract like terms. To find the difference of like terms, find the difference of the coefficients. Then, keep the same variable part. You can use the distributive property to distribute the minus sign to each term of the polynomial. For example:

$$(-2x^2 - x + 5) - (3x^2 - 4x + 1) =$$
$$(-2x^2 - x + 5) - 3x^2 + 4x - 1 =$$
$$(-2x^2 - 3x^2) + (-x + 4x) + (5 - 1) =$$
$$-5x^2 + 3x + 4$$

Review Video: Adding and Subtracting Polynomials
Visit mometrix.com/academy and enter code: 124088

MULTIPLYING POLYNOMIALS

In general, multiplying polynomials is done by multiplying each term in one polynomial by each term in the other and adding the results. In the specific case for multiplying binomials, there is a useful acronym, FOIL, that can help you make sure to cover each combination of terms. The **FOIL method** for $(Ax + By)(Cx + Dy)$ would be:

F	Multiply the *first* terms of each binomial	$(\overbrace{Ax}^{first} + By)(\overbrace{Cx}^{first} + Dy)$	ACx^2
O	Multiply the *outer* terms	$(\overbrace{Ax}^{outer} + By)(Cx + \overbrace{Dy}^{outer})$	$ADxy$
I	Multiply the *inner* terms	$(Ax + \overbrace{By}^{inner})(\overbrace{Cx}^{inner} + Dy)$	$BCxy$
L	Multiply the *last* terms of each binomial	$(Ax + \overbrace{By}^{last})(Cx + \overbrace{Dy}^{last})$	BDy^2

Then, add up the result of each and combine like terms: $ACx^2 + (AD + BC)xy + BDy^2$.

For example, using the FOIL method on binomials $(x + 2)$ and $(x - 3)$:

$$\begin{aligned}
\text{First:}\quad & (\boxed{x} + 2)(\boxed{x} + (-3)) \rightarrow (x)(x) = x^2 \\
\text{Outer:}\quad & (\boxed{x} + 2)(x + \boxed{(-3)}) \rightarrow (x)(-3) = -3x \\
\text{Inner:}\quad & (x + \boxed{2})(\boxed{x} + (-3)) \rightarrow (2)(x) = 2x \\
\text{Last:}\quad & (x + \boxed{2})(x + \boxed{(-3)}) \rightarrow (2)(-3) = -6
\end{aligned}$$

This results in: $(x^2) + (-3x) + (2x) + (-6)$

Combine like terms: $x^2 + (-3 + 2)x + (-6) = x^2 - x - 6$

Review Video: Multiplying Terms Using the FOIL Method
Visit mometrix.com/academy and enter code: 854792

Dividing Polynomials

Use long division to divide a polynomial by either a monomial or another polynomial of equal or lesser degree.

When **dividing by a monomial**, divide each term of the polynomial by the monomial.

When **dividing by a polynomial**, begin by arranging the terms of each polynomial in order of one variable. You may arrange in ascending or descending order, but be consistent with both polynomials. To get the first term of the quotient, divide the first term of the dividend by the first term of the divisor. Multiply the first term of the quotient by the entire divisor and subtract that product from the dividend. Repeat for the second and successive terms until you either get a remainder of zero or a remainder whose degree is less than the degree of the divisor. If the quotient has a remainder, write the answer as a mixed expression in the form:

$$\text{quotient} + \frac{\text{remainder}}{\text{divisor}}$$

For example, we can evaluate the following expression in the same way as long division:

$$\frac{x^3 - 3x^2 - 2x + 5}{x - 5}$$

$$\begin{array}{r|rrrr}
 & x^2 & +2x & +8 & \\
\hline
x - 5 & x^3 & -3x^2 & -2x & +5 \\
 & -\underline{(x^3 - 5x^2)} & & & \\
 & & 2x^2 & -2x & \\
 & & \underline{-(2x^2 - 10x)} & & \\
 & & & 8x & +5 \\
 & & & \underline{-(8x - 40)} & \\
 & & & & 45
\end{array}$$

$$\frac{x^3 - 3x^2 - 2x + 5}{x - 5} = x^2 + 2x + 8 + \frac{45}{x - 5}$$

When **factoring** a polynomial, first check for a common monomial factor, that is, look to see if each coefficient has a common factor or if each term has an x in it. If the factor is a trinomial but not a perfect trinomial square, look for a factorable form, such as one of these:

$$x^2 + (a + b)x + ab = (x + a)(x + b)$$
$$(ac)x^2 + (ad + bc)x + bd = (ax + b)(cx + d)$$

For factors with four terms, look for groups to factor. Once you have found the factors, write the original polynomial as the product of all the factors. Make sure all of the polynomial factors are prime. Monomial factors may be *prime* or *composite*. Check your work by multiplying the factors to make sure you get the original polynomial.

Below are patterns of some special products to remember to help make factoring easier:

- Perfect trinomial squares: $x^2 + 2xy + y^2 = (x + y)^2$ or $x^2 - 2xy + y^2 = (x - y)^2$
- Difference between two squares: $x^2 - y^2 = (x + y)(x - y)$
- Sum of two cubes: $x^3 + y^3 = (x + y)(x^2 - xy + y^2)$
    - Note: the second factor is *not* the same as a perfect trinomial square, so do not try to factor it further.
- Difference between two cubes: $x^3 - y^3 = (x - y)(x^2 + xy + y^2)$
    - Again, the second factor is *not* the same as a perfect trinomial square.
- Perfect cubes: $x^3 + 3x^2y + 3xy^2 + y^3 = (x + y)^3$ and $x^3 - 3x^2y + 3xy^2 - y^3 = (x - y)^3$

Rational Expressions

Rational expressions are fractions with polynomials in both the numerator and the denominator; the value of the polynomial in the denominator cannot be equal to zero. Be sure to keep track of values that make the denominator of the original expression zero as the final result inherits the same restrictions. For example, a denominator of $x - 3$ indicates that the expression is not defined when $x = 3$ and, as such, regardless of any operations done to the expression, it remains undefined there.

To **add or subtract** rational expressions, first find the common denominator, then rewrite each fraction as an equivalent fraction with the common denominator. Finally, add or subtract the numerators to get the numerator of the answer, and keep the common denominator as the denominator of the answer.

When **multiplying** rational expressions, factor each polynomial and cancel like factors (a factor which appears in both the numerator and the denominator). Then, multiply all remaining factors in the numerator to get the numerator of the product, and multiply the remaining factors in the denominator to get the denominator of the product. Remember: cancel entire factors, not individual terms.

To **divide** rational expressions, take the reciprocal of the divisor (the rational expression you are dividing by) and multiply by the dividend.

Review Video: Rational Expressions
Visit mometrix.com/academy and enter code: 415183

SIMPLIFYING RATIONAL EXPRESSIONS

To simplify a rational expression, factor the numerator and denominator completely. Factors that are the same and appear in the numerator and denominator have a ratio of 1. For example, look at the following expression:

$$\frac{x-1}{1-x^2}$$

The denominator, $(1-x^2)$, is a difference of squares. It can be factored as $(1-x)(1+x)$. The factor $1-x$ and the numerator $x-1$ are opposites and have a ratio of -1. Rewrite the numerator as $-1(1-x)$. So, the rational expression can be simplified as follows:

$$\frac{x-1}{1-x^2}=\frac{-1(1-x)}{(1-x)(1+x)}=\frac{-1}{1+x}$$

Note that since the original expression is only defined for $x \neq \{-1, 1\}$, the simplified expression has the same restrictions.

Review Video: Reducing Rational Expressions
Visit mometrix.com/academy and enter code: 788868

QUADRATICS

SOLVING QUADRATIC EQUATIONS

Quadratic equations are a special set of trinomials of the form $y = ax^2 + bx + c$ that occur commonly in math and real-world applications. The **roots** of a quadratic equation are the solutions that satisfy the equation when $y = 0$; in other words, where the graph touches the x-axis. There are several ways to determine these solutions including using the quadratic formula, factoring, completing the square, and graphing the function.

Review Video: Quadratic Equations Overview
Visit mometrix.com/academy and enter code: 476276

Review Video: Solutions of a Quadratic Equation on a Graph
Visit mometrix.com/academy and enter code: 328231

QUADRATIC FORMULA

The **quadratic formula** is used to solve quadratic equations when other methods are more difficult. To use the quadratic formula to solve a quadratic equation, begin by rewriting the equation in standard form $ax^2 + bx +$

$c = 0$, where a, b, and c are coefficients. Once you have identified the values of the coefficients, substitute those values into the quadratic formula

$$x = \frac{-b \pm \sqrt{b^2 - 4ac}}{2a}$$

Evaluate the equation and simplify the expression. Again, check each root by substituting into the original equation. In the quadratic formula, the portion of the formula under the radical $(b^2 - 4ac)$ is called the **discriminant**. If the discriminant is zero, there is only one root: $-\frac{b}{2a}$. If the discriminant is positive, there are two different real roots. If the discriminant is negative, there are no real roots; you will instead find complex roots. Often these solutions don't make sense in context and are ignored.

> **Review Video: Using the Quadratic Formula**
> Visit mometrix.com/academy and enter code: 163102

Factoring

To solve a quadratic equation by factoring, begin by rewriting the equation in standard form, $x^2 + bx + c = 0$. Remember that the goal of factoring is to find numbers f and g such that $(x + f)(x + g) = x^2 + (f + g)x + fg$, in other words $(f + g) = b$ and $fg = c$. This can be a really useful method when b and c are integers. Determine the factors of c and look for pairs that could sum to b.

For example, consider finding the roots of $x^2 + 6x - 16 = 0$. The factors of -16 include, -4 and 4, -8 and 2, -2 and 8, -1 and 16, and 1 and -16. The factors that sum to 6 are -2 and 8. Write these factors as the product of two binomials, $0 = (x - 2)(x + 8)$. Finally, since these binomials multiply together to equal zero, set them each equal to zero and solve each for x. This results in $x - 2 = 0$, which simplifies to $x = 2$ and $x + 8 = 0$, which simplifies to $x = -8$. Therefore, the roots of the equation are 2 and -8.

> **Review Video: Factoring Quadratic Equations**
> Visit mometrix.com/academy and enter code: 336566

Completing the Square

One way to find the roots of a quadratic equation is to find a way to manipulate it such that it follows the form of a perfect square $(x^2 + 2px + p^2)$ by adding and subtracting a constant. This process is called **completing the square**. In other words, if you are given a quadratic that is not a perfect square, $x^2 + bx + c = 0$, you can find a constant d that could be added in to make it a perfect square:

$$x^2 + bx + c + (d - d) = 0; \ \{\text{Let } b = 2p \text{ and } c + d = p^2\}$$

then:

$$x^2 + 2px + p^2 - d = 0 \text{ and } d = \frac{b^2}{4} - c$$

Once you have completed the square you can find the roots of the resulting equation:

$$\begin{aligned} x^2 + 2px + p^2 - d &= 0 \\ (x + p)^2 &= d \\ x + p &= \pm\sqrt{d} \\ x &= -p \pm \sqrt{d} \end{aligned}$$

It is worth noting that substituting the original expressions into this solution gives the same result as the quadratic formula where $a = 1$:

$$x = -p \pm \sqrt{d} = -\frac{b}{2} \pm \sqrt{\frac{b^2}{4} - c} = -\frac{b}{2} \pm \frac{\sqrt{b^2 - 4c}}{2} = \frac{-b \pm \sqrt{b^2 - 4c}}{2}$$

Completing the square can be seen as arranging block representations of each of the terms to be as close to a square as possible and then filling in the gaps. For example, consider the quadratic expression $x^2 + 6x + 2$:

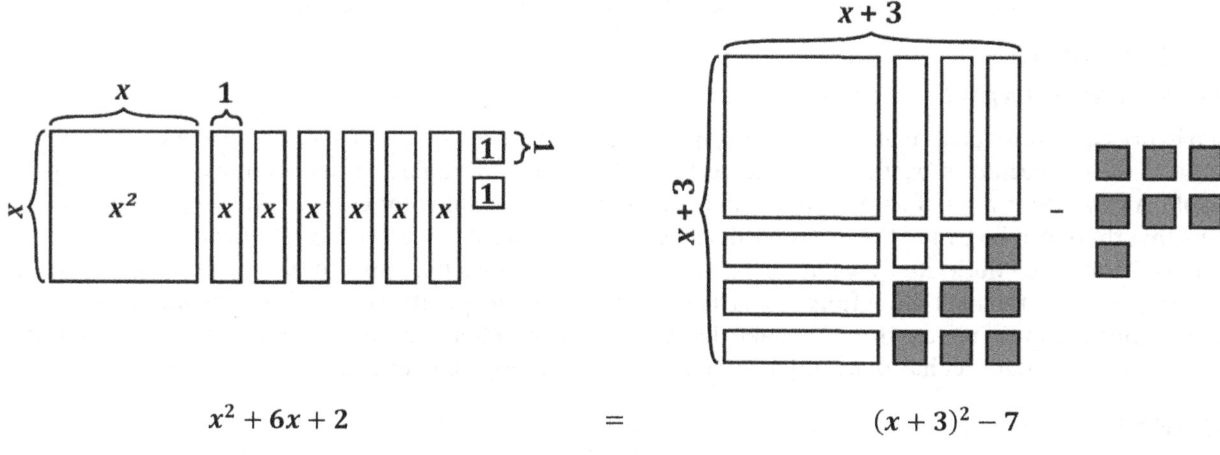

Review Video: Completing the Square
Visit mometrix.com/academy and enter code: 982479

Using Given Roots to Find Quadratic Equation

One way to find the roots of a quadratic equation is to factor the equation and use the **zero product property**, setting each factor of the equation equal to zero to find the corresponding root. We can use this technique in reverse to find an equation given its roots. Each root corresponds to a linear equation which in turn corresponds to a factor of the quadratic equation.

For example, we can find a quadratic equation whose roots are $x = 2$ and $x = -1$. The root $x = 2$ corresponds to the equation $x - 2 = 0$, and the root $x = -1$ corresponds to the equation $x + 1 = 0$.

These two equations correspond to the factors $(x - 2)$ and $(x + 1)$, from which we can derive the equation $(x - 2)(x + 1) = 0$, or $x^2 - x - 2 = 0$.

Any integer multiple of this entire equation will also yield the same roots, as the integer will simply cancel out when the equation is factored. For example, $2x^2 - 2x - 4 = 0$ factors as $2(x - 2)(x + 1) = 0$.

Graphs and Functions

Parabolas

A **parabola** is the set of all points in a plane that are equidistant from a fixed line, called the **directrix**, and a fixed point not on the line, called the **focus**. The **axis** is the line perpendicular to the directrix that passes through the focus.

For parabolas that open up or down, the standard equation is $(x - h)^2 = 4c(y - k)$, where h, c, and k are coefficients. If c is positive, the parabola opens up. If c is negative, the parabola opens down. The vertex is the point (h, k). The directrix is the line having the equation $y = -c + k$, and the focus is the point $(h, c + k)$.

For parabolas that open left or right, the standard equation is $(y - k)^2 = 4c(x - h)$, where k, c, and h are coefficients. If c is positive, the parabola opens to the right. If c is negative, the parabola opens to the left. The vertex is the point (h, k). The directrix is the line having the equation $x = -c + h$, and the focus is the point $(c + h, k)$.

Review Video: Parabolas
Visit mometrix.com/academy and enter code: 129187

Review Video: Vertex of a Parabola
Visit mometrix.com/academy and enter code: 272300

BASIC FUNCTIONS

FUNCTION AND RELATION

When expressing functional relationships, the **variables** x and y are typically used. These values are often written as the **coordinates** (x, y). The x-value is the independent variable and the y-value is the dependent variable. A **relation** is a set of data in which there is not a unique y-value for each x-value in the dataset. This means that there can be two of the same x-values assigned to different y-values. A relation is simply a relationship between the x- and y-values in each coordinate but does not apply to the relationship between the values of x and y in the data set. A **function** is a relation where one quantity depends on the other. For example, the amount of money that you make depends on the number of hours that you work. In a function, each x-value in the data set has one unique y-value because the y-value depends on the x-value.

FUNCTIONS

A function has exactly one value of **output variable** (dependent variable) for each value of the **input variable** (independent variable). The set of all values for the input variable (here assumed to be x) is the domain of the function, and the set of all corresponding values of the output variable (here assumed to be y) is the range of the function. When looking at a graph of an equation, the easiest way to determine if the equation is a function or not is to conduct the vertical line test. If a vertical line drawn through any value of x crosses the graph in more than one place, the equation is not a function.

DETERMINING A FUNCTION

You can determine whether an equation is a **function** by substituting different values into the equation for x. You can display and organize these numbers in a data table. A **data table** contains the values for x and y, which you can also list as coordinates. In order for a function to exist, the table cannot contain any repeating x-values that correspond with different y-values. If each x-coordinate has a unique y-coordinate, the table contains a function. However, there can be repeating y-values that correspond with different x-values. An example of this is when the function contains an exponent. Example: if $x^2 = y$, $2^2 = 4$, and $(-2)^2 = 4$.

Review Video: Definition of a Function
Visit mometrix.com/academy and enter code: 784611

FINDING THE DOMAIN AND RANGE OF A FUNCTION

The **domain** of a function $f(x)$ is the set of all input values for which the function is defined. The **range** of a function $f(x)$ is the set of all possible output values of the function—that is, of every possible value of $f(x)$, for any value of x in the function's domain. For a function expressed in a table, every input-output pair is given explicitly. To find the domain, we just list all the x-values and to find the range, we just list all the values of $f(x)$. Consider the following example:

x	-1	4	2	1	0	3	8	6
$f(x)$	3	0	3	-1	-1	2	4	6

In this case, the domain would be $\{-1, 4, 2, 1, 0, 3, 8, 6\}$ or, putting them in ascending order, $\{-1, 0, 1, 2, 3, 4, 6, 8\}$. (Putting the values in ascending order isn't strictly necessary, but generally makes the set easier to read.) The range would be $\{3, 0, 3, -1, -1, 2, 4, 6\}$. Note that some of these values appear more than once. This is entirely permissible for a function; while each value of x must be matched to a unique value of $f(x)$, the converse is not true. We don't need to list each value more than once, so eliminating duplicates, the range is $\{3, 0, -1, 2, 4, 6\}$, or, putting them in ascending order, $\{-1, 0, 2, 3, 4, 6\}$.

Note that by definition of a function, no input value can be matched to more than one output value. It is good to double-check to make sure that the data given follows this and is therefore actually a function.

> **Review Video: Domain and Range**
> Visit mometrix.com/academy and enter code: 778133
>
> **Review Video: Domain and Range of Quadratic Functions**
> Visit mometrix.com/academy and enter code: 331768

Writing a Function Rule Using a Table

If given a set of data, place the corresponding x- and y-values into a table and analyze the relationship between them. Consider what you can do to each x-value to obtain the corresponding y-value. Try adding or subtracting different numbers to and from x and then try multiplying or dividing different numbers to and from x. If none of these **operations** give you the y-value, try combining the operations. Once you find a rule that works for one pair, make sure to try it with each additional set of ordered pairs in the table. If the same operation or combination of operations satisfies each set of coordinates, then the table contains a function. The rule is then used to write the equation of the function in "$y = f(x)$" form.

Direct and Inverse Variations of Variables

Variables that vary directly are those that either both increase at the same rate or both decrease at the same rate. For example, in the functions $y = kx$ or $y = kx^n$, where k and n are positive, the value of y increases as the value of x increases and decreases as the value of x decreases.

Variables that vary inversely are those where one increases while the other decreases. For example, in the functions $y = \frac{k}{x}$ or $y = \frac{k}{x^n}$ where k and n are positive, the value of y increases as the value of x decreases and decreases as the value of x increases.

In both cases, k is the constant of variation.

Properties of Functions

There are many different ways to classify functions based on their structure or behavior. Important features of functions include:

- **End behavior**: the behavior of the function at extreme values ($f(x)$ as $x \to \pm\infty$)
- ***y*-intercept**: the value of the function at $f(0)$
- **Roots**: the values of x where the function equals zero ($f(x) = 0$)
- **Extrema**: minimum or maximum values of the function or where the function changes direction ($f(x) \geq k$ or $f(x) \leq k$)

CLASSIFICATION OF FUNCTIONS

An **invertible function** is defined as a function, $f(x)$, for which there is another function, $f^{-1}(x)$, such that $f^{-1}(f(x)) = x$. For example, if $f(x) = 3x - 2$ the inverse function, $f^{-1}(x)$, can be found:

$$x = 3(f^{-1}(x)) - 2$$
$$\frac{x+2}{3} = f^{-1}(x)$$

$$f^{-1}(f(x)) = \frac{3x - 2 + 2}{3}$$
$$= \frac{3x}{3}$$
$$= x$$

Note that $f^{-1}(x)$ is a valid function over all values of x.

In a **one-to-one function**, each value of x has exactly one value for y on the coordinate plane (this is the definition of a function) and each value of y has exactly one value for x. While the vertical line test will determine if a graph is that of a function, the horizontal line test will determine if a function is a one-to-one function. If a horizontal line drawn at any value of y intersects the graph in more than one place, the graph is not that of a one-to-one function. Do not make the mistake of using the horizontal line test exclusively in determining if a graph is that of a one-to-one function. A one-to-one function must pass both the vertical line test and the horizontal line test. As such, one-to-one functions are invertible functions.

A **many-to-one function** is a function whereby the relation is a function, but the inverse of the function is not a function. In other words, each element in the domain is mapped to one and only one element in the range. However, one or more elements in the range may be mapped to the same element in the domain. A graph of a many-to-one function would pass the vertical line test, but not the horizontal line test. This is why many-to-one functions are not invertible.

A **monotone function** is a function whose graph either constantly increases or constantly decreases. Examples include the functions $f(x) = x$, $f(x) = -x$, or $f(x) = x^3$.

An **even function** has a graph that is symmetric with respect to the y-axis and satisfies the equation $f(x) = f(-x)$. Examples include the functions $f(x) = x^2$ and $f(x) = ax^n$, where a is any real number and n is a positive even integer.

An **odd function** has a graph that is symmetric with respect to the origin and satisfies the equation $f(x) = -f(-x)$. Examples include the functions $f(x) = x^3$ and $f(x) = ax^n$, where a is any real number and n is a positive odd integer.

Review Video: Even and Odd Functions
Visit mometrix.com/academy and enter code: 278985

Constant functions are given by the equation $f(x) = b$, where b is a real number. There is no independent variable present in the equation, so the function has a constant value for all x. The graph of a constant function is a horizontal line of slope 0 that is positioned b units from the x-axis. If b is positive, the line is above the x-axis; if b is negative, the line is below the x-axis.

Identity functions are identified by the equation $f(x) = x$, where every value of the function is equal to its corresponding value of x. The only zero is the point (0,0). The graph is a line with a slope of 1.

In **linear functions**, the value of the function changes in direct proportion to x. The rate of change, represented by the slope on its graph, is constant throughout. The standard form of a linear equation is $ax + cy = d$, where a, c, and d are real numbers. As a function, this equation is commonly in the form $y = mx + b$ or $f(x) = mx + b$ where $m = -\frac{a}{c}$ and $b = \frac{d}{c}$. This is known as the slope-intercept form, because the coefficients give the slope of the graphed function (m) and its y-intercept (b). Solve the equation $mx + b = 0$ for x to get $x = -\frac{b}{m}$, which is the only zero of the function. The domain and range are both the set of all real numbers.

> **Review Video: Graphing Linear Functions**
> Visit mometrix.com/academy and enter code: 699478

Algebraic functions are those that exclusively use polynomials and roots. These would include polynomial functions, rational functions, square root functions, and all combinations of these functions, such as polynomials as the radicand. These combinations may be joined by addition, subtraction, multiplication, or division, but may not include variables as exponents.

> **Review Video: Common Functions**
> Visit mometrix.com/academy and enter code: 629798

Absolute Value Functions

An **absolute value function** is in the format $f(x) = |ax + b|$. Like other functions, the domain is the set of all real numbers. However, because absolute value indicates positive numbers, the range is limited to positive real numbers. To find the zero of an absolute value function, set the portion inside the absolute value sign equal to zero and solve for x. An absolute value function is also known as a piecewise function because it must be solved in pieces—one for if the value inside the absolute value sign is positive, and one for if the value is negative. The function can be expressed as:

$$f(x) = \begin{cases} ax + b \text{ if } ax + b \geq 0 \\ -(ax + b) \text{ if } ax + b < 0 \end{cases}$$

This will allow for an accurate statement of the range. The graph of an example absolute value function, $f(x) = |2x - 1|$, is below:

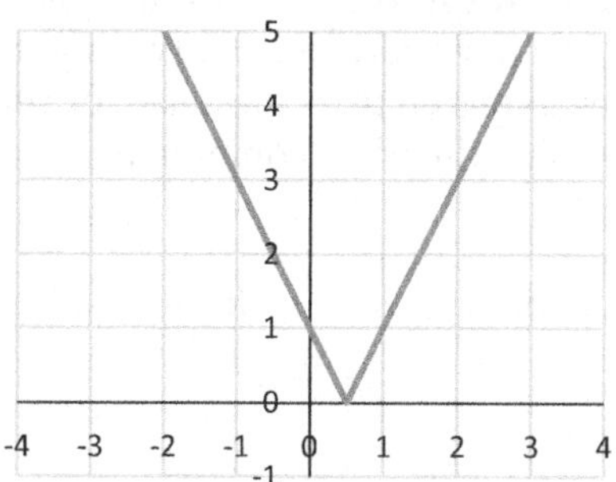

Piecewise Functions

A **piecewise function** is a function that has different definitions on two or more different intervals. The following, for instance, is one example of a piecewise-defined function:

$$f(x) = \begin{cases} x^2, & x < 0 \\ x, & 0 \leq x \leq 2 \\ (x-2)^2, & x > 2 \end{cases}$$

To graph this function, you would simply graph each part separately in the appropriate domain. The final graph would look like this:

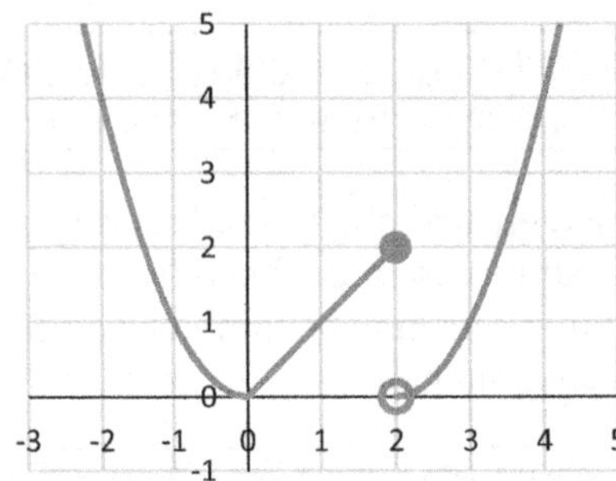

Note the filled and hollow dots at the discontinuity at $x = 2$. This is important to show which side of the graph that point corresponds to. Because $f(x) = x$ on the closed interval $0 \leq x \leq 2$, $f(2) = 2$. The point $(2, 2)$ is therefore marked with a filled circle, and the point (2,0), which is the endpoint of the rightmost $(x - 2)^2$ part of the graph but *not actually part of the function*, is marked with a hollow dot to indicate this.

Review Video: Piecewise Functions
Visit mometrix.com/academy and enter code: 707921

QUADRATIC FUNCTIONS

A **quadratic function** is a function in the form $y = ax^2 + bx + c$, where a does not equal 0. While a linear function forms a line, a quadratic function forms a **parabola**, which is a u-shaped figure that either opens upward or downward. A parabola that opens upward is said to be a **positive quadratic function,** and a parabola that opens downward is said to be a **negative quadratic function**. The shape of a parabola can differ, depending on the values of a, b, and c. All parabolas contain a **vertex**, which is the highest possible point, the **maximum**, or the lowest possible point, the **minimum**. This is the point where the graph begins moving in the opposite direction. A quadratic function can have zero, one, or two solutions, and therefore zero, one, or two x-intercepts. Recall that the x-intercepts are referred to as the zeros, or roots, of a function. A quadratic function will have only one y-intercept. Understanding the basic components of a quadratic function can give you an idea of the shape of its graph.

Example graph of a positive quadratic function, $x^2 + 2x - 3$:

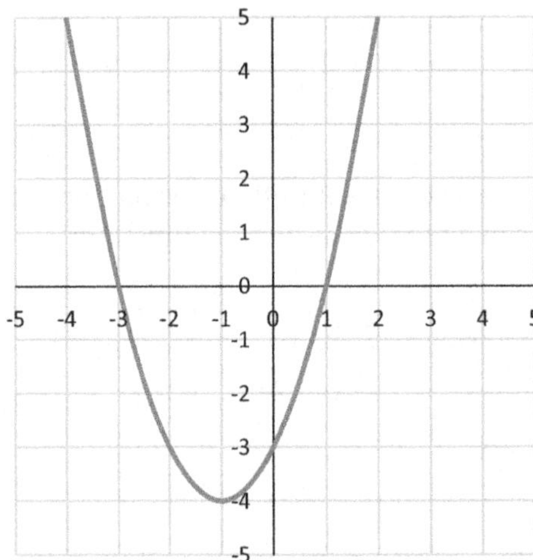

POLYNOMIAL FUNCTIONS

A **polynomial function** is a function with multiple terms and multiple powers of x, such as:

$$f(x) = a_n x^n + a_{n-1}x^{n-1} + a_{n-2}x^{n-2} + \cdots + a_1 x + a_0$$

where n is a non-negative integer that is the highest exponent in the polynomial and $a_n \neq 0$. The domain of a polynomial function is the set of all real numbers. If the greatest exponent in the polynomial is even, the polynomial is said to be of even degree and the range is the set of real numbers that satisfy the function. If the greatest exponent in the polynomial is odd, the polynomial is said to be odd and the range, like the domain, is the set of all real numbers.

RATIONAL FUNCTIONS

A **rational function** is a function that can be constructed as a ratio of two polynomial expressions: $f(x) = \frac{p(x)}{q(x)}$, where $p(x)$ and $q(x)$ are both polynomial expressions and $q(x) \neq 0$. The domain is the set of all real numbers, except any values for which $q(x) = 0$. The range is the set of real numbers that satisfies the function when the domain is applied. When you graph a rational function, you will have vertical asymptotes wherever $q(x) = 0$. If the polynomial in the numerator is of lesser degree than the polynomial in the denominator, the x-axis will also be a horizontal asymptote. If the numerator and denominator have equal degrees, there will be a horizontal asymptote not on the x-axis. If the degree of the numerator is exactly one greater than the degree of the denominator, the graph will have an oblique, or diagonal, asymptote. The asymptote will be along the line $y = \frac{p_n}{q_{n-1}}x + \frac{p_{n-1}}{q_{n-1}}$, where p_n and q_{n-1} are the coefficients of the highest degree terms in their respective polynomials.

SQUARE ROOT FUNCTIONS

A **square root function** is a function that contains a radical and is in the format $f(x) = \sqrt{ax + b}$. The domain is the set of all real numbers that yields a positive radicand or a radicand equal to zero. Because square root values are assumed to be positive unless otherwise identified, the range is all real numbers from zero to infinity. To find the zero of a square root function, set the radicand equal to zero and solve for x. The graph of a square root function is always to the right of the zero and always above the x-axis.

Example graph of a square root function, $f(x) = \sqrt{2x + 1}$:

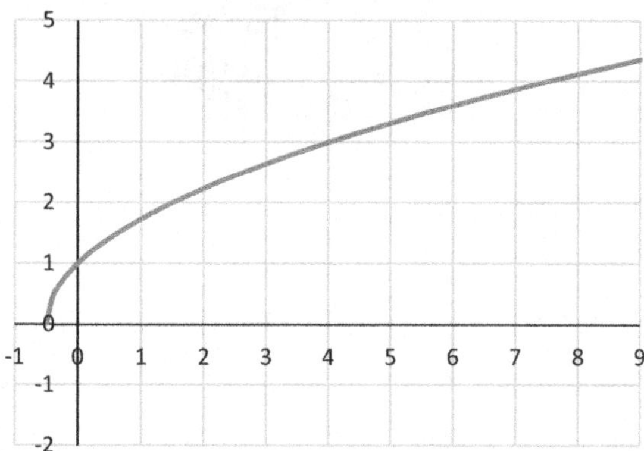

DISPLAYING INFORMATION

FREQUENCY TABLES

Frequency tables show how frequently each unique value appears in a set. A **relative frequency table** is one that shows the proportions of each unique value compared to the entire set. Relative frequencies are given as percentages; however, the total percent for a relative frequency table will not necessarily equal 100 percent due to rounding. An example of a frequency table with relative frequencies is below.

Favorite Color	Frequency	Relative Frequency
Blue	4	13%
Red	7	22%
Green	3	9%
Purple	6	19%
Cyan	12	38%

Review Video: Data Interpretation of Graphs
Visit mometrix.com/academy and enter code: 200439

CIRCLE GRAPHS

Circle graphs, also known as *pie charts*, provide a visual depiction of the relationship of each type of data compared to the whole set of data. The circle graph is divided into sections by drawing radii to create central angles whose percentage of the circle is equal to the individual data's percentage of the whole set. Each 1% of data is equal to 3.6° in the circle graph. Therefore, data represented by a 90° section of the circle graph makes up 25% of the whole. When complete, a circle graph often looks like a pie cut into uneven wedges. The pie chart below shows the data from the frequency table referenced earlier where people were asked their favorite color.

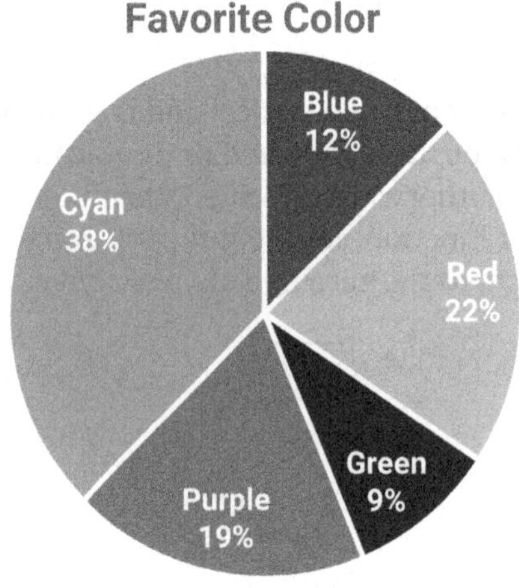

PICTOGRAPHS

A **pictograph** is a graph, generally in the horizontal orientation, that uses pictures or symbols to represent the data. Each pictograph must have a key that defines the picture or symbol and gives the quantity each picture or symbol represents. Pictures or symbols on a pictograph are not always shown as whole elements. In this case, the fraction of the picture or symbol shown represents the same fraction of the quantity a whole picture or symbol stands for. For example, a row with $3\frac{1}{2}$ ears of corn, where each ear of corn represents 100 stalks of corn in a field, would equal $3\frac{1}{2} \times 100 = 350$ stalks of corn in the field.

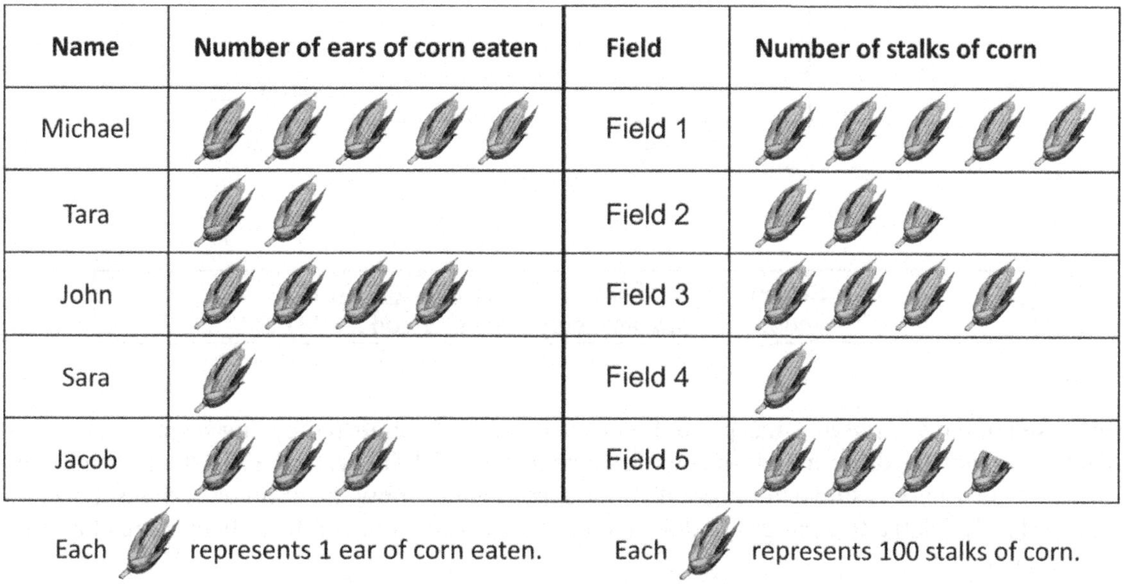

Name	Number of ears of corn eaten	Field	Number of stalks of corn
Michael		Field 1	
Tara		Field 2	
John		Field 3	
Sara		Field 4	
Jacob		Field 5	

Each represents 1 ear of corn eaten. Each represents 100 stalks of corn.

Review Video: Pictographs
Visit mometrix.com/academy and enter code: 147860

LINE GRAPHS

Line graphs have one or more lines of varying styles (solid or broken) to show the different values for a set of data. The individual data are represented as ordered pairs, much like on a Cartesian plane. In this case, the x- and y-axes are defined in terms of their units, such as dollars or time. The individual plotted points are joined by line segments to show whether the value of the data is increasing (line sloping upward), decreasing (line sloping downward), or staying the same (horizontal line). Multiple sets of data can be graphed on the same line graph to give an easy visual comparison. An example of this would be graphing achievement test scores for different groups of students over the same time period to see which group had the greatest increase or decrease in performance from year to year (as shown below).

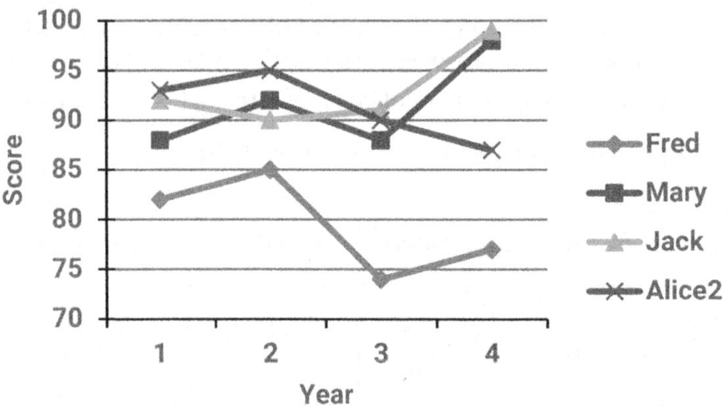

Review Video: How to Create a Line Graph
Visit mometrix.com/academy and enter code: 480147

Line Plots

A **line plot**, also known as a *dot plot*, has plotted points that are not connected by line segments. In this graph, the horizontal axis lists the different possible values for the data, and the vertical axis lists the number of times the individual value occurs. A single dot is graphed for each value to show the number of times it occurs. This graph is more closely related to a bar graph than a line graph. Do not connect the dots in a line plot or it will misrepresent the data.

Review Video: Line Plot
Visit mometrix.com/academy and enter code: 754610

Stem and Leaf Plots

A **stem and leaf plot** is useful for depicting groups of data that fall into a range of values. Each piece of data is separated into two parts: the first, or left, part is called the stem; the second, or right, part is called the leaf. Each stem is listed in a column from smallest to largest. Each leaf that has the common stem is listed in that stem's row from smallest to largest. For example, in a set of two-digit numbers, the digit in the tens place is the stem, and the digit in the ones place is the leaf. With a stem and leaf plot, you can easily see which subset of numbers (10s, 20s, 30s, etc.) is the largest. This information is also readily available by looking at a histogram, but a stem and leaf plot also allows you to look closer and see exactly which values fall in that range. Using a sample set of test scores (82, 88, 92, 93, 85, 90, 92, 95, 74, 88, 90, 91, 78, 87, 98, 99), we can assemble a stem and leaf plot like the one below.

Test Scores

7	4	8							
8	2	5	7	8	8				
9	0	0	1	2	2	3	5	8	9

Review Video: Stem and Leaf Plots
Visit mometrix.com/academy and enter code: 302339

Bar Graphs

A **bar graph** is one of the few graphs that can be drawn correctly in two different configurations - both horizontally and vertically. A bar graph is similar to a line plot in the way the data is organized on the graph. Both axes must have their categories defined for the graph to be useful. Rather than placing a single dot to mark the point of the data's value, a bar, or thick line, is drawn from zero to the exact value of the data, whether it is a number, percentage, or other numerical value. Longer bar lengths correspond to greater data values. To read a bar graph, read the labels for the axes to find the units being reported. Then, look where the bars end in relation to the scale given on the corresponding axis and determine the associated value.

The bar chart below represents the responses from our favorite-color survey.

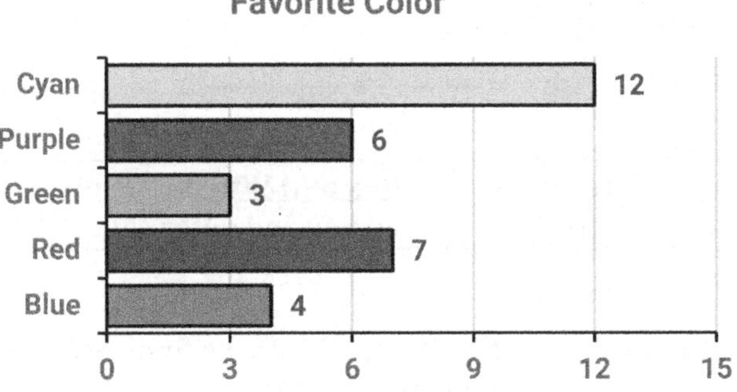

Histograms

At first glance, a **histogram** looks like a vertical bar graph. The difference is that a bar graph has a separate bar for each piece of data and a histogram has one continuous bar for each *range* of data. For example, a histogram may have one bar for the range 0–9, one bar for 10–19, etc. While a bar graph has numerical values on one axis, a histogram has numerical values on both axes. Each range is of equal size, and they are ordered left to right from lowest to highest. The height of each column on a histogram represents the number of data values within that range. Like a stem and leaf plot, a histogram makes it easy to glance at the graph and quickly determine which range has the greatest quantity of values. A simple example of a histogram is below.

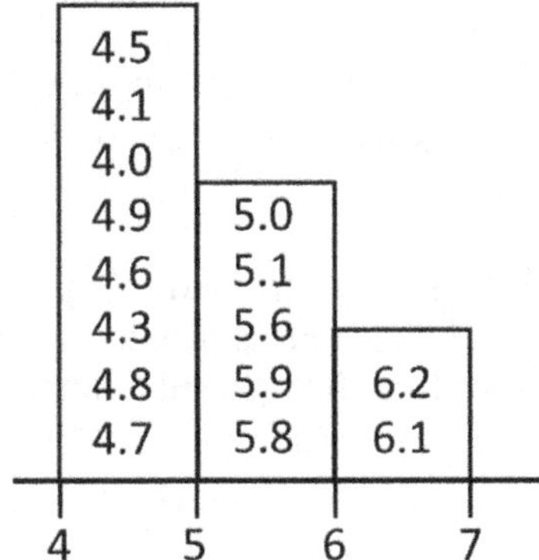

5-Number Summary

The **5-number summary** of a set of data gives a very informative picture of the set. The five numbers in the summary include the minimum value, maximum value, and the three quartiles. This information gives the reader the range and median of the set, as well as an indication of how the data is spread about the median.

BOX AND WHISKER PLOTS

A **box-and-whiskers plot** is a graphical representation of the 5-number summary. To draw a box-and-whiskers plot, plot the points of the 5-number summary on a number line. Draw a box whose ends are through the points for the first and third quartiles. Draw a vertical line in the box through the median to divide the box in half. Draw a line segment from the first quartile point to the minimum value, and from the third quartile point to the maximum value.

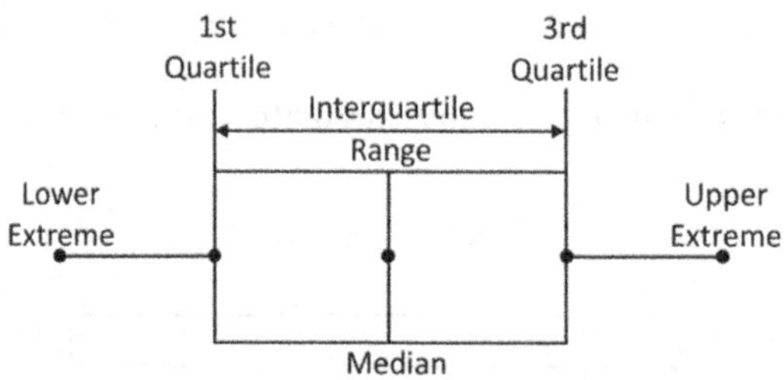

Review Video: Box and Whisker Plots
Visit mometrix.com/academy and enter code: 810817

EXAMPLE

Given the following data (32, 28, 29, 26, 35, 27, 30, 31, 27, 32), we first sort it into numerical order: 26, 27, 27, 28, 29, 30, 31, 32, 32, 35. We can then find the median. Since there are ten values, we take the average of the 5th and 6th values to get 29.5. We find the lower quartile by taking the median of the data smaller than the median. Since there are five values, we take the 3rd value, which is 27. We find the upper quartile by taking the median of the data larger than the overall median, which is 32. Finally, we note our minimum and maximum, which are simply the smallest and largest values in the set: 26 and 35, respectively. Now we can create our box plot:

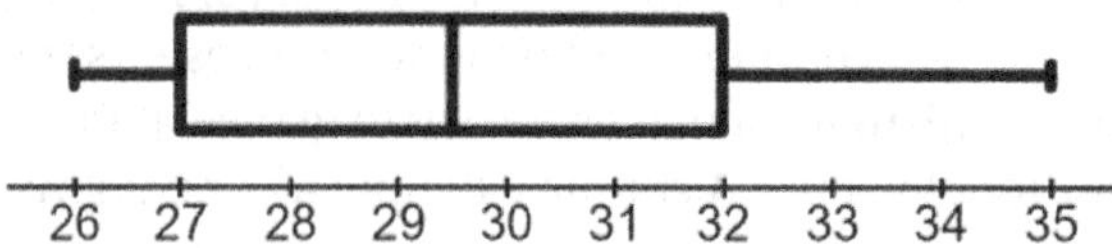

This plot is fairly "long" on the right whisker, showing one or more unusually high values (but not quite outliers). The other quartiles are similar in length, showing a fairly even distribution of data.

INTERQUARTILE RANGE

The **interquartile range, or IQR**, is the difference between the upper and lower quartiles. It measures how the data is dispersed: a high IQR means that the data is more spread out, while a low IQR means that the data is clustered more tightly around the median. To find the IQR, subtract the lower quartile value (Q_1) from the upper quartile value (Q_3).

EXAMPLE

To find the upper and lower quartiles, we first find the median and then take the median of all values above it and all values below it. In the following data set (16, 18, 13, 24, 16, 51, 32, 21, 27, 39), we first rearrange the values in numerical order: 13, 16, 16, 18, 21, 24, 27, 32, 39, 51. There are 10 values, so the median is the average of the 5th and 6th: $\frac{21+24}{2} = \frac{45}{2} = 22.5$. We do not actually need this value to find the upper and lower quartiles. We look at the set of numbers below the median: 13, 16, 16, 18, 21. There are five values, so the 3rd is the median (16), or the value of the lower quartile (Q_1). Then we look at the numbers above the median: 24, 27, 32, 39, 51. Again there are five values, so the 3rd is the median (32), or the value of the upper quartile (Q_3). We find the IQR by subtracting Q_1 from Q_3: $32 - 16 = 16$.

68-95-99.7 RULE

The **68–95–99.7 rule** describes how a normal distribution of data should appear when compared to the mean. This is also a description of a normal bell curve. According to this rule, 68 percent of the data values in a normally distributed set should fall within one standard deviation of the mean (34 percent above and 34 percent below the mean), 95 percent of the data values should fall within two standard deviations of the mean (47.5 percent above and 47.5 percent below the mean), and 99.7 percent of the data values should fall within three standard deviations of the mean, again, equally distributed on either side of the mean. This means that only 0.3 percent of all data values should fall more than three standard deviations from the mean. On the graph below, the normal curve is centered on the y-axis. The x-axis labels are how many standard deviations away from the center you are. Therefore, it is easy to see how the 68-95-99.7 rule can apply.

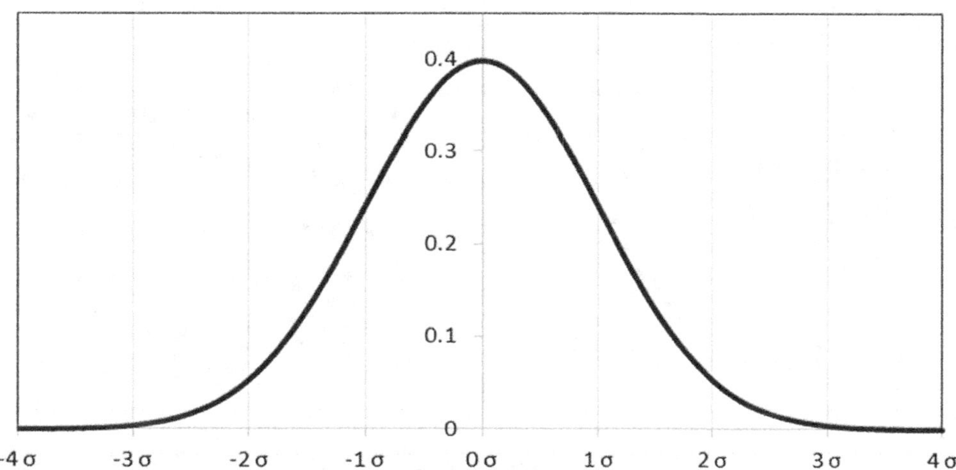

SCATTER PLOTS

BIVARIATE DATA

Bivariate data is simply data from two different variables. (The prefix *bi-* means *two.*) In a *scatter plot*, each value in the set of data is plotted on a grid similar to a Cartesian plane, where each axis represents one of the two variables. By looking at the pattern formed by the points on the grid, you can often determine whether or not there is a relationship between the two variables, and what that relationship is, if it exists. The variables may be directly proportionate, inversely proportionate, or show no proportion at all. It may also be possible to determine if the data is linear, and if so, to find an equation to relate the two variables. The following scatter plot shows the relationship between preference for brand "A" and the age of the consumers surveyed.

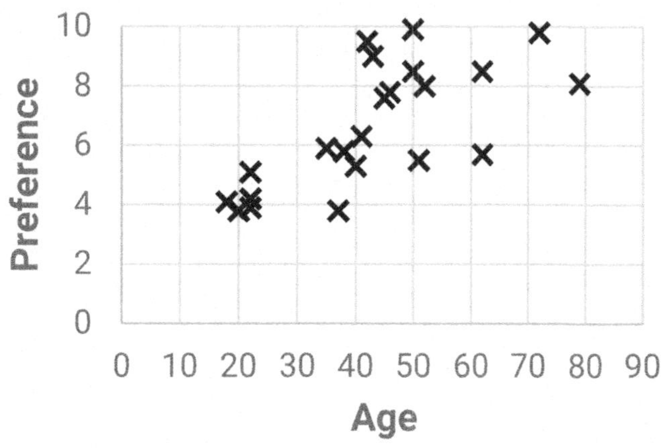

Scatter Plots

Scatter plots are also useful in determining the type of function represented by the data and finding the simple regression. Linear scatter plots may be positive or negative. Nonlinear scatter plots are generally exponential or quadratic. Below are some common types of scatter plots:

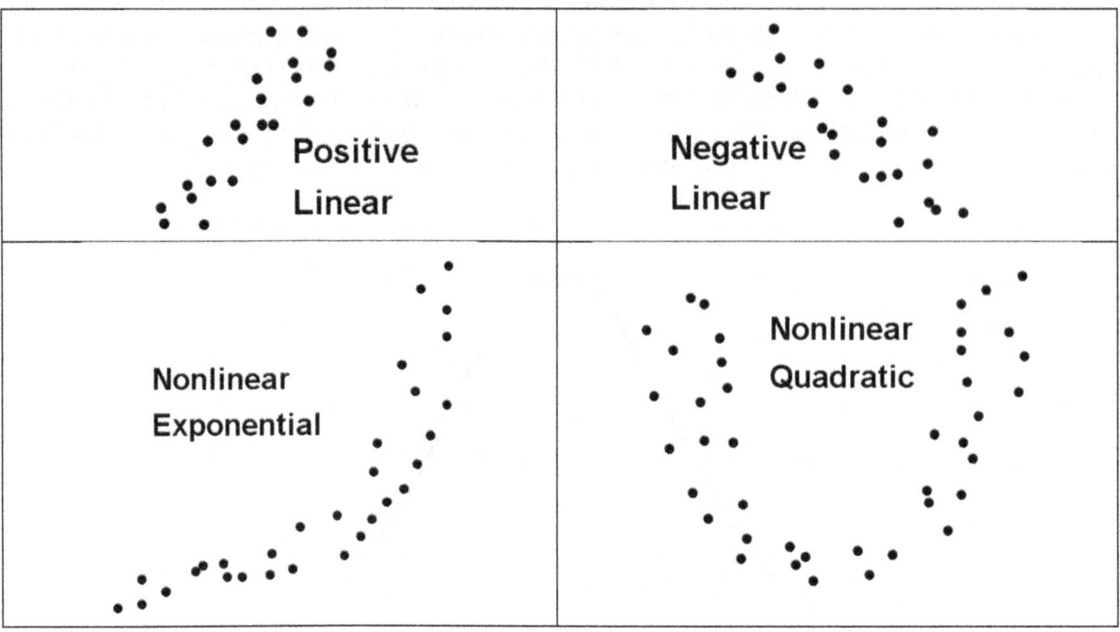

Review Video: Scatter Plot
Visit mometrix.com/academy and enter code: 596526

Reasoning Through Language Arts

Transform passive reading into active learning! After immersing yourself in this chapter, put your comprehension to the test by taking a quiz. The insights you gained will stay with you longer this way. Scan the QR code to go directly to the chapter quiz interface for this study guide. If you're using a computer, simply visit the bonus page at **mometrix.com/bonus948/ged** and click the Chapter Quizzes link.

This section is organized to introduce you to the passages that you will find on your exam. We cover the different types of passages from narrative to persuasive. Then, we move to the reason that a passage is written. As you may know, some texts are written to persuade. Other passages want to inform.

The devices of writers are important to understand as you practice reading passages. The other parts of a passage we focus on are main ideas, supporting details, and themes. Then, we review making inferences and drawing conclusions. With this step-by-step guide, you will move to a higher score on your test.

Careful reading and thinking about a passage are important in every part of life. Work with this information by reading books, magazines, or newspapers. When you read carefully, you can use this information for other passages. With practice you will strengthen your skills for the future. Truly, with this information, you can show others that you know the *secrets* to your exam.

Reading for Meaning

MAIN IDEAS AND SUPPORTING DETAILS

IDENTIFYING TOPICS AND MAIN IDEAS

One of the most important skills in reading comprehension is the identification of **topics** and **main ideas**. There is a subtle difference between these two features. The topic is the subject of a text (i.e., what the text is all about). The main idea, on the other hand, is the most important point being made by the author. The topic is usually expressed in a few words at the most while the main idea often needs a full sentence to be completely defined. As an example, a short passage might be written on the topic of penguins, and the main idea could be written as *Penguins are different from other birds in many ways.* In most nonfiction writing, the topic and the main idea will be **stated directly** and often appear in a sentence at the very beginning or end of the text. When being tested on an understanding of the author's topic, you may be able to skim the passage for the general idea by reading only the first sentence of each paragraph. A body paragraph's first sentence is often—but not always—the main **topic sentence** which gives you a summary of the content in the paragraph.

However, there are cases in which the reader must figure out an **unstated** topic or main idea. In these instances, you must read every sentence of the text and try to come up with an overarching idea that is supported by each of those sentences.

Note: The main idea should not be confused with the thesis statement. While the main idea gives a brief, general summary of a text, the thesis statement provides a **specific perspective** on an issue that the author supports with evidence.

Review Video: Topics and Main Ideas
Visit mometrix.com/academy and enter code: 407801

Supporting Details

Supporting details are smaller pieces of evidence that provide backing for the main point. In order to show that a main idea is correct or valid, an author must add details that prove their point. All texts contain details, but they are only classified as supporting details when they serve to reinforce some larger point. Supporting details are most commonly found in informative and persuasive texts. In some cases, they will be clearly indicated with terms like *for example* or *for instance*, or they will be enumerated with terms like *first, second*, and *last*. However, you need to be prepared for texts that do not contain those indicators. As a reader, you should consider whether the author's supporting details really back up his or her main point. Details can be factual and correct, yet they may not be **relevant** to the author's point. Conversely, details can be relevant, but be ineffective because they are based on opinion or assertions that cannot be proven.

> **Review Video: Supporting Details**
> Visit mometrix.com/academy and enter code: 396297

Common Organizations of Texts

Organization of the Text

The way a text is organized can help readers understand the author's intent and his or her conclusions. There are various ways to organize a text, and each one has a purpose and use. Usually, authors will organize information logically in a passage so the reader can follow and locate the information within the text. However, since not all passages are written with the same logical structure, you need to be familiar with several different types of passage structure.

> **Review Video: Organizational Methods to Structure Text**
> Visit mometrix.com/academy and enter code: 606263
>
> **Review Video: Sequence of Events in a Story**
> Visit mometrix.com/academy and enter code: 807512

Chronological

When using **chronological** order, the author presents information in the order that it happened. For example, biographies are typically written in chronological order. The subject's birth and childhood are presented first, followed by their adult life, and lastly the events leading up to the person's death.

Cause and Effect

One of the most common text structures is **cause and effect**. A **cause** is an act or event that makes something happen, and an **effect** is the thing that happens as a result of the cause. A cause-and-effect relationship is not always explicit, but there are some terms in English that signal causes, such as *since*, *because*, and *due to*. Furthermore, terms that signal effects include *consequently, therefore, this leads to*. As an example, consider the sentence *Because the sky was clear, Ron did not bring an umbrella*. The cause is the clear sky, and the effect is that Ron did not bring an umbrella. However, readers may find that sometimes the cause-and-effect relationship will not be clearly noted. For instance, the sentence *He was late and missed the meeting* does not contain any signaling words, but the sentence still contains a cause (he was late) and an effect (he missed the meeting).

> **Review Video: Cause and Effect**
> Visit mometrix.com/academy and enter code: 868099
>
> **Review Video: Rhetorical Strategy of Cause and Effect Analysis**
> Visit mometrix.com/academy and enter code: 725944

Multiple Effects

Be aware of the possibility for a single cause to have **multiple effects.** (e.g., *Single cause*: Because you left your homework on the table, your dog engulfed the assignment. *Multiple effects*: As a result, you receive a failing grade, your parents do not allow you to go out with your friends, you miss out on the new movie, and one of your classmates spoils it for you before you have another chance to watch it).

Multiple Causes

Also, there is the possibility for a single effect to have **multiple causes.** (e.g., *Single effect*: Alan has a fever. *Multiple causes*: An unexpected cold front came through the area, and Alan forgot to take his multi-vitamin to avoid getting sick.) Additionally, an effect can in turn be the cause of another effect, in what is known as a cause-and-effect chain. (e.g., As a result of her disdain for procrastination, Lynn prepared for her exam. This led to her passing her test with high marks. Hence, her resume was accepted and her application was approved.)

Cause and Effect in Persuasive Essays

Persuasive essays, in which an author tries to make a convincing argument and change the minds of readers, usually include cause-and-effect relationships. However, these relationships should not always be taken at face value. Frequently, an author will assume a cause or take an effect for granted. To read a persuasive essay effectively, readers need to judge the cause-and-effect relationships that the author is presenting. For instance, imagine an author wrote the following: *The parking deck has been unprofitable because people would prefer to ride their bikes.* The relationship is clear: the cause is that people prefer to ride their bikes, and the effect is that the parking deck has been unprofitable. However, readers should consider whether this argument is conclusive. Perhaps there are other reasons for the failure of the parking deck: a down economy, excessive fees, etc. Too often, authors present causal relationships as if they are fact rather than opinion. Readers should be on the alert for these dubious claims.

Problem-Solution

Some nonfiction texts are organized to **present a problem** followed by a solution. For this type of text, the problem is often explained before the solution is offered. In some cases, as when the problem is well known, the solution may be introduced briefly at the beginning. Other passages may focus on the solution, and the problem will be referenced only occasionally. Some texts will outline multiple solutions to a problem, leaving readers to choose among them. If the author has an interest or an allegiance to one solution, he or she may fail to mention or describe accurately some of the other solutions. Readers should be careful of the author's agenda when reading a problem-solution text. Only by understanding the author's perspective and interests can one develop a proper judgment of the proposed solution.

Compare and Contrast

Many texts follow the **compare-and-contrast** model in which the similarities and differences between two ideas or things are explored. Analysis of the similarities between ideas is called **comparison**. In an ideal comparison, the author places ideas or things in an equivalent structure, i.e., the author presents the ideas in the same way. If an author wants to show the similarities between cricket and baseball, then he or she may do so by summarizing the equipment and rules for each game. Be mindful of the similarities as they appear in the passage and take note of any differences that are mentioned. Often, these small differences will only reinforce the more general similarity.

Review Video: Compare and Contrast
Visit mometrix.com/academy and enter code: 798319

Thinking critically about ideas and conclusions can seem like a daunting task. One way to ease this task is to understand the basic elements of ideas and writing techniques. Looking at the ways different ideas relate to each other can be a good way for readers to begin their analysis. For instance, sometimes authors will write about two ideas that are in opposition to each other. Or, one author will provide his or her ideas on a topic, and another author may respond in opposition. The analysis of these opposing ideas is known as **contrast**.

Contrast is often marred by the author's obvious partiality to one of the ideas. A discerning reader will be put off by an author who does not engage in a fair fight. In an analysis of opposing ideas, both ideas should be presented in clear and reasonable terms. If the author does prefer a side, you need to read carefully to determine the areas where the author shows or avoids this preference. In an analysis of opposing ideas, you should proceed through the passage by marking the major differences point by point with an eye that is looking for an explanation of each side's view. For instance, in an analysis of capitalism and communism, there is an importance in outlining each side's view on labor, markets, prices, personal responsibility, etc. Additionally, as you read through the passages, you should note whether the opposing views present each side in a similar manner.

SEQUENCE

Readers must be able to identify a text's **sequence**, or the order in which things happen. Often, when the sequence is very important to the author, the text is indicated with signal words like *first*, *then*, *next*, and *last*. However, a sequence can be merely implied and must be noted by the reader. Consider the sentence *He walked through the garden and gave water and fertilizer to the plants*. Clearly, the man did not walk through the garden before he collected water and fertilizer for the plants. So, the implied sequence is that he first collected water, then he collected fertilizer, next he walked through the garden, and last he gave water or fertilizer as necessary to the plants. Texts do not always proceed in an orderly sequence from first to last. Sometimes they begin at the end and start over at the beginning. As a reader, you can enhance your understanding of the passage by taking brief notes to clarify the sequence.

Review Video: Sequence
Visit mometrix.com/academy and enter code: 489027

PLOT AND STORY STRUCTURE

PLOT AND STORY STRUCTURE

The **plot** includes the events that happen in a story and the order in which they are told to the reader. There are several types of plot structures, as stories can be told in many ways. The most common plot structure is the chronological plot, which presents the events to the reader in the same order they occur for the characters in the story. Chronological plots usually have five main parts, the **exposition**, **rising action**, the **climax**, **falling action**, and the **resolution**. This type of plot structure guides the reader through the story's events as the characters experience them and is the easiest structure to understand and identify. While this is the most common plot structure, many stories are nonlinear, which means the plot does not sequence events in the same order the characters experience them. Such stories might include elements like flashbacks that cause the story to be nonlinear.

Review Video: How to Make a Story Map
Visit mometrix.com/academy and enter code: 261719

EXPOSITION

The **exposition** is at the beginning of the story and generally takes place before the rising action begins. The purpose of the exposition is to give the reader context for the story, which the author may do by introducing one or more characters, describing the setting or world, or explaining the events leading up to the point where the story begins. The exposition may still include events that contribute to the plot, but the **rising action** and main conflict of the story are not part of the exposition. Some narratives skip the exposition and begin the story with the beginning of the rising action, which causes the reader to learn the context as the story intensifies.

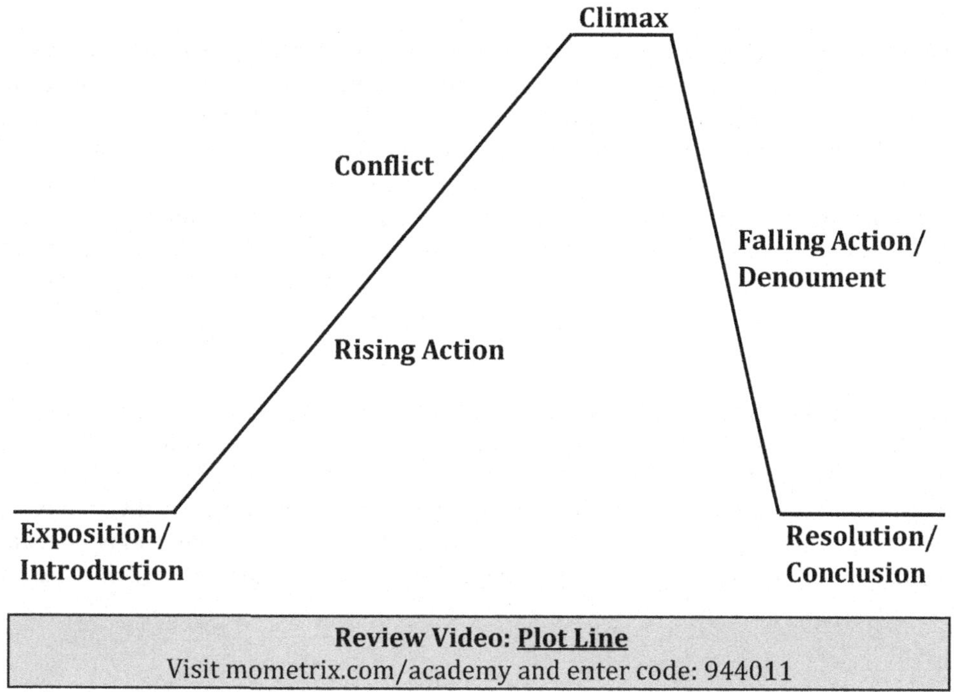

Review Video: Plot Line
Visit mometrix.com/academy and enter code: 944011

Conflict

A **conflict** is a problem to be solved. Literary plots typically include one conflict or more. Characters' attempts to resolve conflicts drive the narrative's forward movement. **Conflict resolution** is often the protagonist's primary occupation. Physical conflicts like exploring, wars, and escapes tend to make plots most suspenseful and exciting. Emotional, mental, or moral conflicts tend to make stories more personally gratifying or rewarding for many audiences. Conflicts can be external or internal. A major type of internal conflict is some inner personal battle, or **man versus self**. Major types of external conflicts include **man versus nature**, **man versus man**, and **man versus society**. Readers can identify conflicts in literary plots by identifying the protagonist and antagonist and asking why they conflict, what events develop the conflict, where the climax occurs, and how they identify with the characters.

Read the following paragraph and discuss the type of conflict present:

> Timothy was shocked out of sleep by the appearance of a bear just outside his tent. After panicking for a moment, he remembered some advice he had read in preparation for this trip: he should make noise so the bear would not be startled. As Timothy started to hum and sing, the bear wandered away.

There are three main types of conflict in literature: **man versus man**, **man versus nature**, and **man versus self**. This paragraph is an example of man versus nature. Timothy is in conflict with the bear. Even though no physical conflict like an attack exists, Timothy is pitted against the bear. Timothy uses his knowledge to "defeat" the bear and keep himself safe. The solution to the conflict is that Timothy makes noise, the bear wanders away, and Timothy is safe.

Review Video: Conflict
Visit mometrix.com/academy and enter code: 559550

Review Video: Determining Relationships in a Story
Visit mometrix.com/academy and enter code: 929925

Rising Action

The **rising action** is the part of the story where conflict **intensifies**. The rising action begins with an event that prompts the main conflict of the story. This may also be called the **inciting incident**. The main conflict generally occurs between the protagonist and an antagonist, but this is not the only type of conflict that may occur in a narrative. After this event, the protagonist works to resolve the main conflict by preparing for an altercation, pursuing a goal, fleeing an antagonist, or doing some other action that will end the conflict. The rising action is composed of several additional events that increase the story's tension. Most often, other developments will occur alongside the growth of the main conflict, such as character development or the development of minor conflicts. The rising action ends with the **climax**, which is the point of highest tension in the story.

Climax

The **climax** is the event in the narrative that marks the height of the story's conflict or tension. The event that takes place at the story's climax will end the rising action and bring about the results of the main conflict. If the conflict was between a good protagonist and an evil antagonist, the climax may be a final battle between the two characters. If the conflict is an adventurer looking for heavily guarded treasure, the climax may be the adventurer's encounter with the final obstacle that protects the treasure. The climax may be made of multiple scenes, but can usually be summarized as one event. Once the conflict and climax are complete, the **falling action** begins.

Falling Action

The **falling action** shows what happens in the story between the climax and the resolution. The falling action often composes a much smaller portion of the story than the rising action does. While the climax includes the end of the main conflict, the falling action may show the results of any minor conflicts in the story. For example, if the protagonist encountered a troll on the way to find some treasure, and the troll demanded the protagonist share the treasure after retrieving it, the falling action would include the protagonist returning to share the treasure with the troll. Similarly, any unexplained major events are usually made clear during the falling action. Once all significant elements of the story are resolved or addressed, the story's resolution will occur. The **resolution** is the end of the story, which shows the final result of the plot's events and shows what life is like for the main characters once they are no longer experiencing the story's conflicts.

Resolution

The way the conflict is **resolved** depends on the type of conflict. The plot of any book starts with the lead up to the conflict, then the conflict itself, and finally the solution, or **resolution**, to the conflict. In **man versus man** conflicts, the conflict is often resolved by two parties coming to some sort of agreement or by one party triumphing over the other party. In **man versus nature** conflicts, the conflict is often resolved by man coming to some realization about some aspect of nature. In **man versus self** conflicts, the conflict is often resolved by the character growing or coming to an understanding about part of himself.

Theme

A **theme** is a central idea demonstrated by a passage. Often, a theme is a lesson or moral contained in the text, but it does not have to be. It also is a unifying idea that is used throughout the text; it can take the form of a common setting, idea, symbol, design, or recurring event. A passage can have two or more themes that convey its overall idea. The theme or themes of a passage are often based on **universal themes**. They can frequently be expressed using well-known sayings about life, society, or human nature, such as "Hard work pays off" or "Good triumphs over evil." Themes are not usually stated **explicitly**. The reader must figure them out by carefully reading the passage. Themes are created through descriptive language or events in the plot. The events of a story help shape the themes of a passage.

EXAMPLE

Explain why "if you care about something, you need to take care of it" accurately describes the theme of the following excerpt.

> Luca collected baseball cards, but he wasn't very careful with them. He left them around the house. His dog liked to chew. One day, Luca and his friend Bart were looking at his collection. Then they went outside. When Luca got home, he saw his dog chewing on his cards. They were ruined.

This excerpt tells the story of a boy who is careless with his baseball cards and leaves them lying around. His dog ends up chewing them and ruining them. The lesson is that if you care about something, you need to take care of it. This is the theme, or point, of the story. Some stories have more than one theme, but this is not really true of this excerpt. The reader needs to figure out the theme based on what happens in the story. Sometimes, as in the case of fables, the theme is stated directly in the text. However, this is not usually the case.

Review Video: Themes in Literature
Visit mometrix.com/academy and enter code: 732074

NARRATOR'S POINT OF VIEW

POINT OF VIEW

Another element that impacts a text is the author's point of view. The **point of view** of a text is the perspective from which a passage is told. An author will always have a point of view about a story before he or she draws up a plot line. The author will know what events they want to take place, how they want the characters to interact, and how they want the story to resolve. An author will also have an opinion on the topic or series of events which is presented in the story that is based on their prior experience and beliefs.

The two main points of view that authors use, especially in a work of fiction, are first person and third person. If the narrator of the story is also the main character, or *protagonist*, the text is written in first-person point of view. In first person, the author writes from the perspective of *I*. Third-person point of view is probably the most common that authors use in their passages. Using third person, authors refer to each character by using *he* or *she*. In third-person omniscient, the narrator is not a character in the story and tells the story of all of the characters at the same time.

Review Video: Point of View
Visit mometrix.com/academy and enter code: 383336

FIRST-PERSON NARRATION

First-person narratives let narrators express inner feelings and thoughts, especially when the narrator is the protagonist as Lemuel Gulliver is in Jonathan Swift's *Gulliver's Travels*. The narrator may be a close friend of the protagonist, like Dr. Watson in Sir Arthur Conan Doyle's *Sherlock Holmes*. Or, the narrator can be less involved with the main characters and plot, like Nick Carraway in F. Scott Fitzgerald's *The Great Gatsby*. When a narrator reports others' narratives, she or he is a "**frame narrator**," like the nameless narrator of Joseph Conrad's *Heart of Darkness* or Mr. Lockwood in Emily Brontë's *Wuthering Heights*. **First-person plural** is unusual but can be effective. Isaac Asimov's *I, Robot*, William Faulkner's *A Rose for Emily*, Maxim Gorky's *Twenty-Six Men and a Girl*, and Jeffrey Eugenides' *The Virgin Suicides* all use first-person plural narration. Author Kurt Vonnegut is the first-person narrator in his semi-autobiographical novel *Timequake*. Also unusual, but effective, is a **first-person omniscient** (rather than the more common third-person omniscient) narrator, like Death in Markus Zusak's *The Book Thief* and the ghost in Alice Sebold's *The Lovely Bones*.

SECOND-PERSON NARRATION

While **second-person** address is very commonplace in popular song lyrics, it is the least used form of narrative voice in literary works. Popular serial books of the 1980s like *Fighting Fantasy* or *Choose Your Own*

Adventure employed second-person narratives. In some cases, a narrative combines both second-person and first-person voices, using the pronouns *you* and *I*. This can draw readers into the story, and it can also enable the authors to compare directly "your" and "my" feelings, thoughts, and actions. When the narrator is also a character in the story, as in Edgar Allan Poe's short story "The Tell-Tale Heart" or Jay McInerney's novel *Bright Lights, Big City,* the narrative is better defined as first-person despite it also addressing "you."

Third-Person Narration

Narration in the third person is the most prevalent type, as it allows authors the most flexibility. It is so common that readers simply assume without needing to be informed that the narrator is not a character in the story, or involved in its events. **Third-person singular** is used more frequently than **third-person plural**, though some authors have also effectively used plural. However, both singular and plural are most often included in stories according to which characters are being described. The third-person narrator may be either objective or subjective, and either omniscient or limited. **Objective third-person** narration does not include what the characters described are thinking or feeling, while **subjective third-person** narration does. The **third-person omniscient** narrator knows everything about all characters, including their thoughts and emotions, and all related places, times, and events. However, the **third-person limited** narrator may know everything about a particular character, but is limited to that character. In other words, the narrator cannot speak about anything that character does not know.

Alternating-Person Narration

Although authors more commonly write stories from one point of view, there are also instances wherein they alternate the narrative voice within the same book. For example, they may sometimes use an omniscient third-person narrator and a more intimate first-person narrator at other times. In J. K. Rowling's series of *Harry Potter* novels, she often writes in a third-person limited narrative, but sometimes changes to narration by characters other than the protagonist. George R. R. Martin's series *A Song of Ice and Fire* changes the point of view to coincide with divisions between chapters. The same technique is used by Erin Hunter (a pseudonym for several authors of the *Warriors, Seekers,* and *Survivors* book series). Authors using first-person narrative sometimes switch to third-person to describe significant action scenes, especially those where the narrator was absent or uninvolved, as Barbara Kingsolver does in her novel *The Poisonwood Bible.*

Setting, Mood, and Tone

Setting and Time Frame

A literary text has both a setting and time frame. A **setting** is the place in which the story as a whole is set. The **time frame** is the period in which the story is set. This may refer to the historical period the story takes place in or if the story takes place over a single day. Both setting and time frame are relevant to a text's meaning because they help the reader place the story in time and space. An author uses setting and time frame to anchor a text, create a mood, and enhance its meaning. This helps a reader understand why a character acts the way he does, or why certain events in the story are important. The setting impacts the **plot** and character **motivations**, while the time frame helps place the story in **chronological context**.

Example

Read the following excerpt from The Adventures of Huckleberry Finn by Mark Twain and analyze the relevance of setting to the text's meaning:

> We said there warn't no home like a raft, after all. Other places do seem so cramped up and smothery, but a raft don't. You feel mighty free and easy and comfortable on a raft.

This excerpt from *The Adventures of Huckleberry Finn* by Mark Twain reveals information about the **setting** of the book. By understanding that the main character, Huckleberry Finn, lives on a raft, the reader can place the story on a river, in this case, the Mississippi River in the South before the Civil War. The information about the setting also gives the reader clues about the **character** of Huck Finn: he clearly values independence and freedom, and he likes the outdoors. The information about the setting in the quote helps the reader to better understand the rest of the text.

Syntax and Word Choice

Authors use words and **syntax**, or sentence structure, to make their texts unique, convey their own writing style, and sometimes to make a point or emphasis. They know that word choice and syntax contribute to the reader's understanding of the text as well as to the tone and mood of a text.

Review Video: Syntax
Visit mometrix.com/academy and enter code: 242280

Mood and Tone

Mood is a story's atmosphere, or the feelings the reader gets from reading it. The way authors set the mood in writing is comparable to the way filmmakers use music to set the mood in movies. Instead of music, though, writers judiciously select descriptive words to evoke certain **moods**. The mood of a work may convey joy, anger, bitterness, hope, gloom, fear, apprehension, or any other emotion the author wants the reader to feel. In addition to vocabulary choices, authors also use figurative expressions, particular sentence structures, and choices of diction that project and reinforce the moods they want to create. Whereas mood is the reader's emotions evoked by reading what is written, **tone** is the emotions and attitudes of the writer that she or he expresses in the writing. Authors use the same literary techniques to establish tone as they do to establish mood. An author may use a humorous tone, an angry or sad tone, a sentimental or unsentimental tone, or something else entirely.

Mood and Tone in The Great Gatsby

To understand the difference between mood and tone, look at this excerpt from F. Scott Fitzgerald's *The Great Gatsby*. In this passage, Nick Caraway, the novel's narrator, is describing his affordable house, which sits in a neighborhood full of expensive mansions.

> "I lived at West Egg, the—well the less fashionable of the two, though this is a most superficial tag to express the bizarre and not a little sinister contrast between them. My house was at the very tip of the egg, only fifty yard from the Sound, and squeezed between two huge places that rented for twelve or fifteen thousand a season ... My own house was an eyesore, but it was a small eyesore, and it had been overlooked, so I had a view of the water, a partial view of my neighbor's lawn, and the consoling proximity of millionaires—all for eighty dollars a month."

In this description, the mood created for the reader does not match the tone created through the narrator. The mood in this passage is one of dissatisfaction and inferiority. Nick compares his home to his neighbors', saying he lives in the "less fashionable" neighborhood and that his house is "overlooked," an "eyesore," and "squeezed between two huge" mansions. He also adds that his placement allows him the "consoling proximity of millionaires." A literal reading of these details leads the reader to have negative feelings toward Nick's house and his economic inferiority to his neighbors, creating the mood.

However, Fitzgerald also conveys an opposing attitude, or tone, through Nick's description. Nick calls the distinction between the neighborhoods "superficial," showing a suspicion of the value suggested by the neighborhoods' titles, properties, and residents. Nick also undermines his critique of his own home by calling it "a small eyesore" and claiming it has "been overlooked." However, he follows these statements with a description of his surroundings, claiming that he has "a view of the water" and can see some of his wealthy neighbor's property from his home, and a comparison between the properties' rent. While the mental image created for the reader depicts a small house shoved between looming mansions, the tone suggests that Nick enjoys these qualities about his home, or at least finds it charming. He acknowledges its shortcomings, but includes the benefits of his home's unassuming appearance.

> **Review Video: Style, Tone, and Mood**
> Visit mometrix.com/academy and enter code: 416961

Historical and Social Context

Fiction that is heavily influenced by a historical or social context cannot be comprehended as the author intended if the reader does not keep this context in mind. Many important elements of the text will be influenced by any context, including symbols, allusions, settings, and plot events. These contexts, as well as the identity of the work's author, can help to inform the reader about the author's concerns and intended meanings. For example, George Orwell published his novel *1984* in the year 1949, soon after the end of World War II. At that time, following the defeat of the Nazis, the Cold War began between the Western Allied nations and the Eastern Soviet Communists. People were therefore concerned about the conflict between the freedoms afforded by Western democracies versus the oppression represented by Communism. Orwell had also previously fought in the Spanish Civil War against a Spanish regime that he and his fellows viewed as oppressive. From this information, readers can infer that Orwell was concerned about oppression by totalitarian governments. This informs *1984*'s story of Winston Smith's rebellion against the oppressive "Big Brother" government, of the fictional dictatorial state of Oceania, and his capture, torture, and ultimate conversion by that government. Some literary theories also seek to use historical and social contexts to reveal deeper meanings and implications in a text.

Character Development and Dialogue

Character Development

When depicting characters or figures in a written text, authors generally use actions, dialogue, and descriptions as characterization techniques. Characterization can occur in both fiction and nonfiction and is used to show a character or figure's personality, demeanor, and thoughts. This helps create a more engaging experience for the reader by providing a more concrete picture of a character or figure's tendencies and features. Characterizations also gives authors the opportunity to integrate elements such as dialects, activities, attire, and attitudes into their writing.

To understand the meaning of a story, it is vital to understand the characters as the author describes them. We can look for contradictions in what a character thinks, says, and does. We can notice whether the author's observations about a character differ from what other characters in the story say about that character. A character may be dynamic, meaning they change significantly during the story, or static, meaning they remain the same from beginning to end. Characters may be two-dimensional, not fully developed, or may be well developed with characteristics that stand out vividly. Characters may also symbolize universal properties. Additionally, readers can compare and contrast characters to analyze how each one developed.

A well-known example of character development can be found in Charles Dickens's *Great Expectations*. The novel's main character, Pip, is introduced as a young boy, and he is depicted as innocent, kind, and humble. However, as Pip grows up and is confronted with the social hierarchy of Victorian England, he becomes arrogant and rejects his loved ones in pursuit of his own social advancement. Once he achieves his social goals, he realizes the merits of his former lifestyle, and lives with the wisdom he gained in both environments and life stages. Dickens shows Pip's ever-changing character through his interactions with others and his inner thoughts, which evolve as his personal values and personality shift.

> **Review Video: Character Changes**
> Visit mometrix.com/academy and enter code: 408719

Dialogue

Effectively written dialogue serves at least one, but usually several, purposes. It advances the story and moves the plot, develops the characters, sheds light on the work's theme or meaning, and can, often subtly, account for the passage of time not otherwise indicated. It can alter the direction that the plot is taking, typically by introducing some new conflict or changing existing ones. **Dialogue** can establish a work's narrative voice and the characters' voices and set the tone of the story or of particular characters. When fictional characters display enlightenment or realization, dialogue can give readers an understanding of what those characters have discovered and how. Dialogue can illuminate the motivations and wishes of the story's characters. By using consistent thoughts and syntax, dialogue can support character development. Skillfully created, it can also represent real-life speech rhythms in written form. Via conflicts and ensuing action, dialogue also provides drama.

Dialogue in Fiction

In fictional works, effectively written dialogue does more than just break up or interrupt sections of narrative. While **dialogue** may supply exposition for readers, it must nonetheless be believable. Dialogue should be dynamic, not static, and it should not resemble regular prose. Authors should not use dialogue to write clever similes or metaphors, or to inject their own opinions. Nor should they use dialogue at all when narrative would be better. Most importantly, dialogue should not slow the plot movement. Dialogue must seem natural, which means careful construction of phrases rather than actually duplicating natural speech, which does not necessarily translate well to the written word. Finally, all dialogue must be pertinent to the story, rather than just added conversation.

Author's Purpose

Author's Purpose

Usually, identifying the author's **purpose** is easier than identifying his or her **position**. In most cases, the author has no interest in hiding his or her purpose. A text that is meant to entertain, for instance, should be written to please the reader. Most narratives, or stories, are written to entertain, though they may also inform or persuade. Informative texts are easy to identify, while the most difficult purpose of a text to identify is persuasion because the author has an interest in making this purpose hard to detect. When a reader discovers that the author is trying to persuade, he or she should be skeptical of the argument. For this reason, persuasive texts often try to establish an entertaining tone and hope to amuse the reader into agreement. On the other hand, an informative tone may be implemented to create an appearance of authority and objectivity.

An author's purpose is evident often in the **organization** of the text (e.g., section headings in bold font points to an informative text). However, you may not have such organization available to you in your exam. Instead, if the author makes his or her main idea clear from the beginning, then the likely purpose of the text is to **inform**. If the author begins by making a claim and provides various arguments to support that claim, then the purpose is probably to **persuade**. If the author tells a story or wants to gain the reader's attention more than to push a particular point or deliver information, then his or her purpose is most likely to **entertain**. As a reader, you must judge authors on how well they accomplish their purpose. In other words, you need to consider the type of passage (e.g., technical, persuasive, etc.) that the author has written and if the author has followed the requirements of the passage type.

Review Video: Understanding the Author's Intent
Visit mometrix.com/academy and enter code: 511819

Informational Texts

An **informational text** is written to educate and enlighten readers. Informational texts are almost always nonfiction and are rarely structured as a story. The intention of an informational text is to deliver information in the most comprehensible way. So, look for the structure of the text to be very clear. In an informational text, the thesis statement is one or two sentences that normally appears at the end of the first paragraph. The author may use some colorful language, but he or she is likely to put more emphasis on clarity and precision.

Informational essays do not typically appeal to the emotions. They often contain facts and figures and rarely include the opinion of the author; however, readers should remain aware of the possibility for bias as those facts are presented. Sometimes a persuasive essay can resemble an informative essay, especially if the author maintains an even tone and presents his or her views as if they were established fact.

Review Video: Informational Text
Visit mometrix.com/academy and enter code: 924964

Persuasive Writing

In a persuasive essay, the author is attempting to change the reader's mind or **convince** him or her of something that he or she did not believe previously. There are several identifying characteristics of **persuasive writing**. One is **opinion presented as fact**. When authors attempt to persuade readers, they often present their opinions as if they were fact. Readers must be on guard for statements that sound factual but which cannot be subjected to research, observation, or experiment. Another characteristic of persuasive writing is **emotional language**. An author will often try to play on the emotions of readers by appealing to their sympathy or sense of morality. When an author uses colorful or evocative language with the intent of arousing the reader's passions, then the author may be attempting to persuade. Finally, in many cases, a persuasive text will give an **unfair explanation of opposing positions**, if these positions are mentioned at all.

Entertaining Texts

The success or failure of an author's intent to **entertain** is determined by those who read the author's work. Entertaining texts may be either fiction or nonfiction, and they may describe real or imagined people, places, and events. Entertaining texts are often narratives or poems. A text that is written to entertain is likely to contain **colorful language** that engages the imagination and the emotions. Such writing often features a great deal of figurative language, which typically enlivens the subject matter with images and analogies.

Though an entertaining text is not usually written to persuade or inform, authors may accomplish both of these tasks in their work. An entertaining text may *appeal to the reader's emotions* and cause him or her to think differently about a particular subject. In any case, entertaining texts tend to showcase the personality of the author more than other types of writing.

Descriptive Text

In a sense, almost all writing is descriptive, insofar as an author seeks to describe events, ideas, or people to the reader. Some texts, however, are primarily concerned with **description**. A descriptive text focuses on a particular subject and attempts to depict the subject in a way that will be clear to readers. Descriptive texts contain many adjectives and adverbs (i.e., words that give shades of meaning and create a more detailed mental picture for the reader). A descriptive text fails when it is unclear to the reader. A descriptive text will certainly be informative and may be persuasive and entertaining as well.

Review Video: Descriptive Texts
Visit mometrix.com/academy and enter code: 174903

Expression of Feelings

When an author intends to **express feelings**, he or she may use **expressive and bold language**. An author may write with emotion for any number of reasons. Sometimes, authors will express feelings because they are describing a personal situation of great pain or happiness. In other situations, authors will attempt to persuade the reader and will use emotion to stir up the passions. This kind of expression is easy to identify when the writer uses phrases like *I felt* and *I sense*. However, readers may find that the author will simply describe feelings without introducing them. As a reader, you must know the importance of recognizing when an author is expressing emotion and not to become overwhelmed by sympathy or passion. Readers should maintain some **detachment** so that they can still evaluate the strength of the author's argument or the quality of the writing.

> **Review Video: Emotional Language in Literature**
> Visit mometrix.com/academy and enter code: 759390

Expository Passage

An **expository** passage aims to **inform** and enlighten readers. Expository passages are nonfiction and usually center around a simple, easily defined topic. Since the goal of exposition is to teach, such a passage should be as clear as possible. Often, an expository passage contains helpful organizing words, like *first, next, for example,* and *therefore*. These words keep the reader **oriented** in the text. Although expository passages do not need to feature colorful language and artful writing, they are often more effective with these features. For a reader, the challenge of expository passages is to maintain steady attention. Expository passages are not always about subjects that will naturally interest a reader, so the writer is often more concerned with **clarity** and **comprehensibility** than with engaging the reader. By reading actively, you can ensure a good habit of focus when reading an expository passage.

> **Review Video: Expository Passages**
> Visit mometrix.com/academy and enter code: 256515

Narrative Passage

A **narrative** passage is a story that can be fiction or nonfiction. However, there are a few elements that a text must have in order to be classified as a narrative. First, the text must have a **plot** (i.e., a series of events). Narratives often proceed in a clear sequence, but this is not a requirement. If the narrative is good, then these events will be interesting to readers. Second, a narrative has **characters**. These characters could be people, animals, or even inanimate objects—so long as they participate in the plot. Third, a narrative passage often contains **figurative language** which is meant to stimulate the imagination of readers by making comparisons and observations. For instance, a *metaphor*, a common piece of figurative language, is a description of one thing in terms of another. *The moon was a frosty snowball* is an example of a metaphor. In the literal sense this is obviously untrue, but the comparison suggests a certain mood for the reader.

Technical Passage

A **technical** passage is written to *describe* a complex object or process. Technical writing is common in medical and technological fields, in which complex ideas of mathematics, science, and engineering need to be explained *simply* and *clearly*. To ease comprehension, a technical passage usually proceeds in a very logical order. Technical passages often have clear headings and subheadings, which are used to keep the reader oriented in the text. Additionally, you will find that these passages divide sections up with numbers or letters. Many technical passages look more like an outline than a piece of prose. The amount of **jargon** or difficult vocabulary will vary in a technical passage depending on the intended audience. As much as possible, technical passages try to avoid language that the reader will have to research in order to understand the message, yet readers will find that jargon cannot always be avoided.

> **Review Video: Technical Passages**
> Visit mometrix.com/academy and enter code: 478923

Persuasion and Rhetoric

Persuasive Techniques

To **appeal using reason**, writers present logical arguments, such as using "If... then... because" statements. To **appeal to emotions**, authors may ask readers how they would feel about something or to put themselves in another's place, present their argument as one that will make the audience feel good, or tell readers how they should feel. To **appeal to character**, **morality**, or **ethics**, authors present their points to readers as the right or most moral choices. Authors cite expert opinions to show readers that someone very knowledgeable about the subject or viewpoint agrees with the author's claims. **Testimonials**, usually via anecdotes or quotations regarding the author's subject, help build the audience's trust in an author's message through positive support from ordinary people. **Bandwagon appeals** claim that everybody else agrees with the author's argument and persuade readers to conform and agree, also. Authors **appeal to greed** by presenting their choice as cheaper, free, or more valuable for less cost. They **appeal to laziness** by presenting their views as more convenient, easy, or relaxing. Authors also anticipate potential objections and argue against them before audiences think of them, thereby depicting those objections as weak.

Authors can use **comparisons** like analogies, similes, and metaphors to persuade audiences. For example, a writer might represent excessive expenses as "hemorrhaging" money, which the author's recommended solution will stop. Authors can use negative word connotations to make some choices unappealing to readers, and positive word connotations to make others more appealing. Using **humor** can relax readers and garner their agreement. However, writers must take care: ridiculing opponents can be a successful strategy for appealing to readers who already agree with the author, but can backfire by angering other readers. **Rhetorical questions** need no answer, but create effect that can force agreement, such as asking the question, "Wouldn't you rather be paid more than less?" **Generalizations** persuade readers by being impossible to disagree with. Writers can easily make generalizations that appear to support their viewpoints, like saying, "We all want peace, not war" regarding more specific political arguments. **Transfer** and **association** persuade by example: if advertisements show attractive actors enjoying their products, audiences imagine they will experience the same. **Repetition** can also sometimes effectively persuade audiences.

Review Video: Using Rhetorical Strategies for Persuasion
Visit mometrix.com/academy and enter code: 302658

CLASSICAL AUTHOR APPEALS

In his *On Rhetoric,* ancient Greek philosopher Aristotle defined three basic types of appeal used in writing, which he called *pathos, ethos*, and *logos*. ***Pathos*** means suffering or experience and refers to appeals to the emotions (the English word *pathetic* comes from this root). Writing that is meant to entertain audiences, by making them either happy, as with comedy, or sad, as with tragedy, uses *pathos*. Aristotle's *Poetics* states that evoking the emotions of terror and pity is one of the criteria for writing tragedy. ***Ethos*** means character and connotes ideology (the English word *ethics* comes from this root). Writing that appeals to credibility, based on academic, professional, or personal merit, uses *ethos*. ***Logos*** means "I say" and refers to a plea, opinion, expectation, word or speech, account, opinion, or reason (the English word *logic* comes from this root.) Aristotle used it to mean persuasion that appeals to the audience through reasoning and logic to influence their opinions.

RHETORICAL DEVICES

- An **anecdote** is a brief story authors may relate to their argument, which can illustrate their points in a more real and relatable way.
- **Aphorisms** concisely state common beliefs and may rhyme. For example, Benjamin Franklin's "Early to bed and early to rise / Makes a man healthy, wealthy, and wise" is an aphorism.
- **Allusions** refer to literary or historical figures to impart symbolism to a thing or person and to create reader resonance. In John Steinbeck's *Of Mice and Men,* protagonist George's last name is Milton. This alludes to John Milton, who wrote *Paradise Lost*, and symbolizes George's eventual loss of his dream.
- **Satire** exaggerates, ridicules, or pokes fun at human flaws or ideas, as in the works of Jonathan Swift and Mark Twain.
- A **parody** is a form of satire that imitates another work to ridicule its topic or style.
- A **paradox** is a statement that is true despite appearing contradictory.
- **Hyperbole** is overstatement using exaggerated language.
- An **oxymoron** combines seeming contradictions, such as "deafening silence."
- **Analogies** compare two things that share common elements.

- **Similes** (stated comparisons using the words *like* or *as*) and **metaphors** (stated comparisons that do not use *like* or *as*) are considered forms of analogy.
- When using logic to reason with audiences, **syllogism** refers either to deductive reasoning or a deceptive, very sophisticated, or subtle argument.
- **Deductive reasoning** moves from general to specific, **inductive reasoning** from specific to general.
- **Diction** is author word choice that establishes tone and effect.
- **Understatement** achieves effects like contrast or irony by downplaying or describing something more subtly than warranted.
- **Chiasmus** uses parallel clauses, the second reversing the order of the first. Examples include T. S. Eliot's "Has the Church failed mankind, or has mankind failed the Church?" and John F. Kennedy's "Ask not what your country can do for you; ask what you can do for your country."
- **Anaphora** regularly repeats a word or phrase at the beginnings of consecutive clauses or phrases to add emphasis to an idea. A classic example of anaphora was Winston Churchill's emphasis of determination: "[W]e shall fight on the beaches, we shall fight on the landing grounds, we shall fight in the fields and in the streets, we shall fight in the hills; we shall never surrender..."

FIGURATIVE LANGUAGE

LITERAL AND FIGURATIVE MEANING

When language is used **literally**, the words mean exactly what they say and nothing more. When language is used **figuratively**, the words mean something beyond their literal meaning. For example, "The weeping willow tree has long, trailing branches and leaves" is a literal description. But "The weeping willow tree looks as if it is bending over and crying" is a figurative description—specifically, a **simile** or stated comparison. Another figurative language form is **metaphor**, or an implied comparison. A good example is the metaphor of a city, state, or city-state as a ship, and its governance as sailing that ship. Ancient Greek lyrical poet Alcaeus is credited with first using this metaphor, and ancient Greek tragedian Aeschylus then used it in *Seven Against Thebes,* and then Plato used it in the *Republic.*

FIGURES OF SPEECH

A **figure of speech** is a verbal expression whose meaning is figurative rather than literal. For example, the phrase "butterflies in the stomach" does not refer to actual butterflies in a person's stomach. It is a metaphor representing the fluttery feelings experienced when a person is nervous or excited—or when one "falls in love," which does not mean physically falling. "Hitting a sales target" does not mean physically hitting a target with arrows as in archery; it is a metaphor for meeting a sales quota. "Climbing the ladder of success" metaphorically likens advancing in one's career to ascending ladder rungs. Similes, such as "light as a feather" (meaning very light, not a feather's actual weight), and hyperbole, like "I'm starving/freezing/roasting," are also figures of speech. Figures of speech are often used and crafted for emphasis, freshness of expression, or clarity.

Review Video: Figures of Speech
Visit mometrix.com/academy and enter code: 111295

FIGURATIVE LANGUAGE

Figurative language extends past the literal meanings of words. It offers readers new insight into the people, things, events, and subjects covered in a work of literature. Figurative language also enables readers to feel they are sharing the authors' experiences. It can stimulate the reader's senses, make comparisons that readers find intriguing or even startling, and enable readers to view the world in different ways. When looking for figurative language, it is important to consider the context of the sentence or situation. Phrases that appear out of place or make little sense when read literally are likely instances of figurative language. Once figurative language has been recognized, context is also important to determining the type of figurative language being used and its function. For example, when a comparison is being made, a metaphor or simile is likely being used. This means the comparison may emphasize or create irony through the things being compared. Seven specific types of figurative language include: alliteration, onomatopoeia, personification, imagery, similes, metaphors, and hyperbole.

> **Review Video: Figurative Language**
> Visit mometrix.com/academy and enter code: 584902

Alliteration and Onomatopoeia

Alliteration describes a series of words beginning with the same sounds. **Onomatopoeia** uses words imitating the sounds of things they name or describe. For example, in his poem "Come Down, O Maid," Alfred Tennyson writes of "The moan of doves in immemorial elms, / And murmuring of innumerable bees." The word "moan" sounds like some sounds doves make, "murmuring" represents the sounds of bees buzzing. Onomatopoeia also includes words that are simply meant to represent sounds, such as "meow," "kaboom," and "whoosh."

> **Review Video: Alliteration in Everyday Expressions**
> Visit mometrix.com/academy and enter code: 462837

Personification

Another type of figurative language is **personification**. This is describing a non-human thing, like an animal or an object, as if it were human. The general intent of personification is to describe things in a manner that will be comprehensible to readers. When an author states that a tree *groans* in the wind, he or she does not mean that the tree is emitting a low, pained sound from a mouth. Instead, the author means that the tree is making a noise similar to a human groan. Of course, this personification establishes a tone of sadness or suffering. A different tone would be established if the author said that the tree was *swaying* or *dancing*. Alfred Tennyson's poem "The Eagle" uses all of these types of figurative language: "He clasps the crag with crooked hands." Tennyson used alliteration, repeating /k/ and /kr/ sounds. These hard-sounding consonants reinforce the imagery, giving visual and tactile impressions of the eagle.

> **Review Video: Personification**
> Visit mometrix.com/academy and enter code: 260066

Similes and Metaphors

Similes are stated comparisons using "like" or "as." Similes can be used to stimulate readers' imaginations and appeal to their senses. Because a simile includes *like* or *as,* the device creates more space between the description and the thing being described than a metaphor does. If an author says that *a house was like a shoebox*, then the tone is different than the author saying that the house *was* a shoebox. Authors will choose between a metaphor and a simile depending on their intended tone.

Similes also help compare fictional characters to well-known objects or experiences, so the reader can better relate to them. William Wordsworth's poem about "Daffodils" begins, "I wandered lonely as a cloud." This simile compares his loneliness to that of a cloud. It is also personification, giving a cloud the human quality loneliness. In his novel *Lord Jim* (1900), Joseph Conrad writes in Chapter 33, "I would have given anything for the power to soothe her frail soul, tormenting itself in its invincible ignorance like a small bird beating about the cruel wires of a cage." Conrad uses the word "like" to compare the girl's soul to a small bird. His description of the bird beating at the cage shows the similar helplessness of the girl's soul to gain freedom.

> **Review Video: Similes**
> Visit mometrix.com/academy and enter code: 642949

A **metaphor** is a type of figurative language in which the writer equates something with another thing that is not particularly similar, instead of using *like* or *as*. For instance, *the bird was an arrow arcing through the sky*. In this sentence, the arrow is serving as a metaphor for the bird. The point of a metaphor is to encourage the reader to consider the item being described in a *different way*. Let's continue with this metaphor for a flying bird. You are asked to envision the bird's flight as being similar to the arc of an arrow. So, you imagine the flight to be swift and bending. Metaphors are a way for the author to describe an item *without being direct and obvious*. This literary device is a lyrical and suggestive way of providing information. Note that the reference for a metaphor will not always be mentioned explicitly by the author. Consider the following description of a forest in winter: *Swaying skeletons reached for the sky and groaned as the wind blew through them*. In this example, the author is using *skeletons* as a metaphor for leafless trees. This metaphor creates a spooky tone while inspiring the reader's imagination.

Literary Examples of Metaphor

A **metaphor** is an implied comparison, i.e., it compares something to something else without using "like", "as", or other comparative words. For example, in "The Tyger" (1794), William Blake writes, "Tyger Tyger, burning bright, / In the forests of the night." Blake compares the tiger to a flame not by saying it is like a fire, but by simply describing it as "burning." Henry Wadsworth Longfellow's poem "O Ship of State" (1850) uses an extended metaphor by referring consistently throughout the entire poem to the state, union, or republic as a seagoing vessel, referring to its keel, mast, sail, rope, anchors, and to its braving waves, rocks, gale, tempest, and "false lights on the shore." Within the extended metaphor, Wordsworth uses a specific metaphor: "the anchors of thy hope!"

Ted Hughes' Animal Metaphors

Ted Hughes frequently used animal metaphors in his poetry. In "The Thought Fox," a model of concise, structured beauty, Hughes characterizes the poet's creative process with succinct, striking imagery of an idea entering his head like a wild fox. Repeating "loneliness" in the first two stanzas emphasizes the poet's lonely work: "Something else is alive / Beside the clock's loneliness." He treats an idea's arrival as separate from himself. Three stanzas detail in vivid images a fox's approach from the outside winter forest at starless midnight—its nose, "Cold, delicately" touching twigs and leaves; "neat" paw prints in snow; "bold" body; brilliant green eyes; and self-contained, focused progress—"Till, with a sudden sharp hot stink of fox," he metaphorically depicts poetic inspiration as the fox's physical entry into "the dark hole of the head." Hughes ends by summarizing his vision of a poet as an interior, passive idea recipient, with the outside world unchanged: "The window is starless still; the clock ticks, / The page is printed."

Review Video: Metaphors in Writing
Visit mometrix.com/academy and enter code: 133295

Metonymy

Metonymy is naming one thing with words or phrases of a closely related thing. This is similar to metaphor. However, the comparison has a close connection, unlike metaphor. An example of metonymy is to call the news media *the press*. Of course, *the press* is the machine that prints newspapers. Metonymy is a way of naming something without using the same name constantly.

Synecdoche

Synecdoche points to the whole by naming one of the parts. An example of synecdoche would be calling a construction worker a *hard hat*. Like metonymy, synecdoche is an easy way of naming something without having to overuse a name. The device allows writers to highlight pieces of the thing being described. For example, referring to businessmen as *suits* suggests professionalism and unity.

Hyperbole

Hyperbole is excessive exaggeration used for humor or emphasis rather than for literal meaning. For example, in *To Kill a Mockingbird*, Harper Lee wrote, "People moved slowly then. There was no hurry, for there was nowhere to go, nothing to buy and no money to buy it with, nothing to see outside the boundaries of Maycomb County." This was not literally true; Lee exaggerates the scarcity of these things for emphasis. In "Old Times on the Mississippi," Mark Twain wrote, "I... could have hung my hat on my eyes, they stuck out so far." This is not literal, but makes his description vivid and funny. In his poem "As I Walked Out One Evening", W. H. Auden wrote, "I'll love you, dear, I'll love you / Till China and Africa meet, / And the river jumps over the mountain / And the salmon sing in the street." He used things not literally possible to emphasize the duration of his love.

UNDERSTATEMENT

Understatement is the opposite of hyperbole. This device discounts or downplays something. Think about someone who climbs Mount Everest. Then, they say that the journey was *a little stroll*. As with other types of figurative language, understatement has a range of uses. The device may show self-defeat or modesty as in the Mount Everest example. However, some may think of understatement as false modesty (i.e., an attempt to bring attention to you or a situation). For example, a woman is praised on her diamond engagement ring. The woman says, *Oh, this little thing?* Her understatement might be heard as stuck-up or unfeeling.

Review Video: Hyperbole and Understatement
Visit mometrix.com/academy and enter code: 308470

LITERARY DEVICES

LITERARY IRONY

In literature, irony demonstrates the opposite of what is said or done. The three types of irony are **verbal irony**, **situational irony**, and **dramatic irony**. Verbal irony uses words opposite to the meaning. Sarcasm may use verbal irony. One common example is describing something that is confusing as "clear as mud." For example, in his 1986 movie *Hannah and Her Sisters,* author, director, and actor Woody Allen says to his character's date, "I had a great evening; it was like the Nuremburg Trials." Notice these employ similes. In situational irony, what happens contrasts with what was expected. O. Henry's short story *The Gift of the Magi* uses situational irony: a husband and wife each sacrifice their most prized possession to buy each other a Christmas present. The irony is that she sells her long hair to buy him a watch fob, while he sells his heirloom pocket-watch to buy her the jeweled combs for her hair she had long wanted; in the end, neither of them can use their gifts. In dramatic irony, narrative informs audiences of more than its characters know. For example, in *Romeo and Juliet,* the audience is made aware that Juliet is only asleep, while Romeo believes her to be dead, which then leads to Romeo's death.

Review Video: Irony
Visit mometrix.com/academy and enter code: 374204

IDIOMS

Idioms create comparisons, and often take the form of similes or metaphors. Idioms are always phrases and are understood to have a meaning that is different from its individual words' literal meaning. For example, "break a leg" is a common idiom that is used to wish someone luck or tell them to perform well. Literally, the phrase "break a leg" means to injure a person's leg, but the phrase takes on a different meaning when used as an idiom. Another example is "call it a day," which means to temporarily stop working on a task, or find a stopping point, rather than literally referring to something as "a day." Many idioms are associated with a region or group. For example, an idiom commonly used in the American South is "'til the cows come home." This phrase is often used to indicate that something will take or may last for a very long time, but not that it will literally last until the cows return to where they reside.

ALLUSION

An allusion is an uncited but recognizable reference to something else. Authors use language to make allusions to places, events, artwork, and other books in order to make their own text richer. For example, an author may allude to a very important text in order to make his own text seem more important. Martin Luther King, Jr. started his "I Have a Dream" speech by saying "Five score years ago..." This is a clear allusion to President Abraham Lincoln's "Gettysburg Address" and served to remind people of the significance of the event. An author may allude to a place to ground his text or make a cultural reference to make readers feel included. There are many reasons that authors make allusions.

Review Video: Allusions
Visit mometrix.com/academy and enter code: 294065

Comic Relief

Comic relief is the use of comedy by an author to break up a dramatic or tragic scene and infuse it with a bit of **lightheartedness**. In William Shakespeare's *Hamlet*, two gravediggers digging the grave for Ophelia share a joke while they work. The death and burial of Ophelia are tragic moments that directly follow each other. Shakespeare uses an instance of comedy to break up the tragedy and give his audience a bit of a break from the tragic drama. Authors sometimes use comic relief so that their work will be less depressing; other times they use it to create irony or contrast between the darkness of the situation and the lightness of the joke. Often, authors will use comedy to parallel what is happening in the tragic scenes.

Review Video: Comic Relief
Visit mometrix.com/academy and enter code: 779604

Foreshadowing

Foreshadowing is a device authors use to give readers **hints** about events that will take place later in a story. Foreshadowing most often takes place through a character's dialogue or actions. Sometimes the character will know what is going to happen and will purposefully allude to future events. For example, consider a protagonist who is about to embark on a journey through the woods. Just before the protagonist begins the trip, another character says, "Be careful, you never know what could be out in those woods!" This alerts the reader that the woods may be dangerous and prompts the reader to expect something to attack the protagonist in the woods. This is an example of foreshadowing through warning. Alternatively, a character may unknowingly foreshadow later events. For example, consider a story where a brother and sister run through their house and knock over a vase and break it. The brother says, "Don't worry, we'll clean it up! Mom will never know!" However, the reader knows that their mother will most likely find out what they have done, so the reader expects the siblings to later get in trouble for running, breaking the vase, and hiding it from their mother.

Symbolism

Symbolism describes an author's use of a **symbol**, an element of the story that **represents** something else. Symbols can impact stories in many ways, including deepening the meaning of a story or its elements, comparing a story to another work, or foreshadowing later events in a story. Symbols can be objects, characters, colors, numbers, or anything else the author establishes as a symbol. Symbols can be clearly established through direct comparison or repetition, but they can also be established subtly or gradually over a large portion of the story. Another form of symbolism is **allusion**, which is when something in a story is used to prompt the reader to think about another work. Many well-known works use **Biblical allusions**, which are allusions to events or details in the Bible that inform a work or an element within it.

Critical Reading Skills

Opinions, Facts, and Fallacies

Critical thinking skills are mastered through understanding various types of writing and the different purposes authors can have for writing different passages. Every author writes for a purpose. When you understand their purpose and how they accomplish their goal, you will be able to analyze their writing and determine whether or not you agree with their conclusions.

Readers must always be aware of the difference between fact and opinion. A **fact** can be subjected to analysis and proven to be true. An **opinion**, on the other hand, is the author's personal thoughts or feelings and may not be altered by research or evidence. If the author writes that the distance from New York City to Boston is about two hundred miles, then he or she is stating a fact. If the author writes that New York City is too crowded, then he or she is giving an opinion because there is no objective standard for overpopulation. Opinions are often supported by facts. For instance, an author might use a comparison between the population density of New York City and that of other major American cities as evidence of an overcrowded population. An opinion supported by facts tends to be more convincing. On the other hand, when authors support their opinions with other opinions, readers should employ critical thinking and approach the argument with skepticism.

Review Video: Distinguishing Fact and Opinion
Visit mometrix.com/academy and enter code: 870899

Reliable Sources

When you read an argumentative passage, you need to be sure that facts are presented to the reader from **reliable sources**. An opinion is what the author thinks about a given topic. An opinion is not common knowledge or proven by expert sources, instead the information is the personal beliefs and thoughts of the author. To distinguish between fact and opinion, a reader needs to consider the type of source that is presenting information, the information that backs-up a claim, and the author's motivation to have a certain point-of-view on a given topic. For example, if a panel of scientists has conducted multiple studies on the effectiveness of taking a certain vitamin, then the results are more likely to be factual than those of a company that is selling a vitamin and simply claims that taking the vitamin can produce positive effects. The company is motivated to sell their product, and the scientists are using the scientific method to prove a theory. Remember, if you find sentences that contain phrases such as "I think...", then the statement is an opinion.

Biases

In their attempts to persuade, writers often make mistakes in their thought processes and writing choices. These processes and choices are important to understand so you can make an informed decision about the author's credibility. Every author has a point of view, but authors demonstrate a **bias** when they ignore reasonable counterarguments or distort opposing viewpoints. A bias is evident whenever the author's claims are presented in a way that is unfair or inaccurate. Bias can be intentional or unintentional, but readers should be skeptical of the author's argument in either case. Remember that a biased author may still be correct. However, the author will be correct in spite of, not because of, his or her bias.

A **stereotype** is a bias applied specifically to a group of people or a place. Stereotyping is considered to be particularly abhorrent because it promotes negative, misleading generalizations about people. Readers should be very cautious of authors who use stereotypes in their writing. These faulty assumptions typically reveal the author's ignorance and lack of curiosity.

Review Video: Bias and Stereotype
Visit mometrix.com/academy and enter code: 644829

Reading Informational Texts

Language Use

Literal and Figurative Language

As in fictional literature, informational text also uses both **literal language**, which means just what it says, and **figurative language**, which imparts more than literal meaning. For example, an informational text author might use a simile or direct comparison, such as writing that a racehorse "ran like the wind." Informational text authors also use metaphors or implied comparisons, such as "the cloud of the Great Depression." Imagery may also appear in informational texts to increase the reader's understanding of ideas and concepts discussed in the text.

Explicit and Implicit Information

When informational text states something explicitly, the reader is told by the author exactly what is meant, which can include the author's interpretation or perspective of events. For example, a professor writes, "I have seen students go into an absolute panic just because they weren't able to complete the exam in the time they were allotted." This explicitly tells the reader that the students were afraid, and by using the words "just because," the writer indicates their fear was exaggerated out of proportion relative to what happened. However, another professor writes, "I have had students come to me, their faces drained of all color, saying 'We weren't able to finish the exam.'" This is an example of implicit meaning: the second writer did not state explicitly that the students were panicked. Instead, he wrote a description of their faces being "drained of all color." From this description, the reader can infer that the students were so frightened that their faces paled.

Review Video: Explicit and Implicit Information
Visit mometrix.com/academy and enter code: 735771

Making Inferences About Informational Text

With informational text, reader comprehension depends not only on recalling important statements and details, but also on reader inferences based on examples and details. Readers add information from the text to what they already know to draw inferences about the text. These inferences help the readers to fill in the information that the text does not explicitly state, enabling them to understand the text better. When reading a nonfictional autobiography or biography, for example, the most appropriate inferences might concern the events in the book, the actions of the subject of the autobiography or biography, and the message the author means to convey. When reading a nonfictional expository (informational) text, the reader would best draw inferences about problems and their solutions, and causes and their effects. When reading a nonfictional persuasive text, the reader will want to infer ideas supporting the author's message and intent.

Structures or Organizational Patterns in Informational Texts

Informational text can be **descriptive**, appealing to the five senses and answering the questions what, who, when, where, and why. Another method of structuring informational text is sequence and order. **Chronological** texts relate events in the sequence that they occurred, from start to finish, while how-to texts organize information into a series of instructions in the sequence in which the steps should be followed. **Comparison-contrast** structures of informational text describe various ideas to their readers by pointing out how things or ideas are similar and how they are different. **Cause and effect** structures of informational text describe events that occurred and identify the causes or reasons that those events occurred. **Problem and solution** structures of informational texts introduce and describe problems and offer one or more solutions for each problem described.

Determining an Informational Author's Purpose

Informational authors' purposes are why they write texts. Readers must determine authors' motivations and goals. Readers gain greater insight into a text by considering the author's motivation. This develops critical reading skills. Readers perceive writing as a person's voice, not simply printed words. Uncovering author motivations and purposes empowers readers to know what to expect from the text, read for relevant details, evaluate authors and their work critically, and respond effectively to the motivations and persuasions of the text. The main idea of a text is what the reader is supposed to understand from reading it; the purpose of the text is why the author has written it and what the author wants readers to do with its information. Authors state some purposes clearly, while other purposes may be unstated but equally significant. When stated purposes contradict other parts of a text, the author may have a hidden agenda. Readers can better evaluate a text's effectiveness, whether they agree or disagree with it, and why they agree or disagree through identifying unstated author purposes.

Identifying Author's Point of View or Purpose

In some informational texts, readers find it easy to identify the author's point of view and purpose, such as when the author explicitly states his or her position and reason for writing. But other texts are more difficult, either because of the content or because the authors give neutral or balanced viewpoints. This is particularly true in scientific texts, in which authors may state the purpose of their research in the report, but never state their point of view except by interpreting evidence or data.

To analyze text and identify point of view or purpose, readers should ask themselves the following four questions:

1. With what main point or idea does this author want to persuade readers to agree?
2. How does this author's word choice affect the way that readers consider this subject?
3. How do this author's choices of examples and facts affect the way that readers consider this subject?
4. What is it that this author wants to accomplish by writing this text?

Review Video: Understanding the Author's Intent
Visit mometrix.com/academy and enter code: 511819

Review Video: Author's Position
Visit mometrix.com/academy and enter code: 827954

Evaluating Arguments Made by Informational Text Writers

When evaluating an informational text, the first step is to identify the argument's conclusion. Then identify the author's premises that support the conclusion. Try to paraphrase premises for clarification and make the conclusion and premises fit. List all premises first, sequentially numbered, then finish with the conclusion. Identify any premises or assumptions not stated by the author but required for the stated premises to support the conclusion. Read word assumptions sympathetically, as the author might. Evaluate whether premises reasonably support the conclusion. For inductive reasoning, the reader should ask if the premises are true, if they support the conclusion, and if so, how strongly. For deductive reasoning, the reader should ask if the argument is valid or invalid. If all premises are true, then the argument is valid unless the conclusion can be false. If it can, then the argument is invalid. An invalid argument can be made valid through alterations such as the addition of needed premises.

Use of Rhetoric in Informational Texts

There are many ways authors can support their claims, arguments, beliefs, ideas, and reasons for writing in informational texts. For example, authors can appeal to readers' sense of **logic** by communicating their reasoning through a carefully sequenced series of logical steps to help "prove" the points made. Authors can appeal to readers' **emotions** by using descriptions and words that evoke feelings of sympathy, sadness, anger, righteous indignation, hope, happiness, or any other emotion to reinforce what they express and share with their audience. Authors may appeal to the **moral** or **ethical values** of readers by using words and descriptions that can convince readers that something is right or wrong. By relating personal anecdotes, authors can supply readers with more accessible, realistic examples of points they make, as well as appealing to their emotions. They can provide supporting evidence by reporting case studies. They can also illustrate their points by making analogies to which readers can better relate.

Organizational Features in Texts

Text Features in Informational Texts

- The **title of a text** gives readers some idea of its content.
- The **table of contents** is a list near the beginning of a text, showing the book's sections and chapters and their coinciding page numbers. This gives readers an overview of the whole text and helps them find specific chapters easily.
- An **appendix**, at the back of the book or document, includes important information that is not present in the main text.
- Also at the back, an **index** lists the book's important topics alphabetically with their page numbers to help readers find them easily.
- **Glossaries**, usually found at the backs of books, list technical terms alphabetically with their definitions to aid vocabulary learning and comprehension. Boldface print is used to emphasize certain words, often identifying words included in the text's glossary where readers can look up their definitions.

- **Headings** separate sections of text and show the topic of each.
- **Subheadings** divide subject headings into smaller, more specific categories to help readers organize information.
- **Footnotes**, at the bottom of the page, give readers more information, such as citations or links.
- **Bullet points** list items separately, making facts and ideas easier to see and understand.
- A **sidebar** is a box of information to one side of the main text giving additional information, often on a more focused or in-depth example of a topic.

VISUAL FEATURES IN TEXTS

- **Illustrations** and **photographs** are pictures that visually emphasize important points in text.
- The **captions** below the illustrations explain what those images show.
- **Charts** and **tables** are visual forms of information that make something easier to understand quickly.
- **Diagrams** are drawings that show relationships or explain a process.
- **Graphs** visually show the relationships among multiple sets of information plotted along vertical and horizontal axes.
- **Maps** show geographical information visually to help readers understand the relative locations of places covered in the text.
- **Timelines** are visual graphics that show historical events in chronological order to help readers see their sequence.

Review Video: Informational Text
Visit mometrix.com/academy and enter code: 924964

TECHNICAL LANGUAGE

TECHNICAL LANGUAGE

Technical language is more impersonal than literary and vernacular language. Passive voice makes the tone impersonal. For example, instead of writing, "We found this a central component of protein metabolism," scientists write, "This was found a central component of protein metabolism." While science professors have traditionally instructed students to avoid active voice because it leads to first-person ("I" and "we") usage, science editors today find passive voice dull and weak. Many journal articles combine both. Tone in technical science writing should be detached, concise, and professional. While one may normally write, "This chemical has to be available for proteins to be digested," professionals write technically, "The presence of this chemical is required for the enzyme to break the covalent bonds of proteins." The use of technical language appeals to both technical and non-technical audiences by displaying the author or speaker's understanding of the subject and suggesting their credibility regarding the message they are communicating.

TECHNICAL MATERIAL FOR NON-TECHNICAL READERS

Writing about **technical subjects** for **non-technical readers** differs from writing for colleagues because authors place more importance on delivering a critical message than on imparting the maximum technical content possible. Technical authors also must assume that non-technical audiences do not have the expertise to comprehend extremely scientific or technical messages, concepts, and terminology. They must resist the temptation to impress audiences with their scientific knowledge and expertise and remember that their primary purpose is to communicate a message that non-technical readers will understand, feel, and respond to. Non-technical and technical styles include similarities. Both should formally cite any references or other authors' work utilized in the text. Both must follow intellectual property and copyright regulations. This includes the author's protecting his or her own rights, or a public domain statement, as he or she chooses.

Review Video: Technical Passages
Visit mometrix.com/academy and enter code: 478923

Non-Technical Audiences

Writers of technical or scientific material may need to write for many non-technical audiences. Some readers have no technical or scientific background, and those who do may not be in the same field as the authors. Government and corporate policymakers and budget managers need technical information they can understand for decision-making. Citizens affected by technology or science are a different audience. Non-governmental organizations can encompass many of the preceding groups. Elementary and secondary school programs also need non-technical language for presenting technical subject matter. Additionally, technical authors will need to use non-technical language when collecting consumer responses to surveys, presenting scientific or para-scientific material to the public, writing about the history of science, and writing about science and technology in developing countries.

Use of Everyday Language

Authors of technical information sometimes must write using non-technical language that readers outside their disciplinary fields can comprehend. They should use not only non-technical terms, but also normal, everyday language to accommodate readers whose native language is different than the language the text is written in. For example, instead of writing that "eustatic changes like thermal expansion are causing hazardous conditions in the littoral zone," an author would do better to write that "a rising sea level is threatening the coast." When technical terms cannot be avoided, authors should also define or explain them using non-technical language. Although authors must cite references and acknowledge their use of others' work, they should avoid the kinds of references or citations that they would use in scientific journals—unless they reinforce author messages. They should not use endnotes, footnotes, or any other complicated referential techniques because non-technical journal publishers usually do not accept them. Including high-resolution illustrations, photos, maps, or satellite images and incorporating multimedia into digital publications will enhance non-technical writing about technical subjects. Technical authors may publish using non-technical language in e-journals, trade journals, specialty newsletters, and daily newspapers.

Types of Technical Writing

Types of Printed Communication

Memo

A memo (short for *memorandum*) is a common form of written communication. There is a standard format for these documents. It is typical for there to be a **heading** at the top indicating the author, date, and recipient. In some cases, this heading will also include the author's title and the name of his or her institution. Below this information will be the **body** of the memo. These documents are typically written by and for members of the same organization. They usually contain a plan of action, a request for information on a specific topic, or a response to such a request. Memos are considered to be official documents, so they are usually written in a **formal** style. Many memos are organized with numbers or bullet points, which make it easier for the reader to identify key ideas.

Posted Announcement

People post **announcements** for all sorts of occasions. Many people are familiar with notices for lost pets, yard sales, and landscaping services. In order to be effective, these announcements need to *contain all of the information* the reader requires to act on the message. For instance, a lost pet announcement needs to include a good description of the animal and a contact number for the owner. A yard sale notice should include the address, date, and hours of the sale, as well as a brief description of the products that will be available there. When composing an announcement, it is important to consider the perspective of the **audience**—what will they need to know in order to respond to the message? Although a posted announcement can have color and decoration to attract the eye of the passerby, it must also convey the necessary information clearly.

Classified Advertisement

Classified advertisements, or **ads**, are used to sell or buy goods, to attract business, to make romantic connections, and to do countless other things. They are an inexpensive, and sometimes free, way to make a brief **pitch**. Classified ads used to be found only in newspapers or special advertising circulars, but there are now online listings as well. The style of these ads has remained basically the same. An ad usually begins with a word or phrase indicating what is being **sold** or **sought**. Then, the listing will give a brief **description** of the product or service. Because space is limited and costly in newspapers, classified ads there will often contain abbreviations for common attributes. For instance, two common abbreviations are *bk* for *black*, and *obo* for *or best offer*. Classified ads will then usually conclude by listing the **price** (or the amount the seeker is willing to pay), followed by **contact information** like a telephone number or email address.

SCALE READINGS OF STANDARD MEASUREMENT INSTRUMENTS

The scales used on **standard measurement instruments** are fairly easy to read with a little practice. Take the **ruler** as an example. A typical ruler has different units along each long edge. One side measures inches, and the other measures centimeters. The units are specified close to the zero reading for the ruler. Note that the ruler does not begin measuring from its outermost edge. The zero reading is a black line a tiny distance inside of the edge. On the inches side, each inch is indicated with a long black line and a number. Each half-inch is noted with a slightly shorter line. Quarter-inches are noted with still shorter lines, eighth-inches are noted with even shorter lines, and sixteenth-inches are noted with the shortest lines of all. On the centimeter side, the second-largest black lines indicate half-centimeters, and the smaller lines indicate tenths of centimeters, otherwise known as millimeters.

VISUAL INFORMATION IN INFORMATIONAL TEXTS

CHARTS, GRAPHS, AND VISUALS

PIE CHART

A pie chart, also known as a circle graph, is useful for depicting how a single unit or category is divided. The standard pie chart is a circle with designated wedges. Each wedge is **proportional** in size to a part of the whole. For instance, consider Shawna, a student at City College, who uses a pie chart to represent her budget. If she spends half of her money on rent, then the pie chart will represent that amount with a line through the center of the pie. If she spends a quarter of her money on food, there will be a line extending from the edge of the circle to the center at a right angle to the line depicting rent. This illustration would make it clear that the student spends twice the amount of money on rent as she does on food.

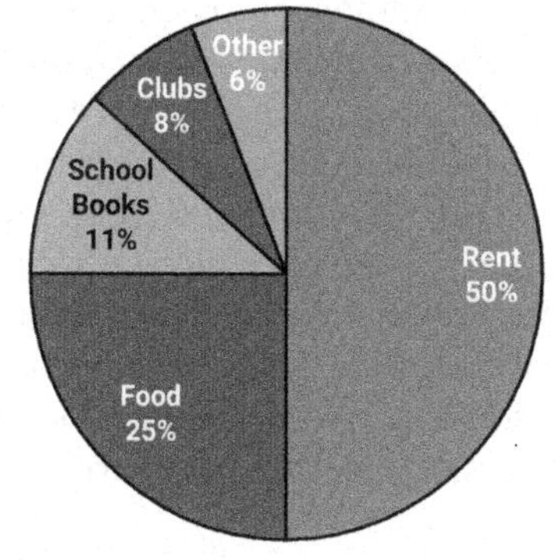

A pie chart is effective at showing how a single entity is divided into parts. They are not effective at demonstrating the relationships between parts of different wholes. For example, an unhelpful use of a pie chart would be to compare the respective amounts of state and federal spending devoted to infrastructure since these values are only meaningful in the context of the entire budget.

Bar Graph

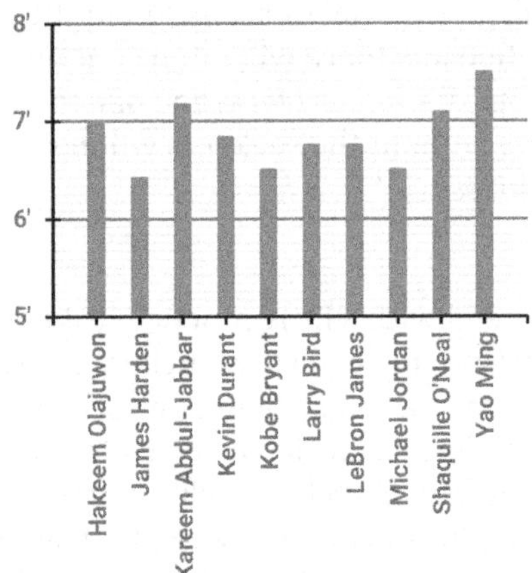

The bar graph is one of the most common visual representations of information. **Bar graphs** are used to illustrate sets of numerical **data**. The graph has a vertical axis (along which numbers are listed) and a horizontal axis (along which categories, words, or some other indicators are placed). One example of a bar graph is a depiction of the respective heights of famous basketball players: the vertical axis would contain numbers ranging from five to eight feet, and the horizontal axis would contain the names of the players. The length of the bar above the player's name would illustrate his height, and the top of the bar would stop perpendicular to the height listed along the left side. In this representation, one would see that Yao Ming is taller than Michael Jordan because Yao's bar would be higher.

Line Graph

A line graph is a type of graph that is typically used for measuring trends over time. The graph is set up along a vertical and a horizontal **axis**. The variables being measured are listed along the left side and the bottom side of the axes. Points are then plotted along the graph as they correspond with their values for each variable. For instance, consider a line graph measuring a person's income for each month of the year. If the person earned $1500 in January, there should be a point directly above January (perpendicular to the horizontal axis) and directly to the right of $1500 (perpendicular to the vertical axis). Once all of the lines are plotted, they are connected with a line from left to right. This line provides a nice visual illustration of the general **trends** of the data, if they exist. For instance, using the earlier example, if the line sloped up, then one would see that the person's income had increased over the course of the year.

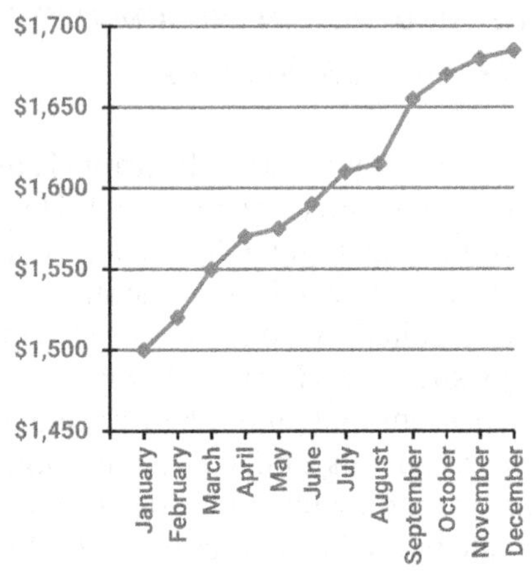

Pictographs

A **pictograph** is a graph, generally in the horizontal orientation, that uses pictures or symbols to represent the data. Each pictograph must have a key that defines the picture or symbol and gives the quantity each picture or symbol represents. Pictures or symbols on a pictograph are not always shown as whole elements. In this case, the fraction of the picture or symbol shown represents the same fraction of the quantity a whole picture or symbol stands for.

Review Video: Pictographs
Visit mometrix.com/academy and enter code: 147860

Reading Argumentative Writing

Author's Argument in Argumentative Writing

In argumentative writing, the argument is a belief, position, or opinion that the author wants to convince readers to believe as well. For the first step, readers should identify the **issue**. Some issues are controversial, meaning people disagree about them. Gun control, foreign policy, and the death penalty are all controversial issues. The next step is to determine the **author's position** on the issue. That position or viewpoint constitutes the author's argument. Readers should then identify the **author's assumptions**: things he or she accepts, believes, or takes for granted without needing proof. Inaccurate or illogical assumptions produce flawed arguments and can mislead readers. Readers should identify what kinds of **supporting evidence** the author offers, such as research results, personal observations or experiences, case studies, facts, examples, expert testimony and opinions, and comparisons. Readers should decide how relevant this support is to the argument.

> **Review Video: Argumentative Writing**
> Visit mometrix.com/academy and enter code: 561544

Evaluating an Author's Argument

The first three reader steps to **evaluate an author's argument** are to identify the **author's assumptions**, identify the **supporting evidence**, and decide **whether the evidence is relevant**. For example, if an author is not an expert on a particular topic, then that author's personal experience or opinion might not be relevant. The fourth step is to assess the **author's objectivity**. For example, consider whether the author introduces clear, understandable supporting evidence and facts to support the argument. The fifth step is evaluating whether the author's **argument is complete**. When authors give sufficient support for their arguments and also anticipate and respond effectively to opposing arguments or objections to their points, their arguments are complete. However, some authors omit information that could detract from their arguments. If instead they stated this information and refuted it, it would strengthen their arguments. The sixth step in evaluating an author's argumentative writing is to assess whether the **argument is valid**. Providing clear, logical reasoning makes an author's argument valid. Readers should ask themselves whether the author's points follow a sequence that makes sense, and whether each point leads to the next. The seventh step is to determine whether the author's **argument is credible**, meaning that it is convincing and believable. Arguments that are not valid are not credible, so step seven depends on step six. Readers should be mindful of their own biases as they evaluate and should not expect authors to conclusively prove their arguments, but rather to provide effective support and reason.

Evaluating an Author's Method of Appeal

To evaluate the effectiveness of an appeal, it is important to consider the author's purpose for writing. Any appeals an author uses in their argument must be relevant to the argument's goal. For example, a writer that argues for the reclassification of Pluto, but primarily uses appeals to emotion, will not have an effective argument. This writer should focus on using appeals to logic and support their argument with provable facts. While most arguments should include appeals to logic, emotion, and credibility, some arguments only call for one or two of these types of appeal. Evidence can support an appeal, but the evidence must be relevant to truly strengthen the appeal's effectiveness. If the writer arguing for Pluto's reclassification uses the reasons for Jupiter's classification as evidence, their argument would be weak. This information may seem relevant because it is related to the classification of planets. However, this classification is highly dependent on the size of the celestial object, and Jupiter is significantly bigger than Pluto. This use of evidence is illogical and does not support the appeal. Even when appropriate evidence and appeals are used, appeals and arguments lose their effectiveness when they create logical fallacies.

Evidence

The term **text evidence** refers to information that supports a main point or minor points and can help lead the reader to a conclusion about the text's credibility. Information used as text evidence is precise, descriptive, and factual. A main point is often followed by supporting details that provide evidence to back up a claim. For example, a passage may include the claim that winter occurs during opposite months in the Northern and Southern hemispheres. Text evidence for this claim may include examples of countries where winter occurs in opposite months. Stating that the tilt of the Earth as it rotates around the sun causes winter to occur at different times in separate hemispheres is another example of text evidence. Text evidence can come from common knowledge, but it is also valuable to include text evidence from credible, relevant outside sources.

> **Review Video: Textual Evidence**
> Visit mometrix.com/academy and enter code: 486236

Evidence that supports the thesis and additional arguments needs to be provided. Most arguments must be supported by facts or statistics. A fact is something that is known with certainty, has been verified by several independent individuals, and can be proven to be true. In addition to facts, examples and illustrations can support an argument by adding an emotional component. With this component, you persuade readers in ways that facts and statistics cannot. The emotional component is effective when used alongside objective information that can be confirmed.

CREDIBILITY

The text used to support an argument can be the argument's downfall if the text is not credible. A text is **credible**, or believable, when its author is knowledgeable and objective, or unbiased. The author's motivations for writing the text play a critical role in determining the credibility of the text and must be evaluated when assessing that credibility. Reports written about the ozone layer by an environmental scientist and a hairdresser will have a different level of credibility.

Review Video: Author Credibility
Visit mometrix.com/academy and enter code: 827257

APPEAL TO EMOTION

Sometimes, authors will appeal to the reader's emotion in an attempt to persuade or to distract the reader from the weakness of the argument. For instance, the author may try to inspire the pity of the reader by delivering a heart-rending story. An author also might use the bandwagon approach, in which he suggests that his opinion is correct because it is held by the majority. Some authors resort to name-calling, in which insults and harsh words are delivered to the opponent in an attempt to distract. In advertising, a common appeal is the celebrity testimonial, in which a famous person endorses a product. Of course, the fact that a famous person likes something should not really mean anything to the reader. These and other emotional appeals are usually evidence of poor reasoning and a weak argument.

Review Video: Emotional Language in Literature
Visit mometrix.com/academy and enter code: 759390

COUNTER ARGUMENTS

When authors give both sides to the argument, they build trust with their readers. As a reader, you should start with an undecided or neutral position. If an author presents only his or her side to the argument, then they are not exhibiting credibility and are weakening their argument.

Building common ground with readers can be effective for persuading neutral, skeptical, or opposed readers. Sharing values with undecided readers can allow people to switch positions without giving up what they feel is important. People who may oppose a position need to feel that they can change their minds without betraying who they are as a person. This appeal to having an open mind can be a powerful tool in arguing a position without antagonizing other views. Objections can be countered on a point-by-point basis or in a summary paragraph. Be mindful of how an author points out flaws in counter arguments. If they are unfair to the other side of the argument, then you should lose trust with the author.

MAKING AND EVALUATING PREDICTIONS

MAKING PREDICTIONS

When we read literature, **making predictions** about what will happen in the writing reinforces our purpose for reading and prepares us mentally. A **prediction** is a guess about what will happen next. Readers constantly make predictions based on what they have read and what they already know. We can make predictions before we begin reading and during our reading. Consider the following sentence: *Staring at the computer screen in shock, Kim blindly reached over for the brimming glass of water on the shelf to her side.* The sentence suggests that Kim is distracted, and that she is not looking at the glass that she is going to pick up. So, a reader might predict that Kim is going to knock over the glass. Of course, not every prediction will be accurate: perhaps Kim will pick the glass up cleanly. Nevertheless, the author has certainly created the expectation that the water might be spilled.

As we read on, we can test the accuracy of our predictions, revise them in light of additional reading, and confirm or refute our predictions. Predictions are always subject to revision as the reader acquires more information. A reader can make predictions by observing the title and illustrations; noting the structure, characters, and subject; drawing on existing knowledge relative to the subject; and asking "why" and "who" questions. Connecting reading to what we already know enables us to learn new information and construct meaning. For example, before third-graders read a book about Johnny Appleseed, they may start a KWL chart—a list of what they *Know*, what they *Want* to know or learn, and what they have *Learned* after reading. Activating existing background knowledge and thinking about the text before reading improves comprehension.

Review Video: Predictive Reading
Visit mometrix.com/academy and enter code: 437248

Test-taking tip: To respond to questions requiring future predictions, your answers should be based on evidence of past or present behavior and events.

Evaluating Predictions

When making predictions, readers should be able to explain how they developed their prediction. One way readers can defend their thought process is by citing textual evidence. Textual evidence to evaluate reader predictions about literature includes specific synopses of the work, paraphrases of the work or parts of it, and direct quotations from the work. These references to the text must support the prediction by indicating, clearly or unclearly, what will happen later in the story. A text may provide these indications through literary devices such as foreshadowing. Foreshadowing is anything in a text that gives the reader a hint about what is to come by emphasizing the likelihood of an event or development. Foreshadowing can occur through descriptions, exposition, and dialogue. Foreshadowing in dialogue usually occurs when a character gives a warning or expresses a strong feeling that a certain event will occur. Foreshadowing can also occur through irony. However, unlike other forms of foreshadowing, the events that seem the most likely are the opposite of what actually happens. Instances of foreshadowing and irony can be summarized, paraphrased, or quoted to defend a reader's prediction.

Review Video: Textual Evidence for Predictions
Visit mometrix.com/academy and enter code: 261070

Making Inferences and Drawing Conclusions

Inferences are logical conclusions that readers make based on their observations and previous knowledge. An inference is based on both what is found in a passage or a story and what is known from personal experience. For instance, a story may say that a character is frightened and can hear howling in the distance. Based on both what is in the text and personal knowledge, it is a logical conclusion that the character is frightened because he hears the sound of wolves. A good inference is supported by the information in a passage.

Implicit and Explicit Information

By inferring, readers construct meanings from text that are personally relevant. By combining their own schemas or concepts and their background information pertinent to the text with what they read, readers interpret it according to both what the author has conveyed and their own unique perspectives. Inferences are different from **explicit information**, which is clearly stated in a passage. Authors do not always explicitly spell out every meaning in what they write; many meanings are implicit. Through inference, readers can comprehend implied meanings in the text, and also derive personal significance from it, making the text meaningful and memorable to them. Inference is a natural process in everyday life. When readers infer, they can draw conclusions about what the author is saying, predict what may reasonably follow, amend these predictions as they continue to read, interpret the import of themes, and analyze the characters' feelings and motivations through their actions.

EXAMPLE OF DRAWING CONCLUSIONS FROM INFERENCES

Read the excerpt and decide why Jana finally relaxed.

> Jana loved her job, but the work was very demanding. She had trouble relaxing. She called a friend, but she still thought about work. She ordered a pizza, but eating it did not help. Then, her kitten jumped on her lap and began to purr. Jana leaned back and began to hum a little tune. She felt better.

You can draw the conclusion that Jana relaxed because her kitten jumped on her lap. The kitten purred, and Jana leaned back and hummed a tune. Then she felt better. The excerpt does not explicitly say that this is the reason why she was able to relax. The text leaves the matter unclear, but the reader can infer or make a "best guess" that this is the reason she is relaxing. This is a logical conclusion based on the information in the passage. It is the best conclusion a reader can make based on the information he or she has read. Inferences are based on the information in a passage, but they are not directly stated in the passage.

Test-taking tip: While being tested on your ability to make correct inferences, you must look for **contextual clues**. An answer can be true, but not the best or most correct answer. The contextual clues will help you find the answer that is the **best answer** out of the given choices. Be careful in your reading to understand the context in which a phrase is stated. When asked for the implied meaning of a statement made in the passage, you should immediately locate the statement and read the **context** in which the statement was made. Also, look for an answer choice that has a similar phrase to the statement in question.

> **Review Video: Inference**
> Visit mometrix.com/academy and enter code: 379203
>
> **Review Video: How to Support a Conclusion**
> Visit mometrix.com/academy and enter code: 281653

READING COMPREHENSION AND CONNECTING WITH TEXTS

COMPARING TWO STORIES

When presented with two different stories, there will be **similarities** and **differences** between the two. A reader needs to make a list, or other graphic organizer, of the points presented in each story. Once the reader has written down the main point and supporting points for each story, the two sets of ideas can be compared. The reader can then present each idea and show how it is the same or different in the other story. This is called **comparing and contrasting ideas**.

The reader can compare ideas by stating, for example: "In Story 1, the author believes that humankind will one day land on Mars, whereas in Story 2, the author believes that Mars is too far away for humans to ever step foot on." Note that the two viewpoints are different in each story that the reader is comparing. A reader may state that: "Both stories discussed the likelihood of humankind landing on Mars." This statement shows how the viewpoint presented in both stories is based on the same topic, rather than how each viewpoint is different. The reader will complete a comparison of two stories with a conclusion.

> **Review Video: How to Compare and Contrast**
> Visit mometrix.com/academy and enter code: 833765

OUTLINING A PASSAGE

As an aid to drawing conclusions, **outlining** the information contained in the passage should be a familiar skill to readers. An effective outline will reveal the structure of the passage and will lead to solid conclusions. An effective outline will have a title that refers to the basic subject of the text, though the title does not need to restate the main idea. In most outlines, the main idea will be the first major section. Each major idea in the passage will be established as the head of a category. For instance, the most common outline format calls for the main ideas of the passage to be indicated with Roman numerals. In an effective outline of this kind, each of the main ideas will be represented by a Roman numeral and none of the Roman numerals will designate minor details or secondary ideas. Moreover, all supporting ideas and details should be placed in the appropriate place on the outline. An outline does not need to include every detail listed in the text, but it should feature all of those that are central to the argument or message. Each of these details should be listed under the corresponding main idea.

Review Video: Outlining as an Aid to Drawing Conclusions
Visit mometrix.com/academy and enter code: 584445

Using Graphic Organizers

Ideas from a text can also be organized using **graphic organizers**. A graphic organizer is a way to simplify information and take key points from the text. A graphic organizer such as a timeline may have an event listed for a corresponding date on the timeline, while an outline may have an event listed under a key point that occurs in the text. Each reader needs to create the type of graphic organizer that works the best for him or her in terms of being able to recall information from a story. Examples include a spider-map, which takes a main idea from the story and places it in a bubble with supporting points branching off the main idea. An outline is useful for diagramming the main and supporting points of the entire story, and a Venn diagram compares and contrasts characteristics of two or more ideas.

Review Video: Graphic Organizers
Visit mometrix.com/academy and enter code: 665513

Making Logical Conclusions about a Passage

A reader should always be drawing conclusions from the text. Sometimes conclusions are **implied** from written information, and other times the information is **stated directly** within the passage. One should always aim to draw conclusions from information stated within a passage, rather than to draw them from mere implications. At times an author may provide some information and then describe a counterargument. Readers should be alert for direct statements that are subsequently rejected or weakened by the author. Furthermore, you should always read through the entire passage before drawing conclusions. Many readers are trained to expect the author's conclusions at either the beginning or the end of the passage, but many texts do not adhere to this format.

Drawing conclusions from information implied within a passage requires confidence on the part of the reader. **Implications** are things that the author does not state directly, but readers can assume based on what the author does say. Consider the following passage: *I stepped outside and opened my umbrella. By the time I got to work, the cuffs of my pants were soaked.* The author never states that it is raining, but this fact is clearly implied. Conclusions based on implication must be well supported by the text. In order to draw a solid conclusion, readers should have **multiple pieces of evidence**. If readers have only one piece, they must be assured that there is no other possible explanation than their conclusion. A good reader will be able to draw many conclusions from information implied by the text, which will be a great help on the exam.

Drawing Conclusions

A common type of inference that a reader has to make is **drawing a conclusion**. The reader makes this conclusion based on the information provided within a text. Certain facts are included to help a reader come to a specific conclusion. For example, a story may open with a man trudging through the snow on a cold winter day, dragging a sled behind him. The reader can logically **infer** from the setting of the story that the man is wearing heavy winter clothes in order to stay warm. Information is implied based on the setting of a story, which is why **setting** is an important element of the text. If the same man in the example was trudging down a beach on a hot summer day, dragging a surf board behind him, the reader would assume that the man is not wearing heavy clothes. The reader makes inferences based on their own experiences and the information presented to them in the story.

Test-taking tip: When asked to identify a conclusion that may be drawn, look for critical "hedge" phrases, such as *likely*, *may*, *can*, and *will often*, among many others. When you are being tested on this knowledge, remember the question that writers insert into these hedge phrases to cover every possibility. Often an answer will be wrong simply because there is no room for exception. Extreme positive or negative answers (such as always or never) are usually not correct. When answering these questions, the reader **should not** use any outside knowledge that is not gathered directly or reasonably inferred from the passage. Correct answers can be derived straight from the passage.

EXAMPLE

Read the following sentence from *Little Women* by Louisa May Alcott and draw a conclusion based upon the information presented:

> *You know the reason Mother proposed not having any presents this Christmas was because it is going to be a hard winter for everyone; and she thinks we ought not to spend money for pleasure, when our men are suffering so in the army.*

Based on the information in the sentence, the reader can conclude, or **infer**, that the men are away at war while the women are still at home. The pronoun *our* gives a clue to the reader that the character is speaking about men she knows. In addition, the reader can assume that the character is speaking to a brother or sister, since the term "Mother" is used by the character while speaking to another person. The reader can also come to the conclusion that the characters celebrate Christmas, since it is mentioned in the **context** of the sentence. In the sentence, the mother is presented as an unselfish character who is opinionated and thinks about the wellbeing of other people.

SUMMARIZING

A helpful tool is the ability to **summarize** the information that you have read in a paragraph or passage format. This process is similar to creating an effective outline. First, a summary should accurately define the main idea of the passage, though the summary does not need to explain this main idea in exhaustive detail. The summary should continue by laying out the most important supporting details or arguments from the passage. All of the significant supporting details should be included, and none of the details included should be irrelevant or insignificant. Also, the summary should accurately report all of these details. Too often, the desire for brevity in a summary leads to the sacrifice of clarity or accuracy. Summaries are often difficult to read because they omit all of the graceful language, digressions, and asides that distinguish great writing. However, an effective summary should communicate the same overall message as the original text.

> **Review Video: Summarizing Text**
> Visit mometrix.com/academy and enter code: 172903

PARAPHRASING

Paraphrasing is another method that the reader can use to aid in comprehension. When paraphrasing, one puts what they have read into their own words by rephrasing what the author has written, or one "translates" all of what the author shared into their own words by including as many details as they can.

EVALUATING A PASSAGE

It is important to understand the logical conclusion of the ideas presented in an informational text. **Identifying a logical conclusion** can help you determine whether you agree with the writer or not. Coming to this conclusion is much like making an inference: the approach requires you to combine the information given by the text with what you already know and make a logical conclusion. If the author intended for the reader to draw a certain conclusion, then you can expect the author's argumentation and detail to be leading in that direction.

One way to approach the task of drawing conclusions is to make brief **notes** of all the points made by the author. When the notes are arranged on paper, they may clarify the logical conclusion. Another way to approach conclusions is to consider whether the reasoning of the author raises any pertinent questions. Sometimes you will be able to draw several conclusions from a passage. On occasion these will be conclusions that were never imagined by the author. Therefore, be aware that these conclusions must be **supported directly by the text**.

Evaluation of Summaries

A summary of a literary passage is a condensation in the reader's own words of the passage's main points. Several guidelines can be used in evaluating a summary. The summary should be complete yet concise. It should be accurate, balanced, fair, neutral, and objective, excluding the reader's own opinions or reactions. It should reflect in similar proportion how much each point summarized was covered in the original passage. Summary writers should include tags of attribution, like "Macaulay argues that" to reference the original author whose ideas are represented in the summary. Summary writers should not overuse quotations; they should only quote central concepts or phrases they cannot precisely convey in words other than those of the original author. Another aspect of evaluating a summary is considering whether it can stand alone as a coherent, unified composition. In addition, evaluation of a summary should include whether its writer has cited the original source of the passage they have summarized so that readers can find it.

Making Connections to Enhance Comprehension

Reading involves thinking. For good comprehension, readers make **text-to-self**, **text-to-text**, and **text-to-world connections**. Making connections helps readers understand text better and predict what might occur next based on what they already know, such as how characters in the story feel or what happened in another text. Text-to-self connections with the reader's life and experiences make literature more personally relevant and meaningful to readers. Readers can make connections before, during, and after reading—including whenever the text reminds them of something similar they have encountered in life or other texts. The genre, setting, characters, plot elements, literary structure and devices, and themes an author uses allow a reader to make connections to other works of literature or to people and events in their own lives. Venn diagrams and other graphic organizers help visualize connections. Readers can also make double-entry notes: key content, ideas, events, words, and quotations on one side, and the connections with these on the other.

Comparing Two Texts

Synthesis of Multiple Texts

Synthesizing, i.e., understanding and integrating, information from multiple texts can at times be among the most challenging skills for some students to succeed with on tests and in school, and yet it is also among the most important. Students who read at the highest cognitive levels can select related material from different text sources and construct coherent arguments that account for these varied information sources. Synthesizing ideas and information from multiple texts actually combines other reading skills that students should have mastered previously in reading one text at a time, and applies them in the context of reading more than one text. For example, students are required to read texts closely, including identifying explicit and implicit meanings; use critical thinking and reading; draw inferences; assess author reasoning; analyze supporting evidence; and formulate opinions they can justify, based on more passages than one. When two paired texts represent opposing sides of the same argument, students can find analyzing them easier; but this is not always the case.

Similarities in Texts

When students are called upon to compare things two texts share in common, the most obvious commonality might be the same subject matter or specific topic. However, two texts need not be about the same thing to compare them. Some other features texts can share include structural characteristics. For example, they may both be written using a sequential format, such as narrating events or giving instructions in chronological order; listing and/or discussing subtopics by order of importance; or describing a place spatially in sequence from each point to the next. They may both use a comparison-contrast structure, identifying similarities and differences between, among, or within topics. They might both organize information by identifying cause-and-effect relationships. Texts can be similar in type, e.g., description, narration, persuasion, or exposition. They can be similar in using technical vocabulary or using formal or informal language. They may share similar tones and/or styles, e.g., humorous, satirical, serious, etc. They can share similar purposes, e.g., to alarm audiences, incite them to action, reassure them, inspire them, provoke strong emotional responses, etc.

CONTRASTS IN TEXTS

When analyzing paired or multiple texts, students might observe differences in tone; for example, one text might take a serious approach while another uses a humorous one. Even within approaches or treatments, style can differ: one text may be humorous in a witty, sophisticated, clever way while another may exercise broad, "lowbrow" humor; another may employ mordant sarcasm; another may use satire, couching outrageous suggestions in a "deadpan" logical voice to lampoon social attitudes and behaviors as Jonathan Swift did in *A Modest Proposal.* Serious writing can range from darkly pessimistic to alarmist to objective and unemotional. Texts might have similar information, yet organize it using different structures. One text may support points or ideas using logical arguments, while another may seek to persuade its audience by appealing to their emotions. A very obvious difference in text is genre: for example, the same mythological or traditional stories have been told as oral folk tales, written dramas, written novels, etc.; and/or set in different times and places (e.g., Shakespeare's *Romeo and Juliet* vs. Laurents, Bernstein, and Sondheim's *West Side Story*).

WORD ROOTS AND PREFIXES AND SUFFIXES

AFFIXES

Affixes in the English language are morphemes that are added to words to create related but different words. Derivational affixes form new words based on and related to the original words. For example, the affix *-ness* added to the end of the adjective *happy* forms the noun *happiness.* Inflectional affixes form different grammatical versions of words. For example, the plural affix *-s* changes the singular noun *book* to the plural noun *books,* and the past tense affix *-ed* changes the present tense verb *look* to the past tense *looked.* Prefixes are affixes placed in front of words. For example, *heat* means to make hot; *preheat* means to heat in advance. Suffixes are affixes placed at the ends of words. The *happiness* example above contains the suffix *-ness.* Circumfixes add parts both before and after words, such as how *light* becomes *enlighten* with the prefix *en-* and the suffix *-en.* Interfixes create compound words via central affixes: *speed* and *meter* become *speedometer* via the interfix *-o-*.

Review Video: Affixes
Visit mometrix.com/academy and enter code: 782422

WORD ROOTS, PREFIXES, AND SUFFIXES TO HELP DETERMINE MEANINGS OF WORDS

Many English words were formed from combining multiple sources. For example, the Latin *habēre* means "to have," and the prefixes *in-* and *im-* mean a lack or prevention of something, as in *insufficient* and *imperfect.* Latin combined *in-* with *habēre* to form *inhibēre,* whose past participle was *inhibitus.* This is the origin of the English word *inhibit,* meaning to prevent from having. Hence by knowing the meanings of both the prefix and the root, one can decipher the word meaning. In Greek, the root *enkephalo-* refers to the brain. Many medical terms are based on this root, such as encephalitis and hydrocephalus. Understanding the prefix and suffix meanings (*-itis* means inflammation; *hydro-* means water) allows a person to deduce that encephalitis refers to brain inflammation and hydrocephalus refers to water (or other fluid) in the brain.

Review Video: Determining Word Meanings
Visit mometrix.com/academy and enter code: 894894

PREFIXES

Knowing common prefixes is helpful for all readers as they try to determining meanings or definitions of unfamiliar words. For example, a common word used when cooking is *preheat*. Knowing that *pre-* means in advance can also inform them that *presume* means to assume in advance, that *prejudice* means advance judgment, and that this understanding can be applied to many other words beginning with *pre-*. Knowing that the prefix *dis-* indicates opposition informs the meanings of words like *disbar, disagree, disestablish,* and many more. Knowing *dys-* means bad, impaired, abnormal, or difficult informs *dyslogistic, dysfunctional, dysphagia,* and *dysplasia.*

SUFFIXES

In English, certain suffixes generally indicate both that a word is a noun, and that the noun represents a state of being or quality. For example, *-ness* is commonly used to change an adjective into its noun form, as with *happy* and *happiness, nice* and *niceness,* and so on. The suffix *–tion* is commonly used to transform a verb into its noun form, as with *converse* and *conversation or move* and *motion*. Thus, if readers are unfamiliar with the second form of a word, knowing the meaning of the transforming suffix can help them determine meaning.

PREFIXES FOR NUMBERS

Prefix	Definition	Examples
bi-	two	bisect, biennial
mono-	one, single	monogamy, monologue
poly-	many	polymorphous, polygamous
semi-	half, partly	semicircle, semicolon
uni-	one	uniform, unity

Prefixes for Time, Direction, and Space

Prefix	Definition	Examples
a-	in, on, of, up, to	abed, afoot
ab-	from, away, off	abdicate, abjure
ad-	to, toward	advance, adventure
ante-	before, previous	antecedent, antedate
anti-	against, opposing	antipathy, antidote
cata-	down, away, thoroughly	catastrophe, cataclysm
circum-	around	circumspect, circumference
com-	with, together, very	commotion, complicate
contra-	against, opposing	contradict, contravene
de-	from	depart
dia-	through, across, apart	diameter, diagnose
dis-	away, off, down, not	dissent, disappear
epi-	upon	epilogue
ex-	out	extract, excerpt
hypo-	under, beneath	hypodermic, hypothesis
inter-	among, between	intercede, interrupt
intra-	within	intramural, intrastate
ob-	against, opposing	objection
per-	through	perceive, permit
peri-	around	periscope, perimeter
post-	after, following	postpone, postscript
pre-	before, previous	prevent, preclude
pro-	forward, in place of	propel, pronoun
retro-	back, backward	retrospect, retrograde
sub-	under, beneath	subjugate, substitute
super-	above, extra	supersede, supernumerary
trans-	across, beyond, over	transact, transport
ultra-	beyond, excessively	ultramodern, ultrasonic

Negative Prefixes

Prefix	Definition	Examples
a-	without, lacking	atheist, agnostic
in-	not, opposing	incapable, ineligible
non-	not	nonentity, nonsense
un-	not, reverse of	unhappy, unlock

EXTRA PREFIXES

Prefix	Definition	Examples
for-	away, off, from	forget, forswear
fore-	previous	foretell, forefathers
homo-	same, equal	homogenized, homonym
hyper-	excessive, over	hypercritical, hypertension
in-	in, into	intrude, invade
mal-	bad, poorly, not	malfunction, malpractice
mis-	bad, poorly, not	misspell, misfire
neo-	new	Neolithic, neoconservative
omni-	all, everywhere	omniscient, omnivore
ortho-	right, straight	orthogonal, orthodox
over-	above	overbearing, oversight
pan-	all, entire	panorama, pandemonium
para-	beside, beyond	parallel, paradox
re-	backward, again	revoke, recur
sym-	with, together	sympathy, symphony

Below is a list of common suffixes and their meanings:

ADJECTIVE SUFFIXES

Suffix	Definition	Examples
-able (-ible)	capable of being	toler*able*, ed*ible*
-esque	in the style of, like	picturesque, grotesque
-ful	filled with, marked by	thankful, zestful
-ific	make, cause	terrific, beatific
-ish	suggesting, like	churlish, childish
-less	lacking, without	hopeless, countless
-ous	marked by, given to	religious, riotous

NOUN SUFFIXES

Suffix	Definition	Examples
-acy	state, condition	accuracy, privacy
-ance	act, condition, fact	acceptance, vigilance
-ard	one that does excessively	drunkard, sluggard
-ation	action, state, result	occupation, starvation
-dom	state, rank, condition	serfdom, wisdom
-er (-or)	office, action	teach*er*, elevat*or*, hon*or*
-ess	feminine	waitress, duchess
-hood	state, condition	manhood, statehood
-ion	action, result, state	union, fusion
-ism	act, manner, doctrine	barbarism, socialism
-ist	worker, follower	monopolist, socialist
-ity (-ty)	state, quality, condition	acid*ity*, civil*ity*, twen*ty*
-ment	result, action	Refreshment
-ness	quality, state	greatness, tallness
-ship	position	internship, statesmanship
-sion (-tion)	state, result	revi*sion*, expedi*tion*
-th	act, state, quality	warmth, width
-tude	quality, state, result	magnitude, fortitude

Reasoning Through Language Arts

Verb Suffixes

Suffix	Definition	Examples
-ate	having, showing	separate, desolate
-en	cause to be, become	deepen, strengthen
-fy	make, cause to have	glorify, fortify
-ize	cause to be, treat with	sterilize, mechanize

Nuance and Word Meanings

Synonyms and Antonyms

When you understand how words relate to each other, you will discover more in a passage. This is explained by understanding **synonyms** (e.g., words that mean the same thing) and **antonyms** (e.g., words that mean the opposite of one another). As an example, *dry* and *arid* are synonyms, and *dry* and *wet* are antonyms.

There are many pairs of words in English that can be considered synonyms, despite having slightly different definitions. For instance, the words *friendly* and *collegial* can both be used to describe a warm interpersonal relationship, and one would be correct to call them synonyms. However, *collegial* (kin to *colleague*) is often used in reference to professional or academic relationships, and *friendly* has no such connotation.

If the difference between the two words is too great, then they should not be called synonyms. *Hot* and *warm* are not synonyms because their meanings are too distinct. A good way to determine whether two words are synonyms is to substitute one word for the other word and verify that the meaning of the sentence has not changed. Substituting *warm* for *hot* in a sentence would convey a different meaning. Although warm and hot may seem close in meaning, warm generally means that the temperature is moderate, and hot generally means that the temperature is excessively high.

Antonyms are words with opposite meanings. *Light* and *dark*, *up* and *down*, *right* and *left*, *good* and *bad*: these are all sets of antonyms. Be careful to distinguish between antonyms and pairs of words that are simply different. *Black* and *gray*, for instance, are not antonyms because gray is not the opposite of black. *Black* and *white*, on the other hand, are antonyms.

Not every word has an antonym. For instance, many nouns do not. What would be the antonym of *chair*? During your exam, the questions related to antonyms are more likely to concern adjectives. You will recall that adjectives are words that describe a noun. Some common adjectives include *purple*, *fast*, *skinny*, and *sweet*. From those four adjectives, *purple* is the item that lacks a group of obvious antonyms.

Review Video: Synonyms and Antonyms
Visit mometrix.com/academy and enter code: 105612

Denotative vs. Connotative Meaning

The **denotative** meaning of a word is the literal meaning. The **connotative** meaning goes beyond the denotative meaning to include the emotional reaction that a word may invoke. The connotative meaning often takes the denotative meaning a step further due to associations the reader makes with the denotative meaning. Readers can differentiate between the denotative and connotative meanings by first recognizing how authors use each meaning. Most non-fiction, for example, is fact-based and authors do not use flowery, figurative language. The reader can assume that the writer is using the denotative meaning of words. In fiction, the author may use the connotative meaning. Readers can determine whether the author is using the denotative or connotative meaning of a word by implementing context clues.

Review Video: Connotation and Denotation
Visit mometrix.com/academy and enter code: 310092

Nuances of Word Meaning Relative to Connotation, Denotation, Diction, and Usage

A word's denotation is simply its objective dictionary definition. However, its connotation refers to the subjective associations, often emotional, that specific words evoke in listeners and readers. Two or more words can have the same dictionary meaning, but very different connotations. Writers use diction (word choice) to convey various nuances of thought and emotion by selecting synonyms for other words that best communicate the associations they want to trigger for readers. For example, a car engine is naturally greasy; in this sense, "greasy" is a neutral term. But when a person's smile, appearance, or clothing is described as "greasy," it has a negative connotation. Some words have even gained additional or different meanings over time. For example, *awful* used to be used to describe things that evoked a sense of awe. When *awful* is separated into its root word, awe, and suffix, -ful, it can be understood to mean "full of awe." However, the word is now commonly used to describe things that evoke repulsion, terror, or another intense, negative reaction.

Review Video: Word Usage in Sentences
Visit mometrix.com/academy and enter code: 197863

Using Context to Determine Meaning

Context Clues

Readers of all levels will encounter words that they have either never seen or have encountered only on a limited basis. The best way to define a word in **context** is to look for nearby words that can assist in revealing the meaning of the word. For instance, unfamiliar nouns are often accompanied by examples that provide a definition. Consider the following sentence: *Dave arrived at the party in hilarious garb: a leopard-print shirt, buckskin trousers, and bright green sneakers.* If a reader was unfamiliar with the meaning of garb, he or she could read the examples (i.e., a leopard-print shirt, buckskin trousers, and bright green sneakers) and quickly determine that the word means *clothing*. Examples will not always be this obvious. Consider this sentence: *Parsley, lemon, and flowers were just a few of the items he used as garnishes.* Here, the word *garnishes* is exemplified by parsley, lemon, and flowers. Readers who have eaten in a variety of restaurants will probably be able to identify a garnish as something used to decorate a plate.

Review Video: Reading Comprehension: Using Context Clues
Visit mometrix.com/academy and enter code: 613660

Using Contrast in Context Clues

In addition to looking at the context of a passage, readers can use contrast to define an unfamiliar word in context. In many sentences, the author will not describe the unfamiliar word directly; instead, he or she will describe the opposite of the unfamiliar word. Thus, you are provided with some information that will bring you closer to defining the word. Consider the following example: *Despite his intelligence, Hector's low brow and bad posture made him look obtuse.* The author writes that Hector's appearance does not convey intelligence. Therefore, *obtuse* must mean unintelligent. Here is another example: *Despite the horrible weather, we were beatific about our trip to Alaska.* The word *despite* indicates that the speaker's feelings were at odds with the weather. Since the weather is described as *horrible*, then *beatific* must mean something positive.

Substitution to Find Meaning

In some cases, there will be very few contextual clues to help a reader define the meaning of an unfamiliar word. When this happens, one strategy that readers may employ is **substitution**. A good reader will brainstorm some possible synonyms for the given word, and he or she will substitute these words into the sentence. If the sentence and the surrounding passage continue to make sense, then the substitution has revealed at least some information about the unfamiliar word. Consider the sentence: *Frank's admonition rang in her ears as she climbed the mountain.* A reader unfamiliar with *admonition* might come up with some substitutions like *vow, promise, advice, complaint,* or *compliment.* All of these words make general sense of the sentence, though their meanings are diverse. However, this process has suggested that an admonition is some sort of message. The substitution strategy is rarely able to pinpoint a precise definition, but this process can be effective as a last resort.

Occasionally, you will be able to define an unfamiliar word by looking at the descriptive words in the context. Consider the following sentence: *Fred dragged the recalcitrant boy kicking and screaming up the stairs.* The words *dragged, kicking,* and *screaming* all suggest that the boy does not want to go up the stairs. The reader may assume that *recalcitrant* means something like unwilling or protesting. In this example, an unfamiliar adjective was identified.

Additionally, using description to define an unfamiliar noun is a common practice compared to unfamiliar adjectives, as in this sentence: *Don's wrinkled frown and constantly shaking fist identified him as a curmudgeon of the first order.* Don is described as having a *wrinkled frown and constantly shaking fist*, suggesting that a *curmudgeon* must be a grumpy person. Contrasts do not always provide detailed information about the unfamiliar word, but they at least give the reader some clues.

Words with Multiple Meanings

When a word has more than one meaning, readers can have difficulty determining how the word is being used in a given sentence. For instance, the verb *cleave*, can mean either *join* or *separate*. When readers come upon this word, they will have to select the definition that makes the most sense. Consider the following sentence: *Hermione's knife cleaved the bread cleanly.* Since a knife cannot join bread together, the word must indicate separation. A slightly more difficult example would be the sentence: *The birds cleaved to one another as they flew from the oak tree.* Immediately, the presence of the words *to one another* should suggest that in this sentence *cleave* is being used to mean *join*. Discovering the intent of a word with multiple meanings requires the same tricks as defining an unknown word: look for contextual clues and evaluate the substituted words.

Context Clues to Help Determine Meanings of Words

If readers simply bypass unknown words, they can reach unclear conclusions about what they read. However, looking for the definition of every unfamiliar word in the dictionary can slow their reading progress. Moreover, the dictionary may list multiple definitions for a word, so readers must search the word's context for meaning. Hence context is important to new vocabulary regardless of reader methods. Four types of context clues are examples, definitions, descriptive words, and opposites. Authors may use a certain word, and then follow it with several different examples of what it describes. Sometimes authors actually supply a definition of a word they use, which is especially true in informational and technical texts. Authors may use descriptive words that elaborate upon a vocabulary word they just used. Authors may also use opposites with negation that help define meaning.

Examples and Definitions

An author may use a word and then give examples that illustrate its meaning. Consider this text: "Teachers who do not know how to use sign language can help students who are deaf or hard of hearing understand certain instructions by using gestures instead, like pointing their fingers to indicate which direction to look or go; holding up a hand, palm outward, to indicate stopping; holding the hands flat, palms up, curling a finger toward oneself in a beckoning motion to indicate 'come here'; or curling all fingers toward oneself repeatedly to indicate 'come on', 'more', or 'continue.'" The author of this text has used the word "gestures" and then followed it with examples, so a reader unfamiliar with the word could deduce from the examples that "gestures" means "hand motions." Readers can find examples by looking for signal words "for example," "for instance," "like," "such as," and "e.g."

While readers sometimes have to look for definitions of unfamiliar words in a dictionary or do some work to determine a word's meaning from its surrounding context, at other times an author may make it easier for readers by defining certain words. For example, an author may write, "The company did not have sufficient capital, that is, available money, to continue operations." The author defined "capital" as "available money," and heralded the definition with the phrase "that is." Another way that authors supply word definitions is with appositives. Rather than being introduced by a signal phrase like "that is," "namely," or "meaning," an appositive comes after the vocabulary word it defines and is enclosed within two commas. For example, an author may write, "The Indians introduced the Pilgrims to pemmican, cakes they made of lean meat dried and mixed with fat, which proved greatly beneficial to keep settlers from starving while trapping." In this example, the appositive phrase following "pemmican" and preceding "which" defines the word "pemmican."

DESCRIPTIONS

When readers encounter a word they do not recognize in a text, the author may expand on that word to illustrate it better. While the author may do this to make the prose more picturesque and vivid, the reader can also take advantage of this description to provide context clues to the meaning of the unfamiliar word. For example, an author may write, "The man sitting next to me on the airplane was obese. His shirt stretched across his vast expanse of flesh, strained almost to bursting." The descriptive second sentence elaborates on and helps to define the previous sentence's word "obese" to mean extremely fat. A reader unfamiliar with the word "repugnant" can decipher its meaning through an author's accompanying description: "The way the child grimaced and shuddered as he swallowed the medicine showed that its taste was particularly repugnant."

OPPOSITES

Text authors sometimes introduce a contrasting or opposing idea before or after a concept they present. They may do this to emphasize or heighten the idea they present by contrasting it with something that is the reverse. However, readers can also use these context clues to understand familiar words. For example, an author may write, "Our conversation was not cheery. We sat and talked very solemnly about his experience and a number of similar events." The reader who is not familiar with the word "solemnly" can deduce by the author's preceding use of "not cheery" that "solemn" means the opposite of cheery or happy, so it must mean serious or sad. Or if someone writes, "Don't condemn his entire project because you couldn't find anything good to say about it," readers unfamiliar with "condemn" can understand from the sentence structure that it means the opposite of saying anything good, so it must mean reject, dismiss, or disapprove. "Entire" adds another context clue, meaning total or complete rejection.

SYNTAX TO DETERMINE PART OF SPEECH AND MEANINGS OF WORDS

Syntax refers to sentence structure and word order. Suppose that a reader encounters an unfamiliar word when reading a text. To illustrate, consider an invented word like "splunch." If this word is used in a sentence like "Please splunch that ball to me," the reader can assume from syntactic context that "splunch" is a verb. We would not use a noun, adjective, adverb, or preposition with the object "that ball," and the prepositional phrase "to me" further indicates "splunch" represents an action. However, in the sentence, "Please hand that splunch to me," the reader can assume that "splunch" is a noun. Demonstrative adjectives like "that" modify nouns. Also, we hand someone some*thing*—a thing being a noun; we do not hand someone a verb, adjective, or adverb. Some sentences contain further clues. For example, from the sentence, "The princess wore the glittering splunch on her head," the reader can deduce that it is a crown, tiara, or something similar from the syntactic context, without knowing the word.

SYNTAX TO INDICATE DIFFERENT MEANINGS OF SIMILAR SENTENCES

The syntax, or structure, of a sentence affords grammatical cues that aid readers in comprehending the meanings of words, phrases, and sentences in the texts that they read. Seemingly minor differences in how the words or phrases in a sentence are ordered can make major differences in meaning. For example, two sentences can use exactly the same words but have different meanings based on the word order:

- "The man with a broken arm sat in a chair."
- "The man sat in a chair with a broken arm."

While both sentences indicate that a man sat in a chair, differing syntax indicates whether the man's or chair's arm was broken.

Review Video: Syntax
Visit mometrix.com/academy and enter code: 242280

Determining Meaning of Phrases and Paragraphs

Like unknown words, the meanings of phrases, paragraphs, and entire works can also be difficult to discern. Each of these can be better understood with added context. However, for larger groups of words, more context is needed. Unclear phrases are similar to unclear words, and the same methods can be used to understand their meaning. However, it is also important to consider how the individual words in the phrase work together. Paragraphs are a bit more complicated. Just as words must be compared to other words in a sentence, paragraphs must be compared to other paragraphs in a composition or a section.

Determining Meaning in Various Types of Compositions

To understand the meaning of an entire composition, the type of composition must be considered. **Expository writing** is generally organized so that each paragraph focuses on explaining one idea, or part of an idea, and its relevance. **Persuasive writing** uses paragraphs for different purposes to organize the parts of the argument. **Unclear paragraphs** must be read in the context of the paragraphs around them for their meaning to be fully understood. The meaning of full texts can also be unclear at times. The purpose of composition is also important for understanding the meaning of a text. To quickly understand the broad meaning of a text, look to the introductory and concluding paragraphs. Fictional texts are different. Some fictional works have implicit meanings, but some do not. The target audience must be considered for understanding texts that do have an implicit meaning, as most children's fiction will clearly state any lessons or morals. For other fiction, the application of literary theories and criticism may be helpful for understanding the text.

Resources for Determining Word Meaning and Usage

While these strategies are useful for determining the meaning of unknown words and phrases, sometimes additional resources are needed to properly use the terms in different contexts. Some words have multiple definitions, and some words are inappropriate in particular contexts or modes of writing. The following tools are helpful for understanding all meanings and proper uses for words and phrases.

- **Dictionaries** provide the meaning of a multitude of words in a language. Many dictionaries include additional information about each word, such as its etymology, its synonyms, or variations of the word.
- **Glossaries** are similar to dictionaries, as they provide the meanings of a variety of terms. However, while dictionaries typically feature an extensive list of words and comprise an entire publication, glossaries are often included at the end of a text and only include terms and definitions that are relevant to the text they follow.
- **Spell Checkers** are used to detect spelling errors in typed text. Some spell checkers may also detect the misuse of plural or singular nouns, verb tenses, or capitalization. While spell checkers are a helpful tool, they are not always reliable or attuned to the author's intent, so it is important to review the spell checker's suggestions before accepting them.
- **Style Manuals** are guidelines on the preferred punctuation, format, and grammar usage according to different fields or organizations. For example, the Associated Press Stylebook is a style guide often used for media writing. The guidelines within a style guide are not always applicable across different contexts and usages, as the guidelines often cover grammatical or formatting situations that are not objectively correct or incorrect.

Identifying and Creating Arguments

The Writing Process

Brainstorming

Brainstorming is a technique that is used to find a creative approach to a subject. This can be accomplished by simple **free-association** with a topic. For example, with paper and pen, write every thought that you have about the topic in a word or phrase. This is done without critical thinking. You should put everything that comes to your mind about the topic on your scratch paper. Then, you need to read the list over a few times. Next, look for patterns, repetitions, and clusters of ideas. This allows a variety of fresh ideas to come as you think about the topic.

Free Writing

Free writing is a more structured form of brainstorming. The method involves taking a limited amount of time (e.g., 2 to 3 minutes) to write everything that comes to mind about the topic in complete sentences. When time expires, review everything that has been written down. Many of your sentences may make little or no sense, but the insights and observations that can come from free writing make this method a valuable approach. Usually, free writing results in a fuller expression of ideas than brainstorming because thoughts and associations are written in complete sentences. However, both techniques can be used to complement each other.

Planning

Planning is the process of organizing a piece of writing before composing a draft. Planning can include creating an outline or a graphic organizer, such as a Venn diagram, a spider-map, or a flowchart. These methods should help the writer identify their topic, main ideas, and the general organization of the composition. Preliminary research can also take place during this stage. Planning helps writers organize all of their ideas and decide if they have enough material to begin their first draft. However, writers should remember that the decisions they make during this step will likely change later in the process, so their plan does not have to be perfect.

Drafting

Writers may then use their plan, outline, or graphic organizer to compose their first draft. They may write subsequent drafts to improve their writing. Writing multiple drafts can help writers consider different ways to communicate their ideas and address errors that may be difficult to correct without rewriting a section or the whole composition. Most writers will vary in how many drafts they choose to write, as there is no "right" number of drafts. Writing drafts also takes away the pressure to write perfectly on the first try, as writers can improve with each draft they write.

Revising, Editing, and Proofreading

Once a writer completes a draft, they can move on to the revising, editing, and proofreading steps to improve their draft. These steps begin with making broad changes that may apply to large sections of a composition and then making small, specific corrections. **Revising** is the first and broadest of these steps. Revising involves ensuring that the composition addresses an appropriate audience, includes all necessary material, maintains focus throughout, and is organized logically. Revising may occur after the first draft to ensure that the following drafts improve upon errors from the first draft. Some revision should occur between each draft to avoid repeating these errors. The **editing** phase of writing is narrower than the revising phase. Editing a composition should include steps such as improving transitions between paragraphs, ensuring each paragraph is on topic, and improving the flow of the text. The editing phase may also include correcting grammatical errors that cannot be fixed without significantly altering the text. **Proofreading** involves fixing misspelled words, typos, other grammatical errors, and any remaining surface-level flaws in the composition.

Recursive Writing Process

However you approach writing, you may find comfort in knowing that the revision process can occur in any order. The **recursive writing process** is not as difficult as the phrase may make it seem. Simply put, the recursive writing process means that you may need to revisit steps after completing other steps. It also implies that the steps are not required to take place in any certain order. Indeed, you may find that planning, drafting, and revising can all take place at about the same time. The writing process involves moving back and forth between planning, drafting, and revising, followed by more planning, more drafting, and more revising until the writing is satisfactory.

Review Video: Recursive Writing Process
Visit mometrix.com/academy and enter code: 951611

Outlining and Organizing Ideas

Essays

Essays usually focus on one topic, subject, or goal. There are several types of essays, including informative, persuasive, and narrative. An essay's structure and level of formality depend on the type of essay and its goal. While narrative essays typically do not include outside sources, other types of essays often require some research and the integration of primary and secondary sources.

The basic format of an essay typically has three major parts: the introduction, the body, and the conclusion. The body is further divided into the writer's main points. Short and simple essays may have three main points, while essays covering broader ranges and going into more depth can have almost any number of main points, depending on length.

An essay's introduction should answer three questions:

1. What is the **subject** of the essay?

   If a student writes an essay about a book, the answer would include the title and author of the book and any additional information needed—such as the subject or argument of the book.

2. How does the essay **address** the subject?

   To answer this, the writer identifies the essay's organization by briefly summarizing main points and the evidence supporting them.

3. What will the essay **prove**?

   This is the thesis statement, usually the opening paragraph's last sentence, clearly stating the writer's message.

The body elaborates on all the main points related to the thesis, introducing one main point at a time, and includes supporting evidence with each main point. Each body paragraph should state the point in a topic sentence, which is usually the first sentence in the paragraph. The paragraph should then explain the point's meaning, support it with quotations or other evidence, and then explain how this point and the evidence are related to the thesis. The writer should then repeat this procedure in a new paragraph for each additional main point.

The conclusion reiterates the content of the introduction, including the thesis, to remind the reader of the essay's main argument or subject. The essay writer may also summarize the highlights of the argument or description contained in the body of the essay, following the same sequence originally used in the body. For example, a conclusion might look like: Point 1 + Point 2 + Point 3 = Thesis, or Point 1 → Point 2 → Point 3 → Thesis Proof. Good organization makes essays easier for writers to compose and provides a guide for readers to follow. Well-organized essays hold attention better and are more likely to get readers to accept their theses as valid.

Main Ideas, Supporting Details, and Outlining a Topic

A writer often begins the first paragraph of a paper by stating the **main idea** or point, also known as the **topic sentence**. The rest of the paragraph supplies particular details that develop and support the main point. One way to visualize the relationship between the main point and supporting information is by considering a table: the tabletop is the main point, and each of the table's legs is a supporting detail or group of details. Both professional authors and students can benefit from planning their writing by first making an outline of the topic. Outlines facilitate quick identification of the main point and supporting details without having to wade through the additional language that will exist in the fully developed essay, article, or paper. Outlining can also help readers to analyze a piece of existing writing for the same reason. The outline first summarizes the main idea in one sentence. Then, below that, it summarizes the supporting details in a numbered list. Writing the paper then consists of filling in the outline with detail, writing a paragraph for each supporting point, and adding an introduction and conclusion.

Introduction

The purpose of the introduction is to capture the reader's attention and announce the essay's main idea. Normally, the introduction contains 50-80 words, or 3-5 sentences. An introduction can begin with an interesting quote, a question, or a strong opinion—something that will **engage** the reader's interest and prompt them to keep reading. If you are writing your essay to a specific prompt, your introduction should include a **restatement or summarization** of the prompt so that the reader will have some context for your essay. Finally, your introduction should briefly state your **thesis or main idea**: the primary thing you hope to communicate to the reader through your essay. Don't try to include all of the details and nuances of your thesis, or all of your reasons for it, in the introduction. That's what the rest of the essay is for!

Review Video: Introduction
Visit mometrix.com/academy and enter code: 961328

Thesis Statement

The thesis is the main idea of the essay. A temporary thesis, or working thesis, should be established early in the writing process because it will serve to keep the writer focused as ideas develop. This temporary thesis is subject to change as you continue to write.

The temporary thesis has two parts: a **topic** (i.e., the focus of your essay based on the prompt) and a **comment**. The comment makes an important point about the topic. A temporary thesis should be interesting and specific. Also, you need to limit the topic to a manageable scope. These three questions are useful tools to measure the effectiveness of any temporary thesis:

- Does the focus of my essay have enough interest to hold an audience?
- Is the focus of my essay specific enough to generate interest?
- Is the focus of my essay manageable for the time limit? Too broad? Too narrow?

The thesis should be a generalization rather than a fact because the thesis prepares readers for facts and details that support the thesis. The process of bringing the thesis into sharp focus may help in outlining major sections of the work. Once the thesis and introduction are complete, you can address the body of the work.

Review Video: Thesis Statements
Visit mometrix.com/academy and enter code: 691033

SUPPORTING THE THESIS

Throughout your essay, the thesis should be **explained clearly and supported** adequately by additional arguments. The thesis sentence needs to contain a clear statement of the purpose of your essay and a comment about the thesis. With the thesis statement, you have an opportunity to state what is noteworthy of this particular treatment of the prompt. Each sentence and paragraph should build on and support the thesis.

When you respond to the prompt, use parts of the passage to support your argument or defend your position. Using supporting evidence from the passage strengths your argument because readers can see your attention to the entire passage and your response to the details and facts within the passage. You can use facts, details, statistics, and direct quotations from the passage to uphold your position. Be sure to point out which information comes from the original passage and base your argument around that evidence.

BODY

In an essay's introduction, the writer establishes the thesis and may indicate how the rest of the piece will be structured. In the body of the piece, the writer **elaborates** upon, **illustrates**, and **explains** the **thesis statement**. How writers arrange supporting details and their choices of paragraph types are development techniques. Writers may give examples of the concept introduced in the thesis statement. If the subject includes a cause-and-effect relationship, the author may explain its causality. A writer will explain or analyze the main idea of the piece throughout the body, often by presenting arguments for the veracity or credibility of the thesis statement. Writers may use development to define or clarify ambiguous terms. Paragraphs within the body may be organized using natural sequences, like space and time. Writers may employ **inductive reasoning**, using multiple details to establish a generalization or causal relationship, or **deductive reasoning**, proving a generalized hypothesis or proposition through a specific example or case.

Review Video: Drafting Body Paragraphs
Visit mometrix.com/academy and enter code: 724590

PARAGRAPHS

After the introduction of a passage, a series of body paragraphs will carry a message through to the conclusion. Each paragraph should be **unified around a main point**. Normally, a good topic sentence summarizes the paragraph's main point. A topic sentence is a general sentence that gives an introduction to the paragraph.

The sentences that follow support the topic sentence. However, though it is usually the first sentence, the topic sentence can come as the final sentence to the paragraph if the earlier sentences give a clear explanation of the paragraph's topic. This allows the topic sentence to function as a concluding sentence. Overall, the paragraphs need to stay true to the main point. This means that any unnecessary sentences that do not advance the main point should be removed.

The main point of a paragraph requires adequate development (i.e., a substantial paragraph that covers the main point). A paragraph of two or three sentences does not cover a main point. This is especially true when the main point of the paragraph gives strong support to the argument of the thesis. An occasional short paragraph is fine as a transitional device. However, a well-developed argument will have paragraphs with more than a few sentences.

METHODS OF DEVELOPING PARAGRAPHS

Common methods of adding substance to paragraphs include examples, illustrations, analogies, and cause and effect.

- **Examples** are supporting details to the main idea of a paragraph or a passage. When authors write about something that their audience may not understand, they can provide an example to show their point. When authors write about something that is not easily accepted, they can give examples to prove their point.

- **Illustrations** are extended examples that require several sentences. Well-selected illustrations can be a great way for authors to develop a point that may not be familiar to their audience.
- **Analogies** make comparisons between items that appear to have nothing in common. Analogies are employed by writers to provoke fresh thoughts about a subject. These comparisons may be used to explain the unfamiliar, to clarify an abstract point, or to argue a point. Although analogies are effective literary devices, they should be used carefully in arguments. Two things may be alike in some respects but completely different in others.
- **Cause and effect** is an excellent device to explain the connection between an action or situation and a particular result. One way that authors can use cause and effect is to state the effect in the topic sentence of a paragraph and add the causes in the body of the paragraph. This method can give an author's paragraphs structure, which always strengthens writing.

TYPES OF PARAGRAPHS

A **paragraph of narration** tells a story or a part of a story. Normally, the sentences are arranged in chronological order (i.e., the order that the events happened). However, flashbacks (i.e., an anecdote from an earlier time) can be included.

A **descriptive paragraph** makes a verbal portrait of a person, place, or thing. When specific details are used that appeal to one or more of the senses (i.e., sight, sound, smell, taste, and touch), authors give readers a sense of being present in the moment.

A **process paragraph** is related to time order (i.e., First, you open the bottle. Second, you pour the liquid, etc.). Usually, this describes a process or teaches readers how to perform a process.

Comparing two things draws attention to their similarities and indicates a number of differences. When authors contrast, they focus only on differences. Both comparing and contrasting may be done point-by-point, noting both the similarities and differences of each point, or in sequential paragraphs, where you discuss all the similarities and then all the differences, or vice versa.

BREAKING TEXT INTO PARAGRAPHS

For most forms of writing, you will need to use multiple paragraphs. As such, determining when to start a new paragraph is very important. Reasons for starting a new paragraph include:

- To mark off the introduction and concluding paragraphs
- To signal a shift to a new idea or topic
- To indicate an important shift in time or place
- To explain a point in additional detail
- To highlight a comparison, contrast, or cause and effect relationship

PARAGRAPH LENGTH

Most readers find that their comfort level for a paragraph is between 100 and 200 words. Shorter paragraphs cause too much starting and stopping and give a choppy effect. Paragraphs that are too long often test the attention span of readers. Two notable exceptions to this rule exist. In scientific or scholarly papers, longer paragraphs suggest seriousness and depth. In journalistic writing, constraints are placed on paragraph size by the narrow columns in a newspaper format.

The first and last paragraphs of a text will usually be the introduction and conclusion. These special-purpose paragraphs are likely to be shorter than paragraphs in the body of the work. Paragraphs in the body of the essay follow the subject's outline (e.g., one paragraph per point in short essays and a group of paragraphs per point in longer works). Some ideas require more development than others, so it is good for a writer to remain flexible. A paragraph of excessive length may be divided, and shorter ones may be combined.

CONCLUSION

Two important principles to consider when writing a conclusion are strength and closure. A strong conclusion gives the reader a sense that the author's main points are meaningful and important, and that the supporting facts and arguments are convincing, solid, and well developed. When a conclusion achieves closure, it gives the impression that the writer has stated all necessary information and points and completed the work, rather than simply stopping after a specified length. Some things to avoid when writing concluding paragraphs include:

- Introducing a completely new idea
- Beginning with obvious or unoriginal phrases like "In conclusion" or "To summarize"
- Apologizing for one's opinions or writing
- Repeating the thesis word for word rather than rephrasing it
- Believing that the conclusion must always summarize the piece

Review Video: Drafting Conclusions
Visit mometrix.com/academy and enter code: 209408

COHERENCE IN WRITING

COHERENT PARAGRAPHS

A smooth flow of sentences and paragraphs without gaps, shifts, or bumps will lead to paragraph **coherence**. Ties between old and new information can be smoothed using several methods:

- **Linking ideas clearly**, from the topic sentence to the body of the paragraph, is essential for a smooth transition. The topic sentence states the main point, and this should be followed by specific details, examples, and illustrations that support the topic sentence. The support may be direct or indirect. In **indirect support**, the illustrations and examples may support a sentence that in turn supports the topic directly.
- The **repetition of key words** adds coherence to a paragraph. To avoid dull language, variations of the key words may be used.
- **Parallel structures** are often used within sentences to emphasize the similarity of ideas and connect sentences giving similar information.
- Maintaining a **consistent verb tense** throughout the paragraph helps. Shifting tenses affects the smooth flow of words and can disrupt the coherence of the paragraph.

Review Video: How to Write a Good Paragraph
Visit mometrix.com/academy and enter code: 682127

SEQUENCE WORDS AND PHRASES

When a paragraph opens with the topic sentence, the second sentence may begin with a phrase like *first of all*, introducing the first supporting detail or example. The writer may introduce the second supporting item with words or phrases like *also*, *in addition*, and *besides*. The writer might introduce succeeding pieces of support with wording like, *another thing*, *moreover*, *furthermore*, or *not only that, but*. The writer may introduce the last piece of support with *lastly*, *finally*, or *last but not least*. Writers get off the point by presenting off-target items not supporting the main point. For example, a main point *my dog is not smart* is supported by the statement, *he's six years old and still doesn't answer to his name*. But *he cries when I leave for school* is not supportive, as it does not indicate lack of intelligence. Writers stay on point by presenting only supportive statements that are directly relevant to and illustrative of their main point.

Review Video: Sequence
Visit mometrix.com/academy and enter code: 489027

Transitions

Transitions between sentences and paragraphs guide readers from idea to idea and indicate relationships between sentences and paragraphs. Writers should be judicious in their use of transitions, inserting them sparingly. They should also be selected to fit the author's purpose—transitions can indicate time, comparison, and conclusion, among other purposes. Tone is also important to consider when using transitional phrases, varying the tone for different audiences. For example, in a scholarly essay, *in summary* would be preferable to the more informal *in short*.

When working with transitional words and phrases, writers usually find a natural flow that indicates when a transition is needed. In reading a draft of the text, it should become apparent where the flow is disrupted. At this point, the writer can add transitional elements during the revision process. Revising can also afford an opportunity to delete transitional devices that seem heavy handed or unnecessary.

Review Video: Transitions in Writing
Visit mometrix.com/academy and enter code: 233246

Types of Transitional Words

Time	afterward, immediately, earlier, meanwhile, recently, lately, now, since, soon, when, then, until, before, etc.
Sequence	too, first, second, further, moreover, also, again, and, next, still, besides, finally
Comparison	similarly, in the same way, likewise, also, again, once more
Contrasting	but, although, despite, however, instead, nevertheless, on the one hand... on the other hand, regardless, yet, in contrast
Cause and Effect	because, consequently, thus, therefore, then, to this end, since, so, as a result, if... then, accordingly
Examples	for example, for instance, such as, to illustrate, indeed, in fact, specifically
Place	near, far, here, there, to the left/right, next to, above, below, beyond, opposite, beside
Concession	granted that, naturally, of course, it may appear, although it is true that
Repetition, Summary, or Conclusion	as mentioned earlier, as noted, in other words, in short, on the whole, to summarize, therefore, as a result, to conclude, in conclusion
Addition	and, also, furthermore, moreover
Generalization	in broad terms, broadly speaking, in general

Review Video: Transition Words
Visit mometrix.com/academy and enter code: 707563

Review Video: How to Effectively Connect Sentences
Visit mometrix.com/academy and enter code: 948325

Writing Style and Form

Writing Style and Linguistic Form

Linguistic form encodes the literal meanings of words and sentences. It comes from the phonological, morphological, syntactic, and semantic parts of a language. **Writing style** consists of different ways of encoding the meaning and indicating figurative and stylistic meanings. An author's writing style can also be referred to as his or her **voice**.

Writers' stylistic choices accomplish three basic effects on their audiences:

- They **communicate meanings** beyond linguistically dictated meanings,
- They communicate the **author's attitude**, such as persuasive or argumentative effects accomplished through style, and
- They communicate or **express feelings**.

Within style, component areas include:

- Narrative structure
- Viewpoint
- Focus
- Sound patterns
- Meter and rhythm
- Lexical and syntactic repetition and parallelism
- Writing genre
- Representational, realistic, and mimetic effects
- Representation of thought and speech
- Meta-representation (representing representation)
- Irony
- Metaphor and other indirect meanings
- Representation and use of historical and dialectal variations
- Gender-specific and other group-specific speech styles, both real and fictitious
- Analysis of the processes for inferring meaning from writing

TONE

Tone may be defined as the writer's **attitude** toward the topic, and to the audience. This attitude is reflected in the language used in the writing. The tone of a work should be **appropriate to the topic** and to the intended audience. While it may be fine to use slang or jargon in some pieces, other texts should not contain such terms. Tone can range from humorous to serious and any level in between. It may be more or less formal, depending on the purpose of the writing and its intended audience. All these nuances in tone can flavor the entire writing and should be kept in mind as the work evolves.

Review Video: Style, Tone, and Mood
Visit mometrix.com/academy and enter code: 416961

WORD SELECTION

A writer's choice of words is a signature of their style. Careful thought about the use of words can improve a piece of writing. A passage can be an exciting piece to read when attention is given to the use of vivid or specific nouns rather than general ones.

Example:

General: His kindness will never be forgotten.

Specific: His thoughtful gifts and bear hugs will never be forgotten.

ACTIVE AND PASSIVE LANGUAGE

Attention should also be given to the kind of verbs that are used in sentences. Active verbs (e.g., run, swim) are about an action. Whenever possible, an **active verb should replace a linking verb** to provide clear examples for arguments and to strengthen a passage overall. When using an active verb, one should be sure that the verb is used in the active voice instead of the passive voice. Verbs are in the active voice when the subject is the one doing the action. A verb is in the passive voice when the subject is the recipient of an action.

Example:

> Passive: The winners were called to the stage by the judges.
>
> Active: The judges called the winners to the stage.

CONCISENESS

Conciseness is writing that communicates a message in the fewest words possible. Writing concisely is valuable because short, uncluttered messages allow the reader to understand the author's message more easily and efficiently. Planning is important in writing concise messages. If you have in mind what you need to write beforehand, it will be easier to make a message short and to the point. Do not state the obvious.

Revising is also important. After the message is written, make sure you have effective, pithy sentences that efficiently get your point across. When reviewing the information, imagine a conversation taking place, and concise writing will likely result.

APPROPRIATE KINDS OF WRITING FOR DIFFERENT TASKS, PURPOSES, AND AUDIENCES

When preparing to write a composition, consider the audience and purpose to choose the best type of writing. Four common types of writing are persuasive, expository, and narrative. **Persuasive**, or argumentative writing, is used to convince the audience to take action or agree with the author's claims. **Expository** writing is meant to inform the audience of the author's observations or research on a topic. **Narrative** writing is used to tell the audience a story and often allows more room for creativity. **Descriptive** writing is when a writer provides a substantial amount of detail to the reader so he or she can visualize the topic. While task, purpose, and audience inform a writer's mode of writing, these factors also impact elements such as tone, vocabulary, and formality.

For example, students who are writing to persuade their parents to grant them some additional privilege, such as permission for a more independent activity, should use more sophisticated vocabulary and diction that sounds more mature and serious to appeal to the parental audience. However, students who are writing for younger children should use simpler vocabulary and sentence structure, as well as choose words that are more vivid and entertaining. They should treat their topics more lightly, and include humor when appropriate. Students who are writing for their classmates may use language that is more informal, as well as age-appropriate.

Review Video: Writing Purpose and Audience
Visit mometrix.com/academy and enter code: 146627

FORMALITY IN WRITING

LEVEL OF FORMALITY

The relationship between writer and reader is important in choosing a **level of formality** as most writing requires some degree of formality. **Formal writing** is for addressing a superior in a school or work environment. Business letters, textbooks, and newspapers use a moderate to high level of formality. **Informal writing** is appropriate for private letters, personal emails, and business correspondence between close associates.

For your exam, you will want to be aware of informal and formal writing. One way that this can be accomplished is to watch for shifts in point of view in the essay. For example, unless writers are using a personal example, they will rarely refer to themselves (e.g., "*I* think that *my* point is very clear.") to avoid being informal when they need to be formal.

Also, be mindful of an author who addresses his or her audience **directly** in their writing (e.g., "Readers, *like you*, will understand this argument.") as this can be a sign of informal writing. Good writers understand the need to be consistent with their level of formality. Shifts in levels of formality or point of view can confuse readers and cause them to discount the message.

CLICHÉS

Clichés are phrases that have been **overused** to the point that the phrase has no importance or has lost the original meaning. These phrases have no originality and add very little to a passage. Therefore, most writers will avoid the use of clichés. Another option is to make changes to a cliché so that it is not predictable and empty of meaning.

Examples:

When life gives you lemons, make lemonade.

Every cloud has a silver lining.

JARGON

Jargon is **specialized vocabulary** that is used among members of a certain trade or profession. Since jargon is understood by only a small audience, writers will use jargon in passages that will only be read by a specialized audience. For example, medical jargon should be used in a medical journal but not in a New York Times article. Jargon includes exaggerated language that tries to impress rather than inform. Sentences filled with jargon are not precise and are difficult to understand.

Examples:

"He is going to *toenail* these frames for us." (Toenail is construction jargon for nailing at an angle.)

"They brought in a *kip* of material today." (Kip refers to 1000 pounds in architecture and engineering.)

SLANG

Slang is an **informal** and sometimes private language that is understood by some individuals. Slang terms have some usefulness, but they can have a small audience. So, most formal writing will not include this kind of language.

Examples:

"Yes, the event was a blast!" (In this sentence, *blast* means that the event was a great experience.)

"That attempt was an epic fail." (By *epic fail*, the speaker means that his or her attempt was not a success.)

COLLOQUIALISM

A colloquialism is a word or phrase that is found in informal writing. Unlike slang, **colloquial language** will be familiar to a greater range of people. However, colloquialisms are still considered inappropriate for formal writing. Colloquial language can include some slang, but these are limited to contractions for the most part.

Examples:

"Can *y'all* come back another time?" (Y'all is a contraction of "you all.")

"Will you stop him from building this *castle in the air*?" (A "castle in the air" is an improbable or unlikely event.)

ACADEMIC LANGUAGE

In educational settings, students are often expected to use academic language in their schoolwork. Academic language is also commonly found in dissertations and theses, texts published by academic journals, and other forms of academic research. Academic language conventions may vary between fields, but general academic language is free of slang, regional terminology, and noticeable grammatical errors. Specific terms may also be used in academic language, and it is important to understand their proper usage. A writer's command of academic language impacts their ability to communicate in an academic or professional context. While it is acceptable to use colloquialisms, slang, improper grammar, or other forms of informal speech in social settings or at home, it is inappropriate to practice non-academic language in academic contexts.

Grammar and Language

PARTS OF SPEECH

NOUNS

A noun is a person, place, thing, or idea. The two main types of nouns are **common** and **proper** nouns. Nouns can also be categorized as abstract (i.e., general) or concrete (i.e., specific).

COMMON NOUNS

Common nouns are generic names for people, places, and things. Common nouns are not usually capitalized.

Examples of common nouns:

> *People*: boy, girl, worker, manager
>
> *Places*: school, bank, library, home
>
> *Things*: dog, cat, truck, car

Review Video: Nouns
Visit mometrix.com/academy and enter code: 344028

PROPER NOUNS

Proper nouns name specific people, places, or things. All proper nouns are capitalized.

Examples of proper nouns:

> *People*: Abraham Lincoln, George Washington, Martin Luther King, Jr.
>
> *Places*: Los Angeles, California; New York; Asia
>
> *Things*: Statue of Liberty, Earth, Lincoln Memorial

Note: Some nouns can be either common or proper depending on their use. For example, when referring to the planet that we live on, *Earth* is a proper noun and is capitalized. When referring to the dirt, rocks, or land on our planet, *earth* is a common noun and is not capitalized.

GENERAL AND SPECIFIC NOUNS

General nouns are the names of conditions or ideas. **Specific nouns** name people, places, and things that are understood by using your senses.

General nouns:

Condition: beauty, strength

Idea: truth, peace

Specific nouns:

People: baby, friend, father

Places: town, park, city hall

Things: rainbow, cough, apple, silk, gasoline

COLLECTIVE NOUNS

Collective nouns are the names for a group of people, places, or things that may act as a whole. The following are examples of collective nouns: *class, company, dozen, group, herd, team,* and *public*. Collective nouns usually require an article, which denotes the noun as being a single unit. For instance, a choir is a group of singers. Even though there are many singers in a choir, the word choir is grammatically treated as a single unit. If we refer to the members of the group, and not the group itself, it is no longer a collective noun.

Incorrect: The *choir are* going to compete nationally this year.

Correct: The *choir is* going to compete nationally this year.

Incorrect: The *members* of the choir *is* competing nationally this year.

Correct: The *members* of the choir *are* competing nationally this year.

PRONOUNS

Pronouns are words that are used to stand in for nouns. A pronoun may be classified as personal, intensive, relative, interrogative, demonstrative, indefinite, and reciprocal.

Personal: *Nominative* is the case for nouns and pronouns that are the subject of a sentence. *Objective* is the case for nouns and pronouns that are an object in a sentence. *Possessive* is the case for nouns and pronouns that show possession or ownership.

Singular

	Nominative	Objective	Possessive
First Person	I	me	my, mine
Second Person	you	you	your, yours
Third Person	he, she, it	him, her, it	his, her, hers, its

Plural

	Nominative	Objective	Possessive
First Person	we	us	our, ours
Second Person	you	you	your, yours
Third Person	they	them	their, theirs

Intensive: I myself, you yourself, he himself, she herself, the (thing) itself, we ourselves, you yourselves, they themselves

Relative: which, who, whom, whose

Interrogative: what, which, who, whom, whose

Demonstrative: this, that, these, those

Indefinite: all, any, each, everyone, either/neither, one, some, several

Reciprocal: each other, one another

> **Review Video: Nouns and Pronouns**
> Visit mometrix.com/academy and enter code: 312073

VERBS

A verb is a word or group of words that indicates action or being. In other words, the verb shows something's action or state of being or the action that has been done to something. If you want to write a sentence, then you need a verb. Without a verb, you have no sentence.

TRANSITIVE AND INTRANSITIVE VERBS

A **transitive verb** is a verb whose action indicates a receiver. **Intransitive verbs** do not indicate a receiver of an action. In other words, the action of the verb does not point to an object.

Transitive: He drives a car. | She feeds the dog.

Intransitive: He runs every day. | She voted in the last election.

A dictionary will tell you whether a verb is transitive or intransitive. Some verbs can be transitive or intransitive.

ACTION VERBS AND LINKING VERBS

Action verbs show what the subject is doing. In other words, an action verb shows action. Unlike most types of words, a single action verb, in the right context, can be an entire sentence. **Linking verbs** link the subject of a sentence to a noun or pronoun, or they link a subject with an adjective. You always need a verb if you want a complete sentence. However, linking verbs on their own cannot be a complete sentence.

Common linking verbs include *appear, be, become, feel, grow, look, seem, smell, sound,* and *taste*. However, any verb that shows a condition and connects to a noun, pronoun, or adjective that describes the subject of a sentence is a linking verb.

Action: He sings. | Run! | Go! | I talk with him every day. | She reads.

Linking:

Incorrect: I am.

Correct: I am John. | The roses smell lovely. | I feel tired.

Note: Some verbs are followed by words that look like prepositions, but they are a part of the verb and a part of the verb's meaning. These are known as phrasal verbs, and examples include *call off, look up*, and *drop off*.

> **Review Video: Action Verbs and Linking Verbs**
> Visit mometrix.com/academy and enter code: 743142

VOICE

Transitive verbs may be in active voice or passive voice. The difference between active voice and passive voice is whether the subject is acting or being acted upon. When the subject of the sentence is doing the action, the verb is in **active voice**. When the subject is being acted upon, the verb is in **passive voice**.

> **Active**: Jon drew the picture. (The subject *Jon* is doing the action of *drawing a picture*.)

> **Passive**: The picture is drawn by Jon. (The subject *picture* is receiving the action from Jon.)

VERB TENSES

Verb **tense** is a property of a verb that indicates when the action being described takes place (past, present, or future) and whether or not the action is completed (simple or perfect). Describing an action taking place in the present (*I talk*) requires a different verb tense than describing an action that took place in the past (*I talked*). Some verb tenses require an auxiliary (helping) verb. These helping verbs include *am, are, is* | *have, has, had* | *was, were, will* (or *shall*).

Present: I talk	Present perfect: I have talked
Past: I talked	Past perfect: I had talked
Future: I will talk	Future perfect: I will have talked

Present: The action is happening at the current time.

> Example: He *walks* to the store every morning.

To show that something is happening right now, use the progressive present tense: I *am walking*.

Past: The action happened in the past.

> Example: She *walked* to the store an hour ago.

Future: The action will happen later.

> Example: I *will walk* to the store tomorrow.

Present perfect: The action started in the past and continues into the present or took place previously at an unspecified time.

> Example: I *have walked* to the store three times today.

Past perfect: The action was completed at some point in the past. This tense is usually used to describe an action that was completed before some other reference time or event.

> Example: I *had eaten* already before they arrived.

Future perfect: The action will be completed before some point in the future. This tense may be used to describe an action that has already begun or has yet to begin.

> Example: The project *will have been completed* by the deadline.

Review Video: Present Perfect, Past Perfect, and Future Perfect Verb Tenses
Visit mometrix.com/academy and enter code: 269472

Conjugating Verbs

When you need to change the form of a verb, you are **conjugating** a verb. The key forms of a verb are present tense (sing/sings), past tense (sang), present participle (singing), and past participle (sung). By combining these forms with helping verbs, you can make almost any verb tense. The following table demonstrate some of the different ways to conjugate a verb:

Tense	First Person	Second Person	Third Person Singular	Third Person Plural
Simple Present	I sing	You sing	He, she, it sings	They sing
Simple Past	I sang	You sang	He, she, it sang	They sang
Simple Future	I will sing	You will sing	He, she, it will sing	They will sing
Present Progressive	I am singing	You are singing	He, she, it is singing	They are singing
Past Progressive	I was singing	You were singing	He, she, it was singing	They were singing
Present Perfect	I have sung	You have sung	He, she, it has sung	They have sung
Past Perfect	I had sung	You had sung	He, she, it had sung	They had sung

Mood

There are three **moods** in English: the indicative, the imperative, and the subjunctive.

The **indicative mood** is used for facts, opinions, and questions.

Fact: You can do this.

Opinion: I think that you can do this.

Question: Do you know that you can do this?

The **imperative** is used for orders or requests.

Order: You are going to do this!

Request: Will you do this for me?

The **subjunctive mood** is for wishes and statements that go against fact.

Wish: I wish that I were famous.

Statement against fact: If I were you, I would do this. (This goes against fact because I am not you. You have the chance to do this, and I do not have the chance.)

ADJECTIVES

An **adjective** is a word that is used to modify a noun or pronoun. An adjective answers a question: *Which one? What kind?* or *How many?* Usually, adjectives come before the words that they modify, but they may also come after a linking verb.

Which one? The *third* suit is my favorite.

What kind? This suit is *navy blue.*

How many? I am going to buy *four* pairs of socks to match the suit.

Review Video: Descriptive Text
Visit mometrix.com/academy and enter code: 174903

ARTICLES

Articles are adjectives that are used to distinguish nouns as definite or indefinite. *A*, *an*, and *the* are the only articles. **Definite** nouns are preceded by *the* and indicate a specific person, place, thing, or idea. **Indefinite** nouns are preceded by *a* or *an* and do not indicate a specific person, place, thing, or idea.

Note: *An* comes before words that start with a vowel sound. For example, "Are you going to get an **u**mbrella?"

Definite: I lost *the* bottle that belongs to me.

Indefinite: Does anyone have *a* bottle to share?

Review Video: Function of Articles in a Sentence
Visit mometrix.com/academy and enter code: 449383

COMPARISON WITH ADJECTIVES

Some adjectives are relative and other adjectives are absolute. Adjectives that are **relative** can show the comparison between things. **Absolute** adjectives can also show comparison, but they do so in a different way. Let's say that you are reading two books. You think that one book is perfect, and the other book is not exactly perfect. It is not possible for one book to be more perfect than the other. Either you think that the book is perfect, or you think that the book is imperfect. In this case, perfect and imperfect are absolute adjectives.

Relative adjectives will show the different **degrees** of something or someone to something else or someone else. The three degrees of adjectives include positive, comparative, and superlative.

The **positive** degree is the normal form of an adjective.

Example: This work is *difficult.* | She is *smart.*

The **comparative** degree compares one person or thing to another person or thing.

Example: This work is *more difficult* than your work. | She is *smarter* than me.

The **superlative** degree compares more than two people or things.

Example: This is the *most difficult* work of my life. | She is the *smartest* lady in school.

Review Video: Adjectives
Visit mometrix.com/academy and enter code: 470154

Adverbs

An **adverb** is a word that is used to **modify** a verb, an adjective, or another adverb. Usually, adverbs answer one of these questions: *When? Where? How?* and *Why?* The negatives *not* and *never* are considered adverbs. Adverbs that modify adjectives or other adverbs **strengthen** or **weaken** the words that they modify.

Examples:

> He walks *quickly* through the crowd.
>
> The water flows *smoothly* on the rocks.

Note: Adverbs are usually indicated by the morpheme *-ly*, which has been added to the root word. For instance, *quick* can be made into an adverb by adding *-ly* to construct *quickly*. Some words that end in *-ly* do not follow this rule and can behave as other parts of speech. Examples of adjectives ending in *-ly* include: *early, friendly, holy, lonely, silly*, and *ugly*. To know if a word that ends in *-ly* is an adjective or adverb, check your dictionary. Also, while many adverbs end in *-ly*, you need to remember that not all adverbs end in *-ly*.

Examples:

> He is *never* angry.
>
> You are *too* irresponsible to travel alone.

Review Video: Adverbs
Visit mometrix.com/academy and enter code: 713951

Review Video: Adverbs that Modify Adjectives
Visit mometrix.com/academy and enter code: 122570

Comparison with Adverbs

The rules for comparing adverbs are the same as the rules for adjectives.

The **positive** degree is the standard form of an adverb.

> Example: He arrives *soon.* | She speaks *softly* to her friends.

The **comparative** degree compares one person or thing to another person or thing.

> Example: He arrives *sooner* than Sarah. | She speaks *more softly* than him.

The **superlative** degree compares more than two people or things.

> Example: He arrives *soonest* of the group. | She speaks the *most softly* of any of her friends.

PREPOSITIONS

A **preposition** is a word placed before a noun or pronoun that shows the relationship between that noun or pronoun and another word in the sentence.

Common prepositions:

about	before	during	on	under
after	beneath	for	over	until
against	between	from	past	up
among	beyond	in	through	with
around	by	of	to	within
at	down	off	toward	without

Examples:

The napkin is *in* the drawer.

The Earth rotates *around* the Sun.

The needle is *beneath* the haystack.

Can you find "me" *among* the words?

Review Video: Prepositions
Visit mometrix.com/academy and enter code: 946763

CONJUNCTIONS

Conjunctions join words, phrases, or clauses and they show the connection between the joined pieces. **Coordinating conjunctions** connect equal parts of sentences. **Correlative conjunctions** show the connection between pairs. **Subordinating conjunctions** join subordinate (i.e., dependent) clauses with independent clauses.

COORDINATING CONJUNCTIONS

The **coordinating conjunctions** include: *and, but, yet, or, nor, for,* and *so*

Examples:

The rock was small, *but* it was heavy.

She drove in the night, *and* he drove in the day.

Correlative Conjunctions

The **correlative conjunctions** are: *either...or* | *neither...nor* | *not only...but also*

Examples:

Either you are coming *or* you are staying.

He *not only* ran three miles *but also* swam 200 yards.

Review Video: Coordinating and Correlative Conjunctions
Visit mometrix.com/academy and enter code: 390329

Review Video: Adverb Equal Comparisons
Visit mometrix.com/academy and enter code: 231291

Subordinating Conjunctions

Common **subordinating conjunctions** include:

after	since	whenever
although	so that	where
because	unless	wherever
before	until	whether
in order that	when	while

Examples:

I am hungry *because* I did not eat breakfast.

He went home *when* everyone left.

Review Video: Subordinating Conjunctions
Visit mometrix.com/academy and enter code: 958913

Interjections

Interjections are words of exclamation (i.e., audible expression of great feeling) that are used alone or as a part of a sentence. Often, they are used at the beginning of a sentence for an introduction. Sometimes, they can be used in the middle of a sentence to show a change in thought or attitude.

Common Interjections: Hey! | Oh, | Ouch! | Please! | Wow!

Agreement and Sentence Structure

Subjects and Predicates

Subjects

The **subject** of a sentence names who or what the sentence is about. The subject may be directly stated in a sentence, or the subject may be the implied *you*. The **complete subject** includes the simple subject and all of its modifiers. To find the complete subject, ask *Who* or *What* and insert the verb to complete the question. The answer, including any modifiers (adjectives, prepositional phrases, etc.), is the complete subject. To find the **simple subject**, remove all of the modifiers in the complete subject. Being able to locate the subject of a sentence helps with many problems, such as those involving sentence fragments and subject-verb agreement.

Examples:

simple subject

The small, red car is the one that he wants for Christmas.

complete subject

simple subject

The young artist is coming over for dinner.

complete subject

Review Video: Subjects in English
Visit mometrix.com/academy and enter code: 444771

In **imperative** sentences, the verb's subject is understood (e.g., [You] Run to the store), but is not actually present in the sentence. Normally, the subject comes before the verb. However, the subject comes after the verb in sentences that begin with *There are* or *There was.*

Direct:

John knows the way to the park.	Who knows the way to the park?	John
The cookies need ten more minutes.	What needs ten minutes?	The cookies
By five o'clock, Bill will need to leave.	Who needs to leave?	Bill
There are five letters on the table for him.	What is on the table?	Five letters
There were coffee and doughnuts in the house.	What was in the house?	Coffee and doughnuts

Implied:

Go to the post office for me.	Who is going to the post office?	You
Come and sit with me, please?	Who needs to come and sit?	You

PREDICATES

In a sentence, you always have a predicate and a subject. The subject tells who or what the sentence is about, and the **predicate** explains or describes the subject. The predicate includes the verb or verb phrase and any direct or indirect objects of the verb, as well as any words or phrases modifying these.

Think about the sentence *He sings.* In this sentence, we have a subject (He) and a predicate (sings). This is all that is needed for a sentence to be complete. Most sentences contain more information, but if this is all the information that you are given, then you have a complete sentence.

Now, let's look at another sentence: *John and Jane sing on Tuesday nights at the dance hall.*

subject — predicate

John and Jane sing on Tuesday nights at the dance hall.

Review Video: Complete Predicate
Visit mometrix.com/academy and enter code: 293942

SUBJECT-VERB AGREEMENT

Verbs must **agree** with their subjects in number and in person. To agree in number, singular subjects need singular verbs and plural subjects need plural verbs. A **singular** noun refers to **one** person, place, or thing. A

plural noun refers to **more than one** person, place, or thing. To agree in person, the correct verb form must be chosen to match the first, second, or third person subject. The present tense ending *-s* or *-es* is used on a verb if its subject is third person singular; otherwise, the verb's ending is not modified.

Review Video: Subject-Verb Agreement
Visit mometrix.com/academy and enter code: 479190

Number Agreement Examples:

singular subject: Dan; singular verb: calls

Single Subject and Verb: Dan calls home.

Dan is one person. So, the singular verb *calls* is needed.

plural subject: Dan and Bob; plural verb: call

Plural Subject and Verb: Dan and Bob call home.

More than one person needs the plural verb *call.*

Person Agreement Examples:

First Person: I *am* walking.

Second Person: You *are* walking.

Third Person: He *is* walking.

Complications with Subject-Verb Agreement

Words Between Subject and Verb

Words that come between the simple subject and the verb have no bearing on subject-verb agreement.

Examples:

singular subject: joy; singular verb: returns

The joy of my life returns home tonight.

The phrase *of my life* does not influence the verb *returns.*

singular subject: question; singular verb: is

The question that still remains unanswered is "Who are you?"

Don't let the phrase "*that still remains...*" trouble you. The subject *question* goes with *is.*

Compound Subjects

A compound subject is formed when two or more nouns joined by *and, or,* or *nor* jointly act as the subject of the sentence.

Joined by And

When a compound subject is joined by *and*, it is treated as a plural subject and requires a plural verb.

Examples:

You and Jon (plural subject) are (plural verb) invited to come to my house.

The pencil and paper (plural subject) belong (plural verb) to me.

Joined by Or/Nor

For a compound subject joined by *or* or *nor*, the verb must agree in number with the part of the subject that is closest to the verb (italicized in the examples below).

Examples:

Today or tomorrow (subject) is (verb) the day.

Stan or Phil (subject) wants (verb) to read the book.

Neither the pen nor the book (subject) is (verb) on the desk.

Either the blanket or pillows (subject) arrive (verb) this afternoon.

Indefinite Pronouns as Subject

An indefinite pronoun is a pronoun that does not refer to a specific noun. Some indefinite pronouns function as only singular, some function as only plural, and some can function as either singular or plural depending on how they are used.

Always Singular

Pronouns such as *each*, *either*, *everybody*, *anybody*, *somebody*, and *nobody* are always singular.

Examples:

Each (singular subject) of the runners has (singular verb) a different bib number.

Is (singular verb) either (singular subject) of you ready for the game?

Note: The words *each* and *either* can also be used as adjectives (e.g., *each* person is unique). When one of these adjectives modifies the subject of a sentence, it is always a singular subject.

singular subject: Everybody; singular verb: grows

Everybody grows a day older every day.

singular subject: Anybody; singular verb: is

Anybody is welcome to bring a tent.

Always Plural

Pronouns such as *both*, *several*, and *many* are always plural.

Examples:

plural subject: Both; plural verb: were

Both of the siblings were too tired to argue.

plural subject: Many; plural verb: have tried

Many have tried, but none have succeeded.

Depend on Context

Pronouns such as *some*, *any*, *all*, *none*, *more*, and *most* can be either singular or plural depending on what they are representing in the context of the sentence.

Examples:

singular subject: All; singular verb: was

All of my dog's food was still there in his bowl.

plural subject: all; plural verb: were

By the end of the night, all of my guests were already excited about coming to my next party.

Other Cases Involving Plural or Irregular Form

Some nouns are **singular in meaning but plural in form**: news, mathematics, physics, and economics.

The *news is* coming on now.

Mathematics is my favorite class.

Some nouns are plural in form and meaning, and have **no singular equivalent**: scissors and pants.

Do these *pants come* with a shirt?

The *scissors are* for my project.

Mathematical operations are **irregular** in their construction, but are normally considered to be **singular in meaning**.

One plus one is two.

Three times three is nine.

Note: Look to your **dictionary** for help when you aren't sure whether a noun with a plural form has a singular or plural meaning.

Complements

A complement is a noun, pronoun, or adjective that is used to give more information about the subject or object in the sentence.

Direct Objects

A direct object is a noun or pronoun that tells who or what **receives** the action of the verb. A sentence will only include a direct object if the verb is a transitive verb. If the verb is an intransitive verb or a linking verb, there will be no direct object. When you are looking for a direct object, find the verb and ask *who* or *what.*

Examples:

I took *the blanket.*

Jane read *books.*

Indirect Objects

An indirect object is a noun or pronoun that indicates what or whom the action had an **influence** on. If there is an indirect object in a sentence, then there will also be a direct object. When you are looking for the indirect object, find the verb and ask *to/for whom or what.*

Examples:

indirect object — direct object

We taught the old dog a new trick.

indirect object — direct object

I gave them a math lesson.

Review Video: Direct and Indirect Objects
Visit mometrix.com/academy and enter code: 817385

Predicate Nominatives and Predicate Adjectives

As we looked at previously, verbs may be classified as either action verbs or linking verbs. A linking verb is so named because it links the subject to words in the predicate that describe or define the subject. These words are called predicate nominatives (if nouns or pronouns) or predicate adjectives (if adjectives).

Examples:

subject — predicate nominative

My father is a lawyer.

subject — predicate adjective

Your mother is patient.

Pronoun Usage

The **antecedent** is the noun that has been replaced by a pronoun. A pronoun and its antecedent **agree** when they have the same number (singular or plural) and gender (male, female, or neutral).

Examples:

Singular agreement: John (antecedent) came into town, and he (pronoun) played for us.

Plural agreement: John and Rick (antecedent) came into town, and they (pronoun) played for us.

To determine which is the correct pronoun to use in a compound subject or object, try each pronoun **alone** in place of the compound in the sentence. Your knowledge of pronouns will tell you which one is correct.

Example:

Bob and (I, me) will be going.

Test: (1) *I will be going* or (2) *Me will be going*. The second choice cannot be correct because *me* cannot be used as the subject of a sentence. Instead, *me* is used as an object.

Answer: Bob and I will be going.

When a pronoun is used with a noun immediately following (as in "we boys"), try the sentence **without the added noun**.

Example:

(We/Us) boys played football last year.

Test: (1) *We played football last ye*ar or (2) *Us played football last year*. Again, the second choice cannot be correct because *us* cannot be used as a subject of a sentence. Instead, *us* is used as an object.

Answer: We boys played football last year.

Review Video: Pronoun Usage
Visit mometrix.com/academy and enter code: 666500

Review Video: Pronoun-Antecedent Agreement
Visit mometrix.com/academy and enter code: 919704

A pronoun should point clearly to the **antecedent**. Here is how a pronoun reference can be unhelpful if it is puzzling or not directly stated.

Unhelpful: Ron and Jim (antecedent) went to the store, and he (pronoun) bought soda.

Who bought soda? Ron or Jim?

Helpful: Jim (antecedent) went to the store, and he (pronoun) bought soda.

The sentence is clear. Jim bought the soda.

Some pronouns change their form by their placement in a sentence. A pronoun that is a **subject** in a sentence comes in the **subjective case**. Pronouns that serve as **objects** appear in the **objective case**. Finally, the pronouns that are used as **possessives** appear in the **possessive case**.

Examples:

Subjective case: *He* is coming to the show.

The pronoun *He* is the subject of the sentence.

Objective case: Josh drove *him* to the airport.

The pronoun *him* is the object of the sentence.

Possessive case: The flowers are *mine*.

The pronoun *mine* shows ownership of the flowers.

The word *who* is a subjective-case pronoun that can be used as a **subject**. The word *whom* is an objective-case pronoun that can be used as an **object**. The words *who* and *whom* are common in subordinate clauses or in questions.

Examples:

He knows who (subject) wants (verb) to come.

He knows the man whom (object) we want (verb) at the party.

Clauses

A clause is a group of words that contains both a subject and a predicate (verb). There are two types of clauses: independent and dependent. An **independent clause** contains a complete thought, while a **dependent (or subordinate) clause** does not. A dependent clause includes a subject and a verb, and may also contain objects or complements, but it cannot stand as a complete thought without being joined to an independent clause. Dependent clauses function within sentences as adjectives, adverbs, or nouns.

Example:

I am running (independent clause) because I want to stay in shape. (dependent clause)

The clause *I am running* is an independent clause: it has a subject and a verb, and it gives a complete thought. The clause *because I want to stay in shape* is a dependent clause: it has a subject and a verb, but it does not express a complete thought. It adds detail to the independent clause to which it is attached.

Review Video: Clauses
Visit mometrix.com/academy and enter code: 940170

Review Video: Independent and Dependent Clauses
Visit mometrix.com/academy and enter code: 556903

Types of Dependent Clauses

Adjective Clauses

An **adjective clause** is a dependent clause that modifies a noun or a pronoun. Adjective clauses begin with a relative pronoun (*who, whose, whom, which,* and *that*) or a relative adverb (*where, when,* and *why*).

Also, adjective clauses usually come immediately after the noun that the clause needs to explain or rename. This is done to ensure that it is clear which noun or pronoun the clause is modifying.

Examples:

independent clause: I learned the reason | adjective clause: why I won the award.

independent clause: This is the place | adjective clause: where I started my first job.

An adjective clause can be an essential or nonessential clause. An essential clause is very important to the sentence. **Essential clauses** explain or define a person or thing. **Nonessential clauses** give more information about a person or thing but are not necessary to define them. Nonessential clauses are set off with commas while essential clauses are not.

Examples:

A person [essential clause: who works hard at first] can often rest later in life.

Neil Armstrong, [nonessential clause: who walked on the moon,] is my hero.

Review Video: Adjective Clauses and Phrases
Visit mometrix.com/academy and enter code: 520888

Adverb Clauses

An **adverb clause** is a dependent clause that modifies a verb, adjective, or adverb. In sentences with multiple dependent clauses, adverb clauses are usually placed immediately before or after the independent clause. An adverb clause is introduced with words such as *after, although, as, before, because, if, since, so, unless, when, where*, and *while*.

Examples:

[adverb clause: When you walked outside,] I called the manager.

I will go with you [adverb clause: unless you want to stay.]

Noun Clauses

A **noun clause** is a dependent clause that can be used as a subject, object, or complement. Noun clauses begin with words such as *how, that, what, whether, which, who,* and *why*. These words can also come with an adjective clause. Unless the noun clause is being used as the subject of the sentence, it should come after the verb of the independent clause.

Examples:

noun clause: The real mystery is how you avoided serious injury.

noun clause: What you learn from each other depends on your honesty with others.

Subordination

When two related ideas are not of equal importance, the ideal way to combine them is to make the more important idea an independent clause and the less important idea a dependent or subordinate clause. This is called **subordination**.

Example:

Separate ideas: The team had a perfect regular season. The team lost the championship.

Subordinated: Despite having a perfect regular season, *the team lost the championship.*

Phrases

A phrase is a group of words that functions as a single part of speech, usually a noun, adjective, or adverb. A **phrase** is not a complete thought and does not contain a subject and predicate, but it adds detail or explanation to a sentence, or renames something within the sentence.

Prepositional Phrases

One of the most common types of phrases is the prepositional phrase. A **prepositional phrase** begins with a preposition and ends with a noun or pronoun that is the object of the preposition. Normally, the prepositional phrase functions as an **adjective** or an **adverb** within the sentence.

Examples:

prepositional phrase: The picnic is on the blanket.

prepositional phrase: I am sick with a fever today.

prepositional phrase: Among the many flowers, John found a four-leaf clover.

Verbal Phrases

A **verbal** is a word or phrase that is formed from a verb but does not function as a verb. Depending on its particular form, it may be used as a noun, adjective, or adverb. A verbal does **not** replace a verb in a sentence.

Examples:

verb: Correct: Walk a mile daily.

This is a complete sentence with the implied subject *you.*

verbal

Incorrect: To walk a mile.

This is not a sentence since there is no functional verb.

There are three types of verbal: **participles, gerunds**, and **infinitives**. Each type of verbal has a corresponding **phrase** that consists of the verbal itself along with any complements or modifiers.

PARTICIPLES

A **participle** is a type of verbal that always functions as an adjective. The present participle always ends with -*ing*. Past participles end with *-d, -ed, -n,* or *-t*. Participles are combined with helping verbs to form certain verb tenses, but a participle by itself cannot function as a verb.

Examples: dance (verb) | dancing (present participle) | danced (past participle)

Participial phrases most often come right before or right after the noun or pronoun that they modify.

Examples:

Shipwrecked on an island (participial phrase), the boys started to fish for food.

Having been seated for five hours (participial phrase), we got out of the car to stretch our legs.

Praised for their work (participial phrase), the group accepted the first-place trophy.

GERUNDS

A **gerund** is a type of verbal that always functions as a **noun**. Like present participles, gerunds always end with -*ing*, but they can be easily distinguished from participles by the part of speech they represent (participles always function as adjectives). Since a gerund or gerund phrase always functions as a noun, it can be used as the subject of a sentence, the predicate nominative, or the object of a verb or preposition.

Examples:

We want to be known for teaching (gerund) the poor (object of preposition).

Coaching (gerund) this team (subject) is the best job of my life.

We like practicing (gerund) our songs (object of verb) in the basement.

INFINITIVES

An **infinitive** is a type of verbal that can function as a noun, an adjective, or an adverb. An infinitive is made of the word *to* and the basic form of the verb. As with all other types of verbal phrases, an infinitive phrase includes the verbal itself and all of its complements or modifiers.

Examples:

infinitive
To join the team is my goal in life.
noun

infinitive
The animals have enough food to eat for the night.
adjective

infinitive
People lift weights to exercise their muscles.
adverb

Review Video: Verbals
Visit mometrix.com/academy and enter code: 915480

Appositive Phrases

An **appositive** is a word or phrase that is used to explain or rename nouns or pronouns. Noun phrases, gerund phrases, and infinitive phrases can all be used as appositives.

Examples:

appositive
Terriers, hunters at heart, have been dressed up to look like lap dogs.

The noun phrase *hunters at heart* renames the noun *terriers*.

appositive
His plan, to save and invest his money, was proven as a safe approach.

The infinitive phrase explains what the plan is.

Appositive phrases can be **essential** or **nonessential**. An appositive phrase is essential if the person, place, or thing being described or renamed is too general for its meaning to be understood without the appositive.

Examples:

essential
Two of America's Founding Fathers, George Washington and Thomas Jefferson, served as presidents.

nonessential
George Washington and Thomas Jefferson, two Founding Fathers, served as presidents.

Absolute Phrases

An absolute phrase is a phrase that consists of **a noun followed by a participle**. An absolute phrase provides **context** to what is being described in the sentence, but it does not modify or explain any particular word; it is essentially independent.

Examples:

noun participle
The alarm ringing, he pushed the snooze button.
absolute phrase

noun participle
The music paused, she continued to dance through the crowd.
absolute phrase

Parallelism

When multiple items or ideas are presented in a sentence in series, such as in a list, the items or ideas must be stated in grammatically equivalent ways. For example, if two ideas are listed in parallel and the first is stated in gerund form, the second cannot be stated in infinitive form. (e.g., *I enjoy reading and to study.* [incorrect]) An infinitive and a gerund are not grammatically equivalent. Instead, you should write *I enjoy reading and studying* OR *I like to read and to study*. In lists of more than two, all items must be parallel.

Example:

> **Incorrect**: He stopped at the office, grocery store, and the pharmacy before heading home.
>
> The first and third items in the list of places include the article *the*, so the second item needs it as well.
>
> **Correct**: He stopped at the office, *the* grocery store, and the pharmacy before heading home.

Example:

> **Incorrect**: While vacationing in Europe, she went biking, skiing, and climbed mountains.
>
> The first and second items in the list are gerunds, so the third item must be as well.
>
> **Correct**: While vacationing in Europe, she went biking, skiing, and *mountain climbing*.

Review Video: Parallel Sentence Construction
Visit mometrix.com/academy and enter code: 831988

Sentence Purpose

There are four types of sentences: declarative, imperative, interrogative, and exclamatory.

A **declarative** sentence states a fact and ends with a period.

> *The football game starts at seven o'clock.*

An **imperative** sentence tells someone to do something and generally ends with a period. An urgent command might end with an exclamation point instead.

> *Don't forget to buy your ticket.*

An **interrogative** sentence asks a question and ends with a question mark.

> *Are you going to the game on Friday?*

An **exclamatory** sentence shows strong emotion and ends with an exclamation point.

> *I can't believe we won the game!*

SENTENCE STRUCTURE

Sentences are classified by structure based on the type and number of clauses present. The four classifications of sentence structure are the following:

Simple: A simple sentence has one independent clause with no dependent clauses. A simple sentence may have **compound elements** (i.e., compound subject or verb).

Examples:

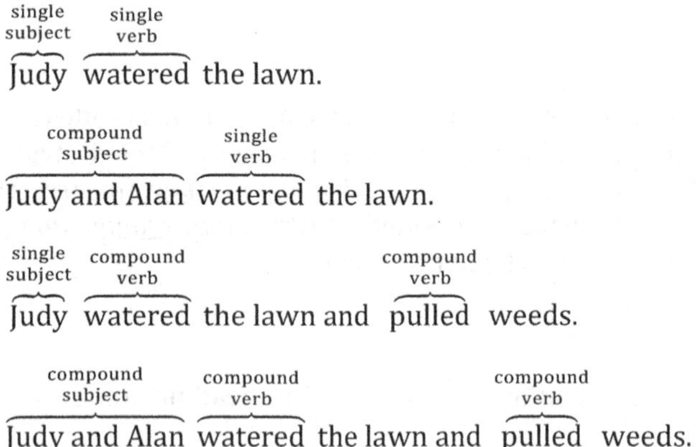

Compound: A compound sentence has two or more independent clauses with no dependent clauses. Usually, the independent clauses are joined with a comma and a coordinating conjunction or with a semicolon.

Examples:

independent clause / independent clause

The time has come, and we are ready.

independent clause / independent clause

I woke up at dawn; the sun was just coming up.

Complex: A complex sentence has one independent clause and at least one dependent clause.

Examples:

dependent clause / independent clause

Although he had the flu, Harry went to work.

independent clause / dependent clause

Marcia got married, after she finished college.

Compound-Complex: A compound-complex sentence has at least two independent clauses and at least one dependent clause.

Examples:

John is my friend (independent clause) who went to India, (dependent clause) and he brought back souvenirs. (independent clause)

You may not realize this, (independent clause) but we heard the music (independent clause) that you played last night. (dependent clause)

Review Video: Sentence Structure
Visit mometrix.com/academy and enter code: 700478

Sentence variety is important to consider when writing an essay or speech. A variety of sentence lengths and types creates rhythm, makes a passage more engaging, and gives writers an opportunity to demonstrate their writing style. Writing that uses the same length or type of sentence without variation can be boring or difficult to read. To evaluate a passage for effective sentence variety, it is helpful to note whether the passage contains diverse sentence structures and lengths. It is also important to pay attention to the way each sentence starts and avoid beginning with the same words or phrases.

Sentence Fragments

Recall that a group of words must contain at least one **independent clause** in order to be considered a sentence. If it doesn't contain even one independent clause, it is called a **sentence fragment**.

The appropriate process for **repairing** a sentence fragment depends on what type of fragment it is. If the fragment is a dependent clause, it can sometimes be as simple as removing a subordinating word (e.g., when, because, if) from the beginning of the fragment. Alternatively, a dependent clause can be incorporated into a closely related neighboring sentence. If the fragment is missing some required part, like a subject or a verb, the fix might be as simple as adding the missing part.

Examples:

Fragment: Because he wanted to sail the Mediterranean.

Removed subordinating word: He wanted to sail the Mediterranean.

Combined with another sentence: Because he wanted to sail the Mediterranean, he booked a Greek island cruise.

Run-on Sentences

Run-on sentences consist of multiple independent clauses that have not been joined together properly. Run-on sentences can be corrected in several different ways:

Join clauses properly: This can be done with a comma and coordinating conjunction, with a semicolon, or with a colon or dash if the second clause is explaining something in the first.

Example:

Incorrect: I went on the trip, we visited lots of castles.

Corrected: I went on the trip, and we visited lots of castles.

Split into separate sentences: This correction is most effective when the independent clauses are very long or when they are not closely related.

Example:

> **Incorrect**: The drive to New York takes ten hours, my uncle lives in Boston.
>
> **Corrected**: The drive to New York takes ten hours. My uncle lives in Boston.

Make one clause dependent: This is the easiest way to make the sentence correct and more interesting at the same time. It's often as simple as adding a subordinating word between the two clauses or before the first clause.

Example:

> **Incorrect**: I finally made it to the store and I bought some eggs.
>
> **Corrected**: When I finally made it to the store, I bought some eggs.

Reduce to one clause with a compound verb: If both clauses have the same subject, remove the subject from the second clause, and you now have just one clause with a compound verb.

Example:

> **Incorrect**: The drive to New York takes ten hours, it makes me very tired.
>
> **Corrected**: The drive to New York takes ten hours and makes me very tired.

Note: While these are the simplest ways to correct a run-on sentence, often the best way is to completely reorganize the thoughts in the sentence and rewrite it.

> **Review Video: Fragments and Run-on Sentences**
> Visit mometrix.com/academy and enter code: 541989

Dangling and Misplaced Modifiers

Dangling Modifiers

A dangling modifier is a dependent clause or verbal phrase that does not have a clear logical connection to a word in the sentence.

Example:

> dangling modifier
>
> **Incorrect**: Reading each magazine article, the stories caught my attention.
>
> The word *stories* cannot be modified by *Reading each magazine article*. People can read, but stories cannot read. Therefore, the subject of the sentence must be a person.
>
> gerund phrase
>
> **Corrected**: Reading each magazine article, I was entertained by the stories.

Example:

dangling modifier

Incorrect: Ever since childhood, my grandparents have visited me for Christmas.

The speaker in this sentence can't have been visited by her grandparents when *they* were children, since she wouldn't have been born yet. Either the modifier should be clarified or the sentence should be rearranged to specify whose childhood is being referenced.

dependent clause

Clarified: Ever since I was a child, my grandparents have visited for Christmas.

adverb phrase

Rearranged: Ever since childhood, I have enjoyed my grandparents visiting for Christmas.

Misplaced Modifiers

Because modifiers are grammatically versatile, they can be put in many different places within the structure of a sentence. The danger of this versatility is that a modifier can accidentally be placed where it is modifying the wrong word or where it is not clear which word it is modifying.

Example:

modifier

Incorrect: She read the book to a crowd that was filled with beautiful pictures.

The book was filled with beautiful pictures, not the crowd.

modifier

Corrected: She read the book that was filled with beautiful pictures to a crowd.

Example:

modifier

Ambiguous: Derek saw a bus nearly hit a man on his way to work.

Was Derek on his way to work or was the other man?

modifier

Derek: On his way to work, Derek saw a bus nearly hit a man.

modifier

The other man: Derek saw a bus nearly hit a man who was on his way to work.

Split Infinitives

A split infinitive occurs when a modifying word comes between the word *to* and the verb that pairs with *to*.

Example: To *clearly* explain vs. *To explain* clearly | To *softly* sing vs. *To sing* softly

Though considered improper by some, split infinitives may provide better clarity and simplicity in some cases than the alternatives. As such, avoiding them should not be considered a universal rule.

Double Negatives

Standard English allows **two negatives** only when a **positive** meaning is intended. (e.g., The team was *not displeased* with their performance.) Double negatives to emphasize negation are not used in standard English.

Negative modifiers (e.g., never, no, and not) should not be paired with other negative modifiers or negative words (e.g., none, nobody, nothing, or neither). The modifiers *hardly, barely*, and *scarcely* are also considered negatives in standard English, so they should not be used with other negatives.

PUNCTUATION

END PUNCTUATION

PERIODS

Use a period to end all sentences except direct questions and exclamations. Periods are also used for abbreviations.

> Examples: 3 p.m. | 2 a.m. | Mr. Jones | Mrs. Stevens | Dr. Smith | Bill, Jr. | Pennsylvania Ave.

Note: An abbreviation is a shortened form of a word or phrase.

QUESTION MARKS

Question marks should be used following a **direct question**. A polite request can be followed by a period instead of a question mark.

> **Direct Question**: What is for lunch today? | How are you? | Why is that the answer?
>
> **Polite Requests**: Can you please send me the item tomorrow. | Will you please walk with me on the track.

Review Video: Question Marks
Visit mometrix.com/academy and enter code: 118471

EXCLAMATION MARKS

Exclamation marks are used after a word group or sentence that shows much feeling or has special importance. Exclamation marks should not be overused. They are saved for proper **exclamatory interjections**.

> Example: We're going to the finals! | You have a beautiful car! | "That's crazy!" she yelled.

Review Video: Exclamation Points
Visit mometrix.com/academy and enter code: 199367

COMMAS

The comma is a punctuation mark that can help you understand connections in a sentence. Not every sentence needs a comma. However, if a sentence needs a comma, you need to put it in the right place. A comma in the wrong place (or an absent comma) will make a sentence's meaning unclear.

These are some of the rules for commas:

Use Case	Example
Before a **coordinating conjunction** joining independent clauses	Bob caught three fish, and I caught two fish.
After an **introductory phrase**	After the final out, we went to a restaurant to celebrate.
After an **adverbial clause**	Studying the stars, I was awed by the beauty of the sky.
Between **items in a series**	I will bring the turkey, the pie, and the coffee.
For **interjections**	Wow, you know how to play this game.
After ***yes* and *no* responses**	No, I cannot come tomorrow.
Separate **nonessential modifiers**	John Frank, who coaches the team, was promoted today.
Separate **nonessential appositives**	Thomas Edison, an American inventor, was born in Ohio.
Separate **nouns of direct address**	You, John, are my only hope in this moment.
Separate **interrogative tags**	This is the last time, correct?
Separate **contrasts**	You are my friend, not my enemy.
Writing **dates**	July 4, 1776, is an important date to remember.
Writing **addresses**	He is meeting me at 456 Delaware Avenue, Washington, D.C., tomorrow morning.
Writing **geographical names**	Paris, France, is my favorite city.
Writing **titles**	John Smith, PhD, will be visiting your class today.
Separate **expressions like *he said***	"You can start," she said, "with an apology."

A comma is also used **between coordinate adjectives** not joined with *and*. However, not all adjectives are coordinate (i.e., equal or parallel). To determine if your adjectives are coordinate, try connecting them with *and* or reversing their order. If it still sounds right, they are coordinate.

Incorrect: The kind, brown dog followed me home.

Correct: The kind, loyal dog followed me home.

Review Video: When to Use a Comma
Visit mometrix.com/academy and enter code: 786797

SEMICOLONS

The semicolon is used to join closely related independent clauses without the need for a coordinating conjunction. Semicolons are also used in place of commas to separate list elements that have internal commas. Some rules for semicolons include:

Use Case	Example
Between closely connected independent clauses **not connected with a coordinating conjunction**	You are right; we should go with your plan.
Between independent clauses **linked with a transitional word**	I think that we can agree on this; however, I am not sure about my friends.
Between items in a **series that has internal punctuation**	I have visited New York, New York; Augusta, Maine; and Baltimore, Maryland.

Review Video: How to Use Semicolons
Visit mometrix.com/academy and enter code: 370605

COLONS

The colon is used to call attention to the words that follow it. When used in a sentence, a colon should only come at the **end** of a **complete sentence**. The rules for colons are as follows:

Use Case	Example
After an independent clause to **make a list**	I want to learn many languages: Spanish, German, and Italian.
For **explanations**	There is one thing that stands out on your resume: responsibility.
To give a **quote**	He started with an idea: "We are able to do more than we imagine."
After the **greeting in a formal letter**	To Whom It May Concern:
Show **hours and minutes**	It is 3:14 p.m.
Separate a **title and subtitle**	The essay is titled "America: A Short Introduction to a Modern Country."

Review Video: Using Colons
Visit mometrix.com/academy and enter code: 868673

PARENTHESES

Parentheses are used for additional information. Also, they can be used to put labels for letters or numbers in a series. Parentheses should be not be used very often. If they are overused, parentheses can be a distraction instead of a help.

Examples:

Extra Information: The rattlesnake (see Image 2) is a dangerous snake of North and South America.

Series: Include in the email (1) your name, (2) your address, and (3) your question for the author.

Review Video: Parentheses
Visit mometrix.com/academy and enter code: 947743

QUOTATION MARKS

Use quotation marks to close off **direct quotations** of a person's spoken or written words. Do not use quotation marks around indirect quotations. An indirect quotation gives someone's message without using the person's exact words. Use **single quotation marks** to close off a quotation inside a quotation.

Direct Quote: Nancy said, "I am waiting for Henry to arrive."

Indirect Quote: Henry said that he is going to be late to the meeting.

Quote inside a Quote: The teacher asked, "Has everyone read 'The Gift of the Magi'?"

Quotation marks should be used around the titles of **short works**: newspaper and magazine articles, poems, short stories, songs, television episodes, radio programs, and subdivisions of books or websites.

Examples:

"Rip Van Winkle" (short story by Washington Irving)

"O Captain! My Captain!" (poem by Walt Whitman)

Although it is not standard usage, quotation marks are sometimes used to highlight **irony** or the use of words to mean something other than their dictionary definition. This type of usage should be employed sparingly, if at all.

Examples:

The boss warned Frank that he was walking on "thin ice."	Frank is not walking on real ice. Instead, he is being warned to avoid mistakes.
The teacher thanked the young man for his "honesty."	The quotation marks around *honesty* show that the teacher does not believe the young man's explanation.

Review Video: Quotation Marks
Visit mometrix.com/academy and enter code: 884918

Periods and commas are put **inside** quotation marks. Colons and semicolons are put **outside** the quotation marks. Question marks and exclamation points are placed inside quotation marks when they are part of a quote. When the question or exclamation mark goes with the whole sentence, the mark is left outside of the quotation marks.

Examples:

Period and comma	We read "The Gift of the Magi," "The Skylight Room," and "The Cactus."
Semicolon	They watched "The Nutcracker"; then, they went home.
Exclamation mark that is a part of a quote	The crowd cheered, "Victory!"
Question mark that goes with the whole sentence	Is your favorite short story "The Tell-Tale Heart"?

Apostrophes

An apostrophe is used to show **possession** or the **deletion of letters in contractions**. An apostrophe is not needed with the possessive pronouns *his, hers, its, ours, theirs, whose,* and *yours.*

Singular Nouns: David's car | a book's theme | my brother's board game

Plural Nouns that end with -*s*: the scissors' handle | boys' basketball

Plural Nouns that end without -*s*: Men's department | the people's adventure

Review Video: When to Use an Apostrophe
Visit mometrix.com/academy and enter code: 213068

Review Video: Punctuation Errors in Possessive Pronouns
Visit mometrix.com/academy and enter code: 221438

HYPHENS

Hyphens are used to **separate compound words**. Use hyphens in the following cases:

Use Case	Example
Compound numbers from 21 to 99 when written out in words	This team needs twenty-five points to win the game.
Written-out fractions that are used as adjectives	The recipe says that we need a three-fourths cup of butter.
Compound adjectives that come before a noun	The well-fed dog took a nap.
Unusual compound words that would be hard to read or easily confused with other words	This is the best anti-itch cream on the market.

Note: This is not a complete set of the rules for hyphens. A dictionary is the best tool for knowing if a compound word needs a hyphen.

Review Video: Hyphens
Visit mometrix.com/academy and enter code: 981632

DASHES

Dashes are used to show a **break** or a **change in thought** in a sentence or to act as parentheses in a sentence. When typing, use two hyphens to make a dash. Do not put a space before or after the dash. The following are the functions of dashes:

Use Case	Example
Set off parenthetical statements or an **appositive with internal punctuation**	The three trees—oak, pine, and magnolia—are coming on a truck tomorrow.
Show a **break or change in tone or thought**	The first question—how silly of me—does not have a correct answer.

ELLIPSIS MARKS

The ellipsis mark has **three** periods (...) to show when **words have been removed** from a quotation. If a **full sentence or more** is removed from a quoted passage, you need to use **four** periods to show the removed text and the end punctuation mark. The ellipsis mark should not be used at the beginning of a quotation. The ellipsis mark should also not be used at the end of a quotation unless some words have been deleted from the end of the final quoted sentence.

Example:

"Then he picked up the groceries...paid for them...later he went home."

BRACKETS

There are two main reasons to use brackets:

Use Case	Example
Placing **parentheses inside of parentheses**	The hero of this story, Paul Revere (a silversmith and industrialist [see Ch. 4]), rode through towns of Massachusetts to warn of advancing British troops.
Adding **clarification or detail to a quotation** that is not part of the quotation	The father explained, "My children are planning to attend my alma mater [State University]."

Review Video: Brackets
Visit mometrix.com/academy and enter code: 727546

Common Usage Mistakes

Word Confusion

Which, That, and Who

The words *which, that,* and *who* can act as **relative pronouns** to help clarify or describe a noun.

Which is used for things only.

Example: Andrew's car, *which is old and rusty,* broke down last week.

That is used for people or things. *That* is usually informal when used to describe people.

Example: Is this the only book *that Louis L'Amour wrote?*

Example: Is Louis L'Amour the author *that wrote Western novels?*

Who is used for people or for animals that have an identity or personality.

Example: Mozart was the composer *who wrote those operas.*

Example: John's dog, *who is called Max,* is large and fierce.

Homophones

Homophones are words that sound alike (or similar) but have different **spellings** and **definitions**. A homophone is a type of **homonym**, which is a pair or group of words that are pronounced or spelled the same, but do not mean the same thing.

To, Too, and Two

To can be an adverb or a preposition for showing direction, purpose, and relationship. See your dictionary for the many other ways to use *to* in a sentence.

Examples: I went to the store. | I want to go with you.

Too is an adverb that means *also, as well, very,* or *in excess.*

Examples: I can walk a mile too. | You have eaten too much.

Two is a number.

Example: You have two minutes left.

There, Their, and They're

There can be an adjective, adverb, or pronoun. Often, *there* is used to show a place or to start a sentence.

Examples: I went there yesterday. | There is something in his pocket.

Their is a pronoun that is used to show ownership.

Examples: He is their father. | This is their fourth apology this week.

They're is a contraction of *they are.*

Example: Did you know that they're in town?

Knew and New

Knew is the past tense of *know*.

Example: I knew the answer.

New is an adjective that means something is current, has not been used, or is modern.

Example: This is my new phone.

Then and Than

Then is an adverb that indicates sequence or order:

Example: I'm going to run to the library and then come home.

Than is special-purpose word used only for comparisons:

Example: Susie likes chips more than candy.

Its and It's

Its is a pronoun that shows ownership.

Example: The guitar is in its case.

It's is a contraction of *it is.*

Example: It's an honor and a privilege to meet you.

Note: The *h* in honor is silent, so *honor* starts with the vowel sound *o*, which must have the article *an*.

Your and You're

Your is a pronoun that shows ownership.

Example: This is your moment to shine.

You're is a contraction of *you are.*

Example: Yes, you're correct.

Saw and Seen

Saw is the past-tense form of *see.*

Example: I saw a turtle on my walk this morning.

Seen is the past participle of *see.*

Example: I have seen this movie before.

Affect and Effect

There are two main reasons that *affect* and *effect* are so often confused: 1) both words can be used as either a noun or a verb, and 2) unlike most homophones, their usage and meanings are closely related to each other. Here is a quick rundown of the four usage options:

Affect (n): feeling, emotion, or mood that is displayed

Example: The patient had a flat *affect.* (i.e., his face showed little or no emotion)

Affect (v): to alter, to change, to influence

Example: The sunshine *affects* the plant's growth.

Effect (n): a result, a consequence

Example: What *effect* will this weather have on our schedule?

Effect (v): to bring about, to cause to be

Example: These new rules will *effect* order in the office.

The noun form of *affect* is rarely used outside of technical medical descriptions, so if a noun form is needed on the test, you can safely select *effect*. The verb form of *effect* is not as rare as the noun form of *affect*, but it's still not all that likely to show up on your test. If you need a verb and you can't decide which to use based on the definitions, choosing *affect* is your best bet.

HOMOGRAPHS

Homographs are words that share the same spelling, but have different meanings and sometimes different pronunciations. To figure out which meaning is being used, you should be looking for context clues. The context clues give hints to the meaning of the word. For example, the word *spot* has many meanings. It can mean "a place" or "a stain or blot." In the sentence "After my lunch, I saw a spot on my shirt," the word *spot* means "a stain or blot." The context clues of "After my lunch" and "on my shirt" guide you to this decision. A homograph is another type of homonym.

BANK

(noun): an establishment where money is held for savings or lending

(verb): to collect or pile up

CONTENT

(noun): the topics that will be addressed within a book

(adjective): pleased or satisfied

(verb): to make someone pleased or satisfied

FINE

(noun): an amount of money that acts a penalty for an offense

(adjective): very small or thin

(adverb): in an acceptable way

(verb): to make someone pay money as a punishment

INCENSE

(noun): a material that is burned in religious settings and makes a pleasant aroma

(verb): to frustrate or anger

LEAD

(noun): the first or highest position

(noun): a heavy metallic element

(verb): to direct a person or group of followers

(adjective): containing lead

OBJECT

(noun): a lifeless item that can be held and observed

(verb): to disagree

PRODUCE

(noun): fruits and vegetables

(verb): to make or create something

REFUSE

(noun): garbage or debris that has been thrown away

(verb): to not allow

SUBJECT

(noun): an area of study

(verb): to force or subdue

TEAR

(noun): a fluid secreted by the eyes

(verb): to separate or pull apart

COMMONLY MISUSED WORDS AND PHRASES

A LOT

The phrase *a lot* should always be written as two words; never as *alot.*

Correct: That's a lot of chocolate!

Incorrect: He does that alot.

CAN

The word *can* is used to describe things that are possible occurrences; the word *may* is used to described things that are allowed to happen.

Correct: May I have another piece of pie?

Correct: I can lift three of these bags of mulch at a time.

Incorrect: Mom said we can stay up thirty minutes later tonight.

COULD HAVE

The phrase *could of* is often incorrectly substituted for the phrase *could have.* Similarly, *could of, may of,* and *might of* are sometimes used in place of the correct phrases *could have, may have,* and *might have.*

Correct: If I had known, I would have helped out.

Incorrect: Well, that could of gone much worse than it did.

Myself

The word *myself* is a reflexive pronoun, often incorrectly used in place of *I* or *me*.

Correct: He let me do it myself.

Incorrect: The job was given to Dave and myself.

Off

The phrase *off of* is a redundant expression that should be avoided. In most cases, it can be corrected simply by removing *of*.

Correct: My dog chased the squirrel off its perch on the fence.

Incorrect: He finally moved his plate off of the table.

Supposed To

The phrase *suppose to* is sometimes used incorrectly in place of the phrase *supposed to*.

Correct: I was supposed to go to the store this afternoon.

Incorrect: When are we suppose to get our grades?

Try To

The phrase *try and* is often used in informal writing and conversation to replace the correct phrase *try to*.

Correct: It's a good policy to try to satisfy every customer who walks in the door.

Incorrect: Don't try and do too much.

Writing

Preparing for an Essay Question

Brainstorm

Spend the first three to five minutes brainstorming for ideas. Write down any ideas that you might have on the topic. The purpose is to pull any helpful information from the depths of your memory. In this stage, anything goes down in a margin for notes regardless of how good or bad the idea may seem at first glance.

Strength Through Different Viewpoints

The best papers will contain several examples and mature reasoning. As you brainstorm, you should consider different perspectives. There are more than two sides to every topic. In an argument, there are countless perspectives that can be considered. On any topic, different groups are impacted and many reach the same conclusion or position. Yet, they reach the same conclusion through different paths. Before writing your essay, try to *see* the topic through as many different *eyes* as you can.

In addition, you don't have to use information on how the topic impacts others. You can draw from your own experience as you wish. If you prefer to use a personal narrative, then explain the experience and your emotions from that moment. Anything that you've seen in your community can be expanded upon to round out your position on the topic.

Once you have finished with your creative flow, you need to stop and review what you brainstormed. *Which idea allowed you to come up with the most supporting information?* Be sure to pick an angle that will allow you to have a thorough coverage of the prompt.

Every garden of ideas has weeds. The ideas that you brainstormed are going to be random pieces of information of different values. Go through the pieces carefully and pick out the ones that are the best. The best ideas are strong points that will be easy to write a paragraph in response.

Now, you have your main ideas that you will focus on. So, align them in a sequence that will flow in a smooth, sensible path from point to point. With this approach, readers will go smoothly from one idea to the next in a reasonable order. Readers want an essay that has a sense of continuity (i.e., Point 1 to Point 2 to Point 3 and so on).

Start Your Engines

Now, you have a logical flow of the main ideas for the start of your essay. Begin by expanding on the first point, then move to your second point. Pace yourself. Don't spend too much time on any one of the ideas that you are expanding on. You want to have time for all of them. Make sure that you watch your time. If you have twenty minutes left to write out your ideas and you have four ideas, then you can only use five minutes per idea. Writing so much information in so little time can be an intimidating task. Yet, when you pace yourself, you can get through all of your points. If you find that you are falling behind, then you can remove one of your weaker arguments. This will allow you to give enough support to your remaining paragraphs.

Once you finish expanding on an idea, go back to your brainstorming session where you wrote out your ideas. You can scratch through the ideas as you write about them. This will let you see what you need to write about next and what you have left to cover.

Your introductory paragraph should have several easily identifiable features.

- First, the paragraph should have a quick description or paraphrasing of the topic. Use your own words to briefly explain what the topic is about.
- Second, you should list your writing points. What are the main ideas that you came up with earlier? If someone was to read only your introduction, they should be able to get a good summary of the entire paper.
- Third, you should explain your opinion of the topic and give an explanation for why you feel that way. What is your decision or conclusion on the topic?

Each of your following paragraphs should develop one of the points listed in the main paragraph. Use your personal experience and knowledge to support each of your points. Examples should back up everything.

Once you have finished expanding on each of your main points, you need to conclude your essay. Summarize what you have written in a conclusion paragraph. Explain once more your argument on the prompt and review why you feel that way in a few sentences. At this stage, you have already backed up your statements. So, there is no need to do that again. You just need to refresh your readers on the main points that you made in your essay.

Don't Panic

Whatever you do during essay, do not panic. When you panic, you will put fewer words on the page and your ideas will be weak. Therefore, panicking is not helpful. If your mind goes blank when you see the prompt, then you need to take a deep breath. Force yourself to go through the steps listed above: brainstorm and put anything on scratch paper that comes to mind.

Also, don't get clock fever. You may be overwhelmed when you're looking at a page that is mostly blank. Your mind is full of random thoughts and feeling confused, and the clock is ticking down faster. You have already brainstormed for ideas. Therefore, you don't have to keep coming up with ideas. If you're running out of time and you have a lot of ideas that you haven't written down, then don't be afraid to make some cuts. Start picking the best ideas that you have left and expand on them. Don't feel like you have to write on all of your ideas.

A short paper that is well written and well organized is better than a long paper that is poorly written and poorly organized. Don't keep writing about a subject just to add sentences and avoid repeating a statement or idea that you have explained already. The goal is 1 to 2 pages of quality writing. That is your target, but you should not mess up your paper by trying to get there. You want to have a natural end to your work without having to cut something short. If your essay is a little long, then that isn't a problem as long as your ideas are clear and flow well from paragraph to paragraph. Remember to expand on the ideas that you identified in the brainstorming session.

Leave time at the end (at least three minutes) to go back and check over your work. Reread and make sure that everything you've written makes sense and flows well. Clean up any spelling or grammar mistakes. Also, go ahead and erase any brainstorming ideas that you weren't able to include. Then, clean up any extra information that you might have written that doesn't fit into your paper.

As you proofread, make sure that there aren't any fragments or run-ons. Check for sentences that are too short or too long. If the sentence is too short, then look to see if you have a specific subject and an active verb. If it is too long, then break up the long sentence into two sentences. Watch out for any "big words" that you may have used. Be sure that you are using difficult words correctly. Don't misunderstand; you should try to increase your vocabulary and use difficult words in your essay. However, your focus should be on developing and expressing ideas in a clear and precise way.

The Short Overview

Depending on your preferences and personality, the essay may be your hardest or your easiest section. You are required to go through the entire process of writing a paper in a limited amount of time which is very challenging.

Stay focused on each of the steps for brainstorming. Go through the process of creative flow first. You can start by generating ideas about the prompt. Next, organize those ideas into a smooth flow. Then, pick out the ideas that are the best from your list.

Create a recognizable essay structure in your paper. Start with an introduction that explains what you have decided to argue. Then, choose your main points. Use the body paragraphs to touch on those main points and have a conclusion that wraps up the topic.

Save a few moments to go back and review what you have written. Clean up any minor mistakes that you might have made and make those last few critical touches that can make a huge difference. Finally, be proud and confident of what you have written!

Chapter Quiz

Ready to see how well you retained what you just read? Scan the QR code to go directly to the chapter quiz interface for this study guide. If you're using a computer, simply visit the bonus page at **mometrix.com/bonus948/ged** and click the Chapter Quizzes link.

Social Studies

Transform passive reading into active learning! After immersing yourself in this chapter, put your comprehension to the test by taking a quiz. The insights you gained will stay with you longer this way. Scan the QR code to go directly to the chapter quiz interface for this study guide. If you're using a computer, simply visit the bonus page at **mometrix.com/bonus948/ged** and click the Chapter Quizzes link.

Reading for Meaning in Social Studies

Main Ideas and Details in Social Studies Readings

When reading a complex text, it's easy to get bogged down in details and minutiae and miss the main idea that the text is trying to convey. If the source in question is a textbook or other reference work with clear sections and headings, those headings generally state the main ideas of the text. It may be helpful to read the headings first, to know the ideas that the text is intended to present. Otherwise, if the main idea of a text is unclear at first read, it may help to break it down a piece at a time.

Look at each paragraph: What is the paragraph about? Is there a topic sentence at the beginning or end or a question raised at the beginning? Is there a particular subject that comes up in nearly every sentence? Is there a detail that's given especial emphasis? Any of those factors points to the main idea of the paragraph. When you know the main topic that each paragraph is meant to convey, put them together and look for a common thread or a repeated idea that keeps coming up. That idea is likely related to the main idea of the text as a whole.

Often, information can be inferred from a text that is not explicitly stated. A text may suggest connections that the writer doesn't call out. If a text relates that a settlement had poor sanitation and later mentions a high prevalence of disease there, it's a reasonable inference that the former caused the latter. A writer's word choice can often allow the reader to make inferences about the writer's attitude toward the subject. If a writer refers to one side in a conflict as brave, the writer probably sympathizes with that side; if the writer refers to that side as reckless, the opposite may be true.

Sometimes inferences can be drawn from what the writer *doesn't* include. If a detailed description of a war between two ancient civilizations only mentions the use of soldiers on horseback by one side, it may be a reasonable inference that the other side didn't have access to horses. Sometimes outside information helps with inferences. A description of a merchant's household by itself may not be illuminating, but by comparison with what the reader knows of the usual standard of living at the time, the reader may infer that the merchant was especially well off.

How Authors Use Language in Social Studies

As with other academic disciplines, social studies has its own form of language that may not be exactly the same as the language used in everyday life outside of the field. Most notably, social studies has its own vocabulary, comprising words that are more or less unique to the discipline (such as oligarchy and populism) and words that have a different meaning than in most other contexts (such as capital and nation). It also has a different emphasis, often focusing more on abstract principles and connections than on concrete details. Even the grammar structures are different: Most social studies texts use a more formal tone and more complicated sentences than are typically found in conversational language.

Social studies, more so than other academic fields such as science and mathematics, makes heavy use of sentence structures referring to sequences of events, to causality, and to other connections between events and ideas. Social studies is heavily concerned with histories and with how concepts and events relate to each other, and the language reflects that. Readers of social studies texts should watch for words, phrases, and sentence structures indicating such temporal and causal relationships, such as "in the following years" or "as a consequence."

Fact Versus Opinion

When reading a historical document or other source, it's important to separate fact from opinion. A **fact** is a relation of an event that happened, or a statement of a condition, without judgment as to whether the event or condition was good or bad, or speculation about its causes and consequences. These judgments and speculations reflect the writer's **opinion**—the writer's own subjective feelings and thoughts about the topic in question.

It's important to separate fact from opinion: The facts about a historical happening may not be in dispute (if the writer is reliable and not lying or stretching the truth), but opinions may differ, and they cannot be taken as truth. That doesn't mean, however, that opinions don't have their place. Although a writer's opinion may not change the facts—and the reader may even disagree with it—it still has value. It helps show the writer's attitudes and thought processes, which help the reader judge the writer's reliability. It may reflect or illuminate common attitudes of the time. And it may possibly provoke further thought on a subject or help the reader to see a different perspective on it.

Claims and Evidence in Social Studies

Not everything you read or hear can be taken at face value. Before believing a claim in a passage, it's important to check whether it's supported by evidence. This is especially important when the passage comes from a highly biased source or if it goes strongly against conventional wisdom—that doesn't necessarily mean that the claim is false, but it definitely suggests that it should be checked.

Is the claim based on facts, rather than just on opinion and emotion? Can those facts be verified? Does the passage cite its sources, and, if so, do those sources really say what the passage says they do? (That's important to check, too; just because a passage cites a source doesn't mean that source really supports its argument.) Look for some other sources about topics related to the claim—do they agree with the facts stated in the passage? Do they provide any important details that the passage omits? Does the passage follow a valid chain of reasoning from the facts to the claim, or does it leap to conclusions or contain an important fallacy?

It may not always be simple to check the evidence behind a claim, but you shouldn't believe every claim without doing so.

Common Fallacies in Arguments

A **fallacy** is a method of argument that might seem superficially convincing but doesn't really lead reliably to the conclusion. There are many different fallacies that are common in arguments in social studies and in other contexts; the following are just a few of the most frequent.

- **Post hoc fallacy**: The assumption that because one event occurred after another, it must have been caused by it.
- **Circular reasoning** (begging the question): An argument that starts by assuming the conclusion must be true.
- **False dichotomy** (excluded middle): An argument based on the assumption that one of two options must be true, ignoring other possibilities.
- **Appeal to ignorance**: An argument that the conclusion must be true just because it hasn't been proven to be false.
- **Argument from authority**: An argument that the conclusion must be true just because some respected person said so.

- **Hasty generalization**: The assumption that something true of a small sample must be true of an entire population.
- **False analogy**: Drawing an analogy between two subjects based on some point of similarity and then assuming that they must be similar in other ways as well.
- **Slippery slope**: The argument that a small allowance must inevitably lead to an extreme consequence.

Sources with Conflicting Information

Historical documents and secondary sources such as textbooks and encyclopedias may contradict each other about social studies topics—or, even if there is no direct contradiction, one source may contain some important details not contained in the other. These differences may be due to bias; one source may be distorting the facts, intentionally or subconsciously, in the interests of pushing a point of view. However, one source may also have an error due to an honest mistake or a misunderstanding. The difference in sources may only be due to their purpose or target audience: A source may omit some facts simply because they weren't relevant to its purpose.

In any case, this possible difference in information between sources is one reason why it's important, where possible, to draw on multiple sources. If two secondary sources contradict each other, it may help to check the primary sources that they draw from. If this isn't possible, or if the primary sources themselves contradict each other, then you can examine the sources for possible bias and check many sources to see which might be outliers. Even when no one source gives full information, with multiple sources it may be possible to arrive at the truth.

Analyzing Historical Events and Arguments in Social Studies

Making Inferences

Inference refers to drawing conclusions based on data—putting together what you know and using logic and analysis to figure out details that aren't explicitly given. Available primary sources may not explicitly state all the facts, and some things may need to be inferred—or sometimes the primary sources actually *mis*state facts due to bias or limited knowledge but there's enough information to infer the truth. Things that are commonly inferred include cause-and-effect relationships, motivations and attitudes of historical individuals, or details about everyday life or environments in ancient civilizations that the people of the time didn't bother to explicitly write down. For instance, if there are a lot of similarities between two civilizations in different places, one might infer that the second civilization was founded by people who emigrated from the first.

Because they go beyond the available facts and rely on some supposition and probability, inferences may be mistaken. For instance, in the example above, the similarities between the two civilizations could be coincidental or they could both have been borrowed from a third civilization. It's useful to look for more evidence to support an inference or to make predictions based on the inference that can be verified.

Review Video: Inference
Visit mometrix.com/academy and enter code: 379203

Connections Between Different Social Studies Elements (People, Events, Places, Processes)

Not only can events be directly caused by prior events, but they can also be influenced by events and ideas. For instance, the founding fathers of the American government did not come up with their revolutionary ideas in a vacuum. They were heavily influenced by the philosophy of the Enlightenment that had recently developed in Europe. Had this philosophy not developed, the Revolution might not have occurred, or at least it may not have proceeded exactly as it did. This goes both ways: Just as events can be influenced by ideas, ideas can form because of or in reaction to events. The Enlightenment itself might not have happened as it did were it not for the Thirty Years' War, which broke the power of the Holy Roman Empire and raised doubts in many writers' minds about nationalism and dogmatism.

Of course, it's rarely correct to say that one event or idea was the *only* cause of another event or idea. Events have many causes, and it's often difficult to determine the main influences leading to a particular event or process. Nevertheless, finding patterns and possible cause-and-effect relationships can lead to a better understanding of the processes involved.

Cause-And-Effect Relationships

History is not a series of disconnected events. Prior events have an influence on future events, and events can be said to be **caused** by events in the past. These relationships are said to be cause-and-effect relationships because the first event is a cause of the second event, which is an **effect** of the first.

The fact that one event comes after another does *not* necessarily mean that the first event caused the second. For example, in the years 735 to 737, an epidemic of smallpox killed about a quarter of the population of Japan. In 739, there was a major rebellion against the oppressive government of northwestern Africa. Did the smallpox epidemic cause the rebellion? It seems very unlikely that there's any connection; they happened in different parts of the world that were not in direct communication. To establish cause and effect, it's important to come up with a plausible explanation as to *how* the first event could have affected the second. The idea can be tested by looking for similar events to the first, and checking whether they led to similar effects. Deciding whether a cause-and-effect relationship exists is not always straightforward, and historians often debate particular examples.

Role of Individuals in History

On a large scale, history may seem like it's mostly about the clashes and relationships of nations and cultures. But those nations and cultures are made up of individual people, and some of those people may have especially large influences. There has been some controversy about to what extent history should be seen as directed by a few exceptional individuals, or to what extent those people were themselves products of their environment and culture, meaning that if they hadn't come around then someone else would inevitably have taken their place. The truth may be somewhere in between; certainly, people are influenced by their cultures, but there are still particular individuals without whom the course of history would not have gone exactly as it did.

The most obvious people of significance are political leaders: kings, emperors, and presidents. But they are not the only people who change the course of history, nor are they even necessarily the most important ones. Writers and philosophers who bring about important changes in ideas, scientists and inventors who pioneer new technologies, revolutionaries who overthrow established orders, and traders and explorers who bring cultures together—all of these and more may have important impacts on world events.

Role of Places in History

Historical events are influenced not only by the people involved in them and the prior events that led up to them, but by the places in which they occur. Different countries and communities have different cultures and traditions that may impact the events that happen there, and different geographical areas may have different environments that likewise have their importance for events.

To understand historical processes, it may be important to know not just where they initially occurred, but also the layout of the surrounding area and the locations and nature of other places nearby. The particular path that an idea took to spread, the route taken by an army, or the course of a trade route that led to important cultural cross-fertilization may all have been constrained by geographical and cultural considerations. To understand why the idea, army, or trade route took the track it did, it may be necessary to know the lay of the land and the characteristics of the places that it passed through—and of the places it did *not* pass through. These routes may have enormous impacts on the course of history.

Role of Available Resources in the Development of a Culture

The availability of resources places important constraints on the development of a culture or a civilization. A place rich with fertile soil ripe for farmland may lead to rapid development and prosperous civilizations, whereas one in which agriculture is difficult will force its people to find other means of acquiring food and is likely to be more sparsely settled. It's no coincidence that the ancient Egyptian civilization was concentrated along the Nile River and not in the open desert. A civilization with considerable mineral wealth that it can exploit will develop differently from one in a forested area that relies instead on wood; each will develop its own types of tools and structures that make the best use of the resources available.

Of course, local limitations in resources can be ameliorated by trade: A settlement rich in one resource but poor in another can trade with another settlement to get the resources it needs. But this itself has a significant impact on the civilizations that are involved in the trade: The necessity of opening and maintaining trade routes may lead to further innovations, and the two civilizations in contact for trade will also engage in cultural exchange and share ideas with each other.

Role of Climate in the Development of a Culture

Climate refers to the prevailing weather and temperature patterns in a particular region. Its effects on the development of cultures and settlements in that region can be profound. Most obviously, it affects the possible agriculture there: Depending on the temperature and rainfall, different crops can be grown, and cultures may develop around the available crops; in extreme climates, agriculture might not be possible at all, and people must find other ways to subsist. Other resources, too, may be affected by climate: For example, wood is only available in climates that permit trees to grow and clay is only available in wet climates.

Extreme climates require special cultural developments to adapt to them. The Inuit of northern Canada must deal with extreme cold, the Bedouins of the Sahara must deal with heat and aridity, and both of these cultures are heavily and clearly shaped by these climate conditions very differently from people of temperate climes. Even today, in our industrial societies, our construction practices are constrained to some degree by climate conditions. In places where hurricanes and tornadoes are frequent, for instance, houses are constructed with storm cellars and reinforced windows to protect against these climatic disasters.

Physical and Cultural Geography

Physical geography refers to the natural characteristics of a region—landforms, climate, water sources, and so on. **Cultural geography** refers to the variation in human customs and cultures in different places. The physical geography of a region can have many important effects on the development of settlements and cultures there. The terrain may affect the available resources: A well-watered lowland may have plenty of wood and clay available, whereas a mountainous highland might have useful stone and ore.

The physical geography, too, constrains the extent of trade and the routes it can take. One reason that major world cities have usually been on seacoasts or on large rivers is because they enable efficient trade by ship. On the other hand, a civilization that arises in a mountainous area is likely to be more isolated due to the difficulty of reaching and trading with other settlements.

But it goes both ways: People can affect the physical geography as well. To create more arable land, people might fill bogs, dig canals for irrigation, and create terraces on slopes. But sometimes the changes can be counterproductive: Careless deforestation, overexploitation, and pollution can devastate the landscape and make it less useful in the future.

Order of Events in a Historical Process

In a complicated process, it may not always be easy to determine the order of events or to remember that order. But most processes in social studies, or in any other endeavor, are not just series of separate events in arbitrary order. There is a reason for the order: one event leads to another. Recognizing that makes it easier to understand the order of events. If you find one event that seems likely to be the cause of another because, for instance, it set up the conditions that the second event required, then the cause must come before the effect. For instance, in 13th-century England, King Henry III called the first parliament and King John signed the Magna Carta. Which came first? Before the Magna Carta, the king's power was more or less absolute, and there would have been no need for a parliament, so King John must have come before King Henry III.

One useful tool in social studies for visualizing the order of events is a **timeline**. In a timeline, events are ordered along a line, with a mark for each event labeled with the event and date. Below is a sample time line of some significant events in 13th-century England.

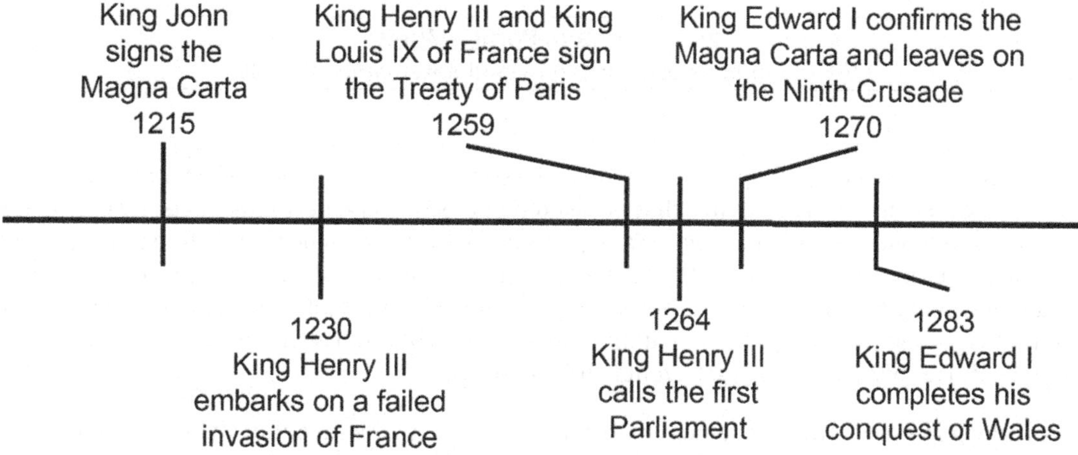

UNDERSTANDING THE STEPS IN A SOCIAL OR GOVERNMENTAL PROCESS

Like the order of historical events, the order of steps in a process is not arbitrary; it relies on cause and effect and on one step setting up the necessary preconditions for the next. Understanding the relationships between the steps, and the reasons for each step, makes it easier to understand their order.

For example, here are some of the main steps in the process of a bill becoming a law in the United States:

- The bill is drafted (written).
- The bill is introduced in the Senate or the House of Representatives.
- The bill goes to a committee.
- The committee votes to accept the bill.
- The entire house debates the bill.
- The members vote to confirm the bill.
- The bill goes to the other house (House or Senate), and the process repeats.
- The bill goes to the president, who has a chance to veto it.

These steps wouldn't really make sense in another order. Clearly, the bill has to be written before anything else can be done. It wouldn't make sense for legislators to debate the bill *after* they've voted on it, and they can't do either until it's been introduced.

THE EFFECT OF DIFFERENT SOCIAL STUDIES CONCEPTS ON AN ARGUMENT OR POINT-OF-VIEW

AUTHOR'S POINT OF VIEW

Primary and secondary sources are written by human beings who have their own points of view that affect their writing. Every author has a point of view, an opinion on the topics that the author writes about, shaped by the author's experiences and environment.

Many authors may be biased toward their own nations and civilizations and may tend to present them in a positive light and rationalize away any shortcomings. Along similar lines, events that negatively affected the authors' civilizations, or the authors themselves, may color their opinion of ideas associated with those events.

An author always has a purpose for writing a passage and an audience in mind for it. Looking into the context of the passage, the situation the author was in when it was written, and events that may have recently affected the author can help give clues as to what the purpose and the audience were. Understanding the author's point of view, the purpose of the passage, and its intended audience helps the reader more reliably interpret the passage.

Review Video: Point of View
Visit mometrix.com/academy and enter code: 383336

EVIDENCE

For primary sources to give compelling evidence toward a conclusion, the evidence must be factual, relevant, and sufficient. **Factual** evidence is evidence that is based on objective and verifiable facts, rather than relying solely or primarily on opinions and emotions. Many persuasive essays may be very light on facts, instead just appealing to the prejudices and feelings of the intended audience, making speculative predictions as to what the author thinks will happen if the author's advice is not followed, and so on. Such passages may show the author's point of view and perhaps give some illumination about common attitudes at the time, but they are not otherwise useful as evidence for actual events and situations.

Some sources may go beyond omitting factual material and may actually invent or distort facts and give misinformation. In the absence of other contemporary sources that provide the correct information, such distortion of facts may be hard to recognize, but it can help to examine sources for possible bias. Highly biased sources are much more likely to misrepresent the facts.

Evidence supporting a particular conclusion is **relevant** if it can be used as part of a reasonable logical argument for or against the conclusion. A passage may present evidence for a point of view that is *factual*, in the sense that it gives correct and verifiable information, but it may not be *relevant*, in the sense that it doesn't actually support the desired conclusion. This doesn't mean that the irrelevant information is out of left field and completely unrelated to the conclusion, but it may be irrelevant because the author assumes a connection that may not be supported. For example, an author may argue that a civilization is in decline and soon to fall by relating an account of an older civilization that shared with the modern civilization certain characteristics of which the author disapproves, and that was destroyed soon after adopting these characteristics. But it may be that there's no reason to believe that those characteristics were a contributing factor to the fall and that there are other features of the older civilization *not* shared by the modern civilization that can be shown to be responsible for its decline. In this case, the account of the older civilization may be *factual*, but not *relevant.*

Evidence supporting a particular conclusion is **sufficient** if it can be used to prove the conclusion beyond a reasonable doubt. It is possible for a passage to supply evidence that is *factual*, in the sense that it gives correct and verifiable information, and *relevant*, in that it does support the conclusion, but not *sufficient*, in that it leaves open the possibility that the conclusion is incorrect. For example, suppose an author wants to argue that a past writer's account of a certain conflict was fabricated. To support this, the author gives evidence that the writer was biased toward one side of the conflict—perhaps the writer had given financial support to the favored side. This may be *factual*; the writer may really have had that bias. It is certainly *relevant*; the writer's bias makes it more likely that the writer distorted the facts. But it is not *sufficient*: Just because the writer was biased toward one side of the conflict, that doesn't necessarily *prove* that the writer lied about it. If, however, other, less-biased contemporary accounts can be found that contradict the writer's account, then that may come closer to being sufficient evidence.

Assessing an Author's Argument

An author's point of view is affected not only directly by events that occurred to or around the author, but by ideas as well, by philosophies and principles that the author came into contact with. Understanding an author's point of view, and so better comprehending the author's argument, may be facilitated by knowing about some of the prevailing ideas that were current in the author's time and place and that may have affected the author's writing. Even the most independent-minded, free-thinking author must be to some extent a product of his or her environment and is not completely unaffected by the ideas of others.

For example, suppose you read a passage from a Chinese writer in the first century BC. This was a time when Confucianism was at its height in China, and had recently become officially adopted by the Chinese government. Certainly, the philosophy of Confucianism would have had some influence on the writer—even if the writer personally disagreed with the philosophy, the passage may represent the writer's reaction *against* this way of thinking that dominated the writer's society. A knowledge of Confucianist thought will therefore be helpful in fully understanding the writer's point of view.

Identifying Bias and Propaganda in Social Studies Readings

Bias refers to the presentation of events in a way that is disproportionately favorable to a person, group, or idea that the presenter favors, or in a way that is disproportionately unfavorable to one that the presenter does not favor. It is not necessarily intentional; writers may let bias creep into their work without realizing it.

Sometimes a writer's bias may be obvious from the language used, with one side always referred to with positive language (heroic, just) and the other with negative language, or even by slurs. But bias isn't always that obvious or easy to identify. Sometimes it can be recognized by comparing different accounts. Do the accounts disagree? Did one writer omit an important fact that changes the impression of a particular group? (Bias can be by omission; a writer may *leave out* a detail that portrays a group in a different light—or may not mention at all a person or group that he or she doesn't like.) It may also be useful to consider the source: a study funded by a company with a financial interest in the result may not *necessarily* be biased, but it is certainly more likely to be. Readers should always be sensitive to the possible presence of bias in a text.

Propaganda is communication designed to manipulate or sway people toward the presenter's point of view. Often it relies more on emotion than on fact, playing on the target's own possible prejudices and beliefs. Propaganda differs from bias in that it is always conscious and intentional; indeed, it is generally the primary purpose of the work in question. Because it is done purposefully, however, propaganda can be carefully planned and worked out to maximize its effectiveness.

Propaganda often uses more obviously charged and inflammatory language than unconsciously biased writing, even using strong symbols and metaphors to demonize or dehumanize the opponent. Nazi propaganda, for instance, often referred to Jews as rats. Other specific propaganda techniques to look out for include bandwagon appeals (trying to convince the targets that *everyone else* already shares the propagandist's point of view), the similar common man or plain folks approach (suggesting that the propagandist's point of view is just what the average person believes anyway and that those who disagree are arrogant elitists), and cults of personality (holding up a charismatic individual who others may be drawn to follow as the face of the propagandist's movement).

Social Studies in Visual Media

Photographs

Photographs are invaluable tools in social studies, showing real records of historical places and events. Like any other primary sources, however, they require skill and care to analyze effectively. Analyzing a photo involves more than just glancing at it and making a snap judgment of what's going on in it. First, spend some time to take a close look at the photograph. Pay attention not just to the foreground elements, but to the background elements as well—including signs and landmarks that may give an indication as to the location, people in the background who may be reacting to foreground events, and so on. Take careful note of all the people and objects in the photograph and all the activities that are going on. Based on what you see in the photograph, including people's clothing, background elements, etc., try to make a guess as to where and when the photograph was likely taken, who the people in it were, and what they were doing. Try to think of a question raised by what you've determined so far, and then look for evidence in the photograph that might point to a possible answer to that question.

POLITICAL CARTOONS

Political cartoons, or editorial cartoons, have been used since the 18th century as a way for artists to comment on contemporary events and prominent figures. Their purpose is not to objectively show what was going on at the time, but rather to express the cartoonist's opinions. They are useful as reflections of prevailing attitudes at the time they were drawn, as well as occasionally providing provocative points of view or hinting at other sides of issues.

Often, political cartoonists explicitly label the elements of their cartoons to clarify what they represent. At other times, they rely on common symbols and on recognizable faces. Symbols and faces that were well known in the past, however, may not be so well known today; we may still recognize elephants and donkeys as representing the Republican and Democratic Parties, and we can identify a drawing of Barack Obama, but we may not recognize John Bull (an old personification of England) or Boss Tweed (a notoriously corrupt 19th-century politician). Therefore, some historical knowledge may be necessary to interpret an old cartoon. Once you know what each symbol or figure represents, look at their relations and interactions to determine what point the cartoonist is trying to make.

Using Numbers and Graphics in Social Studies

USING DATA PRESENTED IN VISUAL FORM, INCLUDING MAPS, CHARTS, GRAPHS, AND TABLES

UNDERSTANDING GRAPHICS

There are many ways that qualitative data may be presented: in words, in graphs, in tables, or in charts. It's straightforward to compare two graphs with each other or two tables. But when two data sets are presented in different ways—when, for instance, one is presented in a table and the other in a graph—then it may not be easy to compare them at a glance.

If you only need to compare a few specific data points, it's relatively straightforward to just pick out those data points from each set and then consider them independently of the rest of the data. However, you may want to compare the data sets as a whole, looking for similarities in trends or behavior and picking out a handful of points isn't enough. In that case, the simplest approach may be to take one of the data sets and represent it in the form of the other. If you want to compare a graph and a table, for instance, take the data from the table and draw it as a graph, or vice versa. That way, you're left with two tables or two graphs that can easily be compared.

ANALYZING INFORMATION FROM A MAP

Maps are a very common and valuable tool in social studies, showing spatial expanses and relationships at a glance. However, effective use of a map requires understanding some key features. First of all, the title of the map may give important indications of what it's supposed to represent, and the main idea it's intended to get across. It's always important to check the **scale** of a map to get an idea of the distances involved. (There are exceptions—special maps that resize states or countries proportional to their populations or other factors do not have consistent scales—but they are unusual.) If there are symbols, patterns, or colors involved, the meanings of which aren't clear, the map should also have a **key** explaining them. A map may also have a **compass rose** showing which way is north; usually the top of the map is north, but not always.

Curved surfaces such as the surface of the earth can't be fit exactly onto flat maps, so be aware of the distortions of shapes and distances in maps, especially maps of large areas. The Mercator projection, long popular for school world maps, is notorious for drastically exaggerating the sizes of landmasses near the poles.

DEPENDENT AND INDEPENDENT VARIABLES

As in science, when you compare two variables in social studies, generally you can consider one as the independent variable and the other as the dependent variable. In a graph, the dependent variable goes on the *x* axis, and the dependent variable goes on the *y* axis.

To see which one is the dependent variable and which one is the independent variable, consider which one can better be said to cause or influence the other. For instance, if one compares the average population of settlements at different elevations, it makes more sense to choose the elevation as the independent variable and the population as the dependent. The elevation may well affect the population, but the population does not affect the elevation—the land will not rise or fall depending on the number of people living in a settlement.

Sometimes two variables may be interdependent, each affecting the other in a feedback loop. Suppose you're comparing families' wealth to their education levels. Wealthier families are better able to send their children to good universities, but more highly educated people may have a better opportunity to accrue wealth. So, which is the cause and which is the effect? In cases such as these, the choice may be arbitrary and may depend on the specific relationship you're looking for.

ANALYZING INFORMATION FROM A TABLE

Tables are simple, compact, and widely used methods of conveying information that falls into different categories. They're especially common and useful when there are two sets of categories according to which the data can be arranged—one set of categories then makes up the rows of the table, and the other makes up the columns—or when there are discrete data sets with multiple values that can be arranged in rows.

To make effective use of a table, first check the title of the table, if one is provided, to get a big picture of the table's purpose and then look at the labels of the rows and columns. Each cell of the table gives a quantity or quality associated with the categories in the corresponding row and column. Consider the following sample table:

Crop Yields in Provinces of Tabolia (in hundreds of tons)

Province / Season	Ablia	Betal	Catabel	Datia	Elbatia
Spring	23	33	55	29	20
Summer	35	46	60	40	33
Autumn	65	87	93	66	59
Winter	11	15	22	13	12

The title tells what the table is about: crop yields in the provinces of the (fictitious) nation of Tabolia. Each cell represents the yields in a particular province and season; thus, for instance, the intersection of the first row and third column gives the yield in Catabel during the spring, which is 55 (i.e., according to the units given in the title, 5,500 tons).

ANALYZING A PIE CHART

A **pie chart** is one common kind of chart often used in social studies in which different categories are represented as sectors of a circle. As with other charts and graphs, it's important to first read the title of the chart to see an overview of what it is about. The sectors may be labeled directly with the corresponding categories, or they may be given different colors or patterns, in which case you should look for a key to see what each represents. The percentage of the circle occupied by each sector also may or may not be explicitly labeled. If it is not, it can be estimated visually: Half the circle is 50%, a quarter is 25%, and so on.

Consider the following sample pie chart:

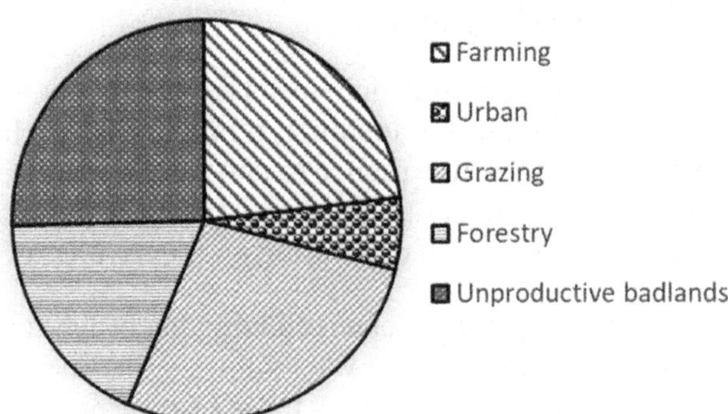

According to the title, this chart shows land use in the (fictitious) country of Picharat. The key to the right shows what each sector represents: The blue striped sector in the upper right, for instance, represents the percentage of the land used for farming. Although the percentages are not explicitly given in the chart, we can estimate them: The farming sector takes up a little less than a quarter of the circle, so it looks like around 23%.

INTERPRETING A LINE GRAPH

A **line graph** is a type of graph that shows a relationship between two variables, the dependent variable on the *y* axis and the independent variable on the *x*. In interpreting a line graph, it's useful to first look at the title to observe the overall relationship that it is intended to convey and then look at the labels of the axes to see what two variables are involved. The overall shape of the graph shows the general relationship between the variables. For instance, if the graph slopes upward, the variables are positively correlated: As one increases, so does the other. If the graph slopes downward, they are negatively correlated: An increase in one accompanies a decrease in the other.

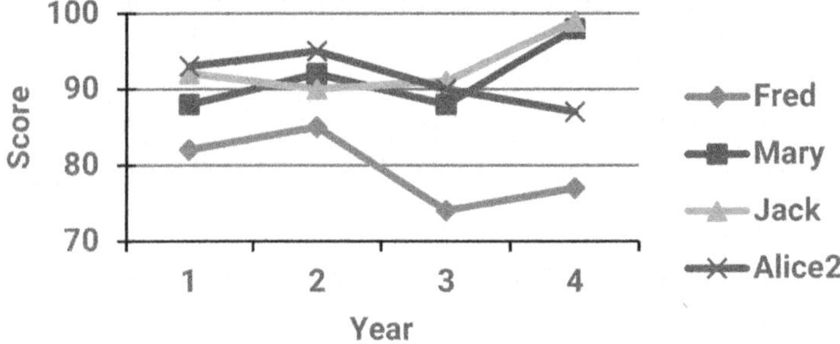

To find the value of the dependent variable for a specific value of the independent variable, find the appropriate value of the independent variable on the *x* axis, interpolating between labels if necessary. Trace a line straight upward until you hit the graph, and then trace a line from there left to the *y* axis; the position on which gives the value of the dependent variable. The reverse process can provide the value of the independent variable for a specific value of the dependent variable.

INTERPRETING A BAR GRAPH

A **bar graph** is a graph showing the relationship between two variables in which the height of a bar for each value of the independent variable indicates the corresponding value of the dependent variable. Unlike for a line graph, the independent variable need not be quantitative, but it may represent qualitative values such as countries or types of terrain.

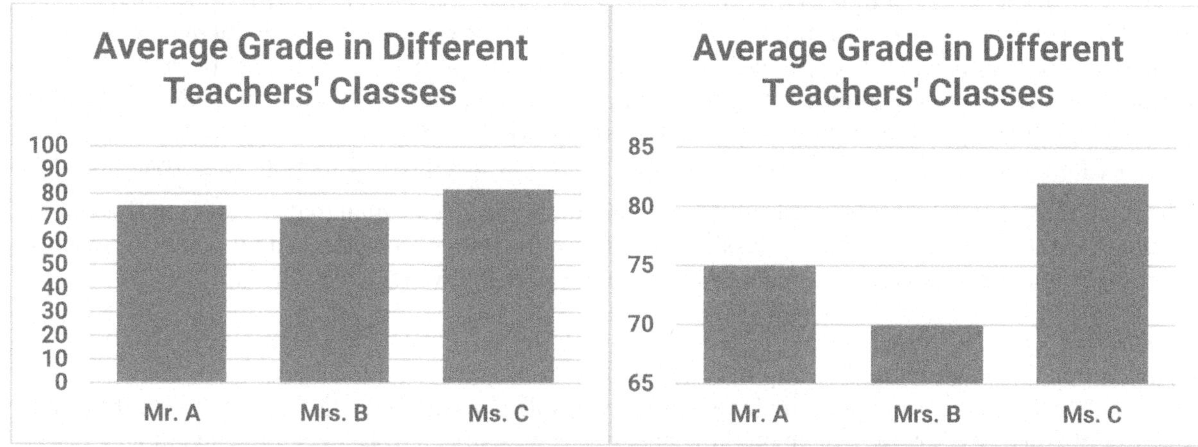

Interpreting a bar graph is relatively straightforward. To find the value of the dependent variable corresponding to a particular value of the independent variable, first find the appropriate value on the *x* axis and then look at the height of the corresponding bar, checking it against the scale of the *y* axis. One pitfall to look out for, however, is that if the scale of the *y* axis does not start at 0, the difference between values may be exaggerated. Compare the following two graphs, which show the same data, but with the *y* axis starting at 0 on the left graph and starting at 65 on the right. If you don't look carefully, you could get the mistaken impression from the graph on the right that the average grade of students in Ms. C's class is more than three times that in Mrs. B's!

UTILIZING GRAPHICS

MAKING A TABLE

A table is a convenient way to concisely display data that depend on two different variables or that depend on one variable but include several different quantities. In the former case, the independent variable usually goes in the columns and the dependent variable goes in the rows, although this rule isn't as hard and fast as it is for graphs. In the latter case, the independent variable goes in the first column and each other quantity in its own column.

For instance, suppose that you want to record the population, elevation, and area of several different cities. Each city would get its own row in the table, and the first column would be the name of the city because the city is effectively the independent variable. Then the second column could hold the population of each city, the third could hold the elevation, and the fourth could hold the area, with each going in the appropriate row.

As with any other form of data presentation, it's important that a table be clearly labeled so the reader can easily see what each value represents. For instance, the table described above might look as follows:

City	Population (thousands)	Elevation (feet)	Area (square miles)
A-Ville	39	1,200	1.2
B-Town	220	30	5.0
C-Burg	45	-200	2.5
D-Grad	23	330	0.8
...	...	...	...

Social Studies

Creating a Pie Chart

A pie chart is a circular chart showing the relative quantity of various categories, each category being represented by a sector or wedge of the circle with its size proportional to its value. Many utilities such as Microsoft Excel can generate pie charts automatically, but it's useful to know how to create them yourself. To draw a pie chart, the first step is to represent each of the values as a percentage of the whole; these percentages must add to 100%. The simplest way to do this is to total all the values and then divide each value by the total; these quotients give the fraction or percentage of the whole that each value represents. For instance, if your values are 40, 20, 15, and 5, then the percentages are $\frac{40}{80} = 50\%$, $\frac{20}{80} = 25\%$, $\frac{15}{80} \approx 19\%$, and $\frac{5}{80} \approx 6\%$. Then draw a circle where each category is allotted a fraction of the circle equal to its fraction of the whole. Either label the values directly on the chart, or assign a color or pattern to each value and fill in the appropriate sectors accordingly, making sure you also include a key so the reader knows which is which.

Drawing a Line Graph

To create a line graph to show the relationship between two variables, first decide on your axes. The dependent variable goes on the *y* axis, and the independent variable goes on the *x* axis. Be sure to label the axes with the appropriate quantities. Now, decide on the scale for the axes. In general, you want to avoid leaving too much blank space on any side of the graph, so the scale should start shortly before to the minimum value of the variable and end shortly after the maximum. Grid lines and labels should be evenly spaced at round intervals, such as 5 or 10, not at arbitrary intervals such as 2.4 or 7.

Once you have set up and labeled the axes and the scale, you're ready to plot points. For each point on the graph, trace a vertical line up from the value of the independent variable on the *x* axis and a horizontal line right from the value of the dependent variable on the *y* axis and plot the point where those two lines cross. Once you've plotted all the points, you can connect them to produce the line graph.

Making a Bar Graph

Bar graphs are useful when you want to show how a quantitative variable differs for various values of a qualitative variable—they can also be used to show the relationship between two quantitative variables, but generally a line graph is better for that. The qualitative variable (or the independent variable, if they're both quantitative) goes on the *x* axis, and the other goes on the *y* axis. The value at the top of the *y* axis should be not much more than the maximum value of the dependent variable, but for the bottom you have a decision to make. Starting the scale at zero may wash out small differences between values, but starting the scale just below the minimum value may exaggerate the differences. The latter is usually preferable; the onus is on the reader to interpret the graph correctly.

Above each value of the independent variable, draw a bar with its top at the appropriate value of the dependent variable. You can extend a horizontal line to the right from the value on the *y* axis to find where to put the top of the bar. The bars should be evenly spaced and of uniform width; only their heights should differ.

Using a Graph to Predict Trends

Bar graphs and especially line graphs can be used to predict possible trends in data—that is, to make predictions of how the dependent variable will behave past the range of the independent variable that is represented in the graph. In the simplest form, you can look at whether the line seems to be going up or down—that is, whether the variable is increasing or decreasing—and predict that it will continue to do the same. If the value of the dependent variable consistently increases as the independent variable increases, then that represents a probable trend, and you can predict that it will continue to do so.

However, you can also predict more complex trends than that. What if the graph doesn't consistently increase or decrease, but has a more complex shape, such as a sine wave? Or, if it is increasing or decreasing, *how fast* is it increasing or decreasing? Linearly? Quadratically? Exponentially? Again, you can roughly predict the trend just by observing what the graph is doing during its range and assuming that it will continue to do the same. There are mathematical methods to find patterns in data more precisely, but they may not be necessary.

Correlation Versus Causation

Correlation refers to how closely the changes in two quantities tend to be connected. If the changes in one quantity closely mirror changes in the other—as one quantity rises, the other always rises as well, or as one rises the other always falls—then the two quantities are said to be highly correlated. (Correlation can be quantified by statistical techniques.) **Causation** refers to one event directly causing another or to the change in one quantity causing a change in another.

There is a common saying in statistics that correlation is not causation. What this means is that just because two quantities are correlated, it is not necessarily the case that one causes the other. Even if the correlation is a real phenomenon and not a coincidence, there could be some third factor behind both changes. For example, suppose that a survey of students at a K–12 school shows that taller students have larger vocabularies. Does a large vocabulary cause students to grow taller? Or does height make it easier to learn words? Neither: Older students tend to be taller, and older students tend to have larger vocabularies. The two quantities are correlated, but neither one causes the other.

Using Statistics in Social Studies

Mean, Median, Mode, and Range of a Set of Data

The **mean** of a set of data is what is usually meant by the average. To find the mean, add all the elements of the set together and divide by the number of elements. For example, consider the data set {48, 50, 55, 56, 60, 63, 68, 72, 77}. The sum of the elements is 549. There are nine elements, so the mean is $\frac{549}{9} = 61$. Note that, as in this example, the mean is not necessarily one of the elements itself.

The **median** of a set of data is the value in the middle of the set, when its elements are put in order. To find the median, you first order the elements of the set and then count them and find the element in the middle. For example, consider the data set {56, 22, 42, 99, 14, 22, 45, 40, 12}. Put in order, these elements are {12, 14, 22, 22, 40, 42, 45, 56, 99}. There are nine elements, so the middle element is the fifth, 40. Therefore, the median of this data set is 40.

In the case of a data set with an even number of elements, the median is the average of the two middle elements. For example, consider the data set {200, 150, 209, 222, 180, 184, 210, 190}. Put in order, this data set becomes {150, 180, 184, 190, 200, 209, 210, 222}. There are eight elements, so the middle elements are the fourth and fifth, 190 and 200, and the median is their average, 195.

The mean and median are both **measures of central tendency**: They both measure in some sense the center of a collection of data, or an average value—in fact, usually when people speak of the average, they're referring to the mean. For symmetrically distributed data sets such as classic bell curves, the mean and median are the same, but for other data sets, this may not be true. The mean has the advantage of accounting for all the data: A change in any element will change the mean. However, the median is less affected by **outliers**—unusual data points far from the other values—and may be more representative of a typical value for highly skewed data sets.

For example, suppose in a small village of 100 people, 33 people have a monthly income of $1,500, 33 people have a monthly income of $2,000, and 33 people have a monthly income of $2,500, and 1 very wealthy resident has a monthly income of $1,000,000. The *mean* income of the residents is:

$$\frac{33 \times 1{,}500 + 33 \times 2{,}000 + 33 \times 2{,}500 + 1{,}000{,}000}{100} = \$11{,}980$$

All but one of the residents earn much less than this. In this case, the *median* of $2,000 better represents the income of a typical resident.

The **mode** of a set of data is the value that appears most often. For instance, in the data set {2, 4, 5, 5, 6, 6, 7, 9, 9, 9, 10, 11, 11, 12, 14, 16, 18}, the value 9 appears three times; 5, 6, and 11 each appear twice; and each of the other values in the data set only appears once. The mode of the data set is 9.

It is possible for a data set not to have a mode. For instance, in the data set {22, 24, 26, 27, 31, 33, 36, 38, 41, 49}, each value appears exactly once; no value appears more than any other. It is also possible for a data set to have multiple modes; in the data set {5, 6, 6, 7, 10, 13, 15, 16, 16, 18, 20}, the values 6 and 16 each appear twice, while each other value appears once, so 6 and 16 are both modes. A data set with two modes is said to be **bimodal**.

The **range** of a set of data is the difference between the largest and the smallest values. To find the range, just subtract the smallest value in the data set from the largest. For example, for the data set {5, 7, 8, 8, 10, 12, 15, 17, 19, 30, 45}, the range is $45 - 5 = 40$.

The range is a rough measurement of the spread, or **dispersion**, of a set of data. It has the disadvantage, however, that it's very sensitive to **outliers**—individual data points far from the rest. For instance, in the data set {3, 5, 6, 7, 8, 11, 13, 13, 20,003}, the range is $20{,}003 - 3 = 20{,}000$—but most of that range is just due to the last data point, 20,003. Take out that single point, and the range shrinks to $13 - 3 = 10$. There are other measurements of dispersion that are less affected by outliers, but they can be more complicated to calculate.

Qualitative and Quantitative Data Sets

A **quantitative** data set is a data set of numerical values. These values may or may not have units; what is important is that they can be compared and mathematically manipulated. A **qualitative** data set is a data set of properties or objects that cannot be meaningfully ranked or added. For instance, {1950, 1952, 1977, 2002, 2005} is a set of quantitative data. So is {30 km, 35 km, 44 km, 62 km}. {Red, red, blue, white, green, white, red} is a set of qualitative data. The values—red, blue, white, and green—are not numerical, cannot be ranked (it doesn't make sense to say that red is greater than white, or vice versa), and cannot be added or otherwise combined mathematically.

Qualitative data sets do not have means, medians, or ranges; all of these properties depend on comparisons or arithmetical operations that cannot be carried out on unranked, nonnumeric values. Qualitative data sets *can*, however, have modes; the mode depends only on which values appear the most often, and it does not depend on any comparison or operation between values.

US History

Colonial Period (1607-1765)

The **colonial period** describes a time in which several European countries attempted to settle and colonize the Americas to expand their territories. The earliest attempts to colonize were by Spain and France, who conquered and settled much of what are now the southern and central parts of the United States of America. In the process of colonizing the Americas, many Native American groups were displaced or killed by disease and territorial expansion. The main focus of the colonial period in what is now the United States is often placed on the **thirteen English colonies**, which were located on the east coast. The primary reasons for the English colonization in the Americas were in response to England's policy of mercantilism and colonists' desire to be free from **religious persecution**. **Mercantilism** in England required the colonies to provide raw materials to England to continue to grow and support the mother country while also limiting trade with other nations. The other primary motivation for settlement included escape from persecution by the Church of England toward Catholic and other religious groups.

The 13 Colonies

The **thirteen colonies** were a group of English colonies that were overtly similar in their political and religious beliefs. The thirteen colonies were comprised of:

New England Colonies:

- New Hampshire
- Massachusetts
- Rhode Island
- Connecticut

Chesapeake Bay Colonies:

- Virginia
- Maryland

Review Video: The English Colony of Virginia
Visit mometrix.com/academy and enter code: 537399

Middle Colonies:

- New York
- Pennsylvania
- New Jersey
- Delaware

Southern Colonies:

- North Carolina
- South Carolina
- Georgia

Review Video: The Southern Colonies
Visit mometrix.com/academy and enter code: 703830

French and Indian War

The **French and Indian War** was essentially a war over territory between the English colonies and the French colonies. Rising competition between the English and French empires brought more British military support into the colonies, which created a stronger feeling of unity between the colonies and England than ever before. In 1763, the **Treaty of Paris** brought an end to the war, as France relinquished some of its Eastern territory to England, including the territory east of modern-day Louisiana all the way to the Great Lakes. In the aftermath of the war, **tensions** rose between the colonies and England because of unequal investment in the war. British taxpayers had supplied the majority of funding for the war, while the colonists were forced to fight in a war that served the monarchy's interests rather than their own interests. These tensions, along with continued British occupation, were the foundation for the coming revolution.

American Revolution (1765-1783)

The Intolerable Acts

Following the French and Indian War, Britain increased taxes and continued to impose quartering on the colonies. The most famous of these included the Stamp Acts, the Tea Acts, and the Quartering Acts. The purpose of these laws was to force the colonies to be dependent on Britain, and to help restore the British economy following the wars of the previous years. These laws were known to the British as the **Coercive Acts**. In America, they were called the **Intolerable Acts,** due to the offensive nature of England's attempt to control and stifle the colonies. As tensions rose, members of the colonies began organizing rebellious protests, such as the Boston Tea Party, in response to particular tax laws that were passed. These inciting reasons and protests led up to the official start of the **American Revolution.**

IMPORTANT EVENTS AND GROUPS LEADING UP TO AMERICAN REVOLUTION

Over several years, various events and groups contributed to the rebellion that became a revolution:

- **Sons of Liberty** – This was the protest group headed by Samuel Adams that incited the Revolution.
- **Boston Massacre** – On March 5, 1770, British soldiers fired on a crowd and killed five people.
- **Committees of Correspondence** – These were set up throughout the colonies to transmit revolutionary ideas and create a unified response.
- **The Boston Tea Party** – On December 6, 1773, the Sons of Liberty, dressed as Mohawks, dumped tea into the harbor from a British ship to protest the tea tax. The harsh British response further aggravated the situation.
- **First Continental Congress** – This was held in 1774 to list grievances and develop a response, including boycotts. It was attended by all the colonies with the exception of Georgia.
- **The Shot Heard Round the World** – In April, 1775, English soldiers on their way to confiscate arms in Concord passed through Lexington, Massachusetts and met the colonial militia called the Minutemen. A fight ensued. In Concord, a larger group of Minutemen forced the British to retreat.

Review Video: The First and Second Continental Congress
Visit mometrix.com/academy and enter code: 835211

ORIGINAL 13 COLONIES AND MAJOR TURNING POINTS OF THE REVOLUTION

The original **13 colonies** were: Connecticut, Delaware, Georgia, Maryland, Massachusetts, New Hampshire, New Jersey, New York, North Carolina, Pennsylvania, Rhode Island, South Carolina, and Virginia. Delaware was the first state to ratify the **constitution**.

The major turning points of the American Revolution were:

- The actions of the **Second Continental Congress** – This body established the Continental Army and chose George Washington as its commanding general. They allowed printing of money and created government offices.
- "**Common Sense**" – Published in 1776 by Thomas Paine, this pamphlet calling for independence was widely distributed.
- The **Declaration of Independence** – Written by Thomas Jefferson, it was ratified on July 4, 1776 by the Continental Congress assembled in Philadelphia.
- **Alliance with France** – Benjamin Franklin negotiated an agreement with France to fight with the Americans in 1778.
- **Treaty of Paris** – Signaled the official end of the war in 1782, granted independence to the colonies, and gave them generous territorial rights.

Review Video: Declaration of Independence
Visit mometrix.com/academy and enter code: 256838

Review Video: European Colonization of the Americas
Visit mometrix.com/academy and enter code: 438412

FOUNDING OF A NATION

Each of the colonies overthrew the British representation within their own colonies and established their own state constitutions. The newly formed 13 states, with the guidance and primary authorship of Thomas Jefferson, unanimously adopted the **Declaration of Independence,** which officially separated the colonies from British rule. Shortly thereafter, the **Second Continental Congress**, made up of state representatives, met together to ratify the **Articles of Confederation**, which was the original constitution for the United States of America, outlining how sovereignty would be shared among the states in the new country. With the assistance of the French, the Americans were able to fend off a large scale naval and military invasion from the British and secure their revolution.

Review Video: Founding Fathers and Mothers
Visit mometrix.com/academy and enter code: 704562

Confederation Period

The **Confederation Period** (1783-1788) was the period in US history directly following the American Revolution. The Articles of Confederation held the states loosely, and the states were largely self-governing and did not have much political unity. In this format, the federal government was very weak, with no chief executive or judicial system. The weak federal government was bound to continue degrading in unity and would eventually fail if left without reform. In 1787, political leaders met to write a new constitution with more thoroughly written policies that would establish federal powers, while still sharing power with the state governments. This new constitution ended the confederation period and led the way into the Federalist Era.

Federalist Era (1788-1801)

The 1787 convention that wrote the new **Constitution of the United States of America** established three government branches, the **legislative** (making laws) the **executive** (enforcing laws), and the **judicial** (interpreting and judging laws). Having three branches with separate powers helped to provide what is known as **checks and balances** in government, so that no one branch will have too much power. This was meant to maintain liberty and state powers, while giving the federal government enough power to effectively govern the new country. The new constitution also established voting practices on the individual and state level, including the controversial topic of slavery and voting practices for states that did not abolish slavery. At this point, some northern states had made slavery illegal, but the constitution of the time allowed for the states to determine their own laws on the matter. The Federalist Era placed more power in the hands of the federal government, but also established a place for political parties to advocate for the rights of the people.

Bill of Rights and Amendments

Over the next few years, the need for revision to the constitution was made clear. In 1789, congress adopted several **amendments** to the constitution, mostly dealing with individual rights, such as the right to freedom of speech, the right to bear arms, and several others. The first ten amendments are called "**The Bill of Rights**." In the process of instituting these amendments, it was also laid out that any declarations (such as rights or laws) not specifically granted in the constitution or amendments to the constitution are reserved for the states or lower jurisdictions to establish.

Jeffersonian Era (1801-1817)

The **Jeffersonian Era** is defined by the influences of Thomas Jefferson and his political activism. In the Federalist Era, many of the political voices advocated for power going to those with wealth and property, rather than the equal rights of all people. Jefferson's political outlook was called **American Republicanism** (now the Democratic-Republican Party), which opposed aristocracy, elitism, and corruption in government. During Jefferson's presidency, he made significant strides toward a more inclusive voting system. He also managed to purchase Louisiana from France at an extremely reasonable price, thus roughly doubling the size of the United States at the time. From 1812-1815, a war ensued between the United Kingdom and the United States due to the British cutting off trade routes and fostering hostility between the Native Americans and the United States. The war concluded with no changes to boundaries, leading to the beginning of the **Era of Good Feelings.**

Era of Good Feelings and the Jacksonian Era

The **Era of Good Feelings** (1817-1825) followed the Jeffersonian Era, and was marked by the collapse of the Federalist system. President James Monroe attempted to deter the partisan political system and prevent political parties from driving national politics. During the Era of Good Feelings, there was a **temporary sense of national security** and a **desire for unity** in America following the war of previous years. Following

Monroe's presidency, votes were largely split between the two major parties of the time, the **Whigs** and the **Democrats**.

During the **Jacksonian Era** (1825-1849), **voting rights** were extended to most white men over 21 years old and revised other federal policies. The policy favored the idea of election by the "common man," which expanded voting rights, while continuing to deny rights to women, Native Americans and African Americans. This period also saw an increase in **expansionism**, encouraging territorial expansion to the west in the name of manifest destiny. During this period, issues of slavery were largely avoided at first, though they grew over the coming years, leading into the Civil War Era.

Review Video: Andrew Jackson - Key Events and Major Issues
Visit mometrix.com/academy and enter code: 739251

Civil War Era (1850-1865)

The **Civil War Era** began with continued push from the northern states to expand democratic rights to Black people. The constitution of the time allowed for slavery to be a state's right to determine and enforce. Eleven states (with two to join later) determined to secede from the United States of America and become their own nation. In these eleven states, slavery was a major mode and means for the economy, and despite the overt ethical issues with slavery, these southern states were adamant about maintaining their way of life. The official Confederacy was formed in 1861 and continued until the end of the civil war in 1865.

Review Video: Overview of the American Civil War
Visit mometrix.com/academy and enter code: 239557

Reconstruction Era (1865-1877) and the 13th, 14th, and 15th Amendments

Reconstruction was the period from 1865 to 1877, during which the South was under strict control of the US government. In March, 1867, all state governments of the former Confederacy were terminated, and **military occupation** began. Military commanders called for constitutional conventions to reconstruct the state governments, to which delegates were to be elected by universal male suffrage. After a state government was in operation and the state had **ratified the 14th Amendment**, its representatives were admitted to Congress. Three constitutional amendments from 1865 to 1870, which tried to rectify the problems caused by slavery, became part of the Reconstruction effort. The **13th Amendment** declared slavery illegal. The **14th Amendment** made all persons born or naturalized in the country US citizens, and forbade any state to interfere with their fundamental civil rights. The **15th Amendment** made it illegal to deny individuals the right to vote on the grounds of race. In his 1876 election campaign, President **Rutherford B. Hayes** promised to withdraw troops from the South, and did so in 1877.

Review Video: The Reconstruction Era
Visit mometrix.com/academy and enter code: 790561

Major Changes in Industry in the Late 1800s

Important events during this time of enormous business growth and large-scale exploitation of natural resources include:

- **Industrialization** – Like the rest of the world, the United States' entry into the Industrial Age was marked by many new inventions and the mechanization of factories.
- **Railroad expansion** – The Transcontinental Railroad was built from 1865 to 1969. Railroad tracks stretched over 35,000 miles in 1865, but that distance reached 240,000 miles by 1910. The raw materials and manufactured goods needed for the railroads kept mines and factories very busy.
- **Gold and silver mining** – Mines brought many prospectors to the West from 1850 to about 1875, but mining corporations soon took over.

- **Cattle ranching** - This was a large-scale enterprise beginning in the late 1860s, but by the 1880s open ranges were being fenced and plowed for farming and pastures. Millions of farmers moved into the high plains, establishing the "Bread Basket," which was the major wheat growing area of the country.

Gilded Age (1877-1895)

The **Gilded Age**, from the 1870s to 1890, was so named because of the enormous wealth and grossly opulent lifestyle enjoyed by a handful of powerful families. This was the time when huge mansions were built as summer "cottages" in Newport, Rhode Island, and great lodges were built in mountain areas for the pleasure of families such as the Vanderbilts, Ascots, and Rockefellers.

Control of the major industries was held largely by the following men:

- Jay Gould—railroads
- Andrew Carnegie—steel
- John D. Rockefeller Sr.—oil
- Philip Danforth Armour—meatpacking
- J. P. Morgan—banking
- John Jacob Astor—fur pelts
- Cornelius Vanderbilt—steamboat shipping

These men were were known as **Robber Barons** for their ruthless business practices and exploitation of workers. Of course, all of these heads of industry diversified and became involved in multiple business ventures. To curb cutthroat competition, particularly among the railroads, and to prohibit restrained trade, Congress created the **Interstate Commerce Commission** and the **Sherman Anti-Trust Act**. Neither of these, however, was enforced.

Review Video: The Gilded Age: An Overview
Visit mometrix.com/academy and enter code: 684770

Review Video: The Gilded Age: Chinese Immigration
Visit mometrix.com/academy and enter code: 624166

Immigration Trends in Late 1800s

The population of the United States doubled between 1860 and 1890, with the arrival of 10 million immigrants. Most lived in the north. Cities and their **slums** grew tremendously because of immigration and industrialization. While previous immigrants had come from Germany, Scandinavia, and Ireland, the 1880s saw a new wave of immigrants from Italy, Poland, Hungary, Bohemia, and Greece, as well as Jewish groups from central and eastern Europe, especially Russia. The Roman Catholic population grew from 1.6 million in 1850 to 12 million in 1900, a growth that ignited an anti-Catholic backlash from the anti-Catholic Know-Nothing Party of the 1880s and the Ku Klux Klan. Exploited immigrant workers started **labor protests** in the 1870s, and the **Knights of Labor** was formed in 1878, calling for sweeping social and economic reform. Its membership reached 700,000 by 1886. Eventually, this organization was replaced by the **American Federation of Labor**, headed by Samuel Gompers.

Progressive Era (1896–1916)

The **Progressive Era**, which was the time period from the 1890s to the 1920s, got its name from progressive, reform-minded political leaders who wanted to export a just and rational social order to the rest of the world while increasing trade with foreign markets. Consequently, the United States interfered in a dispute between Venezuela and Britain. America invoked the **Monroe Doctrine** and sided with Cuba in its struggle for independence from Spain. The latter resulted in the **Spanish-American Wars** in 1898 that ended with Cuba, Puerto Rico, the Philippines, and Guam becoming American protectorates at the same time the United States annexed Hawaii. In 1900, America declared an **Open Door policy** with China to support its independence and open markets. In 1903, Theodore Roosevelt helped Panama become independent of Colombia, and then secured the right to build the **Panama Canal**. Roosevelt also negotiated the peace treaty to end the Russo-Japanese War, which earned him the Nobel Peace prize. He then sent the American fleet on a world cruise to display his country's power.

Review Video: An Overview of American Imperialism
Visit mometrix.com/academy and enter code: 629170

Domestic Accomplishments of the Progressive Era

To the Progressives, promoting law and order meant cleaning up city governments to make them honest and efficient, bringing more democracy and humanity to state governments, and establishing a core of social workers to improve slum housing, health, and education. Also during the **Progressive Era**, the national government strengthened or created the following regulatory agencies, services, and acts to oversee business enterprises:

- Passed in 1906, the **Hepburn A**ct reinforced the Interstate Commerce Commission. In 1902, Roosevelt used the Justice Department and lawsuits to try to break monopolies and enforce the **Sherman Anti-Trust Act**. The **Clayton Anti-Trust Act** was added in 1914.
- From 1898 to 1910, the **Forest Service** guided lumber companies in the conservation and more efficient use of woodland resources under the direction of Gifford Pinchot.
- In 1906, the **Pure Food and Drug Act** was passed to protect consumers from fraudulent labeling and adulteration of products.
- In 1913, the **Federal Reserve System** was established to supervise banking and commerce. In 1914, the **Fair Trade Commission** was established to ensure fair competition.

World War I (1917–1919)

When World War I broke out in 1914, America declared **neutrality**. The huge demand for war goods by the Allies broke a seven-year industrial stagnation and gave American factories full-time work. The country's sympathies lay mostly with the Allies, and before long American business and banking were heavily invested in an Allied victory. In 1916, **Woodrow Wilson** campaigned on the slogan "He kept us out of war." However, when the British ship the ***Lusitania*** was torpedoed in 1915 by a German submarine and many Americans were killed, the United States broke its neutrality and directly entered the war. Eventually, when it was proven that Germany was trying to incite Mexico and Japan into attacking the United States, Wilson declared war in 1917, even though America was unprepared. Nonetheless, America quickly armed and transferred sufficient troops to Europe, bringing the **Allies** to victory in 1918.

Review Video: WWI Overview
Visit mometrix.com/academy and enter code: 659767

Roaring Twenties and the Great Depression

The **Roaring Twenties** (1920–1929) refers to the economically successful period of time following World War I. New technologies such as automobiles, new forms of media such as films, and new communication technology became widely available. In the wake of industrial growth and revolution, culture shifted toward more modern sentiments, and moved toward a more **practical** approach to life. New forms of art and music were born and thrived during this period, and during this timeframe civil rights were expanded to allow **women to vote**. In 1929, the stock market crashed and caused the end of the Roaring Twenties and the beginning of the **Great Depression**, which lasted from 1930 until 1941. The Great Depression was characterized by high unemployment rates and a slow-moving market with little profit to be made. Many banks failed during this time, and there was no governmental protection against bank failures. As a result, many depositors withdrew their money from banks to protect themselves, removing much of the money from the economy in an effect called economic contraction.

> **Review Video: 1920's**
> Visit mometrix.com/academy and enter code: 124996
>
> **Review Video: What Caused the Great Depression**
> Visit mometrix.com/academy and enter code: 635912

World War II (1939–1945)

World War II began in 1939. As with World War I, the United States tried to stay out of World War II, even though the **Lend-Lease program** transferred munitions to Great Britain. However, on December 7, 1941, Japan attacked **Pearl Harbor** in Hawaii. Since Japan was an ally of Germany, the United States declared war on all the Axis powers. Although there was fighting in both Europe and the Pacific, the decision was made to concentrate on defeating Hitler first. Since it did not have combat within its borders, the United States became the great manufacturer of goods and munitions for the war effort. Women went to work in the factories, while the men entered the military. All facets of American life were centered on the war effort, including rationing, metal collections, and buying war bonds. The benefit of this production was an **end to the economic depression**. The influx of American personnel and supplies eventually brought victory in Europe in April of 1945, and in Asia the following August.

> **Review Video: World War II**
> Visit mometrix.com/academy and enter code: 759402

Major Programs and Events Resulting from the Cold War

After World War II, the Soviet Union kept control of Eastern Europe, including half of Germany. **Communism** spread around the world. Resulting fears led to:

- The **Truman Doctrine** (1947) – This was a policy designed to protect free peoples everywhere against oppression.
- The **Marshall Plan** (1948) – This devoted $12 billion to rebuild Western Europe and strengthen its defenses.
- The **Organization of American States** (1948) – This was established to bolster democratic relations in the Americas.
- The **Berlin Blockade** (1948-49) – The Soviets tried to starve out West Berlin, so the United States provided massive supply drops by air.
- The **North Atlantic Treaty Organization** (1949) – This was formed to militarily link the United States and western Europe so that an attack on one was an attack on both.
- The **Korean War** (1950-53) – This divided the country into the communist North and the democratic South.
- The **McCarthy era** (1950-54) – Senator Joseph McCarthy of Wisconsin held hearings on supposed Communist conspiracies that ruined innocent reputations and led to the blacklisting of suspected sympathizers in the government, Hollywood, and the media.

Major Events of the 1960s

The 1960s were a tumultuous time for the United States. Major events included:

- The **Cuban Missile Crisis** (1961) – This was a stand-off between the United States and the Soviet Union over a build-up of missiles in Cuba. Eventually, the Soviets stopped their shipments and a nuclear war was averted.
- The **assassinations** of President Kennedy (1963), Senator Robert Kennedy (1968), and Dr. Martin Luther King, Jr. (1968).
- The **Civil Rights Movement** – Protest marches were held across the nation to draw attention to the plight of Black citizens. From 1964 to 1968, race riots exploded in more than 100 cities.

- The **Vietnam War** (1964-73) – This resulted in a military draft. There was heavy involvement of American personnel and money. There were also protest demonstrations, particularly on college campuses. At Kent State, several students died after being shot by National Guardsmen.
- **Major legislation** – Legislation passed during this decade included the Civil Rights Act, the Clean Air Act, and the Water Quality Act. This decade also saw the creation of the Peace Corps, Medicare, and the War on Poverty, in which billions were appropriated for education, urban redevelopment, and public housing.

Presidents and Vice Presidents from 1972 to 1974

In a two-year time span, the United States had two presidents and two vice presidents. This situation resulted first from the resignation of Vice President **Spiro T. Agnew** in October of 1973 because of alleged kickbacks. President **Richard M. Nixon** then appointed House Minority Leader **Gerald R. Ford** to be vice president. This was accomplished through Senate ratification, a process that had been devised after Harry Truman succeeded to the presidency upon the death of Franklin Roosevelt and went through nearly four years of his presidency without a vice president. Nixon resigned the presidency in August of 1974 because some Republican party members broke into Democratic headquarters at the **Watergate** building in Washington, DC, and the president participated in covering up the crime. Ford succeeded Nixon, and had to appoint another vice president. He chose **Nelson Rockefeller**, former governor of New York.

Post-war Era and the Civil Rights Era

The **Post-War Era** (1945-1964) was a time of **economic recovery** and general growth in America. The wars of the past several decades inspired a more active foreign policy to deter such violent wars from occurring again. This largely focused on the Soviet Union and the expansion of Communism around the world. Several countries at this time participated in both a space race and an **arms race**, a rush to develop and accumulate more powerful weapons, particularly nuclear weapons, to become the world's strongest military power. The political differences and concerns over powerful armaments eventually led to the Cold War, Vietnam War, and Korean War. The 60s were also a major pivot-point for civil rights, leading into the **Civil Rights Era** (1965-1980). Due to the protesting and activism of several groups, including **Dr. Martin Luther King Jr**. and the **NAACP**, civil rights landmarks were made regarding racial equality, including laws dealing with **segregation**, **employment opportunity**, and **voting** rights.

Reagan Era (1981–1991)

The **Reagan Era** is an era largely describing the foreign policy of the United States during the 1980s and sometimes viewed as extending through the 1990s or early-2000s. During this period, conservative reforms worked to **increase military spending** while also **cutting taxes** and reducing or restricting the involvement of the national government. Ronald Reagan's financial policy revolved around the idea that if the government stepped back, the economy could grow, which would in turn help to reduce national debt.

1990s and Early-2000s

The 1990s and early-2000s were characterized largely by new economic developments surrounding the availability of computers and the development of the internet, allowing new technology to drive the economy in new ways. The economy boomed in the late 1990s leading into the early 2000s. Amid all of the economic success, the United States faced attacks by terrorist groups such as al-Qaeda, which caused alarm and greater restriction to national security and border control. The most influential of these terror attacks was the September 11, 2001 airliner hijacking, where al-Qaeda members took over four airplanes and used them as weapons to crash into key governmental and trade buildings. These attacks triggered a focus of American attention on terrorist groups, and led to several wars in Afghanistan and Iraq.

2008 to Present

Following the economic success of the 1990s and 2000s, the housing industry collapsed, leading to what is known as the **Great Recession** in 2008. In 2008, President Barack Obama was elected as the country's first

African-American president. The war on terror continued until 2011, when Obama announced the death of Osama bin Laden, the al-Qaeda leader of the time. Obama's primary focus during his presidency included large stimulus packages and reforms to health insurance programs, an attempt to make healthcare affordable and available to all Americans. In 2016, President Donald Trump took office. His campaigns centered around immigration laws and tax reforms. Other major trends within this time period include a new wave of social equality issues surrounding same-sex rights and racial tension issues within America.

World History

Pre-Historical and Pre-Modern Periods

The earliest history of the human race is known as **pre-historical** due to the lack of record keeping. The earliest writing did not appear until the Sumerian civilization in Mesopotamia. In addition to the overt lack of writing from early civilizations, historical records were much more localized than more modern historical records. Ancient history can be broken down many ways, but a common distinction is the **pre-modern period**, including early civilizations such as Egypt, Babylon, and the Greek and Roman Empires. These early civilizations saw invention of technologies such as wood and early metalwork and the domestication of animals. Early civilizations were heavily dependent on agriculture and usually needed access to rivers for a consistent water source. The pre-modern period is viewed as ending with the connection of mainland Europe and some of Africa and Asia by the Greek and Roman Empires. The growth of these empires during this period also saw the worldwide spread of religions such as Judaism and Christianity.

Important Contributions of the Ancient Civilizations of Sumer, Egypt, and Indus Valley

These three ancient civilizations are distinguished by their unique contributions to the development of world civilization:

- **Sumer** used the first known writing system, which enabled the Sumerians to leave a sizeable written record of their myths and religion, advanced the development of the wheel and irrigation, and urbanized their culture.
- **Egypt** was united by the Nile River. Egyptians originally settled in villages on its banks, had a national religion that held their pharaohs as gods, had a central government that controlled civil and artistic affairs, and had writing and libraries.
- The **Indus Valley** was also called Harappan after the city of Harappa. This civilization started in the 3rd and 4th centuries BC and was widely dispersed over 400,000 square miles. It had a unified culture of luxury and refinement, no known national government, an advanced civic system, and prosperous trade routes.

Review Video: Early Mesopotamia: The Sumerians
Visit mometrix.com/academy and enter code: 939880

Review Video: Ancient Egypt
Visit mometrix.com/academy and enter code: 398041

Common Traits and Cultural Identifiers of the Early Empires of Mesopotamia, Egypt, Greece, and Rome

These empires all had: a strong military; a centralized government; control and standardization of commerce, money, and taxes; a weight system; and an official language.

- **Mesopotamia** had a series of short-term empires that failed because of their oppression of subject peoples.

- **Egypt** also had a series of governments after extending its territory beyond the Nile area. Compared to Mesopotamia, these were more stable and long-lived because they blended different peoples to create a single national identity.
- **Greece** started as a group of city-states that were united by Alexander the Great and joined to create an empire that stretched from the Indus River to Egypt and the Mediterranean coast. Greece blended Greek values with those of the local cultures, which collectively became known as Hellenistic society.
- **Rome** was an Italian city-state that grew into an empire extending from the British Isles across Europe to the Middle East. It lasted for 1,000 years and became the foundation of the Western world's culture, language, and laws.

Review Video: Ancient Greece
Visit mometrix.com/academy and enter code: 800829

CHARACTERISTICS OF CHINESE AND INDIAN EMPIRES

While the Chinese had the world's longest lasting and continuous empires, the Indians had more of a cohesive culture than an empire system. Their distinct characteristics are as follows:

- **China** – Since the end of the Warring States period in 221 BC, China has functioned as an empire. Although the dynasties changed several times, the basic governmental structure remained the same into the 20th century. The Chinese also have an extensive written record of their culture which heavily emphasizes history, philosophy, and a common religion.
- **India** – The subcontinent was seldom unified in terms of government until the British empire controlled the area in the 19th and 20th centuries. In terms of culture, India has had persistent institutions and religions that have loosely united the people, such as the caste system and guilds. These have regulated daily life more than any government.

MIDDLE AGES IN EUROPEAN HISTORY

The **Middle Ages**, or Medieval times, was a period that ran from approximately 500-1500 AD. The fall of the Greek and Roman civilizations marks the beginning of this period, allowing for the rise of new independent countries, largely relying on the feudal system of government, with kings who allotted power and territory to governors. During this time, the centers of European civilization moved from the Mediterranean countries to France, Germany, and England, where strong national governments were developing. Key events of this time include:

- **Roman Catholicism** was the cultural and religious center of medieval life, extending into politics and economics.
- **Knights**, with their systems of honor, combat, and chivalry, were loyal to their king.
- **Peasants**, or serfs, served a particular lord and his lands.
- Many **universities** were established that still function in modern times.
- The **Crusades**, the recurring wars between European Christians and Middle East Muslims, raged over the Holy Lands.
- Charles the Great, or **Charlemagne**, created an empire across France and Germany around 800 AD.
- The **Black Death plague** swept across Europe from 1347-1350, leaving between one third and one half of the population dead.

Review Video: The Middle Ages
Visit mometrix.com/academy and enter code: 413133

Review Video: Trade in the Middle Ages
Visit mometrix.com/academy and enter code: 650839

PROTESTANT REFORMATION

The dominance of the **Catholic Church** during the Middle Ages in Europe gave it immense power, which encouraged corrupt practices such as the selling of indulgences and clerical positions. The **Protestant Reformation** began as an attempt to reform the Catholic Church, but eventually led to separation from it. In 1517, Martin Luther posted his *Ninety-Five Theses* on the door of a church in Saxony, which criticized unethical practices, various doctrines, and the authority of the pope. Other reformers such as John Calvin and John Wesley soon followed, but disagreed among themselves and divided along doctrinal lines. Consequently, the Lutheran, Reformed, Calvinist, and Presbyterian churches were founded, among others. In England, King Henry VIII was denied a divorce by the pope, so he broke away and established the **Anglican Church**. The Protestant reformation caused the Catholic Church to finally reform itself, but the Protestant movement continued, resulting in a proliferation of new denominations.

RENAISSANCE

Renaissance is the French word for rebirth, and is used to describe the renewal of interest in ancient Greek and Latin art, literature, and philosophy that occurred in Europe, especially Italy, from the 14th through the 16th centuries. Historically, it was also a time of great scientific inquiry, the rise of individualism, extensive geographical exploration, and the rise of secular values.

Notable figures of the Renaissance include:

- **Petrarch** – An Italian scholar, writer, and key figure in northern Italy, which is where the Renaissance started and where chief patrons came from the merchant class
- **Leonardo da Vinci** – Artist and inventor
- **Michelangelo** and **Raphael** – Artists
- **Desiderius Erasmus** – Applied historical scholarship to the New Testament and laid the seeds for the Protestant Reformation
- **Sir Thomas More** – A lawyer and author who wrote *Utopia*
- **Niccolò Machiavelli** – Author of *The Prince* and *Discourses*, which proposed a science of human nature and civil life
- **William Shakespeare** – A renowned playwright and poet

Review Video: The Renaissance
Visit mometrix.com/academy and enter code: 123100

AGE OF DISCOVERY AND COLONIALISM

Throughout world history, there have been several waves of so-called **new imperialism**, in which established countries attempted to **colonize** territories that had not been explored by European nations. This was called the **Age of Discovery** largely because of the overseas exploration, "discovering" new lands, even though many of the explored lands were already populated. This colonialism was largely driven by the desire for increased wealth and resources, though many participants also sought after religious freedoms. Some of the earliest colonization attempts came from Spain and Portugal, who launched expeditions into Africa and Asia. These early colonial missions established the slave trade throughout Europe and for future colonial expansions. Later waves of colonialism included exploration of the **Americas** by Britain, France, and Spain. Other countries, such as China, Japan, and Russia, practiced imperialism in Asia. The process of colonizing many of these territories led to great injustices, such as the slave trade, and the horrific spread of disease and massacres of people groups such as the Aztecs in central Mexico and many Native American tribes in North America.

DECOLONIZATION

Following the powerful race for colonization throughout the world, many of the territories secured by European imperialism fought for their own **freedoms** and **independence**. Supporting these colonial missions was extremely costly and oftentimes, the colonials and the people from the ruling countries had very different priorities, which led to many disagreements. This was the case in the British colonies. Britain enacted many invasive and overcontrolling policies on the 13 established colonies. Tensions grew until the colonials revolted and declared their independence beginning the American Revolutionary War, which would solidify the United States of America as an independent nation. Several other countries worldwide followed suit and eventually secured their own independence. Decolonization largely began in the Americas and ended as late as 1960 in many African countries.

Worldwide Abolition of Slavery

Slavery has been accepted in various forms throughout most of known history. Contemporary to the decolonization period, the issue of slavery started to gain attention as an ethical matter worldwide. The movement to end slavery worldwide is known as **abolitionism** and roughly began in the late 1700s, however, anti-slavery sentiment was a slow-moving cause. The profitability of the slave trade and the use of slaves as the primary workforce for much of agriculture and shipping was a huge deterrent to change. In America, slavery was largely left as a states' right until tensions grew, leading into the American Civil War. Slavery was abolished progressively throughout the world, though at varying rates. Eventually, the United Nations adopted a firm doctrine on slavery, known as the Universal Declaration of Human Rights in 1948, which abolished slavery internationally.

Industrial Revolution

The **Industrial Revolution** started in England with the construction of the first **cotton mill** in 1733. Other inventions and factories followed in rapid succession. The **steel industry** grew exponentially when manufacturers realized that cheap, abundant English coal could be used instead of wood for melting metals. The **steam engine**, which revolutionized transportation and work power, came next. Around 1830, a factory-based, **technological era** was ushered into the rest of Europe. Society changed from agrarian to urban. A need for cheap, unskilled labor resulted in the extensive employment and abuse of women and children, who worked up to 14 hours a day, six days a week in deplorable conditions. Expanding populations brought crowded, unsanitary conditions to the cities, and the factories created air and water pollution. Societies had to deal with these new situations by enacting **child labor laws** and creating **labor unions** to protect the safety of workers.

Review Video: The Industrial Revolution
Visit mometrix.com/academy and enter code: 372796

Participants of World War I and World War II

World War I, which began in 1914, was fought by the **Allies** including Britain, France, Russia, Greece, Italy, Romania, and Serbia. They fought against the **Central Powers** of Germany, Austria-Hungary, Bulgaria, and Turkey. In 1917, the United States joined the Allies, and Russia withdrew to pursue its own revolution. World War I ended in 1918.

World War II was truly a world war, with fighting occurring on nearly every continent. Germany occupied most of Europe and Northern Africa. It was opposed by the countries of the British Empire, free France and its colonies, Russia, and various national resistance forces. Japan, an **Axis** ally of Germany, had been forcefully expanding its territories in Korea, China, Indonesia, the Philippines, and the South Pacific for many years. When Japan attacked Pearl Harbor in 1941, the United States joined the **Allied** effort. Italy changed from the Axis to the Allied side mid-war after deposing its own dictator. The war ended in Europe in April 1945, and in Japan in August 1945.

Importance of Cross-Cultural Comparisons in World History Instruction

It is important to make **cross-cultural comparisons** when studying world history so that the subject is **holistic** and not oriented to just Western civilization. Not only are the contributions of civilizations around the world important, but they are also interesting and more representative of the mix of cultures present in the United States. It is also critical to the understanding of world relations to study the involvement of European countries and the United States in international commerce, colonization, and development. **Trade routes** from ancient times linked Africa, Asia, and Europe, resulting in exchanges and migrations of people, philosophies, and religions, as well as goods. While many civilizations in the Americas thrived, and some became very sophisticated, many were eventually overcome or even erased by **European expansion**. The historic isolation of China and the modern industrialization of Japan have had huge impacts on their relations with the rest of the world. The more students understand this history and its effects on the modern world, the better they will able to function in their own spheres.

US Government and Citizenship

Principles of the Constitution

The six basic principles of the Constitution are:

1. **Popular Sovereignty** – The people establish government and give power to it; the government can function only with the consent of the people.
2. **Limited Government** – The Constitution specifies limits on government authority, and no official or entity is above the law.
3. **Separation of Powers** – Power is divided among three government branches: the legislative (Congress), the executive (President), and the judicial (federal courts).
4. **Checks and Balances** – This is a system that enforces the separation of powers and ensures that each branch has the authority and ability to restrain the powers of the other two branches, thus preventing tyranny.
5. **Judicial Review** – Judges in the federal courts ensure that no act of government is in violation of the Constitution. If an act is unconstitutional, the judicial branch has the power to nullify it.
6. **Federalism** – This is the division of power between the central government and local governments, which limits the power of the federal government and allows states to deal with local problems.

Classic Forms of Government

Forms of government that have appeared throughout history include:

- **Feudalism** – This is based on the rule of local lords who are loyal to the king and control the lives and production of those who work on their land.
- **Classical republic** – This form is a representative democracy. Small groups of elected leaders represent the interests of the electorate.
- **Absolute monarchy** – A king or queen has complete control of the military and government.
- **Authoritarianism** – An individual or group has unlimited authority. There is no system in place to restrain the power of the government.
- **Dictatorship** – Those in power are not held responsible to the people.
- **Autocracy** – This is rule by one person (despot), not necessarily a monarch, who uses power tyrannically.
- **Oligarchy** – A small, usually self-appointed elite rules a region.
- **Liberal democracy** – This is a government based on the consent of the people that protects individual rights and freedoms from any intolerance by the majority.
- **Totalitarianism** – All facets of the citizens' lives are controlled by the government.

Influences of Philosophers on Political Study

Ancient Greek philosophers **Aristotle** and **Plato** believed political science would lead to order in political matters, and that this scientifically organized order would create stable, just societies.

Thomas Aquinas adapted the ideas of Aristotle to a Christian perspective. His ideas stated that individuals have certain rights, but also certain duties, and that these rights and duties should determine the type and extent of government rule. In stating that laws should limit the role of government, he laid the groundwork for ideas that would eventually become modern constitutionalism.

Niccolò Machiavelli, author of *The Prince*, was a proponent of politics based solely on power.

Parliamentary and Democratic Systems of Government

In a **parliamentary system**, government involves a legislature and a variety of political parties. The head of government, usually a Prime Minister, is typically the head of the dominant party. A head of state can be elected, or this position can be taken by a monarch, such as in Great Britain's constitutional monarchy system.

In a **democratic system** of government, the people elect their government representatives. The term democracy is a Greek term that means "for the rule of the people." There are two forms of democracy—direct and indirect. In a direct democracy, each issue or election is decided by a vote where each individual is counted separately. An indirect democracy employs a legislature that votes on issues that affect large number of people whom the legislative members represent. Democracy can exist as a Parliamentary system or a Presidential system. The US is a presidential, indirect democracy.

Bill of Rights

The **United States Bill of Rights** was based on principles established by the **Magna Carta** in 1215, the 1688 **English Bill of Rights**, and the 1776 **Virginia Bill of Rights**. In 1791, the federal government added 10 amendments to the United States Constitution that provided the following **protections**:

- Freedom of speech, religion, peaceful assembly, petition of the government, and petition of the press
- The right to keep and bear arms
- No quartering of soldiers on private property without the consent of the owner
- Regulations on government search and seizure
- Provisions concerning prosecution
- The right to a speedy, public trial and the calling of witnesses
- The right to trial by jury
- Freedom from excessive bail or cruel punishment
- These rights are not necessarily the only rights
- Powers not prohibited by the Constitution are reserved to the states

Review Video: Bill of Rights
Visit mometrix.com/academy and enter code: 585149

Making a Formal Amendment to the Constitution

So far, there have been only **27 amendments** to the federal Constitution. There are four different ways to change the constitution: two methods for proposal and two methods for ratification:

1. An amendment is proposed by a two-thirds vote in each house of Congress and ratified by three-fourths of the state legislatures.
2. An amendment is proposed by a two-thirds vote in each house of Congress and ratified by three-fourths of the states in special conventions called for that purpose.
3. An amendment is proposed by a national convention that is called by Congress at the request of two-thirds of the state legislatures and ratified by three-fourths of the state legislatures.
4. An amendment is proposed by a national convention that is called by Congress at the request of two-thirds of the state legislatures and ratified by three-fourths of the states in special conventions called for that purpose.

Division of Powers

The **division of powers** in the federal government system is as follows:

- **National** – This level can coin money, regulate interstate and foreign trade, raise and maintain armed forces, declare war, govern United States territories and admit new states, and conduct foreign relations.
- **Concurrent** – This level can levy and collect taxes, borrow money, establish courts, define crimes and set punishments, and claim private property for public use.
- **State** – This level can regulate trade and business within the state, establish public schools, pass license requirements for professionals, regulate alcoholic beverages, conduct elections, and establish local governments.

There are three types of **delegated powers** granted by the Constitution:

1. **Expressed or enumerated powers** – These are specifically spelled out in the Constitution.
2. **Implied** – These are not expressly stated, but are reasonably suggested by the expressed powers.
3. **Inherent** – These are powers not expressed by the Constitution but ones that national governments have historically possessed, such as granting diplomatic recognition.

Powers can also be classified as reserved or exclusive. **Reserved powers** are not granted to the national government, but not denied to the states. **Exclusive powers** are those reserved to the national government, including concurrent powers.

Stages of Extending Suffrage in the US

Originally, the Constitution of 1789 provided the right to vote only to white male property owners. Through the years, suffrage was extended through the following five stages.

1. In the early 1800s, states began to eliminate **property ownership** and **tax payment qualifications**.
2. By 1810, there were no more **religious tests** for voting. In the late 1800s, the 15th Amendment protected citizens from being denied the right to vote because of **race or color**.
3. In 1920, the 19th Amendment prohibited the denial of the right to vote because of **gender**, and women were given the right to vote.
4. Passed in 1961 and ratified in 1964, the 23rd Amendment added the voters of the **District of Columbia** to the presidential electorate and eliminated the poll tax as a condition for voting in federal elections. The **Voting Rights Act of 1965** prohibited disenfranchisement through literacy tests and various other means of discrimination.
5. In 1971, the 26th Amendment set the minimum voting age at **18 years of age**.

Major Supreme Court Cases

Out of the many Supreme Court rulings, several have had critical historical importance. These include:

- **Marbury v. Madison** (1803) – This ruling established judicial review as a power of the Supreme Court.
- **Dred Scott v. Sandford** (1857) – This decision upheld property rights over human rights in the case of a slave who had been transported to a free state by his master, but was still considered a slave.
- **Brown v. Board of Education** (1954) – The Court ruled that segregation was a violation of the Equal Protection Clause and that the "separate but equal" practice in education was unconstitutional. This decision overturned the 1896 Plessy v. Ferguson ruling that permitted segregation if facilities were equal.

- **Miranda v. Arizona** (1966) – This ruling compelled the reading of Miranda rights to those arrested for crimes the law. It ensured that confessions could not be illegally obtained and that citizen rights to fair trials and protection under the law would be upheld.

Review Video: Marbury vs. Madison
Visit mometrix.com/academy and enter code: 573964

Famous Speeches in US History that Defined Government Policy, Foreign Relations, and American Spirit

Among the best-known speeches and famous lines known to modern Americans are the following:

- The **Gettysburg Address** – Made by Abraham Lincoln on November 19, 1863, it dedicated the Gettysburg battleground's cemetery.
- The **Fourteen Points** – Made by Woodrow Wilson on January 18, 1918, this outlined Wilson's plans for peace and the League of Nations.
- **Address to Congress** – Made by Franklin Roosevelt on December 8, 1941, it declared war on Japan and described the attack on Pearl Harbor as "a day which will live in infamy."
- **Inaugural Address** – Made by John F. Kennedy on January 20, 1961, it contained the famous line: "Ask not what your country can do for you, ask what you can do for your country."
- **Berlin Address** – Made by John F. Kennedy on June 26, 1963, it contained the famous line "Ich bin ein Berliner," which expressed empathy for West Berliners in their conflict with the Soviet Union.
- "**I Have a Dream**" and "**I See the Promised Land**" – Made by Martin Luther King, Jr. on August 28, 1963 and April 3, 1968, respectively, these speeches were hallmarks of the Civil Rights Movement.
- **Brandenburg Gate speech** – Made by Ronald Reagan on June 12, 1987, this speech was about the Berlin Wall and the end of the Cold War. It contained the famous line "Tear down this wall."

Closed and Open Primaries in a Direct Primary System

The **direct primary system** is a means for members of a political party to participate in the selection of a candidate from their party to compete against the other party's candidate in a general election. A **closed primary** is a party nominating election in which only declared party members can vote. Party membership is usually established by registration. Currently, 26 states and the District of Columbia use this system. An **open primary** is a party nominating election in which any qualified voter can take part. The voter makes a public choice at the polling place about which primary to participate in, and the choice does not depend on any registration or previous choices. A **blanket primary**, which allowed voters to vote in the primaries of both parties, was used at various times by three states. The Supreme Court ruled against this practice in 2000.

Important Documents in United States History and Government

The following are among the greatest **American documents** because of their impact on foreign and domestic policy:

- Declaration of Independence (1776)
- The Articles of Confederation (1777)
- The Constitution (1787) and the Bill of Rights (1791)
- The Northwest Ordinance (1787)
- The Federalist Papers (1787-88)
- George Washington's Inaugural Address (1789) and Farewell Address (1796)
- The Alien and Sedition Act (1798)
- The Louisiana Purchase Treaty (1803)
- The Monroe Doctrine (1823); The Missouri Compromise (1830)
- The Compromise of 1850
- The Kansas-Nebraska Act (1854)

- The Homestead Act (1862)
- The Emancipation Proclamation (1863)
- The agreement to purchase Alaska (1866)
- The Sherman Anti-Trust Act (1890)
- Theodore Roosevelt's Corollary to the Monroe Doctrine (1905)
- The Social Security Act (1935) and other acts of the New Deal in the 1930s; The Truman Doctrine (1947); The Marshall Plan (1948)
- The Civil Rights Act (1964)

FEDERAL TAXES

The four types of **federal taxes** are:

- **Income taxes on individuals** – This is a complex system because of demands for various exemptions and rates. Further, the schedule of rates can be lowered or raised according to economic conditions in order to stimulate or restrain economic activity. For example, a tax cut can provide an economic stimulus, while a tax increase can slow down the rate of inflation. Personal income tax generates about five times as much as corporate taxes. Rates are based on an individual's income, and range from 10 to 35 percent.
- **Income taxes on corporations** – The same complexity of exemptions and rates exists for corporations as individuals. Taxes can be raised or lowered according to the need to stimulate or restrain the economy.
- **Excise taxes** – These are taxes on specific goods such as tobacco, liquor, automobiles, gasoline, air travel, and luxury items, or on activities such as highway usage by trucks.
- **Customs duties** – These are taxes imposed on imported goods. They serve to regulate trade between the United States and other countries.

UNITED STATES CURRENCY SYSTEM

The Constitution of 1787 gave the United States Congress the central authority to **print or coin money** and to **regulate its value**. Before this time, states were permitted to maintain separate currencies. The currency system is based on a **modified gold standard**. There is an enormous store of gold to back up United States currency housed at Fort Knox, Kentucky. Paper money is actually **Federal Reserve notes** and coins. It is the job of the Bureau of Engraving and Printing in the Treasury Department to design plates, special types of paper, and other security measures for bills and bonds. This money is put into general circulation by the Treasury and Federal Reserve Banks, and is taken out of circulation when worn out. Coins are made at the Bureau of the Mint in Philadelphia, Denver, and San Francisco.

EMPLOYMENT ACT OF 1946

The **Employment Act of 1946** established the following entities to combat unemployment:

- The **Council of Economic Advisers** (CEA) – Composed of a chair and two other members appointed by the President and approved by the Senate, this council assists the President with the development and implementation of US economic policy. The Council members and their staff, located in the Executive Office, are professionals in economics and statistics who forecast economic trends and provide analysis based on evidence-based research.
- The **Economic Report of the President** – This is presented every January by the President to Congress. Based on the work of the Council, the report recommends a program for maximizing employment, and may also recommend legislation.
- **Joint Economic Committee** (JEC) – This is a committee composed of 10 members of the House and 10 members of the Senate that makes a report early each year on its continuous study of the economy. Study is conducted through hearings and research, and the report is made in response to the president's recommendations.

Qualifications of a US Citizen

Anyone born in the US, born abroad to a US citizen, or who has gone through a process of **naturalization** to become a citizen, is considered a **citizen** of the United States. It is possible to lose US citizenship as a result of conviction of certain crimes such as treason. Citizenship may also be lost if a citizen pledges an oath to another country or serves in the military of a country engaged in hostilities with the US. A US citizen can also choose to hold dual citizenship, work as an expatriate in another country without losing US citizenship, or even renounce citizenship if he or she so chooses.

Rights, Duties, and Responsibilities Granted to or Expected from US Citizens

Citizens are granted certain rights under the US government. The most important of these are defined in the **Bill of Rights**, and include freedom of speech, religion, assembly, and a variety of other rights the government is not allowed to remove.

Duties of a US citizen include:

- Paying taxes
- Loyalty to the government, though the US does not prosecute those who criticize or seek to change the government
- Support and defend the Constitution
- Serve in the Armed Forces as required by law
- Obeying laws as set forth by the various levels of government.

Responsibilities of a US citizen include:

- Voting in elections
- Respecting one another's rights and not infringing upon them
- Staying informed about various political and national issues
- Respecting one another's beliefs

United States Political Systems

Representative Democracy

In a system of government characterized as a representative democracy, voters elect **representatives** to act in their interests. Typically, a representative is elected by and responsible to a specific subset of the total population of eligible voters; this subset of the electorate is referred to as a representative's constituency. A **representative democracy** may foster a more powerful legislature than other forms of government systems; to compensate for a strong legislature, most constitutions stipulate that measures must be taken to balance the powers within government, such as the creation of a separate judicial branch. Representative democracy became popular in post-industrial nations where increasing numbers of people expressed an interest in politics, but where technology and census counts remained incompatible with systems of direct democracy. Today, the majority of the world's population resides in representative democracies, including constitutional monarchies that possess a strong representative branch.

Democracy

Democracy, or rule by the people, is a form of government in which power is vested in the people and in which policy decisions are made by the majority in a decision-making process such as an election that is open to all or most citizens. Definitions of democracy have become more generalized and include aspects of society and political culture in democratic societies that do not necessarily represent a form of government. What defines a democracy varies, but some of the characteristics of a democracy could include the presence of a middle class, the presence of a civil society, a free market, political pluralism, universal suffrage, and specific rights and freedoms. In practice however, democracies do have limits on specific freedoms, which are justified as being necessary to maintain democracy and ensure democratic freedoms. For example, freedom of association is limited in democracies for individuals and groups that pose a threat to government or to society.

Presidential/Congressional System

In a **presidential system**, also referred to as a **congressional system**, the legislative branch and the executive branches are elected separately from one another. The features of a presidential system include a *president* who serves as both the head of state and the head of the government, who has no formal relationship with the legislative branch, who is not a voting member, who cannot introduce bills, and who has a fixed term of office. *Elections* are held at scheduled times. The president's *cabinet* carries out the policies of the executive branch and the legislative branch.

Political Parties

A **political party** is an organization that advocates a particular ideology and seeks to gain power within government. The tendency of members of political parties to support their party's policies and interests relative to those of other parties is referred to as partisanship. Often, a political party is comprised of members whose positions, interests and perspectives on policies vary, despite having shared interests in the general ideology of the party. As such, many political parties will have divisions within them that have differing opinions on policy. Political parties are often placed on a political spectrum, with one end of the spectrum representing conservative, traditional values and policies and the other end of the spectrum representing radical, progressive value and policies.

Types of Party Systems

There is a variety of **party systems**, including single-party systems, dominant-party systems, and dual-party systems. In a **single-party system**, only one political party may hold power. In this type of system, minor parties may be permitted, but they must accept the leadership of the dominant party. **Dominant-party systems** allow for multiple parties in opposition of one another, however the dominant party is the only party considered to have power. A **two-party system**, such as in the United States, is one in which there are two dominant political parties. In such a system, it is very difficult for any other parties to win an election. In most two-party systems, there is typically one right wing party and one left wing party.

Democratic Party

The **Democratic Party** was founded in 1792. In the United States, it is one of the two dominant political parties, along with the Republican Party. The Democratic Party is to the left of the Republican Party. The Democratic Party began as a conservative party in the mid-1800s, shifting to the left during the 1900s. There are many factions within the Democratic Party in the United States. The **Democratic National Committee (DNC)** is the official organization of the Democratic Party, and it develops and promotes the party's platform and coordinates fundraising and election strategies. There are Democratic committees in every US state and most US counties. The official symbol of the Democratic Party is the donkey.

Republican Party

The **Republican Party** is often referred to as the **GOP**, which stands for *Grand Old Party*. The Republican Party is considered socially conservative and economically neoliberal relative to the Democratic Party. Like the Democratic Party, there are factions within the Republic Party that agree with the party's overall ideology, but disagree with the party's positions on specific issues. The official symbol of the Republican Party is the elephant. The **Republican National Committee (RNC)** is the official organization of the Republican Party, and it develops and promotes the party's platform and coordinates fundraising and election strategies. There are Republican committees in every US state and most US counties.

Political Campaigns

A **political campaign** is an organized attempt to influence the decisions of a particular group of people. Examples of campaigns could include elections or efforts to influence policy changes. One of the first steps in a campaign is to develop a **campaign message**. The message must then be delivered to the individuals and groups that the campaign is trying to reach and influence through a campaign plan. There are various ways for a campaign to communicate its message to the intended audience, including public media; paid media such as television, radio and newspaper ads, billboards and the internet; public events such as protests and rallies; meetings with speakers; mailings; canvassing; fliers; and websites. Through these efforts, the campaign attempts to attract additional support and, ultimately, to reach the goal of the campaign.

VOTING

Voting is a method of decision making that allows people to express their opinion or preference for a candidate or for a proposed resolution of an issue. In a democratic system, voting typically takes place as part of an **election**. An individual participates in the voting process by casting a vote, or a **ballot**; ballots are produced by states A *secret ballot* can be used at polls to protect voters' privacy. Individuals can also vote via *absentee ballot*. In some states voters can write-in a name to cast a vote for a candidate that is not on the ballot. Some states also use *straight ticket voting*, allowing the voter to vote for one party for all the elected positions on the ballot.

US ELECTIONS

In the United States, **officials** are elected at the federal, state and local levels. The first two articles of the Constitution, as well as various amendments, establish how **federal elections** are to be held. The **President** is elected indirectly, by electors of an electoral college. Members of the electoral college nearly always vote along the lines of the popular vote of their respective states. Members of **Congress** are directly elected. At the state level, state law establishes most aspects of how elections are held. There are many elected offices at the state level, including a governor and state legislature. There are also elected offices at the local level.

VOTER ELIGIBILITY

The United States Constitution establishes that individual people are permitted to **vote** in elections if they are citizens of the United States and are at least eighteen years old. The **fifteenth** and **nineteenth amendments** of the United States Constitution stipulate that the right to vote cannot be denied to any United States citizen based on race or sex, respectively. States regulate voter eligibility beyond the minimum qualifications stipulated by the United States Constitution. Depending on the regulations of individual states, individuals may be denied the right to vote if they are convicted criminals.

ADVANTAGES AND DISADVANTAGES TO TWO-PARTY SYSTEM

Advocates of the **two-party system** argue that its advantages are that they are stable because they enable policies and government to change slowly rather than rapidly due to the relative lack of influence from small parties representing unconventional ideologies. In addition, they seem to drive voters toward a middle ground and are less susceptible to revolutions, coups, or civil wars. Among the critiques of the two-party system is the claim that stability in and of itself is not necessarily desirable, as it often comes at the expense of democracy. Critics also argue that the two-party system promotes negative political campaigns, in which candidates and their respective parties only take positions on issues that will differentiate themselves from their opponents, rather than focusing on policy issues that are of significance to citizens. Another concern is that if one of the two major parties becomes weak, a dominant-party system may develop.

CAMPAIGN MESSAGE

Political campaigns consist of three main elements, which are the campaign message, the money that is necessary to run the campaign, and the "machine," or the capital that is necessary to run the campaign. A campaign message is a succinct statement expressing why voters should support the campaign and the individual or policy associated with that campaign. The message is one of the most significant aspects of a political campaign, and a considerable amount of time, money and effort is invested in devising a successful campaign message, as it will be repeated throughout the campaign and will be one of the most identifying factors of the campaign.

Modern Election Campaigns in the US

Political campaigns in the US have changed and continue to change as advances in technology permit varied campaign methods. Campaigns represent a civic practice, and today they are a high profit industry. The US has an abundance of professional political consultants that employ highly sophisticated campaign management strategies and tools. The election process varies widely between the federal, state and local levels. Campaigns are typically controlled by individual candidates, rather than by the parties that they are associated with. Larger campaigns utilize a vast array of media to reach their targeted audiences, while smaller campaigns are typically limited to direct contact with voters, direct mailings and other forms of low-cost advertising to reach their audiences. In addition to fundraising and spending done by individual candidates, party committees and political action committees also raise money and spend it in ways that will advance the cause of the particular campaign they are associated with.

Voter Registration

Individuals have the responsibility of **registering to vote**. Every state except North Dakota requires citizens to register to vote. In an effort to increase voter turnout, Congress passed the **National Voter Registration Act** in 1993. This Act is also known as "Motor Voter," because it required states to make the voter registration process easier by providing registration services through drivers' license registration centers, as well as through disability centers, schools, libraries, and mail-in registration. Some states are exempt because they permit same-day voter registration, which enables voters to register to vote on the day of the election.

Presidential Elections

The President of the United States is elected **indirectly**, by members of an **electoral college**. Members of the electoral college nearly always vote along the lines of the popular vote of their respective states. The winner of a presidential election is the candidate with at least 270 electoral college votes. It is possible for a candidate to win the electoral vote, and lose the popular vote. Incumbent Presidents and challengers typically prefer a balanced ticket, where the President and Vice President are elected together and generally balance one another with regard to geography, ideology, or experience working in government. The nominated Vice Presidential candidate is referred to as the President's *running mate*.

Electoral College

Electoral college votes are cast by state by a group of electors; each elector casts one electoral college vote. State law regulates how states cast their electoral college votes. In all states except Maine and Nebraska, the candidate winning the most votes receives all the state's electoral college votes. In Maine and Nebraska two electoral votes are awarded based on the winner of the statewide election, and the rest go to the highest vote-winner in each of the state's congressional districts. Critics of the electoral college argue that it is undemocratic because the President is elected indirectly as opposed to directly, and that it creates inequality between voters in different states because candidates focus attention on voters in swing states who could influence election results. Critics argue that the electoral college provides more representation for voters in small states than large states, where more voters are represented by a single electoral than in small states and discriminates against candidates that do not have support concentrated in a given state.

Congressional Elections

Congressional elections are every two years. Members of the **House of Representatives** are elected for a two year term and elections occur every two years on the first Tuesday after November 1st in even years. A Representative is elected from each of the 435 House districts in the US House elections usually occur in the same year as Presidential elections. Members of the **Senate** are elected to six year terms; one-third of the Senate is elected every two years. Per the Seventeenth Amendment to the Constitution, which was passed in 1913, Senators are elected by the electorate of states. The country is divided into **Congressional districts**. Critics argue that this division eliminates voter choice, sometimes creating areas in which Congressional races are uncontested. Every ten years **redistricting** of Congressional districts occurs. However, redistricting is often partisan and therefore reduces the number of competitive districts. The division of voting districts resulting in an unfair advantage to one party in elections is known as gerrymandering. Gerrymandering has been criticized as being undemocratic.

State and Local Elections

State elections are regulated by state laws and constitutions. In keeping with the ideal of separation of powers, the legislature and the executive are elected separately at the state level, as they are at the federal level. In each state, a **Governor** and a **Lieutenant Governor** are elected. In some states, the Governor and Lieutenant Governor are elected on a joint ticket, while in other states they are elected separately from one another. In some states, executive positions such as Attorney General and Secretary of State are also elected offices. All members of state legislatures are elected, including state senators and state representatives. Depending on the state, members of the state supreme court and other members of the state judiciary may be chosen in elections. Local government can include the governments of counties and cities. At this level, nearly all government offices are filled through an election process. Elected local offices may include sheriffs, county school boards, and city mayors.

Campaign Finance and Independent Expenditures

An individual or group is legally permitted to make unlimited **independent expenditures** in association with federal elections. An independent expenditure is an expenditure that is made to pay for a form of communication that supports the election or defeat of a candidate; the expenditure must be made independently from the candidate's own campaign. To be considered independent, the communication may not be made with the cooperation or consultation with, or at the request or suggestion of, any candidate, any committees or political party associated with the candidate, or any agent that acts on behalf of the candidate. There are no restrictions on the amount that anyone may spend on an independent expenditure, however, any individual making an independent expenditure must report it and disclose the source of the funds they used.

Campaign Finance and Activities of Political Parties

Political parties participate in federal elections at the local, state and national levels. Most **party committees** must register with the **Federal Election Committee** and file reports disclosing federal campaign activities. While party committees may contribute funds directly to federal candidates, the amounts that they contribute are restricted by the campaign finance contribution limits. National and state party committees are permitted to make additional **coordinated expenditures**, within limits, to assist their nominees in general elections. However, national party committees are not permitted to make unlimited **independent expenditures**, also known as soft money, to support or oppose federal candidates. State and local party committees are also not permitted to use soft money for the purpose of supporting or opposing federal candidates, but they are allowed to spend soft money, up to a limit of $10,000 per source, on voter registration and on efforts aimed at increasing voter participation. All party committees are required to register themselves and file disclosure reports with the Federal Election Committee once their federal election activities exceed specified monetary limits.

Public Opinion

Public opinion represents the collective attitudes of individual members of the adult population in the United States of America. There are many varied forces that may influence public opinion. These forces include *public relations efforts* on the part of political campaigns and political parties. Another force affecting political opinion is the *political media* and the *mass media*. Public opinion is very important during elections, particularly Presidential elections, as it is an indicator of how candidates are perceived by the public and of how well candidates are doing during their election campaigns. Public opinion is often measured and evaluated using survey sampling.

Mass Media and Public Opinion

The **mass media** is critical in developing public opinion. In the short term people generally evaluate information they receive relative to their own beliefs; in the long term the media may have a considerable impact on people's beliefs. Due to the impact of the media on an individual's beliefs, some experts consider the effects of the media on an individual's independence and autonomy to be negative. Others view the impact of the media on individuals as a positive one, because the media provides information that expands worldviews and enriches lives, and fosters the development of opinions that are informed by many sources of information. A critical aspect of the relationship between the media and public opinion is who is in control of the knowledge and information that is disseminated through the media. Whoever controls the media can propagate their own agenda. The extent to which an individual interprets and evaluates information received through the media can influence behaviors such as voting patterns, consumer behavior, and social attitudes.

Economics

Effects Economy Can Have on Purchasing Decisions of Consumers

The **economy** plays an important role in how careful consumers are when using their resources. It also affects what they perceive as needs as opposed to what they perceive as wants. When the economy is doing well, unemployment figures are low, which means that people can easily attain their basic necessities. As a result, consumers are typically more willing to spend their financial resources. Consumers will also be more willing to spend their resources on products and services that are not necessary to their survival, but are instead products and services that they enjoy having and believe increase their quality of life. On the other hand, when the economy is in a slump, consumers are much more likely to cut back on their spending because they perceive a significantly higher risk of being unable to acquire basic necessities due to a lack of financial resources.

Common Terminology in Economics

- **Supply** is the amount of a product or service available to consumers.
- **Demand** is how much consumers are willing to pay for the product or service. These two facets of the market determine the price of goods and services. The higher the demand, the higher the price the supplier will charge; the lower the demand, the lower the price.
- **Scarcity** is a measure of supply. Demand is high when there is a scarcity, or low supply, of an item.
- **Choice** is related to scarcity and demand in that when an item in demand is scarce, consumers have to make difficult choices. They can pay more for an item, go without it, or go elsewhere for the item.
- **Money** is the cash or currency available for payment.
- **Resources** are the items one can barter in exchange for goods. Money is the cash reserves of a nation, while resources are the minerals, labor force, armaments, and other raw materials or assets a nation has available for trade.
- **Taxes** are legally required payments to the government for income, goods bought, or property owned. Taxes are categorized as direct or indirect.
- **Tariffs** are taxes specifically imposed on imports from another country.

Effects of Economic Downturn or Recession

When a **recession** happens, people at all levels of society feel the economic effects. For example:

- High **unemployment** results because businesses have to cut back to keep costs low, and may no longer have the work for the labor force they once did.
- **Mortgage rates** go up on variable-rate loans as banks try to increase their revenues, but the higher rates cause some people who cannot afford increased housing costs to sell or suffer foreclosure.
- **Credit** becomes less available as banks try to lessen their risk. This decreased lending affects business operations, home and auto loans, etc.
- **Stock market prices** drop, and the lower dividends paid to stockholders reduce their income. This is especially hard on retired people who rely on stock dividends.
- **Psychological depression and trauma** may occur in those who suffer bankruptcy, unemployment, or foreclosure during a depression.

Economic Effects of Abundant Natural Resources

The **positive economic aspects** of abundant natural resources are an increase in **revenue and new jobs** where those resources have not been previously accessed. For example, the growing demand for oil, gas, and minerals has led companies to venture into new regions.

The **negative economic aspects** of abundant natural resources are:

- **Environmental degradation**, if sufficient regulations are not in place to counter strip mining, deforestation, and contamination.
- **Corruption**, if sufficient regulations are not in place to counter bribery, political favoritism, and exploitation of workers as greedy companies try to maximize their profits.
- **Social tension**, if the resources are privately owned such that the rich become richer and the poor do not reap the benefits of their national resources. Class divisions become wider, resulting in social unrest.
- **Dependence**, if income from the natural resources is not used to develop other industries as well. In this situation, the economy becomes dependent on one source, and faces potential crises if natural disasters or depletion take away that income source.

Economics and Kinds of Economies

Economics is the study of the buying choices that people make, the production of goods and services, and how our market system works. The two kinds of economies are command and market. In a **command economy**, the government controls what and how much is produced, the methods used for production, and the distribution of goods and services. In a **market economy**, producers make decisions about methods and distribution on their own. These choices are based on what will sell and bring a profit in the marketplace. In a market economy, consumers ultimately affect these decisions by choosing whether or not to buy certain goods and services. The United States has a market economy.

Market Economy

The five characteristics of a **market economy** are:

- **Economic freedom** – There is freedom of choice with respect to jobs, salaries, production, and price.
- **Economic incentives** – A positive incentive is to make a profit. However, if the producer tries to make too high a profit, the consequences might be that no one will purchase the item at that price. A negative incentive would be a drop in profits, causing the producer to decrease or discontinue production. A boycott, which might cause the producer to change business practices or policies, is also a negative economic incentive.
- **Competition** – There is more than one producer for any given product. Consumers thereby have choices about what to buy, which are usually made based on quality and price. Competition is an incentive for a producer to make the best product at the best price. Otherwise, producers will lose business to the competition.
- **Private ownership** – Production and profits belong to an individual or to a private company, not to the government.
- **Limited government** – Government plays no role in the economic decisions of its individual citizens.

Factors of Production and Types of Markets That Create Economic Flow

The factors of **production** are:

- **Land** – This includes not only actual land, but also forests, minerals, water, etc.
- **Labor** – This is the work force required to produce goods and services, including factors such as talent, skills, and physical labor.

- **Capital** – This is the cash and material equipment needed to produce goods and services, including buildings, property, tools, office equipment, roads, etc.
- **Entrepreneurship** – Persons with initiative can capitalize on the free market system by producing goods and services.

The two types of markets are factor and product markets. The **factor market** consists of the people who exchange their services for wages. The people are sellers and companies are buyers. The **product market** is the selling of products to the people who want to buy them. The people are the buyers and the companies are the sellers. This exchange creates a circular economic flow in which money goes from the producers to workers as wages, and then flows back to producers in the form of payment for products.

Economic Impact of Technology

At the start of the 21st century, the role of **information and communications technologies** (ICT) grew rapidly as the economy shifted to a knowledge-based one. Output is increasing in areas where ICT is used intensively, which are service areas and knowledge-intensive industries such as finance; insurance; real estate; business services; health care; environmental goods and services; and community, social, and personal services. Meanwhile, the economic share for manufacturers is declining in medium- and low-technology industries such as chemicals, food products, textiles, gas, water, electricity, construction, and transport and communication services. Industries that have traditionally been high-tech, such as aerospace, computers, electronics, and pharmaceuticals are remaining steady in terms of their economic share. Technology has become the strongest factor in determining **per capita income** for many countries. The ease of technology investments as compared to industries that involve factories and large labor forces has resulted in more foreign investments in countries that do not have natural resources to call upon.

Geography

Geography involves learning about the world's primary **physical and cultural patterns** to help understand how the world functions as an interconnected and dynamic system. Combining information from different sources, geography teaches the basic patterns of climate, geology, vegetation, human settlement, migration, and commerce. Thus, geography is an **interdisciplinary** study of history, anthropology, and sociology. **History** incorporates geography in discussions of battle strategies, slavery (trade routes), ecological disasters (the Dust Bowl of the 1930s), and mass migrations. Geographic principles are useful when reading **literature** to help identify and visualize the setting, and also when studying **earth science**, **mathematics** (latitude, longitude, sun angle, and population statistics), and **fine arts** (song, art, and dance often reflect different cultures). Consequently, a good background in geography can help students succeed in other subjects as well.

Themes of Geography

The five themes of geography are:

- **Location** – This includes relative location (described in terms of surrounding geography such as a river, sea coast, or mountain) and absolute location (the specific point of latitude and longitude).
- **Place** – This includes physical characteristics (deserts, plains, mountains, and waterways) and human characteristics (features created by humans, such as architecture, roads, religion, industries, and food and folk practices).
- **Human-environmental interaction** – This includes human adaptation to the environment (using an umbrella when it rains), human modification of the environment (building terraces to prevent soil erosion), and human dependence on the environment for food, water, and natural resources.
- **Movement** –Interaction through trade, migration, communications, political boundaries, ideas, and fashions.

- **Regions** – This includes formal regions (a city, state, country, or other geographical organization as defined by political boundaries), functional regions (defined by a common function or connection, such as a school district), and vernacular regions (informal divisions determined by perceptions or one's mental image, such as the "Far East").

Review Video: Regional Geography
Visit mometrix.com/academy and enter code: 350378

Areas Covered by Geography

Geography is connected to many issues and provides answers to many everyday questions. Some of the areas covered by geography include:

- Geography investigates global climates, landforms, economies, political systems, human cultures, and migration patterns.
- Geography answers questions not only about where something is located, but also why it is there, how it got there, and how it is related to other things around it.
- Geography explains why people move to certain regions (climate, availability of natural resources, arable land, etc.).
- Geography explains world trade routes and modes of transportation.
- Geography identifies where various animals live and where various crops and forests grow.
- Geography identifies and locates populations that follow certain religions.
- Geography provides statistics on population numbers and growth, which aids in economic and infrastructure planning for cities and countries.

Physical and Cultural Geography and Physical and Political Locations

- **Physical geography** is the study of climate, water, and land and their relationships with each other and humans. Physical geography locates and identifies the earth's surface features and explores how humans thrive in various locations according to crop and goods production.
- **Cultural geography** is the study of the influence of the environment on human behaviors as well as the effect of human activities such as farming, building settlements, and grazing livestock on the environment. Cultural geography also identifies and compares the features of different cultures and how they influence interactions with other cultures and the earth.
- **Physical location** refers to the placement of the hemispheres and the continents.
- **Political location** refers to the divisions within continents that designate various countries. These divisions are made with borders, which are set according to boundary lines arrived at by legal agreements.

Both physical and political locations can be precisely determined by geographical surveys and by latitude and longitude.

Spatial Organization

Spatial organization in geography refers to how things or people are grouped in a given space anywhere on earth. Spatial organization applies to the **placement of settlements**, whether hamlets, towns, or cities. These settlements are located to make the distribution of goods and services convenient. For example, in farm communities, people come to town to get groceries, to attend church and school, and to access medical services. It is more practical to provide these things to groups than to individuals. These settlements, historically, have been built close to water sources and agricultural areas. Lands that are topographically difficult, have few resources, or experience extreme temperatures do not have as many people as temperate zones and flat plains, where it is easier to live. Within settlements, a town or city will be organized into commercial and residential neighborhoods, with hospitals, fire stations, and shopping centers centrally located. All of these organizational considerations are spatial in nature.

Important Terms Related to Maps

The most important terms used when describing items on a map or globe are:

- **Latitude and longitude** – Latitude and longitude are the imaginary lines (horizontal and vertical, respectively) that divide the globe into a grid. Both are measured using the 360 degrees of a circle.
- **Coordinates** – These are the latitude and longitude measures for a place.
- **Absolute location** – This is the exact spot where coordinates meet. The grid system allows the location of every place on the planet to be identified.
- **Equator** – This is the line at 0° latitude that divides the earth into two equal halves called hemispheres.
- **Parallels** – This is another name for lines of latitude because they circle the earth in parallel lines that never meet.
- **Meridians** – This is another name for lines of longitude. The Prime Meridian is located at 0° longitude, and is the starting point for measuring distance (both east and west) around the globe. Meridians circle the earth and connect at the Poles.

Review Video: Elements of a Map
Visit mometrix.com/academy and enter code: 437727

Types of Maps

- A **physical map** is one that shows natural features such as mountains, rivers, lakes, deserts, and plains. Color is used to designate the different features.
- A **topographic map** is a type of physical map that shows the relief and configuration of a landscape, such as hills, valleys, fields, forest, roads, and settlements. It includes natural and human-made features.
- A **topological map** is one on which lines are stretched or straightened for the sake of clarity, but retain their essential geometric relationship. This type of map is used, for example, to show the routes of a subway system.
- A **political map** uses lines for state, county, and country boundaries; points or dots for cities and towns; and various other symbols for features such as airports and roads.

Map Styles

There are three basic styles of maps:

- **Base maps** – Created from aerial and field surveys, base maps serve as the starting point for topographic and thematic maps.
- **Topographic maps** – These show the natural and human-made surface features of the earth, including mountain elevations, river courses, roads, names of lakes and towns, and county and state lines.
- **Thematic maps** – These use a base or topographic map as the foundation for showing data based on a theme, such as population density, wildlife distribution, hill-slope stability, economic trends, etc.

Scale is the size of a map expressed as a ratio of the actual size of the land (for example, 1 inch on a map represents 1 mile on land). In other words, it is the proportion between a distance on the map and its corresponding distance on earth. The scale determines the level of detail on a map. **Small-scale maps** depict larger areas, but include fewer details. **Large-scale maps** depict smaller areas, but include more details.

Time Zones

Time is linked to **longitude** in that a complete rotation of the Earth, or 360° of longitude, occurs every 24 hours. Each hour of time is therefore equivalent to 15° of longitude, or 4 minutes for each 1° turn. By the agreement of 27 nations at the 1884 International Meridian Conference, the time zone system consists of **24 time zones** corresponding to the 24 hours in a day. Although high noon technically occurs when the sun is directly above a meridian, calculating time that way would result in 360 different times for the 360 meridians.

Using the 24-hour system, the time is the same for all locations in a 15° zone. The 1884 conference established the meridian passing through Greenwich, England, as the zero point, or **prime meridian**. The halfway point is found at the 180th meridian, a half day from Greenwich. It is called the **International Date Line**, and serves as the place where each day begins and ends on earth.

CARTOGRAPHY

Cartography is the art and science of **mapmaking**. Maps of local areas were drawn by the Egyptians as early as 1300 BC, and the Greeks began making maps of the known world in the 6th century BC. Cartography eventually grew into the field of geography. The first step in modern mapmaking is a **survey**. This involves designating a few key sites of known elevation as benchmarks to allow for measurement of other sites. **Aerial photography** is then used to chart the area by taking photos in sequence. Overlapping photos show the same area from different positions along the flight line. When paired and examined through a stereoscope, the cartographer gets a three-dimensional view that can be made into a **topographical map**. In addition, a field survey (on the ground) is made to determine municipal borders and place names. The second step is to compile the information and **computer-draft** a map based on the collected data. The map is then reproduced or printed.

GLOBE AND MAP PROJECTIONS

A **globe** is the only accurate representation of the earth's size, shape, distance, and direction since it, like the earth, is **spherical**. The flat surface of a map distorts these elements. To counter this problem, mapmakers use a variety of "**map projections**," a system for representing the earth's curvatures on a flat surface through the use of a grid that corresponds to lines of latitude and longitude. Some distortions are still inevitable, though, so mapmakers make choices based on the map scale, the size of the area to be mapped, and what they want the map to show. Some projections can represent a true shape or area, while others may be based on the equator and therefore become less accurate as they near the poles. In summary, all maps have some distortion in terms of the shape or size of features of the spherical earth.

TYPES OF MAP PROJECTIONS

There are three main types of map projections:

- **Conical** – This type of projection superimposes a cone over the sphere of the earth, with two reference parallels secant to the globe and intersecting it. There is no distortion along the standard parallels, but distortion increases further from the chosen parallels. A Bonne projection is an example of a conical projection, in which the areas are accurately represented but the meridians are not on a true scale.
- **Cylindrical** – This is any projection in which meridians are mapped using equally spaced vertical lines and circles of latitude (parallels) are mapped using horizontal lines. A Mercator's projection is a modified cylindrical projection that is helpful to navigators because it allows them to maintain a constant compass direction between two points. However, it exaggerates areas in high latitudes.
- **Azimuthal** – This is a stereographic projection onto a plane centered so that a straight line from the center to any other point represents the shortest distance. This distance can be measured to scale.

Review Video: Map Projections
Visit mometrix.com/academy and enter code: 327303

HEMISPHERES AND PARALLELS ON THE WORLD MAP

The definitions for these terms are as follows:

- **Northern Hemisphere** – This is the area above, or north, of the equator.
- **Southern Hemisphere** – This is the area below, or south, of the equator.
- **Western Hemisphere** – This is the area between the North and South Poles. It extends west from the Prime Meridian to the International Date Line.

- **Eastern Hemisphere** – This is the area between the North and South Poles. It extends east from the Prime Meridian to the International Date Line.
- **North and South Poles** – Latitude is measured in terms of the number of degrees north and south from the equator. The North Pole is located at 90°N latitude, while the South Pole is located at 90°S latitude.
- **Tropic of Cancer** – This is the parallel, or latitude, 23½° north of the equator.
- **Tropic of Capricorn** – This is the parallel, or latitude, 23½° south of the equator. The region between these two parallels is the tropics. The subtropics is the area located between 23½° and 40° north and south of the equator.
- **Arctic Circle** – This is the parallel, or latitude, 66½° north of the equator.
- **Antarctic Circle** – This is the parallel, or latitude, 66½° south of the equator.

Review Video: Geographical Features
Visit mometrix.com/academy and enter code: 773539

GPS

Global Positioning System (GPS) is a system of satellites that orbit the Earth and communicate with mobile devices to pinpoint the mobile device's position. This is accomplished by determining the distance between the mobile device and at least three satellites. A mobile device might calculate a distance of 400 miles between it and the first satellite. The possible locations that are 400 miles from the first satellite and the mobile device will fall along a circle. The possible locations on Earth relative to the other two satellites will fall somewhere along different circles. The point on Earth at which these three circles intersect is the location of the mobile device. The process of determining position based on distance measurements from three satellites is called **trilateration**.

Physical and Cultural Features of Geographic Locations and Countries

Physical Features

- **Vegetation zones, or biomes** – Forests, grasslands, deserts, and tundra are the four main types of vegetation zones.
- **Climate zones** – Tropical, dry, temperate, continental, and polar are the five different types of climate zones. Climate is the long-term average weather conditions of a place.

Cultural Features

- **Population density** – This is the number of people living in each square mile or kilometer of a place. It is calculated by dividing population by area.
- **Religion** – This is the identification of the dominant religions of a place, whether Christianity, Hinduism, Judaism, Buddhism, Islam, Shinto, Taoism, or Confucianism. All of these originated in Asia.
- **Languages** – This is the identification of the dominant or official language of a place. There are 12 major language families. The Indo-European family (which includes English, Russian, German, French, and Spanish) is spoken over the widest geographic area, but Mandarin Chinese is spoken by the most people.

Geomorphology

The study of landforms is call **geomorphology** or physiography, a science that considers the relationships between *geological structures* and *surface landscape features*. It is also concerned with the processes that change these features, such as erosion, deposition, and plate tectonics. Biological factors can also affect landforms. Examples are when corals build a coral reef or when plants contribute to the development of a salt marsh or a sand dune. Rivers, coastlines, rock types, slope formation, ice, erosion, and weathering are all part of geomorphology. A **landform** is a landscape feature or geomorphological unit. These include hills, plateaus, mountains, deserts, deltas, canyons, mesas, marshes, swamps, and valleys. These units are categorized according to elevation, slope, orientation, stratification, rock exposure, and soil type. Landform elements include pits, peaks, channels, ridges, passes, pools, and plains. The highest order landforms are continents and oceans. Elementary landforms such as segments, facets, and relief units are the smallest homogenous divisions of a land surface at a given scale or resolution.

Oceans, Seas, Lakes, Rivers, and Canals

- **Oceans** are the largest bodies of water on earth and cover nearly 71% of the earth's surface. There are five major oceans: Atlantic, Pacific (largest and deepest), Indian, Arctic, and Southern (surrounds Antarctica).
- **Seas** are smaller than oceans and are somewhat surrounded by land like a lake, but lakes are fresh water and seas are salt water. Seas include the Mediterranean, Baltic, Caspian, Caribbean, and Coral.
- **Lakes** are bodies of water in a depression on the earth's surface. Examples of lakes are the Great Lakes and Lake Victoria.
- **Rivers** are a channeled flow of water that start out as a spring or stream formed by runoff from rain or snow. Rivers flow from higher to lower ground, and usually empty into a sea or ocean. Great rivers of the world include the Amazon, Nile, Rhine, Mississippi, Ganges, Mekong, and Yangtze.
- **Canals** are artificial waterways constructed by humans to connect two larger water bodies. Examples of canals are the Panama and the Suez.

Mountains, Hills, Foothills, Valleys, Plateaus, and Mesas

The definitions for these geographical features are as follows:

- **Mountains** are elevated landforms that rise fairly steeply from the earth's surface to a summit of at least 1,000-2,000 feet (definitions vary) above sea level.
- **Hills** are elevated landforms that rise 500-2,000 feet above sea level.
- **Foothills** are a low series of hills found between a plain and a mountain range.
- **Valleys** are a long depression located between hills or mountains. They are usually products of river erosion. Valleys can vary in terms of width and depth, ranging from a few feet to thousands of feet.
- **Plateaus** are elevated landforms that are fairly flat on top. They may be as high as 10,000 feet above sea level and are usually next to mountains.
- **Mesas** are flat areas of upland. Their name is derived from the Spanish word for table. They are smaller than plateaus and often found in arid or semi-arid areas.

Formation of Mountains

Mountains are formed by the movement of geologic plates, which are rigid slabs of rocks beneath the earth's crust that float on a layer of partially molten rock in the earth's upper mantle. As the plates collide, they push up the crust to form mountains. This process is called **orogeny**. There are three basic forms of orogeny:

- If the collision of continental plates causes the crust to buckle and fold, a chain of **folded mountains**, such as the Appalachians, the Alps, or the Himalayas, is formed.
- If the collision of the plates causes a denser oceanic plate to go under a continental plate, a process called **subduction**; strong horizontal forces lift and fold the margin of the continent. A mountain range like the Andes is the result.
- If an oceanic plate is driven under another oceanic plate, **volcanic mountains** such as those in Japan and the Philippines are formed.

Coral Reefs

Coral reefs are formed from millions of tiny, tube-shaped **polyps**, an animal life form encased in tough limestone skeletons. Once anchored to a rocky surface, polyps eat plankton and miniscule shellfish caught with poisonous tentacles near their mouth. Polyps use calcium carbonate absorbed from chemicals given off by algae to harden their body armor and cement themselves together in fantastic shapes of many colors. Polyps reproduce through eggs and larvae, but the reef grows by branching out shoots of polyps. There are three types of coral reefs:

- **Fringing reefs** – These surround, or "fringe," an island.
- **Barrier reefs** – Over the centuries, a fringe reef grows so large that the island sinks down from the weight, and the reef becomes a barrier around the island. Water trapped between the island and the reef is called a lagoon.
- **Atolls** – Eventually, the sinking island goes under, leaving the coral reef around the lagoon.

Plains, Deserts, Deltas, and Basins

- **Plains** are extensive areas of low-lying, flat, or gently undulating land, and are usually lower than the landforms around them. Plains near the seacoast are called lowlands.
- **Deserts** are large, dry areas that receive less than 10 inches of rain per year. They are almost barren, containing only a few patches of vegetation.
- **Deltas** are accumulations of silt deposited at river mouths into the seabed. They are eventually converted into very fertile, stable ground by vegetation, becoming important crop-growing areas. Examples include the deltas of the Nile, Ganges, and Mississippi River.
- **Basins** come in various types. They may be low areas that catch water from rivers; large hollows that dip to a central point and are surrounded by higher ground, as in the Donets and Kuznetsk basins in Russia; or areas of inland drainage in a desert when the water can't reach the sea and flows into lakes or evaporates in salt flats as a result. An example is the Great Salt Lake in Utah.

Marshes and Swamps and Tundra and Taiga

Marshes and swamps are both **wet lowlands**. The water can be fresh, brackish, or saline. Both host important ecological systems with unique wildlife. There are, however, some major differences. **Marshes** have no trees and are always wet because of frequent floods and poor drainage that leaves shallow water. Plants are mostly grasses, rushes, reeds, typhas, sedges, and herbs. **Swamps** have trees and dry periods. The water is very slow-moving, and is usually associated with adjacent rivers or lakes.

Both taiga and tundra regions have many plants and animals, but they have few humans or crops because of their harsh climates. **Taiga** has colder winters and hotter summers than tundra because of its distance from the Arctic Ocean. Taiga is the world's largest forest region, located just south of the tundra line. It contains huge mineral resources and fur-bearing animals. **Tundra** is a Russian word describing marshy plain in an area that has a very cold climate but receives little snow. The ground is usually frozen, but is quite spongy when it is not.

Humid Continental, Prairie, Subtropical, and Marine Climates

- A **humid continental climate** is one that has four seasons, including a cold winter and a hot summer, and sufficient rainfall for raising crops. Such climates can be found in the United States, Canada, and Russia. The best farmlands and mining areas are found in these countries.
- **Prairie climates**, or steppe regions, are found in the interiors of Asia and North America where there are dry flatlands (prairies that receive 10-20 inches of rain per year). These dry flatlands can be grasslands or deserts.

- **Subtropical climates** are very humid areas in the tropical areas of Japan, China, Australia, Africa, South America, and the United States. The moisture, carried by winds traveling over warm ocean currents, produces long summers and mild winters. It is possible to produce a continuous cycle of a variety of crops.
- A **marine climate** is one near or surrounded by water. Warm ocean winds bring moisture, mild temperatures year-round, and plentiful rain. These climates are found in Western Europe and parts of the United States, Canada, Chile, New Zealand, and Australia.

Review Video: Climates
Visit mometrix.com/academy and enter code: 991320

Adaptation to Environmental Conditions

The environment influences the way people live. People **adapt** to **environmental conditions** in ways as simple as putting on warm clothing in a cold environment; finding means to cool their surroundings in an environment with high temperatures; building shelters from wind, rain, and temperature variations; and digging water wells if surface water is unavailable. More complex adaptations result from the physical diversity of the earth in terms of soil, climate, vegetation, and topography. Humans take advantage of opportunities and avoid or minimize limitations. Examples of environmental limitations are that rocky soils offer few opportunities for agriculture and rough terrain limits accessibility. Sometimes, **technology** allows humans to live in areas that were once uninhabitable or undesirable. For example, air conditioning allows people to live comfortably in hot climates; modern heating systems permit habitation in areas with extremely low temperatures, as is the case with research facilities in Antarctica; and airplanes have brought people to previously inaccessible places to establish settlements or industries.

Natural Resources, Renewable Resources, Nonrenewable Resources, and Commodities

Natural resources are things provided by nature that have commercial value to humans, such as minerals, energy, timber, fish, wildlife, and the landscape. **Renewable resources** are those that can be replenished, such as wind, solar radiation, tides, and water (with proper conservation and clean-up). Soil is renewable with proper conservation and management techniques, and timber can be replenished with replanting. Living resources such as fish and wildlife can replenish themselves if they are not over-harvested. **Nonrenewable resources** are those that cannot be replenished. These include fossil fuels such as oil and coal and metal ores. These cannot be replaced or reused once they have been burned, although some of their products can be recycled. **Commodities** are natural resources that have to be extracted and purified rather than created, such as mineral ores.

Review Video: Renewable vs. Nonrenewable Resources
Visit mometrix.com/academy and enter code: 840194

Harmful or Potentially Harmful Interaction with Environment

Wherever humans have gone on the earth, they have made **changes** to their surroundings. Many are harmful or potentially harmful, depending on the extent of the alterations. Some of the changes and activities that can harm the **environment** include:

- Cutting into mountains by machine or blasting to build roads or construction sites
- Cutting down trees and clearing natural growth
- Building houses and cities
- Using grassland to graze herds
- Polluting water sources
- Polluting the ground with chemical and oil waste
- Wearing out fertile land and losing topsoil

- Placing communication lines cross country using poles and wires or underground cable
- Placing railway lines or paved roads cross country
- Building gas and oil pipelines cross country
- Draining wetlands
- Damming up or re-routing waterways
- Spraying fertilizers, pesticides, and defoliants
- Hunting animals to extinction or near extinction

CARRYING CAPACITY AND NATURAL HAZARDS

Carrying capacity is the maximum, sustained level of use of an environment can incur without sustaining significant environmental deterioration that would eventually lead to environmental destruction. Environments vary in terms of their carrying capacity, a concept humans need to learn to measure and respect before harm is done. Proper **assessment of environmental conditions** enables responsible decision making with respect to how much and in what ways the resources of a particular environment should be consumed. **Energy and water conservation** as well as recycling can extend an area's carrying capacity. In addition to carrying capacity limitations, the physical environment can also have occasional extremes that are costly to humans. **Natural hazards** such as hurricanes, tornadoes, earthquakes, volcanoes, floods, tsunamis, and some forest fires and insect infestations are processes or events that are not caused by humans, but may have serious consequences for humans and the environment. These events are not preventable, and their precise timing, location, and magnitude are not predictable. However, some precautions can be taken to reduce the damage.

APPLYING GEOGRAPHY TO INTERPRETATION OF THE PAST

Space, environment, and chronology are three different points of view that can be used to study history. Events take place within **geographic contexts**. If the world is flat, then transportation choices are vastly different from those that would be made in a round world, for example. Invasions of Russia from the west have normally failed because of the harsh winter conditions, the vast distances that inhibit steady supply lines, and the number of rivers and marshes to be crossed, among other factors. Any invading or defending force anywhere must make choices based on consideration of space and environmental factors. For instance, lands may be too muddy or passages too narrow for certain equipment. Geography played a role in the building of the Panama Canal because the value of a shorter transportation route had to outweigh the costs of labor, disease, political negotiations, and equipment, not to mention a myriad of other effects from cutting a canal through an isthmus and changing a natural land structure as a result.

APPLYING GEOGRAPHY TO INTERPRETATION OF THE PRESENT AND PLANS FOR THE FUTURE

The decisions that individual people as well as nations make that may **affect the environment** have to be made with an understanding of spatial patterns and concepts, cultural and transportation connections, physical processes and patterns, ecosystems, and the impact, or "footprint," of people on the physical environment. Sample issues that fit into these considerations are recycling programs, loss of agricultural land to further urban expansion, air and water pollution, deforestation, and ease of transportation and communication. In each of these areas, present and future uses have to be balanced against possible harmful effects. For example, wind is a clean and readily available resource for electric power, but the access roads to and noise of wind turbines can make some areas unsuitable for livestock pasture. Voting citizens need to have an understanding of **geographical and environmental connections** to make responsible decisions.

Cultural Studies

CULTURE

A **culture** is a comprehensive style of living that is developed in a society and maintained from generation to generation. Culture is manifested in a group's traditions, rituals, language, social norms, technology, and economic structures. Broadly speaking, culture is everything that is learned by a member of a particular society, though it may include things that an individual learns but which are never made explicit either in the individual's mind or in his or her social interactions. For this reason, many sociologists feel it is difficult to properly study one's own culture; they suggest that only the unclouded eyes of a foreign observer can perceive a society's most fundamental values.

Sociology, Psychology, and Anthropology

There are three branches of cultural studies known as psychology, sociology, and anthropology. Each of these categories deals with some form of studying humans and human behavior. **Anthropology** is the most material of the branches, as it deals with studying past and present ways of life for humans. It is an intersection between history, geography, technology, and art. Anthropology is the broadest of cultural studies and contains overlap with countless other disciplines. **Sociology** deals with social interaction and the cultures of human civilizations. Often, sociologists bring ethical, political, and historical matters into question. Sociology largely derives its viewpoints from principles of human interaction and external matters of life. **Psychology,** on the other hand, focuses mainly on the internal workings of the mind and the mental and biological processes involved in thinking.

Material Culture

A society's **material culture** is the set all of the physical objects that the people of that society have either created or to which they assign cultural meaning. Hence, material culture may include objects like books, jewelry, buildings, and furniture; but it may also include natural areas if those areas are assigned significance by the members of the society. As an example of this latter kind of material culture, a sociologist might point to the Native American society, in which the land itself held immense cultural value. Along with **verbal culture**, material culture makes up the sum total of what sociologists have at their disposal for study.

Nonmaterial Culture

Nonmaterial culture is all of a society's customs, beliefs, political structures, languages, and ways of using material objects. In the United States, for instance, the emphasis placed on religious freedom and individual liberty might be considered an example of nonmaterial culture. The boundary between material and nonmaterial culture is never altogether clear; how, for instance, should one separate the American flag and what it stands for, namely the idea of freedom? **Values** and **norms**, as opposed to the physical things that are used to express values and norms, are what make up a society's nonmaterial culture. Typically, nonmaterial culture is more difficult to change than material culture, and its change is more difficult to observe.

Values

The **values** of a culture are its highest ideals. In the United States, for example, we would say that freedom and equality are two of our most important values. Values are usually very general concepts. They may be complementary, as for example the values of hard work and material success seem to go together. Values are quite fluid, and a major focus of sociology is observing how they change over time. Values may come into conflict with one another, which can create social conflict and disorganization. An example of this is the conflict in mid-twentieth-century America between the values of equal rights and segregation; ultimately, it was clear that only one of these values could remain.

Sanctions

In sociological terms, **sanctions** are any rewards or consequences given to an individual or group to pursue or renounce a certain course of behavior. Sanctions may be positive, as when a reward is promised for something done properly, or negative, as when a punishment is promised for something done improperly. Although the most common use of the word refers to *international economic pressures* (as in, for instance, the economic restrictions placed on Iraq during the 1990s), all societies place sanctions on their members in order to elicit approved behavior. People who uphold the values and norms of the society are rewarded with preferential treatment from their fellows, while those who transgress can be punished socially, economically, or legally.

Norms

Norms are specific rules regulating behavior in a culture. Norms may or may not be directly codified in the law of a society, but they are intended to encourage behavior that promotes the society's values. Taking again the example of the United States, one might say that treating men and women equally is a social norm, insofar as equality between the sexes is a value aspired to by our culture. Norms, then, depend on values for their justification, and values depend on norms for their enactment. Norms may vary greatly from society to society, such that the same behavior may be approved or condemned depending on where it is performed. Most of the time, norms are so customary for the members of a society that they are performed automatically.

Formal Norms and Informal Norms

Norms may be considered formal or informal, depending on whether they are codified in the laws of the society in which they apply. **Formal norms** are written law; examples of formal norms include the prohibition of murder, the forced payment of taxes, and the sanctity of marriage. **Informal norms**, on the other hand, are unwritten codes of conduct. Examples of informal norms might include the prohibition of spitting in public or the encouragement of deference to women. Typically, a society formalizes the norms which are most important, and for which violators should be punished. Formal norms tend to be much more consistent among different societies than informal norms.

Social Markers, Laws, and Folkways

A **social marker** is any part of behavior that indicates the identity, character, or way of understanding of a particular group of people. Social markers can be laws, folkways, traditions, or other patterns of behavior. **Laws** are simply social norms that have been made explicit and are enforced by the government. There are plenty of norms, though, that are encoded in law but are also internalized-- the prohibition of murder, for instance. **Folkways** are social norms that have become habitual or traditional in a society. In the United States, we are accustomed to tipping a waiter or waitress for their service: that this is so ingrained in our daily life makes it an American folkway.

Cultural Pluralism and Subculture

Cultural pluralism exists when multiple distinct cultures exist within the same society after a process of accommodation. These self-contained cultures should not be confused with **subcultures**, which are smaller cultures within a large culture. Subcultures usually have a set of norms and values that are different from those held by the larger society of which they are a member. In the United States, we might consider punk rockers or hippies as subcultures, because they have different values than Americans on the whole, but do not really have a self-sustaining or separate society of their own.

Countercultures

A **counterculture** is any group whose values and norms challenge and seek to alter the values and norms of the dominant culture in their society. Although the term when used today evokes memories of the 1960s youth rebellion in Western Europe and the United States, earlier countercultural movements include the Bohemians in nineteenth century France, or even the early Christians. Countercultures typically appear at a time when traditional norms and values are felt to no longer be appropriate or helpful in making sense of the world. As in the case of a social movement, a counterculture tends to have more and stronger adherents at the beginning of its life; once the counterculture's norms have been partially co-opted by the larger society, countercultures tend to lose steam.

Dominant Culture and Ethnocentrism

In any society, the **dominant culture** is the group whose norms, values, and behavior patterns are most widespread and influential on the rest of the society. Many nations, including the United States, have laws to restrain the dominant culture from extinguishing minority cultures. **Ethnocentrism** describes the tendency to view one's own cultural patterns as superior and to judge all others only as they relate to one's own. This philosophy has been at the root of some of humanity's worst atrocities, including the Holocaust, which was perpetrated by Germans who believed they must maintain the purity of their race, and colonial conquests, in which Western nations brutally imposed their customs on various indigenous peoples.

Chapter Quiz

Ready to see how well you retained what you just read? Scan the QR code to go directly to the chapter quiz interface for this study guide. If you're using a computer, simply visit the bonus page at **mometrix.com/bonus948/ged** and click the Chapter Quizzes link.

Science

Transform passive reading into active learning! After immersing yourself in this chapter, put your comprehension to the test by taking a quiz. The insights you gained will stay with you longer this way. Scan the QR code to go directly to the chapter quiz interface for this study guide. If you're using a computer, simply visit the bonus page at **mometrix.com/bonus948/ged** and click the Chapter Quizzes link.

Reading for Meaning in Science

Claims and Evidence in Science

When you carry out a scientific investigation and draw conclusions based on the results, the investigation itself is evidence of the validity of your finding. However, it may not be enough evidence by itself to be fully convincing. There are ways to find more evidence to support your finding. Have other scientists done similar investigations and obtained similar results? You can search through past publications to check (scientists often refer to the body of previously published scientific papers as the literature). Is there some theoretical basis that could explain why you got the results you did? If not, that doesn't necessarily mean you're wrong—maybe you discovered something completely new—but it does set a higher bar for the quality of the evidence that must be gathered.

One of the most important pieces of evidence to support a finding is if you and others can replicate your results. This is why scientific papers include not only the results of a study, but also a detailed explanation of how the study was carried out—so that other scientists can judge its validity and can in principle try to carry out the experiment for themselves.

Scientific Papers

Scientific papers are a specialized form of writing that must be approached differently from other literature. You can't read a scientific paper the way you can a novel or an article in the newspaper and expect to get much out of it. Generally, a scientific paper is not just read once from beginning to end: It requires a different approach.

A scientific paper starts with an **abstract**—a summary of the paper briefly explaining its purpose, its main results, and its conclusion. It's worth reading the abstract first because it gives you the big idea of what the paper is about. After that, it might be useful to *skim* the entire paper, not reading it closely but just looking it over for the main ideas. You may want to pay particular attention to graphs and other visuals that portray the data and the relationships between variables in a comprehensible way. After skimming the paper, you can go back and read in more detail the parts that seem especially relevant to what you're looking for or that you didn't understand from your skimming.

Conflicting Sources

At times, you may run into science sources that may seem to give contradictory information. The most obvious explanation is that one of these sources is incorrect. Do both sources explain the basis for their conclusions, and are the conclusions warranted from their results? Has the information in either of the sources been tested and validated by the greater scientific community? (If one source disagrees with the vast majority of other scientific sources, it could be that the writers of that source are trying to push an idiosyncratic, unsupported point of view.) If one of the sources is a secondary source, check the primary source that it is based on—is it being accurately represented?

However, it could also be that both sources are valid, but they're not as contradictory as they seem. Are they really discussing the same circumstances, or are they discussing phenomena under different conditions? If one source discusses the behavior of a chemical at room temperature and one discusses very different behavior of the same chemical at very cold temperatures, that's not necessarily a contradiction—the chemical may behave differently at different temperatures.

Primary and Secondary Sources

In the sciences and in social science, there is a distinction between primary and secondary sources. A **primary source** is a source that gives information based on direct observation or on the writer's own ideas. In science, the main primary sources are scientific papers. In social science, the primary sources may include journals, letters, and newspaper articles from the time period being studied. A **secondary source** is a source that draws from primary sources, summarizing or restating the information. Articles in popular magazines and on websites are secondary sources as are textbooks and encyclopedias. (Because textbooks and encyclopedias may draw from other secondary sources, they are sometimes considered to be at yet another level, **tertiary sources**, but not everyone makes that distinction.)

Review Video: Primary and Secondary Sources
Visit mometrix.com/academy and enter code: 383328

Because primary sources are where the information ultimately comes from, they are in a sense more reliable; they represent the original source of the information without passing through further layers of bias, rewording, and possible misrepresentation. However, primary sources can be difficult to acquire, and even if you can acquire them, they can be difficult to understand and properly interpret, so secondary (and even tertiary) sources remain useful to comprehend the information.

Science Vocabulary, Terms, and Phrases

Scientific Writing

Scientific writing is different from popular writing in many ways, and to someone not used to reading scientific writing, it may be difficult to understand. One hurdle is the vocabulary: science writing often uses specialist words not used in everyday life, or they are used with different meaning. If there's a word in the passage that you don't understand, skim through the passage to see if it's defined elsewhere in the text. If it's not, it's often possible to guess the meaning from the context.

Even if you understand all the important words in a passage, the dense and technical writing may still be difficult to understand. You can approach a passage of scientific writing similarly to a whole scientific paper. First, skim the passage, not trying yet to understand every detail, but just to grasp the main ideas. Pay particular attention to any figures or diagrams, which may provide crucial information or explanations. Then you can go back and look for specific details you're interested in.

Explaining Scientific Information

When relaying scientific information, it's important to be able to convey that information clearly. In the professional scientific world, information is conveyed primarily through research papers published in scientific journals. These papers have a set formula: first, an **abstract** that summarizes the whole paper; next, an **introduction** that lays out the goals of the study the paper describes and discusses prior work on the subject; then a description of the **methods** used in the study; after that, a relation of the **results** that were obtained; and, finally, a **discussion** of those results and any conclusions drawn from them.

Even outside of the context of formal scientific papers, though, there are still important factors in scientific communication. It's important to choose your words and phrasing carefully to avoid ambiguity; make sure you know what scientific terms mean before you use them. Clarity and explicitness are more important in science communication than brevity or style. Graphs and diagrams are often helpful to convey information.

Variables and Constants in Science

It's often useful in scientific writing to use symbols to represent certain **variables**—i.e., quantities that may change during an investigation or between an investigation—and **constants**—values that are expected to remain the same. As long as these variables are clearly defined, they can make text and formulas much clearer and easier to read than if the quantities had to be spelled out and described every time they were referred to.

Variables and constants are usually symbolized by letters in the Latin or Greek alphabets. Some symbols are standard and widely used: c is an accepted symbol for the speed of light (a constant), and λ, the Greek letter lambda, is often used to represent wavelength (a variable). Other symbols may be defined as the author decides in particular papers. In any case, it is important that any new or nonstandard symbols be explicitly defined in the paper or other passage where they appear. When reading a scientific text, make sure to look for the definitions of any symbols in it.

Scientific Terminology

Like any field of study, science has specialized terminology—i.e., words and phrases that have a particular meaning in that field. This is true not just of science in general, but of particular subfields; chemistry has special terms particular to it, for example, and organic chemistry has further terminology, and so do still more specific fields within organic chemistry.

This specialized terminology aids in comprehension for readers familiar with the field. These scientific terms can concisely but precisely convey concepts that would be difficult or impractically lengthy to express in common language, and they may have unambiguous meanings. However, for nonspecialists who have not encountered these terms before, they can be an obstacle for comprehension; this is one of the factors that makes scientific papers hard for nonscientists to understand. If you run across a scientific term that you don't understand, you can look it up, preferably in a glossary or textbook dedicated to the subject rather than a general dictionary. Sometimes you may be able to determine the gist of the term's meaning from the context, but this may be unreliable or miss important nuances in the meaning that may not be obvious.

There are many words that have specialized meanings in science that may not match their meanings in other contexts. When you're reading a scientific paper, it's important to keep those specialized meanings in mind. Following are just a few of many examples.

Theory: In everyday life, the word "theory" is often used to refer to a guess or a supposition, but in science that's a *hypothesis*—a *theory* is a detailed explanatory framework.

Medium: In biology or chemistry, a *medium* is a substrate in which cell cultures are grown. In physics, it refers to the substance through which a sound wave or other signal travels.

Plant: Often people use the word "plant" to refer to nonmobile organisms including fungi and algae. Biologically, however, fungi and most algae are *not* plants; they belong to different kingdoms (another word with a distinct scientific meaning).

Radiation: To a scientist, radiation is anything that radiates—travels outward from a source. Nuclear radiation is one kind of radiation, but sound and light are also forms of radiation.

Chemical: Though people often think of chemicals as being artificial and potentially harmful, scientifically speaking anything made up of atoms is a chemical. Air and water are chemicals.

Designing and Interpreting Science Experiments

Science Investigations

To design a good scientific investigation, it's useful to define specifically what kinds of effects the investigator is looking for and how they will be measured. Quantitative measurements are more reliable than poorly defined, subjective impressions. For example, if investigating the effect of a chemical on plant growth, deciding that we'll just add the chemical to the plants and see what happens is vague and unhelpful; the height of the plants is a measurable value, and it is a more useful observable quantity.

Generally, in an effective investigation, only one variable is changed at a time. In the plant growth example, all the plants should be kept at the same temperature, given the same amount of water, etc.—the only difference should be the concentration of the chemical. When possible, an experiment should be **controlled**: There should be other samples (called **controls**) that are *not* tampered with, to make sure that the observed effect really is due to the factor being changed. This means that our example investigation should include some plants that have *not* been treated with the chemical.

A good scientific investigation also takes measures to account for and minimize random and systematic error.

Independent and Dependent Variables

In a scientific experiment, generally the investigator is going to change some property of a system and determine what effect this change has on a different property. The property that is changed directly by the experimenter is the **independent variable**; the property having the change that the experimenter is observing is called the **dependent variable**. For instance, if the experimenter wants to test the response time of some insect at different temperatures, the independent variable is the temperature and the dependent variable is the insect's response time.

Review Video: Identifying Independent and Dependent Variables
Visit mometrix.com/academy and enter code: 627181

In some investigations, the investigator may not change anything directly but may still want to observe how some property changes based on another property. In this case, there is still an independent variable and a dependent variable because one variable still depends on the other. Suppose someone wants to investigate how the acidity of a lake changes over time. The investigator is changing neither the acidity of the lake nor the time, but the acidity is the dependent variable and the time is the independent variable because it makes more sense to say that the acidity of the lake depends on the time rather than that the time depends on the acidity of the lake.

Developing a Good Hypothesis for a Scientific Investigation

In a scientific investigation, the **hypothesis** is a prediction of what the investigator expects to happen. The experiment may either **confirm** the hypothesis—i.e., show it to be true—or **falsify** the hypothesis—i.e., show it to be false. Even though it may not turn out to be correct, it's still important to have a hypothesis, because it helps guide the investigation and give the investigator something specific to look for.

A hypothesis should have some reasoning behind it; there should be some rationale why the investigator expects it to happen. It may be an educated guess, but it shouldn't be just a wild guess made at random with no basis whatsoever.

A good hypothesis should be specific and observable. Suppose that an investigator wants to test the effect of a chemical on the growth of a bacterial culture. "The chemical will affect the growth of the bacteria" is not a good hypothesis; it's so vague that it says almost nothing. "The chemical will slow the growth of the bacteria" is a little better, but it is still not very specific. "The bacterial cultures treated with the chemical will grow to only half the normal size" is a good hypothesis because it is specific and measurable.

Minimizing Error and Bias

Random error, also called statistical error, is one of the two main types of error that arise in a scientific investigation. It gets its name from the fact that it is not consistent but may randomly cause the measured value to be either higher or lower than the actual value.

Random error comes about due to unavoidable variability in measurements. For instance, if you're measuring the diameter of a wire with a micrometer (an instrument for measuring very small distances), you may not get exactly the same measurement each time—perhaps because it's hard to tell when the micrometer is firmly in contact with the wire but not so firmly that you're compressing it, or because the wire isn't perfectly round. If your measurements vary from 0.12 mm to 0.14 mm, we may write that as 0.13 mm $\pm$ 0.01 mm.

Random error can be minimized by taking many measurements and using the average value. Because random error can make the measurement either larger or smaller than the actual value, on average, for many measurements, it tends to cancel out. Although the random error can't be completely eliminated, the more measurements you take, the smaller it tends to become.

Systematic error is the other main type of error that arises in a scientific investigation. Unlike the first main type of error, random error, systematic error has a consistent effect on all measurements, making all the measurements off in the same direction and by about the same amount.

Systematic error comes about due to often-subtle defects in the measuring instrument or measurement process. For example, suppose you want to measure the amount of liquid in a cup, and you do so by pouring the liquid into a graduated cylinder. It may be, however, that each time you pour the liquid into the cylinder, a few drops are left behind in the cup. All your measurements are then lower than they should be by the volume of those drops.

There is no universal way to avoid systematic error, but it can often be accounted for by careful consideration of the experimental procedure and calibration of measuring instruments. It may also help to try to measure quantities by two or more different methods; if different methods of measuring the same quantity give consistently different results, then at least one of those methods probably has some systematic error.

A scientific investigation is said to have **experimental bias**—or simply to be **biased**—if researchers or experimental subjects influence the recorded observations toward the results they want or expect. This doesn't necessarily mean that they are deliberately and dishonestly fudging the values. Bias is frequently unconscious; the investigators may not be aware that they are letting their preconceptions influence their observations.

Experimental bias is especially likely in investigations with subjective observations. In a medical trial to test whether a drug can alleviate some symptoms, experimental subjects who expect the drug to help them might convince themselves they're feeling better even if the drug actually has no effect. However, even in studies with more objective measurements, investigators have been known to record wrong values due to unconscious bias.

One way to eliminate bias is to make sure, if possible, that the experiment is **blinded**—the investigator doesn't know which of the subjects have been treated and which are untreated controls, so the investigator *can't* change the observations in favor of a particular result. An investigation involving human subjects can be **double-blinded**, so that neither the investigator nor the subjects know which subjects are receiving treatment and which are controls.

Types of Scientific Investigations

In an **experimental investigation**, the investigator changes something about an object or system and observes how that change affects it. For example, if a drug company wishes to know whether a newly developed drug has any side effects, it may arrange for a clinical trial to be carried out in which some of the participants are given the drug and others are given a placebo and the health of the participants is monitored to determine whether those participants who are given the drug experience different symptoms.

Experimental investigations are in many ways the most informative kind of investigation because they can be carefully controlled and directed toward answering specific questions. However, it is not always practical or even possible to carry out an experimental investigation. Astronomers observing distant stars, for example, can't really affect those stars directly, so they cannot carry out an experimental investigation on them. To study how the stars are affected by different factors, they would have to carry out a different kind of investigation, such as a comparative investigation.

In a **descriptive investigation**, the investigator carefully observes an object or system, without necessarily changing it. Descriptive investigations may not include a hypothesis, but they should still include an experimental question. For example, suppose a paleontologist discovers a fossil of a previously unknown animal. The paleontologist is likely to perform a descriptive investigation of the fossil, studying it and trying to draw conclusions from the fossil about what kind of animal it was, what other animals it was related to, what it may have eaten, and other characteristics.

Descriptive investigations are useful for studying little-known phenomena, generating new questions, and laying the groundwork for other investigations later. When limited data sets are available and the scientist cannot directly alter the variables of interest, a descriptive investigation may be the only type of investigation possible. However, it may not be possible to answer specific questions through descriptive investigations, and investigators may be limited in what they can discover.

Comparative investigations involve observations and comparisons of different populations. For example, suppose an investigator wants to study the effects of childhood malnutrition on people's later lives. Obviously, it would not be ethical to select a group of children and intentionally induce malnutrition to carry out an experimental investigation. However, the investigators could locate people who had experienced malnutrition in childhood and study their development and their health as adults, comparing them with those of people who had not experienced such malnutrition and controlling for appropriate variables.

Like descriptive investigations, comparative investigations can be carried out on phenomena that the investigator cannot manipulate directly, and, like experimental investigations, they can include dependent and independent variables and can be used to study specific questions. However, the fact that the investigator is not setting the variables directly may make it difficult to find controls or hold other variables constant.

Using Evidence to Draw Conclusions or Make Predictions

Drawing conclusions from collected data is a central step in scientific investigations, but it's important not to reach too far and draw conclusions that aren't warranted by the data. When reading over the conclusions of an investigation, it's useful to check to make sure there wasn't an error.

This isn't just a matter of verifying that the data show what the conclusion claims—that if the conclusion is that a chemical helps plant growth, for instance, the data don't really show the plants treated with the chemical doing worse. It's possible that such a simple mistake was made, of course, but subtler issues are more likely. Did the investigator take care to eliminate obvious sources of error and bias? If applicable, was the experiment blinded or double-blinded? Reliable conclusions cannot be drawn from biased data.

If the data seem to show a relationship between two variables, is this relationship really statistically significant, or is it likely to be just an artifact of random error? Did the investigator take into account *all* of the data collected, or did the investigator cherry-pick data that led to the desired conclusion, while ignoring other data that might contradict this conclusion?

Statistical Significance

An experimental finding is said to be **statistically significant** if it is significant enough that it is unlikely to be just the result of random error. For example, suppose you wanted to know how temperature affected the rate of a certain chemical change. You timed the change 10 times at each of two different temperatures and took the average time at each temperature, and found that the average was higher at the cold temperature—the change took longer to occur at cold temperatures. Or did it? If the average time was 30 seconds at the high temperature and 90 seconds at the low temperature, then yes; that's a dramatic difference, and it is unlikely to be the result of random error. But if the average time was 30.2 seconds at the high temperature and 30.3

seconds at the low temperature, you can't draw a reliable conclusion; that tiny difference could easily be due to random error in the measurements.

Conclusions from a Graph of Scientific Data

A graph is a useful tool for analyzing data, finding relationships, and drawing conclusions. Sometimes a relationship that is not obvious from looking at the numerical data may become much clearer from looking at a graph. This may be as simple as noticing that one variable tends to increase or decrease as another variable increases—the graph tends to generally slope upward or downward. But it's possible to be more precise. Based on the shape of the graph—whether the data points seem to lie close to a line, to a parabola, or to some other particular kind of curve—it may be possible to infer whether the relationship between the variables is linear, quadratic, etc.

If the relationship is linear, we can draw quantitative conclusions by using a **linear fit**, or a best-fit line. This involves drawing a straight line through the data that come closest to the data points, even if it doesn't exactly pass through all of them. (There are more precise mathematical methods of finding a best-fit line, but drawing it by eye can be a useful approximation.) The equation of this line gives a mathematical formula for the relationship between the variables.

Errors in Conclusions

Although it's important to be able to analyze the results of an investigation and draw conclusions from it, there are a number of possible errors that must be avoided. Some of them have to do with the investigation itself; if the investigation was biased or had systematic errors that are not being taken into account, then no reliable conclusions can be drawn. But even if the investigation was carried out properly, it's easy to leap to unsupported conclusions. It's important to look out for hidden assumptions: Are your conclusions predicated on an assumption that was not tested by the experiment? (One special case of this is assuming that because two variables are correlated, one must have caused the other.) It's also easy to overgeneralize: If your investigation covered a specific case or category, it's not necessarily the case that your results hold more broadly (for example, if you did an investigation using mice, you can't necessarily conclude that your results hold for all mammals). And it's often tempting to introduce new ideas in the conclusion, but that isn't the place for them; you should draw conclusions only based on the investigation that you performed.

Empirical and Theoretical Results

Empirical and theoretical describe two different sources of data, both of which are important for different reasons. **Empirical** results are derived directly from experiment and observation. The researchers obtaining empirical results may not understand *why* they obtain the results they do; they are only recording what they observe. These empirical results may then serve as a basis for later theoretical developments. For example, physicists observed empirically that excited atoms tended to emit light preferentially at certain wavelengths long before quantum theory was developed and explained this phenomenon. **Theoretical** results are predictions as to what one would expect to observe given particular circumstances, based on some established theory. It may not be trivial to obtain these results; theoretical results may come about through detailed calculations and modeling.

Ideally, of course, empirical and theoretical results should match. If they do not, then it indicates that either something was done wrong in the experiment (perhaps, for example, there was some confounding variable that was overlooked) or that the theory used was invalid or had some unrecognized limitations. Either way, this can be an impetus for further research.

Extending Results

In the context of a scientific investigation, a **prediction** is an expression of what you would expect to happen if certain conditions are met. It is not a blanket statement of the future; when you make a scientific prediction, you are not necessarily stating what *will* happen, only what would happen *if* certain conditions hold. For example, we can predict based on what we know about its chemical properties that *if* we place an apple in a solution of concentrated sulfuric acid, it will dissolve.

Predictions are important in science for two reasons: (1) because they permit application of scientific theories—if a theory predicts what will happen under certain circumstances, then we may be able to use that to our benefit—and (2) because they allow hypotheses and theories to be tested—if a theory predicts that something should happen under particular circumstances, and we put that to the test and the event does occur as predicted, that provides further evidence of the validity of the theory. If, on the other hand, the event does *not* match the prediction, the theory may be falsified. A theory that has been validated by numerous successful predictions may come to be widely accepted as valid.

Interpolation is the estimation of the expected value of a dependent variable for a particular value of an independent variable. This estimation is based on the measured value of the dependent variable at values of the independent variable both smaller and larger than the value in question. For example, suppose we know that the height of a tree was 10 meters in 1960 and 20 meters in 1980; by interpolation, we can guess that it may have been 15 meters tall in 1970.

The preceding example assumes a linear relationship and is therefore a case of **linear interpolation**. However, of course not all relationships are linear, and interpolation can take that into account. Interpolation may be done graphically: We can draw a curve through the known data points and use that curve to estimate the value of the dependent variable (y) at some other value of the independent variable (x). If we have many data points, interpolation tends to be fairly reliable, though not completely; it could still be the case that there is some large spike or other change that we don't know about between the measured data points.

Extrapolation is the estimation of the expected value of a dependent variable for a particular value of an independent variable, based on the measured value of the dependent variable at values of the independent variable either smaller or larger than the value in question, but not both. For example, suppose we know that the population of a town was 5,000 in the year 1990, 6,000 in the year 2000, and 7,000 in the year 2010; by extrapolation we can guess that its population may be 8,000 in the year 2020.

Like interpolation, extrapolation does not necessarily assume a linear relationship, and it may be done graphically. However, extrapolation may be less reliable than interpolation. Frequently, a relationship that holds for some range of variables breaks down at higher and lower values. For instance, suppose we note that hanging a 1 kg mass on a spring stretches it by 1 cm, a 2 kg mass by 2 cm, and a 3 kg mass by 3 cm. We extrapolate that a 10 kg mass would stretch the spring by 10 cm. But that isn't necessarily true: There's a limit to the weight a spring can hold before it breaks or is damaged, and 10 kg may exceed that limit.

Science Theories and Processes

In everyday language, the word "theory" is often used to refer to a guess or speculation. In science, however, a **theory** is a verifiable explanatory framework that accounts for a set of observations. In science, the word "theory" does not imply that an idea is uncertain or unsupported—though it doesn't necessarily imply the opposite, either. Some theories have made many predictions that have been confirmed by observations and are considered strongly supported, such as gravitational theory, the theory of relativity, and evolutionary theory. Other theories remain somewhat speculative and not fully confirmed, such as string theory. Still other theories have been falsified by observations and are today obsolete, such as ether theory, the idea that light was a wave in a pervasive substance called ether.

A **hypothesis** corresponds more to the nonscientific use of the word "theory"—a hypothesis is a speculative proposal that has not yet been fully tested. If further experiment and observation confirm the hypothesis, it may become a basis of a theory. A scientific **law** is a description of some phenomenon that has been repeatedly confirmed by observation. Unlike a theory, a scientific law does not attempt to *explain* the phenomenon in question, only to describe it.

MAIN PROCESSES OF A SCIENTIFIC INVESTIGATION

Scientific investigation involves a number of processes, not all of which are necessarily a part of every investigation. A scientific investigation usually begins with formulating a question—a good investigation is not just a directionless set of observations with no particular goal in mind, but it is designed to answer a specific question. The investigator may also propose a hypothesis, a prediction as to the expected result, to help guide the investigation. The investigator then gathers data, either through observation—i.e., measuring and recording different properties of the system—or through experiment— i.e., making changes to the system and measuring the effects—or a combination of the two.

Once the investigator has collected specific data, another step is to analyze the data. This may involve a qualitative comparison between different sets of data, or it may involve detailed quantitative analysis including graphs and/or statistical methods. Based on the results of the data analysis, the investigator then draws conclusions from the data and uses them to formulate a (perhaps tentative) answer to the initial question and, if applicable, to judge whether the hypothesis is confirmed or falsified.

PROCESS OF OBSERVATION

In a scientific investigation, **observation** refers to more than simply looking at something. In a preliminary descriptive investigation, the investigator may just be observing the object or phenomenon generally to look for any interesting features that might be worth investigating in more detail, but in most investigations the observation will be guided by an experimental question that the investigator wants to answer and the investigator will be focusing his or her attention on some specific quantity or quality to be observed. The observations should be carefully recorded for later reference and analysis.

If the investigator is observing a measurable quantity, then measurement of that quantity is also part of the observation. An investigator observing the evaporation of the liquid in a beaker over time, for example, will not merely record that the amount of liquid is decreasing. As part of the observation, the investigator will record quantitative measurements of the amount of liquid at different times, such as by weighing the beaker or measuring the depth of the liquid within it.

PROCESS OF INFERENCE

Inference is the process of drawing conclusions based on observations. This is an important part of the process of science as well as social studies. It could even be said that the goal of most scientific investigations is to infer an answer to the experimental question.

Often, drawing an inference involves noticing a trend in the data and assuming that the trend continues. For example, if every time an investigator puts a particular chemical in a bacterial culture the bacteria die, it is a reasonable inference that that chemical is deadly to the bacteria. The trend may be more subtle, involving, for example, a relationship between two quantities. An investigator may observe that a certain type of tree tends to be taller at lower altitudes and infer that there is something about higher altitudes that inhibits the trees' growth.

An inference is not necessarily a sure thing, especially if only a few observations have been made; it could be that the relationship on which the inference is based is coincidental, and the inference is not valid. The inference may be used to create a hypothesis that can be tested in further investigations.

PROCESS OF COMMUNICATION

Communication is a frequently overlooked but very important part of a scientific investigation. Investigators must be able to relate the results and conclusions of their investigation to others. If the investigators are unable to effectively communicate their results, then their investigation is ultimately fruitless; even if the investigators themselves are convinced of their results, if no one else knows about them, then they can have no further impact.

Communication in science is more than just telling other investigators what you found. It is also important to relate *how* you found your results. A good scientific report, like those found in published science journals, will describe in detail how the investigation was carried out, include any possible sources of error or uncertainty that the investigators were aware of, and explain precisely how the investigators arrived at their conclusions. Ideally, other investigators should be able to follow every step of the investigators' reasoning and should be provided with enough information in principle to repeat the investigation themselves.

It is also helpful to be able to clearly communicate the gist of the results of an investigation to nonspecialists. This is a separate matter from communication to other knowledgeable investigators but is also important.

Using Numbers and Graphics in Science

Exponential, Linear, and Quadratic Relationships

Exponential, linear, and quadratic relationships are different kinds of possible relationships between two variables. An **exponential relationship** is a relationship in which one variable is proportional to a constant raised to the power of the other variable, as in $y = 2^x$. Although outside of science people may informally refer to any large increase as exponential, the term does have a precise mathematical meaning. A **linear relationship** is a relationship in which one variable increases at a constant rate as the other increases: The two variables obey the equation $y = mx + b$ for some constants m and b. The graph of a linear relationship will be a straight line. A **quadratic relationship** is a relationship in which one variable increases with the *square* of the other variable; the general equation is $y = ax^2 + bx + c$ for some constants a, b, and c. The graph of a quadratic relationship will be a parabola. These three cases do not exhaust all of the possible types of relationship between variables, but they are among the most common.

Scientific Formulas and Statistics

Scientific Formulas

The first step in solving a problem using a scientific formula is to determine which formula to use. Generally, you want to find a formula that includes the unknown that you want to solve for and that otherwise includes only known values. Be careful that you know the context of the formula and that you know what the symbols represent because the same symbol may have multiple meanings. For instance, in the formula for the velocity of a wave in a string, $v = \sqrt{\frac{T}{m/L}}$, T stands for tension, but in the formula for the frequency of a wave, $f = \frac{1}{T}$, T stands for period. Once you have found the appropriate formula, you can put in the known values and solve for your unknown (being careful to convert the units if appropriate).

For example, suppose we're told that the centripetal force on a ball being swung in a circle of 50-cm radius is 16 N, the mass of the ball is 500 g, and we want to know its velocity. An appropriate formula is $F_C = \frac{mv^2}{r}$. For consistency in the units, we should convert the radius to meters and the mass to kilograms; then $16\text{ N} = \frac{(0.500\text{ kg})v^2}{0.50\text{ m}}$, and $v = \sqrt{\frac{(16\text{ N})(0.50\text{ m})}{0.500\text{ kg}}} = 4.0\frac{\text{m}}{\text{s}}$.

Sometimes, no single known formula is sufficient to solve a problem because every formula that includes the unknown quantity that we're trying to solve for also includes another unknown quantity as well. In such a case, it may be necessary to use two or more formulas to solve the problem, using one formula to solve for a variable that we then use in another formula. To determine which formulas to use, it's often useful to work backwards; that is, we figure out what other unknown variables the formula that we want to use includes and then we look for another formula that we can use to solve for those variables.

For example, suppose we are told that an electron is accelerated over a given distance by an electric field of given strength and we are asked for its final velocity. No single equation from a typical textbook will give this quantity. However, there is a well-known equation for velocity given distance and acceleration: $v^2 = v_0^2 +$

$2a\Delta x$. We don't know the acceleration, but we know it relates to force: $F = ma$. Therefore, if we can find the force on the electron, we can find its acceleration. Finally, there is an equation for the force due to an electric field: $F = qE$.

Descriptive Statistics

When there are large numbers of data points, it's useful to present them in a summarized way that takes all the data into account but is easier to use and understand than just the raw data points themselves. **Statistics** is a method for doing this: The point of statistics is to take many data points and find trends and properties that describe the data set as a whole, or patterns within it. Common statistical properties of a data set include the **mean**, or average, and the **standard deviation**, a measure of the variability of the data set—how much the data points tend to differ. In addition to describing single data sets, statistics can also be used to characterize the relationships between two or more variables. One statistical property that serves this purpose is **correlation**, which describes to what extent the changes in one variable tend to be mirrored by the other.

Conclusions drawn from statistics are generally not absolute, but they are probabilistic: A statistical analysis can only establish that it is *probable* that a particular relationship holds. However, for very large data sets and repeated trials, this probability can be very high.

Precision and Accuracy

Most scientific measurements have some uncertainty or error in them, and the precision and accuracy are some ways of describing the extent: The higher the precision or accuracy, the smaller the error or uncertainty. However, precision and accuracy are not the same thing. **Precision** refers to the *consistency* of the measurements: If multiple measurements all yield values that are close to each other, the measurements are *precise*. **Accuracy** refers to how close the measurements are to the real value of the quantity being measured. Significant random error can lead to low precision; *systematic* error leads to low accuracy.

It is possible for measurements to be precise but not accurate or vice versa. Suppose an object has a mass of 50.0 g. One investigator tries to measure its mass and obtains measurements of 39.9, 40.0, 39.8, and 40.1 g. These measurements are precise, but not accurate: They are close to each other, but not to the actual value. Another obtains measurements of 40.5, 46.2, 51.8, and 61.1 g. These measurements are accurate, but not precise: There is a wide spread, but their average is close to the actual value.

Review Video: Precision, Accuracy, and Error
Visit mometrix.com/academy and enter code: 520377

Probability and Sampling in Science

Experimental Probability

As the name implies, an **experimental probability**, or empirical probability, is the probability of an event as determined by experiment. (This contrasts with the **theoretical probability**, the expected probability that an event should occur based on known principles.) An experimental probability can be found by repeating an experiment multiple times (the more the better) and counting how many times the event occurs. The probability is the number of times the event occurred divided by the number of experiments run. For a simple example, suppose we have a six-sided die, and we want to know the probability that it will come up 6 if we roll it. The theoretical probability, assuming that the die is fair, is 1/6. But suppose we don't know for sure that it's fair, and want to check the probability experimentally. If we roll the die 1,000 times, and it comes up 6 for 230 times, then the experimental probability is 230/1,000, or 0.23—significantly higher than 1/6 (about 0.17), so this is probably not a fair die.

Probabilities—whether experimental or theoretical—are always between 0 and 1. A probability of 0 means that the event has no chance of happening; a probability of 1 means that it always happens.

Joint Probability

The **joint probability** of two events is the probability that *both* events will occur. By definition, the joint probability must be less than or equal to the probability of each event separately, but beyond that it could have any value. There are, however, two important special cases. If the joint probability of two events is zero, then the events are said to be **mutually exclusive**. For example, if you flip a coin, the joint probability of it coming up heads *and* tails is 0—those can't both happen at once.

Another important special case is that in which the joint probability is equal to the products of the probabilities of each event:

$$P(A \text{ and } B) = P(A) \times P(B)$$

This is true when the events are **independent**—whether or not one event happens does not affect whether the other event happens. For instance, if you flip *two* coins, the probability of their both coming up heads is $\left(\frac{1}{2}\right) \times \left(\frac{1}{2}\right) = \frac{1}{4}$.

The joint probability can be used to find the probability that *at least one* event will happen:

$$P(A \text{ or } B) = P(A) + P(B) - P(A \text{ and } B)$$

For mutually exclusive events, this reduces to:

$$P(A \text{ or } B) = P(A) + P(B)$$

Conditional Probability

The **conditional probability** is the probability that one event will occur, given that we know another event has occurred. The conditional probability that event A will occur if event B occurred is written $P(A|B)$, and it can be read as the probability of *A* given *B*. If the two events are independent—if whether one occurs has no effect on whether the other occurs—then $P(A|B) = P(A)$; the conditional probability of event A given B is the same as the probability of event A by itself. Otherwise, $P(A|B)$ could have any value from zero (if event A *never* occurs if event B happens) through one (if event A *always* occurs when event B happens). For instance, suppose that event A is the probability that a student will pass the first exam in a class and event B is the probability that a student will pass the second exam. A student who passed the first exam is more likely to also pass the second, so we'd expect that $P(B|A) > P(B)$.

The conditional probability can be used to find the joint probability of the events—the probability that they will both occur:

$$P(A \text{ and } B) = P(B|A) \times P(A)$$

Review Video: Conditional Probability
Visit mometrix.com/academy and enter code: 397924

Sampling

Populations and Samples

In a scientific study, a **sample** is the collection of subjects that are being directly analyzed or measured. This contrasts with the **population**, which is the total collection of all such subjects that exist. The results of the experiment on the sample are extrapolated and assumed to apply to the population as a whole. For example, if a scientist wishes to study the effects of an experimental drug on people with insomnia, it's certainly not possible (or necessarily desirable) to test the drug on everyone in the world who has insomnia. The drug will be tested on a relatively small number of volunteers. These volunteers are the *sample*; the collection of everyone in the world with insomnia is the *population*. In general, the larger the sample, the more reliable the results of the experiment, although the method in which the sample was chosen is also significant.

Sampling is used not only in the natural sciences, but it is used in social studies as well, and even in fields such as politics. Surveys to gauge public opinion, for example, use sampling; the people conducting the survey can't call everyone in the country, so they survey a sample of the population and extrapolate the results.

Random Sample

A **random sample** is a sample chosen from the population completely at random in such a way that no member of the population has any greater chance of being included in the sample than any other member, and the fact that one particular member of the population is chosen for the sample does not affect the chances of any other particular member being chosen.

Because there is no bias in the selection of the sample and there are no assumptions necessary, a random sample is considered to be the kind of sample that is most likely to be representative of the population and most likely to give reliable results. (There is, of course a chance that the sample is unrepresentative just by coincidence—that the random sample just happened to include only members with certain characteristics—but for large samples, this chance is extremely small.) However, truly random sampling can be impractical for large populations. For small populations, one could, for instance, put a slip of paper representing each member of the population in a bowl and draw the desired number of slips, but this clearly wouldn't be feasible for populations with thousands of members.

Systematic Sample

A **systematic sample** is a sample chosen from the population by arranging the members of the population in some order and then choosing at fixed intervals from a random starting place—choosing every 10th member, for example, or every 100th member, or some other interval depending on the desired size of the sample. For instance, the sample could consist of every 100th student chosen from an alphabetical list by name of students at a particular school, or every 20th house on a long street. Systematic samples are often simpler to carry out than random samples, though they still may not be practical for large populations that cannot be ordered in any straightforward way. As with a random sample, each member of the population has an equal chance of being chosen. However, unlike with a random sample, the probabilities of choosing different members are not independent, and if there is some correlation between the ordering of the members and the characteristics being studied then the systematic sample may cause some unforeseen biases—although in most cases this is unlikely and a systematic sample may be as representative of the population as a random sample would be.

Convenience Sample

A **convenience sample** is a sample chosen simply from those members of the population that are readily available or easily reached. One common type of convenience sample for human subjects is a **voluntary response sample**—a sample consisting of those people who volunteered to participate in a particular study or who voluntarily answered a survey.

The main advantage of a convenience sample is that, as the name implies, it is convenient; it is in general much easier to put together a convenience sample than a random sample or a systematic sample. In some cases, it may not be possible to get a truly random sample and a convenience sample may be the only practical option. However, because of the nature of the convenience sample, it may not be well representative of the population as a whole. Although scientists may have methods of trying to account for possible bias in a convenience sample, those methods are imperfect, and conclusions drawn from a convenience sample are considered less reliable than those from a random sample or a systematic sample.

Fundamental Counting Principle

If an event has N equally likely (and mutually exclusive) possible outcomes, then the probability that any one outcome will occur is $1/N$. For instance, suppose you roll a fair six-sided die. (Fair in this context just means that any side of the die is equally likely to come up.) There are six possible outcomes, so the probability of rolling any particular number is $1/6$.

The **fundamental counting principle** comes into play when you have two or more independent events, each with its own set of outcomes. The principle states that the total number of possible outcomes is the product of the numbers of outcomes of each event. For instance, suppose that you simultaneously roll a six-sided die, flip a coin, and draw a tile representing a letter of the alphabet. (Assume that there is one tile for each letter, so each letter is equally likely to be drawn.) There are six possible outcomes of the die roll, 2 for the coin, and 26 for the letters, so the total number of possible outcomes is $6 \times 2 \times 26 = 312$, and the probability of obtaining any one outcome—such as 3-tails-Q—is 1/312.

Permutations and Combinations

Permutations and combinations refer to the number of ways of choosing a number of objects from a larger set. In a **permutation**, the order matters: *A, B, C* is considered distinct from *B, C, A*. In a **combination**, only which objects are chosen matters; the order is ignored.

The number of distinct ways of choosing k objects from a set of n, when the order of the objects matters, is written ${}_nP_k$ (P for permutation), and it is equal to:

$$\frac{n!}{(n-k)!} \text{ where } n! = n \times (n-1) \times (n-2) \times \ldots \times 3 \times 2 \times 1$$

So, for example, the number of ways of choosing 4 out of 7objects in order is:

$${}_7P_4 = \frac{7!}{(7-4)!} = \frac{7 \cdot 6 \cdot 5 \cdot 4 \cdot 3 \cdot 2 \cdot 1}{3 \cdot 2 \cdot 1} = \frac{5{,}040}{6} = 840$$

The probability of choosing any particular ordered set of four is 1/840.

The number of distinct ways of choosing k objects from a set of n and order of the objects *doesn't* matter is written as ${}_nC_k$ (C for combination), and it is equal to:

$$\frac{n!}{k!\,(n-k)!}$$

Therefore, the number of ways of choosing 4 out of 7 objects ignoring order is:

$${}_7C_4 = \frac{7!}{4!\,3!} = \frac{5{,}040}{(24)(6)} = 35$$

The probability of choosing any particular unordered set of four is 1/35.

Review Video: Probability: Permutation and Combination
Visit mometrix.com/academy and enter code: 907664

Presenting Science Information Using Numbers, Symbols, and Graphics

Using Graphics

Graphics can often hold a reader's interest better than long text passages, and they can convey information more compactly. One obvious use of a graphic is to display what something *looks* like, either the object under study or the apparatus used to study it. This is common even in technical papers: a paper about a newly discovered fossil would be incomplete without a photograph or drawing of the fossil in question. More abstract schematic diagrams are also useful to show how things fit together, such as a circuit diagram showing the makeup of an electrical circuit. A map is another example of a useful graphic, to show where phenomena were found or where discoveries were made.

These uses of graphics show information that arguably could not be adequately conveyed in any other way; however, visually pleasing graphics are also sometimes used as a more eye-catching alternative to a graph or table. These graphics are often known as infographics, and they involve creative use of images that relate to the data being displayed. Instead of a simple bar graph of the amount of oil produced by different countries, for example, an infographic could use scaled images of oil derricks.

Using Symbols

A symbol is a figure that represents some other object or concept. Symbols allow information to be conveyed much more concisely than they could be in words (although technically words are a kind of symbol themselves). For example, chemists use a one- or two-letter symbol for each element; carbon is C, sodium is Na, and so on. This makes chemical equations much more compact and readable than if the full name of the element were written out each time it appears.

Different fields of science have established symbols that are known to everyone working in the field and can be used without explanation, such as the aforementioned chemical symbols, or the use in physics of c for the speed of light and G for the gravitational constant. Sometimes in a particular study, however, it may be necessary to modify a symbol to specify what it applies to: v is an accepted symbol for velocity, but you may want to use the symbols v_A and v_B to refer to the velocities of two specific objects in your study. Sometimes it may be necessary to define brand-new symbols. It's important to clearly and unambiguously define what each new symbol represents.

Using Numbers

Uncertainty

Scientific papers and presentations are often full of numbers, showing the sizes of objects, the duration of events, and many other measurable quantities. However, any measurement or calculation has some uncertainty, and the presentation should reflect that as well. The uncertainty can be given explicitly, either as a range of values (the result is between 0.32 and 0.52 ms) or with a plus-or-minus sign (0.42 ± 0.10 ms). Such explicit uncertainties are the norm in technical papers, but even in more informal contexts, the uncertainty is implied by the place value of the last digit of the number. For instance, if you are measuring a length with a tape measure that has markings to the nearest millimeter, and the length is right on the 2 m mark, you would write the length as 2.000 m—not just 2 m, because this implies that you don't know the length any more precisely than that, and not 2.0000 m, because that implies that you know the length down to the nearest tenth of a millimeter, which you don't. The digits of a number that carry meaning—excluding any leading zeros, but including following zeros after a decimal point—are called **significant figures**.

Units

Most quantitative values in a scientific report are incomplete if they do not include units. If you write that something has a duration of 3.0, that's meaningless—is it 3.0 seconds? 3.0 minutes? 3.0 years? There are some exceptions—ratios of quantities, for example, where the units cancel, and the final value is unitless—but in general each quantity should be accompanied by appropriate units. In science, it's most common to use metric units—meters, kilograms, and so on. Although in everyday life in the United States other units such as pounds and feet are common, these are seldom used in scientific contexts.

Units should be chosen that are appropriate to the scale of the measurement. If you're discussing the distances between stars, kilometers may be an appropriate unit, or even light-years. If you're discussing the width of an atom, it may be more appropriate to use nanometers. Each unit has a standard abbreviation that should be used: m for meters, s for seconds, and so on. Some measurements have a **compound unit** that combines different basic quantities: velocities, for example, can be measured in meters per second, or m/s.

Comparing Different Methods of Presenting Scientific Information

There are many ways of presenting scientific data that each have their advantages and disadvantages, any of which may be more suitable than others in specific contexts. The most obvious method of presentation is just text: simple statements of data or results. This is particularly appropriate for qualitative explanations or for simple data sets that only involve one or two quantities. For more complicated data sets, however, other methods of presentation may make it easier for the reader to visualize data.

Tables are useful if the data consist of multiple sets that can be compared but each set is relatively simple on its own. Each data set would make up a row of the table. Tables can also be used for data sets with two variables, as long as those data sets are relatively small; one can be the rows of the table, and one can be the columns. However, for large data sets or data sets in which it's important to visually convey the relationship between the variables, it may be more appropriate to use a graph, which can depict large data sets in a compact way at a cost of not including the exact numerical values.

Scientific Inquiry and Reasoning

Scientific Inquiry

The concept of **scientific inquiry** refers to the idea of how one thinks and asks questions in a logical way to gain trustworthy information. The underlying motivation of science is to try to understand the natural world. Much of human thought is based on assumptions about how things work that may or may not be true. The goal of scientific inquiry is to test those assumptions to gain a greater understanding of the world with good questions and objective tests, and then re-use what was learned to ask better questions. The more we understand about the natural world, the better the questions we can ask, and that is the general idea behind scientific inquiry. The applied practice of scientific inquiry is to ask questions in a systematic method, called the scientific method.

Scientific Knowledge

Scientific knowledge refers to any topic that is studied **empirically**, meaning that it is based on observation of a **phenomenon** in an objective way. The body of **scientific knowledge** is often broken down into several domains including biology, ecology, Earth science, space science, physics, and chemistry. These each have further subdomains and are overlapping in many ways. For instance, ecology is the study of ecosystems, which are made up of biological factors and geological factors, so it contains elements of both biology and Earth science. Each of these domains is subject to the concepts of scientific inquiry, such as the scientific method, scientific facts, hypotheses, and scientific laws.

Important Terminology

- A **phenomenon** is an event or effect that is observed.
- A **scientific fact** is considered an objective and verifiable observation. Usually, a fact can be repeated or demonstrated to others.
- A **scientific theory** is a proposition explaining why or how something happens and is built on scientific facts and laws. Scientific theories can be tested, but are not fully proven. If new evidence is found that disproves the theory, it is no longer considered true.
- A **hypothesis** is an educated guess that is not yet proven. It is used to predict the outcome of an experiment in an attempt to solve a problem or answer a question.
- A **law** is an explanation of events that always leads to the same outcome. It is a fact that an object falls. The law of gravity explains why an object falls. The theory of relativity, although generally accepted, has been neither proven nor disproved.
- A **model** is used to explain something on a smaller scale or in simpler terms to provide an example. It is a representation of an idea that can be used to explain events or applied to new situations to predict outcomes or determine results.

History of Scientific Knowledge

When one examines the history of **scientific knowledge**, it is clear that it is constantly **evolving**. The body of facts, models, theories, and laws grows and changes over time. In other words, one scientific discovery leads to the next. Some advances in science and technology have important and long-lasting effects on science and society. Some discoveries were so alien to the accepted beliefs of the time that not only were they rejected as wrong, but were also considered outright blasphemy. Today, however, many beliefs once considered incorrect have become an ingrained part of scientific knowledge, and have also been the basis of new advances. Examples of advances include: Copernicus's heliocentric view of the universe, Newton's laws of motion and planetary orbits, relativity, geologic time scale, plate tectonics, atomic theory, nuclear physics, biological evolution, germ theory, industrial revolution, molecular biology, information and communication, quantum theory, galactic universe, and medical and health technology.

Scientific Inquiry and Scientific Method

Scientists use a number of generally accepted techniques collectively known as the **scientific method**. The scientific method generally involves carrying out the following steps:

- Identifying a problem or posing a question
- Formulating a hypothesis or an educated guess
- Conducting experiments or tests that will provide a basis to solve the problem or answer the question
- Observing the results of the test
- Drawing conclusions

An important part of the scientific method is using acceptable experimental techniques. Objectivity is also important if valid results are to be obtained. Another important part of the scientific method is peer review. It is essential that experiments be performed and data be recorded in such a way that experiments can be reproduced to verify results. Historically, the scientific method has been taught with a more linear approach, but it is important to recognize that the scientific method should be a cyclical or **recursive process**. This means that as hypotheses are tested and more is learned, the questions should continue to change to reflect the changing body of knowledge. One cycle of experimentation is not enough.

Review Video: The Scientific Method
Visit mometrix.com/academy and enter code: 191386

Metric and International System of Units

The **metric system** is the accepted standard of measurement in the scientific community. The **International System of Units (SI)** is a set of measurements (including the metric system) that is almost globally accepted. The United States, Liberia, and Myanmar have not accepted this system. **Standardization** is important because it allows the results of experiments to be compared and reproduced without the need to laboriously convert measurements. The SI is based partially on the **meter-kilogram-second (MKS) system** rather than the **centimeter-gram-second (CGS) system**. The MKS system considers meters, kilograms, and seconds to be the basic units of measurement, while the CGS system considers centimeters, grams, and seconds to be the basic units of measurement. Under the MKS system, the length of an object would be expressed as 1 meter instead of 100 centimeters, which is how it would be described under the CGS system.

Review Video: Metric System Conversions
Visit mometrix.com/academy and enter code: 163709

Basic Units of Measurement

Using the **metric system** is generally accepted as the preferred method for taking measurements. Having a **universal standard** allows individuals to interpret measurements more easily, regardless of where they are located. The basic units of measurement are: the **meter**, which measures length; the **liter**, which measures volume; and the **gram**, which measures mass. The metric system starts with a base unit and increases or decreases in units of 10. The prefix and the base unit combined are used to indicate an amount. For example, deka- is 10 times the base unit. A dekameter is 10 meters; a dekaliter is 10 liters; and a dekagram is 10 grams. The prefix hecto- refers to 100 times the base amount; kilo- is 1,000 times the base amount. The prefixes that indicate a fraction of the base unit are deci-, which is $\frac{1}{10}$ of the base unit; centi-, which is $\frac{1}{100}$ of the base unit; and milli-, which is $\frac{1}{1,000}$ of the base unit.

Common Prefixes

The prefixes for multiples are as follows:

Deka	(da)	**10^1** (deka is the American spelling, but deca is also used)
Hecto	(h)	10^2
Kilo	(k)	10^3
Mega	(M)	10^6
Giga	(G)	10^9
Tera	(T)	10^{12}

The prefixes for subdivisions are as follows:

Deci	(d)	**10^{-1}**
Centi	(c)	10^{-2}
Milli	(m)	10^{-3}
Micro	(μ)	10^{-6}
Nano	(n)	10^{-9}
Pico	(p)	10^{-12}

The rule of thumb is that prefixes greater than 10^3 are capitalized when abbreviating. Abbreviations do not need a period after them. A decimeter (dm) is a tenth of a meter, a deciliter (dL) is a tenth of a liter, and a decigram (dg) is a tenth of a gram. Pluralization is understood. For example, when referring to 5 mL of water, no "s" needs to be added to the abbreviation.

Basic SI Units of Measurement

SI uses **second(s)** to measure time. Fractions of seconds are usually measured in metric terms using prefixes such as millisecond ($\frac{1}{1,000}$ of a second) or nanosecond ($\frac{1}{1,000,000,000}$ of a second). Increments of time larger than a second are measured in **minutes** and **hours**, which are multiples of 60 and 24. An example of this is a swimmer's time in the 800-meter freestyle being described as 7:32.67, meaning 7 minutes, 32 seconds, and 67 one-hundredths of a second. One second is equal to $\frac{1}{60}$ of a minute, $\frac{1}{3,600}$ of an hour, and $\frac{1}{86,400}$ of a day. Other SI base units are the **ampere** (A) (used to measure electric current), the **kelvin** (K) (used to measure thermodynamic temperature), the **candela** (cd) (used to measure luminous intensity), and the **mole** (mol) (used to measure the amount of a substance at a molecular level). **Meter** (m) is used to measure length and **kilogram** (kg) is used to measure mass.

Significant Figures

The mathematical concept of **significant figures** or **significant digits** is often used to determine the accuracy of measurements or the level of confidence one has in a specific measurement. The significant figures of a measurement include all the digits known with certainty plus one estimated or uncertain digit. There are a number of rules for determining which digits are considered "important" or "interesting." They are: all non-zero digits are *significant*, zeros between digits are *significant*, and leading and trailing zeros are *not significant* unless they appear to the right of the non-zero digits in a decimal. For example, in 0.01230 the significant digits are 1230, and this number would be said to be accurate to the hundred-thousandths place. The zero indicates that the amount has actually been measured as 0. Other zeros are considered place holders, and are not important. A decimal point may be placed after zeros to indicate their importance (in 100. for example).

Estimating, on the other hand, involves approximating a value rather than calculating the exact number. This may be used to quickly determine a value that is close to the actual number when complete accuracy does not matter or is not possible. In science, estimation may be used when it is impossible to measure or calculate an exact amount, or to quickly approximate an answer when true calculations would be time consuming.

Graphs and Charts

Graphs and charts are effective ways to present scientific data such as observations, statistical analyses, and comparisons between dependent variables and independent variables. On a line chart, the **independent variable** (the one that is being manipulated for the experiment) is represented on the horizontal axis (the x-axis). Any **dependent variables** (the ones that may change as the independent variable changes) are represented on the y-axis. An **XY** or **scatter plot** is often used to plot many points. A "best fit" line is drawn, which allows outliers to be identified more easily. Charts and their axes should have titles. The x and y interval units should be evenly spaced and labeled. Other types of charts are **bar charts** and **histograms**, which can be used to compare differences between the data collected for two variables. A **pie chart** can graphically show the relation of parts to a whole.

Review Video: Identifying Variables
Visit mometrix.com/academy and enter code: 627181

Review Video: Data Interpretation of Graphs
Visit mometrix.com/academy and enter code: 200439

Data Presentation

Data collected during a science lab can be organized and **presented** in any number of ways. While **straight narrative** is a suitable method for presenting some lab results, it is not a suitable way to present numbers and quantitative measurements. These types of observations can often be better presented with **tables** and **graphs**. Data that is presented in tables and organized in rows and columns may also be used to make graphs quite easily. Other methods of presenting data include illustrations, photographs, video, and even audio formats. In a **formal report**, tables and figures are labeled and referred to by their labels. For example, a picture of a bubbly solution might be labeled Figure 1, Bubbly Solution. It would be referred to in the text in the following way: "The reaction created bubbles 10 mm in size, as shown in Figure 1, Bubbly Solution." Graphs are also labeled as figures. Tables are labeled in a different way. Examples include: Table 1, Results of Statistical Analysis, or Table 2, Data from Lab 2.

Statistical Precision and Errors

Errors that occur during an experiment can be classified into two categories: random errors and systematic errors. **Random errors** can result in collected data that is wildly different from the rest of the data, or they may result in data that is indistinguishable from the rest. Random errors are not consistent across the data set. In large data sets, random errors may contribute to the variability of data, but they will not affect the average. Random errors are sometimes referred to as noise. They may be caused by a student's inability to take the same measurement in exactly the same way or by outside factors that are not considered variables, but influence the data. A **systematic error** will show up consistently across a sample or data set, and may be the result of a flaw in the experimental design. This type of error affects the average, and is also known as bias.

Scientific Notation

Scientific notation is used because values in science can be very large or very small, which makes them unwieldy. A number in **decimal notation** is 93,000,000. In **scientific notation**, it is 9.3×10^7. The first number, 9.3, is the **coefficient**. It is always greater than or equal to 1 and less than 10. This number is followed by a multiplication sign. The base is always 10 in scientific notation. If the number is greater than ten, the exponent is positive. If the number is between zero and one, the exponent is negative. The first digit of the number is followed by a decimal point and then the rest of the number. In this case, the number is 9.3, and the decimal point was moved seven places to the right from the end of the number to get 93,000,000. The number of places moved, seven, is the exponent.

STATISTICAL TERMINOLOGY

Mean - The average, found by taking the sum of a set of numbers and dividing by the number of numbers in the set.

Median - The middle number in a set of numbers sorted from least to greatest. If the set has an even number of entries, the median is the average of the two in the middle.

Mode - The value that appears most frequently in a data set. There may be more than one mode. If no value appears more than once, there is no mode.

Range - The difference between the highest and lowest numbers in a data set.

Standard deviation - Measures the dispersion of a data set or how far from the mean a single data point is likely to be.

Regression analysis - A method of analyzing sets of data and sets of variables that involves studying how the typical value of the dependent variable changes when any one of the independent variables is varied and the other independent variables remain fixed.

Review Video: Mean, Median, and Mode
Visit mometrix.com/academy and enter code: 286207

Review Video: Standard Deviation
Visit mometrix.com/academy and enter code: 419469

Physics

LAWS OF THERMODYNAMICS

The **laws of thermodynamics** are generalized principles dealing with energy and heat.

- The **zeroth law** of thermodynamics states that two objects in thermodynamic equilibrium with a third object are also in equilibrium with each other. Being in thermodynamic equilibrium basically means that different objects are at the same temperature.
- The **first law** deals with conservation of energy. It states that neither mass nor energy can be destroyed; only converted from one form to another.
- The **second law** states that the entropy (the amount of energy in a system that is no longer available for work or the amount of disorder in a system) of an isolated system can only increase. The second law also states that heat is not transferred from a lower-temperature system to a higher-temperature one unless additional work is done.
- The **third law** of thermodynamics states that as temperature approaches absolute zero, entropy approaches a constant minimum. It also states that a system cannot be cooled to absolute zero.

Review Video: Laws of Thermodynamics
Visit mometrix.com/academy and enter code: 253607

HEAT AND TEMPERATURE

Heat is energy transfer (other than direct work) from one body or system to another due to thermal contact. Everything tends to become less organized and less orderly over time (**entropy**). In all energy transfers, therefore, the overall result is that the energy is spread out uniformly. This transfer of heat energy from hotter to cooler objects is accomplished by conduction, radiation, or convection. **Temperature** is a measurement of an object's stored heat energy. More specifically, temperature is the average kinetic energy of an object's particles. When the temperature of an object increases and its atoms move faster, kinetic energy also increases. Temperature is not energy since it changes and is not conserved. Thermometers are used to measure temperature.

Mass, Weight, Volume, Density, and Specific Gravity

Mass — Mass is a measure of the amount of substance in an object.

Weight — Weight is a measure of the gravitational pull of Earth on an object.

Volume — Volume is a measure of the amount of space occupied. There are many formulas to determine volume. For example, the volume of a cube is the length of one side cubed (a^3) and the volume of a rectangular prism is length times width times height ($l \times w \times h$). The volume of an irregular shape can be determined by how much water it displaces.

Density — Density is a measure of the amount of mass per unit volume. The formula to find density is mass divided by volume (D = m/V). It is expressed in terms of mass per cubic unit (e.g., grams per cubic centimeter $\frac{g}{cm^3}$).

Specific gravity — This is a measure of the ratio of a substance's density compared to the density of water.

Review Video: Mass, Weight, Volume, Density, and Specific Gravity
Visit mometrix.com/academy and enter code: 920570

Thermal Contact

Thermal contact refers to energy transferred to a body by a means other than work. A system in thermal contact with another can exchange energy with it through the process of heat transfer. Thermal contact does not necessarily involve direct physical contact. **Heat** is energy that can be transferred from one body or system to another without work being done. Everything tends to become less organized and less useful over time (entropy). In all energy transfers, therefore, the overall result is that the heat is spread out so that objects are in thermodynamic equilibrium and the heat can no longer be transferred without additional work.

Models for Flow of Electric Charge

Models that can be used to explain the **flow of electric current, potential, and circuits** include water, gravity, and roller coasters. For example, just as a mass can have a potential for energy based on its location, so can a charge within an electrical field. Just as a force is required to move an object uphill, a force is also required to move a charge from a low to high potential. Another example is water. Water does not flow when it is level. If it is lifted to a point and then placed on a downward path, it will flow. A roller coaster car requires work to be performed to transport it to a point where it has potential energy (the top of a hill). Once there, gravity provides the force for it to flow (move) downward. If either path is broken, the flow or movement stops or is not completed.

Atomic Structures

Magnetic Fields

The motions of subatomic structures (nuclei and electrons) produce a **magnetic field**. It is the direction of the spin and orbit that indicates the direction of the field. The strength of a magnetic field is known as the **magnetic moment**. As electrons spin and orbit a nucleus, they produce a magnetic field. Pairs of electrons that spin and orbit in opposite directions cancel each other out, creating a net magnetic field of zero. Materials that have an unpaired electron are magnetic. Those with a weak attractive force are referred to as paramagnetic materials, while ferromagnetic materials have a strong attractive force. A diamagnetic material has electrons that are paired and, therefore, does not typically have a magnetic moment. There are, however, some diamagnetic materials that have a weak magnetic field.

Electric Charges

The attractive force between the electrons and the nucleus is called the **electric force**. A positive (+) charge or a negative (−) charge creates a field of sorts in the empty space around it, which is known as an **electric field**. The direction of a positive charge is away from the electric field and the direction of a negative charge is towards it. An electron within the force of the field is pulled towards a positive charge because an electron has a negative charge. A particle with a positive charge is pushed away, or repelled, by another positive charge. Like charges repel each other and opposite charges attract. Lines of force show the paths of charges. The **electric force** between two objects is directly proportional to the product of the charge magnitudes and inversely proportional to the square of the distance between the two objects. **Electric charge** is measured with the unit Coulomb (C). It is the amount of charge moved in one second by a steady current of one ampere (1C = 1A × 1s).

Review Video: Electric Charge
Visit mometrix.com/academy and enter code: 323587

Electric Current Movement Through Circuits

Electric current is the sustained flow of electric charge along a path in a circuit. This differs from a static electric charge, which is a constant non-moving charge rather than a continuous flow. The **rate of flow of electric charge** is expressed using the ampere (amp or A) and can be measured using an ammeter. A current of 1 ampere means that 1 coulomb of charge passes through a given area every second. Electric charges typically only move from areas of high electric potential to areas of low electric potential. To get charges to flow into a high potential area, you must connect it to an area of higher potential by introducing a battery or other voltage source.

Simple Circuits

Movement of electric charge along a path between areas of high electric potential and low electric potential, with a resistor or load device between them, is the definition of a **simple circuit**. It is a closed conducting path between the high and low potential points, such as the positive and negative terminals on a battery. One example of a circuit is the flow from one terminal of a car battery to the other. The electrolyte solution of water and sulfuric acid provides work in chemical form to start the flow. A frequently used classroom example of circuits involves using a D cell (1.5 V) battery, a small light bulb, and a piece of copper wire to create a circuit to light the bulb.

Review Video: Resistance of Electric Currents
Visit mometrix.com/academy and enter code: 668423

Magnets

A **magnet** is any object or material, such as iron, steel, or magnetite (lodestone), that can affect another substance within its **field of force** that has like characteristics. Magnets can either attract or repel other substances. Magnets have two **poles**: north and south. Like poles repel and opposite poles (pairs of north and south) attract. The magnetic field is a set of invisible lines representing the paths of attraction and repulsion. Magnetism can occur naturally, or ferromagnetic materials can be magnetized. Certain matter that is magnetized can retain its magnetic properties indefinitely and become a permanent magnet. Other matter can lose its magnetic properties. For example, an iron nail can be temporarily magnetized by stroking it repeatedly in the same direction using one pole of another magnet. Once magnetized, it can attract or repel other magnetically inclined materials, such as paper clips. Dropping the nail repeatedly will cause it to lose its charge.

Review Video: Magnets
Visit mometrix.com/academy and enter code: 570803

Magnetic Fields, Current, and Magnetic Domains

A **magnetic field** can be formed not only by a magnetic material, but also by electric current flowing through a wire. When a coiled wire is attached to the two ends of a battery, for example, an electromagnet can be formed by inserting a ferromagnetic material such as an iron bar within the coil. When electric current flows through the wire, the bar becomes a magnet. If there is no current, the magnetism is lost. A **magnetic domain** occurs when the magnetic fields of atoms are grouped and aligned. These groups form what can be thought of as miniature magnets within a material. This is what happens when an object like an iron nail is temporarily magnetized. Prior to magnetization, the organization of atoms and their various polarities are somewhat random with respect to where the north and south poles are pointing. After magnetization, a significant percentage of the poles are lined up in one direction, which is what causes the magnetic force exerted by the material.

Motion and Displacement

Motion is a change in the location of an object and is the result of an unbalanced net force acting on the object. Understanding motion requires an understanding of three basic quantities: displacement, velocity, and acceleration.

When something moves from one place to another, it has undergone **displacement**. Displacement along a straight line is a very simple example of a vector quantity. If an object travels from position $x = -5$ cm to $x = 5$ cm, it has undergone a displacement of 10 cm. If it traverses the same path in the opposite direction, its displacement is -10 cm. A vector that spans the object's displacement in the direction of travel is known as a displacement vector.

Review Video: Displacement in Physics
Visit mometrix.com/academy and enter code: 236197

Gravitational Force

Gravitational force is a universal force that causes every object to exert a force on every other object. The gravitational force between two objects can be described by the formula, $F = Gm_1m_2/r^2$, where m_1 and m_2 are the masses of two objects, r is the distance between them, and G is the gravitational constant, $G = 6.672 \times 10^{-11}\ \text{N m}^2/\text{kg}^2$. In order for this force to have a noticeable effect, one or both of the objects must be extremely large, so the equation is generally only used in problems involving planetary bodies. For problems involving objects on the earth being affected by earth's gravitational pull, the force of gravity is simply calculated as $F = mg$, where g is 9.81 m/s^2 toward the ground.

Review Video: Newton's Law of Gravitation
Visit mometrix.com/academy and enter code: 709086

NEWTON'S FIRST TWO LAWS OF MOTION

NEWTON'S FIRST LAW

An object at rest or in motion will remain at rest or in motion unless acted upon by an external force.

This phenomenon is commonly referred to as **inertia**, the tendency of a body to remain in its present state of motion. In order for the body's state of motion to change, it must be acted on by an unbalanced force.

> **Review Video: Newton's First Law of Motion**
> Visit mometrix.com/academy and enter code: 590367

NEWTON'S SECOND LAW

An object's acceleration is **directly proportional** to the net force acting on the object and **inversely proportional** to the object's mass.

This law is generally written in equation form $F = ma$, where F is the net force acting on a body, m is the mass of the body, and a is its acceleration. Note that since the mass is always a positive quantity, the acceleration is always in the same direction as the force.

> **Review Video: Newton's Second Law of Motion**
> Visit mometrix.com/academy and enter code: 737975

SIMPLE MACHINES

Simple machines include the inclined plane, lever, wheel and axle, and pulley. These simple machines have no internal source of energy. More complex or compound machines can be formed from them. Simple machines provide a mechanical advantage to make it easier to accomplish a task. The **inclined plane** enables a force less than the object's weight to be used to push an object to a greater height. A **lever** enables a multiplication of force. The wheel and axle allows for movement with less resistance. Single or double **pulleys** allow for easier direction of force. The wedge and screw are forms of the inclined plane. A **wedge** turns a smaller force working over a greater distance into a larger force. The **screw** is similar to an incline that is wrapped around a shaft.

> **Review Video: Simple Machines**
> Visit mometrix.com/academy and enter code: 950789
>
> **Review Video: Simple Machines - Wheel and Axle**
> Visit mometrix.com/academy and enter code: 574045

FRICTION

Friction is a force that arises as a **resistance to motion** where two surfaces are in contact. The maximum magnitude of the frictional force (f) can be calculated as $f = F_c\mu$, where F_c is the contact force between the two objects and μ is a coefficient of friction based on the surfaces' material composition. Two types of friction are static and kinetic. To illustrate these concepts, imagine a book resting on a table. The force of its weight (W) is equal and opposite to the force of the table on the book, or the normal force (N). If we exert a small force (F) on the book, attempting to push it to one side, a frictional force (f) would arise, equal and opposite to our force. At this point, it is a **static frictional force** because the book is not moving. If we increase our force on the book, we will eventually cause it to move. At this point, the frictional force opposing us will be a **kinetic frictional force**. Generally, the kinetic frictional force is lower than static frictional force (because the frictional coefficient for static friction is larger), which means that the amount of force needed to maintain the movement of the book will be less than what was needed to start it moving.

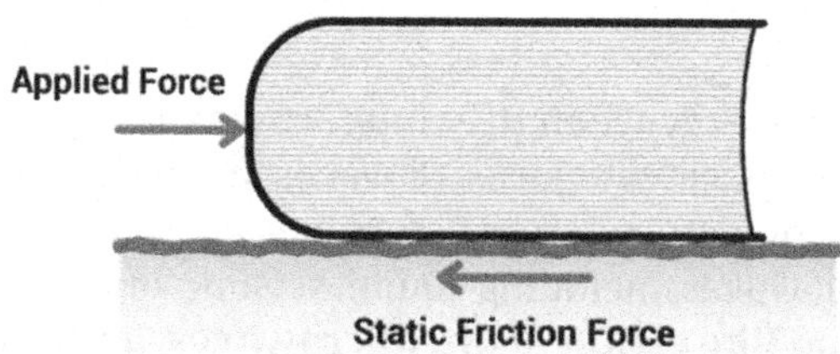

Review Video: Friction
Visit mometrix.com/academy and enter code: 716782

Review Video: Push and Pull Forces
Visit mometrix.com/academy and enter code: 104731

SOUND

Sound is a pressure disturbance that moves through a medium in the form of mechanical waves, which transfer energy from one particle to the next. Sound requires a medium to travel through, such as air, water, or other matter since it is the chain reaction of collisions that transfers energy to adjacent particles, not the actual movement of particles over a great distance. Sound is transferred through the movement of particles, which can be atoms or molecules. Waves of sound energy move outward in all directions from the source. Sound waves consist of compressions (particles are forced together) and rarefactions (particles move farther apart and their density decreases). A wavelength consists of one compression and one rarefaction. Different sounds have different wavelengths. Sound is a form of kinetic energy.

Review Video: Sound
Visit mometrix.com/academy and enter code: 562378

PITCH, LOUDNESS, SOUND INTENSITY, TIMBRE, AND OSCILLATION

Pitch — Pitch is the quality of sound determined by frequency. For example, a musical note can be tuned to a specific frequency. A, for instance, has a frequency of 440 Hz, which is a higher frequency than middle C. Humans can detect frequencies between about 20 Hz to 20,000 Hz.

Loudness — Loudness is a human's perception of sound intensity.

Sound intensity — Sound intensity is measured as the sound power per unit area and can be expressed in decibels.

Timbre — This is a human's perception of the type or quality of sound.

Oscillation — This is a measurement, usually of time, against a basic value, equilibrium, or rest point.

DOPPLER EFFECT

The **Doppler effect** refers to the effect the relative motion of the source of the wave and the location of the observer has on waves. The Doppler effect is easily observable in sound waves. What a person hears when a train approaches or a car honking its horn passes by are examples of the Doppler effect. The pitch of the sound is different not because the *emitted frequency* has changed, but because the *received frequency* has changed. The frequency is higher (as is the pitch) as the train approaches, the same as emitted just as it passes, and lower as the train moves away. This is because the wavelength changes. The Doppler effect can occur when an observer is stationary, and can also occur when two trains approach and pass each other. **Electromagnetic**

waves are also affected in this manner. The motion of the medium can also affect the wave. For waves that do not travel in a medium, such as light waves, it is the difference in velocity that determines the outcome.

WAVES

Waves have energy and can transfer energy when they interact with matter. Although waves transfer energy, they do not transport matter. The two basic categories of waves are mechanical and electromagnetic. Mechanical waves are a disturbance of matter that transfers energy from one particle to an adjacent particle. There are many types of mechanical waves, including sound, seismic, and water. **Electromagnetic waves can transmit energy through a vacuum like visible light, microwaves, and radio waves**. A **transverse wave** provides a good illustration of the features of a wave, which include crests, troughs, amplitude, and wavelength.

ELECTROMAGNETIC SPECTRUM

The electromagnetic spectrum is defined by frequency (f) and wavelength (λ). Frequency is typically measured in hertz and wavelength is usually measured in meters. Because light travels at a fairly constant speed, frequency is inversely proportional to wavelength, a relationship expressed by the formula $f = c/\lambda$, where c is the speed of light (about 3.0×10^8 m/s). Frequency multiplied by wavelength equals the speed of the wave; for electromagnetic waves, this is the speed of light, with some variance for the medium in which it is traveling. Electromagnetic waves include (from largest to smallest wavelength) radio waves, microwaves, infrared radiation (radiant heat), visible light, ultraviolet radiation, x-rays, and gamma rays. The energy of electromagnetic waves is carried in packets that have a magnitude inversely proportional to the wavelength. Radio waves have a range of wavelengths, from about 10^{-3} to 10^5 meters, while their frequencies range from 10^3 to about 10^{11} Hz.

Review Video: Electromagnetic Spectrum
Visit mometrix.com/academy and enter code: 771761

VISIBLE LIGHT

Visible light is defined as the portion of the electromagnetic spectrum that stimulates the human retina. It is absorbed and emitted by electrons, atoms, and molecules that move from one energy level to another. Visible light interacts with matter through molecular electron excitation (which occurs in the human retina) and through plasma oscillations (which occur in metals). Visible light is between ultraviolet and infrared light on the spectrum. The wavelengths of visible light cover a range from 380 nm (violet) to 760 nm (red). Different wavelengths correspond to different colors.

Review Video: Light
Visit mometrix.com/academy and enter code: 900556

REFLECTION AND REFRACTION

Reflection is the rebounding of a light wave from a surface back toward the medium from where it came. A light wave that hits a reflecting surface at a 90-degree angle retraces its original path back to its source. Striking the surface at any other angle results in reflection of the wave at an angle in the opposite direction. Reflectance is the amount of light a material reflects; metals have high reflectance. The smoother a surface, the higher its reflectance. **Refraction is the change in the direction of a light wave as it passes between transparent mediums with different optical densities**. This results in a change in the wave's velocity. The ratio of the sine of the angle of the incoming ray to the sine of the angle of refraction is equal to the ratio of the speed of light in the original medium to the speed of light in the refracting medium.

$$\frac{\sin\theta_{in}}{\sin\theta_{ref}} = \frac{v_{in}}{v_{ref}}$$

Review Video: Reflection, Transmission, and Absorption of Light
Visit mometrix.com/academy and enter code: 109410

Chemistry

Past Atomic Models and Theories

There have been many revisions to theories regarding the structure of **atoms** and their **particles**. Part of the challenge in developing an understanding of matter is that atoms and their particles are too small to be seen. It is believed that the first conceptualization of the atom was developed by **Democritus** in 400 B.C. Some of the more notable models are the solid sphere or billiard ball model postulated by John Dalton, the plum pudding or raisin bun model by J.J. Thomson, the planetary or nuclear model by Ernest Rutherford, the Bohr or orbit model by Niels Bohr, and the electron cloud or quantum mechanical model by Louis de Broglie and Erwin Schrodinger. Rutherford directed the alpha scattering experiment that discounted the plum pudding model. The shortcoming of the Bohr model was the belief that electrons orbited in fixed rather than changing ecliptic orbits.

Review Video: Atomic Models
Visit mometrix.com/academy and enter code: 434851

Models of Atoms

Atoms are extremely small. A hydrogen atom is about 5×10^{-8} mm in diameter. According to some estimates, five trillion hydrogen atoms could fit on the head of a pin. **Atomic radius** refers to the average distance between the nucleus and the outermost electron. Models of atoms that include the proton, nucleus, and electrons typically show the electrons very close to the nucleus and revolving around it, similar to how the Earth orbits the sun. However, another model relates the Earth as the nucleus and its atmosphere as electrons, which is the basis of the term "**electron cloud**." Another description is that electrons swarm around the nucleus. It should be noted that these atomic models are not to scale. A more accurate representation would be a nucleus with a diameter of about 2 cm in a stadium. The electrons would be in the bleachers. This model is similar to the not-to-scale solar system model. In reference to the periodic table, atomic radius increases as energy levels are added and decreases as more protons are added (because they pull the electrons closer to the nucleus). Essentially, atomic radius increases toward the left and toward the bottom of the periodic table.

Structure of Atoms

All matter consists of **atoms**. Atoms consist of a nucleus and electrons. The **nucleus** consists of protons and neutrons. The properties of these are measurable; they have mass and an electrical charge. The nucleus is positively charged due to the presence of protons. **Electrons** are negatively charged and orbit the nucleus. The nucleus has considerably more mass than the surrounding electrons. Atoms can bond together to make

molecules. Atoms that have an equal number of protons and electrons are electrically neutral. If the number of protons and electrons in an atom is not equal, the atom has a positive or negative charge and is an ion.

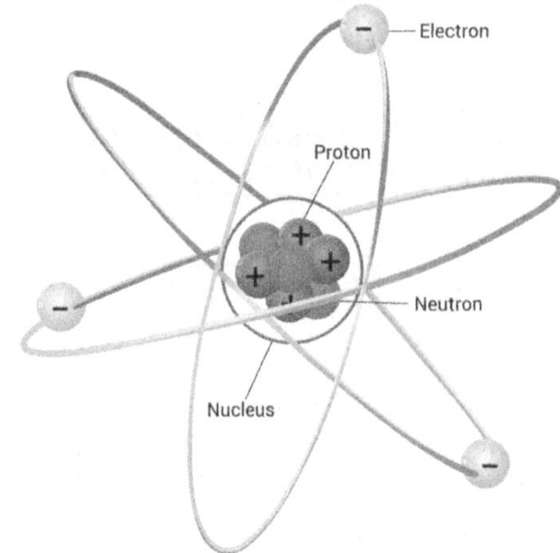

Atomic Number, Neutrons, Nucleon, and Element

- **Atomic number** (proton number) — The atomic number of an element refers to the number of protons in the nucleus of an atom. It is a unique identifier. It can be represented as Z. Atoms with a neutral charge have an atomic number that is equal to the number of electrons.
- **Neutrons** — Neutrons are the uncharged atomic particles contained within the nucleus. The number of neutrons in a nucleus can be represented as "N."
- **Nucleon** — This refers collectively to both neutrons and protons.
- **Element** — An element is matter with one particular type of atom. It can be identified by its atomic number or the number of protons in its nucleus. There are approximately 118 elements currently known, 94 of which occur naturally on Earth. Elements from the periodic table include hydrogen, carbon, iron, helium, mercury, and oxygen.

Molecules

Electrons in an atom can orbit different levels around the nucleus. They can absorb or release energy, which can change the location of their orbit or even allow them to break free from the atom. The outermost layer is the **valence layer**, which contains the valence electrons. The valence layer tends to have or share eight electrons. **Molecules** are formed by a chemical bond between atoms, a bond that occurs at the valence level. Two basic types of bonds are covalent and ionic. A **covalent bond** is formed when atoms share electrons. An **ionic bond** is formed when an atom transfers an electron to another atom. A cation or positive ion is formed when an atom loses one or more electrons. An anion or negative ion is formed when an atom gains one or more electrons. A **hydrogen bond** is a weak bond between a hydrogen atom of one molecule and an electronegative atom (such as nitrogen, oxygen, or fluorine) of another molecule. The **Van der Waals force** is a weak force between molecules. This type of force is much weaker than actual chemical bonds between atoms.

Review Video: Molecules
Visit mometrix.com/academy and enter code: 349910

Review Video: Anion, Cation, and Octet Rule
Visit mometrix.com/academy and enter code: 303525

Review Video: Ionic Bonding
Visit mometrix.com/academy and enter code: 116546

Interaction of Atoms to Form Compounds

Atoms interact by **transferring** or sharing the electrons furthest from the nucleus. Known as the outer or **valence electrons**, they are responsible for the chemical properties of an element. **Bonds** between atoms are created when electrons are paired up by being transferred or shared. If electrons are transferred from one atom to another, the bond is ionic. If electrons are shared, the bond is covalent. Atoms of the same element may bond together to form molecules or crystalline solids. When two or more different types of atoms bind together chemically, a compound is made. The physical properties of compounds reflect the nature of the interactions among their molecules. These interactions are determined by the structure of the molecule, including the atoms they consist of and the distances and angles between them.

Matter

Matter refers to substances that have mass and occupy space (or volume). The traditional definition of matter describes it as having three states: solid, liquid, and gas. These different states are caused by differences in the distances and angles between molecules or atoms, which result in differences in the energy that binds them. **Solid** structures are rigid or nearly rigid and have strong bonds. Molecules or atoms of **liquids** move around and have weak bonds, although they are not weak enough to readily break. Molecules or atoms of **gases** move almost independently of each other, are typically far apart, and do not form bonds. The current definition of matter describes it as having four states. The fourth is **plasma**, which is an ionized gas that has some electrons that are described as free because they are not bound to an atom or molecule.

Review Video: States of Matter
Visit mometrix.com/academy and enter code: 742449

Most Abundant Elements in the Universe and on Earth

Aside from dark energy and dark matter, which are thought to account for all but four percent of the universe, the two most abundant elements in the universe are **hydrogen** (H) and **helium** (He). After hydrogen and helium, the most abundant elements are oxygen, neon, nitrogen, carbon, silicon, and magnesium. The most abundant isotopes in the solar system are hydrogen-1 and helium-4. Measurements of the masses of elements in the Earth's crust indicate that oxygen (O), silicon (Si), and aluminum (Al) are the most abundant on Earth. Hydrogen in its plasma state is the most abundant chemical element in stars in their main sequences but is relatively rare on planet Earth.

Energy Transformations

The following are some examples of energy transformations:

- **Electric to mechanical**: Ceiling fan
- **Chemical to heat**: A familiar example of a chemical to heat energy transformation is the internal combustion engine, which transforms the chemical energy (a type of potential energy) of gas and oxygen into heat. This heat is transformed into propulsive energy, which is kinetic. Lighting a match and burning coal are also examples of chemical to heat energy transformations.
- **Chemical to light**: Phosphorescence and luminescence (which allow objects to glow in the dark) occur because energy is absorbed by a substance (charged) and light is re-emitted comparatively slowly. This process is different from the one involved with glow sticks. They glow due to chemiluminescence, in which an excited state is created by a chemical reaction and transferred to another molecule.
- **Heat to electricity**: Examples include thermoelectric, geothermal, and ocean thermal.
- **Nuclear to heat**: Examples include nuclear reactors and power plants.
- **Mechanical to sound**: Playing a violin or almost any instrument
- **Sound to electric**: Microphone
- **Light to electric**: Solar panels
- **Electric to light**: Light bulbs

Relationship Between Conservation of Matter and Atomic Theory

Atomic theory is concerned with the characteristics and properties of atoms that make up matter. It deals with matter on a *microscopic level* as opposed to a *macroscopic level*. Atomic theory, for instance, discusses the kinetic motion of atoms in order to explain the properties of macroscopic quantities of matter. John Dalton (1766-1844) is credited with making many contributions to the field of atomic theory that are still considered valid. This includes the notion that all matter consists of atoms and that atoms are indestructible. In other words, atoms can be neither created nor destroyed. This is also the theory behind the conservation of matter, which explains why chemical reactions do not result in any detectable gains or losses in matter. This holds true for chemical reactions and smaller-scale processes. When dealing with large amounts of energy, however, atoms can be destroyed by nuclear reactions. This can happen in particle colliders or atom smashers.

Review Video: John Dalton
Visit mometrix.com/academy and enter code: 565627

Difference Between Atoms and Molecules

Elements from the periodic table such as hydrogen, carbon, iron, helium, mercury, and oxygen are **atoms**. Atoms combine to form molecules. For example, two atoms of hydrogen (H) and one atom of oxygen (O) combine to form one molecule of water (H_2O).

Chemical and Physical Properties

Matter has both physical and chemical properties. **Physical properties** can be seen or observed without changing the identity or composition of matter. For example, the mass, volume, and density of a substance can be determined without permanently changing the sample. Other physical properties include color, boiling point, freezing point, solubility, odor, hardness, electrical conductivity, thermal conductivity, ductility, and malleability. **Chemical properties** cannot be measured without changing the identity or composition of matter. Chemical properties describe how a substance reacts or changes to form a new substance. Examples of chemical properties include flammability, corrosivity, oxidation states, enthalpy of formation, and reactivity with other chemicals.

Chemical and Physical Changes

Physical changes do not produce new substances. The atoms or molecules may be rearranged, but no new substances are formed. Phase changes or changes of state such as melting, freezing, and sublimation are physical changes. For example, physical changes include the melting of ice, the boiling of water, sugar dissolving into water, and the crushing of a piece of chalk into a fine powder. **Chemical changes** involve a chemical reaction and do produce new substances. When iron rusts, iron oxide is formed, indicating a chemical change. Other examples of chemical changes include baking a cake, burning wood, digesting a cracker, and mixing an acid and a base.

Physical and Chemical Properties and Changes

Both physical changes and chemical reactions are everyday occurrences. **Physical changes** do not result in different substances. For example, when water becomes ice it has undergone a physical change, but not a chemical change. It has changed its form, but not its composition. It is still H_2O. **Chemical properties** are concerned with the constituent particles that make up the physicality of a substance. Chemical properties are apparent when **chemical changes** occur. The chemical properties of a substance are influenced by its electron configuration, which is determined in part by the number of protons in the nucleus (the atomic number). Carbon, for example, has 6 protons and 6 electrons. It is an element's outermost valence electrons that mainly determine its chemical properties. Chemical reactions may release or consume energy.

Review Video: Chemical and Physical Properties of Matter
Visit mometrix.com/academy and enter code: 717349

Elements, Compounds, Solutions, and Mixtures

- **Elements** — These are substances that consist of only one type of atom.
- **Compounds** — These are substances containing two or more elements. Compounds are formed by chemical reactions and frequently have different properties than the original elements. Compounds are decomposed by a chemical reaction rather than separated by a physical one.
- **Solutions** — These are homogeneous mixtures composed of two or more substances that have become one.
- **Mixtures** — Mixtures contain two or more substances that are combined but have not reacted chemically with each other. Mixtures can be separated using physical methods, while compounds cannot.

Heat, Energy, Work, and Thermal Energy

- **Heat** — Heat is the transfer of energy from a body or system as a result of thermal contact. Heat consists of random motion and the vibration of atoms, molecules, and ions. The higher the temperature is, the greater the atomic or molecular motion will be.
- **Energy** — Energy is the capacity to do work.
- **Work** — Work is the quantity of energy transferred by one system to another due to changes in a system that is the result of external forces, or macroscopic variables. Another way to put this is that work is the amount of energy that must be transferred to overcome a force. Lifting an object in the air is an example of work. The opposing force that must be overcome is gravity. Work is measured in joules (J). The rate at which work is performed is known as power.
- **Thermal energy** — Thermal energy is the energy present in a system due to temperature.

Types of Energy

Some discussions of energy consider only two types of energy: **kinetic energy** (the energy of motion) and **potential energy** (which depends on relative position or orientation). There are, however, other types of energy. **Electromagnetic waves**, for example, are a type of energy contained by a field. Another type of potential energy is electrical energy, which is the energy it takes to pull apart positive and negative electrical charges. **Chemical energy** refers to the manner in which atoms form into molecules, and this energy can be released or absorbed when molecules regroup. **Solar energy** comes in the form of visible light and non-visible light, such as infrared and ultraviolet rays. **Sound energy** refers to the energy in sound waves.

Review Video: Potential and Kinetic Energy
Visit mometrix.com/academy and enter code: 491502

Chemical Reactions

Chemical reactions measured in human time can take place quickly or slowly. They can take fractions of a second or billions of years. The rates of chemical reactions are determined by how frequently reacting atoms and molecules interact. Rates are also influenced by the temperature and various properties (such as shape) of the reacting materials. **Catalysts** accelerate chemical reactions, while inhibitors decrease reaction rates. Some types of reactions release energy in the form of heat and light. Some types of reactions involve the transfer of either electrons or hydrogen ions between reacting ions, molecules, or atoms. In other reactions, chemical bonds are broken down by heat or light to form reactive radicals with electrons that will readily form new bonds. Processes such as the formation of ozone and greenhouse gases in the atmosphere and the burning and processing of fossil fuels are controlled by radical reactions.

Review Video: Understanding Chemical Reactions
Visit mometrix.com/academy and enter code: 579876

Review Video: Catalysts
Visit mometrix.com/academy and enter code: 288189

READING CHEMICAL EQUATIONS

Chemical equations describe chemical reactions. The reactants are on the left side before the arrow. The products are on the right side after the arrow. The arrow is the mark that points to the reaction or change. The coefficient is the number before the element. This gives the ratio of reactants to products in terms of moles.

The equation for making water from hydrogen and oxygen is $2H_{2(g)} + O_{2(g)} \rightarrow 2H_2O_{(l)}$. The number 2 before hydrogen and water is the coefficient. This means that there are 2 moles of hydrogen and 2 of water. There is 1 mole of oxygen. This does not need to have the number 1 before the symbol for the element. For additional information, the following subscripts are often included to indicate the state of the substance: (g) stands for gas, (l) stands for liquid, (s) stands for solid, and (aq) stands for aqueous. Aqueous means the substance is dissolved in water. Charges are shown by superscript for individual ions, not for ionic compounds. Polyatomic ions are separated by parentheses. This is done so the kind of ion will not be confused with the number of ions.

Review Video: The Process of a Reaction
Visit mometrix.com/academy and enter code: 808039

BALANCING EQUATIONS

An **unbalanced equation** is one that does not follow the **law of conservation of mass**, which states that matter can only be changed, not created or destroyed. If an equation is unbalanced, the numbers of atoms indicated by the stoichiometric coefficients on each side of the arrow will not be equal. Start by writing the formulas for each species in the reaction. Count the atoms on each side and determine if the number is equal. Coefficients must be whole numbers. Fractional amounts, such as half a molecule, are not possible. Equations can be balanced by adjusting the coefficients of each part of the equation to the smallest possible whole number coefficient. $H_2 + O_2 \rightarrow H_2O$ is an example of an unbalanced equation. The balanced equation is $2H_2 + O_2 \rightarrow 2H_2O$, which indicates that it takes two moles of hydrogen and one of oxygen to produce two moles of water.

Review Video: Balancing Chemical Equations
Visit mometrix.com/academy and enter code: 341228

PERIODIC TABLE

The **periodic table** groups elements with similar chemical properties together. The grouping of elements is based on **atomic structure**. It shows periodic trends of physical and chemical properties and identifies families of elements with similar properties. It is a common model for organizing and understanding elements. In the periodic table, each element has its own cell that includes varying amounts of information presented in symbol form about the properties of the element. Cells in the table are arranged in **rows** (periods) and **columns** (groups or families). At minimum, a cell includes the symbol for the element and its atomic number. The cell for hydrogen, for example, which appears first in the upper left corner, includes an "H" and a "1" above the letter. Elements are ordered by atomic number, left to right, top to bottom.

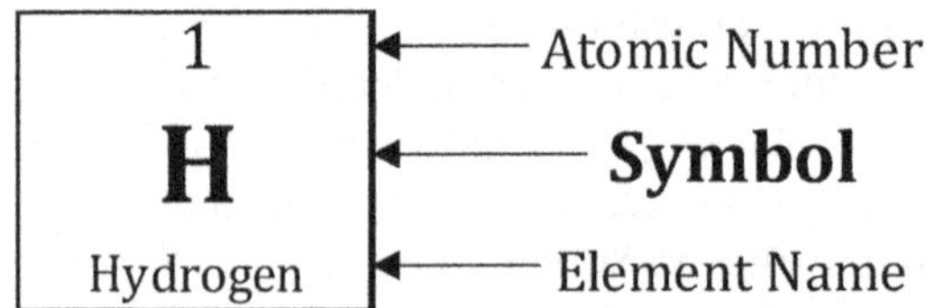

Review Video: The Periodic Table
Visit mometrix.com/academy and enter code: 154828

SOLUTIONS

A solution is a homogeneous mixture, meaning that it is uniform in composition. Solutions consist of a solute (the substance that is dissolved) and a solvent (the substance that does the dissolving). For example, in sugar water the solvent is the water and the solute is the sugar. The intermolecular attraction between the solvent and the solute is called solvation. **Hydration** refers to solutions in which water is the solvent. Solutions are formed when the forces between the molecules of the solute and the solvent are as strong as the forces holding the solute together. An example is that salt (NaCl) dissolves in water to create a solution. The Na^+ and the Cl^- ions in salt interact with the molecules of water and vice versa to overcome the intramolecular forces of the solute.

Review Video: Solutions
Visit mometrix.com/academy and enter code: 995937

Review Video: Volume Percent of a Solution
Visit mometrix.com/academy and enter code: 400152

MIXTURES, SUSPENSIONS, COLLOIDS, EMULSIONS, AND FOAMS

A **mixture** is a combination of two or more substances that are not bonded. **Suspensions** are mixtures of heterogeneous materials. Particles in suspensions are usually larger than those found in true solutions. Dirt mixed vigorously with water is an example of a suspension. The dirt is temporarily suspended in water, but it settles to the bottom of the container once the mixing is ceased. A mixture of large (1 nm to 500 nm) particles is called a **colloidal suspension**. The particles are termed dispersants and the dispersing medium is similar to the solvent in a solution. Sol refers to a liquid or a solid that also has solids dispersed through it, such as milk or gelatin. An aerosol spray is a colloid suspension of gas and the solid or liquid being dispersed. An **emulsion** refers to a liquid or a solid that has small droplets of another liquid dispersed through it. A **foam** is a liquid that has gas dispersed through it.

PH

The **potential of hydrogen** (pH) is a measurement of the concentration of hydrogen ions in a substance in terms of the number of moles of H^+ per liter of solution. All substances fall between 0 and 14 on the pH scale. A lower pH indicates a higher H^+ concentration, while a higher pH indicates a lower H^+ concentration. Pure water has a neutral pH, which is 7. Anything with a pH lower than water (<7) is considered acidic. Anything with a pH higher than water (>7) is a base. Drain cleaner, soap, baking soda, ammonia, egg whites, and sea water are common bases. Urine, stomach acid, citric acid, vinegar, hydrochloric acid, and battery acid are acids. A pH indicator is a substance that acts as a detector of hydrogen or hydronium ions. It is halochromic, meaning it changes color to indicate that hydrogen or hydronium ions have been detected.

Review Video: Overview of pH Levels
Visit mometrix.com/academy and enter code: 187395

PROPERTIES OF ACIDS

When they are dissolved in aqueous solutions, some properties of **acids** are that they conduct electricity, change blue litmus paper to red, have a sour taste, react with bases to neutralize them, and react with active metals to free hydrogen. A **weak acid** is one that does not donate all of its protons or disassociate completely. **Strong acids** include hydrochloric, hydriodic, hydrobromic, perchloric, nitric, and sulfuric. They ionize completely. **Superacids** are those that are stronger than 100 percent sulfuric acid. They include fluoroantimonic, magic, and perchloric acids. Acids can be used in pickling, a process used to remove rust and corrosion from metals. They are also used as catalysts in the processing of minerals and the production of salts and fertilizers. Phosphoric acid (H_3PO_4) is added to sodas and other acids are added to foods as preservatives or to add taste.

Review Video: Properties of Acids and Bases
Visit mometrix.com/academy and enter code: 645283

Properties of Bases

When they are dissolved in aqueous solutions, some properties of **bases** are that they conduct electricity, change red litmus paper to blue, feel slippery, and react with acids to neutralize their properties. A **weak base** is one that does not completely ionize in an aqueous solution, and usually has a low pH. **Strong bases** can free protons in very weak acids. Examples of strong bases are hydroxide compounds such as potassium, barium, and lithium hydroxides. Most are in the first and second groups of the periodic table. A **superbase** is extremely strong compared to sodium hydroxide and cannot be kept in an aqueous solution. Superbases are organized into organic, organometallic, and inorganic classes. Bases are used as insoluble catalysts in heterogeneous reactions and as catalysts in hydrogenation.

Properties of Salts

Some properties of **salts** are that they are formed from acid base reactions, are ionic compounds consisting of metallic and nonmetallic ions, dissociate in water, and are comprised of tightly bonded ions. Some common salts are sodium chloride (NaCl), sodium bisulfate ($NaHSO_4$), potassium dichromate ($K_2Cr_2O_7$), and calcium chloride ($CaCl_2$). Calcium chloride is used as a drying agent, and may be used to absorb moisture when freezing mixtures. Potassium nitrate (KNO_3) is used to make fertilizer and in the manufacturing of explosives. Sodium nitrate ($NaNO_3$) is also used in the making of fertilizer. Baking soda [sodium bicarbonate ($NaHCO_3$)] is a salt, as are Epsom salts [magnesium sulfate ($MgSO_4$)]. Salt and water can react to form a base and an acid. This is called a **hydrolysis reaction**.

Unique Properties of Water

The important properties of water (H_2O) are high polarity, hydrogen bonding, cohesiveness, adhesiveness, high specific heat, high latent heat, and high heat of vaporization. Water is vital to life as we know it. The reason is that water is one of the main parts of many living things.

Water is a liquid at room temperature. The high specific heat of water means that it does not easily break its hydrogen bonds. Also, it resists heat and motion. This is why it has a high boiling point and high vaporization point.

Most substances are denser in their solid forms. However, water is different because its solid-state floats in its liquid state. Water is cohesive. This means that it is drawn to itself. It is also adhesive. This means that it draws in other molecules. If water will attach to another substance, the substance is said to be hydrophilic. Because of its cohesive and adhesive properties, water makes a good solvent. Substances with polar ions and molecules easily dissolve in water.

Kinetic Theory of Gases

The **kinetic theory of gases** assumes that gas molecules are small compared to the distances between them and that they are in constant random motion. The attractive and repulsive forces between gas molecules are negligible. Their kinetic energy does not change with time as long as the temperature remains the same. The higher the temperature is, the greater the motion will be. As the temperature of a gas increases, so does the kinetic energy of the molecules. In other words, gas will occupy a greater volume as the temperature is increased and a lesser volume as the temperature is decreased. In addition, the same amount of gas will occupy a greater volume as the temperature increases, but pressure remains constant. At any given temperature, gas molecules have the same average kinetic energy. The **ideal gas law** is derived from the kinetic theory of gases.

Review Video: Ideal Gas vs. Real Gas
Visit mometrix.com/academy and enter code: 619477

Organic Compounds

Two of the main characteristics of organic compounds are that they generally include carbon and are formed by covalent bonds. Carbon can form long chains, double and triple bonds, and rings. While inorganic compounds tend to have high melting points, organic compounds tend to melt at temperatures below 300° C. They also tend to boil, sublimate, and decompose below this temperature. Unlike inorganic compounds, they are not very water-soluble. Organic molecules are organized into functional groups based on their specific atoms, which helps determine how they will react chemically. A few groups are alkanes, nitro, alkenes, sulfides, amines, and carbolic acids. The hydroxyl group (−OH) consists of alcohols. These molecules are polar, which increases their solubility. By some estimates, there are more than 16 million organic compounds.

Review Video: Organic Compounds
Visit mometrix.com/academy and enter code: 264922

Hydrogen Bonds

Hydrogen bonds are weaker than covalent and ionic bonds and refer to the type of attraction in an electronegative atom such as oxygen, fluorine, or nitrogen. Hydrogen bonds can form within a single molecule or between molecules. A water molecule is **polar**, meaning it is partially positively charged on one end (the hydrogen end) and partially negatively charged on the other (the oxygen end). This is because the hydrogen atoms are arranged around the oxygen atom in a close tetrahedron. Hydrogen is **oxidized** (its number of electrons is reduced) when it bonds with oxygen to form water. Hydrogen bonds tend not only to be weak but also short-lived. They also tend to be numerous. Hydrogen bonds give water many of its important properties, including its high specific heat and high heat of vaporization, its solvent qualities, its adhesiveness and cohesiveness, its hydrophobic qualities, and its ability to float in its solid form. Hydrogen bonds are also an important component of proteins, nucleic acids, and DNA.

Inorganic Compounds

The main trait of inorganic compounds is that they generally lack carbon. Inorganic compounds include mineral salts, alloys, non-metallic compounds such as phosphate, and metal complexes. A metal complex has a central atom (or ion) bonded to surrounding ligands (molecules or anions). The ligands sacrifice the donor atoms (in the form of at least one pair of electrons) to the central atom. Many inorganic compounds are ionic, meaning they form ionic bonds rather than share electrons. They may have high melting points because of this. They may also be colorful, but this is not an absolute identifier of an inorganic compound. Salts, which are inorganic compounds, are an example of inorganic bonding of cations and anions. Some examples of salts are magnesium chloride ($MgCl_2$) and sodium oxide (Na_2O). Oxides, carbonates, sulfates, and halides are classes of inorganic compounds. They are typically poor conductors, are very water soluble, and crystallize easily. Minerals and silicates are also inorganic compounds.

Biology

Subfields of Biology

There are a number of subfields of biology:

- **Zoology** – The study of animals
- **Botany** – The study of plants

- **Biophysics** – The application of the laws of physics to the processes of organisms and the application of the facts about living things to human processes and inventions
- **Biochemistry** – The study of the chemistry of living organisms, including diseases and the pharmaceutical drugs used to cure them
- **Cytology** – The study of cells
- **Histology** – The study of the tissues of plants and animals
- **Organology** – The study of tissues organized into organs
- **Physiology** – The study of the way organisms function, including metabolism, the exchange of matter and energy in nutrition, the senses, reproduction and development, and the work of the nervous system and brain
- **Genetics** – The study of heredity as it relates to the transmission of genes
- **Ethology** – The study of animal behavior
- **Ecology** – The study of the relationship of living organisms to their environments

Classification of Life Forms

All living creatures can be classified into one of three domains and then into one of six kingdoms:

- Domain Bacteria
  - **Kingdom Eubacteria**—single celled prokaryotes with little internal complexity, contains peptidoglycan. Members have just one chromosome, reproduce asexually, may have flagella, and are very simple in form.
- Domain Archaea
  - **Kingdom Archaebacteria**—single celled prokaryotes with little internal complexity, does not contain peptidoglycan. Members have just one chromosome, reproduce asexually, may have flagella, and are very simple in form.
- Domain Eukarya
  - **Kingdom Protista**—single celled eukaryotes with greater internal complexity than Bacteria or Archaea. They have a true nucleus surrounded by a membrane that separates it from the cytoplasm. Most are one-celled and have no complex tissues like plants.
  - **Kingdom Fungi**—single celled or multicellular with considerable variation and complexity. Members have no chlorophyll, so they don't make their own food like plants. They reproduce using spores. Fungi are made up of filaments called hyphae that, in larger fungi, can interlace to form a tissue called mycelium.
  - **Kingdom Plantae**—multicellular with great variation and complexity, rigid cell walls. This group consists of organisms that have chlorophyll and make their own food. Plants have differentiated tissues and reproduce either sexually or asexually.
  - **Kingdom Animalia**—multicellular with much variation and complexity, cell membrane. This group consists of organisms that move around and have to feed on existing organic material.

Review Video: Kingdom Animalia
Visit mometrix.com/academy and enter code: 558413

Review Video: Kingdom Fungi
Visit mometrix.com/academy and enter code: 315081

Review Video: Kingdom Plantae
Visit mometrix.com/academy and enter code: 710084

Characteristics of Invertebrates

Invertebrates are animals with no internal skeletons. They can be divided into three groups:

1. **Marine Invertebrates** – Members of this group live in oceans and seas. Marine invertebrates include sponges, corals, jellyfish, snails, clams, octopuses, squids, and crustaceans, none of which live on the surface.
2. **Freshwater Invertebrates** – Members of this group live in lakes and rivers. Freshwater invertebrates include worms on the bottom, microscopic crustaceans, and terrestrial insect larvae that live in the water column, but only where there is no strong current. Some live on the surface of the water.
3. **Terrestrial Invertebrates** – Members of this group live on dry ground. Terrestrial invertebrates include insects, mollusks (snails, slugs), arachnids, and myriapods (centipedes and millipedes). Terrestrial invertebrates breathe through a series of tubes that penetrate into the body (trachea) and deliver oxygen into tissues. Underground terrestrial invertebrates are generally light-colored with atrophied eyes and no cuticle to protect them from desiccation. They include worms that live underground and in caves and rock crevices. This group also includes insects such as ants that create colonies underground.

Characteristics of Vertebrate Groups

The **vertebrates**, animals with an internal skeleton, are divided into four groups:

1. **Fish** – This group is the most primitive, but is also the group from which all other groups evolved. Fish live in water, breathe with gills, are cold-blooded, have fins and scales, and are typically oviparous, which means they lay eggs. Fish typically have either cartilaginous skeletons (such as rays and sharks) or bony skeletons.
2. **Amphibians** – The skin of animals in this group is delicate and permeable, so they need water to keep it moist. Amphibians are oviparous. The young start out in water with gills, but the adults use lungs.
3. **Reptiles and birds** – The skin of animals in this group has very hard, horn-like scales. Birds have exchanged scales for feathers. Reptiles and birds are oviparous, although birds care for their eggs and reptiles do not. Members have a cloaca, an excretory and reproductive cavity that opens to the outside. Reptiles are cold-blooded, but birds are warm-blooded.
4. **Mammals** – Mammals have bodies covered with fur; are warm-blooded; are viviparous, meaning they give birth to live young which are fed with milk from female mammary glands; and are tetrapods (four-legged). Most live on the ground (except whales and dolphins) and a few fly (bats).

Hunters and Prey Animals

The interaction between **predators** and their **prey** is important to controlling the balance of an ecosystem. **Hunters** are **carnivorous** animals at the top of the ecological pyramid that eat other animals. Hunters tend to be territorial, leaving signs to warn others to stay out or risk a fight. Hunters are equipped to capture with claws, curved beaks, spurs, fangs, etc. They try to use a minimum amount of energy for each capture, so they prey upon the more vulnerable (the old, ill, or very young) when given a choice. Predators never kill more than they can eat. Some hunters have great speed, some stalk, and some hunt in groups. **Prey** animals are those that are captured by predators for food. They are usually **herbivores** further down the ecological pyramid. Prey animals have special characteristics to help them flee from predators. They may hide in nests or caves, become totally immobile to escape detection, have protective coloration or camouflage, have warning coloration to indicate being poisonous, or have shells or quills for protection.

LIFE PROCESSES THAT ALL LIVING THINGS HAVE IN COMMON

Living things share many **processes** that are necessary to survival, but the ways these processes and interactions occur are highly diverse. Processes include those related to:

- **Nutrition** – the process of obtaining, ingesting, and digesting foods; excreting unused or excess substances; and extracting energy from the foods to maintain structure.
- **Transport** (circulation) – the process of circulating essential materials such as nutrients, cells, hormones, and gases (oxygen and hydrogen) to the places they are needed by moving them through veins, arteries, and capillaries. Needed materials do not travel alone, but are "piggybacked" on transporting molecules.
- **Respiration** – the process of breathing, which is exchanging gases between the interior and exterior using gills, trachea (insects), or lungs.
- **Regulation** – the process of coordinating life activities through the nervous and endocrine systems.
- **Reproduction and growth** – the process of producing more of one's own kind and growing from birth to adulthood. The more highly evolved an animal is, the longer its growth time is.
- **Locomotion** (in animals) – the process of moving from place to place in the environment by using legs, flight, or body motions.

ORGANISMS THAT INTERFERE WITH CELL ACTIVITY

Viruses, bacteria, fungi, and other parasites may infect plants and animals and interfere with normal life functions, create imbalances, or disrupt the operations of cells.

- **Viruses** – These enter the body by inhalation (airborne) or through contact with contaminated food, water, or infected tissues. They affect the body by taking over the cell's protein synthesis mechanism to make more viruses. They kill the host cell and impact tissue and organ operations. Examples of viruses include measles, rabies, pneumonia, and AIDS.
- **Bacteria** – These enter the body through breaks in the skin or contaminated food or water, or by inhalation. They reproduce rapidly and produce toxins that kill healthy host tissues. Examples include diphtheria, bubonic plague, tuberculosis, and syphilis.
- **Fungi** – These feed on healthy tissues of the body by sending rootlike tendrils into the tissues to digest them extracellularly. Examples include athlete's foot and ringworm.
- **Parasites** – These enter the body through the skin, via insect bites, or through contaminated food or water. Examples include tapeworms, malaria, or typhus.

HYDROCARBONS AND CARBOHYDRATES

Carbon is an element found in all living things. Two types of carbon molecules that are essential to life are hydrocarbons and carbohydrates. **Hydrocarbons**, composed only of hydrogen and carbon, are the simplest organic molecules. The simplest of these is methane, which has one carbon atom and four hydrogen atoms. Methane is produced by the decomposition of animal or vegetable matter, and is part of petroleum and natural gas. **Carbohydrates** are compounds made of hydrogen, carbon, and oxygen. There are three types of these macromolecules (large molecules):

1. **Sugars** are soluble in water and, although they have less energy than fats, provide energy more quickly.
2. **Starches**, insoluble in water, are long chains of glucose that act as reserve substances. Potatoes and cereals are valuable foods because they are rich in starch. Animals retain glucose in their cells as glycogen, a special type of starch.
3. **Cellulose**, composed of glucose chains, makes up the cells and tissues of plants. It is one of the most common organic materials.

Lipids, Proteins, and Nucleic Acids

Besides hydrocarbons and carbohydrates, there are three other types of carbon molecules that are essential to life: lipids, proteins, and nucleic acids. **Lipids** are compounds that are insoluble or only partially soluble in water. There are three main types: fats, which act as an energy reserve for organisms; phospholipids, which are one of the essential components of cell membranes; and steroids such as cholesterol and estrogen, which are very important to metabolism. **Proteins** are complex substances that make up almost half the dry weight of animal bodies. These molecules contain hydrogen, carbon, oxygen, and other elements, chiefly nitrogen and sulfur. Proteins make up muscle fibers and, as enzymes, act as catalysts. **Nucleic acids** are large molecules (polymers) composed of a large number of simpler molecules (nucleotides). Each one has a sugar containing five carbons (pentose), a phosphorous compound (phosphate group), and a nitrogen compound (nitrogenated base). Nucleic acids facilitate perpetuation of the species because they carry genetic information as DNA and RNA.

Cell

The **cell** is the basic organizational unit of all living things. Each component within a cell has a function that helps organisms grow and survive. There are many different types of cells, and they are unique to each type of organism. The one thing that all cells have in common is a **membrane**, which is comparable to a semi-permeable plastic bag. The membrane is composed of phospholipids. There are also some **transport holes**, which are proteins that help certain molecules and ions move in and out of the cell. The cell is filled with a fluid called **cytoplasm** or cytosol. Within the cell are a variety of **organelles**, groups of complex molecules that help a cell survive, each with its own unique membrane that has a different chemical makeup from the cell membrane. The larger the cell, the more organelles it will need to live.

Review Video: Difference Between Plant and Animal Cells
Visit mometrix.com/academy and enter code: 115568

Review Video: Cell Structure
Visit mometrix.com/academy and enter code: 591293

Nucleus and Mitochondria in Eukaryotic Cells

Eukaryotic cells have a nucleus, a big dark spot floating somewhere in the center that acts like the brain of the cell by controlling eating, movement, and reproduction. A **nuclear envelope** surrounds the nucleus and its contents, but allows RNA and proteins to pass through. **Chromatin**, made up of DNA, RNA, and nuclear proteins, is present in the nucleus. The nucleus also contains a nucleolus made of RNA and protein. **Mitochondria** are very small organelles that take in nutrients, break them down, and create energy for the cell through a process called cellular respiration. There might be thousands of mitochondria depending on the cell's purpose. A muscle cell needs more energy for movement than a cell that transmits nerve impulses, for example. Mitochondria have two membranes: a **cover** and the **inner cristae** that folds over many times to increase the surface work area. The fluid inside the mitochondria, the matrix, is filled with water and enzymes that take food molecules and combine them with oxygen so they can be digested.

Review Video: Mitochondria
Visit mometrix.com/academy and enter code: 444287

Chloroplasts of Plant Cells

Chloroplasts, which make plants green, are the food producers of a plant cell. They differ from an animal cell's mitochondria, which break down sugars and nutrients. **Photosynthesis** occurs when the energy from the sun hits a chloroplast and the chlorophyll uses that energy to combine carbon dioxide and water to make sugars and oxygen. The nutrition and oxygen obtained from plants makes them the basis of all life on earth. A chloroplast has two membranes to contain and protect the inner parts. The **stroma** is an area inside the chloroplast where reactions occur and starches are created. A **thylakoid** has chlorophyll molecules on its surface, and a stack of thylakoids is called a granum. The stacks of sacs are connected by **stromal lamellae**, which act like the skeleton of the chloroplast, keeping all the sacs a safe distance from each other and maximizing the efficiency of the organelle.

Passive and Active Transport

Passive transport within a cell does not require additional energy or active work. For example, when there is a large concentration difference between the outside and the inside of a cell, the pressure of the greater concentration, not energy, will move molecules across the lipid bilayer into the cell. Another example of passive transport is osmosis, which is the movement of water across a membrane. Too much water in a cell can cause it to burst, so the cell moves ions in and out to help equalize the amount of water. **Active transport** is when a cell uses energy to move individual molecules across the cell membrane. **Proteins** embedded in the lipid bilayer do most of the transport work. There are hundreds of different types of proteins because they are specific. For instance, a protein that moves glucose will not move calcium. The activity of these proteins can be stopped by inhibitors or poisons, which can destroy or plug up a protein.

Review Video: Passive Transport: Diffusion and Osmosis
Visit mometrix.com/academy and enter code: 642038

Mitotic Cell Replication

Mitosis is the duplication of a cell and all its parts, including the DNA, into two identical daughter cells. There are five phases in the life cycle of a cell:

1. **Prophase** – This is the process of duplicating everything in preparation for division.
2. **Metaphase** – The cell's different pieces align themselves for the split. The DNA lines up along a central axis and the centrioles send out specialized tubules that connect to the centromere. The centromere has two strands of a chromosome (condensed DNA) attached to it.
3. **Anaphase** – Half of the chromosomes go one way and half go another.
4. **Telophase** – When the chromosomes get to the side of the cell, the cell membrane closes in and splits the cell into two pieces. This results in two separate cells, each with half of the original DNA.
5. **Interphase** – This is the normal state of the cell, or the resting stage between divisions. During this stage, the cell duplicates nucleic acids in preparation for the next division.

Review Video: Mitosis
Visit mometrix.com/academy and enter code: 849894

Microbes

Microbes are the smallest, simplest, and most abundant organisms on earth. Their numbers are incalculable, and a microscope is required to see them. There is a huge variety of microbes, including bacteria, fungi, some algae, and protozoa. Microbes can be harmful or helpful.

Microbes can be **heterotrophic** (eat other things) or **autotrophic** (make food for themselves). They can be solitary or colonial, sexual or asexual. Examples include mold, a multi-cellular type of fungus, and yeasts, which are single-celled (but may live in colonies). A **mushroom** is a fungus that lives as a group of strands underground called hyphae that decompose leaves or bark on the ground. When it reproduces, it develops a mushroom whose cap contains spores. **Mold** is a type of zygote fungi that reproduces with a stalk, but releases zygospores. **Good bacteria** can be those that help plants absorb the nitrogen needed for growth or help grazing animals break down the cellulose in plants. Some **bad bacteria** are killed by the penicillin developed from a fungus.

Roots, Stems, and Leaves

Roots are structures designed to pull water and minerals from soil or water. In large plants such as trees, the roots usually go deep into the ground to not only reach the water, but also to support and stabilize the tree.

There are some plant species that have roots above ground, and there are also plants called epiphytes that live in trees with their roots clinging to the branches. Some roots, like carrots and turnips, serve as food. Roots are classified as **primary** and **lateral** (like a trunk and branches). The **apical meristem** is the tip of a root or shoot that helps the plant increase in length. **Root hairs** are fuzzy root extensions that help with the absorption of water and nutrients. The majority of the plant above ground is made up of the stems (trunk and branches) and leaves. **Stems** transport food and water and act as support structures. **Leaves** are the site for photosynthesis, and are connected to the rest of the plant by a vascular system.

Gymnosperms, Cycads, and Conifers

Gymnosperms are plants with vascular systems and seeds but no flowers (flowers are an evolutionary advancement). The function of the seed is to ensure offspring can be produced by the plant by providing a protective coating that lets the plant survive for long periods until it germinates. It also stores food for the new plant to use until it can make its own. Seeds can be spread over a wide area. **Cycads** are sturdy plants with big, waxy fronds that make them look like ferns or palms. They can survive in harsh conditions if there is warm weather. For reproduction, they have big cones located in the center of the plant. The female plant grows a fruit in the middle of the stem. **Conifers** are trees that thrive in northern latitudes and have cones. Examples of conifers are pine, cedar, redwood, and spruce. Conifers are evergreens because they have needles that take full advantage of the sun year-round. They are also very tall and strong because of the chemical substance xylem in their systems.

Angiosperms

Angiosperms are plants that have flowers. This is advantageous because the plant's seeds and pollen can be spread not only by gravity and wind, but also by insects and animals. Flowers are able to attract organisms that can help pollinate the plant and distribute seeds. Some flowering plants also produce fruit. When an animal eats the fruit, the plant seeds within will be spread far and wide in the animal's excrement. There are two kinds of angiosperm seeds: monocotyledons (monocots) and dicotyledons (dicots). A **cotyledon** is the seed leaf or food package for the developing plant. **Monocots** are simple flowering plants such as grasses, corn, palm trees, and lilies. They always have three petals on their flowers, and their leaves are long strands (like a palm frond). A **dicot** has seeds with two cotyledons, or two seed leaves of food. Most everyday flowers are dicots with four or five petals and extremely complex leaves with veins. Examples include roses, sunflowers, cacti, and cherry trees.

Arthropods

Arthropods have a number of unique characteristics:

- They have an **exoskeleton** (outside instead of inside).
- They **molt**. As the arthropod grows, it must shed its old shell and grow a new one.
- They have several **legs**, which are jointed.
- Their advanced **nervous systems** allow for hunting, moving around, finding a mate, and learning new behaviors for adaptation.
- They develop through **metamorphosis**. As arthropods develop, they change body shape. There are two types of metamorphosis:
    - *Complete* – The entire body shape changes. An example is butterflies, which change from worm-like larvae to insects with wings.
    - *Gradual* – The arthropod starts off small with no wings, and then molts and grows wings. Example: Grasshoppers.

Arthropods include spiders, crustaceans, and the enormous insect species (26 orders) called uniramians. Ranging from fleas to mosquitoes, beetles, dragonflies, aphids, bees, flies, and many more, uniramians have exoskeletons made of chitin, compound eyes, complex digestive systems, and usually six legs. This group is extremely diverse. Some can fly, some have toxins or antennae, and some can make wax, silk, or honey.

Reptiles

One group of vertebrates is the **reptile**. This group includes:

- **Crocodilia** – This is a group of reptiles that can grow quite large, and includes alligators and crocodiles. Normally found near the water in warmer climates, Crocodilia might be more closely related to birds than other reptiles.
- **Squamata** – This is the order of reptiles that includes snakes and lizards. Snakes are special because they have no legs and no ears. They feel vibrations, smell with their tongues, have specialized scales, and can unhinge their jaws to swallow prey that is larger than they are. Like snakes, lizards have scales, but they differ in that they have legs, can dig, can climb trees, and can grab things.
- **Chelonia** – This is the order of reptiles that includes turtles and tortoises. It is a special group because its members have shells. Different varieties live in forests, water, and deserts, or anywhere the climate is warm enough. They also live a long time, up to hundreds of years. Turtles are typically found near water and tortoises on land, even dry areas.

Reproduction in Mammals

When classified according to how they reproduce, there are three types of mammals:

1. **Monotremes** are rare mammals that lay eggs. These were the first mammals, and are more closely related to reptiles than other mammals. Examples include the duck-billed platypus and the spiny anteater.
2. **Marsupials** are special mammals. They give birth to live young, but the babies mature in pouches, where they are carried and can feed on milk. Many are found in Australia. The isolation of this island continent prevented placental mammals from taking hold. Examples of marsupials include kangaroos, possums, and koalas.
3. **Placental mammals** give birth from the females' placenta to live young. The young may be able to walk immediately, or they may need to be carried. They are still dependent on parental care for at least a short time. Placental mammals are the dominant form of mammals. Members of this group include cetaceans such as whales and dolphins, which are mammals that evolved but returned to the ocean.

Respiratory System

The **respiratory system** exchanges gases with the environment. Amphibians exchange gases through their moist skin, and fish use gills, but mammals, birds, and reptiles have lungs. The human respiratory system is made up of the nose, mouth, pharynx, trachea, and two lungs. The purpose of the respiratory system is to bring oxygen into the body and expel carbon dioxide. The respiratory system can inhale viruses, bacteria, and dangerous chemicals, so it is vulnerable to toxins and diseases such as pneumonia, which causes the lungs to fill with fluid until they cannot take in enough oxygen to support the body. **Emphysema**, often caused by smoking tobacco, destroys the tissues in the lungs, which cannot be regenerated. The respiratory system interacts with the **digestive system** in that the mouth and pharynx are used to swallow food and drink, as well as to breathe. It interacts with the circulatory system in that it provides fresh oxygen through blood vessels that pass through the lungs. This oxygen is then carried by the circulatory system throughout the body.

Review Video: Respiratory System
Visit mometrix.com/academy and enter code: 783075

Skeletal System

The human body has an **endoskeleton**, meaning it is inside the body. It is made up of bones instead of the hard plate of exoskeletons or fluids in tubes, which comprise the hydrostatic system of the starfish. The purpose of the skeleton is to support the body, provide a framework to which the muscles and organs can connect, and protect the inner organs. The skull protects the all-important brain and the ribs protect the internal organs from impact. The skeletal system interacts with the muscular system to help the body move, and softer cartilage works with the calcified bone to allow smooth movement of the body. The skeletal system also interacts with the circulatory system in that the marrow inside the bones helps produce both white and red blood cells.

Review Video: Skeletal System
Visit mometrix.com/academy and enter code: 256447

Nervous System

The **nervous system** is divided into two parts: the **central nervous system** (brain and spinal cord) and the **peripheral nervous system** (a network of billions of neurons of different types throughout the entire body). The neurons are connected end to end, and transmit electrical impulses to each other. **Efferent neurons** send impulses from the central system to the limbs and organs. **Afferent neurons** receive sensory information and transmit it back to the central system. The nervous system is concerned with **senses and action**. In other words, it senses something and then acts upon it. An example is a predator sensing prey and attacking it. The nervous system also automatically senses activity inside the body and reacts to stimuli. For example, the first bite of a meal sets the whole digestive system into motion. The nervous system **interacts** with every other system in the body because all the tissues and organs need instruction, even when individuals are not aware of any activity occurring. For instance, the endocrine system is constantly working to produce hormones or adrenaline as needed.

Review Video: Function of the Nervous System
Visit mometrix.com/academy and enter code: 708428

Genetics, Genes, and Chromosomes

Genetics is the science devoted to the study of how characteristics are transmitted from one generation to another. In the 1800s, Gregor Mendel outlined the three laws of heredity that explain how genetics works. Genes are the hereditary units of material that are transmitted from one generation to the next. They are capable of undergoing mutations, can be recombined with other genes, and can determine the nature of an organism, including its color, shape, and size. **Genotype** is the genetic makeup of an individual based on one or more characteristics, while phenotype is the external manifestation of the genotype. For example, genotype determines hair color genes, whereas phenotype is the actual color of the hair observed. **Chromosomes** are the structures inside the nucleus of a cell made up primarily of deoxyribonucleic acid (DNA) and proteins. The chromosomes carry the genes. The numbers vary according to the species, but they are always the same for each species. For example, the human has 46 chromosomes, and the water lily has 112.

Review Video: Chromosomes
Visit mometrix.com/academy and enter code: 132083

Mendel's Contributions to Genetics

Johann Gregor Mendel is known as the father of **genetics**. Mendel was an Austrian monk who performed thousands of experiments involving the breeding of the common pea plant in the garden of his monastery. Mendel kept detailed records including seed color, pod color, seed type, flower color, and plant height for eight years and published his work in 1865. Unfortunately, his work was largely ignored until the early 1900s. Mendel's work showed that genes come in pairs and that dominant and recessive traits are inherited independently of each other. His work established the law of segregation, the law of independent assortment, and the law of dominance.

Darwin's Contributions to the Theory of Evolution

Charles Darwin's theory of evolution is the unifying concept in biology today. From 1831 to 1836, Darwin traveled as a naturalist on a five-year voyage on the *H.M.S. Beagle* around the tip of South America and to the Galápagos Islands. He studied finches, took copious amounts of meticulous notes, and collected thousands of plant and animal specimens. He collected 13 species of finches each with a unique bill for a distinct food source, which led him to believe, due to similarities between the finches, that the finches shared a common ancestor. The similarities and differences of fossils of extinct rodents and modern mammal fossils led him to believe that the mammals had changed over time. Darwin believed that these changes were the result of random genetic changes called mutations. He believed that mutations could be beneficial and eventually result in a different organism over time. In 1859, in his first book, *On the Origin of Species*, Darwin proposed that natural selection was the means by which adaptations would arise over time. He coined the term "natural selection" and said that it is the mechanism of evolution. Because variety exists among individuals of a species, he stated that those individuals must compete for the same limited resources. Some would die, and others would survive. According to Darwin, evolution is a slow, gradual process. In 1871, Darwin published his second book, *Descent of Man, and Selection in Relation to Sex*, in which he discussed the evolution of man.

Contribution to Genetics Made by Alfred Hershey and Martha Chase

Alfred Hershey and Martha Chase did a series of experiments in 1952 known as the **Hershey-Chase experiments**. These experiments showed that deoxyribonucleic acid (DNA), not protein, is the genetic material that transfers information for inheritance. The Hershey-Chase experiments used a bacteriophage, a virus that infects bacteria, to infect the bacteria *Escherichia coli.* The bacteriophage T2 is basically a small piece of DNA enclosed in a protein coating. The DNA contains phosphorus, and the protein coating contains sulfur. In the first set of experiments, the T2 was marked with radioactive phosphorus-32. In the second set of experiments, the T2 was marked with radioactive sulfur-35. For both sets of experiments, after the *E. coli* was infected by the T2, the *E. coli* was isolated using a centrifuge. In the first set of experiments, the radioactive isotope (P-32) was found in the *E. coli*, showing that the genetic information was transferred by the DNA. In the second set of experiments, the radioactive isotope (S-35) was not found in the *E. coli*, showing that the genetic information was not transferred by the protein as was previously thought. Hershey and Chase conducted further experiments allowing the bacteria from the first set of experiments to reproduce, and the offspring was also found to contain the radioactive isotope (P-32) further confirming that the DNA transferred the genetic material.

Ecology

Autotrophs, Producers, Herbivores, Carnivores, Omnivores, and Decomposers

Energy flows in one direction: from the sun, through photosynthetic organisms such as green plants (producers) and algae (autotrophs), and then to herbivores, carnivores, and decomposers. **Autotrophs** are organisms capable of producing their own food. The organic molecules they produce are food for all other organisms (heterotrophs). **Producers** are green plants that manufacture food by photosynthesis. **Herbivores** are animals that eat only plants (deer, rabbits, etc.). Since they are the first animals to receive the energy captured by producers, herbivores are called primary consumers. **Carnivores**, or secondary consumers, are animals that eat the bodies of other animals for food. Predators (wolves, lions, etc.) kill other animals, while scavengers consume animals that are already dead from predation or natural causes (buzzards). **Omnivores** are animals that eat both plants and other animals (humans). **Decomposers** include saprophytic fungi and bacteria that break down the complex structures of the bodies of living things into simpler forms that can be used by other living things. This recycling process releases energy from organic molecules.

ABIOTIC FACTORS AND BIOTIC FACTORS

Abiotic factors are the physical and chemical factors in the environment that are nonliving but upon which the growth and survival of living organisms depends. These factors can determine the types of plants and animals that will establish themselves and thrive in a particular area. Abiotic factors include:

- Light intensity available for photosynthesis
- Temperature range
- Available moisture
- Type of rock substratum
- Type of minerals
- Type of atmospheric gases
- Relative acidity (pH) of the system

Biotic factors are the living components of the environment that affect, directly or indirectly, the ecology of an area, possibly limiting the type and number of resident species. The relationships of predator/prey, producer/consumer, and parasite/host can define a community. Biotic factors include:

- Population levels of each species
- The food requirements of each species
- The interactions between species
- The wastes produced

HOW PLANTS MANUFACTURE FOOD

Plants are the only organisms capable of transforming **inorganic material** from the environment into **organic matter** by using water and solar energy. This transformation is made possible by chloroplasts, flat structures inside plant cells. **Chloroplasts**, located primarily in leaves, contain chlorophyll (the pigment capable of absorbing light and storing it in chemical compounds), DNA, ribosomes, and numerous enzymes. Chloroplasts are surrounded by a membrane. The leaves of plants are the main producers of oxygen, which helps purify the air. The **chlorophyll** in chloroplasts is responsible for the light, or luminous, phase of photosynthesis. The energy it absorbs breaks down water absorbed through the roots into hydrogen and oxygen to form ATP molecules that store energy. In the dark phase, when the plant has no light, the energy molecules are used to attach carbon dioxide to water and form glucose, a sugar.

PRODUCERS, CONSUMERS, AND DECOMPOSERS

The **food chain**, or food web, is a series of events that happens when one organism consumes another to survive. Every organism is involved in dozens of connections with others, so what happens to one affects the environment of the others. In the food chain, there are three main categories:

- **Producers** – Plants and vegetables are at the beginning of the food chain because they take energy from the sun and make food for themselves through photosynthesis. They are food sources for other organisms.
- **Consumers** – There are three levels of consumers: the organisms that eat plants (primary consumers, or herbivores); the organisms that eat the primary consumers (secondary consumers, or carnivores); and, in some ecosystems, the organisms that eat both plants and animals (tertiary consumers, or omnivores).
- **Decomposers** – These are the organisms that eat dead things or waste matter and return the nutrients to the soil, thus returning essential molecules to the producers and completing the cycle.

Review Video: Food Webs
Visit mometrix.com/academy and enter code: 853254

System of Classification for Living Organisms

The main characteristic by which living organisms are classified is the degree to which they are **related**, not the degree to which they resemble each other. The science of classification is called **taxonomy**. This classification is challenging since the division lines between groups is not always clear. Some animals have characteristics of two separate groups. The current system of taxonomy involves placing an organism into a **domain** (Bacteria, Archaea, and Eukarya), and then into a **kingdom** (Eubacteria, Archaeabacteria, Protista, Fungi, Plantae, and Animalia). The kingdoms are divided into phyla, then classes, then orders, then families, and finally genuses and species. For example, the family cat is in the domain of eukaryotes, the kingdom of animals, the phylum of chordates, the class of mammals, the order of carnivores, the family of felidae, and the genus of felis. All species of living beings can be identified with Latin scientific names that are assigned by the worldwide binomial system. The genus name comes first, and is followed by the name of the species. The family cat is *felis domesticus*.

> **Review Video: Biological Classification Systems**
> Visit mometrix.com/academy and enter code: 736052

Properties That Contribute to Earth's Life-Sustaining System

Life on earth is dependent on:

- All three states of **water** – gas (water vapor), liquid, and solid (ice)
- A variety of forms of **carbon**, the basis of life (carbon-based units)
- In the atmosphere, carbon dioxide, in the forms of methane and black carbon soot, produces the **greenhouse effect** that provides a habitable atmosphere.
- The earth's **atmosphere and electromagnetic field**, which shield the surface from harmful radiation and allow useful radiation to go through.
- The **earth's relationship to the sun and the moon**, which creates the four seasons and the cycles of plant and animal life.
- The combination of **water, carbon, and nutrients** that provides sustenance for life and regulates the climate system in a habitable temperature range with non-toxic air.

Geology

Earth System Science

The complex and interconnected dynamics of the continents, atmosphere, oceans, ice, and life forms are the subject of Earth system science. These interconnected dynamics require an interdisciplinary approach that includes chemistry, physics, biology, mathematics, and applied sciences in order to study the Earth as an integrated system and determine (while considering human impact and interaction) the past, present, and future states of the Earth. Scientific inquiry in this field includes exploration of:

- Extreme weather events as they pertain to a changing climate
- Earthquakes and volcanic eruptions as they pertain to tectonic shifts
- Losses in biodiversity in relation to the changes in the Earth's ecosystems
- Causes and effects in the environment
- The Sun's solar variability in relation to the Earth's climate
- The atmosphere's increasing concentrations of carbon dioxide and aerosols
- Trends in the Earth's systems in terms of changes and their consequences

Traditional Earth Science Disciplines

Modern science is approaching the study of the Earth in an integrated fashion that sees the Earth as an interconnected system that is impacted by humankind and, therefore, must include social dimensions. Traditionally, though, the following were the Earth science disciplines:

- **Geology** – This is the study of the origin and structure of the Earth and of the changes it has undergone and is in the process of undergoing. Geologists work from the crust inward.
- **Meteorology** – This is the study of the atmosphere, including atmospheric pressure, temperature, clouds, winds, precipitation, etc. It is also concerned with describing and explaining weather.
- **Oceanography** – This is the study of the oceans, which includes studying their extent and depth, the physics and chemistry of ocean waters, and the exploitation of their resources.
- **Ecology** – This is the study of living organisms in relation to their environment and to other living things. It is the study of the interrelations between the different components of the ecosystem.

Geological Eras

Geologists divide the history of the Earth into units of time called eons, which are divided into **eras**, then into **periods**, then into **epochs** and finally into **ages**. Dates are approximate of course, and there may be variations of a few million years. (Million years ago is abbreviated as Ma.) Some of the most commonly known time periods are:

- **Hadean Eon** – About 4.5 to 3.8 billion years ago
- **Archaean Eon** – 3.8 to 2.5 billion years ago
- **Proterozoic Eon** – 2.5 billion to 542 Ma
- **Phanerozoic Eon** – 542 Ma to the present
    - **Paleozoic Era** – 542 Ma to 251 Ma
        - **Cambrian Period** – 542 to 488 Ma
        - **Ordovician Period** – 488 to 443 Ma
        - **Silurian Period** – 443 to 416 Ma
        - **Devonian Period** – 416 to 359 Ma
        - **Carboniferous Period** – 359 to 290 Ma
        - **Permian Period** – 290 to 252 Ma
    - **Mesozoic Era** – 252 to 65 Ma
        - **Triassic Period** – 252 to 200 Ma
        - **Jurassic Period** – 200 to 150 Ma
        - **Cretaceous Period** – 150 to 65 Ma
    - **Cenozoic Era** – 65 Ma to the present
        - **Paleogene Period** – 65 to 28 Ma
        - **Neogene Period** – 28 to 2 Ma
        - **Quaternary Period** – about 2 Ma to the present

Development of Life on Earth According to Time Periods

The evolution of life on Earth is believed to have occurred as follows:

- Igneous rocks formed. (Hadean Eon)
- The continents formed. (Archaean Eon)
- The first multi-cellular creatures such as hydras, jellyfish, and sponges appeared about 600 Ma.
- Flatworms, roundworms, and segmented worms appeared about 550 Ma.
- Moss, arthropods, octopus, and eels appeared. (Cambrian Period)
- Mushrooms, fungi, and other primitive plants appeared; sea animals began to use calcium to build bones and shells. (Ordovician Period)

- Fish with jaws appeared. (Silurian Period)
- Fish developed lungs and legs (frogs) and went on land; ferns appeared. (Devonian period)
- Reptiles developed the ability to lay eggs on land and pine trees appeared. (Carboniferous Period)
- Dinosaurs dominated the land during the Triassic and Jurassic Periods.
- Flying insects, birds, and the first flowering plants appeared; dinosaurs died out. (Cretaceous Period)
- Mammals evolved and dominated; grasses became widespread. (50 Ma)
- Hominids appeared more than 2 Ma.

Hydrosphere and Hydrologic Cycle

The **hydrosphere** is anything on Earth that is related to water, whether it is in the air, on land, or in a plant or animal system. A water molecule consists of only two atoms of hydrogen and one of oxygen, yet it is what makes life possible. Unlike any other planets that have been discovered, Earth is able to sustain water in a liquid state most of the time. Water vapor and ice are of no use to living organisms. The **hydrologic cycle** is the journey water takes as it proceeds through different forms. Liquid surface water evaporates to form the gaseous state of a cloud, and then becomes liquid again in the form of rain. This process takes about 10 days. This cycle is for surface water only: rivers, lakes, groundwater, ocean surface, etc. Water in the deep ocean and in the heart of glaciers is typically sequestered from the cycle for many thousands of years.

Review Video: Hydrologic Cycle
Visit mometrix.com/academy and enter code: 426578

Aquifers

An **aquifer** is an underground water reservoir formed from groundwater that has infiltrated from the surface by passing through the soil and permeable rock layers to whereever the rock layer is impermeable. The section of permeable layers with water present is called the zone of saturation, and the area above that (with no water) is the zone of aeration. There are two types of aquifers. In one, the water is under pressure (**confined**) as the supply builds up between layers of impermeable rocks and has to move back towards the surface, resulting in a spring or artesian well. The second type of aquifer is called "**unconfined**" because it has room to expand and contract, and the water has to be pumped out. The highest level of the aquifer is called the water table. If water is pumped out of the aquifer such that the water table dips in a specific area, that area is called a cone of depression.

Biosphere

Biosphere is the term used by physical geographers to describe the living world of trees, bugs, and animals. It refers to any place where life exists on Earth, and is the intersection of the hydrosphere, the atmosphere, the land, and the energy that comes from space. The biosphere includes the upper areas of the atmosphere where birds and insects can travel, areas deep inside caves, and hydrothermal vents at the bottom of the ocean.

Factors that affect the biosphere include:

- The **distance and tilt** between the Earth and the Sun – This produces temperatures that are conducive to life and causes the seasons.
- **Climate, daily weather, and erosion** – These change the land and the organisms on and in it.
- Earthquakes, tornadoes, volcanoes, tsunamis, and other **natural phenomena** – These all change the land.
- **Chemical erosion** – This changes the composition of rocks and organic materials.
- **Biological erosion** – This is bacteria and single-celled organisms breaking down organic and inorganic materials.

Ecological System and Biome

An **ecological system**, or ecosystem, is the community of all the living organisms in a specific area interacting with non-living factors such as temperature, sunlight, atmospheric pressure, weather patterns, wind, types of nutrients, etc. An ecosystem's development depends on the energy that passes in and out of it. The boundaries of an ecosystem depend on the use of the term, whether it refers to an ecosystem under a rock or in a valley, pond, or ocean.

A **biome** is a general ecosystem type defined by the plants and animals that live there and the local climate patterns. Examples include tropical rainforests or savannas, deserts, grasslands, deciduous forests, tundra, woodlands, and ice caps. There can be more than one type of biome within a larger climate zone. The transition area between two biomes is an ecotone, which may have characteristics of both biomes.

Erosion

Erosion is the process that breaks down matter, whether it is a rock that is broken into pebbles or mountains that are blown by wind and rained on until they become hills. . The erosion of land by weather or breaking waves is called **denudation**. **Mass wasting** is the movement of masses of dirt and rock from one place to another. This can occur in two ways: **mechanical** (such as breaking a rock with a hammer) or **chemical** (such as pouring acid on a rock to dissolve it). If the material changes color, it indicates that a break down was chemical in nature. Whatever is broken down must go somewhere, so erosion eventually builds something up. For example, an eroded mountain ends up in a river that carries the sediment towards the ocean, where it builds up and creates a wetland or delta at the mouth of the river.

Climates

Scientists have determined the following different types of **climates**:

- Polar (ice caps)
- Polar (tundra)
- Subtropical (dry summer)
- Subtropical (dry winter)
- Subtropical (humid)
- Subtropical (marine west coast)
- Subtropical (Mediterranean)
- Subtropical (wet)
- Tropical (monsoon)
- Tropical (savannah/grasslands)
- Tropical (wet)

Several factors make up and affect climates. These include:

- Temperature
- Atmospheric pressure
- The number of clouds and the amount of dust or smog
- Humidity
- Winds

The moistest and warmest of all the climates is that of the tropical rainforest. It has daily convection thunderstorms caused by the surface daytime heat and the high humidity, which combine to form thunderclouds.

Review Video: Climates
Visit mometrix.com/academy and enter code: 991320

LAYERS OF THE EARTH

The Earth has several distinct layers, each with its own properties:

- **Crust** – This is the outermost layer of the Earth that is comprised of the continents and the ocean basins. It has a variable thickness (35-70 km in the continents and 5-10 km in the ocean basins) and is composed mostly of alumino-silicates.
- **Mantle** – This is about 2900 km thick, and is made up mostly of ferro-magnesium silicates. It is divided into an upper and lower mantle. Most of the internal heat of the Earth is located in the mantle. Large convective cells circulate heat, and may cause plate tectonic movement.
- **Core** – This is separated into the liquid outer core and the solid inner core. The outer core is 2300 km thick (composed mostly of nickel-iron alloy), and the inner core (almost entirely iron) is 12 km thick. The Earth's magnetic field is thought to be controlled by the liquid outer core.

COMPOSITION OF EARTH'S ATMOSPHERE

The Earth's atmosphere is 79% nitrogen, 20% oxygen, and 1% other gases. The oxygen was originally produced almost entirely by algae-type plants. The atmosphere has four layers:

- **Troposphere** – This is the layer closest to the Earth where all weather takes place. It is the region that contains rising and falling packets of air. Air pressure at sea level is 0.1 atmospheres, but the top of the troposphere is about 10% of that amount.
- **Stratosphere** – In this layer, air flow is mainly horizontal. The upper portion has a thin layer of concentrated ozone (a reactive form of oxygen) that is largely responsible for absorbing the Sun's ultraviolet rays.
- **Mesosphere** – This is the coldest layer. Temperatures drop to -100°C at the top.
- **Thermosphere** – This is divided into the lower ionosphere and the higher exosphere. This layer is very thin and has many ionized atoms with a net electrical charge. The aurora and Van Allen Belts are here. This layer also absorbs the most energetic photons from the Sun and reflects radio waves, enabling long distance radio communication.

Review Video: Earth's Atmosphere
Visit mometrix.com/academy and enter code: 417614

PALEONTOLOGY

Paleontology is the study of prehistoric plant and animal life through the analysis of **fossil remains**. These fossils reveal the ecologies of the past and the path of evolution for both extinct and living organisms. A historical science, paleontology seeks information about the identity, origin, environment, and evolution of past organisms and what they can reveal about the past of the Earth as a whole. Paleontologists seek to explain causes rather than conduct experiments to observe effects. It is related to the fields of biology, geology, and archaeology, and is divided into several sub-disciplines concerned with the types of fossils studied, the process of fossilization, and the ecology and climate of the past. Paleontologists also help identify the composition of the Earth's rock layers by the fossils that are found, thus identifying potential sites for oil, mineral, and water extraction.

DETERMINING THE ORDER IN WHICH GEOLOGIC EVENTS OCCURRED USING THE ROCK RECORD

The **Law of Superposition** logically assumes that the bottom layer of a series of sedimentary layers is the oldest, unless it has been overturned or older rock has been pushed over it. In addition, igneous intrusions can cut through or flow above already present rocks (e.g., lava flows). This is a further indication that the lower rock layers are older. Another guideline for the rock record is that **rock layers** are older than the folds and faults in them because the rocks must exist before they can be folded or faulted. If a rock contains **atomic nuclei**, reference tables of the half-lives of commonly used radio isotopes can be used to match the decay rate of known substances to the nuclei in a rock, and thereby determine its age. Ages of rocks can also be determined from **contact metamorphism**, the re-crystallization of pre-existing rocks due to changes in physical and chemical conditions, such as heat, pressure, and chemically active fluids that might be present in lava or polluted waters.

Matching Rocks and Geologic Events in One Place with Those of Another

Geologists physically follow rock layers from one location to another by a process called "walking the outcrop." Geologists walk along the outcropping to see where it goes and what the differences and similarities of the neighboring locations they cross are. Similar rock **types** or **patterns** of rock layers that are similar in terms of thickness, color, composition, and fossil remains tell geologists that two locations have a similar geologic history. Fossils are found all over the Earth, but are from a relatively **small time period** in Earth's history. Therefore, fossil evidence helps date a rock layer, regardless of where it occurs. **Volcanic ash** is a good time indicator since ash is deposited quickly over a widespread area. Matching the date of an eruption to the ash allows for a precise identification of time. Similarly, the **meteor impact** at the intersection of the Cretaceous and Tertiary Periods left a time marker. Wherever the meteor's iridium content is found, geologists are able to date rock layers.

Sequencing the Earth's Geologic History from the Fossil and Rock Record

Reference tables are used to match specimens and time periods. For example, the fossil record has been divided into time units of the Earth's history. Rocks can therefore be dated by the fossils found with them. There are also reference tables for dating plate motions and mountain building events in geologic history. Since humans have been around for a relatively short period of time, **fossilized human remains** help to affix a date to a location. Some areas have missing **geologic layers** because of erosion or other factors, but reference tables specific to a region will list what is complete or missing. The theory of **uniformitarianism** assumes that geologic processes have been the same throughout history. Therefore, the way erosion or volcanic eruptions happen today is the same as the way these events happened millions of years ago because there is no reason for them to have changed. Therefore, knowledge about current events can be applied to the past to make judgments about events in the rock record.

Revealing Changes in Earth's History by the Fossil and Rock Records

Fossils can show how animal and plant life have changed or remained the same over time. For example, fossils have provided evidence of the existence of dinosaurs even though they no longer roam the Earth, and have also been used to prove that certain insects have been around for hundreds of millions of years. Fossils have been used to identify four basic eras: **Proterozoic**, the age of primitive life; **Paleozoic**, the age of fishes; **Mesozoic**, the age of dinosaurs; and **Cenozoic**, the age of mammals. Most ancient forms of life have disappeared, and there are reference tables that list when this occurred. Fossil records also show the evolution of certain life forms, such as the horse from the eohippus. However, the majority of changes do not involve evolution from simple to complex forms, but rather an increase in the variety of forms.

Mountains

A **mountain** is a portion of the Earth that has been raised above its surroundings by volcanic action or tectonic plate movement. Mountains can be made of any type of rock and most lie along active plate boundaries. There are two major mountain systems. The **Circum-Pacific** encircles the entire Pacific Ocean, from New Guinea up across Japan and the Aleutians and down to southern South America. The **Alpine-Himalaya** stretches from northern Africa across the Alps and to the Himalayas and Indonesia. **Orogeny** is the term for the process of natural mountain formation. Therefore, physical mountains are orogens. **Folded mountains** are created through the folding of rock layers when two crustal plates come together. The Alps and Himalayas are folded mountains. The latter was formed by the collision of India with Asia. **Fault-block mountains** are created from the tension forces of plate movements. These produce faults that vertically displace one section to form a mountain. **Dome mountains** are created from magma pushing up through the Earth's crust.

Volcanoes and Volcanic Mountains

Volcanoes are classified according to their activity level. An **active** volcano is in the process of erupting or building to an eruption; a dormant volcano has erupted before and may erupt again someday, but is not currently active; and an **extinct** volcano has died out volcanically and will not erupt ever again. Active volcanoes endanger plant and animal life, but lava and ash add enriching minerals to the soil. There are three types of volcanic mountains:

- **Shield volcanoes** are the largest volcanic mountains because of a repeated, viscous lava flow from small eruptions over a long period of time that cause the mountain to grow.
- **Cinder cone volcanoes**, or linear volcanoes, are small in size, but have massive explosions through linear shafts that spread cinders and ash around the vent. This results in a cone-shaped hill.
- **Composite volcanoes** get their name from the mix of lava and ash layers that build the mountain.

Subdivisions of Rock

The three major subdivisions of rock are:

- **Igneous** (magmatites) – This type is formed from the cooling of liquid magma. In the process, minerals crystallize and amalgamate. If solidification occurs deep in the Earth (plutonic rock), the cooling process is slow. This allows for the formation of large crystals, giving rock a coarse-grained texture (granite). Quickly cooled magma has a glassy texture (obsidian).
- **Metamorphic** – Under conditions of high temperature and pressure within the Earth's crust, rock material melts and changes structure, transitioning or metamorphosing into a new type of rock with different minerals. If the minerals appear in bands, the rock is foliated. Examples include marble (unfoliated) and slate (foliated).
- **Sedimentary** – This is the most common type of rock on Earth. It is formed by sedimentation, compaction, and then cementation of many small particles of mineral, animal, or plant material. There are three types of sedimentary rocks: clastic, clay, and sand that came from disintegrated rocks; chemical (rock salt and gypsum), formed by evaporation of aqueous solutions; and biogenic (coal), formed from animal or plant remnants.

Review Video: Igneous, Sedimentary, and Metamorphic Rocks
Visit mometrix.com/academy and enter code: 689294

Glaciers

Glaciers start high in the mountains, where snow and ice accumulate inside a cirque (a small semicircular depression). The snow becomes firmly packed into masses of coarse-grained ice that are slowly pulled down a slope by gravity. Glaciers grow with large amounts of snowfall and retreat (diminish) if warm weather melts more ice than can be replaced. Glaciers once covered large areas of both the northern and southern hemispheres with mile-thick ice that carved out valleys, fjords, and other land formations. They also moved plants, animals, and rocks from one area to another. There were two types of glaciers: **valley**, which produced U-shaped erosion and sharp-peaked mountains; and **continental**, which moved over and rounded mountain tops and ridges. These glaciers existed during the ice ages, the last of which occurred from 2.5 million years ago to 12,000 years ago.

Earth Science and Weather

Layers Above the Surface of Earth

The **ozone layer**, although contained within the stratosphere, is determined by ozone (O_3) concentrations. It absorbs the majority of ultraviolet light from the Sun. The ionosphere is part of both the exosphere and the thermosphere. It is characterized by the fact that it is a plasma, a partially ionized gas in which free electrons and positive ions are attracted to each other, but are too energetic to remain fixed as a molecule. It starts at about 50 km above Earth's surface and goes to 1,000 km. It affects radio wave transmission and auroras. The ionosphere pushes against the inner edge of the Earth's magnetosphere, which is the highly magnetized, non-spherical region around the Earth. The homosphere encompasses the troposphere, stratosphere, and mesosphere. Gases in the homosphere are considered well mixed. In the heterosphere, the distance that particles can move without colliding is large. As a result, gases are stratified according to their molecular weights. Heavier gases such as oxygen and nitrogen occur near the bottom of the heterosphere, while hydrogen, the lightest element, is found at the top.

Review Video: Earth's Atmosphere
Visit mometrix.com/academy and enter code: 417614

Tropospheric Circulation

Most weather takes place in the **troposphere**. Air circulates in the atmosphere by convection and in various types of "cells." Air near the equator is warmed by the Sun and rises. Cool air rushes under it, and the higher, warmer air flows toward Earth's poles. At the poles, it cools and descends to the surface. It is now under the hot air, and flows back to the equator. Air currents coupled with ocean currents move heat around the planet, creating winds, weather, and climate. Winds can change direction with the seasons. For example, in Southeast Asia and India, summer monsoons are caused by air being heated by the Sun. This air rises, draws moisture from the ocean, and causes daily rains. In winter, the air cools, sinks, pushes the moist air away, and creates dry weather.

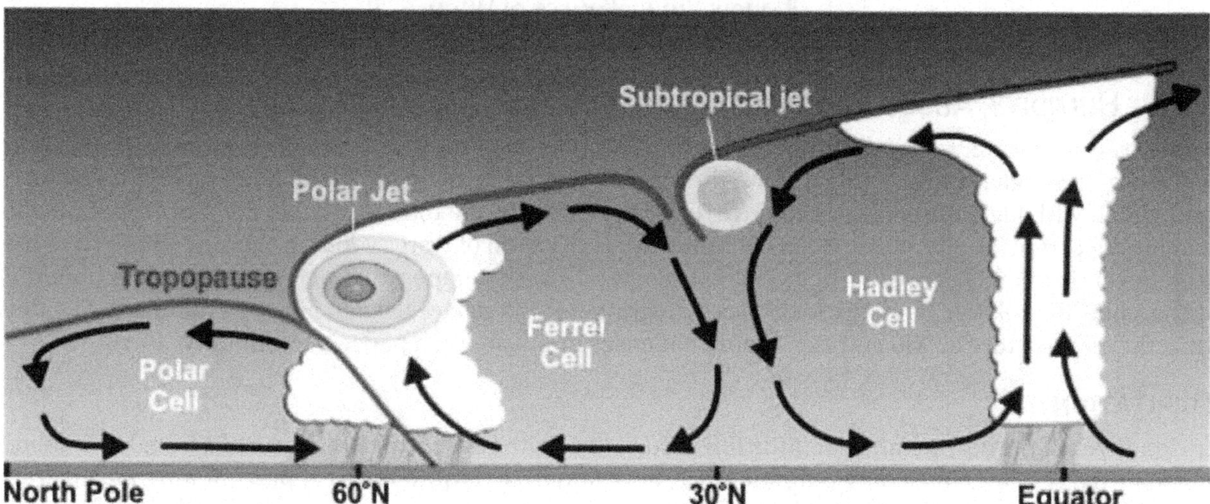

Common Weather Phenomena and Equipment to Measure Them

Common **atmospheric conditions** that are frequently measured are temperature, precipitation, wind, and humidity. These weather conditions are often measured at permanently fixed **weather stations** so weather data can be collected and compared over time and by region. Measurements may also be taken by ships, buoys, and underwater instruments. Measurements may also be taken under special circumstances. Common instruments used and measurements taken include:

- A **thermometer** for measuring temperature
- A **barometer** for measuring barometric/air pressure
- A **hygrometer** for measuring humidity
- An **anemometer** for measuring wind speed
- A **weather vane** for measuring wind direction
- A **rain gauge** for measuring precipitation

WEATHER, CLIMATE, AND METEOROLOGY

Meteorology is the study of the atmosphere, particularly as it pertains to forecasting the weather and understanding its processes. **Weather** is the condition of the atmosphere at any given moment. Most weather occurs in the troposphere and includes changing events such as clouds, storms, and temperature, as well as more extreme events such as tornadoes, hurricanes, and blizzards. **Climate** refers to the average weather for a particular area over time, typically at least 30 years. Latitude is an indicator of climate. Changes in climate occur over long time periods.

WINDS AND GLOBAL WIND BELTS

Winds are the result of air moving by convection. Masses of warm air rise, and cold air sweeps into their place. The warm air also moves, cools, and sinks. The term "prevailing wind" refers to the wind that usually blows in an area in a single direction. **Dominant winds** are the winds with the highest speeds. Belts or bands that run latitudinally and blow in a specific direction are associated with **convection cells. Hadley cells** are formed directly north and south of the equator. The **Farrell cells** occur at about 30° to 60°. The jet stream runs between the Farrell cells and the polar cells. At the higher and lower latitudes, the direction is easterly. At mid latitudes, the direction is westerly. From the North Pole to the south, the surface winds are Polar High Easterlies, Subpolar Low Westerlies, Subtropical High or Horse Latitudes, North-East Trade winds, Equatorial Low or Doldrums, South-East Trades, Subtropical High or Horse Latitudes, Subpolar Low Easterlies, and Polar High.

Review Video: Source of Wind
Visit mometrix.com/academy and enter code: 451712

RELATIVE HUMIDITY, ABSOLUTE HUMIDITY, AND DEW POINT TEMPERATURE

Humidity refers to water vapor contained in the air. The amount of moisture contained in air depends upon its temperature. The higher the air temperature, the more moisture it can hold. These higher levels of moisture are associated with higher humidity. **Absolute humidity** refers to the total amount of moisture air is capable of holding at a certain temperature. **Relative humidity** is the ratio of water vapor in the air compared to the amount the air is capable of holding at its current temperature. As temperature decreases, absolute humidity stays the same and relative humidity increases. A hygrometer is a device used to measure humidity. The **dew point** is the temperature at which water vapor condenses into water at a particular humidity.

PRECIPITATION

After clouds reach the dew point, **precipitation** occurs. Precipitation can take the form of a liquid or a solid. It is known by many names, including rain, snow, ice, dew, and frost. **Liquid** forms of precipitation include rain and drizzle. Rain or drizzle that freezes on contact is known as freezing rain or freezing drizzle. **Solid or frozen** forms of precipitation include snow, ice needles or diamond dust, sleet or ice pellets, hail, and graupel or snow pellets. Virga is a form of precipitation that evaporates before reaching the ground. It usually looks like sheets or shafts falling from a cloud. The amount of rainfall is measured with a rain gauge. Intensity can be measured according to how fast precipitation is falling or by how severely it limits visibility. Precipitation plays a major role in the water cycle since it is responsible for depositing much of the Earth's fresh water.

CLOUDS

Clouds form when air cools and warm air is forced to give up some of its water vapor because it can no longer hold it. This vapor condenses and forms tiny droplets of water or ice crystals called clouds. Particles, or aerosols, are needed for water vapor to form water droplets. These are called **condensation nuclei**. Clouds are created by surface heating, mountains and terrain, rising air masses, and weather fronts. Clouds precipitate, returning the water they contain to Earth. Clouds can also create atmospheric optics. They can scatter light, creating colorful phenomena such as rainbows, colorful sunsets, and the green flash phenomenon.

Review Video: Types of Clouds
Visit mometrix.com/academy and enter code: 803166

High, Middle, and Low Cloud Types

Most clouds can be classified according to the altitude of their base above Earth's surface. **High clouds** occur at altitudes between 5,000 and 13,000 meters. **Middle clouds** occur at altitudes between 2,000 and 7,000 meters. **Low clouds** occur from the Earth's surface to altitudes of 2,000 meters. Types of high clouds include cirrus (Ci), thin wispy mare's tails that consist of ice; cirrocumulus (Cc), small, pillow-like puffs that often appear in rows; and cirrostratus (Cs), thin, sheet-like clouds that often cover the entire sky. Types of middle clouds include altocumulus (Ac), gray-white clouds that consist of liquid water; and altostratus (As), grayish or blue-gray clouds that span the sky. Types of low clouds include stratus (St), gray and fog-like clouds consisting of water droplets that take up the whole sky; stratocumulus (Sc), low-lying, lumpy gray clouds; and nimbostratus (Ns), dark gray clouds with uneven bases that indicate rain or snow. Two types of clouds, cumulus (Cu) and cumulonimbus (Cb), are capable of great vertical growth. They can start at a wide range of altitudes, from the Earth's surface to altitudes of 13,000 meters.

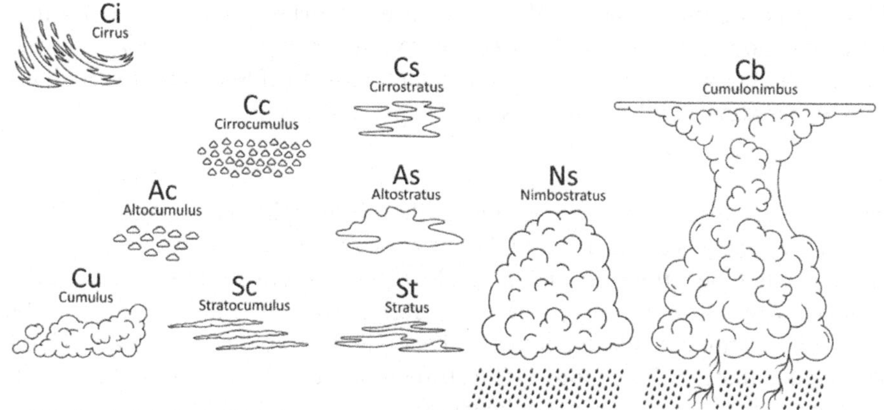

Air Masses

Air masses are large volumes of air in the troposphere of the Earth. They are categorized by their temperature and by the amount of water vapor they contain:

- **Arctic** and **Antarctic** air masses are cold
- **Polar** air masses are cool
- **Tropical** and **equatorial** air masses are hot
- **Maritime** and **monsoon** air masses are moist and unstable
- **Continental** and **superior** air masses are dry

Weather Fronts and Weather Maps

A **weather front** is the area between two differing masses of air that affects weather. Movement of a front is influenced by the jet stream and other high winds as well as the type of front; cold fronts move up to twice as fast as warm ones. It is in the turbulent frontal area that weather events take place, both commonplace and dramatic. This area also creates temperature changes. Weather phenomena include rain, thunderstorms, high winds, tornadoes, cloudiness, clear skies, and hurricanes. Different fronts can be plotted on weather maps using a set of designated symbols. Surface weather maps can also include symbols representing clouds, rain, temperature, air pressure, and fair weather.

Space Science

Astronomy

Astronomy is the scientific study of celestial objects and their positions, movements, and structures. *Celestial* does not refer to the Earth by itself, but does include its movement through space. Other celestial objects include the Sun, the Moon, planets, satellites, asteroids, meteors, comets, stars, galaxies, the universe, and other space phenomena. The term astronomy has its roots in the Greek words *astro* and *nomos*, which means "laws of the stars."

Review Video: Astronomy
Visit mometrix.com/academy and enter code: 640556

Universe

Origin

The **universe** can be said to consist of everything and nothing. The universe contains all of space, matter, energy, and time. There are likely still phenomena that have yet to be discovered. The universe can also be thought of as nothing, since a vast portion of the known universe is empty space. It is believed that the universe is expanding. The **Big Bang** is a core part of a theory developed to explain the origin of the universe. It is widely accepted among astronomers, though there are other theories regarding the origin of the universe, such as the **Steady-State theory** and the **Creationist theory**. According to the Big Bang model, all the matter in the universe was once in one place. This matter underwent a huge explosion that spread it into space. Galaxies formed from, this material and the universe is still expanding.

Structure

What can be seen of the universe is believed to be at least 93 billion light years across. To put this into perspective, the Milky Way galaxy is about 100,000 light years across. Our view of matter in the universe is that it forms into clumps which become stars, galaxies, clusters of galaxies, superclusters, and the Great Wall of galaxies. **Galaxies** consist of stars, some with planetary systems. Some estimates state that the universe is about 13 billion years old. It is not considered dense and is believed to consist of 73% dark energy, 23% cold dark matter, and 4% regular matter. Cosmology is the study of the universe. Interstellar medium (ISM) is the gas and dust in the interstellar space between a galaxy's stars.

Review Video: Dark Matter
Visit mometrix.com/academy and enter code: 251909

Galaxies

Galaxies consist of stars, stellar remnants, and dark matter. **Dwarf galaxies** contain as few as 10 million stars, while giant galaxies contain as many as 1 trillion stars. Galaxies are gravitationally bound, meaning that stars, star systems, other gases, and dust orbit the galaxy's center. The Earth exists in the **Milky Way galaxy** and the nearest galaxy to ours is the **Andromeda galaxy**. Galaxies can be classified by their visual shape into elliptical, spiral, irregular, and starburst galaxies. It is estimated that there are more than 100 billion galaxies in the universe ranging from 1,000 to 100,000 parsecs in diameter. Galaxies can be megaparsecs apart. Intergalactic space consists of a gas with an average density of less than one atom per cubic meter. Galaxies are organized into clusters which form superclusters. Dark matter may account for up to 90% of the mass of galaxies. Dark matter is still not well understood.

Planets

In order of their distance from the Sun (closest to furthest away), the **planets** are: Mercury, Venus, Earth, Mars, Jupiter, Saturn, Uranus, and Neptune (Pluto is now considered to be a dwarf planet). All the planets revolve around the Sun, which is an average-sized star in the spiral Milky Way galaxy. They revolve in the same direction in nearly circular orbits. If the planets were viewed by looking down from the Sun, they would rotate in a counter-clockwise direction. All the planets are in, or near, the same plane, called the ecliptic, and their axis of rotation is nearly perpendicular to the ecliptic. The only exception is Uranus, which is tipped on its side.

Terrestrial Planets, Jovian Planets, and Mass of Planets

The **Terrestrial Planets** are: Mercury, Venus, Earth, and Mars. These are the four planets closest to the Sun. They are called terrestrial because they all have a compact, rocky surface similar to the Earth's. Venus, Earth, and Mars have significant atmospheres, but Mercury has almost no atmosphere.

The **Jovian Planets** are: Jupiter (the largest planet), Saturn, Uranus, and Neptune. They are called Jovian (Jupiter-like) because of their huge sizes in relation to that of the Earth, and because they all have a gaseous nature like Jupiter. Although gas giants, some or all of the Jovian Planets may have small, solid cores.

The Sun represents 99.85% of all the matter in our solar system. Combined, the planets make up only 0.135% of the mass of the solar system, with Jupiter having twice the mass of all the other planets combined. The remaining 0.015% of the mass comes from comets, planetary satellites, asteroids, meteoroids, and interplanetary medium.

Review Video: Terrestrial Planets
Visit mometrix.com/academy and enter code: 100346

Definition of Planet

On August 24, 2006, the International Astronomical Union redefined the criteria a body must meet to be classified as a planet, stating that the following conditions must be met:

- "A planet orbits around a star and is neither a star nor a moon."
- "Its shape is spherical due to its gravity."
- "It has 'cleared' the space of its orbit."

A **dwarf planet** such as Pluto does not meet the third condition. Small solar system bodies such as asteroids and comets meet only the first condition.

Solar System

The **solar system** developed about 4.6 billion years ago out of an enormous cloud of dust and gas circling around the Sun. Four rocky planets orbit relatively close to the Sun. Their inside orbits are separated from the outside orbits of the four, larger gaseous planets by an asteroid belt. Pluto, some comets, and several small objects circle in the Kuiper belt outside Neptune's orbit. The Oort cloud, composed of icy space objects, encloses the planetary system like a shell.

Review Video: The Solar System
Visit mometrix.com/academy and enter code: 273231

Earth's Moon

The Moon is the closest celestial body to Earth. Its proximity has allowed it to be studied since the invention of the telescope. As a result, its landforms have been named after astronomers, philosophers, and other scholars. Its surface has many craters created by asteroids since it has no protective atmosphere. These dark lowlands looked like seas to early astronomers, so many have been given names like the Sea of Tranquility, even though there is virtually no water on the Moon except possibly in its polar regions. These impact craters and depressions actually contain solidified lava flows. The bright highlands were thought to be continents, and were named terrae. The rocks of the Moon have been pounded by asteroids so often that there is a layer of rubble and dust called the regolith. Also, because there is no protective atmosphere, temperatures on the Moon vary widely, from 265°F to -255°F.

EARTH'S SUN AND OTHER STARS

A **star** begins as a cloud of hydrogen and some heavier elements drawn together by their own mass. As the matter coalesces due to its own gravity, it begins to rotate. Once there is sufficient mass, the core heats up to several million degrees Fahrenheit, which causes the hydrogen atoms to lose their shells and their nuclei to fuse. This releases enormous amounts of energy, generates an outward pressure that is balanced by the pull of gravity, and enables the star to become stable. At this point the star is in a stage called the **main sequence**. This is the stage our Sun is in, and it will remain in this stage until its supply of hydrogen fuel runs out. Stars are not always alone like our Sun, and may exist in pairs or groups. The hottest stars shine blue-white; medium-hot stars like our Sun glow yellow; and cooler stars appear orange. The Sun is an **average star** in terms of mass, light production, and size. All stars, including our Sun, have a **core** where fusion happens; a **photosphere** (surface) that produces sunspots (cool, dark areas); a red **chromosphere** that emits solar (bright) flares and shooting gases; and a **corona**, the transparent area only seen during an eclipse.

Review Video: The Sun
Visit mometrix.com/academy and enter code: 699233

COMETS, ASTEROIDS, AND METEOROIDS

Comets are celestial bodies composed of dust, rock, frozen gases, and ice. Invisible until they near the Sun, comets emit volatile components in jets of gas and dust when exposed to the Sun's heat. The **coma** is the comet's fog-like envelope that glows as it reflects sunlight and releases radiation. **Solar winds** blow a comet away from the Sun and give it a tail of dust or electrically charged molecules. Each orbit of a comet causes it to lose matter until it breaks up or vaporizes into the Sun.

Asteroids are irregularly-shaped boulders, usually less than 60 miles in diameter, that orbit the Sun. Most are made of graphite; about 25% are silicates, or iron and nickel. Collisions or gravitational forces can cause them to fly off and possibly hit a planet.

Meteoroids are fragments of asteroids of various sizes. If they come through Earth's atmosphere, they are called meteors or shooting stars. If they land on Earth, they are called meteorites, and create craters on impact (the Barringer Crater in Arizona).

Chapter Quiz

Ready to see how well you retained what you just read? Scan the QR code to go directly to the chapter quiz interface for this study guide. If you're using a computer, simply visit the bonus page at **mometrix.com/bonus948/ged** and click the Chapter Quizzes link.

GED Practice Test #1

Want to take this practice test in an online interactive format?
Check out the bonus page, which includes interactive practice questions and much more: **mometrix.com/bonus948/ged**

Reasoning Through Language Arts—Reading

Refer to the following for questions 1–6:

History of England

by Charles Dickens

If you look at a Map of the World, you will see, in the left-hand upper corner of the Eastern Hemisphere, two Islands lying in the sea. They are England and Scotland, and Ireland. England and Scotland form the greater part of these Islands. Ireland is the next in size. The little neighbouring islands, which are so small upon the Map as to be mere dots, are chiefly little bits of Scotland, —broken off, I dare say, in the course of a great length of time, by the power of the restless water.

In the old days, a long, long while ago..., these Islands were in the same place, and the stormy sea roared round them, just as it roars now. But the sea was not alive, then, with great ships and brave sailors, sailing to and from all parts of the world. It was very lonely. The Islands lay solitary, in the great expanse of water. The foaming waves dashed against their cliffs, and the bleak winds blew over their forests; but the winds and waves brought no adventurers to land upon the Islands, and the savage Islanders knew nothing of the rest of the world, and the rest of the world knew nothing of them.

It is supposed that the Phoenicians, who were an ancient people, famous for carrying on trade, came in ships to these Islands, and found that they produced tin and lead; both very useful things, as you know, and both produced to this very hour upon the sea-coast. The most celebrated tin mines in Cornwall are, still, close to the sea. One of them, which I have seen, is so close to it that it is hollowed out underneath the ocean; and the miners say, that in stormy weather, when they are at work down in that deep place, they can hear the noise of the waves thundering above their heads. So, the Phœnicians, coasting about the Islands, would come, without much difficulty, to where the tin and lead were.

The Phœnicians traded with the Islanders for these metals, and gave the Islanders some other useful things in exchange. The Islanders were, at first, poor savages, going almost naked, or only dressed in the rough skins of beasts, and staining their bodies, as other savages do, with coloured earths and the juices of plants. But the Phœnicians, sailing over to the opposite coasts of France and Belgium, and saying to the people there, 'We have been to those white cliffs across the water, which you can see in fine weather, and from that country, which is called Britain, we bring this tin and lead,' tempted some of the French and Belgians to come over also. These people settled themselves on the south coast of England, which is now called Kent; and, although they were a rough people too, they taught the savage Britons some useful arts, and improved that part of the Islands. It is probable that other people came over from Spain to Ireland, and settled there.

Thus, by little and little, strangers became mixed with the Islanders, and the savage Britons grew into a wild, bold people; almost savage, still, especially in the interior of the country away from the sea where the foreign settlers seldom went; but hardy, brave, and strong.

The whole country was covered with forests, and swamps. The greater part of it was very misty and cold. There were no roads, no bridges, no streets, no houses that you would think deserving of the name. A town was nothing but a collection of straw-covered huts, hidden in a thick wood, with a ditch all round, and a low wall, made of mud, or the trunks of trees placed one upon another. The people planted little or no corn, but lived upon the flesh of their flocks and cattle. They made no coins, but used metal rings for money. They were clever in basket-work, as savage people often are; and they could make a coarse kind of cloth, and some very bad earthenware. But in building fortresses they were much more clever.

They made boats of basket-work, covered with the skins of animals, but seldom, if ever, ventured far from the shore. They made swords, of copper mixed with tin; but, these swords were of an awkward shape, and so soft that a heavy blow would bend one. They made light shields, short pointed daggers, and spears—which they jerked back after they had thrown them at an enemy, by a long strip of leather fastened to the stem. The butt-end was a rattle, to frighten an enemy's horse. The ancient Britons, being divided into as many as thirty or forty tribes, each commanded by its own little king, were constantly fighting with one another, as savage people usually do; and they always fought with these weapons.

1. According to the author, why did the ancient Britons regularly fight with each other?

a. They had many weapons.
b. They disliked the Phoenicians.
c. There were no roads or bridges.
d. They were divided into many tribes.

2. Which phrase best shows the change Dickens believes the Phœnicians caused in the ancient Britons?

a. "The Phoenicians traded with the Islanders..."
b. "They were clever in basket-work..."
c. "These people settled themselves on the south coast of England..."
d. "...the savage Britons grew into a wild, bold people..."

3. Which sentence or phrase best expresses the isolation of the islands of England and Scotland and Ireland?

a. "...which are so small upon the Map as to be mere dots"
b. "The Islands lay solitary, in the great expanse of water."
c. "they can hear the noise of the waves thundering above their heads."
d. "Thus, by little and little, strangers became mixed with the Islanders..."

4. Read this phrase from paragraph 7:

But seldom, if ever, ventured far from the shore.

Why does the author include this phrase?

a. To show the ways in which the people used boats
b. To highlight the irony of making boats
c. To show where the people used weapons
d. To explain why the people built fortresses

5. Why does the author begin the passage by describing a map?

a. To explain the location of the islands
b. To show the roads that run through England, Scotland, and Ireland
c. To show how the little bits of Scotland broke away from the main island
d. To show the size of the islands in relation to France and Belgium

6. What sentence or phrase best describes the lands in the interior of the islands? In other words, these lands are the parts away from the coast.

a. "These people settled themselves on the south coast of England, which is now called Kent..."
b. "Especially in the interior of the country away from the sea where the foreign settlers seldom went..."
c. The whole country was covered with forests and swamps.
d. "The ancient Britons, being divided into as many as thirty or forty tribes, each commanded by its own little king..."

Refer to the following for questions 7–12:

"The Gift of the Magi"

by O. Henry

[Jim and Della are a young husband and wife. They are very poor, and it is Christmas Eve. Della has been able to save $1.87 for a Christmas present. To buy a better gift for her husband, she decides to sell her beautiful hair to buy a fob for Jim. The fob will be for Jim's watch which is his most prized possession.]

When Della reached home her intoxication gave way a little to prudence and reason. She got out her curling irons and lighted the gas and went to work repairing the ravages made by generosity added to love. Which is always a tremendous task, dear friends--a mammoth task.

Within forty minutes her head was covered with tiny, close-lying curls that made her look wonderfully like a truant schoolboy. She looked at her reflection in the mirror long, carefully, and critically.

"If Jim doesn't kill me," she said to herself, "before he takes a second look at me, he'll say I look like a Coney Island chorus girl. But what could I do—oh! What could I do with a dollar and eighty-seven cents?"

At seven o'clock the coffee was made and the frying pan was on the back of the stove hot and ready to cook the chops.

Jim was never late. Della doubled the fob chain in her hand and sat on the corner of the table near the door that he always entered. Then she heard his step on the stairway down on the first flight, and she turned white for just a moment. She had a habit of saying little silent prayers about the simplest everyday things and now she whispered: "Please God, make him think I am still pretty."

* * *

Jim stopped inside the door, as immovable as a setter at the scent of quail. His eyes were fixed upon Della, and there was an expression in them that she could not read, and it terrified her. It was not anger, nor surprise, nor disapproval, nor horror, nor any of the sentiments that she had been prepared for. He simply stared at her fixedly with that peculiar expression on his face.

Della wriggled off the table and went for him.

"Jim, darling," she cried, "don't look at me that way. I had my hair cut off and sold it because I couldn't have lived through Christmas without giving you a present. It'll grow out again—you won't mind, will you? I just had to do it. My hair grows awfully fast. Say 'Merry Christmas!' Jim, and let's be happy. You don't know what a nice—what a beautiful, nice gift I've got for you."

"You've cut off your hair?" asked Jim, laboriously, as if he had not arrived at that patent fact yet even after the hardest mental labor.

"Cut it off and sold it," said Della. "Don't you like me just as well, anyhow? I'm me without my hair, ain't I?"

Jim looked about the room curiously.

"You say your hair is gone?" he said, with an air almost of idiocy.

"You needn't look for it," said Della. "It's sold, I tell you—sold and gone, too. It's Christmas Eve, boy. Be good to me, for it went for you. Maybe the hairs of my head were numbered," she went on with a sudden serious sweetness, "but nobody could ever count my love for you. Shall I put the chops on, Jim?"

Out of his trance Jim seemed quickly to wake. He enfolded his Della.

* * *

Jim drew a package from his overcoat pocket and threw it upon the table.

"Don't make any mistake, Dell," he said, "about me. I don't think there's anything in the way of a haircut or a shave or a shampoo that could make me like my girl any less. But if you'll unwrap that package you may see why you had me going a while at first." White fingers and nimble tore at the string and paper. And then an ecstatic scream of joy; and then, alas! a quick, feminine change to hysterical tears and wails, necessitating the immediate employment of all the comforting powers of the lord of the flat.

For there lay the Combs—the set of combs, side and back, that Della had worshipped for long in a Broadway window. Beautiful combs, pure tortoise shell, with jeweled rims—just the shade to wear in the beautiful vanished hair. They were expensive combs, she knew, and her heart had simply craved and yearned over them without the least hope of possession. And now, they were hers, but the tresses that should have adorned the coveted adornments were gone. But she hugged them to her bosom, and at length she was able to look up with dim eyes and a smile and say: "My hair grows so fast, Jim!"

And then Della leaped up like a little singed cat and cried, "Oh, oh!"

Jim had not yet seen his beautiful present. She held it out to him eagerly upon her open palm. The dull precious metal seemed to flash with a reflection of her bright and ardent spirit.

"Isn't it a dandy, Jim? I hunted all over town to find it. You'll have to look at the time a hundred times a day now. Give me your watch. I want to see how it looks on it."

Instead of obeying, Jim tumbled down on the couch and put his hands under the back of his head and smiled.

"Della," said he, "let's put our Christmas presents away and keep 'em a while. They're too nice to use just at present. I sold the watch to get the money to buy your combs. And now suppose you put the chops on."

7. What is the meaning of the word *ardent*?

a. procrastinate
b. passionate
c. lukewarm
d. uncaring

8. What is the chronological order of these events: ?

(1) Jim gives Della's present to her | (2) Della prepares dinner | (3) Jim assures Della that he is not upset | (4) Della prepares her hair | (5) Della prays for Jim's reaction | (6) Jim receives his present from Della

a. 4, 3, 2, 1, 5, 6
b. 6, 1, 4, 3, 2, 5
c. 4, 2, 1, 5, 3, 6
d. 4, 2, 5, 3, 1, 6

9. In the passage, O. Henry uses several similes. Which of the following is not an example of a simile?

a. "her head was covered with tiny, close-lying curls that made her look wonderfully like a truant schoolboy."
b. "Jim stopped inside the door, as immovable as a setter at the scent of quail."
c. "'I hunted all over town to find it.'"
d. "And then Della leaped up like a little singed cat and cried, 'Oh, oh!'."

10. Which of the following best shows how O. Henry builds tension in the story?

a. "It was even worthy of The Watch. As soon as she saw it she knew that it must be Jim's."
b. "The door opened and Jim stepped in and closed it. He looked very thin and very serious."
c. "Jim looked about the room curiously. 'You say your hair is gone?' he said, with an air almost of idiocy."
d. "Jim was never late. Della doubled the fob chain in her hand and sat on the corner of the table near the door that he always entered."

11. What is the theme of this passage?

a. True love leads to the sacrifice of one's most precious possessions.
b. Christmas is the representation of the love and sacrifice needed by all.
c. The love between two people eventually leads to frustration.
d. People should not try to surprise each other gifts.

12. Who is the narrator of this passage?

a. Della
b. Jim
c. O. Henry
d. None of the above

Refer to the following for questions 13–23:

The Story of My Life

by Helen Keller

Have you ever been at sea in a dense fog, when it seemed as if a tangible white darkness shut you in, and the great ship, tense and anxious, groped her way toward the shore with plummet and sounding-line, and you waited with beating heart for something to happen? I was like that ship before my education began...

I felt approaching footsteps. I stretched out my hand as I supposed to my mother. Someone took it, and I was caught up and held close in the arms of her who had come to reveal all things to me, and, more than all things else, to love me.

[One afternoon] we walked down the path to the well-house, attracted by the fragrance of the honeysuckle with which it was covered. Someone was drawing water and my teacher placed my hand under the spout. As the cool stream gushed over one hand she spelled into the other the word water, first slowly, then rapidly. I stood still, my whole attention fixed upon the motions of her fingers. Suddenly I felt a misty consciousness as of something forgotten–a thrill of returning thought; and somehow the mystery of language was revealed to me. I knew then that "w-a-t-e-r" meant the wonderful cool something that was flowing over my hand. That living word awakened my soul, gave it light, hope, joy, set it free! There were barriers still, it is true, but barriers that could in time be swept away. I left the well-house eager to learn. Everything had a name, and each name gave birth to a new thought.

I recall many incidents of the summer of 1887 that followed my soul's sudden awakening. I did nothing but explore with my hands and learn the name of every object that I touched; and the more I handled things and learned their names and uses, the more joyous and confident grew my sense of kinship with the rest of the world.

I had my first lessons in the beneficence of nature. I learned how the sun and the rain make to grow out of the ground every tree that is pleasant to the sight and good for food, how birds build their nests and live and thrive from land to land, how the squirrel, the deer, the lion and every other creature finds food and shelter. As my knowledge of things grew I felt more and more the delight of the world I was in. Long before I learned to do a sum in arithmetic or describe the shape of the earth, Miss Sullivan had taught me to find beauty in the fragrant woods, in every blade of grass, and in the curves and dimples of my baby sister's hand. She linked my earliest thoughts with nature, and made me feel that "birds and flowers and I were happy peers."

But about this time I had an experience which taught me that nature is not always kind. One day my teacher and I were returning from a long ramble. The morning had been fine, but it was growing warm and sultry when at last we turned our faces homeward. Two or three times we stopped to rest under a tree by the wayside. Our last halt was under a wild cherry tree a short distance from the house. The shade was grateful, and the tree was so easy to climb that with my teacher's assistance I was able to scramble to a seat in the branches. It was so cool up in the tree that Miss Sullivan proposed that we have our luncheon there. I promised to keep still while she went to the house to fetch it.

Suddenly a change passed over the tree. All the sun's warmth left the air. I knew the sky was black, because all the heat, which meant light to me, had died out of the atmosphere. A strange odour came up from the earth. I knew it, it was the odour that always precedes a thunderstorm, and a nameless fear clutched at my heart. I felt absolutely alone, cut off from my friends and the firm earth. The immense, the unknown, enfolded me. I remained still and expectant; a chilling terror crept over me. I longed for my teacher's return; but above all things I wanted to get down from that tree.

There was a moment of sinister silence, then a multitudinous stirring of the leaves. A shiver ran through the tree, and the wind sent forth a blast that would have knocked me off had I not clung to the branch with might and main. The tree swayed and strained. The small twigs snapped and fell about me in showers. A wild impulse to jump seized me, but terror held me fast. I crouched down in the fork of the tree. The branches lashed about me. I felt the intermittent jarring that came now and then, as if something heavy had fallen and the shock had traveled up till it reached the limb I sat on. It worked my suspense up to the highest point, and just as I was thinking the tree and I should fall together, my teacher seized my hand and helped me down. I clung to her, trembling with joy to feel the earth under my feet once more. I had learned a new lesson–that nature "wages open war against her children, and under softest touch hides treacherous claws."

13. What is the meaning of the word *beneficence*?

a. Duties
b. Generosity
c. Stinginess
d. Danger

14. Paragraph 3 is mainly about the narrator...

a. Learning to write words with a pencil
b. Learning the difference between cold and hot water
c. Learning the location of the well-house
d. Learning that words have meaning

15. Why did Helen hold out her hand in paragraph 2?

a. She thought the visitor was her mother
b. She wanted to greet the visitor
c. She wanted to please her mother
d. She loved the approaching person

16. In paragraphs 7 and 8, Helen felt nervous because...

a. she was lost.
b. she was alone.
c. it was raining.
d. it was windy.

17. Which sentence best explains what Helen learned from Miss Sullivan?

a. "I learned how the sun and the rain make to grow out of the ground every tree that is pleasant to the sight..."
b. "There were barriers still, it is true, but barriers that could in time be swept away."
c. "Everything had a name, and each name gave birth to a new thought."
d. "...nature 'wages open war against her children, and under softest touch hides treacherous claws.'"

18. Which aspect of the selection best shows the close bond between Helen and Miss Sullivan?

a. The moment when Miss Sullivan spelled "w-a-t-e-r" into Helen's hand
b. When Helen learned to find beauty in nature
c. When Miss Sullivan proposed eating lunch by the cherry tree
d. The moment when Miss Sullivan pulled Helen from the tree

19. What is a major theme of the passage?

a. Family ties
b. Discovery
c. Disappointment
d. Youth

20. In paragraph 8, the narrator uses the phrase "hides treacherous claws" to explain that...

a. Miss Sullivan, beneath her kind exterior, is very mean
b. Helen continues to have violent temper tantrums
c. Climbing trees can be very dangerous.
d. Nature can be cruel.

21. By telling the story in the order that events occur, the author helps you understand...

a. The change that Helen went through after meeting Miss Sullivan
b. The way in which Helen learned to be brave
c. The strategies Miss Sullivan used to teach Helen
d. The confusion that Helen felt when she was with Miss Sullivan

22. Based on the passage, you can conclude that Helen...

a. Disliked Miss Sullivan
b. Is scared of nature
c. Didn't understand words before Miss Sullivan arrived
d. Never learned how to read or write

23. What tool of figurative language is used in the phrase: "...each name gave birth to a new thought."?

a. Metaphor
b. Hyperbole
c. Simile
d. Personification

Refer to the following for questions 24–29:

[In 1906, Elinore Pruitt Stewart moved to Denver for housework to support her daughter, Jerrine. Her employer in Denver was Mrs. Juliet Coney. A few years later, she moved to Wyoming to be a housekeeper for a rancher. The following passage is one of many letters that Stewart wrote to Mrs. Coney on life as a homesteader in Wyoming.]

A Letter of Elinore Pruitt Stewart

January 23, 1913

When I read of the hard times among the Denver poor, I feel like urging them every one to get out and file on land. I am very enthusiastic about women homesteading. It really requires less strength and labor to raise plenty to satisfy a large family than it does to go out to wash, with the added satisfaction of knowing that their job will not be lost to them if they care to keep it. Even if improving the place does go slowly, it is that much done to stay done. Whatever is raised is the homesteader's own, and there is no house-rent to pay. This year Jerrine cut and dropped enough potatoes to raise a ton of fine potatoes. She wanted to try, so we let her, and you will remember that she is but six years old.... Any woman strong enough to go out by the day could have done every bit of the work and put in two or three times that much, and it would have been so much more pleasant than to work so hard in the city and be on starvation rations all winter.

To me, homesteading is the solution of all poverty's problems, but I realize that temperament has much to do with success in any undertaking, and persons afraid of coyotes and work and loneliness had better let ranching alone. At the same time, any woman who can stand her own company, can see the beauty of the sunset, loves growing things, and is willing to put in as much time at careful labor as she does over the washtub, will certainly succeed; will have independence, plenty to eat all the time, and a home of her own in the end.

Experimenting need cost the homesteader no more than the work, because by applying to the Department of Agriculture at Washington he can get enough of any seed and as many kinds as he wants to make a thorough trial, and it doesn't even cost postage. Also one can always get bulletins from there and from the Experiment Station of one's own State concerning any problem or as many problems as may come up. I would not, for anything, allow Mr. Stewart to do anything toward improving my place, for I want the fun and the experience myself. And I want to be able to speak from experience when I tell others what they can do. Theories are very beautiful, but facts are what must be had, and what I intend to give some time.

24. The writer of this letter is suggesting that women should own land and farm rather than

a. cook in a restaurant.
b. open a bed and breakfast.
c. do laundry for others.
d. teach in a one-room schoolhouse.

25. Stewart mentions her daughter's potato crop. She does this to show

a. that child labor is acceptable.
b. that there are no schools in the area.
c. that women work just as hard as men do.
d. how easy it is to raise crops.

26. What do you think Mrs. Coney's reaction to the letter might have been?

a. She was probably glad to be rid of such a lazy worker.
b. She may be glad to know that Mrs. Stewart is enjoying her time with homesteading.
c. She may have been sorry that she too did not homestead.
d. She was likely angry that Mrs. Stewart had written.

27. Which of the following does Stewart NOT give as an advantage of homesteading?

a. It takes less strength and work than doing laundry for others
b. The worker cannot lose her job if she wants to keep it.
c. No one has to pay rent.
d. One can always find good company.

28. Which of the following is a risk for the poor in Denver?

a. The possibility of losing their jobs
b. The likelihood of a strike
c. The probability of a landslide
d. Losing their homes to fire

29. The tone of the letter is

a. complaining and bitter.
b. sad and lonely.
c. positive and encouraging.
d. hopeless and despairing.

Refer to the following for questions 30–35:

Forest Manager: Salvage logging is removing dead or dying forest stands that are left behind by a fire or disease. This practice has been used for several decades. These dead or dying trees become fuel that feeds future fires. The best way to lower the risk of forest fires is to remove the dead timber from the forest floor. Salvage logging followed by replanting ensures the reestablishment of desirable tree species.

For example, planting conifers accelerates the return of fire-resistant forests. Harvesting timber helps forests by reducing fuel load, thinning the forest stands, and relieving competition between trees. Burned landscapes leave black surfaces and ash layers that have very high soil temperatures. These high soil temperatures can kill many plant species. Logging mixes the soil. So, this lowers surface temperatures to more normal levels. The shade from material that is left behind by logging also helps to lower surface temperatures. After an area has been salvage logged, seedlings in the area start to grow almost immediately. However, this regrowth can take several years in areas that are not managed well.

Ecology professor: Salvage logging moves material like small, broken branches to the forest floor. These pieces can become fuel for more fires. The removal of larger, less flammable trees leaves behind small limbs and increases the risk of forest fires. In unmanaged areas, these pieces are found more commonly on the tops of trees where they are unavailable to fires. Logging destroys old forests that are more resistant to wildfires. So, this creates younger forests that are more open to fires. In old forests, branches of bigger trees are higher above the floor where fires may not reach.

Replanting after wildfires creates monoculture plantations where only a single crop is planted. This monoculture allows less biological diversity. Also, it allows plants to be less resistant to disease. So, this increases the chance of fire. Salvage logging also upsets natural forest regrowth by killing most of the seedlings that grow after a wildfire. It breaks up the soil and increases erosion. Also, it removes most of the shade that is needed for young seedlings to grow.

30. According to the professor, why are the broken branches in unmanaged forests preferable to those in logged areas for wildfire resistance?

a. They are left on the forest floor and bring nutrients to the soil.
b. They are left on the forest floor and serve as fuel for fires.
c. They are left on the tops of trees where fires cannot reach.
d. They are spread more evenly across the forest floor.

31. Which of the following is NOT a supporting detail for the forest manager's argument?

a. "This practice has been used for decades."
b. "Logging mixes the soil. So, this lowers surface temperatures to more normal levels."
c. "After an area has been salvage logged, seedlings in the area start to grow almost immediately."
d. "Salvage logging is removing dead or dying forest stands that are left behind by a fire or disease."

32. A study compared two plots of land that were managed differently after a fire. Plot A was salvage logged. Plot B was left unmanaged. After a second fire, they compared two plant groups between Plots A and B. They found that both plant groups burned worse in Plot A than in Plot B. Whose viewpoint do these results support?

a. Only the manager
b. Only the professor
c. Both the manager and professor
d. Neither the manager nor the professor

33. What is the main idea of the forest manager's argument?

a. Salvage logging is helpful because it removes dead or dying timber from the forest floor. So, this lowers the risk of future fires.
b. Salvage logging is helpful because it has been practiced for many decades.
c. Salvage logging is harmful because it raises soil temperatures above normal levels. So, this threatens the health of plant species.
d. Salvage logging is helpful because it gives shade for seedlings to grow after a wildfire.

34. Which of the following statements does NOT agree with the professor?

a. In younger forests, small branches are closer to the forest floor and more available for fires.
b. Old growth forests have taller trees, so branches are high up and fires cannot reach them.
c. Monoculture forests have less biological diversity and fewer disease-resistant trees.
d. Larger trees are common in old growth forests and serve as the main fuel source for fires.

35. Whose viewpoints would potentially be confirmed by a future study looking at the spreading out and regrowth of seedlings for many years after a wildfire in managed and unmanaged forests?

a. only the manager
b. only the professor
c. both the manager and professor
d. neither the manager nor professor

Refer to the following for questions 36–40:

Section 1: Improving Diets

A healthier diet is something that many people want for themselves. However, this can be a struggle to put into practice for many people. This does not mean that just because it's hard and frustrating doesn't mean that people should stop trying.

A powerful and easy approach to improving diets is to know that some foods are so good for us that we can almost think of them as medicine. Some foods help to fight heart disease, cancer, or depression. Other foods help to lower cholesterol or blood pressure. Broccoli is high in vitamin K and vitamin C which help build strong bones and fight off cancers. Avocadoes can lower cholesterol and help reduce the risk of heart disease. Sweet potatoes are full of cancer-fighting and immune system-boosting vitamin A. Garlic can slow down the growth of bacteria and has been shown to lower cholesterol and blood pressure. Spinach is a great cancer fighter and has immune-boosting antioxidants important for eye health. Beans help lower risk of heart disease and breast cancer.

At some point, people want to give themselves the full treatment: diet, exercise, and general health overhaul. In the meantime, they can take the baby step of adding in one or more healthy food a week. This step is quick, easy, and painless. It couldn't be simpler to implement. Also, it will make their switch to healthy eating much easier to accomplish when they finally get there.

Section 2: Dietary Guidelines for Americans

The Dietary Guidelines for Americans is put together by the US Department of Health and Human Services and the US Department of Agriculture. The guidelines offer advice to people about food choices that advance good health and lower the risk of certain diseases (e.g., hypertension, anemia, and osteoporosis). In addition, this form offers a detailed outline on the kinds of foods that people should have in their diets. The outline is given so that additional supplements or vitamins may not be necessary. The form also has information on the types of exercise that are necessary for someone to stay healthy. Also, there is information on to handle and prepare certain foods to lower the risk of foodborne illness.

The Food Pyramid gave recommendations for the number of daily servings from each group. The USDA's Food Pyramid was heavily criticized for being unclear and confusing. In 2011, MyPlate replaced the Food Pyramid. MyPlate is much easier to understand because it has a picture of a dinner plate that is divided into four sections. So, this shows how our daily diet should be spread out among the different food groups. Vegetables and grains each take up 30% of the plate. Fruits and proteins each make up 20% of the plate. In the corner of the image is a cup that is marked as Dairy.

Most experts consider MyPlate to be a great improvement over the Food Pyramid. However, some it has still come under criticism from some quarters. Many believe too much emphasis is placed on protein, and some say the dairy recommendation should be eliminated altogether. The Harvard School of Public Health created its own Healthy Eating Plate to address what it sees as shortcomings in MyPlate. Harvard's guide adds healthy plant-based oils to the mix, stresses whole grains instead of merely grains, recommends drinking water or unsweetened coffee or tea instead of milk, and adds a reminder that physical activity is important.

Section 3: Preparing Better Meals in the Food Industry

People in the food industry that want to prepare a healthy meal for their customers should first decide on the nutritional goals of their menu. Once these goals have been set up, you should continue to plan by researching foods. These foods need to meet your goals without going beyond the available time and resource limits. Then, you can put together a meal plan that list several details. These details should have what foods will be included, the average time it takes to prepare and cook each of these meals, and the cost of preparing these meals. The next step is to decide on the best way of preparing the food for these meals. Think about which foods should be prepared first and the best ways to handle or prepare your food to lower the risk of illness. Also, think about methods that can be used to lower the cooking time. Finally, you can prepare the meal according to your plans.

When you need to decide on what foods to prepare, you need to think about several things. You should consider the food's nutritional value, the time it takes to prepare each food, the number of people to be served, and the cost of preparing each food. Each food has its own cooking time and has different nutrients. So, it is important to prepare foods that meet people's nutritional goals without using too much time for cooking the meal. Since you will likely have a budget for the meal, you need to review the number of people to be served and the cost of preparing each food. If the cost is too high, some meals may not be good choices to serve to large groups. For example, you are interested in serving a good source of protein for a meal. So, steak may be a good option for a small group of people. However, that would probably be too expensive for a larger group.

36. What is the main idea of Section 1?

a. Preparing a menu requires thorough research.
b. Some foods are healthier than others.
c. Positive diet changes can be simple.
d. Some people can make dietary changes and some cannot.

37. What is the purpose of including Section 2 in this passage?

a. To explain how the Food Pyramid was poorly designed
b. To cover the government's influence on the dietary recommendations for Americans
c. To show that there is no perfect system for coming up with dietary recommendations
d. To share information on generally accepted nutrition guidelines

38. What is the purpose of including Harvard's Healthy Eating Plate in Section 2?

a. To support the assertion MyPlate has received criticism
b. To suggest Healthy Eating Plate may replace current USDA dietary guidelines
c. It shows another option as a dietary guideline
d. To highlight the influence of an Ivy League school

39. According to the text, when preparing food for customers, all of the following are important EXCEPT which?

a. Foodborne illness
b. Calories in a meal
c. Layering the flavors in a dish
d. Preparation time

40. What is the tone of the three sections?

a. Condemning
b. Informative
c. Serious
d. Pretentious

Reasoning Through Language Arts—Writing

Refer to the following for questions 1–9:

How Do You Prepare Your Vehicle for Winter?

A

(1) Anyone who live in a climate which brings snow during the winter knows how important it is to have a working vehicle. (2) Before winter begins, get the car or truck serviced. (3) Consider the following tips. (4) Few things are worst than being unable to see in snow or sleet. (5) Most wiper blades do not last no longer than a year. (6) Be sure that while you are at it, the windshield washer reservoir has fluid. (7) First of all, do the windshield wipers work properly? (8) Do not fill it with water because plain water won't work in the winter since it freezes.

B

(9) Now, you need to check a few things under the hood. (10) Are belts and hoses in good shape is the battery in good working order? (11) When was the last oil change? (12) Make sure you have the right blend of antifreeze and water in the radiator. (13) Add to your vehicle's emergency kit extra food water and warm clothes or a blanket. (14) In winter, carry an ice scraper and a small shovel. (15) Consider tire chains and salt, sand, or non-clumping kitty litter to give your vehicle traction if needed.

C

(16) Have a plan if you are stranded. (17) You leave only the car because you know exactly where you are and how far you are from help. (18) Following these precautions will help to keep you and your loved ones safe in winter driving.

1. What correction should be made to sentence (1)?

a. make live singular
b. place commas around which brings snow
c. set during the winter off in dashes
d. change which to that

2. What correction should be made to sentence (4)?

a. NO CHANGE
b. change Few to Fewer
c. change worst to worse
d. change are to is

3. Consider the following excerpt from the passage.

Sentence (5): "Most wiper blades do not last no longer than a year."

Select the best version of the underlined portion.

a. NO CHANGE
b. do not last longer
c. do not lasted no longer
d. have not last no longer

4. What correction should be made to sentence (6)?

a. move while you are at it to the front of the sentence and place a comma after it
b. move Be sure to the end of the sentence
c. place a question mark at the end of the sentence
d. no correction is necessary

5. Which revision should be made to sentence (7) to improve the organization of the paragraph?

a. move sentence (7) to the beginning of paragraph A
b. move sentence (7) after sentence (3).
c. move sentence (7) to the end of paragraph A
d. move sentence (7) to the beginning of paragraph B

6. What correction should be made to sentence (9)?

a. NO CHANGE
b. delete under the hood from the sentence
c. change a few to one
d. place have between to and note

7. Consider the following excerpt from the passage.

Sentence (10): "Are belts and hoses in good shape is the battery in good working order?"

Select the best version of the underlined portion.

a. NO CHANGE
b. good shape, is the
c. good shape and is the
d. good shape; is the

8. What correction should be made to sentence (13)?

a. remove the apostrophe from vehicle's
b. change the spelling of emergency to emergancy
c. place commas after the words food and water
d. no correction is necessary

9. What correction should be made to sentence (17)?

a. move only to come between You and leave
b. delete exactly
c. put a comma before and
d. no correction is necessary

Refer to the following for questions 10–18:

How Slow Is Your Food?

A

(1) A growing grassroots movement is taking place around the world. (2) Developed nations have spent the past half-century creating fast food products, which are designed more for ease and availability than for taste. (3) Today, people worry more over genetically modified crops, food safety, and the cost of shipping food across the nation. (4) So, slow foods is making a comeback.

B

(5) Slow food puts the emphasize on community and sharing. (6) A major concern is to support local farmers and artisans. (7) Examples are those who are trying to save endangered species of animals, grains, the fruits, and the vegetables. (8) A new interest in heirloom varieties has reawakened palates that were used to food which had lost nutritional appeal and

flavor. (9) Slow food also seeks to fully use sustainable agriculture. (10) This way soils can be replenished without the use of chemicals.

C

(11) Slow food usa has taken the program to students in elementary and secondary schools through its Garden to Table program. (12) Focusing on pleasure, tradition, and sustainability, the projects offer young people a chance to be involved in hands-on gardening and cooking. (13) I once had a garden in my backyard. (14) Students learn where their food comes from and they find out who grows it and how to cook it and the need to share with others. (15) A similar program, Slow Food on Campus, is conducted by the college and university students. (16) All programs adhere to the basic ideas of slow food: a good, clean, and fair food system.

10. Consider the following excerpt from the passage.

Sentence (2): "Developed nations have spent the past half-century creating fast <u>food products, which are</u> designed more for ease and availability than for taste."

Select the best version of the underlined portion.

a. NO CHANGE
b. food products which are
c. food product, which are
d. food products, which is

11. What correction should be made to sentence (4)?

a. remove the extra comma
b. change is to are
c. capitalize slow foods
d. put a hyphen between *come* and *back*

12. Consider the following excerpt from the passage.

Sentence (5): "Slow food <u>puts the emphasize</u> on community and sharing."

Select the best version of the underlined portion.

a. NO CHANGE
b. places the emphasize
c. put the emphasize
d. puts the emphasis

13. Consider the following excerpt from the passage.

Sentence (7): "Examples are those who are trying to save <u>endangered species of animals, grains, the fruits and the vegetables."</u>

Select the best version of the underlined portion.

a. endangered species of animals, grains, the fruits and the vegetables
b. endangered specie of animals, grains, the fruits and the vegetables
c. endangered species of animal, grain, the fruit and the vegetable
d. endangered species of animals, grains, fruits and vegetables

14. What correction should be made to sentence (9)?

a. change seeks to plural
b. put a dash between replenished and without
c. delete fully
d. no correction is needed

15. What correction should be made to sentence (11)?

a. remove capital letters from Garden and Table
b. capitalize food usa
c. change the spelling of through to thru
d. no correction is needed

16. Which revision should be made to sentence (13) to improve the organization of this paragraph?

a. move the sentence to the beginning of the paragraph
b. use the sentence as the concluding statement of the article
c. delete sentence (13)
d. move the sentence to the previous paragraph

17. What correction should be made to sentence (14)?

a. add commas
b. make the terms parallel
c. change their to they're
d. make two sentences

18. What correction should be made to sentence (15)?

a. make college and university students the subject
b. remove the commas
c. remove the capital letters on Slow, Food, and Campus
d. change the spelling of similar to simular

Refer to the following for questions 19–28:

Are You SAD?

A

(1) For many healthy people, the coming of winter gets them down. (2) Some hibernation tendencies are common. (3) If you notice true depression a sense of hopelessness less energy, or anxiety, you may be suffering from seasonal affective disorder or SAD. (4) Some people experience SAD during spring and summer for most people, however, winter is the season to be SAD.

B

(5) Researchers are not certainly what causes SAD. (6) One suggestion is that having our regular body rhythms disrupted when less sunlight is available is the culprit. (7) Another study blames increased production of melatonin: a hormone related to sleep. (8) During the dark winter months, the body makes more melatonin. (9) At the same time, it makes less serotonin: the brain chemical that effects our moods. (10) Fewer sunlight means less serotonin. (11) So far, risk factors has not been identified.

C

(12) Most people with SAD just tough it out and waiting for spring. (13) If you have symptoms that last more than two weeks, it is time to see a doctor. (14) People with mild cases of SAD need to spend time outside, exercise regularly, and go to social events or travel. (15) The good news is that spring always comes?

19. Consider the following excerpt from the passage.

Sentence 1: For many healthy people, the coming of winter gets them down.

What correction should be made to this sentence?

a. NO CHANGE
b. change gets to plural form
c. change healthy to healthly
d. delete the comma

20. Consider the following excerpt from the passage.

Sentence 3: If you notice true depression a sense of hopelessness less energy, or anxiety, you may be suffering from seasonal affective disorder or SAD.

What correction should be made to this sentence?

a. NO CHANGE
b. place a comma after hopelessness
c. capitalize seasonal affective disorder
d. remove the comma after disorder

21. Consider the following excerpt from the passage.

Sentence (4): Some people experience SAD during spring and summer for most people, however, winter is the season to be SAD.

Select the best version of the underlined portion.

a. NO CHANGE
b. and summer, for most
c. and summer: for most
d. and summer. For most

22. Consider the following excerpt from the passage.

Sentence 5: Researchers are not certainly what causes SAD.

What correction should be made to this sentence?

a. NO CHANGE
b. do not use capital letters for SAD
c. end the sentence with a question mark
d. change certainly to certain

23. Consider the following excerpt from the passage.

Sentence 8: During the dark winter months, the body makes more melatonin.

What correction should be made to this sentence?

a. NO CHANGE
b. change more to much
c. capitalize melatonin
d. put a comma between dark and winter

24. Consider the following excerpt from the passage.

Sentence 9: At the same time, it makes less serotonin: the brain chemical that effects our moods.

What correction should be made to this sentence?

a. NO CHANGE
b. move the first phrase to after serotonin
c. change less to fewer
d. change effects to affects

25. Consider the following excerpt from the passage.

Sentence 10: Fewer sunlight means less serotonin.

What correction should be made to this sentence?

a. change means to mean
b. capitalize serotonin
c. change less to fewer
d. change Fewer to Less

26. Consider the following excerpt from the passage.

Sentence (11): "So far, risk factors has not been identified."

Select the best version of the underlined portion.

a. NO CHANGE
b. so far, risk factors has not
c. So far, risk factor have not
d. So far, risk factors have not

27. Consider the following excerpt from the passage.

Sentence 12: Most people with SAD just tough it out and waiting for spring.

What correction should be made to this sentence?

a. NO CHANGE
b. change tough to toughing
c. change waiting to wait
d. write SAD as sad

28. Consider the following excerpt from the passage.

Sentence 15: The good news is that spring always comes?

What correction should be made to this sentence?

a. NO CHANGE
b. change the question mark to a period
c. capitalize spring
d. change good to well

Refer to the following for questions 29–37:

Only Temporary

A

(1) Many businesses in the United States regularly hire "temps" or temporary workers. (2) Now known as the staffing industry, temp work employs nearly 3 million people and generating more than $40 billion annually. (3) Because jobs are no longer secure, many people find that moving from job to job is a good way to improve they're skills. (4) They sometimes find the perfect job and are hired as a full-time employee. (5) Businesses love temps, they save the company money because temps do not receive benefits.

B

(6) Would temp work be a good move for you? (7) If you are the kind of worker who bores quickly and needs new challenges, temping may be the way to go. (8) Temp work may offer a more flexible schedule and it gives a changing work environment. (9) On the down side, you will not get benefits like paid vacations or health insurance. (10) You may not always be treated very well because temp workers come and go.

C

(11) If you're looking for a job, temp work can add valuable experience to your résumé. (12) It also allows you time to look for and interviewing for a new and permanent job. (13) In addition, temp work is a great way to explore different careers. (14) Many temp jobs are temp-to-hire because the company needs to fill a position and is looking among temp workers for a permanant hire. (15) You may be just the employee they are seeking!

29. Consider the following excerpt from the passage.

Sentence 1: Many businesses in the United States regularly hire "temps" or temporary workers.

What correction should be made to this sentence?

a. remove the quotation marks from temps
b. remove or temporary workers from the sentence
c. change the spelling of temporary to temparary
d. place a comma after temps

30. Consider the following excerpt from the passage.

Sentence 2: Now known as the staffing industry, temp work employs nearly 3 million people and generating more than $40 billion annually.

What correction should be made to this sentence?

a. change industry to industries
b. change work to works
c. change employs to employing
d. change generating to generates

31. Consider the following excerpt from the passage.

Sentence 3: Because jobs are no longer secure, many people find that moving from job to job is a good way to improve they're skills.

What correction should be made to this sentence?

a. change Because to Since
b. remove the comma after secure
c. change skills to skill
d. change they're to their

32. Consider the following excerpt from the passage.

Sentence (4): "They sometimes find the perfect job and are hired as a full-time employee."

Select the best version of the underlined portion.

a. NO CHANGE
b. are hired as full-time employees.
c. is hired as a full-time employee.
d. is hired as a fulltime employee.

33. Consider the following excerpt from the passage.

Sentence (5): "Businesses love temps, they save the company money, because temps do not receive benefits."

Select the best version of the underlined portion.

a. NO CHANGE
b. Businesses love temps, it saves
c. Businesses love temps; they save
d. Businesses love temps, they saves

34. Consider the following excerpt from the passage.

Sentence (8): "Temp work may offer a more flexible schedule and it gives a changing work environment."

Select the best version of the underlined portion.

a. NO CHANGE
b. flexible schedule and it give
c. flexible schedules and it gives
d. flexible schedule, and it gives

35. Consider the following excerpt from the passage.

Sentence 11: If you're looking for a job, temp work can add valuable experience to your résumé.

What correction should be made to this sentence?

a. NO CHANGE
b. change you're to your
c. change valueable to valuable
d. put a hyphen between temp and work

36. What correction should be made to sentence (12)?

a. NO CHANGE
b. change look to looking
c. change interviewing to interview
d. change permanent to permanant

37. Consider the following excerpt from the passage.

Sentence (14): Many temp jobs are temp-to-hire because the company needs to fill a position and is looking among temp workers for a permanant hire.

Select the best version of the underlined portion.

a. NO CHANGE
b. workers for a permanent hire
c. a worker for a permanant hire
d. workers for permanant hires

Refer to the following for questions 38–43:

Picking the Perfect Pet

A

(1) Today's choices for pets go beyond the question of whether to get a cat or a dog? (2) Gerbils, rabbits, and amphibians is all popular options. (3) Before heading to an animal shelter, you need to know what pet makes sense for your home or classroom. (4) An obvious question to answer if you rent is if pets are permitted. (5) Some apartment complex places weight and size limits on pets or charge fees. (6) After gaining permission from the manager, your pet needs to be considered for other issues.

B

(7) If allergies effect someone in your home, be sure to select a pet that will not aggravate the condition. (8) Some dog breeds like the schnauzer and the poodle are acceptable pets for those who are sensitive to fur and dander.

C

(9) Irregardless of the pet you choose, think about other costs such as veterinary care and vaccinations, food costs, licensing, and equipment. (10) Does the pet need a special kind of

home? (11) Who will be responsible for feeding and cleaning up after the animal? (12) Taking time to do a little research can save you a lot of heartache and expense later.

38. Consider the following excerpt from the passage.

Sentence 1: "Today's choices for pets go beyond the question of whether to get a cat or a dog?"

Select the best version of the underlined portion.

a. NO CHANGE
b. change Today's to Todays
c. change question to questions
d. change the question mark to a period

39. What correction should be made to sentence (2)?

a. remove the comma after Gerbils
b. change amphibians to amfibians
c. change is to are
d. change Gerbils to Hamsters

40. Consider the following excerpt from the passage.

Sentence 5: "Some apartment complex places weight and size limits on pets or charge fees."

Select the best version of the underlined portion.

a. NO CHANGE
b. Some apartment complex places wait
c. Some apartment complexes places weight
d. Some apartment complexes place weight

41. What correction should be made to sentence (6)?

a. delete the comma
b. change permission to permision
c. rewrite the independent clause
d. No correction is needed

42. Consider the following excerpt from the passage.

Sentence (7): "If allergies effect someone in your home, be sure to select a pet that will not aggravate the condition."

Select the best version of the underlined portion.

a. NO CHANGE
b. If allergies affect someone
c. If allergies affects someone
d. If allergies effects someone

43. Consider the following excerpt from the passage.

Sentence (9): "Irregardless of the pet you choose, think about other costs such as veterinary care and vaccinations, food costs, licensing and equipment."

What correction should be made to sentence (9)?

a. change Irregardless to Regardless
b. change licensing to lisencing
c. remove the extra commas
d. no correction is needed

Refer to the following for questions 44–50:

Madame President

A

(1) Before they had the right to vote, women have attempted to gain the nations highest executive office. (2) Victoria Woodhull ran as a third party candidate in 1872. (3) Although she did not win, she became the first woman who owned an investment firm on wall street. (4) In 1884 and 1888, the lawyer Belva Lockwood also ran as a third party candidate. (5) Margaret Chase Smith (who served in both houses of Congress) was the first woman nominated by a major party: the Republicans.

B

(6) Nine other women have seeked for the presidency since the 1970s. (7) Five of them were Democrats and one was a Republican and three represented third parties. (8) I think it's about time this country had a woman as president. (9) Only two women have been nominated as vice president: Democrat Geraldine Ferraro in 1984 and Republican Sarah Palin in 2008. (10) Many people believe that soon the United States will join countries such as Britain, India, Germany, Chile, and Liberia, that have women heads of state.

44. What correction should be made to sentence (1)?

a. NO CHANGE
b. change nations to nation's
c. put *finally* between to and gain
d. capitalize executive office

45. What correction should be made to sentence (3)?

a. change became to become
b. capitalize wall street
c. change Although to Though
d. capitalize investment firm

46. What correction should be made to sentence (5)?

a. NO CHANGE
b. do not capitalize Republicans
c. change woman to women
d. change the parentheses to commas

47. What correction should be made to sentence (6)?

a. NO CHANGE
b. woman have seeked for
c. women have seek for
d. women have sought

48. What correction should be made to sentence (7)?

a. NO CHANGE
b. change them to those
c. change were to was
d. add a comma after Democrats and delete the and after Democrats

49. Which revision would improve the overall organization of this article?

a. switch paragraphs A and B
b. place the final sentence at the beginning of paragraph B
c. delete sentence (8)
d. place sentence (2) at the end of paragraph A

50. What correction should be made to sentence (10)?

a. NO CHANGE
b. remove the unnecessary commas
c. change the spelling of believe to beleive
d. remove the comma after Liberia

Reasoning Through Language Arts—Extended Response

1. The study summary below outlines a problem that has been in America for decades. The next article gives one possible solution to the problem. Analyze the arguments made by the author of the article. Then, decide if his reasoning is sound. Be sure to give evidence from the passage. Also, give evidence from your own knowledge and experience. Explain why you would predict that his idea would succeed or fail.

Study Summary from the Education Resources Information Center

Student scores on standardized tests have steadily declined since 1965. Researchers conducted a literature review and completed data analysis to determine the reasons for this decrease, assessing trends for the period from 1965 to 1983. The reasons for the declining student scores include changes in the composition of test-takers, decreases in the quantity of schooling which students experience, curriculum changes, declines in student motivation, and deterioration of the family system and social environment. These factors, in combination, have contributed to the test score decline for more than fifteen years. Efforts to end the decreases must address the curricular and school climate factors identified.

Excerpt from an article by Roger Sipher

"So That Nobody Has To Go To School If They Don't Want To"

A decline in standardized test scores is but the most recent indicator that American education is in trouble. One reason for the crisis is that present mandatory-attendance laws force many to attend school who have no wish to be there. Such children have little desire to learn and are so antagonistic to school that neither they nor more highly motivated students receive the quality education that is the birthright of every American. The solution to this problem is simple: Abolish compulsory-attendance laws and allow only those who are committed to getting an education to attend.

Most parents want a high school education for their children. Unfortunately, compulsory attendance hampers the ability of public school officials to enforce legitimate educational and disciplinary policies and thereby make the education a good one. Private schools have no such problem. They can fail or dismiss students, knowing such students can attend public school. Without compulsory attendance, public schools would be freer to oust students whose academic or personal behavior undermines the educational mission of the institution.

Abolition of archaic attendance laws would produce enormous dividends:

- First, it would alert everyone that school is a serious place where one goes to learn. Schools are neither day-care centers nor indoor street corners. Young people who resist learning should stay away; indeed, an end to compulsory schooling would require them to stay away.
- Second, students opposed to learning would not be able to pollute the educational atmosphere for those who want to learn. Teachers could stop policing recalcitrant students and start educating.
- Third, grades would show what they are supposed to: how well a student is learning. Parents could again read report cards and know if their children were making progress.
- Fourth, public esteem for schools would increase. People would stop regarding them as way stations for adolescents and start thinking of them as institutions for educating America's youth.
- Fifth, elementary schools would change because students would find out early they had better learn something or risk flunking out later. Elementary teachers would no longer have to pass their failures on to junior high and high school.
- Sixth, the cost of enforcing compulsory education would be eliminated. Despite enforcement efforts, nearly 15 percent of the school-age children in our largest cities are almost permanently absent from school.

Communities could use these savings to support institutions to deal with young people not in school. If, in the long run, these institutions prove more costly, at least we would not confuse their mission with that of schools. Schools should be for education. At present, they are only tangentially so. They have attempted to serve an all-encompassing social function, trying to be all things to all people. In the process they have failed miserably at what they were originally formed to accomplish.

Mathematics—No Calculator

1. A metal rod used in manufacturing must be as close as possible to 15 inches in length. The tolerance of the length, L, in inches, is specified by the inequality $|L - 15| \leq 0.01$. What is the minimum length permissible for the rod?

a. 14.9 inches
b. 14.99 inches
c. 15.01 inches
d. 15.1 inches

2. A bullet travels at 5×10^6 feet per hour. If it strikes its target in 2×10^{-4} hours, how far has it traveled?

a. 50 feet
b. 100 feet
c. 200 feet
d. 1,000 feet

3. What is $4^6 \div 2^8$?

a. 2
b. 8
c. 16
d. 32

4. A function $f(x)$ is defined by $f(x) = 2x^2 + 7$. What is the value of $2f(x) - 3$?

a. $4x^2 + 11$
b. $4x^4 + 11$
c. $x^2 + 11$
d. $4x^2 + 14$

5. Simplify: $|7 - 5| - |5 - 7|$

a. -2
b. 0
c. 2
d. 4

Mathematics—Calculator

Refer to the following for question 6:

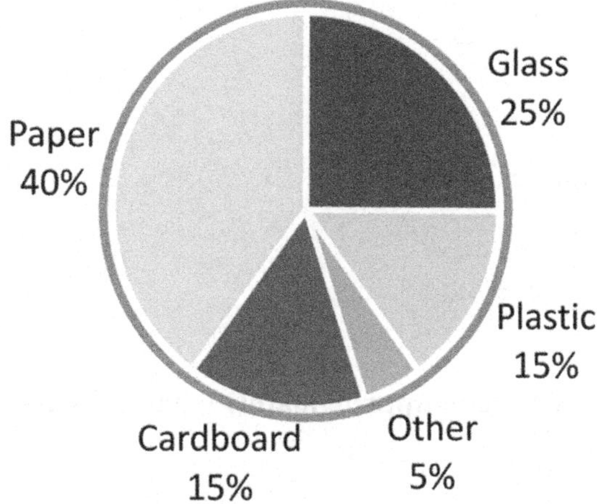

6. The Charleston Recycling Company collects 50,000 tons of recyclable material every month. The chart shows the kinds of materials that are collected by the company's five trucks. What is the second most common material that is recycled?

a. Cardboard
b. Glass
c. Paper
d. Plastic

7. Which of the following expressions represents the ratio of the area of a circle to its circumference?

a. πr^2
b. $\frac{\pi r^2}{2\pi}$
c. $\frac{2\pi r}{r^2}$
d. $\frac{r}{2}$

8. Francine can ride 16 miles on her bicycle in 45 minutes. At this speed, how many minutes would it take Francine to ride 60 miles?

9. If $a = 4$, $b = 3$, and $c = 1$, then what is the value of $\frac{a(b-c)}{b(a+b+c)}$?

a. $\frac{4}{13}$
b. $\frac{1}{3}$
c. $\frac{1}{4}$
d. $\frac{1}{6}$

10. John buys 100 shares of stock at $100 per share. The price goes up by 10%, and he sells 50 shares. Then, prices drop by 10%, and he sells his remaining 50 shares. How much did he get for the last 50 shares?

a. $4,900
b. $4,950
c. $5,000
d. $5,500

11. Which of the following expressions is equivalent to the equation $3x^2 + 4x - 15$?

a. $(x-3)(x+5)$
b. $(x+5)(3+x^2)$
c. $x(3x^2+4-15)$
d. $(3x-5)(x+3)$

12. Factor the following expression: $x^2 + x - 12$

a. $(x-2)(x+6)$
b. $(x+6)(x-2)$
c. $(x-4)(x+3)$
d. $(x+4)(x-3)$

13. A circle has a circumference of 35 feet. Approximately what is its diameter?

a. 3.5 feet
b. 5.57 feet
c. 6.28 feet
d. 11.14 feet

14. A circle is inscribed within a square, as shown. What is the difference between the area of the square and that of the circle, where r is the radius of the circle?

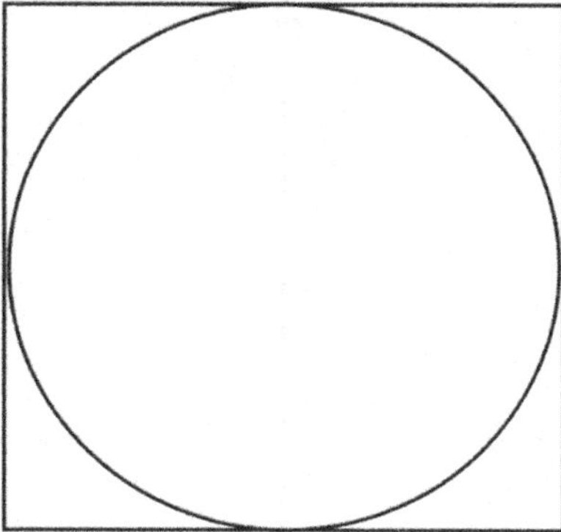

a. 2π
b. $\frac{4}{3}\pi r^3$
c. $r^2(4 - \pi)$
d. $2\pi r$

15. A taxi service charges $5.50 for the first $\frac{1}{5}$ of a mile, $1.50 for each additional $\frac{1}{5}$ of a mile, and 20¢ per minute of waiting time. Joan took a cab from her place to a flower shop 8 miles away, where she bought a bouquet, then another 3.6 miles to her mother's place. The driver had to wait 9 minutes while she bought the bouquet. What was the fare?

a. $20
b. $91
c. $92.80
d. $120.20

16. A satellite in a circular orbit revolves around Earth every 120 minutes. If Earth's radius is 4,000 miles at sea level, and the satellite's orbit is 400 miles above sea level, approximately what distance does the satellite travel in 40 minutes? Use 3.14 for π.

a. 4,121 miles
b. 4,400 miles
c. 8,000 miles
d. 9,211 miles

GED Practice Test #1

17. Select the points that are located at $(3, -2)$ and $(-1, 4)$.

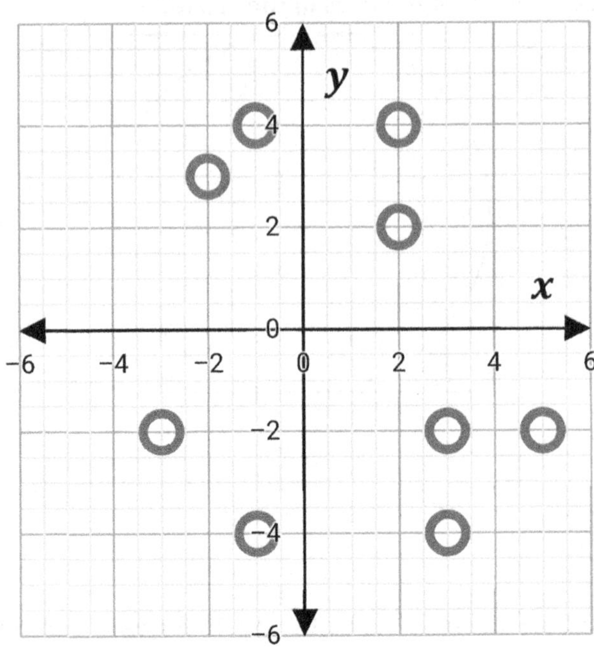

18. If x and y are positive integers, which of the following expressions is equivalent to $(xy)^{7y} - (xy)^{y}$?

a. $(xy)^{6y}$
b. $(xy)^{7y-1}$
c. $(xy)^{y}[(xy)^{7} - 1]$
d. $(xy)^{y}[(xy)^{6y} - 1]$

19. It rained every day last week except Friday. If it rained twice as much on Monday as it did on Thursday, which of the following graphs could model the week's rainfall in inches?

a. 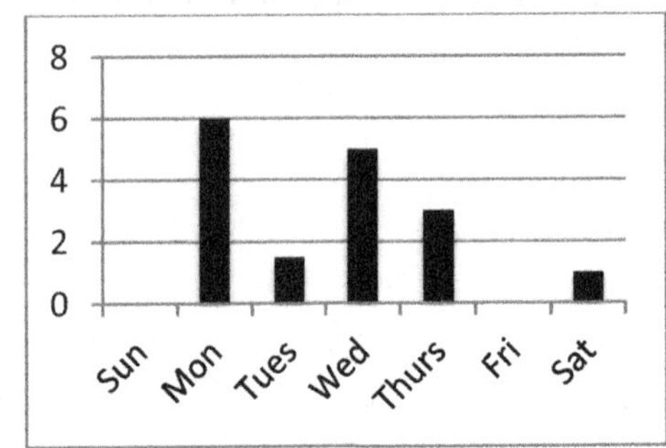

c. 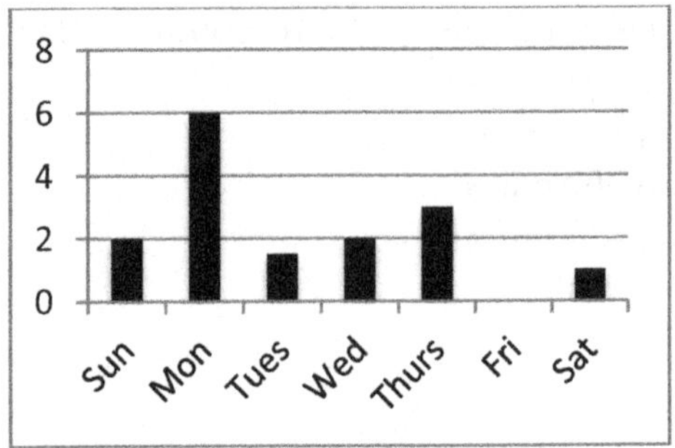

b. 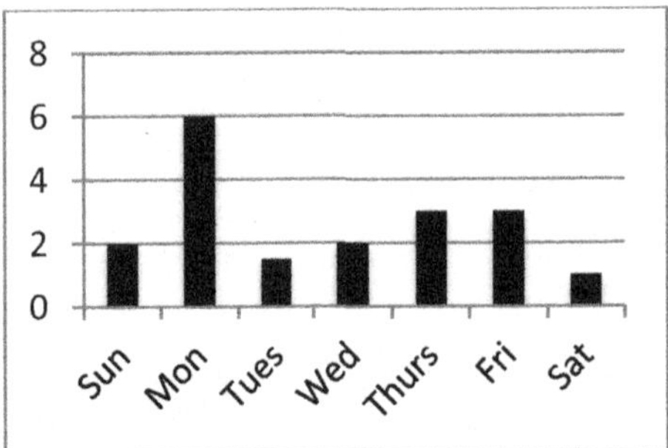

d. 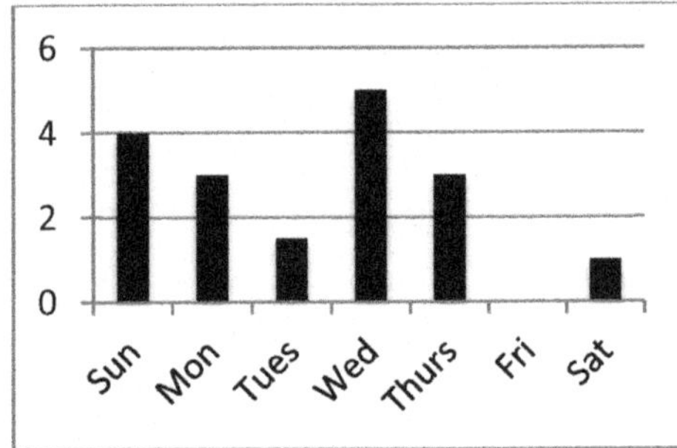

20. If $3a + 5b = 98$ and $a = 11$, what is the value of $a + b$?

21. Jamie had $6.50 in his wallet when he left home. He spent $4.25 on drinks and $2.00 on a magazine. Later, his friend repaid him $2.50 that he had borrowed the previous day. How much money does Jamie have in his wallet now?

a. $2.75
b. $3.25
c. $12.25
d. $14.25

22. If 24 people tried to climb a mountain and 6 people completed the climb, what percentage of people didn't climb the mountain?

23. A regular deck of cards has 52 cards. What is the probability of drawing three aces in a row?

a. 1 in 52
b. 1 in 156
c. 1 in 5,525
d. 1 in 132,600

24. The distance traveled by a moving object is found with the formula: $d = rt$, where r is the rate of travel (speed) and t is the time of travel. A major league pitcher throws a fastball at a speed of 125 ft/sec. The distance from the pitching rubber to home plate is 60.5 feet. How long, in seconds, does it take a fastball to travel this distance? Write your answer to the nearest hundredth of a second.

25. The two shortest sides of a right triangle are 6 and 8 units long, respectively. What is the perimeter of the triangle?

a. 10 units
b. 14 units
c. 18 units
d. 24 units

26. A company has been asked to design a building for an athletic event. The building is in the shape of a square pyramid. The pyramid has a height of 481 feet, and the length of each side of the base is 756 feet. What is the approximate volume of the pyramid?

a. 1.21×10^5 ft^3
b. 4.85×10^5 ft^3
c. 9.16×10^7 ft^3
d. 2.75×10^8 ft^3

27. In the graph shown below, what is the slope of a line that passes through the origin and will intercept the line $y = f(x)$ at the point where $y = 2$?

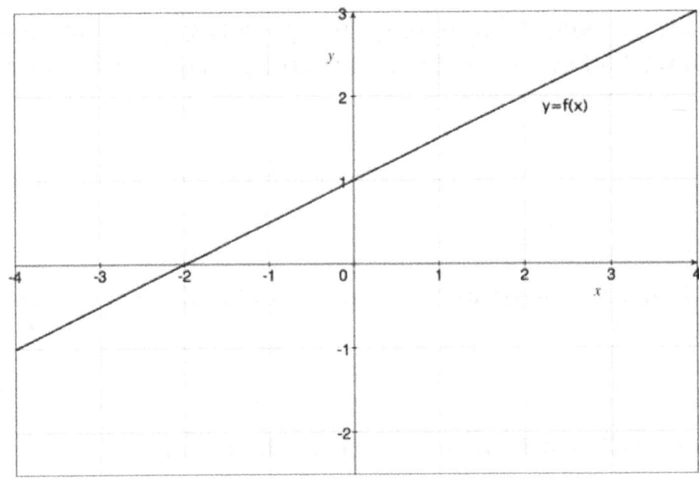

28. Put the following numbers in order from the least to greatest: $2^3, 4^2, 6^0, 9, 10^1$.

a. $2^3, 4^2, 6^0, 9, 10^1$
b. $6^0, 9, 10^1, 2^3, 4^2$
c. $10^1, 2^3, 6^0, 9, 4^2$
d. $6^0, 2^3, 9, 10^1, 4^2$

29. The table below shows the height of a fruit tree over time. Plot the points that represent the height of the tree after 2 years and 3 years.

Time (years)	0	1	2	3	4	5
Height (cm)	0	6	12	18	24	30

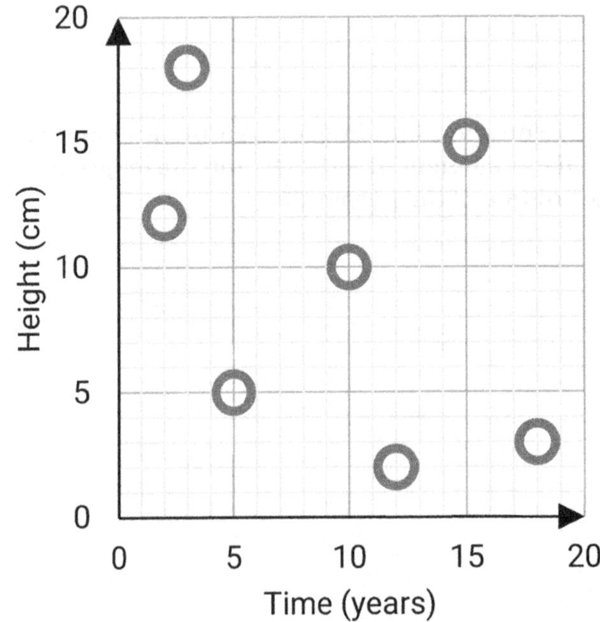

30. Which of the following expressions is equal to x^3x^5?

a. x^2
b. x^8
c. $2x^8$
d. x^{15}

31. Which equation is represented by the graph shown below?

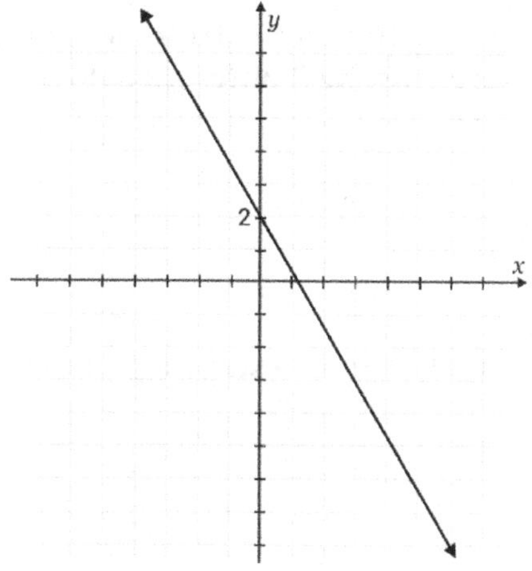

a. $y = \frac{5}{3}x + 2$
b. $y = -\frac{5}{3}x - 2$
c. $y = -\frac{5}{3}x + 2$
d. $y = \frac{5}{3}x - 2$

Refer to the following for question 32:

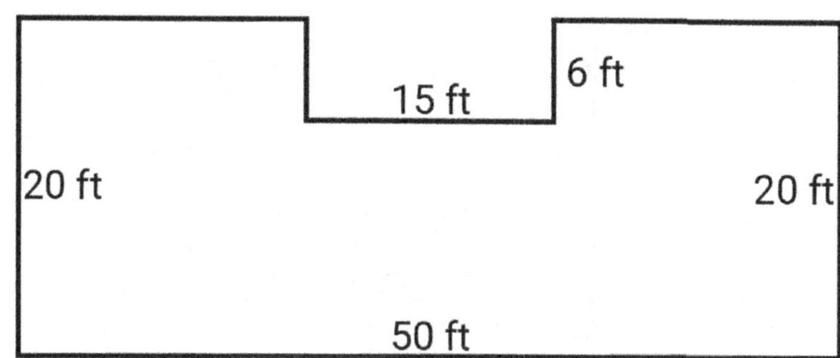

32. What is the area of the figure shown above? Give your answer in square feet.

33. There are 400 fish in a tank. 150 are blue, 150 are red, and the remainder are brown. Tranh dips a net into the tank and pulls out one fish. The probability of pulling out any single fish is the same. What is the probability, as a percentage, that the fish he pulls out is brown?

34. Lauren had \$80 in her savings account. When she received her paycheck, she put some money in her savings account. This brought the balance up to \$120. By what percentage did the total amount in her account increase by putting this amount in her savings account?

a. 35%
b. 40%
c. 50%
d. 80%

35. Carrie wants to decorate her party with bundles of balloons containing 3 balloons each. Balloons are available in 4 different colors. There must be 3 different colors in each bundle. How many different kinds of bundles can she make?

a. 18
b. 12
c. 6
d. 4

36. A line that passes through the point $(1, 4)$ with a slope of 3, can be expressed in slope-intercept form as ____________.

a. $y = 3x + 1$
b. $x = 3y + 1$
c. $y = 3x - 1$
d. $y = 4x + 1$

37. A rectangle has a width of 7 cm and a length of 9 cm. What is its perimeter?

a. 16 cm
b. 32 cm
c. 48 cm
d. 62 cm

38. Select 2 points that are on the graphed line of $y - 6 = \frac{1}{3}x$?

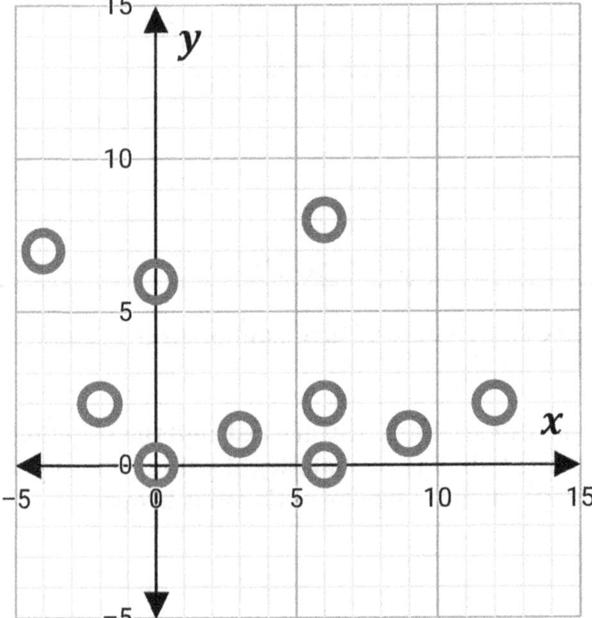

39. How many 3-inch segments can a 4.5-yard line be divided into?

a. 15
b. 45
c. 54
d. 64

40. The equation of the line, in slope-intercept form, that passes through the points $(-2,-3)$ and $(4,-4)$ is __________.

a. $y = -\frac{1}{6}x + \frac{10}{3}$
b. $y = -\frac{1}{6}x - \frac{10}{3}$
c. $y = \frac{1}{6}x - \frac{10}{3}$
d. $y = -6x - \frac{10}{3}$

41. How many identical cubes, each with edges of 3 inches, can fit in a box measuring 15 inches by 9 inches by 6 inches?

42. A jar contains pennies and nickels. The ratio of nickels to pennies is 6:2. What percentage of the coins are pennies?

43. The two legs of a right triangle have side lengths of 5 and 12. What is the length of the hypotenuse?

a. 13
b. 17
c. $\sqrt{60}$
d. $\sqrt{119}$

Refer to the following for question 44:

A ticket agency finds that demand for tickets for a concert in a 25,000-seat stadium falls if the price is raised. The number of tickets sold, N, varies with the dollar price, p, according to the relationship $N = 25{,}000 - 0.1p^2$.

44. What is the lowest price at which they will sell no tickets at all?

a. \$10
b. \$25
c. \$50
d. \$500

45. Chan receives a bonus from his job. He pays 30% in taxes, gives 30% to charity, and uses another 25% to pay off an old debt. He has \$600 remaining from his bonus. What was the total amount of Chan's bonus?

46. For the number set $\{7, 12, 5, 16, 23, 44, 18, 9, Z\}$, which of the following values could be equal to Z if Z is the median of the set?

a. 11
b. 12
c. 14
d. 17

47. The equations $y = 8x - 4$ and __________ will form parallel lines when graphed.

a. $y = \frac{1}{8}x - 4$
b. $y = 2x - 1$
c. $y = \frac{1}{8}x - 4$
d. $y = 8x - 1$

48. If $a = -6$ and $b = 7$, then what is the value of $4a(3b + 5) + 2b$?

a. -610
b. 610
c. 624
d. 638

49. If the two lines $2x + y = 0$ and $y = 3$ are plotted on a typical xy-coordinate grid, at which point will they intersect?

a. $\left(-\frac{3}{2}, 0\right)$
b. $\left(-\frac{3}{2}, 3\right)$
c. $\left(\frac{3}{2}, 3\right)$
d. $(4, 1)$

Refer to the following for question 50:

Kyle bats third in the batting order for the Badgers baseball team. The table below shows the number of hits that Kyle had in each of 7 consecutive games played during one week in July.

Day	Monday	Tuesday	Wednesday	Thursday	Friday	Saturday	Sunday
Hits	1	2	3	1	1	4	2

50. What is the mean of the numbers in the distribution shown in the table?

a. 1
b. 2
c. 3
d. 4

Science

1. The chart below shows the daily high temperature (in Fahrenheit) in Miami, FL during one week in February.

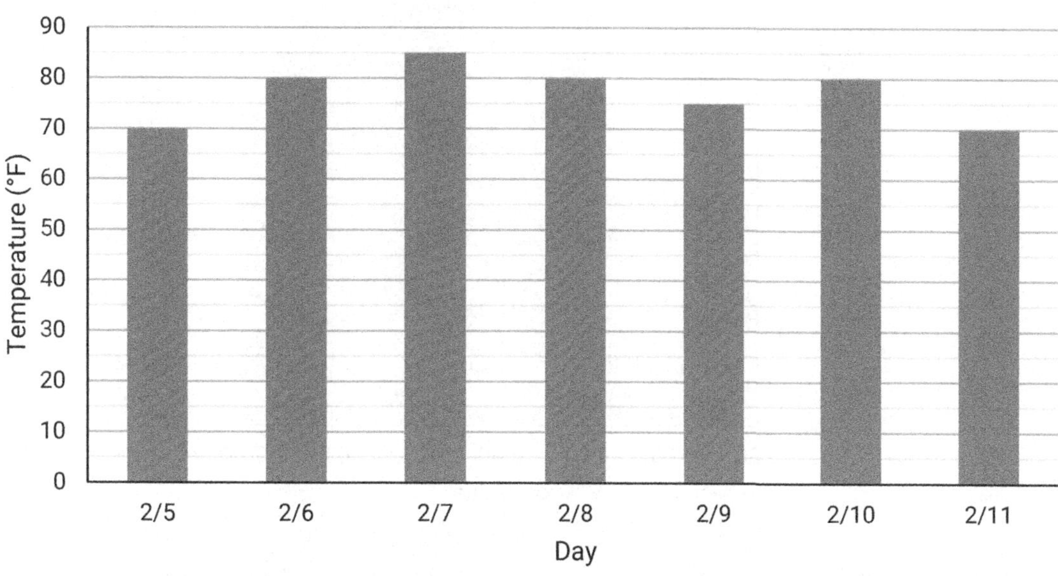

What is the average high temperature for this week, rounded to the nearest whole number? You may use your calculator.

a. 77 °F
b. 79 °F
c. 82 °F
d. 84 °F

2. In ladybugs, there are two alleles for the gene for spot color: s for black spots, and S for red spots. SS and Ss result in a ladybug with red spots, and ss results in a ladybug with black spots.

If a population of 100 ladybugs includes 33 with an SS genotype, 38 with an Ss genotype, and 29 with an ss genotype, what percentage of those 100 ladybugs will have red spots?

a. 33%
b. 38%
c. 71%
d. 29%

3. Select the data chart that most accurately matches the graph shown below.

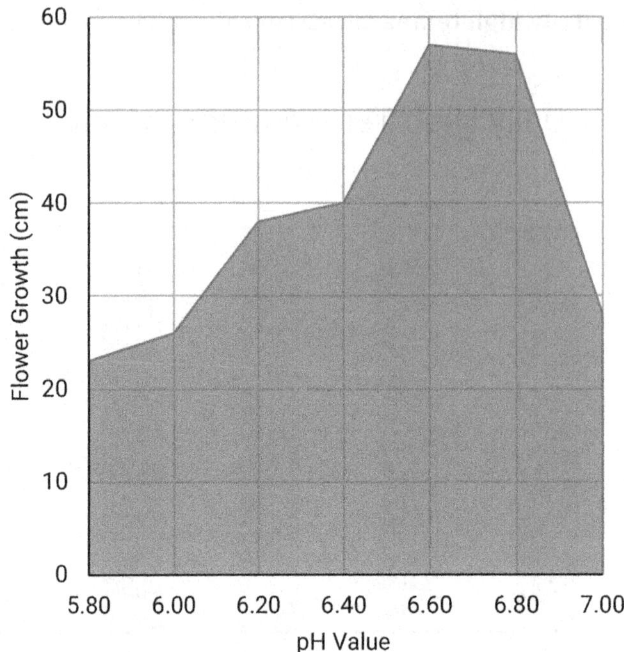

a.

pH Value	Flower Growth (cm)
23	5.8
36	6
38	6.2
40	6.4
57	6.6
56	6.8
28	7

b.

pH Value	Flower Growth (cm)
5.8	33
6	46
6.2	48
6.4	50
6.6	67
6.8	66
7	38

c.

pH Value	Flower Growth (cm)
6	23
8	26
8.2	38
8.4	40
8.6	57
8.8	56
9	28

d.

pH Value	Flower Growth (cm)
5.8	23
6	26
6.2	38
6.4	40
6.6	57
6.8	56
7	28

4. A biome is an area that is classified by the vegetation and wildlife that lives within it. The following information is specifically about desert and rainforest biomes.

Average annual precipitation in a desert biome: 100 mm
Average annual precipitation in a rainforest biome: 2,000 mm

Average temperature in a desert biome: 30 °C
Average temperature in a rainforest biome: 25 °C

Biodiversity index in a desert biome: 2.5
Biodiversity index in a rainforest biome: 8.0

Primary vegetation in a desert biome: cacti, succulents
Primary vegetation in a rainforest biome: tall trees, dense undergrowth

Based on this data, which of the following conclusions about these biomes is most likely accurate?

a. Due to the lower annual precipitation, the desert biome also has lower biodiversity as well as vegetation that can survive in drier climates.
b. Due to the similar average temperatures of the desert and rainforest biomes, the vegetation and wildlife are also similar.
c. Due to the higher biodiversity in the rainforest biome, the vegetation does not need as much precipitation.
d. Due to the denser vegetation in the rainforest biome, biodiversity is low since there is less room for wildlife to thrive.

5. John is conducting an experiment to see how different amounts of fertilizer affect plant growth. He is conducting the experiment in a covered greenhouse, and two of his friends are assisting him.

Which of the following would be considered an independent variable in this experiment?

a. The number of people conducting the experiment
b. The amount of fertilizer used
c. The temperature of the air in the greenhouse
d. The weather outside of the greenhouse

6. Velocity is a fundamental concept used in physics. If a train is moving at a velocity of 60 kilometers per hour toward the east, this means that it is traveling at a speed of 60 km/hr and the direction is east. Velocity plays a role in understanding phenomena such as the movement of celestial bodies, the behavior of subatomic particles, and the movement of vehicles, spacecraft, and aircraft. Scientists use velocity to analyze and predict the motion of objects across our universe.

Using the paragraph above, which of the following is the best definition of velocity?

a. The speed and direction of an object
b. The behavior of subatomic particles
c. The height of spacecraft
d. The flight path of aircraft

7. This map shows the average change in temperature worldwide versus the baseline temperatures recorded from 1951 to 1980. Which of the following conclusions could be made based on this map?

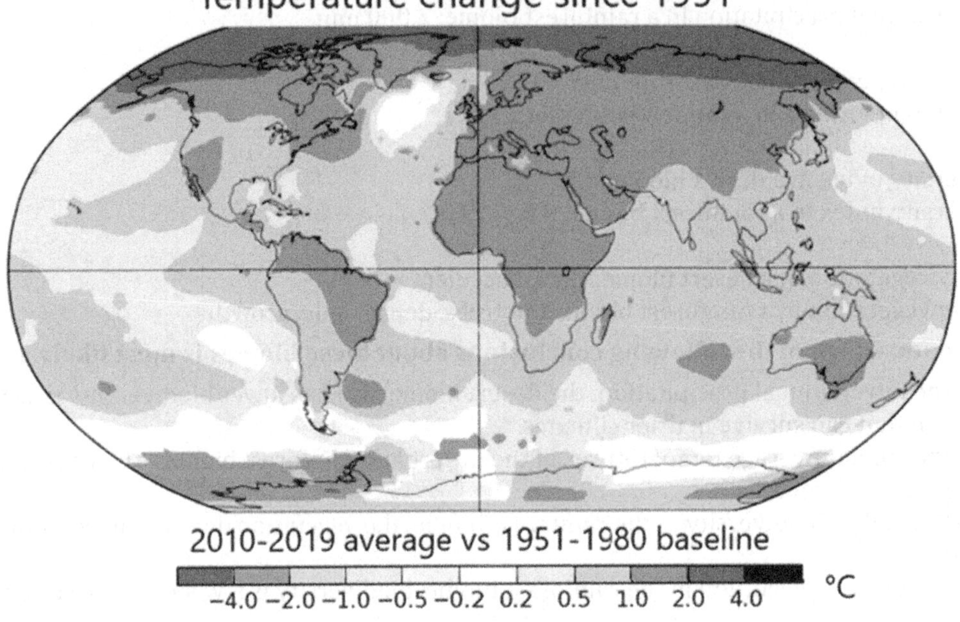

a. Areas near the equator have had the lowest increases in temperature.
b. Areas north of the equator have had the highest increases in temperature.
c. Increases in temperature have been fairly even throughout the map.
d. Increases in temperature have mostly been less than 0.5 °C

Refer to the following for questions 8–9:

Gravity is an invisible force in which objects pull on each other. Ancient scholars looked for an explanation of why objects fall to the ground, and the Greek philosopher Aristotle believed that this happened because Earth was the center of the universe, attracting objects toward it. Later, Plutarch observed that this phenomenon was not limited to Earth.

Gravity gives objects on Earth their weight. The gravity on Earth comes from its mass (a measurement of how much matter is in the object), and that mass pulls on the mass of other objects. This pull keeps objects that are on the ground from floating away and causes objects in the air to fall toward the ground. Gravity has nearly no effect on subatomic particles due to their miniscule size.

Gravity holds planets in their orbits and holds the moon in its orbit of the Earth. The moon's gravitational pull causes the tides of the oceans. Gravity even affects light, although this is only seen on a large scale, such as with a star. Black holes are thought to have so much mass that not even light can escape them.

8. Select the answer that best describes a conclusion about gravity that could be reached based on the information in the passage.

a. An object on the moon will float due to the moon having no gravity.
b. Objects close to a black hole will be pushed away.
c. A person's weight would be lower on a smaller planet than on Earth.
d. The force of gravity increases when objects are farther apart.

9. Based on this passage, which of the following is true?

a. Gravity is a force that only exists on planets
b. Gravity is an attractive force between objects
c. Gravity causes objects in the solar system to rotate
d. Gravity is a force that pushes objects away from each other

Refer to the following for questions 10–12:

Of the 4,000 species of frogs in the world, 427 are found in the Amazon rainforest. The Amazon rainforest is in South America, covering parts of Brazil, Peru, Colombia, and other countries. The climate is rainy, hot, and humid, which makes the area a perfect location for many species.

One type of frog found in the Amazon is the giant cane toad. This large toad is gray, yellow, or brown with dry and warty textured skin. In addition to living in the Amazon rainforest, this toad has been introduced to various other regions worldwide. The giant cane toad is primarily active during the night. It is omnivorous, but its preference is to feed on small animals and insects. The name *cane toad* arose from the use of these toads to eliminate sugarcane pests. The giant cane toad secretes a fluid from its skin that is highly toxic to most animals. If an animal catches a giant cane toad in its mouth, that animal can die from the highly toxic poison. The toxin can be irritating to humans. The giant cane toad also excretes white venom from its back.

Another type of frog found in the Amazon is the poison dart frog. These frogs are known for their bright colors, usually orange, red, or green. These small frogs are active during the day rather than at night. They are usually found on the rainforest floor. The poison dart frog feeds on small arthropods and insects. Poison dart frogs, as their name suggests, excrete a poison through their skin that is potent enough to kill an adult human. The name arose from the practice of a nearby indigenous people who would cover the ends of their darts in the poison from these frogs.

10. Select the answer that best describes a logical conclusion that could be made from the passage above.

a. Poisonous frogs can be found in different sizes and colors.
b. Poisonous frogs are located in areas where humans and other animals will not encounter them.
c. Poisonous frogs all have bright colors so humans and other animals know to avoid them.
d. Poisonous frogs tend to be very small so animals can avoid them more easily.

11. Based on the passage, which statement is true?

a. The poison dart frog and the giant cane toad have both been used for the advantage of humans.
b. The poison dart frog and the giant cane toad are both endangered species.
c. The poison dart frog and the giant cane toad both excrete toxins that cause death in humans and other animals.
d. The poison dart frog and the giant cane toad are both herbivores.

12. The northern glass frog is another frog that can be found in the Amazon rainforest. Like the giant cane toad, this frog is nocturnal. Which of the following best describes what *nocturnal* means?

a. The northern glass frog is mainly active at night.
b. The northern glass frog is active during the day and inactive at night.
c. The northern glass frog is mainly active during twilight.
d. The northern glass frog is active during both day and night.

13. A student is conducting a research project on the effects of a certain medication. The student discovered three research studies that report contradictory findings. Study A reports that the medication has been found to be ineffective compared to a placebo. Study B reports that the medication is only effective for people of a certain age range. Study C reports that the medication leads to an increased risk of gastrointestinal issues.

Which of the following best describes how the student can reconcile these findings?

a. Disregard Studies A and B and use the information from Study C to support his or her own findings.
b. Analyze the sample sizes and methodologies, as well as study findings, of all three studies to identify the factors that affected the outcomes.
c. Use the parts of each study that best support the conclusion that he or she is leading toward.
d. Disregard Study A, since the other studies show levels of effectiveness, and combine the findings of Studies B and C.

14. In an experiment investigating the relationship between temperature (T) and the rate of enzyme activity (R), the following data was found:

Temperature (°C)	Enzyme Activity (R: units/min)
30	65
40	85
50	105
60	125
70	145

Which of the following shows the numerical relationship between the temperature (T) and rate of enzyme activity (R)?

a. $R = 2T + 5$
b. $R = 2T - 5$
c. $R = T + 20$
d. $R = 5T - 5$

15. During a migratory bird count, the following data was gathered:

Flock number	Number of birds
1	1,320
2	408
3	793
4	1,254
5	681
6	590

Which of the following best describes a reason to find the mean of the number of birds in each flock?

a. To find the most common number of birds in a flock
b. To find the difference between the largest and smallest flocks
c. To find the total number of birds
d. To get an idea of how big a typical group is

16. In one type of pea plant, one gene determines the color of the plant. There are two different alleles for this gene. Each plant has two copies of the gene, one from each of its parents. When the plant has one or two copies of the dominant allele (Y), the plant will be yellow. When the plant has only the recessive allele (y), the plant will be green. The pair of alleles each plant has is called its genotype.

	y	y
Y	Yy	Yy
y	yy	yy

Use the Punnett square to determine the probability that an offspring of a yellow pea plant with a genotype of Yy and a green pea plant with a genotype of yy would be yellow.

a. 25%
b. 100%
c. 75%
d. 50%

Refer to the following for questions 17–18:

Forces are a fundamental concept in physics. Forces affect how objects behave and how celestial bodies move. The interactions of forces are vectors, meaning they have both magnitude and direction. These forces play a major role in Isaac Newton's Laws of Motion, as they help scientists understand the dynamics of the physical world.

Newton's First Law of Motion states that an object at rest will stay at rest and that an object in motion will remain in motion until another force is applied to it. This is also called the Law of Inertia. Objects are resistant to changes in their state of motion, whether the object is stationary or in motion. If an object is already moving at a constant speed in a certain direction, it will continue moving at that same speed and direction until an outside force is applied to it. The greater an object's mass, the greater its inertia, or resistance to an outside force.

Newton's Second Law of Motion is also known as the Law of Acceleration. This law states that the force acting on an object equals its mass times its acceleration. This law outlines the relationship between force, mass, and acceleration. It helps to predict the behavior of objects when forces are applied to them. According to this law, when a force is applied to an object, that object will accelerate in the direction of the force.

Newton's Third Law of Motion states that every action results in an equal but opposite reaction. This law helps to illustrate the dynamics of the physical world and shows the symmetry of forces in nature. This law shows how forces occur in pairs, and how bodies apply forces upon each other in equal magnitude and in opposite directions.

17. Based on this passage, which of the following is the best example of Newton's First Law of Motion?

a. A ball being propelled through the air
b. A rocket increasing its speed after launching from the ground
c. A passenger lurching forward when a car comes to a sudden stop
d. A person walking on the sidewalk

18. According to Newton's Third Law of Motion, what happens when a book is sitting on a chair?

a. The book cannot resist a change in its state of motion.
b. The book is applying a force to the chair, and the chair is applying an equal force to the book.
c. A force applied to the book will cause it to accelerate in the opposite direction of that force.
d. The chair is applying a large force to the book, and the book is applying a much smaller force to the chair.

Refer to the following for questions 19–20:

The relative position that an organism occupies within a food chain or food web is called its trophic level. An organism's trophic level is based on how it obtains its energy. All food chains or food webs have at least three trophic levels, with the primary producer at the lowest level and the top consumer at the highest level.

Primary producers are usually plants, algae, or phytoplankton, and they get their energy from the sun. These primary producers are considered trophic level 1, and they perform photosynthesis to create their own food supply. The organisms at trophic level 1 are food for the next trophic level.

Primary consumers form trophic level 2. These organisms are herbivores. They feed on the primary producers that capture energy from the sun through photosynthesis. Examples of primary consumers include cows, sheep, mice, and grasshoppers.

Secondary consumers form trophic level 3. These organisms are carnivores, and they feed on the primary consumers. Examples of secondary consumers include snakes, foxes, and lions. In a marine ecosystem, any animal that consumes zooplankton is a secondary consumer. Animals that eat zooplankton include jellyfish, crabs, and some whales.

Animals can be on more than one level in a food web. Some secondary consumers are omnivores. Omnivores feed on both primary producers and primary consumers. This means that omnivores are also primary consumers. For example, grizzly bears are omnivores that eat berries (primary producers) and salmon (primary consumers), so they can be considered both primary consumers (level 2) and secondary consumers (level 3).

Many food chains have tertiary consumers, on trophic level 4, who consume secondary consumers. Some food chains or webs have a fifth trophic level of quaternary consumers. There are even cases of food webs with six levels.

At the top of a food chain are apex predators, which do not have natural predators of their own. Apex predators are usually on trophic level 3, 4, or 5, depending on the food web. Lions, wolves, and sharks are examples of apex predators. Through predation, apex predators keep the populations of the lower trophic levels under control.

19. If an apex predator population were to disappear, which of the following is a likely outcome for the ecosystem?

a. The health of the overall ecosystem would improve.
b. There would be no impact to the ecosystem.
c. Their prey species would experience a population explosion and lack enough food to eat.
d. Any carnivores in the lower trophic levels would become herbivores.

20. Krill are small crustaceans that feed on zooplankton, and they are preyed upon by some fish and whales. Which trophic level do krill belong to?

a. Primary consumer
b. Secondary consumer
c. Tertiary consumer
d. Apex predatory

Refer to the following for questions 21–22:

Johanna is conducting an experiment on the relationship between the angle of a ramp and the distance that a ball will roll. She sets up a ramp on a flat surface as shown in the drawing below. The angle of the ramp ranges from 10 to 60 degrees. She pushes the ball down the ramp from the top and repeats this five times for every 10° change in angle. She measures the distance that the ball rolls past the end of the ramp with a tape measure.

21. Which of the following is a potential flaw in this experimental design?

a. Observer bias about the experiment's outcome
b. Lack of control over experimental conditions
c. Lack of randomization
d. Publication bias

22. Which of the following aspects of the experimental design helps to ensure the reliability of the results?

a. Using ramps of different angles
b. Using a tape measure to record the ball's distance
c. Repeating the process five times for each angle
d. Using ramps of different lengths.

Refer to the following for questions 23–24:

Malik is conducting an experiment to find out the effect of different liquids on plant growth. He is using three plants: basil, marigold, and aloe. The liquids for the experiment are lemon juice mixed with tap water, milk mixed with tap water, and vinegar mixed with tap water. To conduct the experiment, Malik applies 4 oz. of lemon juice mixed with tap water to the basil plant, 4 oz. of milk mixed with tap water to the marigold, and 4 oz. of vinegar mixed with tap water to the aloe plant every other day. He records plant growth, in centimeters, for a total of six weeks. He also records the number of leaves on each plant, as well as any other visible changes such as discoloration.

23. Which of the following aspects of the experimental design creates a confounding variable?

a. The use of three different types of plants
b. The duration of recording plant growth
c. The measurement the plant growth in centimeters
d. The application of liquid every other day

24. Which of the following could be included in the experiment to strengthen the design and provide a baseline for the results?

a. The measurement of the pH values of the liquids
b. Variations in the depth of soil for each plant
c. The measurement of plant growth in inches instead of centimeters
d. The addition of a control group

25. The chart shows the number of hours a train has traveled for on certain days and the number of kilometers it has traveled in that time.

Hours	Distance (km)
12	540
11	473
13	572
11	440
12	564
12	492
10	420
12	504

The scientific formula for calculating speed (s) is s = distance (d) divided by time (t).

What is the average speed that the train travels on days that it has traveled for at least 12 hours? Round to the nearest tenth of a kilometer per hour.

a. 43.2 km/hr
b. 48 km/hr
c. 43.8 km/hr
d. 44.7 km/hr

Refer to the following for questions 26–28:

A chemical reaction is a fundamental process in chemistry that involves the changing of one or more substances, or reactants, into new substances called products. During a chemical reaction, the bonds between atoms are formed or broken, and new products are created. The product is a new substance that has different properties than the original reactants.

Chemical reactions are governed by the law of conservation of mass. This law states that the total mass of the reactants must equal the total mass of the products. No atoms are created or destroyed in the process of a chemical reaction. The number of protons and neutrons in an atom's nucleus remains the same during a chemical reaction. The atoms are rearranged to create the new product. Chemical reactions are expressed by chemical equations, which have the same number of atoms of each element on each side of the equation.

Signs of a chemical change include color change, formation of a precipitate (solids forming within a liquid), formation of a gas, odor change, and temperature change. Some examples of chemical reactions include rust formation, the tarnishing of metal, baking, and combustion.

26. During a chemical reaction, the atomic number of the elements involved does not change. Based on the passage, which is the best definition of atomic number?

a. The color of the resulting product of the reaction
b. The number of protons and neutrons in an atom's nucleus
c. The number of products from the reactants
d. The temperature of the original reactants

27. Based on the passage, which of the following is a chemical reaction?

a. Paper being cut into smaller pieces
b. Salt dissolving in water
c. Mixing equal amounts of sand and dirt together
d. An apple turning brown when exposed to air

28. Based on the passage, which of the following is a key characteristic of a chemical reaction?

a. The resulting product has the same number of atoms as the reactants but different properties than the reactants.
b. The resulting product has a different number of atoms than the reactants but the same mass as the reactants.
c. The resulting product has a different mass than the reactants but the same properties as the reactants.
d. The resulting product has a different color than the reactants and a different number of atoms than the reactants.

Refer to the following for questions 29–30:

An experiment is conducted measuring the salinity of ocean water at different depths.

The salinity of each water sample is measured using a salinometer, which measures the concentration of dissolved salts in water. This experiment is conducted on a cloudless day, when the air temperature is 70 °F. The salinometer is calibrated regularly throughout the experiment. The water is collected in the same amount at each depth using the same collection device, and the salinity is recorded for each measured depth. The water is collected six times per depth at the same location in the ocean. The results are noted in the chart below.

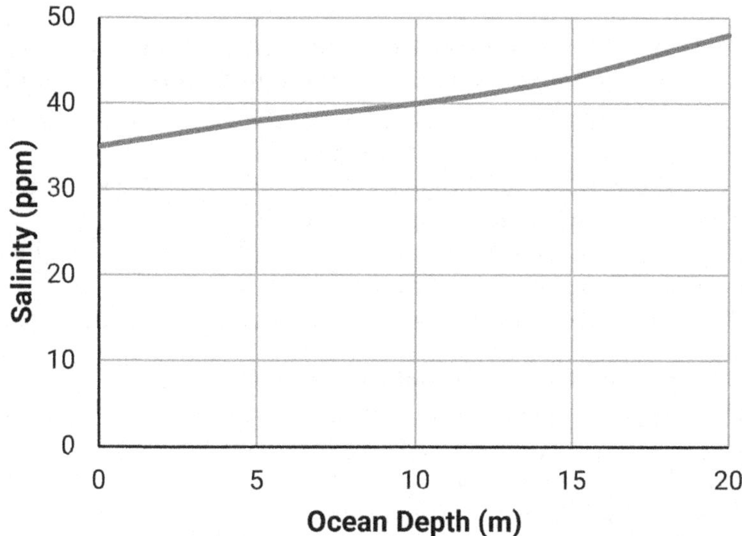

29. What conclusion can be drawn from this experiment?

a. Salinity levels are highest at the ocean's surface and decrease at lower depths.
b. Salinity levels remain constant at all depths of the ocean due to the constant movement of water.
c. As the depth of the ocean increases, the salinity of the water increases.
d. The salinity of the ocean does not change in a predictable way.

30. Which of the following would strengthen the design of this experiment?

a. Measuring the pH level of the ocean water in addition to the salinity
b. Repeating the same experiment multiple times at different locations in the ocean
c. Measuring the salinity of the water on an overcast day
d. Using a different collection device for each ocean depth

GED Practice Test #1

Refer to the following for questions 31–32:

This chart shows the average daily precipitation in Puyo, Ecuador by month versus the average daily precipitation in Valparaiso, Chile by month.

Month	Precipitation (mm)	Month	Precipitation (mm)
January	300	January	0
February	280	February	0
March	375	March	5
April	485	April	15
May	325	May	55
June	340	June	85
July	350	July	110
August	340	August	60
September	345	September	25
October	365	October	10
November	370	November	8
December	380	December	1

31. If summer in South America occurs between December and February, and winter occurs between June and August, which of the following best describes the significance of the modes in this data set?

a. The mode in each set shows that Puya, Ecuador has consistent rainfall in summer months, while Valparaiso, Chile has consistent rainfall in winter months.
b. The mode in each set shows that Puya, Ecuador has consistent rainfall in winter months, while Valparaiso, Chile has consistent rainfall in summer months.
c. The mode in each set shows that Puya, Ecuador has the highest amount of rainfall in the fall, and Valparaiso, Chile has the highest amount of rainfall in the winter.
d. The mode in each set shows that Puya, Ecuador has a higher total rainfall than that of Puya, Ecuador.

32. Which best describes what the range of the data set shows?

a. Valparaiso has less rain during the winter than Puya.
b. Puya has higher totals of rainfall during some months than Valparaiso.
c. Valparaiso has a higher total rainfall than Puya.
d. Puya has a larger variability in its data set than Valparaiso.

Refer to the following for questions 33–34:

Liz is examining the plant growth of two different plant species under controlled conditions. After collecting data, she found that plant A has a 50% chance of sprouting within the first 14 days after planting, and plant B has a 70% chance of sprouting within the first 14 days after planting.

33. If Liz plants one of each type of seed, what is the probability that both plants will sprout within the first 14 days?

a. 35%
b. 75%
c. 60%
d. 45%

34. What is the probability that neither of the plants will sprout within the first 14 days?

a. 70%
b. 65%
c. 40%
d. 15%

Refer to the following for questions 35–37:

Jupiter, the fifth planet from the sun and the largest planet in the solar system, is 11 times larger than Earth. Jupiter has a mainly gaseous composition, and the main gases that compose Jupiter are hydrogen and helium. Due to this, Jupiter does not have a solid surface. The outer layers of the planet transition to its dense atmosphere, which is composed mainly of hydrogen and helium.

The swirls and stripes of Jupiter are made up of clouds of ammonia and water driven by powerful jet streams in its atmosphere. The well-known Great Red Spot is actually a giant storm that is bigger than Earth. This storm has raged for centuries, but it has been slowly diminishing in size over the past few decades. Scientists are trying to understand the underlying cause of the storm.

Jupiter has intricate rings that are much fainter than Saturn's. The tiny particles composing the rings are most likely remnants of asteroids and shattered moons. Jupiter has more than 80 moons with diverse characteristics, including one that has volcanic activity and a subsurface ocean. Due to Jupiter's massive size, its gravitational pull is strong enough to hold its large number of moons in orbit and its ring particles in proximity.

Saturn is the sixth planet from the sun and is about 15% smaller than Jupiter. It is best known for its iconic ring system. Saturn is a gas giant. The planet and its atmosphere are composed mainly of hydrogen and helium.

Saturn's seven rings vary in thickness and are composed mostly of dust and ice crystals. The rings have several gaps between them. Scientists think that Saturn's rings are either leftover material from when Saturn was formed or that a moon got too close to the planet and was ripped apart into tiny chunks. The ring particles are expected to be absorbed into Saturn within about 300 million years.

Saturn has the most moons of any planet in the solar system at well over one hundred. Its largest moon, Titan, is bigger than Mercury and has a surface similar to Earth. However, the mountains on Titan are formed from ice instead of rock, and the lakes and oceans are composed of methane and ethane instead of water.

35. Based on this passage, what can be concluded about the size of Earth compared to Jupiter and Saturn?

a. Earth is smaller than both Jupiter and Saturn.
b. Earth is larger than Saturn but smaller than Jupiter.
c. Earth is larger than Jupiter but smaller than Saturn.
d. Earth is larger than both Jupiter and Saturn.

36. Which of the following conclusions can be made from this passage?

a. The ice crystal chunks composing Saturn's rings help to hold the planet in its orbit.
b. The Great Red Spot holds Jupiter's moons in orbit.
c. A strong gravitational pull due to Saturn's large size holds its moon and ring particles in its orbit.
d. The helium in Jupiter's atmosphere helps to hold its moons and ring particles in its orbit.

37. Which of the following is a conclusion that could be made based on the evidence provided?

a. The number of ring fragments around Saturn is slowly increasing.
b. Jupiter's Great Red Spot will continue to shrink over the next several decades.
c. The moons around Saturn have water on their surface.
d. Jupiter's surface has volcanoes composed of rocky formations.

Refer to the following for questions 38–39:

Jaden notices that the milkweed plants in his front yard, where there are no other large plants, grow taller than the milkweed plants in his back yard, where there are also several shade trees. He investigates the link between plant growth and sunlight, and he reads about photosynthesis, which powers energy production and fuels cellular growth in plants. He then sets up a test at school with two identical groups of milkweeds. Group A is placed in a location that receives full sun, and Group B is placed in a shady location nearby. After several weeks of recording plant growth, Jaden finds that the plants in Group A have grown taller than the plants in Group B.

38. Which of the following steps of the scientific process is missing from this scenario?

a. Data collection
b. Hypothesis
c. Research
d. Experiment

39. Which of the following is a reasonable conclusion for Jaden to reach after his experiment?

a. Sunlight negatively affects the growth of milkweed.
b. Shade is inappropriate for all types of plants.
c. Photosynthesis does not affect plant growth.
d. Sunlight positively affects the growth of milkweed.

Refer to the following for questions 40–42:

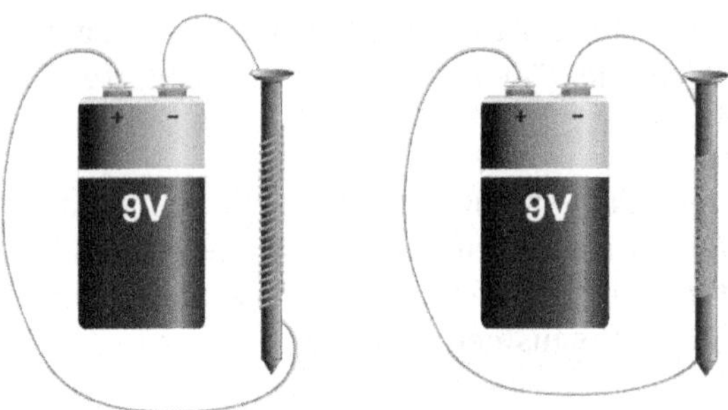

Nadia is creating an electromagnet to explore how electricity and magnetism are connected. She wraps copper wire around an iron nail in tight coils, leaving the ends of the nail exposed on each side of the copper. She then connects one end of the wire to one terminal of a 9-volt battery and the other end of the wire to the other terminal of the battery. Nadia places several small metal objects on her desk to test the magnetic properties of the electromagnet. She is able to use the electromagnet to pick up paper clips and steel washers. She tries to use it to pick up some large screws but is unable to.

Next, Nadia wraps some copper wire around a different iron nail of the same size, making fewer and looser coils as she wraps. She then connects the copper wire ends to the 9-volt battery and is able to pick up the paper clips but not the steel washers. Finally, Nadia connects this more loosely wrapped copper wire to a battery with higher voltage. The electromagnet is able to pick up the paper clips, the steel washers, and some large screws. She removes one side of the copper wire from the battery, and the electromagnet is no longer able to pick up the metal objects.

40. Based on this experiment, which of the following combinations would result in the highest level of magnetism?

a. Loose copper wire on the nail and a low voltage power source
b. Tight copper wire on the nail and a high voltage power source
c. Loose copper wire on the nail and a high voltage power source
d. Tight copper wire on the nail and a low voltage power source

41. Which of the following conclusions can be made about electromagnetism based on Nadia's experiment?

a. The magnetic field disappears once the power source is disconnected.
b. The nail remains magnetic even without a power source.
c. The magnetic field is strengthened by wrapping the coils more loosely on the nail.
d. The steel washers become magnetic after exposure to a magnetic field.

42. Which of the following would be the most appropriate way for Nadia to present her findings?

a. A live demonstration of the electromagnet's capabilities
b. A detailed essay explaining the process of the experiment
c. A bar graph showing the results of the collected data
d. A series of sketches showing which objects were attracted to the electromagnet

Refer to the following for questions 43–44:

Planet	Escape Velocity (km/s)	Length of Day Relative to Earth	Mass Relative to Earth	Diameter (km)	Gravity (m/s^2)
Mercury	4.3	175.94	0.055	4,879	3.7
Venus	10.4	116.75	0.815	12,104	8.9
Earth	11.2	1	1.0	12,756	9.8
Mars	5	1.029	0.108	6,792	3.9
Jupiter	59.5	9.9	317.8	142,984	23.1
Saturn	35.5	0.4125	95.2	120,536	9
Uranus	21.3	0.716	14.6	51,118	10.1
Neptune	23.5	0.67	17.2	49,528	11

43. Which of these planets in the chart is the exception in the general positive correlation between escape velocity and gravity?

a. Mercury
b. Earth
c. Jupiter
d. Saturn

44. Using the data from the chart, what is the length of a day on Venus, in hours?

a. 2,802 hours
b. 4.86 hours
c. 9.73 hours
d. 233.5 hours

Refer to the following for questions 45–46:

Photosynthesis is a chemical reaction that takes place in chloroplasts in plants. It is how plants turn carbon dioxide (CO_2) and water (H_2O) into glucose ($C_6H_{12}O_6$), which the plants use as food, and oxygen (O_2), which they send into the air as a waste product. This reaction occurs only when energy is added. The plants get this energy from light.

45. In a chemical equation, each side of the equation should contain the same number of atoms. Select the number below that balances the reactants and products in this equation for photosynthesis.

$$6\,CO_2 + 6\,H_2O \rightarrow C_6H_{12}O_6 + \_\_\ O_2$$

a. 2
b. 4
c. 6
d. 12

46. A tree can use 496 moles of carbon dioxide in one year. The atomic mass of carbon is 12, and the atomic mass of oxygen is 16. How many kilograms of carbon dioxide does this tree use in one year, rounded to the nearest kilogram? You may use your calculator.

a. 22
b. 14
c. 6
d. 8

Refer to the following for questions 47–50:

The Respiratory System

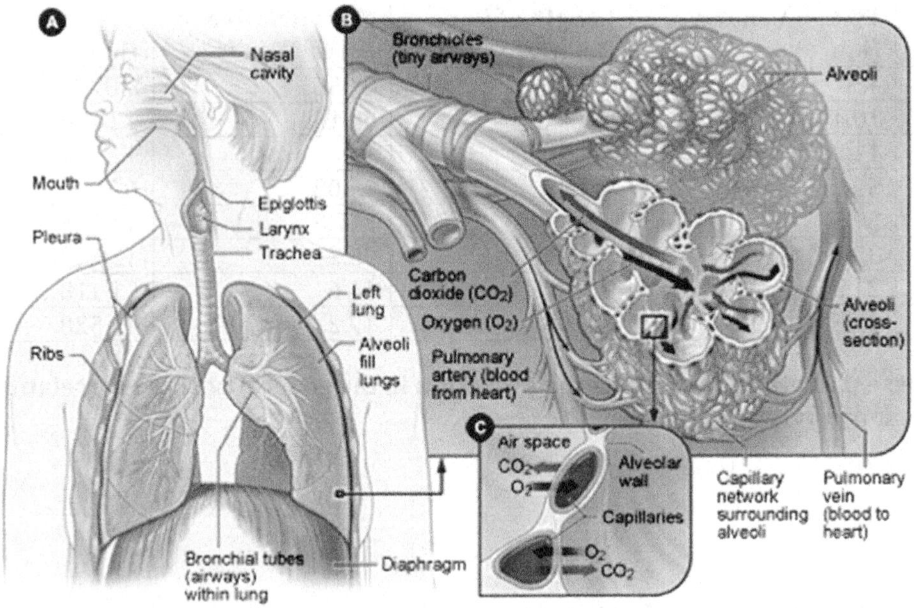

The human body's respiratory system works with the circulatory system to provide oxygen to the body and to remove waste products of metabolism. The respiratory system is made up of several components as shown in the diagram. The process includes both internal and external respiration. External respiration involves the processes through which the body takes in oxygen-rich air and delivers it to the alveoli. Internal respiration involves the processes that take place at a cellular level, where red blood cells carry oxygen to other cells around the body. The oxygen is used during cellular respiration, and the red blood cells transport waste products back to the lungs. The respiratory process is important for the production of energy and enables the tissues and cells throughout the body to function properly.

47. Which of the following is the correct sequence of components used during respiration?

a. Alveoli – nose and mouth – larynx – trachea – bronchioles
b. Larynx – alveoli – trachea – nose and mouth – bronchioles
c. Trachea – bronchioles – nose and mouth – larynx – alveoli
d. Nose and mouth – larynx – trachea – bronchioles – alveoli

48. Which of the following components is involved in internal respiration?

a. Larynx
b. Red blood cells
c. Trachea
d. Bronchioles

49. Which of the following is the waste product that is removed from the body by the process of respiration?

a. Carbon dioxide
b. Oxygen
c. Alveoli
d. Pharynx

50. Which of the following is the source of the red blood cells used during internal respiration?

a. Bronchioles
b. Pulmonary artery
c. Pulmonary vein
d. Alveolar wall

Social Studies

Refer to the following for questions 1–3:

The following is an excerpt from a speech about the nation's space effort given by President John F. Kennedy at Rice University in 1962.

"We set sail on this new sea because there is new knowledge to be gained, and new rights to be won, and they must be won and used for the progress of all people. For space science, like nuclear science and all technology, has no conscience of its own. Whether it will become a force for good or ill depends on man, and only if the United States occupies a position of pre-eminence can we help decide whether this new ocean will be a sea of peace or a new terrifying theater of war. I do not say that we should or will go unprotected against the hostile misuse of space any more than we go unprotected against the hostile use of land or sea, but I do say that space can be explored and mastered without feeding the fires of war, without repeating the mistakes that man has made in extending his writ around this globe of ours.

There is no strife, no prejudice, no national conflict in outer space as yet. Its hazards are hostile to us all. Its conquest deserves the best of all mankind, and its opportunity for peaceful cooperation may never come again. But why, some say, the moon? Why choose this as our goal? And they may well ask, why climb the highest mountain? Why, 35 years ago, fly the Atlantic? Why does Rice play Texas?

We choose to go to the moon. We choose to go to the moon in this decade and do the other things, not because they are easy, but because they are hard, because that goal will serve to organize and measure the best of our energies and skills, because that challenge is one that we are willing to accept, one we are unwilling to postpone, and one which we intend to win, and the others, too.

It is for these reasons that I regard the decision last year to shift our efforts in space from low to high gear as among the most important decisions that will be made during my incumbency in the office of the Presidency."

1. One of Kennedy's strategies during his speech was to characterize space as a beckoning frontier. Which of the following phrases falls within this strategy?

a. "We choose to go to the moon in this decade and do the other things, not because they are easy..."
b. "There is no strife, no prejudice, no national conflict in outer space as yet."
c. "It is for these reasons that I regard the decision last year to shift our efforts in space from low to high gear..."
d. "Whether it will become a force for good or ill depends on man..."

2. Which of the following describes the purpose of Kennedy's repetition in this speech?

a. To explain that there is no real reason to travel to the moon
b. To emphasize the presence of hazards in space
c. To highlight the urgency and importance of his message
d. To stress the concept that space travel is like mountain climbing

3. Kennedy used loaded language in his speech as a method of persuasion. Which of these phrases is an example of loaded language?

a. "For space science, like nuclear science and all technology, has no conscience of its own."
b. "...that challenge is one that we are willing to accept, one we are unwilling to postpone, and one which we intend to win..."
c. "There is no strife, no prejudice, no national conflict in outer space as yet."
d. "And they may well ask, why climb the highest mountain? Why, 35 years ago, fly the Atlantic?"

Refer to the following for questions 4–5:

"I DID NOT RAISE MY GIRL TO BE A VOTER"
SOPRANO SOLO WITH VOCIFEROUS SUPPORTING CHORUS OF MALE VOICES

4. Which of the following best characterizes the artist's opinion of the topic of this political cartoon?

a. Women should be allowed to vote.
b. Girls should not be raised to be voters.
c. Men should be in control of voting.
d. Labor practices should be controlled by men.

5. Which of the following is a conclusion that could be made from this cartoon?

a. Labor leaders support women's right to vote.
b. Women are in agreement with not being able to vote.
c. Political bosses should control both women's rights and labor practices.
d. If women were allowed to vote, they would vote against poor labor practices.

Refer to the following for questions 6–8:

The following excerpts are from Articles V and VI of the Articles of Confederation, which were adopted by the Continental Congress in 1777 and used as the first Constitution of the United States from 1781 until they were replaced by the modern Constitution in 1789.

Article V. For the more convenient management of the general interests of the united states, delegates shall be annually appointed in such manner as the legislature of each state shall direct, to meet in Congress on the first Monday in November, in every year, with a power reserved to each state to recall its delegates, or any of them, at any time within the year, and to send others in their stead, for the remainder of the Year.

No State shall be represented in Congress by less than two, nor by more than seven Members; and no person shall be capable of being delegate for more than three years, in any term of six years; nor shall any person, being a delegate, be capable of holding any office under the united states, for which he, or another for his benefit receives any salary, fees or emolument of any kind.

Each State shall maintain its own delegates in a meeting of the states, and while they act as members of the committee of the states.

In determining questions in the united states, in Congress assembled, each state shall have one vote.

Freedom of speech and debate in Congress shall not be impeached or questioned in any Court, or place out of Congress, and the members of congress shall be protected in their persons from arrests and imprisonments, during the time of their going to and from, and attendance on congress, except for treason, felony, or breach of the peace.

Article VI (excerpt):

No vessels of war shall be kept up in time of peace, by any state, except such number only, as shall be deemed necessary by the united states, in congress assembled, for the defence of such state, or its trade; nor shall any body of forces be kept up, by any state, in time of peace, except such number only as, in the judgment of the united states, in congress assembled, shall be deemed requisite to garrison the forts necessary for the defence of such state; but every state shall always keep up a well regulated and disciplined militia, sufficiently armed and accoutred, and shall provide and constantly have ready for use, in public stores, a due number of field pieces and tents, and a proper quantity of arms, ammunition, and camp equipage.

6. Which of the following was a weakness of Article V?

a. Small states had a disproportionate amount of power in Congress.
b. Some delegates received compensation for their term in Congress.
c. Freedom of speech and debate could be stifled within Congress.
d. Not every state was able to send a delegate as a representative to Congress.

7. Which of the following issues could arise from Article VI?

a. Troops would not be ready to assemble unless a conflict arose.
b. States would need to always keep forts and vessels of war ready.
c. States could have a disproportionate number of military supplies.
d. The federal government could have a difficult time defending itself.

8. What does the word *recall* in Article V most closely mean?

a. Order to come back to Congress
b. Decide between two options
c. Remove a person from their position
d. Remember a previous fact

Refer to the following for questions 9–11:

The following is an excerpt from President Woodrow Wilson's speech to Congress on April 2, 1917.

With a profound sense of the solemn and even tragical character of the step I am taking and of the grave responsibilities which it involves, but in unhesitating obedience to what I deem my constitutional duty, I advise that the Congress declare the recent course of the Imperial German government to be in fact nothing less than war against the government and people of the United States; that it formally accept the status of belligerent which has thus been thrust upon it; and that it take immediate steps, not only to put the country in a more thorough state of defense but also to exert all its power and employ all its resources to bring the government of the German Empire to terms and end the war.

While we do these things, these deeply momentous things, let us be very clear, and make very clear to all the world, what our motives and our objects are. ...

Our object now, as then, is to vindicate the principles of peace and justice in the life of the world as against selfish and autocratic power and to set up among the really free and self-governed peoples of the world such a concert of purpose and of action as will henceforth ensure the observance of those principles. Neutrality is no longer feasible or desirable where the peace of the world is involved and the freedom of its peoples, and the menace to that peace and freedom lies in the existence of autocratic governments backed by organized force which is controlled wholly by their will, not by the will of their people. We have seen the last of neutrality in such circumstances. We are at the beginning of an age in which it will be insisted that the same standards of conduct and of responsibility for wrong done shall be observed among nations and their governments that are observed among the individual citizens of civilized states.

The following is an excerpt from a New York Times article describing President Wilson's speech to Congress:

Before an audience that cheered him as he has never been cheered in the Capitol in his life, the President cast in the lot of Americans unreservedly with the Allies and declared for a war that must not end until the issue between autocracy and democracy has been fought out. He recited our injuries at Germany's hands, but he did not rest our cause on those; he went on from that point to range us with the Allies as a factor in an irrepressible conflict between the autocrat and the people. He showed that peace was impossible for the democracies of the world while this power remained on earth. "The world," he said, "must be made safe for democracy."

...

When he came to this part of his address the first big cheer he got was when, painting the battle of democracy and autocracy, and the difference between the two, he said that democracies "do not fill other countries with spies or set upon a course of intrigue" -and would have said more but for the cheering that split his sentence at that word.

GED Practice Test #1

9. What was the main purpose of President Wilson's speech?

a. To implore Americans to spread peace and justice to other countries
b. To convince Congress that America must go to war against Germany
c. To explain the stance of the US in the current political climate
d. To describe to Congress the standards of conduct in the US

10. Which of these words best describes the *New York Times'* coverage of President Wilson's speech?

a. Biased
b. Objective
c. Symbolic
d. Analytical

11. Which of the following is the most accurate comparison of President Wilson's speech excerpt and the *New York Times* article excerpt?

a. The purpose of the speech was to inform Congress, while the purpose of the article was to inform the American people.
b. The purpose of the speech was to entertain Congress, while the purpose of the article was to educate the American people.
c. The purpose of the speech was to persuade Congress, while the purpose of the article was to persuade the American people.
d. The purpose of the speech was to educate Congress, while the purpose of the article was to entertain the American people.

Refer to the following for questions 12–13:

This graph shows an increase of demand (D1 to D2) for the supply at the Island Coffee Company. In this graph, S represents supply.

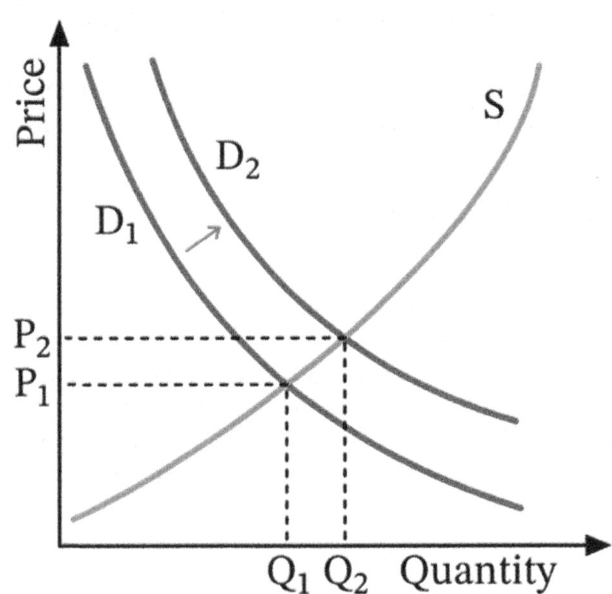

12. Which of the following is a result of the increased demand on the supply of coffee?

a. Price decreases with increased demand.
b. Quantity remains the same with increased demand.
c. Quantity decreases with increased demand.
d. Price increases with increased demand.

13. Which of the following could lead to an increase in supply while not affecting the price?

a. The company expands to a second manufacturing facility.
b. The company hires several new employees.
c. The company exchanges their equipment for new, more-efficient equipment.
d. The company switches to a certified organic supplier.

Refer to the following for questions 14–16:

The following is an excerpt of President Roosevelt's speech to Congress the day after Japan's attack on Pearl Harbor.

> Yesterday, December 7, 1941—a date which will live in infamy—the United States of America was suddenly and deliberately attacked by naval and air forces of the Empire of Japan.
>
> The United States was at peace with that Nation and, at the solicitation of Japan, was still in conversation with its Government and its Emperor looking toward the maintenance of peace in the Pacific. Indeed, one hour after Japanese air squadrons had commenced bombing in the American Island of Oahu, the Japanese Ambassador to the United States and his colleague delivered to our Secretary of State a formal reply to a recent American message. And while this reply stated that it seemed useless to continue the existing diplomatic negotiations, it contained no threat or hint of war or of armed attack.
>
> It will be recorded that the distance of Hawaii from Japan makes it obvious that the attack was deliberately planned many days or even weeks ago. During the intervening time the Japanese Government has deliberately sought to deceive the United States by false statements and expressions of hope for continued peace.

The following is an excerpt of an announcement by the Japanese government to the people of Japan after the attack.

> What an uproar! Japan's Imperial Forces got things off to a quick start with one splendid strike then another in historic surprise attacks on Pearl Harbor, where the bravado of the US Asia fleet met with sudden defeat, and off the Malaya Coast, where the main forces of the British Asia fleet were utterly annihilated. Word has it that Roosevelt and Churchill were shaken up and went pale upon hearing of the defeats. In a third strike, Hong Kong Island, England's strategic base for its 100-year exploitation of East Asia, fell into ruin in only a matter of ten days. During this time, Churchill was sent reeling, cutting off contact with others and showing up in Washington.
>
> What these two headstrong countries are striving for will only lead them on a downhill path to military defeat. Our barbaric enemies are already cowering in fear in the Pacific, and the fall of Manila shall mark the day of the Philippines' subjugation and reversion back to Greater East Asia. The enemy power of Singapore, which was—alas—boasting of its impenetrable stronghold before the Imperial Forces penetrated the jungle area of the Malay Peninsula and advanced southward like a raging tide, shall also vanish into nothingness in the midst of this glorious chapter in history.

14. Which of the following is a similarity between Roosevelt's address and Japan's announcement?

a. They both characterized the Japanese military as victorious.
b. They both described the attack as a surprise.
c. They both explained the attack's effect on England.
d. They both portrayed the Philippines as allies.

15. Which of the following sentences or phrases from these excerpts does not contain any opinions?

a. "Japan's Imperial Forces got things off to a quick start with one splendid strike then another in historic surprise attacks on Pearl Harbor..."
b. "What these two headstrong countries are striving for will only lead them on a downhill path to military defeat."
c. "...one hour after Japanese air squadrons had commenced bombing in the American Island of Oahu, the Japanese Ambassador to the United States and his colleague delivered to our Secretary of State a formal reply to a recent American message."
d. The enemy power of Singapore, which was—alas—boasting of its impenetrable stronghold before the Imperial Forces penetrated the jungle area of the Malay Peninsula and advanced southward like a raging tide, shall also vanish into nothingness in the midst of this glorious chapter in history.

16. How did these two excerpts portray the same event differently?

a. The president's address described the attack as an event of ongoing conflict, while the announcement to Japan described the attack as unforeseen.
b. The president's address described the attack as a minor event, while the announcement to Japan described the attack as a historic event.
c. The president's address described the attack as an accident, while the announcement to Japan described the attack as deliberate.
d. The president's address described the attack as a threat that will lead to conflict, while the announcement to Japan described the attack as leading to a decisive victory.

Refer to the following for questions 17–19:

For a bill to become law, the bill must first be introduced by a member of the Senate or the House of Representatives. The bill can be related to a wide range of issues, including policies or budget considerations. The bill is then assigned a code that depends on where it originated. After the bill is assigned a code, it is referred to the relevant focused committee in that house of Congress based on the type of issue it involves. The focused committee analyzes the bill and gathers input and testimony from experts on the topic. The committee can amend, rewrite, or reject the bill before it gets any further. If a majority of the committee members approve of the bill, it moves to the full chamber.

Once the bill is introduced to the full chamber, it is discussed and debated. Amendments can be proposed. Once the debate has ended, the chamber votes on the bill. If the majority of the chamber is in favor, the bill will advance. When a bill is approved by either the Senate or House of Representatives, it then goes to the other house for debate and approval. If either house fails to pass the bill, it will die. If the bill is passed by both houses of Congress, it goes forward to the final phase, in which the president acts on the bill.

Once the bill reaches the president, it becomes law either if he immediately signs it or if he lets it sit 10 days without signing it. If Congress adjourns before 10 days have passed, and the president has not signed the bill yet, it will not become law. This cannot be overridden. The president also has the option of vetoing the bill. If this happens, the bill will be sent back to Congress. Congress can either revise the bill and try to get it passed again, or they can override the president's veto with two-thirds of their votes in favor of the bill in both houses.

17. Suppose a bill called H.R.4365 is introduced. What are the next three steps that the bill could follow?

a. The bill is referred to a committee in the House of Representatives. The committee analyzes the bill and then revises it prior to the next step.
b. The bill is voted upon by the Senate. Then, it is approved by the House of Representatives and sent to the President to act upon.
c. The bill is referred to a committee in the Senate. It is voted upon by the full chamber and then debated in the House of Representatives.
d. The bill is debated in the House of Representatives. If the House of Representatives approves of the bill, it is then sent to the Senate for approval.

18. Which of the following is an example of the checks and balances built into the process?

a. The committee analyzes bills, and then they can approve them.
b. The bill is introduced by a member of the Senate or House of Representatives, and it is assigned a code.
c. The Senate and House of Representatives create bills, and the president can veto them.
d. A bill is introduced within the full chamber, and it is debated and discussed.

19. What does the word *override* most closely mean in this passage?

a. To advance a bill through Congress
b. To approve a decision by majority vote
c. To send a bill for further consideration
d. To use authority to cancel or reject a decision

Refer to the following for questions 20–22:

Article II Section 1 of the Constitution of the United States:

The executive Power shall be vested in a President of the United States of America.

He shall hold his Office during the Term of four Years, and, together with the Vice President, chosen for the same Term, be elected, as follows:

Each State shall appoint, in such Manner as the Legislature thereof may direct, a Number of Electors, equal to the whole Number of Senators and Representatives to which the State may be entitled in the Congress: but no Senator or Representative, or Person holding an Office of Trust or Profit under the United States, shall be appointed an Elector.

...

In Case of the Removal of the President from Office, or of his Death, Resignation, or Inability to discharge the Powers and Duties of the said Office, the Same shall devolve on the Vice President, and the Congress may by Law provide for the Case of Removal, Death, Resignation or Inability, both of the President and Vice President, declaring what Officer shall then act as President, and such Officer shall act accordingly, until the Disability be removed, or a President shall be elected.

The President shall, at stated Times, receive for his Services, a Compensation, which shall neither be increased nor diminished during the Period for which he shall have been elected, and he shall not receive within that Period any other Emolument from the United States, or any of them.

25th Amendment to the Constitution:

Section 1

In case of the removal of the President from office or of his death or resignation, the Vice President shall become President.

Section 2

Whenever there is a vacancy in the office of the Vice President, the President shall nominate a Vice President who shall take office upon confirmation by a majority vote of both Houses of Congress.

Section 3

Whenever the President transmits to the President pro tempore of the Senate and the Speaker of the House of Representatives his written declaration that he is unable to discharge the powers and duties of his office, and until he transmits to them a written declaration to the contrary, such powers and duties shall be discharged by the Vice President as Acting President.

20. Which part of Article II of the Constitution does Section 1 of the 25th Amendment reiterate?

a. "The executive Power shall be vested in a President of the United States of America."
b. "...the Congress may by Law provide for the Case of Removal, Death, Resignation or Inability, both of the President and Vice President, declaring what Officer shall then act as President..."
c. "In Case of the Removal of the President from Office, or of his Death, Resignation, or Inability to discharge the Powers and Duties of the said Office, the Same shall devolve on the Vice President..."
d. "no Senator or Representative, or Person holding an Office of Trust or Profit under the United States, shall be appointed an Elector..."

21. Which of the following does the word *emolument*, as used in Article II, most closely mean?

a. Classified information from the government
b. Appointment of a new person to office
c. The powers given to the elected president
d. A payment or fee from serving in office

22. Which of the following is the main purpose of Sections 1 and 2 of the 25th Amendment?

a. It establishes the next steps if a president or vice president cannot or will not perform his or her duties any longer.
b. It describes Congress's responsibilities in choosing a replacement for the vice president.
c. It confirms that while the president might leave office due to death, he or she cannot resign.
d. It relays the steps that the vice president might take to choose his or her own replacement.

Refer to the following for questions 23–24:

The first map shows major cities in Canada, and the darker area on the second map indicates the high population around the Toronto area.

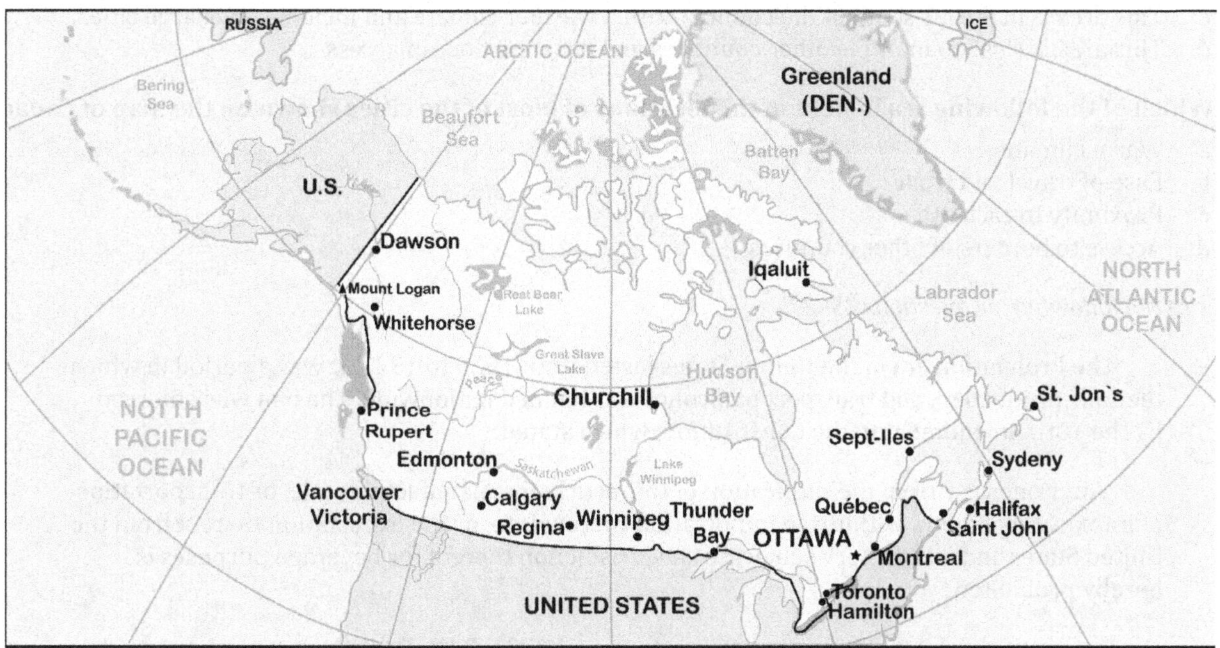

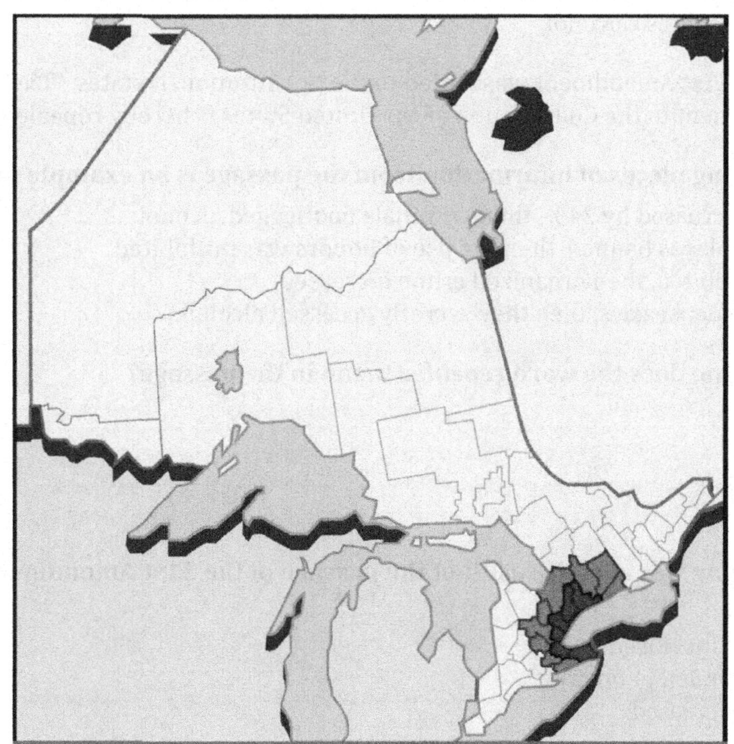

23. Approximately 26% of the population of Canada lives in the darker-colored region shown in the second map. Which of the following are likely reasons for this?

a. This area is easy to get to from the rest of Canada and has access to multiple lakes.
b. This area has ample space for expansion and can use nearby water for entertainment.
c. This area is in the far south of the country with a warmer climate and includes two large cities.
d. This area is close to multiple other countries and has direct ocean access.

24. Which of the following is a benefit of the locations of most of the cities shown on the map of Canada?

a. Warm climate
b. Ease of travel and trade
c. Proximity to each other
d. Access to borders of other countries

Refer to the following for questions 25–27:

The Prohibition era in the United States lasted from 1920 to 1933. It was a period in which the sale, production, and transport of alcohol was banned nationwide. The ban was enforced by the 18th Amendment to the Constitution, which stated:

"After one year from the ratification of this article the manufacture, sale, or transportation of intoxicating liquors within, the importation thereof into, or the exportation thereof from the United States and all territory subject to the jurisdiction thereof for beverage purposes is hereby prohibited."

During the Prohibition era, the crime rate increased by 24%. Organized crime increased, and criminal syndicates operated an illegal alcohol trade. Those participating in organized crime profited from bootlegging alcohol and transporting it to speakeasies, where people could still secretly access alcohol.

In 1933, the 21st Amendment was added to the Constitution. It states, "The eighteenth article of amendment to the Constitution of the United States is hereby repealed."

25. Which of the following pieces of information from the passage is an example of causation?

a. The crime rate increased by 24%, then criminals bootlegged alcohol.
b. The sale of alcohol was banned, then the use of liquors was prohibited.
c. Alcohol was prohibited, then organized crime increased.
d. People drank in speakeasies, then they secretly accessed alcohol.

26. Which of the following does the word *repealed* mean in the passage?

a. Revoked
b. Extended
c. Enforced
d. Initiated

27. Which of the following was a likely result of the passage of the 21st Amendment?

a. People protested.
b. Crime syndicates increased.
c. Speakeasies continued to operate.
d. The crime rate decreased.

Refer to the following for questions 28–29:

This chart illustrates the population of Washington, D.C. by race from 1810 to 2010.

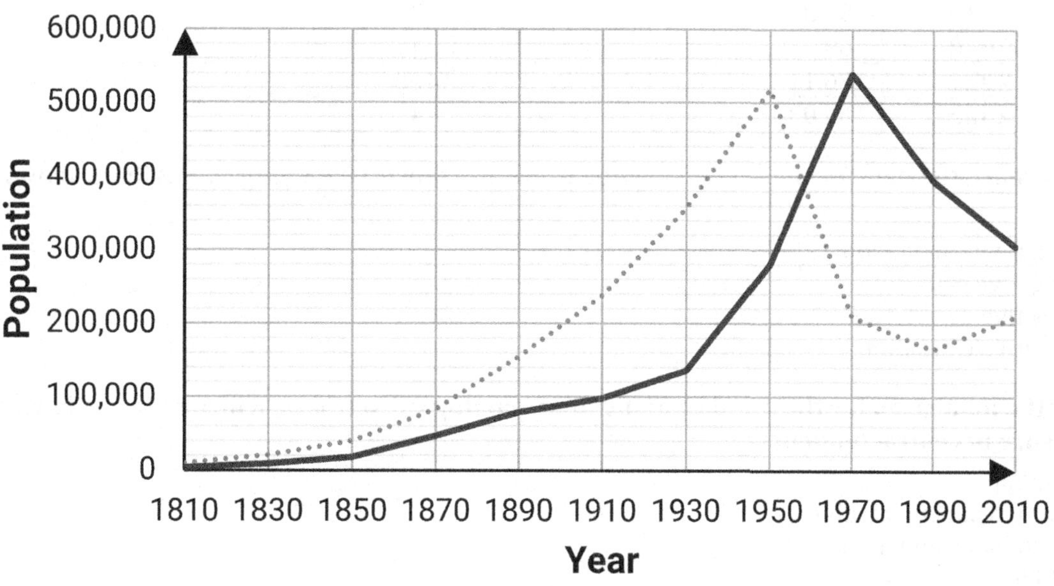

Washington, DC was founded in 1790. Its population grew slowly for the first 70 years. In 1800, Washington, DC became the capital of the United States. In 1860, most of the population of the city was white. At the start of the Civil War, the population increased significantly. The population continued to increase after World War I and World War II. After the wars, many white Americans began an exodus to the suburbs. After Martin Luther King Jr. was assassinated, black Americans also began leaving for the suburbs.

28. During which of the following years did black Americans begin to leave the city?

a. 1950
b. 1970
c. 1990
d. 2000

29. By the year 2020, Washington, DC had a population of about 713,000. White Americans made up about 40% of that population. What was the increase in the number of white Americans in Washington, DC compared to that in 2010?

a. About 75,000
b. About 130,000
c. About 210,000
d. About 285,000

Refer to the following for questions 30–31:

Year	Number of Digital Video Game Users (in millions)	Number of Music Streaming Subscribers in US (in millions)
2017	145.28	198.6
2018	148.95	229.5
2019	153.85	304.9
2020	169.7	341
2021	176.11	400
2022	169.03	443

30. In this chart, the data for digital video game users and music streaming subscribers shows a mostly ____.

a. negative correlation
b. negative causation
c. positive correlation
d. positive causation

31. Using the data given for the number of music streaming subscribers, which of the following is the best measure of central tendency?

a. Median
b. Both mean and median
c. Both mean and mode
d. Mode

Refer to the following for questions 32–34:

The following is an excerpt from a Time magazine article titled "Nation: A War at War," which ran on May 18th, 1970. At this time, the Nixon administration was reducing the number of troops in Vietnam while relying more heavily on South Vietnam's military. Two weeks earlier, on May 4, thirteen unarmed students at Kent State University had been shot by the Ohio National Guard during an anti-war protest. Four died.

Both the eruption of protest and the reaction to it mocked Nixon's still unfulfilled promise to lead the nation "forward together." Not only were there rending, sometimes bloody clashes between peace demonstrators and peace officers, but a scattering of vicious brawls set citizen against citizen as well.

Not long ago, the Administration was considered an artful, managerial mechanism, oiled with serenity, unanimity and self-confidence. Now it showed symptoms of severe internal distress. Interior Secretary Walter Hickel's letter of criticism to the President (see box, page 10) and the abrupt resignation of two young Administration staffers were among the most tangible signs of strain. There were also hints of basic disagreement in the Cabinet over the Cambodian decision—hints that Nixon declined to deny at a hastily called press conference. On Capitol Hill dissension increased daily.

The President had carefully calculated the diplomatic and military hazards of invading the Cambodian sanctuaries. But the more important risk involved the response at home—and in that crucial area he has proved to be dangerously wrong. Nixon, to be sure, could not have foreseen the Kent State shootings.

But he was sadly slow in recognizing their impact. After the four students were gunned down, he found no reason to censure the Guardsmen. All he could bring himself to say was:

"When dissent turns to violence, it invites tragedy." That much was obvious. It seemed equally clear that even if the Cambodian expedition should accomplish more than now appears likely, it has already destroyed far more American resources of morale and cohesion than any North Vietnamese supplies could be worth.

32. Which of the following best characterizes how the evolving situation of the Vietnam War shaped this author's point of view?

a. The president's decision to invade Cambodia increased public support of the war and gave the author a favorable view of the war effort.
b. Nixon's response to the lack of support at home regarding the war created a decline in morale and gave the author an unfavorable view of the war effort.
c. Nixon's reaction to the Kent State shootings bolstered morale at home and gave the author a favorable view of the war effort.
d. The public's positive reactions toward Nixon's policies regarding the war encouraged the president to show more confidence, and gave the author an unfavorable view of the war effort.

33. Which of the following is an example of the author using a solely factual statement?

a. "But he was sadly slow in recognizing their impact."
b. "...the Administration was considered an artful, managerial mechanism..."
c. "...four students were gunned down..."
d. "...in that crucial area he has proved to be dangerously wrong."

34. Which of the following statements shows the author's bias?

a. "The President had carefully calculated the diplomatic and military hazards of invading the Cambodian sanctuaries."
b. "...he found no reason to censure the Guardsmen."
c. "There were also hints of basic disagreement in the Cabinet over the Cambodian decision."
d. "...the eruption of protest and the reaction to it mocked Nixon's still unfulfilled promise to lead the nation 'forward together.'"

Refer to the following for questions 35–37:

In many states, the state legislature has control over redistricting both state legislative and congressional districts. A majority vote is required to pass district lines, and the first draft of the redistricting legislation is created by a committee. These bills can be overridden by legislators and vetoed by the governor. A few states—Maryland, Mississippi, and Florida—leave the gubernatorial veto out of the process.

Redistricting is completed every 10 years, after the decennial census. The way in which these district lines are drawn can have a big impact on elections, including how communities are represented and how political power is spread out. Because communities and populations change over time, the redistricting process is important for ensuring that districts are equally populated and representative of the population of the state. A technique called "gerrymandering" can be used in favor of or opposition to one party or politician. One method of gerrymandering is to split up groups of people who have similar characteristics into different districts so that their voting power is weakened. A district that has been gerrymandered sometimes looks irregular, but this is not always the case.

Most cases of gerrymandering are partisan. One method is racial gerrymandering, used to minimize the voting impact of particular racial groups. "Negative racial gerrymandering" is redistricting that is used to keep racial minorities from electing their preferred candidate. The Voting Rights Act of 1980 is meant to make districts redraw their lines if they have a discriminatory effect. Computers can be used to create fair district lines, but they can also be used to create gerrymandered districts using the information from the census.

35. Which of the following is another technique that would cause gerrymandering?

a. Drawing district lines to include smaller groups of people
b. Leaving the entire state as one large district
c. Redistricting the state every two years instead of every 10 years
d. Putting certain groups of voters into as few districts as possible

36. Which of the following would be a likely result of creating an even grid of district lines throughout a state rather than creating district lines based on the census?

a. The districts would alternate between the two major political parties.
b. The districts would be representative of the demographics of the state.
c. The districts would all have different populations.
d. The districts would include all minorities in one grid square.

37. Which of the following is the best definition of the word *partisan*?

a. Favoring a particular political party or candidate
b. Legal to enact in most states
c. Ethical to arrange depending on the motivation
d. Generated by computers to create fair divisions

Refer to the following for questions 38–39:

An economist is researching the causes of recent inflation in the US. She decides to look at the unemployment rate as a potential factor.

Year	Employment (%)	Inflation (%)
1981	59	4
1982	57.8	3.8
1983	57.9	3.9
1984	59.5	3.9
1985	60.1	4
1986	60.7	4.4
1987	61.5	4.4
1988	62.3	4.6
1989	63	6.1
1990	62.8	3.1
1991	61.7	2.9
1992	61.5	2.7

38. Which of the following best characterizes the relationship between the inflation rate and the unemployment rate in this chart?

a. Positive correlation
b. Inverse correlation
c. Absolute correlation
d. Non-linear correlation

39. Which of the following describes why the unemployment rate is an independent variable in this research?

a. The unemployment rate is unrelated to the inflation rate.
b. The unemployment rate is what the economist is trying to find the cause of.
c. The unemployment rate is potentially causing the changes in the inflation rate.
d. The unemployment rate is impacted by changes in the inflation rate.

Refer to the following for questions 40–43:

The Lewis and Clark Expedition began in Camp Wood, IL in May 1804. The expedition was led by Meriwether Lewis and William Clark. Joseph Whitehouse was a private in the expedition and also served as the group's tailor. The following accounts are from March 23, 1806.

William Clark:

This morning proved So raney and uncertain that we were undeturmined for Some time whether we had best Set out & risque the [river?] which appeared to be riseing or not. Jo. Colter returned haveing killed an Elk about 3 miles towards Point Adams. the rained Seased and it became fair about Meridean, at which time we loaded our Canoes & at 1 P. M. left Fort Clatsop on our homeward bound journey. at this place we had wintered and remained from the 7th of Decr. 1805 to this day and have lived as well as we had any right to expect, and we can Say that we were never one day without 3 meals of Some kind a day either pore Elk meat or roots, not withstanding the repeeted fall of rain which has fallen almost Constantly Since we passed the long narrows on the [blank] of Novr. last indeed w[e] have had only [blank] days fair weather since that time. Soon after we had Set out from Fort Clatsop we were met by De lash el wilt & 8 men of the Chinnooks, and Delashelwilts wife the old boud and his Six Girls, they had, a Canoe, a Sea otter Skin, Dried fish and hats for Sale, we purchased a Sea otter Skin, and proceeded on, thro' Meriwethers Bay, there was a Stiff breese from the S. W. which raised Considerable Swells around Meriwethers point which was as much as our Canoes Could ride. above point William we came too at the Camp of Drewyer & the 2 Field's. they had killed 2 Elk which was about 1½ miles distant. here we Encampd. for the night having made 16 miles.

Joseph Whitehouse:

Sunday March 23d At 1 o'Clock P. M. we embarked, on board our Canoes from Fort Clatsop, on our homeward bound Voyage. We proceeded on up the South side of the Columbia River, when we were met by a party of the Chin-ook tribe of Indians, who belong to the Flatt head nation. These Indians were in Canoes, & were on their way to Fort Clatsop in Order to trade with us; they had with them a Canoe & a Sea Otter Skin, which they Intended trading with us. We halted a short time, & Captain Lewis purchased the Sea Otter skin from them. We then continued on our Voyage, and went round a point of land called by our officers Merryweather point (the Sirname of Captain Lewis) when the wind rose & blew hard from the South West, & the waves ran very high. We proceeded on, & passed another point of land called point William by our officers the Sirname of Captain Clark. We halted a short distance above this last point, at a Camp where the two hunters that were sent on ahead of us were. These two hunters had killed 2 Elk, which they informed us lay 1½ Miles from this place. We encamped at that place having come 16 Miles this day.

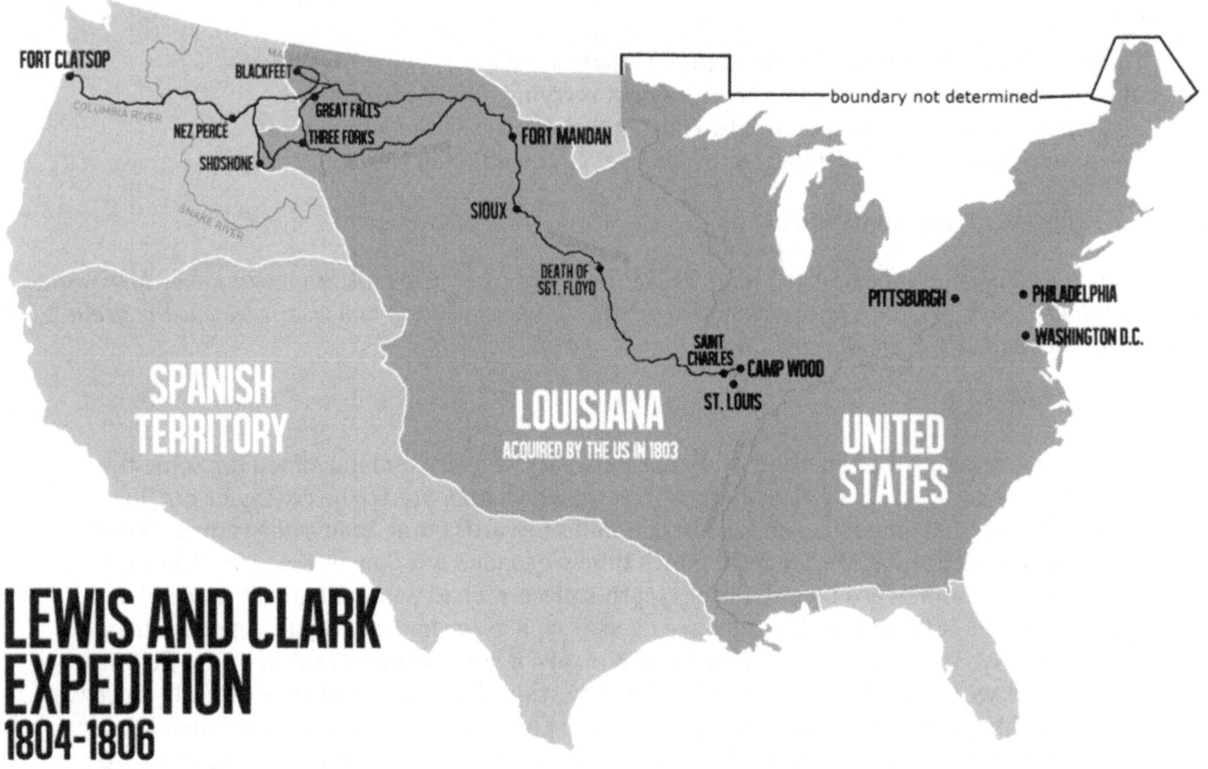

40. According to these accounts, which location on the map will be the next stop in their journey?

a. Sioux
b. St. Louis
c. Great Falls
d. Nez Perce

41. Which of the following describes how an author's account of events was shaped by his point of view?

a. Whitehouse served as a tailor, so he was looking forward to getting fabrics in trade from the Native Americans.
b. Clark was a leader of the expedition, so he was concerned about the safety of his team leaving that morning.
c. Because Whitehouse was mainly documenting their encounters with Native American tribes, he left out any mention of distances.
d. Clark was in charge of the food supplies for the expedition, so he documented the details of additions to their supply.

42. Which of the following best indicates whether Clark documented a reliable account of the day?

a. The similarities with Whitehouse's account of the day
b. The explanation that it will be their homeward journey
c. The use of Meriwether's name for landmarks
d. The omission of any mention of the rest of the crew on the journey

43. Which of the following was a result of the Lewis and Clark Expedition that benefited the United States?

a. The discovery of elk as food
b. The ability to travel in inclement weather
c. Geographic knowledge of the Spanish Territory
d. Trade and diplomacy with Native Americans

Refer to the following for questions 44–45:

This chart shows the number of internet users per 100 people and GDP per capita, as of 2017. Economists believe that widespread internet use in any country has a strong positive effect on the country's economic growth. Internet usage drives business growth, job creation, and economic modernization. The chart shows that countries with a higher percentage of internet users also have a higher GDP per capita.

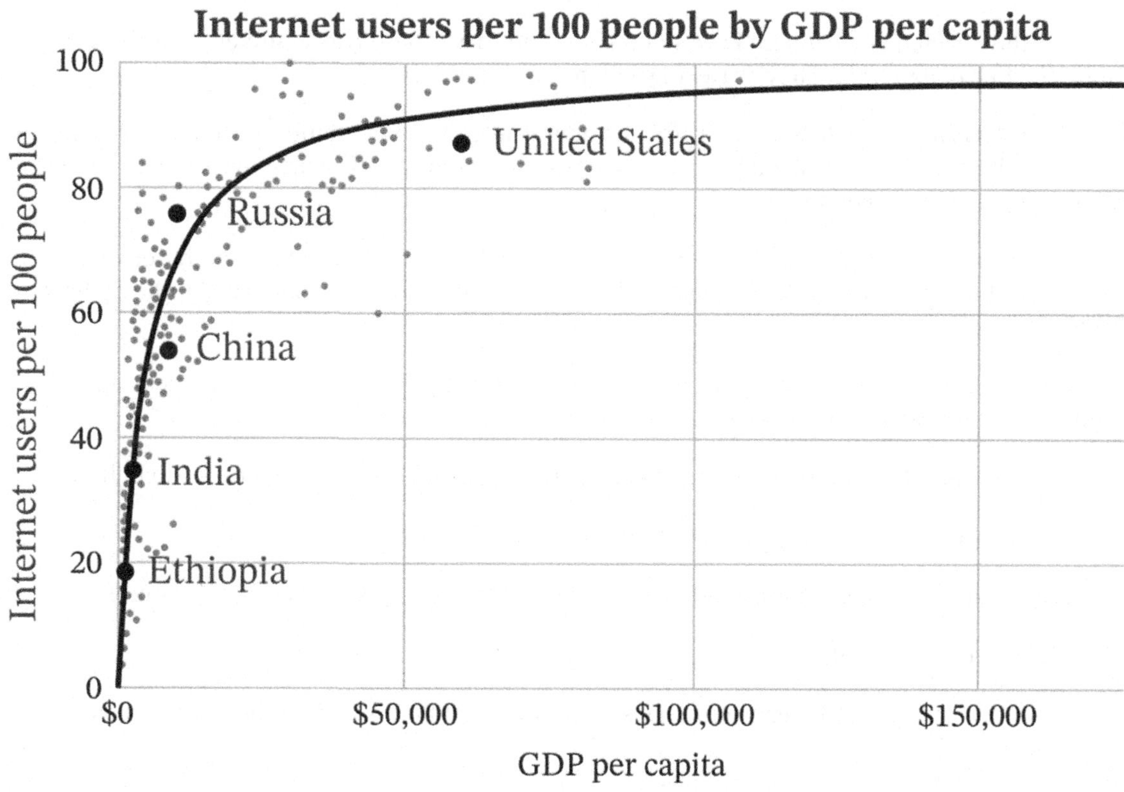

44. According to the chart, what level of internet usage has the strongest effect on GDP?

a. 40-60%
b. 10-30%
c. 70-90%
d. 0-10%

45. Which of the following best describes the range and its significance for the number of internet users per 100 people for the countries named on the chart?

a. The range is about 70 and shows the variation in the number of internet users in this data.
b. The range is about 30 and shows the number of internet users that occurs most in the data.
c. The range is about 80 and shows the sum of the number of internet users for these countries.
d. The range is about 50 and shows the average numbers of internet users for these countries.

Refer to the following for questions 46–47:

The following speech is one in a series of four-minute speeches organized by the Committee of Public Information in 1917 during World War I.

"Ladies and Gentlemen, I have just received the information that there is a German spy among us—a German spy watching us.

He is around, here somewhere, reporting upon you and me—sending reports about us to Berlin and telling the Germans just what we are doing with the Liberty Loan.

From every section of the country these spies have been getting reports over to Potsdam—not general reports but details—where the loan is going well and where its success seems weak, and what people are saying in each community.

For the German government is worried about our great loan. Those Junkers fear its effect upon the German morale. They're raising a loan this month, too.

If the American people lend their billions now, one and all with a hip-hip-hurrah, it means that America is united and strong. While, if we lend our money half-heartedly, America seems weak and autocracy remains strong.

Money means everything now; it means a quicker victory and therefore less bloodshed. We are in the war, and now Americans can have but one opinion, only one wish in the Liberty Loan.

Well, I hope these spies are getting their messages straight, letting Potsdam know that America is hurling back to the autocrats these answers:

For treachery here, attempted treachery in Mexico, treachery everywhere—one billion.

For murder of American women and children—one billion more.

For broken faith and promise to murder more Americans—billions and billions more.

And then we will add:

In the world fight for Liberty, our share—billions and billions and billions and endless billions.

Do not let the German spy hear and report that you are a slacker."

46. Which of the following best describes the purpose of this speech?

a. It is an entreaty to help the speaker find the spy in their presence.
b. It is propaganda meant to raise money for the war.
c. It is a warning to beware of the actions of Germany.
d. It is an appeal to assist with raising German morale.

47. Which of the following excerpts from this speech is considered a glittering generality?

a. "...billions and billions and billions and endless billions."
b. "...telling the Germans just what we are doing with the Liberty Loan."
c. "...these spies have been getting reports over to Potsdam..."
d. "...it means that America is united and strong..."

Refer to the following for questions 48–50:

The following was written as an opinion on campaign finance reform:

> "When candidates run for office, they raise money to fund their campaigns. These funds are used for advertising, travel, staff salaries, supplies, equipment, and more fundraising. When a candidate receives donations, he or she can spend the money to gain familiarity with voters, and since voters are more likely to vote for people with recognizable names, the candidate can also gain popularity among voters. Campaign finance laws currently dictate how much and in what ways a candidate can receive from individuals, political action committees (PACs), and political party committees. Despite these laws, the amount of money raised and spent by candidates is often disparate, with a few candidates gaining a major advantage with their large sum of campaign funds. To even out the playing field, campaign funding should be limited to small donors, and a cap should be placed on how much a campaign can spend. Even better, each candidate should be provided with a set amount to spend on their campaign, and no more."

The chart shows the 2004 candidates for president, as well as their total spending on campaigns. Bush and Kerry became the Republican and Democratic nominees, respectively.

Candidate	Total Spending	% of Popular Vote
George W. Bush	$367,228,819	50.73%
John Kerry	$328,479,256	48.27%
Ralph Nader	$4,572,638	0.38%
Michael Badnarik	$1,093,018	0.32%
Michael Peroutka	$709,091	0.12%
David Cobb	$493,727	0.10%

48. According to the author, which of the following best describes the relationship between campaign spending and the popular vote?

a. Higher spending leads to more votes.
b. Higher spending leads to fewer votes.
c. Popularity leads to a lower need for spending without losing votes.
d. There is no relationship between spending and percent of popular vote.

49. Which of the following best describes whether the mean is a good measure of central tendency for the candidates' total spending?

a. It is, because it accurately represents spending for a typical candidate.
b. It is, because it shows the amount that most campaigns spend.
c. It is not, because the mean is skewed by the significantly higher numbers from the candidates with the highest spending.
d. It is not, because it only shows the difference between the highest and lowest amounts of spending.

50. This chart shows campaign spending for an upcoming election. Candidates A, B, and C are Democrats, while candidates D, E, and F are Republicans. Based on the information in the passage and chart above, which two of these candidates would most likely become the presidential nominees?

Candidate	Amount Spent
A	$234,309
B	$358,008,447
C	$238,968
D	$1,345,202
E	$760,370,195
F	$4,187,628

a. D and E
b. C and F
c. A and B
d. B and E

Answer Key and Explanations #1

Reasoning Through Language Arts—Reading

1. D: The correct answer is D because the author says that the ancient Britons were divided into many tribes and each had a king. The passage does say Choice A is incorrect because the passage says the ancient Britons had weapons, however, it doesn't say the weapons were the reason they fought. Choice B is incorrect because the text says the ancient Britons fought each other. It does not mention them fighting the Phoenicians. Choice C is incorrect because paragraph 6 says that there were no roads or bridges. The author gives this detail in order to describe the land. This detail does not support paragraph 7 which says that the ancient Britons regularly fought.

2. D: The correct answer is D because the word *grew* shows that the ancient Britons changed after the Phoenicians arrived. Choice A is incorrect because the answer choice only shows something that the Phoenicians did with the Britons; however, it does not describe how the Britons changed. Choice B is incorrect because basket-work is something the ancient Britons did before the Phœnicians interacted with them. Choice C is incorrect because it refers to the French and Belgians who moved to England.

3. B: The word *solitary* refers to isolation or being alone. Also, the sentence says that the islands are alone in a great expanse of water. So, this shows that other lands do not surround the islands. Choice A is incorrect because the sentence only talks about the size of the small islands around Scotland. It does not talk about where the islands are in relation to larger lands. Choice C is incorrect because it refers to people on the island, not the island in relation to the rest of the world. Choice D is incorrect because it shows the opposite of isolation; the sentence shows how the people who came to the islands (e.g., the French, Belgians, and Spanish) mixed with the ancient Britons.

4. B: The phrase "But seldom, if ever, ventured far from the shore" means that the boats didn't go far from shore. This implies that the boats may not have had much use in spite of the effort to build them. Choice A is incorrect because the text does not explain specifically how the boats were used. The author does describe weapons in the same paragraph. However, the phrase in the question focuses on the boats that the people made. The paragraph only moves onto weapons in the second sentence. Choice D is incorrect because the author does not connect the boats (discussed in paragraph 7) to the fortresses (discussed at the end of paragraph 6).

5. A: Choice A is the best answer because the first paragraph describes the location of the islands on the map. Choice B is incorrect because there were no roads that ran through England, Scotland, or Ireland during the time period that the passage is describing. Choice C is incorrect because the details about the small islands are only a small part of the first paragraph. Most of the paragraph describes how the islands appear on the map. Choice D is incorrect because the paragraph does not mention the size of the main islands. Also, the paragraph does not mention France or Belgium. Those countries are first mentioned in paragraph 4.

6. C: Choice C is the correct answer because this answer choice describes the lands by mentioning swamps and forests. Choice A is incorrect because it describes the coast, not the interior land of the island. Choice B is incorrect. It is about the interior of the island, but does not describe the land. Choice D is incorrect because it discusses the tribes and the people rather than the features of the lands (e.g., the swamps and forests).

7. B: The word *ardent* means passionate or devoted. Look at the word in the context of the sentence: "The dull precious metal seemed to flash with a reflection of her bright and ardent spirit," and think about Della's actions. Choice A is not correct because Della has planned and saved to buy her husband a Christmas present. So, she has not procrastinated (i.e., waited too long to start on something). Choices C and D are synonyms. They are wrong because Della shows over and over again that she cares very much for her husband.

8. D: The first event in the story is Della preparing her hair (4). The next event in the story is Della preparing a meal for the night (2). Then, Della prays about the reaction that Jim will have to her hair (5). The next event is Jim assuring Della that he is not upset about her decision to cut her hair (3). Then, Jim gives the combs to Della (1). Finally, Della gives the fob chain to Jim (6).

9. C: The sentence "'I hunted all over town to find it.'" is an exaggeration or hyperbole. The other answer choices have similes.

10. C: In the beginning of the story, Della has her hair cut off. She does this so she can get money for Jim's gift. However, she is worried about how she will appear to her husband and is concerned that he will be very angry or worse. When Jim keeps asking about Della's hair, it almost seems as if he is angry about it.

11. A: The entire story is about how Della and Jim are deeply in love. They sell a prized possession to buy a present for the other. Choice B is wrong because the overall meaning of this passage is not about a holiday. Choice C is wrong because it fails to recognize how Della and Jim overcome difficulty and have a deeper love for each other after giving their gifts. Choice D is wrong because the focus of the passage is not on buying the right gift for a loved one. Instead, the focus is on giving up a thing that you care about to show how much you love someone.

12. D: The narrator of the passage is not named. Della and Jim are simply characters in the story. O. Henry is the author of the story, not the narrator.

13. B: The word *beneficence* is used to show how nature helps the plants and animals on Earth. For example, nature provides sunlight and rain to help trees grow. Choice A is incorrect because duties and beneficence are not synonymous. Choice C is incorrect because nature gives the sunlight and the rain. This makes it the opposite of stingy. Later, Keller experiences the dangers of nature. However, choice D is incorrect because paragraph 5 is about the generosity of nature.

14. D: The paragraph shows the narrator's discovery that words have meaning. Choice A is incorrect because the narrator and Miss Sullivan do not use a pencil. Instead, Miss Sullivan uses her fingers to spell words into the narrator's hand. Choice B is incorrect because the narrator does not focus on the distinction between hot and cold water. Choice C is incorrect because the focus of the paragraph is not on learning the locations of places.

15. A: Helen says in the second sentence that she stretches out her hand to who she thinks is her mother. Choice B is incorrect because Helen is not aware that a visitor is coming. Choice C is incorrect because there is no mention that she wants to please her mother. Choice D is incorrect. Helen assumes the person approaching is her mother, but she does not mention loving her mother in the passage.

16. B: Helen is alone and defenseless as the storm approaches. Choice A is incorrect because Helen is not lost. She knows where she is, but she is unable to get out of the tree to go home. The wind and approaching rain make Helen uncomfortable, however, choices C and D are incorrect. We know Helen is upset about being alone because of the relief she expresses in Miss Sullivan's presence later.

17. C: Miss Sullivan opens up Helen's world by showing her that words have meaning and every object has a name. Choice A is incorrect because Helen is only able to learn about nature through the words taught by Miss Sullivan. Choice B is incorrect because the observation about barriers is not what she learned from Miss Sullivan. Choice D is incorrect because the sentence is not about what Helen learned. Instead, it is about the idea of learning.

18. D: Helen describes "[longing]" for Miss Sullivan's return and clings to her upon being rescued. Choice A is incorrect because Miss Sullivan teaches Helen water early in their relationship before they had developed a bond. Choice B is incorrect because that is a personal growth in Helen, not a growth in the relationship of

Helen and Miss Sullivan. Choice C is incorrect because it does not show the bond between Helen and Miss Sullivan. Instead, this moment simply shows something Helen and Miss Sullivan are doing together.

19. B: The passage shows Helen's discoveries about language and nature. While Helen develops a close tie with Miss Sullivan, Miss Sullivan is not Helen's family. So, choice A is incorrect. Choice C is incorrect because the passage never mentions or implies disappointment. Choice D is incorrect because the text does not emphasize Helen's youth.

20. D: This phrase is used to explain how nature, although generous and peaceful, can be violent and dangerous. Choice A is incorrect because Miss Sullivan does not show any cruelty towards Helen. Choice B is incorrect because this paragraph shows Helen feeling nervous but does not show her having a temper tantrum. Choice C is incorrect because Helen was in danger from being alone in the tree as the storm approached. The phrase "treacherous claws" is about the danger of being alone in the tree rather than the danger of climbing the tree.

21. A: The narrator describes her life before the arrival of Miss Sullivan, then she explains her life after and all the changes she experiences. Helen may have become braver with Miss Sullivan, but this is not the focal point of the story. This makes choice B incorrect. Choice C is incorrect because only part of the passage shows the strategies that Miss Sullivan uses to teach Helen. Choice D is incorrect because Helen feels security rather than confusion when she is with Miss Sullivan.

22. C: The passage is about how Miss Sullivan teaches Helen words have meaning. Choice A is incorrect because Helen expresses a clear fondness for Miss Sullivan. Choice B is incorrect because Helen is not scared of nature; rather, she realizes that nature can be generous and dangerous. The passage does not clearly say that Helen learns to read or write. Instead, it shows the beginning of her relationship with words and implies that Helen will continue to learn.

23. D: A non-human thing (e.g., a name) is described with a human quality or action (e.g., birth). Choice A is not correct because there is not a comparison being made. Choice B is not correct because there is no exaggeration in the sentence. Choice C is not correct because there is not a comparison being made with the words *like* or *as*.

24. C: The question asks which job is less desirable than homesteading according to the writer. Choice C is correct because Stewart speaks of going out to wash as less preferable than homesteading. Choice A is incorrect because the letter does not mention cooking or restaurants. Choice B is also incorrect. The reason is that there is no mention of opening a bed and breakfast in the letter. Choice D is also wrong because the letter shares nothing about teaching.

25. D: Growing potatoes is so simple that her six-year-old can do so with little help. The issue is not child labor. So, choice A is incorrect. Stewart does not mention schooling. So, this makes choice B incorrect. Stewart's point has nothing to do with whether women work as hard as men. So, choice C is not the correct response.

26. B: Stewart mentions the hard work of laundry, but she does not speak of any enjoyment of it as she does about homesteading. Choice A cannot be correct because Stewart does not seem to be lazy. Choice C is possible, but there is no evidence to support that idea. Choice D cannot be correct because no reason for anger is given.

27. D: Stewart says that homesteading is a lonely task. For example, she mentions that "persons afraid of ...loneliness had better let ranching alone." Stewart explains in the letter that her work uses less strength than washing. So, choice A is wrong. Choice B is also incorrect because it is addressed in the first paragraph of the letter. Choice C is incorrect because it is mentioned as an advantage in the first paragraph.

28. A: Stewart directly states that women would have "the added satisfaction of knowing that their job will not be lost to them if they care to keep it." Although going on strike was common at the time, Stewart does not mention it. So, choice B is incorrect. Denver is in the Rocky Mountains, but landslides are not mentioned as a risk. So, choice C cannot be the correct answer. Fire is always a risk, but Stewart does not bring it up in the letter. So, choice D is not the correct answer.

29. C: The letter is very positive and full of reasons on why homesteading is a good choice. Choice A is incorrect. The reason is that there is no complaint of hard work, weather, or loneliness. Choice B is also not correct because the letter does not speak of sadness or loneliness. Instead, Stewart rejoices in the good success of the homestead. Also, choice D is not correct because there is no hopelessness expressed in the letter.

30. C: The professor argues that small, woody material is left on the tops of trees and is less likely to be reached by fire.

31. D: Choice D is not a supporting detail because it is a definition of salvage logging. The other choices are supporting details of the Forest Manager's argument.

32. B: Plot A was salvage logged and burned worse than the unmanaged plot (Plot B). This study supports the professor's view that salvage logging increases the risk and severity of fire.

33. A: The question asks which option is the chief argument regarding fire prevention. Choices B and D are not helpful for fire prevention. Choice C is incorrect because logging decreases soil temperature. Choice B is a supporting detail from the passage but is not the main idea. Choice C contradicts the passage. Choice D is not mentioned in the passage.

34. D: The professor says the larger trees in old growth forests are more resistant to fire than smaller, younger trees. Answers A, B, and C all agree with the professor.

35. C: Both the manager and the professor discuss the importance of seedling growth after a fire. So, a study looking at the regrowth of seedlings in logged and unmanaged forests would potentially provide support for both arguments (as well as possibly showing problems with both arguments).

36. C: The first section covers how people want to change and the options that are available to them. As people move towards a healthier lifestyle, they can work at small steps on their way to better health. Choice A is incorrect because the first section does not mention menus. Choice B is incorrect because the paragraph lists benefits of certain foods but does not suggest any are better than others. Choice D is incorrect because the passage mentions that the process is a struggle for many, not an impossible task.

37. D: The overall passage is information for someone who is interested in the food industry. So, choice A is not correct. The reason is that there is not much of a comparison or contrast between the Food Pyramid and MyPlate. Choice B is incorrect because the focus of the passage is not on government involvement. Choice C is incorrect because the text says some groups disagree about certain dietary suggestions but does not make recommendations.

38. A: Choice B is wrong because there is no mention of Harvard's guidelines replacing MyPlate. Choice C is also incorrect. It is another approach to dietary guidelines, but it was included to support a claim, not provide diet options. Choice D is wrong because Harvard is included for their material, not their Ivy League status.

39. C: This passage was written for people who have an interest in the food industry. So, choice A is wrong because the passage is not meant for those who are new to dieting. Choice B is wrong because experienced professionals don't need introductory-level material on preparing food. Choice D is incorrect because there is no mention of parents or children in the passage.

40. B: Each section of the passage has the tone of educating readers. So, choice A is wrong because the tone is not blaming readers. Choice C is close, but it is not the best answer choice. Choice D is wrong because the tone of the material is not snobbish or cocky.

Reasoning Through Language Arts—Writing

1. A: The problem in this sentence is subject-verb agreement. Remember that the indefinite pronouns are always singular. Choice B is incorrect because the clause is essential to the sentence. So, commas are not needed. Choice C is wrong because the prepositional phrase does not need punctuation. Choice D is incorrect because there is no need to change *which* to *that.*

2. C: The question tests you on the correct word for comparison with adjectives. The correct adjective is the comparative form of the adjective *bad* which is *worse*, not the superlative form *worst.* Choice D will create a problem with subject-verb agreement. So, it is incorrect. Choice B is wrong as well. The reason is that it creates an adjective comparison problem, and this is the problem you want to correct. Choice A is incorrect because there is a problem that needs to be corrected.

3. B: The sentence is written as a double negative. Choice B is the only choice that corrects the problem. So, choice A is incorrect because the sentence needs to be changed. Choice C is incorrect because it does not solve the problem of the double negative and makes another problem with verb tense. Also, choice D does not solve the problem of the double negative. So, it can be eliminated.

4. A: The sentence has a clarity problem. The dependent clause should come at the beginning of the sentence rather than interrupting the independent clause. Choice B does not make a correction to the sentence. Choice C makes the sentence into a question which is not necessary. Choice D is incorrect because the sentence needs to be reworded to have clarity.

5. B: This sentence should come after the third sentence because it is the first "tip" to consider. Choice A is incorrect because this sentence is only one part to a working vehicle. Choice C is not correct because a sentence that begins with *First of all* should not be the concluding sentence. Choice D is wrong because the sentence belongs with paragraph A. In paragraph B, the focus is on working under the hood and the inside of the vehicle.

6. A: The sentence is written correctly. Choice D is incorrect because splitting the infinitive will be a mistake, not a correction. Choice B is not correct because you need to know which area of the car needs to be checked. Choice C is incorrect because that would only create a problem in agreement.

7. D: Sentence (10) is a run-on sentence and needs correct punctuation. The use of a semicolon between two sentences that are connected in thought is the only acceptable answer choice. You cannot leave the sentence alone. So, choice A is not the correct choice. Choice C places a conjunction between the two sentences. However, it does not include the necessary comma before the conjunction. So, it is an incorrect choice.

8. C: These words are three items in a series. So, commas are needed to separate them. Choice A is not correct because the apostrophe shows possession, and it is used correctly. Choice B is also wrong because the word *emergency* is spelled correctly in the sentence. Choice D is incorrect because the sentence needs commas.

9. A: This sentence has a misplaced modifier. Currently, you can read the sentence and think that you should take everything with you except the car. When you move the word, you understand the reason that you are leaving the car is that you know where you are going and what you are doing. Choice B is not correct because the word is important to the sentence. Choice C is wrong because there is no need for a comma. Choice D is not correct as well. The reason is that there is an error in the sentence.

10. A: There is nothing wrong with the sentence. So, choice A is the correct choice. Everything after the comma could be removed without harming the independent clause at the beginning of the sentence. So, the nonessential adjective clause needs a comma. Choice B is incorrect because it suggests removing the comma. Choice C makes *products* singular. This is incorrect because it creates a problem with subject-verb agreement. The same problem is in choice D; however, the verb is singular.

11. B: This question is about subject-verb agreement. *Slow foods* is plural and needs the plural form of *to be* which is *are*. When you change *is* to *are*, the sentence is corrected. Choice A is not correct because there is not an extra comma in the sentence. Choice C is also wrong because *slow foods* is not a proper noun. So, it does not need capitalization. Choice D is incorrect because *comeback* is one word.

12. D: The question reviews correct spelling. *Emphasize* is the verb, and *emphasis* is the noun which is needed here. Choice A is incorrect because it does not address the problem. Choice B changes the verb from *puts* to *places*, yet there is no problem with the verb choice. Choice C makes the verb plural, but this only adds to the problem.

13. D: This sentence contains an error related to parallel structure. Placing the definite article *the* in front of the final two terms in the series hurts the structure, so choice A is incorrect. Removing *the* makes all the items parallel. Choice B is also incorrect because *specie* is not the singular form of *species*. Additionally, using a singular noun in place of *species* would be inaccurate, as the author is referring to multiple species. Choice C is incorrect because making all nouns singular does not improve the structure of the sentence.

14. C: The error in this sentence is a split infinitive. The adverb *fully* comes between the words *to* and *use*, and this is not correct grammar. Choice A is incorrect because the change would cause a subject-verb disagreement. Choice B is wrong because the prepositional phrase is not an aside. Also, choice D is wrong because there is an error in the sentence.

15. B: *Slow Food USA* is the name of an organization. So, this makes it a proper noun that needs capitalization. Choice A is not correct because this is the proper name of a specific program. So, the capital letters are correct. Choice C is also wrong because *thru* is a shortcut spelling, but *through* is Standard English. Choice D is incorrect because the sentence has an error.

16. C: Sentence (13) is not important to the article. The writer's garden is not a concern. Choice A is wrong. The reason is that placing the sentence at the beginning of the paragraph makes readers think that the paragraph will be a narrative about the writer's garden. Choice B is incorrect because the last sentence of an essay should be related to the rest of the essay. Choice D is not correct because the sentence should be removed from this passage.

17. D: The sentence is a run-on. So, the best answer choice is to make two sentences of the run-on sentence. Choice A is incorrect because adding commas does not correct the run-on. For choice C, the original word is the correct word. So, this is not correct. Choice B is incorrect because it suggests that the terms are not parallel.

18. B: The proper noun *Slow Food on Campus* is an essential appositive. So, the commas can be removed. Now, the sentence is in passive voice. Choice A would help move the sentence to active voice which is preferred over passive voice. However, this is not the error of the sentence. So, choice A is incorrect. Choice C is wrong because *Slow Food on Campus* is a proper noun that needs capital letters. Choice D is also wrong because *similar* is the correct spelling.

19. A: This sentence is written correctly. Choice D is wrong because the introductory prepositional phrase needs a comma. Choice B is not correct because the verb needs to stay in singular form. Choice C is incorrect because *healthy* is spelled correctly.

20. B: Items in a series need commas between each item. Choice D is wrong because there are no commas for this series. There is no need to capitalize the name of a disease. So, choice C is incorrect. There is an error in the sentence. So, choice A cannot be correct.

21. D: This sentence is a run-on. The sentence has two independent clauses. So, you can place a period between them and capitalize the word *for*. Choice A is wrong because the original sentence is not correct. Choice B is wrong as well. The reason is that a comma between two independent clauses does not correct the problem. Choice C is wrong because a colon cannot be used to separate independent clauses.

22. D: The sentence does not need an adverb. Instead, it needs a predicate adjective to modify the subject *researchers*. Choice B is incorrect because SAD is an acronym that should have capital letters. The sentence is not a question. So, choice C is wrong because it does not need a question mark. Choice A is not correct because there is a mistake in the sentence.

23. A: The sentence is written correctly. So, choice D is not correct because the adjectives are not coordinate. Choice B is not correct because the sentence is making a comparison to months that are not during the winter. In other words, the body makes less melatonin in the summer months. Choice C is wrong because *melatonin* does not need to be capitalized.

24. D: The question tests on the use of *effect* and *affect*. In this sentence, you are looking for the verb that means *influence*. So, affect is the correct word in this sentence. Choice B is wrong because the prepositional phrase should not come after *serotonin*. Choice C is incorrect because *Less* is for amounts which is true for this sentence. *Fewer* is for numbers and applies to things that can be counted. So, the correct adverb is being used in this sentence. Choice A is wrong because the sentence has an error.

25. D: Again, *fewer* is for numbers and applies to things that can be counted. Sunlight cannot be counted. *Less* is for an amount which is true for this sentence. Also, making the change brings back the intended parallelism of the sentence. Choice A is incorrect because the subject and verb agree as they are written. Choice B is also incorrect because the word is not a proper noun and does not need capitalization. Choice C is incorrect. The reason is given in the explanation above for choice D.

26. D: *Factors* is plural and needs a plural verb. The verb *has* is singular. So, this makes a disagreement between subject and verb. *Have* is the plural form of *has* and needs to be used here. Choice A is incorrect because the sentence has an error with subject-verb agreement. Choice B is wrong because removing the capital letter causes another error. Choice C is incorrect. The change simply switches the problem in agreement rather than eliminating it.

27. C: The sentence has a problem with parallel structure. The verbs *tough* and *wait* need to be parallel. Choice D is incorrect because SAD is an acronym and needs capital letters. Choice B is also incorrect. There is an attempt to correct the problem of parallelism. However, *toughing* needs an auxiliary verb. Choice A is wrong because there is an error that needs to be corrected.

28. B: The sentence is not interrogative; it is declarative. In other words, it needs a period at the end, not a question mark. Choice D is incorrect because *well* is an adverb, and the noun *news* needs an adjective modifier. Choice C is incorrect because the seasons are not capitalized. Choice A is wrong because there is an error that needs to be corrected.

29. A: Choice A is correct because the word is not being used in a different way from a dictionary definition. Choice B is not correct because readers need an explanation of the word *temp*. Choice C is wrong because *temporary* is spelled correctly. Choice D is incorrect because a comma is not needed.

30. D: This question is about parallel structure. *Employs* and *generating* are verbs that need to be changed to be parallel. The best way to make them parallel is by putting both in the present tense. Choice A is incorrect because *the staffing industry* is a single unit. So, it does not need the plural form. Choice B is incorrect because the noun is singular and needs a singular verb. Choice C cannot be done without adding more words.

31. D: The problem in the sentence is the wrong homonym. The word *their* is possessive and is needed in this sentence. *They're* is a contraction of *they are*. So, this is the wrong word. In this sentence, *because* is used correctly. So, this makes choice A incorrect. Choice C makes *skills* singular; however, this is not the correct choice. After all, an employer wants a worker who has more than one skill.

32. B: The problem in this question is with antecedent agreement. The pronoun *they* needs a plural noun: *employees*. Choice A is incorrect because of the problem with antecedent agreement. Choice C is incorrect because it has disagreement between subject and verb. Choice D is also wrong. The hyphen in *full-time* does not need to be removed. Also, choice D has disagreement between subject and verb. So, choice D is not correct.

33. C: The problem with the sentence is a comma splice. A semicolon shows that the thoughts of both sentences are related. So, the problem is corrected with the semicolon. Choice A cannot be correct because the original has a comma splice. Choice B is also wrong. The reason is that it has a pronoun-antecedent agreement problem. Choice D is incorrect because it creates a subject-verb agreement problem.

34. D: Adding a comma eliminates the problem of the run-on sentence. Choice A is wrong because there is an error in the sentence. Choice B is also incorrect because it creates a problem with subject-verb agreement. Choice C is incorrect because it creates a subject-verb disagreement in a different part of the sentence.

35. C: The problem in this sentence is a misspelling of valuable. Choice D is wrong because a hyphen is not needed to connect the two words. Choice B cannot be correct because *you're* is the right homonym. Choice A is not correct because there is an error in the sentence.

36. C: This sentence has no parallelism. *To look for* and *interviewing* can be made parallel by making this change. Choice D is not correct because the word *permanent* is spelled correctly. Choice B is not correct. The reason is that it tries to correct the problem, but it fails. Choice A cannot be correct because of the error with parallel structure in the sentence.

37. B: The problem is a misspelled word. Choice B corrects the problem. So, choice A cannot be correct because of the spelling error. Choice C is incorrect because the preposition *among* suggests that there is more than one worker who is being considered for a position. Choice D corrects the spelling error. However, it changes *workers* from plural to singular. So, it is incorrect.

38. D: The sentence is declarative, not interrogative. So, the sentence needs a period as the end mark. Choice B is not correct because the apostrophe is needed to show possession. Choice C is incorrect because it does not solve the problem, and it creates a problem of agreement. Choice A is incorrect as well. The reason is that the sentence has an error that needs to be corrected.

39. C: The sentence contains a disagreement between the compound subject, which is considered plural, and the singular verb. Changing *is* to *are* solves the problem. Choice A is incorrect; the comma is needed for items in a series. Choice B is not correct; the word is correctly spelled as written. Choice D, likewise, is incorrect; it offers only a cosmetic change, not a solution to the problem of subject-verb agreement.

40. D: The problem in the sentence as written is one of subject-verb agreement and colloquial or substandard English. *Some* indicates that more than one apartment complex is being discussed. It, therefore, is necessary to change both the subject and verb to plural. Choice A is incorrect; the sentence as written clearly contains an error to be remedied. Choice B is not correct; choosing an alternative spelling for the homonym does not solve the problem. Choice C is incorrect as well; it creates instead a different subject-verb agreement problem.

41. C: The problem in this sentence is a dangling modifier. To correct the problem, you can write the independent clause as "*you need to consider the other issues about keeping your pet at your apartment.*" Choice A is wrong because the comma needs to come after the introductory prepositional phrase. Choice B is not correct because the word is spelled correctly. Choice D cannot be correct because there is an error in the sentence.

42. B: This question is on the use of *affect* and *effect*. *Affect* is the verb that means to influence, and it is needed here. *Effect* is the noun that points to the influence. Choice A is incorrect because there is a problem in the sentence. Choice C is also incorrect because it creates a subject-verb agreement problem. Choice D is not correct because it does not address the word choice and creates a subject-verb agreement problem.

43. A: *Irregardless* is used very often in informal communication. However, it is not an acceptable word in Standard English. The correct word is *regardless*. Choice B is not correct because the word *licensing* is spelled correctly. Choice C is not correct because the sentence does not have extra commas. The first comma separates the dependent clause. The other commas are needed for the items in a series. Choice D is incorrect as well because the sentence does have an error.

44. B: The apostrophe is needed in *nations* to show possession of the *highest executive office*. Choice D is not correct because executive office is not a proper noun that needs capitalization. Choice C is wrong because you do not want to separate an infinitive. Also, choice A is wrong because there is an error in the sentence.

45. B: *Wall Street* is the name of a street in New York. So, it needs capitalization. Choice A is wrong because this would make an error in verb tense. Choice C is incorrect because the words *although* and *though* are nearly synonyms. So, choosing *although* is not an error. Choice D is incorrect as well because *investment firm* is a common noun. It is not the name of a certain investment firm. So, no capitalization is needed.

46. D: The information in the parentheses is not necessary information. However, the information is closely connected to the sentence. So, commas should be used instead of parentheses. Choice B is wrong because *Republicans* is the name of a certain political party and needs capitalization. Choice C is incorrect because the sentence needs a singular noun for *Margaret Chase Smith*. Choice A is not correct because there is a mistake in the sentence.

47. D: The question tests on irregular verb forms. The sentence needs the past participle of *seek* which is *sought*. So, choice A is incorrect. Choice B is also wrong because the singular subject causes a problem with subject-verb agreement. Choice C is incorrect because the problem is not with the verb tense.

48. D: This is a run-on sentence that can be corrected with a comma between the short independent clauses. Choice B is not correct because the pronoun *them* is correct. Choice C is incorrect. If you made the change, then you would have an error in subject-verb agreement. Choice A is wrong because there is an error in the sentence.

49. C: Sentence (8) is a personal opinion that does not help this passage. Choice A is incorrect. Changing the order of the paragraphs only hurts the chronological order of the passage. Choices B and D are incorrect. The reason is that moving these sentences upsets the unity and coherence of the piece.

50. D: The sentence places a comma after each country correctly because they are items in a series. However, a comma is not needed after Liberia because it is the last item in the series. Choice B is incorrect because the commas are necessary for the items in the series. The exception is the comma after Liberia. Choice A is incorrect because believe is spelled correctly and there is an error in the sentence.

Reasoning Through Language Arts—Extended Response

1. Essay question graders commonly look for the following elements in a strong response: strong content knowledge, clear organization, and effective arguments or examples. Language and usage are not usually strictly graded, but can make a big impact on the clarity of your ideas.

Please use the provided rubric to make sure your response meets these common criteria. Try to have a friend or family member grade your response for you or take a break after writing your response and return to grade it with fresh eyes.

CONSTRUCTED RESPONSE RUBRIC

Domain	Description
Content Knowledge	• The response directly addresses every part of the prompt. • The response demonstrates independent knowledge of the topic. • The response discusses the topic at an appropriate depth.
Organization	• The response introduces the topic, usually with a thesis statement or by restating the prompt. • The response directly addresses the prompt by providing a clear and concise answer or solution. • The answer or solution is supported by logical arguments or evidence. • The response restates the main idea in the conclusion.
Arguments and Examples	• The response provides a reasonable answer to the prompt. • The answer is supported by strong reasoning or evidence. • The response develops ideas logically and connects ideas to one another. • The reasoning and evidence provided act to support a unified main idea.
Language and Usage	• The response demonstrates effective use of grammar and uses varied sentence structure throughout the response. • The response demonstrates correct use of spelling, punctuation, and capitalization. • The response demonstrates strong and varied use of vocabulary relevant to the topic and appropriate for the intended audience.

Mathematics—No Calculator

1. B: The inequality specifies that the difference between L and 15 inches must be less or equal to 0.01. Note that $|14.99 - 15| = |-0.01| = 0.01$, which is equal to the specified tolerance and therefore meets the condition.

2. D: Distance is the product of velocity and time.

$$\begin{aligned}(5 \times 10^6) \times (2 \times 10^{-4}) &= (5 \times 2) \times (10^6 \times 10^{-4}) \\ &= 10 \times 10^{6-4} \\ &= 10 \times 10^2 \\ &= 10^3 \\ &= 1{,}000\end{aligned}$$

Therefore, the bullet traveled 1,000 feet.

3. C: Since 4 is the same as 2^2, $4^6 = (2^2)^6 = 2^{12}$. When dividing exponents with the same base, simply subtract the exponent in the denominator from the exponent in the numerator.

$$2^{12} \div 2^8 = 2^{12-8} = 2^4 = 16$$

4. A: Start by substituting the function $f(x)$ into the expression $2f(x) - 3$.

$$2(2x^2 + 7) - 3$$

From here, simplify the expression using the distributive property.

$$4x^2 + 14 - 3$$

Finally, combine like terms.

$$4x^2 + 11$$

5. B: The vertical operators indicate absolute values, which are always positive. Start by simplifying the expressions inside the absolute value bars.

$$|7 - 5| - |5 - 7|$$
$$|2| - |-2|$$

Then, evaluate the absolute values and subtract. Since absolute value is always positive, both $|2|$ and $|-2|$ are equal to 2.

$$2 - 2 = 0$$

Mathematics—Calculator

6. B: This pie chart shows the percentage of the total recyclable material that each material represents. The larger percentages have larger slices of the circle. Also, the percentage for each material is shown next to each slice. In this chart, paper is the most recycled material because it has the largest slice. This is 40% of the total. The next most common is glass at 25% of the total. All of the other materials stand for smaller portions of the total.

7. D: The area of the circle is πr^2, while the circumference is $2\pi r$. Taking the ratio of these two expressions gives $\frac{\pi r^2}{2\pi r}$. To reduce the ratio, cancel the common π and r from both the numerator and denominator. This results in the ratio $\frac{r}{2}$.

8. 168.75: Solve this problem using a proportion.

$$\frac{16 \text{ miles}}{45 \text{ min}} = \frac{60 \text{ miles}}{x \text{ min}}$$

From here, cross multiply.

$$16x = 2{,}700$$

Then, divide each side by 16.

$$x = 168.75$$

Therefore, it would take Francine 168.75 minutes to ride 60 miles.

9. B: Substitute the given values and solve. Simplify the operations inside parentheses first.

$$\frac{a(b-c)}{b(a+b+c)} = \frac{4(3-1)}{3(4+3+1)}$$
$$= \frac{4(2)}{3(8)}$$
$$= \frac{8}{24}$$
$$= \frac{1}{3}$$

10. B: The stock first increased by 10%, or \$10 (10% of \$100), to \$110 per share. Then, the price decreased by \$11 (10% of \$110), so that the sell price was \$110 – \$11 = \$99 per share, and the sell price for 50 shares was 99 × \$50 = \$4,950.

11. D: To factor this equation, we need to think of things using the reverse of the FOIL method. Start by setting up two empty parentheses.

$$3x^2 + 4x - 15 = (\quad)(\quad)$$

First, determine what goes in the first part of each set of parentheses. The only way to multiply with integers and get $3x^2$ is $3x \cdot x$. Put these terms in each of the first parts of the sets of parentheses.

$$3x^2 + 4x - 15 = (3x\quad)(x\quad)$$

Next, determine what numbers multiply to –15 and will make the middle term of the multiplied expression equal to $4x$.

$$3x^2 + 4x - 15 = (3x - 5)(x + 3)$$

Notice that it is important to make sure –5 goes in the left set of parentheses and +3 goes in the right set of parentheses. If they were switched, using the FOIL method on the two binomials would result in $(3x + 3)(x - 5) = 3x^2 - 12x - 15$, which is not the desired expression. Therefore, the correct factorization of the expression is $(3x - 5)(x + 3)$.

12. D: Recall that the general form of a quadratic expression is $ax^2 + bx + c$. A great way to factor quadratic expression like this, where $a = 1$ and all the answer choices are integer factors, would be to consider the factors of the last term, c. Specifically, any two factors of c that would add to b. Essentially: $f_1 \times f_2 = -12$ and $f_1 + f_2 = 1$. We can check the factors of –12.

f_1	f_2	$f_1 + f_2$
12	-1	11
6	-2	4
4	-3	1
3	-4	-1
2	-6	-4
1	-12	-11

From this the only option that works is 4 and –3, which means the expression factors as $(x + 4)(x - 3)$.

13. D: The circumference of a circle can be found using the formula $C = \pi d$, where d is the diameter of the circle.

$$35 = \pi d$$

$$d = \frac{35}{\pi} \approx 11.14$$

Therefore, the diameter of the circle is approximately 11.14 feet.

14. C: The side of the square is equal to the diameter of the circle, or twice the radius, $2r$. The area of the square is this quantity squared, or $4r^2$. The area of the circle is πr^2. Subtracting the area of the circle from the area of the square gives the difference between the two areas.

$$4r^2 - \pi r^2$$

A common r^2 can be factored out of each term to get the expression $r^2(4 - \pi)$.

15. C: The total distance traveled was 8 miles + 3.6 miles = 11.6 miles. The first $\frac{1}{5}$ of a mile is charged at the higher rate. Since $\frac{1}{5} = 0.2$, the remainder of the trip is 11.4 miles. Thus, the fare for the distance traveled is computed as $\$5.50 + 5 \times 11.4 \times \$1.50 = \$91$. The charge for waiting time is added next, which is simply $9 \times 20¢ = 180¢ = \$1.80$. Finally, add the two charges, $\$91 + \$1.80 = \$92.80$.

16. D: The radius, R, of the satellite's orbit is the sum of Earth's radius plus the satellite's orbital altitude, or $R = 4{,}400$ mi. The circumference of the circular orbit is therefore $C = 2\pi r = 2\pi(4{,}400) = 8{,}800\pi$ mi. Since 40 minutes is one-third of the satellite's 120-minute orbital time, it traverses one-third of this distance in that time.

$$D = \frac{1}{3} \times 8{,}800(3.14) \approx 9{,}210.67$$

Therefore, the distance the satellite travels is approximately 9,211 miles.

17. The following graph demonstrates the correct points:

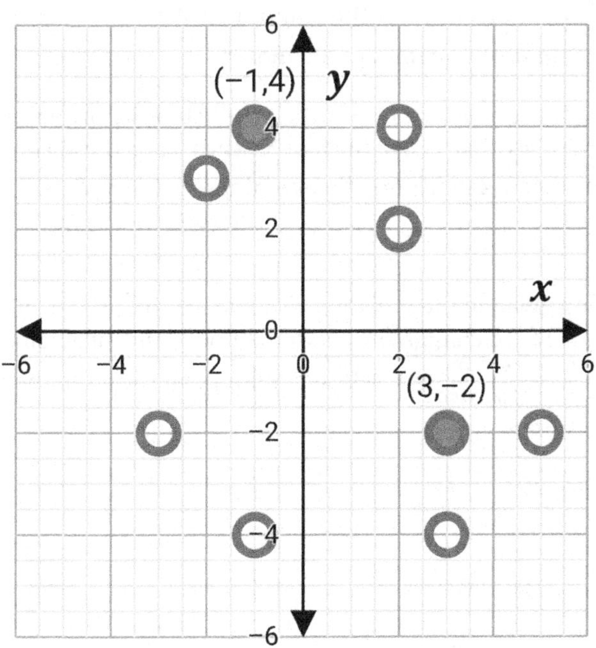

Ordered pairs take the form (x, y). The variable x represents the distance from the origin along the x-axis, and the variable y represents the distance from the origin along the y-axis. The point $(3, -2)$ indicates 3 units to the right along the x-axis and 2 units down along the y-axis. These directions intersect at the point $(3, -2)$. The point $(-1, 4)$ indicates 1 unit left along the x-axis, and 4 units up along the y-axis. These directions intersect at the point $(-1,4)$.

18. D: Remember that when you multiply like bases, you add the exponents, and when you divide like bases, you subtract the exponents.

$$(xy)^{7y} - (xy)^{y} = (xy)^{y}[(xy)^{7y-y} - 1] = (xy)^{y}[(xy)^{6y} - 1]$$

19. C: We are looking for a graph with two key pieces of information: rainfall every day except Friday, and an amount of rain on Monday double the rain on Thursday. Answer choice A is incorrect because it shows no rain on Sunday. Answer choice B is incorrect because it shows rain on Friday. Answer choice D is incorrect because the amount of rain on Monday is equal to the amount of rain on Thursday. Only answer choice C is correct because it shows no rain on Friday, 6 inches on Monday, and 3 inches on Thursday.

20. 24 First solve for b. If $3a + 5b = 98$ and $a = 11$:

$$\begin{aligned} 3(11) + 5b &= 98 \\ 33 + 5b &= 98 \\ 5b &= 65 \\ b &= 13 \end{aligned}$$

Therefore, $a + b = 11 + 13 = 24$.

21. A: Jamie had \$6.50 in his wallet. To solve this problem, you subtract \$4.25 and \$2.00 from that amount: \$6.50 − \$4.25 − \$2.00 = \$0.25. So, you are left with \$0.25. Then, you add the \$2.50 that your friend had borrowed: \$0.25 + \$2.50 = \$2.75. Therefore, Jamie currently has \$2.75 in his wallet.

22. 75: Of the 24 people that set out to climb, only 6 made it to the top so 18 people did not complete the climb because $24 - 6 = 18$. This means that $\frac{18}{24}$, which can be simplified to $\frac{3}{4}$ by dividing both the numerator and denominator by 6, of the people did not complete the climb. The fraction $\frac{3}{4}$ is equivalent to the percentage 75%. So, 75% of the people did not complete the climb up the mountain.

23. C: The probability of getting three aces in a row is the product of the probabilities for each draw. For the first ace, that is 4 in 52, since there are 4 aces in a deck of 52 cards. For the second, it is 3 in 51, since 3 aces and 51 cards remain; and for the third, it is 2 in 50. So, the overall probability, P, is $P = \frac{4}{52} \times \frac{3}{51} \times \frac{2}{50} = \frac{24}{132{,}600} = \frac{1}{5{,}525}$.

24. 0.48: Modify the relationship given in the question to solve for the time. You know that the distance is the product of the rate and time: $d = rt$. To change the relationship for this problem, you need to put time (t) by itself. So, this will look like: $t = \frac{d}{r} = \frac{60.5\text{ ft}}{125\text{ ft/sec}} = 0.484$ sec. When you round to the nearest hundredth of a second, you have the answer of 0.48 seconds.

25. D: The longest side of a right triangle, called the hypotenuse, H, can be calculated using the Pythagorean theorem, together with the lengths of the other two sides, which are given as 6 and 8 units.

$$H^2 = (S_1)^2 + (S_2)^2$$
$$H^2 = 6^2 + 8^2$$
$$H^2 = 36 + 64$$
$$H^2 = 100$$
$$\sqrt{H^2} = \sqrt{100}$$
$$H = 10$$

Therefore, using $H = 10$, the perimeter, P, can be calculated as follows: $P = 10 + 6 + 8 = 24$. The perimeter of the triangle is 24 units.

26. C: The formula for the volume of a pyramid is $V = \frac{1}{3}Bh$, where B is the area of the base and h is the height of the pyramid. The base is a square with a length of 756 feet on each side. So, the area of the base is $A = s^2 = (756\text{ ft})^2 = 571{,}536\text{ ft}^2$. With a base of $571{,}536\text{ ft}^2$ and a height of 481 ft, the volume of the pyramid is $V = \frac{1}{3}(571{,}536\text{ ft}^2)(481\text{ ft}) \approx 9.16 \times 10^7\text{ ft}^3$.

27. 1: At $y = 2$, we see that $x = 2$ for the plotted line. The equation for a straight line is of the form $y = mx + b$, where m is the slope of the line and b is the y-intercept. If the new line passes through the origin, then $b = 0$. Substitute the values for x, y, and b in the equation and solve for m.

$$2 = m(2) + 0$$
$$2 = 2m$$
$$1 = m$$

Therefore, the slope of the line that passes through the origin and the point (2,2) is 1.

28. D: When a number is raised to a power, you multiply the number by itself the number of times indicated by the power. For example, $2^3 = 2 \times 2 \times 2 = 8$. A number raised to the power of 0 is always equal to 1. So, 6^0 is the smallest number shown. Similarly, for the other numbers:

$$9 = 9;\ 10^1 = 10;\ 4^2 = 4 \times 4 = 16$$

Since $1 < 8 < 9 < 10 < 16$, we can write the order as $6^0, 2^3, 9, 10^1, 4^2$.

29. The following graph demonstrates the correct points:

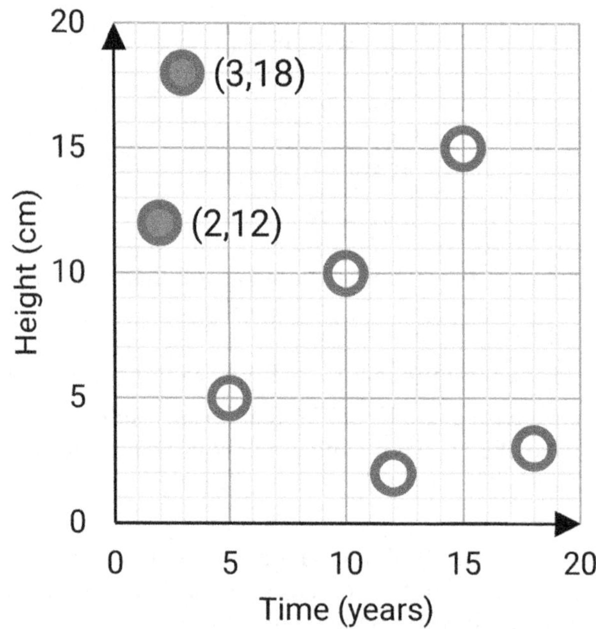

The graph shows that the number of years is the independent variable x, and the tree height is the dependent variable y. The height of the tree after 2 years is 12 cm. This can be represented with the ordered pair (2,12). The height of the tree after 3 years is 18 cm. This can be represented with the ordered pair (3,18).

30. B: To multiply two powers that have the same base, you need to add their exponents. This is represented by the property $x^m \cdot x^n = x^{m+n}$. So, $x^3x^5 = x^{3+5} = x^8$.

31. C: The line in the graph has a negative slope and a positive y-axis intercept, so the factor multiplying the variable x, or the slope, must be negative, and the constant, or y-intercept, must be positive. To find the slope, m, use the slope formula and the two points (0,2) and (3,−3).

$$m = \frac{y_2 - y_1}{x_2 - x_1} = \frac{-3 - 2}{3 - 0} = \frac{-5}{3}$$

Therefore, the slope of the line is $m = -\frac{5}{3}$. The y-intercept is the point where the line crosses the y-axis, which is (0,2). Therefore, the value of b, the y-coordinate of the y-intercept is 2. Substitute these values into the slope-intercept form of a line, $y = mx + b$.

$$y = -\frac{5}{3}x + 2$$

32. 910: One way to determine the answer is by computing the area of the large rectangle as well as the area of the rectangular cutout. Then, the area of the cutout is subtracted from that of the larger rectangle. The area of the rectangle is the product of its length and width, $A_{\text{rect}} = 20 \text{ ft} \times 50 \text{ ft} = 1{,}000 \text{ ft}^2$. Since the cutout is rectangular as well, its area is computed in the same way: $A_{\text{cutout}} = 6 \text{ ft} \times 15 \text{ ft} = 90 \text{ ft}^2$. Then subtract the two areas: $1{,}000 \text{ ft}^2 - 90 \text{ ft}^2 = 910 \text{ ft}^2$.

33. 25: Start by adding the number of blue and red fish together: $150 + 150 = 300$. This leaves only 100 brown fish. Since the probability of pulling out any single fish is the same, he has a $\frac{100}{400} = \frac{1}{4} = 25\%$ chance of getting a brown fish.

34. C: To solve, use the percentage increase formula.

$$\text{Percentage Increase} = \frac{\text{new} - \text{initial}}{\text{initial}} \times 100$$

In this case, the initial value is \$80, and the new value is \$120.

$$\text{Percentage Increase} = \frac{120 - 80}{80} \times 100 = \frac{40}{80} \times 100 = 50\%$$

Therefore, the total amount in her account increased by 50%.

35. D: There are four different colors. So, one color must be held back from each balloon bundle. So, there is one color set for each excluded color or four in all.

When the order of the individual parts is not important, this is called a combination. The number of combinations of n objects taken k at a time is given by $C = \frac{n!}{r!(n-r)!}$. The ! notation is for a factorial product where $n! = 1 \times 2 \times 3 \times \ldots \times (n-1) \times n$. In this case, $n = 4$ colors, and $k = 3$ balloons per bundle. Substitute these values into the equation above and simplify.

$$C = \frac{4!}{(4-3)! \times 3!} = \frac{1 \times 2 \times 3 \times 4}{(1)(1 \times 2 \times 3)} = 4$$

Carrie can make 4 different kinds of bundles of balloons.

36. A: An equation can be expressed in slope-intercept form if the slope and a point are provided. In this case, the slope is 3 and the point is (1,4). Start by substituting 3 in for the slope, m, in the equation $y = mx + b$.

$$y = 3x + b$$

Then, substitute the point (1,4) in for x and y.

$$4 = 3(1) + b$$

Now, solve for the variable b, which represents the y-intercept.

$$4 = 3(1) + b$$
$$4 = 3 + b$$
$$1 = b$$

Now that the slope, m, and the y-intercept, b, are determined, the equation can be expressed in slope-intercept form.

$$y = 3x + 1$$

37. B: The perimeter of a figure is the sum of all its sides. Since a rectangle's width and length will be the same on opposite sides, the perimeter of a rectangle can be calculated by using the following formula.

$$P = 2w + 2l$$

Substitute the numbers given in the question.

$$P = 2(7) + 2(9)$$
$$P = 14 + 18$$
$$P = 32$$

Therefore, the perimeter of the rectangle is 32 cm.

38. (0, 6) and (6, 8):

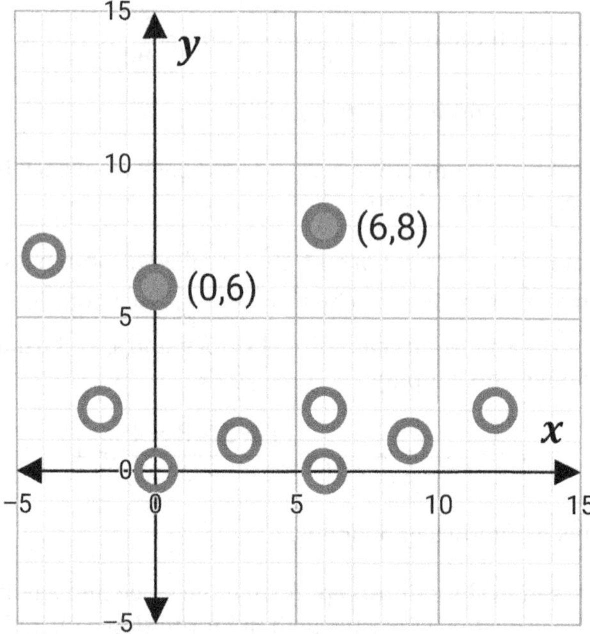

The equation $y - 6 = \frac{1}{3}x$ is almost in slope-intercept form. Add 6 to both sides of the equation to get $y = \frac{1}{3}x + 6$. Now the equation is in slope-intercept form, $y = mx + b$, where m represents the slope and b represents the y-intercept. In the equation $y = \frac{1}{3}x + 6$, the slope is $\frac{1}{3}$ and the y-intercept is 6.

A y-intercept of 6 indicates that the graphed line intersects the y-axis at $y = 6$. This point is located at (0,6).

Use the slope and the y-intercept to identify another point on the graphed line. The slope is $\frac{1}{3}$, which indicates a "rise" of 1 and a "run" of 3. From the point (0,6), "rise" 1 unit vertically, and "run" 3 units horizontally. The new location is (3,7). This point is not presented on the graph. Apply the slope again. From the point (3,7), "rise" 1 unit vertically, and "run" 3 units horizontally. The new location is (6,8).

39. C: For this problem there are 3 inches in each segment, 12 inches in a foot, and 3 feet in a yard. Set up a conversion problem and simplify.

$$4.5\ \cancel{\text{yd}} \times \frac{3\ \cancel{\text{ft}}}{1\ \cancel{\text{yd}}} \times \frac{12\ \cancel{\text{in}}}{1\ \cancel{\text{ft}}} \times \frac{1\ \text{segment}}{3\ \cancel{\text{in}}} = 4.5 \times 12\ \text{segments} = 54\ \text{segments}$$

Therefore, a 4.5-yard line can be divided into 54 3-inch segments.

40. B: The equation of the line can be expressed in slope-intercept form, $y = mx + b$, when m and b are determined. Start by solving for m, the slope, using the slope formula: $m = \frac{y_2 - y_1}{x_2 - x_1}$. Use the points $(-2, -3)$ and $(4, -4)$ to substitute x- and y-values into the formula.

$$m = \frac{y_2 - y_1}{x_2 - x_1} = \frac{-4 - (-3)}{4 - (-2)} = -\frac{1}{6}$$

Now solve for b, the y-intercept. Substitute in values for x, y, and m into the slope-intercept formula, $y = mx + b$. Use either pair of (x, y) coordinates. For example, when $(-2, -3)$ is used, $y = mx + b$ becomes $-3 = \left(-\frac{1}{6}\right)(-2) + b$. Now solve for the value of b.

$$-3 = \left(-\frac{1}{6}\right)(-2) + b$$
$$-3 = \frac{2}{6} + b$$
$$-\frac{10}{3} = b$$

We know that $m = -\frac{1}{6}$ and $b = -\frac{10}{3}$. Now the equation of the line can be expressed in slope-intercept form.

$$y = -\frac{1}{6}x - \frac{10}{3}$$

41. 30: The answer is found by dividing the volume of the box by the volume of the cube:

$$\frac{V_{box}}{V_{cube}} = \frac{(15 \text{ in}) \times (9 \text{ in}) \times (6 \text{ in})}{(3 \text{ in}) \times (3 \text{ in}) \times (3 \text{ in})} = \frac{810 \text{ in}^3}{27 \text{ in}^3} = 30$$

42. 25 If the ratio of pennies to nickels is 2:6, the ratio of the pennies to the combined coins is 2:2+6, or 2:8. This is ¼ or, expressed as a percentage, 25%.

43. A: The legs and hypotenuse of a right triangle are related through the Pythagorean theorem, $a^2 + b^2 = c^2$, where a and b are the lengths of the legs and c is the length of the hypotenuse. In this case, $a = 5$ and $b = 12$ (or vice-versa; it doesn't matter which leg we call a and which leg we call b). Substitute these values into the Pythagorean theorem and solve for c.

$$(5)^2 + (12)^2 = c^2$$
$$25 + 144 = c^2$$
$$169 = c^2$$
$$13 = c$$

Therefore, the length of the hypotenuse is 13.

44. D: When no tickets are sold, $N = 0$. The following equation can be created and solved for p.

$$0 = 25{,}000 - 0.1p^2$$
$$0.1p^2 = 25{,}000$$
$$p^2 = \frac{25{,}000}{0.1}$$
$$p^2 = 250{,}000$$
$$p = 500$$

Therefore, the lowest price at which they will sell no tickets at all is \$500.

45. \$4,000: Besides the \$600 he has remaining, Chan has paid out a total of 85% (30% + 30% + 25%) of his bonus for the expenses described in the question. Therefore, the \$600 represents the remaining 15%. Remember that 15% can be written as $\frac{15}{100}$. To determine his total bonus, solve $\frac{15}{100}x = 600$. So, $x = \frac{100}{15} \times 600 = 4{,}000$, and Chan's total bonus is \$4,000.

46. C: The median of a set of numbers is one for which the set contains an equal number of greater and lesser values. Besides Z, there are 8 numbers in the set, so that 4 must be greater and 4 lesser than Z. The 4 smallest values are 5, 7, 9, and 12. The 4 largest are 16, 18, 23, and 44. So Z must fall between 12 and 16. Therefore, the correct answer choice is 14.

47. D: Lines with the same slope will be parallel. The equation $y = 8x - 4$ is in slope-intercept form, $y = mx + b$, where m represents the slope and b represents the y-intercept. The slope in the equation $y = 8x - 4$ is 8. The only equation listed with a slope of 8 is $y = 8x - 1$. The lines $y = 8x - 1$ and $y = 8x - 4$ will be parallel when graphed.

48. A: Substitute the given values for the variables into the expression.

$$4(-6)\,(3(7) + 5) + 2(7)$$

Using order of operations, find the expression in the parentheses first. Remember that first you must multiply 3 by 7. Then, add 5 to follow the order of operations.

$$4(-6)(21 + 5) + 2(7)$$
$$4(-6)(26) + 2(7)$$

Next, multiply in order from left to right.

$$-24(26) + 2(7)$$
$$-624 + 14$$

Finally, add.

$$-610$$

49. B: Since the second line, $y = 3$, is horizontal, the intersection must occur at a point where $y = 3$. Substitute $y = 3$ into the equation and solve for x.

$$2x + (3) = 0$$
$$2x = -3$$
$$x = -\frac{3}{2}$$

Therefore, the point where these two lines will intersect is at $\left(-\frac{3}{2}, 3\right)$.

50. B: The mean, or average, is the sum of the numbers in a data set divided by the total number of items in the set. This data set has 7 items (one for each day of the week). The total number of hits that Kyle had during the week is the sum of the numbers in the right-hand column. The sum is 14, so the mean is 2 because $14 \div 7 = 2$.

Science

1. A: The average of a set of numbers is calculated by adding the numbers in the set together and then dividing by the total number of values in the set. In this case, you are given a set of temperatures and asked to find the average. Each temperature is shown on the chart, one per day. To find the average high temperature for the week, start by adding all seven temperatures from the chart: $70 + 80 + 85 + 80 + 75 + 80 + 70 = 540$. Next, divide by the number of days, which is 7: $540 \div 7 = 77.14$. Finally, round to the nearest whole number: 77.14 rounds to 77.

2. C: According to the information given, the genotypes SS and Ss will both result in red spots. Since there are 33 ladybugs with the SS genotype and 38 with the Ss genotype out of 100, add 33 to 38 to get 71. To get the percentage, divide 71 by the total number of ladybugs (100) to get 0.71, then multiply that by 100 to get the percentage: 0.71 times 100 is 71%.

3. D: The graph provided shows that the line for the flower growth data starts just above 20 cm at a pH of 5.8, then rises as the pH rises to 38 cm at a pH of approximately 6.2. Flower growth reaches 40 cm at a pH of approximately 6.4. The line then rises rapidly, reaching a maximum of 57 cm at a pH of approximately 6.6. It drops slowly until a pH of approximately 6.8, and then quickly drops to 28 cm before the graph ends at a pH of 7. This aligns most closely with the flower growth data set shown in choice D. The data for the pH value and flower growth are reversed in choice A. In choice B, the values for the flower growth data are too high and do not align with the graph. In choice C, the pH values are too high and do not align with the graph.

4. A: Since the desert biome has much lower annual precipitation, it is reasonable to conclude that this leads to lower biodiversity, which is supported by the data. It is also reasonable to conclude that the lack of rainfall necessitates vegetation that can survive in the drier climate. Choice B does accurately note that the average temperatures are close, but the data for the vegetation and wildlife shows that they are different in the two biomes. Choice C accurately notes the higher biodiversity in the rainforest biome but does not account for the higher annual precipitation. Choice D accurately notes the denser vegetation of the rainforest biome but fails to also note the higher biodiversity.

5. B: The independent variable in this case is the amount of fertilizer being used. An independent variable is one that the person or people conducting the experiment manipulate to find out what effect it has on something else; the something else, which in this case is plant growth, is called the dependent variable. In this case, John and his friends are changing or manipulating the amount of fertilizer used to find out its effect on the plants. The number of people conducting the experiment is not something they are changing or manipulating. The temperature of the air in the greenhouse, as well as the weather outside of the greenhouse, are also not being manipulated to conduct the experiment.

6. A: Using the context clues within the paragraph, specifically relating to the movement of the train, you can see that velocity refers to the speed and direction of an object. Velocity might be one of the behaviors of a subatomic particle that is analyzed, but particle behavior is not just velocity. The height of an aircraft is also incorrect because it is not related to the object's speed and direction. The flight path of an aircraft is incorrect because the flight path does not refer to the aircraft's speed, only its direction.

7. B: The equator is the line that goes horizontally across the center of the map. According to the key, the highest increases in temperature are indicated with dark red, red, and orange colors, which are mostly concentrated above, or north of, the equator line. Choice A is incorrect because it states that these changes are concentrated near the equator, and choice C is incorrect because it states that the changes are even throughout the map. According to the key, the blues, green, white, and yellow colors show temperature increases of less than 0.5 °C. Choice D is incorrect because it states that these colors take up most of the map.

8. C: The passage states that gravity has nearly no effect on subatomic particles due to their miniscule, or very small, size. This leads to the conclusion that an object of larger mass has a stronger gravitational pull.

The passage also mentions that gravity is what gives objects weight on Earth. This leads to the conclusion that on a smaller planet, which has less gravitational pull, a person would have a lower weight than he or she does on Earth.

9. B: The passage states that gravity is a force that causes objects with mass to pull on, or attract, each other. Throughout the passage, there are examples of how objects of different mass are affected by the attractive force of gravity. The passage also mentions that gravity affects the moon, so it is not a force that exists only on planets.

10. A: According to the passage, the giant cane toad is a large frog species that can be found in a variety of colors, including shades of brown. The poison dart frog is small and has bright colors. The conclusion is that poisonous frogs can be found in different sizes and colors. Since the passage mentions that the poison from the poison dart frog has been used by humans, it can be assumed that they are in areas where humans will encounter them, so choice B is incorrect. Choice C states that all poisonous frogs have bright colors, and while this is true of the poison dart frog, the giant cane toad does not have bright colors. The giant cane toad is very large, meaning choice D is incorrect since it states that poisonous frogs tend to be very small.

11. A: The poison dart frog has been used by humans who add the frogs' poison to the end of dart tips. The giant cane toad has been used by humans to eat the pests on sugarcane. There is no mention in the passage of either being endangered, and the giant cane toad's toxin will cause skin irritation, not death, in humans. They eat insects and arthropods, so they are not herbivores.

12. A: When the northern glass frog is described as nocturnal, this means that it is mainly active at night. The giant cane toad is also described as nocturnal, and the passage indicates that the giant cane toad is primarily active during the night. When an animal is active during the day and inactive at night, it is diurnal (choice B). An animal that is mostly active during twilight is crepuscular (choice C). Cathemeral describes a pattern of activity during both daylight and darkness (choice D).

13. B: When research shows contradictory findings, the best approach is to analyze the sample sizes, methodologies, and study findings to look for the factors that affected those outcomes. A small sample size can lead to a less-reliable result. Different research designs and different participant demographics can lead to different results. Choice A is incorrect because disregarding this research does not take into consideration the insights it might offer. Choice C is incorrect because all of the research must be considered, not only the parts that support a predetermined conclusion. Choice D is similarly incorrect because it disregards a study that does not support the predetermined conclusion.

14. A: To find the numerical relationship between T and R, it is necessary to find the pattern in the data. Enzyme activity increases when temperature increases, and they both increase at a steady rate (20 units/min per 10 °C), so the numerical relationship will show a steady rate of change and can be expressed as a linear equation as given in the answer options.

To determine which equation is correct, plug the numbers from the chart into each of the answer options. Using the data from the chart, choice A works when 105 is plugged in for R, and 50 for T: $105 = 2(50) + 5$. This will work using any line of data from the chart. Choice B subtracts 5, which is incorrect. Choice C adds 20 to each data point for T, which is also incorrect. For choice D, multiplying the data points for T by 5 will result in values that are too high for R.

15. D: The mean is a measure of central tendency of a data set. The measures of central tendency help to smooth out outliers and represent the set as a whole. The mean, or average, is a number that represents the data set's general magnitude at a glance. It is the sum of the values in the data set divided by the number of values in the data set. Here, the mean number of birds per flock is $(1320 + 408 + 793 + 1254 + 681 + 590) \div 6 = 841$. While no flock has exactly 841 species, the number 841 is a good indicator of how big a typical flock is.

16. D: There is a 50% chance that the yellow (Yy) and green (yy) plants will produce a yellow (Yy) plant. The Punnett square shows this possibility in 2 out of 4 of the boxes, since the dominant allele (Y) is present in two boxes. This is 2/4 or 50%. The other 50% of the time, the plant will be green (yy).

17. C: Since Newton's First Law of Motion is the Law of Inertia, a passenger will lurch forward when a car comes to a sudden stop because the passenger, already in motion, will stay in motion at their original speed until stopped by the force exerted by their seatbelt. A ball being propelled through the air is an example of Newton's Second Law. If the force and mass are known quantities, acceleration can be calculated. A rocket increasing its speed after launching is also an example of Newton's Second Law of Motion, since acceleration is involved. A person walking on the sidewalk is an example of Newton's Third Law of Motion, as the sidewalk exerts an equal opposing force on the person who is walking.

18. B: Newton's Third Law of Motion states that every action has an equal but opposite reaction. According to the passage, objects apply forces upon each other that are in the same amount, or equal in magnitude, but in opposite directions. In this example, the book is applying a downward force to the chair, and the chair is applying an equal force upward in the opposite direction. Choice A refers to Newton's First Law of Motion, in which objects are resistant to a change in motion. Choice C refers to Newton's Second Law of Motion, which describes the relationship between force, mass, and acceleration. Choice D describes unequal forces applied by the book and the chair, but Newton's Third Law of Motion states that forces are applied in equal magnitude and opposite directions.

19. C: Without the apex predators, their prey would experience a population explosion, which would then cause the prey to not have enough food to eat. The lack of apex predators would affect the ecosystem negatively.

20. B: According to the passage, any animal that feeds on zooplankton is a secondary consumer. A secondary consumer will be preyed upon by larger animals that are considered tertiary consumers. Zooplankton are considered a primary consumer.

21. B: In this experiment, the potential flaw is the lack of control of experimental conditions. As Johanna pushes the ball, the strength of the push will vary each time, changing how far the ball rolls. The differences in the initial condition of the ball's release can affect the outcome of the experiment. Without controlling these conditions, the outcome of the experiment may vary in unexpected ways that are not solely due to the ramp angle. Observer bias happens when the observer's prejudices or opinions affect the experiment, and this should not happen when measuring a distance. Randomization occurs when participants are assigned to random conditions within the experiment. Publication bias is when the decision of whether to publish the findings of a study depends on the results.

22. C: By repeating the process five times for each angle, Johanna is helping to ensure the reliability of the results. This repetition creates a more robust data set and helps to ensure that the results are both consistent and reliable. Using a variety of ramp angles and measuring the distance with a tape measure are important aspects of the experiment, but the repetition will help to increase confidence in the results that are recorded. This experiment did not involve using ramps with different lengths, which could affect the outcome and make the results less reliable.

23. A: To improve the validity of the design of this experiment, Malik should use three of the same type of plant. Since the three plants used in the experiment have different growth patterns and nutritional needs, the variation in plant types is a confounding factor that will lead to unreliable results. Using the same plant types will minimize the effect that the inherent plant differences have on the results.

24. D: To improve the design of the experiment, and to provide a baseline for the results, Malik should add a control group to the experiment. In this case, he should use the same type of plant for each liquid tested, along with a fourth plant that receives only plain tap water. This would determine a baseline of the expected growth of the plant without the addition of other types of liquid, and the growth of the other plants could be compared to this baseline to determine the effects of the other liquids.

25. C: Start by adding the hours of all the days in which the train traveled at least 12 hours: $12 + 13 + 12 + 12 + 12 = 61$. Then, add the distances the train traveled on those days: $540 + 572 + 564 + 492 + 504 = 2672$. Finally, divide the distance by the time: $2672 \div 61 = 43.803$, which rounds to 43.8.

26. B: Since the passage refers to the number of protons and neutrons in the atom's nucleus remaining the same during a chemical reaction, this is the best definition of atomic number. The color of the resulting product can change in a chemical reaction, and a change in temperature can also be the result of a chemical reaction. The number of products from the reactants is not related to the definition of an atomic number.

27. D: The oxidation of an apple, or turning brown when exposed to air, is an example of a chemical reaction. The enzymes from the apple react to the oxygen in the air, resulting in a brown color. The change in color is one of the possible signs of a chemical reaction. The other options are physical processes that do result in the mixing or changing of the object's physical state but do not form new substances with different chemical properties.

28. A: A key characteristic of a chemical reaction is that the resulting product retains the same number of atoms as the reactants, but the properties are changed during the reaction. The total mass of the reactants and the product will be the same due to the law of conservation of mass. The resulting product may have a different color than the reactants, since that is a possible sign of a chemical reaction, but the reaction may produce other changes instead.

29. C: According to the data on the chart, the salinity of the water increases as the depth of the ocean increases. It does not show that the salinity levels are highest at the ocean's surface and decrease at lower depths, as the salinity is at 35 ppm at the ocean's surface and 45 ppm at 20 m. The data does not indicate that salinity levels remain constant at all depths of the ocean. It does appear to change in a predictable way, which is seen by the steady change shown on the graph.

30. B: If the experimenter repeats the same experiment multiple times at different locations in the ocean, they will account for the natural variability of the salinity in the ocean and increase the reliability of the final results. The measurement of the pH level could give additional data, but it would not strengthen the design of the experiment. The measurement should be conducted with consistent environmental variables, but the environmental factors are already consistent for the experiment. Using a different collection device for each ocean depth could confound the results and introduce a potential source of error.

31. B: The mode of the data set for Puya, Ecuador is 340 mm, which shows a consistent pattern of rainfall in June and August. This is during the winter months in Ecuador. The mode is the number that occurs the most in a data set. The mode of the data set for Valparaiso, Chile is 0 mm, which occurs during this country's summer months.

32. D: The range of the data set shows its variability. The range is the difference between the maximum and minimum values in the data set. For Puya, Ecuador, the range is $485 - 280 = 205$ mm. For Valparaiso, Chile, the range is $110 - 0 = 110$ mm. Puya has a larger variability in its rainfall amounts than Valparaiso.

33. A: To find the probability of both plants sprouting, multiply the probabilities of each event occurring. First convert the percentages to decimals: $50\% = 0.50$ and $70\% = 0.70$. Then, multiply the decimals and convert back to a percentage: $0.50 \times 0.70 = 0.35$, or 35%. The probability that both plant species sprout within the first 14 days after planting the seeds is 35%.

34. D: To find the probability that neither of the plants will sprout within the first 14 days, first find the probability that each individual plant will not sprout. Convert the probabilities of the plants spouting from percentages to decimals, then subtract this number from 1 to get the decimal probability that the plant will not sprout. For plant A, this is $1 - 0.50 = 0.50$. For plant B, it is $1 - 0.70 = 0.30$. Next, multiply these probabilities together and convert back to a percentage: $0.50 \times 0.30 = 0.15$, or 15%.

35. A: The passage states that Jupiter is the largest planet in our solar system and about 11 times the size of Earth. It also states that Saturn is about 15% smaller than Jupiter, which means that it is more than 9 times the size of Earth: $11 \times (1 - 0.15) = 9.35$. This means that Earth is smaller than both Jupiter and Saturn.

36. C: The passage states that Jupiter's massive size gives it a strong gravitational pull, and this is what holds the ring particles and moons in its orbit. Since Jupiter is the largest planet in the solar system and Saturn is only 15% smaller, the conclusion can be made that it also has a strong gravitational pull holding ring particles and moons in orbit.

37. B: Since the passage states that the Great Red Spot of Jupiter has slowly been diminishing in size over the past few decades, it is reasonable to conclude that it will continue to shrink over the next several decades. The passage mentions that the ring fragments around Saturn are slowly being absorbed into the planet, so the number is not increasing. One of the moons of Saturn is described to have gases instead of bodies of water, but there is no mention of other moons with water on their surfaces. Jupiter is composed of gases and does not have volcanoes or rocky formations on its surface.

38. B: Jaden did not form a hypothesis before proceeding with his experiment. The hypothesis is an assumption that can be tested to see if it is true. A hypothesis for this scenario could be, "If the plants receive more sunlight, they will grow taller due to photosynthesis." Jaden performed data collection when he recorded plant growth. He researched when he investigated the link between plant growth and sunlight. He set up an experiment with the scenario of two groups of plants, one in full sun and one in the shade.

39. D: In Jaden's experiment, sunlight positively affects the growth of milkweed. His experiment did not involve other types of plants, so it does not lead to a conclusion about all plants. Since he had researched how plants produce energy through photosynthesis, which fuels a plant's cellular growth, it would not be a reasonable conclusion that photosynthesis does not affect plant growth.

40. B: When Nadia wraps the copper wire more tightly with the same 9-volt battery, she is able to pick up more objects than when the copper wire is wrapped more loosely. When she connects that same loosely wrapped copper wire to a higher voltage power source, the magnetism increases. It is reasonable to conclude that both a tightly wrapped copper wire on the nail and a higher power source will result in a higher level of magnetism.

41. A: Once Nadia disconnects the power source, the magnetic field disappears, and she is no longer able to pick up metal objects with the electromagnet. This leads to the conclusion that the power source is necessary for the magnetic field to be present. The nail does not remain magnetic without its power source.

42. C: A bar graph is an effective tool to present qualitative data such as the information collected from this experiment. This type of graph will allow the viewer to easily observe the data and compare any trends from the data. A bar graph can help to convey the magnitude of differences in data, and it presents the data in a way that is easy to understand.

43. D: A positive correlation occurs when two variables either increase or decrease together. For most of the planets, when the escape velocity is higher, gravity is mostly higher as well. The exception is Saturn, which has the second-highest escape velocity (35.5 m/s) but only the fifth-highest gravity (9 m/s^2).

44. A: The length of days for planets are listed relative to one Earth day. One day on Earth is 24 hours, so multiplying 24 times 116.75 will result in 2,802 hours.

45. C: To balance a chemical equation, the same number of each type of atom is needed on the left and right of the arrow. In this example, the number of oxygen atoms on the left is calculated by adding the number of oxygen atoms in CO_2 to the number of oxygen atoms in H_2O. First, multiply the coefficient (6) and the subscript (2) in 6 CO_2: $6 \times 2 = 12$. Then, in 6 H_2O, the coefficient is 6 and there is no subscript, so there are 6 oxygen atoms. The total number of oxygen atoms on the left is 18. On the right, $C_6H_{12}O_6$ = 6 oxygen atoms, and O_2 = 2 oxygen atoms. Adding a coefficient of 6 in front of O_2 will result in 12 oxygen atoms. Add that to the 6 in $C_6H_{12}O_6$ and the total on the right will be 18.

46. A. The atomic mass of an element is the weight, in grams, of one mole of its atoms, and the atomic mass of a compound is the weight, in grams, of one mole of its molecules. One mole of carbon dioxide (CO_2) contains one mole of carbon and two moles of oxygen, so the atomic mass of carbon dioxide is $12 + (2 \times 16) = 44$. Multiply the number of moles of carbon dioxide by its atomic weight to get the weight of the carbon dioxide used by the tree: $496 \times 44 = 21{,}824$ grams. Then, convert grams to kilograms by dividing by 1,000 to get 21.824 kilograms. Finally, round to the nearest kilogram.

47. D: The correct sequence of components used during respiration starts with the nose and mouth, which brings air into the body. Next the air passes through the larynx and moves on through the trachea. The trachea brings the air to the bronchioles, which have alveoli at the ends of them.

48. B: Internal respiration involves the processes that take place at a cellular level. During internal respiration, the red blood cells use oxygen and then transport waste back to the lungs. The larynx, trachea, and bronchioles are all components of external respiration.

49. A: During respiration, gas is exchanged within the lungs by alveoli, and the alveoli then move carbon dioxide from the bloodstream so it can be exhaled. Oxygen is taken into the bloodstream by the alveoli, which are the tiny air sacs at the ends of the bronchioles. The pharynx is a part of the respiratory system that is used to carry air to the larynx.

50. B: The pulmonary artery brings blood away from the heart and into the alveoli, where internal respiration takes place. The pulmonary vein then takes the blood back away from the alveoli to the heart. The bronchioles are the airways that lead to the alveoli.

Social Studies

1. B: When President Kennedy described outer space as having no strife, no prejudice, and no national conflict, he painted it as a beckoning, or appealing, destination that is free from these negative characteristics. Kennedy described space in a positive light while attempting to invoke the pioneering attitudes of the American people.

2. C: The use of repetition in Kennedy's speech served to highlight the urgency and importance in his message. Kennedy stated, "We choose to go to the moon. We choose to go to the moon in this decade and do the other things, not because they are easy, but because they are hard, because that goal will serve to organize and measure the best of our energies and skills, because that challenge is one that we are willing to accept..." This repetition was used to implore the audience to consider the importance of space travel for Americans.

3. B: Kennedy used loaded language within his speech to appeal to the emotions of the audience and persuade the audience toward his point of view. Loaded language is an appeal to emotions, using words with strong positive or negative connotations, in contrast with an appeal to logic. In this example, Kennedy used deeply emotional language to convince the audience that it was their duty as a country to support the moon mission.

4. A: This political cartoon portrays women who oppose their own right to vote as on the same side as child-labor employers and sweatshop owners. The nefarious expressions of the male chorus characterize them as bad people, and the political boss conductor is leading them all as a group. The caption also emphasizes that the male chorus of poor labor practices supports the female soloist who does not vote. Therefore, it can be concluded that the artist believes, unlike the people in the cartoon, that women should be allowed to vote.

5. D: According to the cartoon, as long as women are not voting, they are in accord with the poor labor practices. The men representing the labor leaders are happy that the woman is unable to vote. If women were allowed to vote, it would impact the labor bosses negatively because women would be able to vote against poor labor practices.

6. A: According to Article V, each state had one vote in Congress on issues affecting the United States. This means that a more populated state like Virginia, which in 1790 had a population of 747,000 people, and a less populated state like Delaware, which had a population of about 59,000 people, had the same amount of power despite the population disparity. The same situation exists today, as all states have two senators no matter what their populations are. The article states that no delegate would receive compensation for their term, and no state would be represented by less than two members. Freedom of speech could not be stifled within Congress.

7. D: According to this excerpt of Article IV, the responsibility of having a well-regulated militia ready at all times fell to the states rather than the federal government. Due to this lack of federal armed forces, the federal government could have a difficult time defending itself.

8. C: If a delegate of Congress is recalled, they are removed from office. Article V states that the delegates can be recalled by their states at any time within the year, and someone else can be sent in their place. If a delegate is recalled, or removed from office, the state would be able to substitute a different delegate instead.

9. B: In this speech, President Wilson asked Congress to consider Germany's action as an act of war and to take defensive action. Throughout the speech, Wilson described the objectives of the US as to protect peace and justice. He characterized Germany as a menace and said that it was the end to the United States' neutrality in the war.

10. A: In this excerpt, the *New York Times* article gave a biased account of Wilson's speech, emphasizing the applause and cheers he received when delivering the message to Congress. By leading with the line that the "audience that cheered him as he has never been cheered in the Capitol in his life," the article set up the speech as an overwhelmingly positive interaction with Congress. An objective account would present the facts without bias. If the excerpt was symbolic, it would use words to symbolize specific concepts or events. An analytical account would interpret the facts of the situation.

11. C: President Wilson's speech used loaded language to persuade Congress that there was no other option than to declare war on Germany. Germany was described as a selfish and autocratic power, while the US was described as free and self-governed. Wilson referred multiple times to Germany as threatening peace. The *New York Times* article described Wilson's speech in a wholly positive light, focusing on the applause and acceptance he gained from Congress, and again invoking the threat to peace in the world. The article was mean to persuade the American people that Wilson's declaration was rightful and unavoidable.

12. D: According to the chart, when demand for the coffee is increased (D1 to D2), price will also increase (P1 to P2). This can be seen easily where the D1 and D2 lines intersect with the S line.

13. C: Exchanging existing equipment for more-efficient equipment would allow more coffee to be ground and supplied to the market with little to no cost increase. Expanding to a second manufacturing facility would increase supply, but would likely increase cost as well. Hiring several new employees would not increase supply. Switching to a certified-organic supplier would increase cost but not affect supply.

14. B: In his speech, President Roosevelt stated that the US was "suddenly and deliberately attacked," alluding to the surprise nature of the attack. The announcement from Japan described the incident as "historic surprise attacks on Pearl Harbor." The President's speech did not characterize Japan's military as victorious, while the announcement described Japan's military as landing a "splendid" strike in which the US fleet "met with sudden defeat." The announcement described the attack's effect on England and portrayed the Philippines as an enemy.

15. C: President Roosevelt's address to Congress stated that the Japanese Ambassador delivered a formal reply to the US one hour after the bombing had commenced. This sentence does not contain opinions. The sentence from the Japanese announcement describing the two countries as headstrong used opinionated descriptions of both the countries and their future paths. The sentence describing the Imperial Forces' action included a description of a "splendid" strike, which is an opinion. The prediction of Singapore vanishing into nothing was an unverifiable prediction, and the description of the chapter in history as "glorious" was an opinion.

16. D: President Roosevelt's address described the US as at peace with Japan and described the attack as a "day which will live in infamy" since it was such a major event. The president described the attack as deliberate and goes on to allude that the threat will lead to conflict since there is no hope in continued diplomatic talks. The announcement to Japan described the attack as premeditated, deliberate, and a "historic surprise attack." It also described the attack as leading to a decisive victory, saying, "What these two headstrong countries are striving for will only lead them on a downhill path to military defeat."

17. A: Bills are given a code that corresponds to the house of Congress where it originated. A bill starting with the code H.R. originated in the House of Representatives. Once the bill is introduced, it is then referred to a committee within that house. The committee will analyze the bill and could revise it prior to the next step.

18. C: The checks and balances built into the process of turning a bill into a law involve each branch of government making sure that the other branches do not have too much power. In this case, the legislative branch, which is made up of the Senate and the House of Representatives, is balanced by the power of the executive branch, which includes the president. If the legislative branch approves a law, the president can still veto it if he disagrees with it.

19. D: In this passage, the word *override* is used to describe what Congress can do to counteract the president's veto. If Congress still passes a bill through a majority vote after the president's veto, they are using their authority to reject the president's decision. If the president lets a bill sit for 10 days and Congress adjourns during that time, the bill will not pass and Congress cannot override the bill's failure. In other words, they are not able to use their authority to reject the president's decision to not approve the bill.

20. C: Article II Section 1 of the Constitution states that in case of a president leaving office, the powers and duties of the office of president will devolve on, or be transferred to, the vice president. Section 1 of the 25th Amendment also says that if the president leaves office, the vice president will become president.

21. D: An emolument is some form of payment, such as a salary or fee. Article II states that the president's compensation, or pay, for serving as president is a fixed amount that cannot be changed during the presidency, and that the president may not "receive any other Emolument." This means that the salary is a form of emolument, and the only one that the president is allowed to receive.

22. A: These sections of the 25th Amendment establish what happens if a president or vice president cannot or will not perform their duties any longer. In the case of the president's death or resignation, the vice president will become president. if the vice president needs to be replaced, the president will nominate a replacement.

23. C: The larger map of Canada shows that this small area of Ontario is further south than most of the country, so it has a warmer climate than most of the country. The area includes the large and populous cities Toronto and Hamilton and their suburbs. It does have multiple lakes, but it is far away from much of the northern and western regions of Canada. Expansion is limited by the lakes on either side and the neighboring US state of New York.

24. B: The cities marked on the first map of Canada are mostly located near oceans, lakes, or rivers. Cities are commonly located near water for ease of travel and trade. The marked cities are fairly evenly distributed throughout the eastern and western sides of the country and are not close to each other. There are more cities in the southern area, due to the colder climate of the northern parts of Canada, but there are many in the northern areas as well. Some of the cities are located along the border with the US, but many are not.

25. C: Causation is when one action causes another action. In this case, prohibiting the manufacture, sale, or transportation of alcohol caused organized crime to increase. Criminals bootlegging alcohol was not caused by an increase in the crime rate, but rather was a factor contributing to the increase in crime. The sale of alcohol being banned and the use of liquor being prohibited both describe parts of Prohibition, not a causal relationship. People who drank in speakeasies were secretly accessing alcohol, but this is not a causal relationship.

26. A: In 1933, the 21st Amendment repealed the 18th Amendment. The passage states that Prohibition, which was instituted by the 18th Amendment, lasted until 1933. It was at this time that the 21st Amendment revoked the 18th Amendment so that the sale, production, and transport of alcohol was no longer prohibited.

27. D: Because the crime rate increased in response to the passage of the 18th Amendment and the prohibition of alcohol, once the 21st Amendment repealed the 18th Amendment it is likely that the crime rate decreased again. Crime syndicates would no longer have a need to trade in illegal alcohol once it was available to the public again.

28. B: Black Americans began to leave the city in large numbers in about 1970, after Martin Luther King Jr. was assassinated in 1968 and the city suffered significant damage in the riots that followed. Until then, the population of black Americans had steadily increased throughout the city's history.

29. A: In 2020, the white population of the city was 40% of 713,000, or approximately 285,000. The chart shows a population of approximately 210,000 white Americans in Washington, DC in 2010. The population of white Americans in Washington, DC rose by approximately $285{,}000 - 210{,}000 = 75{,}000$ from 2010 to 2020.

30. C: The data for the two categories in the chart show a mostly positive correlation. A positive correlation is when two variables increase or decrease together. In this case, the number of music streaming subscribers has generally increased, aside from a small decrease from 2021 to 2022, and the number of digital video game users has increased steadily in the years shown in the chart. There is no reason to think that the number of video game users caused the number of music streaming subscribers to change or that the number of music streaming subscribers caused the number of video game users to change.

31. B: To calculate the mean, or average, of this data set, add the numbers together to get 1,917 million (which is 1.917 billion):

$$198.6 + 229.5 + 304.9 + 341 + 400 + 443 = 1{,}917$$

Then divide by 6, which is the number of items in the dataset.

$$1{,}917 \div 6 = 319.5$$

The mean is 319.5 million. The median for this data set is 322.95 million, which is the average of the two middle numbers when the numbers in the dataset are ordered from smallest to largest:

$$(304.9 + 341) \div 6 = 322.95$$

The values for mean and median are very close to one another, so they are both good measures of central tendency for this data set. Mode is the number that occurs the most often in a data set. There is no number in the data set that repeats, so this data set has no mode.

32. B: According to the article, Nixon was slow in recognizing the impact of the Kent State shooting, in which anti-war protestors were killed, and did not censure the Guardsmen involved. His response was feeble, and it lowered morale at home. The author used strong language to condemn the shooting and stated that Nixon's response to the shooting was slow and consisted only of an obvious comment. The author characterized Nixon's judgment as "dangerously wrong" in assessing the risk in the response at home, which implies that his judgement in the war itself may also be disastrously wrong. These factors led the author to have unfavorable view of the war effort.

33. C: This statement simply reports that four students were gunned down at Kent State. The other choices include opinionated and loaded language. The author characterized Nixon's recognition of the Kent State shootings' impact as "sadly slow," called the administration an "artful, managerial mechanism," and described Nixon as "dangerously wrong" in his assessment of the risk involved in the response at home.

34. D: The author's characterization of Nixon's unfulfilled promise to the nation as "mocked" shows that the author does not hold Nixon's word in high regard. The article overall projects an negative opinion of how Nixon handled public protests, and this biased line reinforces the author's opinion.

35. D: When certain groups of voters are put into as few districts as possible, this is considered to be a gerrymandering technique known as "packing." This technique groups voters together to concentrate their voting strength and preference for a particular candidate or party in the packed district and to dilute or eliminate their voting power in other districts.

36. C: When district lines are created, each district should represent the population of the state, and each should have an equal number of people. This means that some districts might be large where the population is spread out, such as in rural areas, and small where the state is more densely populated, like in cities. If an even grid was created for the district lines, the districts would have very different populations with different demographics.

37. A: The word *partisan* means in favor of a particular political party or candidate. The passage states that most instances of gerrymandering are partisan, then goes on to explain that racial gerrymandering is enacted to keep minorities from electing their preferred candidate. These lines would be drawn by the party in power to keep themselves in power.

38. B: In an inverse correlation, also called a negative correlation, the two variables move in opposite directions. This is evident throughout most of the chart, as the unemployment rate went down until 2019, while the inflation rate mostly rose. In 2020, the unemployment rate rose sharply, and the inflation rate went down. Then, in 2021-2022, the two rates moved opposite directions again as the unemployment rate dropped and the inflation rate rose.

39. C: In this research, the economist is looking for causes of changes to the inflation rate. The inflation rate is the dependent variable. The independent variable is the unemployment rate, which potentially causes the inflation rate to change. The economist could check other independent variables, such as the exchange rate, to see their impact on and relationship with changes in the inflation rate.

40. D: Both accounts mention leaving Fort Clatsop on their return journey. The accounts were written on March 23, 1806, which Joseph Whitehouse noted was the day they left Fort Clatsop. Since the expedition began in Camp Wood, Fort Clatsop was their turnaround point, and from here they returned through the location marked as Nez Perce. This is where the expedition encountered a Native American tribe called the Nez Perce.

41. B: As a leader of the expedition, Clark documented his concern about the safety of the team leaving on the morning of March 23rd, 1806. He noted that the morning was so "raney and uncertain" that they were not sure whether it was a good time to leave for their journey back. The decision to leave during bad weather could impact the expedition and the safety of the men, so it was natural for Clark to express concern over the inclement weather and initial indecision.

42. A: Since Clark and Whitehouse documented the day with many similar details, the journal entries corroborate each other, and it is likely that they are reliable accounts of the day. Although Clark and Whitehouse had different positions and different perspectives, they often described events in a similar way, which strengthens the reliability of each account.

43. D: During the expedition, Lewis and Clark met and traded with Native Americans, including the Chinook tribe described in the journal entries. This trade and diplomacy benefited the United States, as the people were natives of the newly acquired territory and good relations with them would benefit the nation. There was no mention that elk was a new discovery, although they did eat elk on the expedition. The journey did not reach into the Spanish Territory, as shown on the map. The ability to travel in inclement weather was not new.

44. C: According to the graph, when less than 70% of the population (70 out of 100 people) has internet access, the GDP is not significantly affected by internet usage. When between 70% and 90% of the population has internet access, GDP grows rapidly along with internet usage. When internet usage is above 90%, the graph of the GDP becomes almost entirely horizontal, which means that there is growth in GDP that is not related to internet usage.

45. A: The range of a set of data can be found by subtracting the smallest number in the data set from the largest number in the data set. In the chart, the US is at close to 90 internet users per 100, the highest of the named countries, while Ethiopia is at about 20, the lowest of the named countries. Using these numbers, the range is about 70. This shows that there is a lot of variation in the percentage of the population that has access to the internet in countries around the world.

46. B: This speech, part of a series, was meant as propaganda to help raise money, in the form of Liberty Loans, to fund the war. The speaker talks of a spy watching the audience, and describes what they should do to appear as a united and strong country in the face of the enemy: lend more money to the government so as to outspend and defeat the Germans.

47. D: A glittering generality is a propaganda technique where the speaker uses words with positive connotations to prompt approval without further thought. In this case, presenting America as "united and strong" gives the listeners a positive view of their country, without a need for evidence or facts. This type of phrase is an appeal to emotion rather than to logic.

48. A: The author claims that spending a lot of money on campaign activities allows voters to become more familiar with the candidate, and that voters tend to prefer candidates that they are familiar with. In other words, the author claims that higher spending totals directly lead to greater popularity and therefore more votes.

49. C: When aet contains skewed data, the mean (average) is not a good measure of central tendency. In this case, two candidates have significantly higher total spending than the other candidates, so the average will be much higher than what most candidates spend. Because the mean does not accurately represent spending for a typical candidate, it is not a useful number for understanding campaign spending in general.

50. D: The candidates with the highest campaign spending will most likely become the presidential nominees. Similar to the chart above, this chart shows two candidates with significantly higher campaign spending than the rest of the candidates, one Democrat and one Republican. These candidates are able to spend far more on voter outreach and other campaign activities than the other candidates, and will therefore gain more voters through these activities and win the primary (nomination) elections.

GED Practice Tests #2 and #3

To take these additional GED practice tests, visit our bonus page:
mometrix.com/bonus948/ged

How to Overcome Test Anxiety

Just the thought of taking a test is enough to make most people a little nervous. A test is an important event that can have a long-term impact on your future, so it's important to take it seriously and it's natural to feel anxious about performing well. But just because anxiety is normal, that doesn't mean that it's helpful in test taking, or that you should simply accept it as part of your life. Anxiety can have a variety of effects. These effects can be mild, like making you feel slightly nervous, or severe, like blocking your ability to focus or remember even a simple detail.

If you experience test anxiety—whether severe or mild—it's important to know how to beat it. To discover this, first you need to understand what causes test anxiety.

Causes of Test Anxiety

While we often think of anxiety as an uncontrollable emotional state, it can actually be caused by simple, practical things. One of the most common causes of test anxiety is that a person does not feel adequately prepared for their test. This feeling can be the result of many different issues such as poor study habits or lack of organization, but the most common culprit is time management. Starting to study too late, failing to organize your study time to cover all of the material, or being distracted while you study will mean that you're not well prepared for the test. This may lead to cramming the night before, which will cause you to be physically and mentally exhausted for the test. Poor time management also contributes to feelings of stress, fear, and hopelessness as you realize you are not well prepared but don't know what to do about it.

Other times, test anxiety is not related to your preparation for the test but comes from unresolved fear. This may be a past failure on a test, or poor performance on tests in general. It may come from comparing yourself to others who seem to be performing better or from the stress of living up to expectations. Anxiety may be driven by fears of the future—how failure on this test would affect your educational and career goals. These fears are often completely irrational, but they can still negatively impact your test performance.

Elements of Test Anxiety

As mentioned earlier, test anxiety is considered to be an emotional state, but it has physical and mental components as well. Sometimes you may not even realize that you are suffering from test anxiety until you notice the physical symptoms. These can include trembling hands, rapid heartbeat, sweating, nausea, and tense muscles. Extreme anxiety may lead to fainting or vomiting. Obviously, any of these symptoms can have a negative impact on testing. It is important to recognize them as soon as they begin to occur so that you can address the problem before it damages your performance.

The mental components of test anxiety include trouble focusing and inability to remember learned information. During a test, your mind is on high alert, which can help you recall information and stay focused for an extended period of time. However, anxiety interferes with your mind's natural processes, causing you to blank out, even on the questions you know well. The strain of testing during anxiety makes it difficult to stay focused, especially on a test that may take several hours. Extreme anxiety can take a huge mental toll, making it difficult not only to recall test information but even to understand the test questions or pull your thoughts together.

Effects of Test Anxiety

Test anxiety is like a disease—if left untreated, it will get progressively worse. Anxiety leads to poor performance, and this reinforces the feelings of fear and failure, which in turn lead to poor performances on subsequent tests. It can grow from a mild nervousness to a crippling condition. If allowed to progress, test anxiety can have a big impact on your schooling, and consequently on your future.

Test anxiety can spread to other parts of your life. Anxiety on tests can become anxiety in any stressful situation, and blanking on a test can turn into panicking in a job situation. But fortunately, you don't have to let anxiety rule your testing and determine your grades. There are a number of relatively simple steps you can take to move past anxiety and function normally on a test and in the rest of life.

Physical Steps for Beating Test Anxiety

While test anxiety is a serious problem, the good news is that it can be overcome. It doesn't have to control your ability to think and remember information. While it may take time, you can begin taking steps today to beat anxiety.

Just as your first hint that you may be struggling with anxiety comes from the physical symptoms, the first step to treating it is also physical. Rest is crucial for having a clear, strong mind. If you are tired, it is much easier to give in to anxiety. But if you establish good sleep habits, your body and mind will be ready to perform optimally, without the strain of exhaustion. Additionally, sleeping well helps you to retain information better, so you're more likely to recall the answers when you see the test questions.

Getting good sleep means more than going to bed on time. It's important to allow your brain time to relax. Take study breaks from time to time so it doesn't get overworked, and don't study right before bed. Take time to rest your mind before trying to rest your body, or you may find it difficult to fall asleep.

Along with sleep, other aspects of physical health are important in preparing for a test. Good nutrition is vital for good brain function. Sugary foods and drinks may give a burst of energy but this burst is followed by a crash, both physically and emotionally. Instead, fuel your body with protein and vitamin-rich foods.

Also, drink plenty of water. Dehydration can lead to headaches and exhaustion, especially if your brain is already under stress from the rigors of the test. Particularly if your test is a long one, drink water during the breaks. And if possible, take an energy-boosting snack to eat between sections.

Along with sleep and diet, a third important part of physical health is exercise. Maintaining a steady workout schedule is helpful, but even taking 5-minute study breaks to walk can help get your blood pumping faster and clear your head. Exercise also releases endorphins, which contribute to a positive feeling and can help combat test anxiety.

When you nurture your physical health, you are also contributing to your mental health. If your body is healthy, your mind is much more likely to be healthy as well. So take time to rest, nourish your body with healthy food and water, and get moving as much as possible. Taking these physical steps will make you stronger and more able to take the mental steps necessary to overcome test anxiety.

Mental Steps for Beating Test Anxiety

Working on the mental side of test anxiety can be more challenging, but as with the physical side, there are clear steps you can take to overcome it. As mentioned earlier, test anxiety often stems from lack of preparation, so the obvious solution is to prepare for the test. Effective studying may be the most important weapon you have for beating test anxiety, but you can and should employ several other mental tools to combat fear.

First, boost your confidence by reminding yourself of past success—tests or projects that you aced. If you're putting as much effort into preparing for this test as you did for those, there's no reason you should expect to fail here. Work hard to prepare; then trust your preparation.

Second, surround yourself with encouraging people. It can be helpful to find a study group, but be sure that the people you're around will encourage a positive attitude. If you spend time with others who are anxious or cynical, this will only contribute to your own anxiety. Look for others who are motivated to study hard from a desire to succeed, not from a fear of failure.

Third, reward yourself. A test is physically and mentally tiring, even without anxiety, and it can be helpful to have something to look forward to. Plan an activity following the test, regardless of the outcome, such as going to a movie or getting ice cream.

When you are taking the test, if you find yourself beginning to feel anxious, remind yourself that you know the material. Visualize successfully completing the test. Then take a few deep, relaxing breaths and return to it. Work through the questions carefully but with confidence, knowing that you are capable of succeeding.

Developing a healthy mental approach to test taking will also aid in other areas of life. Test anxiety affects more than just the actual test—it can be damaging to your mental health and even contribute to depression. It's important to beat test anxiety before it becomes a problem for more than testing.

Study Strategy

Being prepared for the test is necessary to combat anxiety, but what does being prepared look like? You may study for hours on end and still not feel prepared. What you need is a strategy for test prep. The next few pages outline our recommended steps to help you plan out and conquer the challenge of preparation.

Step 1: Scope Out the Test

Learn everything you can about the format (multiple choice, essay, etc.) and what will be on the test. Gather any study materials, course outlines, or sample exams that may be available. Not only will this help you to prepare, but knowing what to expect can help to alleviate test anxiety.

Step 2: Map Out the Material

Look through the textbook or study guide and make note of how many chapters or sections it has. Then divide these over the time you have. For example, if a book has 15 chapters and you have five days to study, you need to cover three chapters each day. Even better, if you have the time, leave an extra day at the end for overall review after you have gone through the material in depth.

If time is limited, you may need to prioritize the material. Look through it and make note of which sections you think you already have a good grasp on, and which need review. While you are studying, skim quickly through the familiar sections and take more time on the challenging parts. Write out your plan so you don't get lost as you go. Having a written plan also helps you feel more in control of the study, so anxiety is less likely to arise from feeling overwhelmed at the amount to cover.

Step 3: Gather Your Tools

Decide what study method works best for you. Do you prefer to highlight in the book as you study and then go back over the highlighted portions? Or do you type out notes of the important information? Or is it helpful to make flashcards that you can carry with you? Assemble the pens, index cards, highlighters, post-it notes, and any other materials you may need so you won't be distracted by getting up to find things while you study.

If you're having a hard time retaining the information or organizing your notes, experiment with different methods. For example, try color-coding by subject with colored pens, highlighters, or post-it notes. If you learn better by hearing, try recording yourself reading your notes so you can listen while in the car, working out, or simply sitting at your desk. Ask a friend to quiz you from your flashcards, or try teaching someone the material to solidify it in your mind.

Step 4: Create Your Environment

It's important to avoid distractions while you study. This includes both the obvious distractions like visitors and the subtle distractions like an uncomfortable chair (or a too-comfortable couch that makes you want to fall asleep). Set up the best study environment possible: good lighting and a comfortable work area. If background music helps you focus, you may want to turn it on, but otherwise keep the room quiet. If you are using a computer to take notes, be sure you don't have any other windows open, especially applications like social media, games, or anything else that could distract you. Silence your phone and turn off notifications. Be sure to keep water close by so you stay hydrated while you study (but avoid unhealthy drinks and snacks).

Also, take into account the best time of day to study. Are you freshest first thing in the morning? Try to set aside some time then to work through the material. Is your mind clearer in the afternoon or evening? Schedule your study session then. Another method is to study at the same time of day that you will take the test, so that your brain gets used to working on the material at that time and will be ready to focus at test time.

Step 5: Study!

Once you have done all the study preparation, it's time to settle into the actual studying. Sit down, take a few moments to settle your mind so you can focus, and begin to follow your study plan. Don't give in to distractions or let yourself procrastinate. This is your time to prepare so you'll be ready to fearlessly approach the test. Make the most of the time and stay focused.

Of course, you don't want to burn out. If you study too long you may find that you're not retaining the information very well. Take regular study breaks. For example, taking five minutes out of every hour to walk briskly, breathing deeply and swinging your arms, can help your mind stay fresh.

As you get to the end of each chapter or section, it's a good idea to do a quick review. Remind yourself of what you learned and work on any difficult parts. When you feel that you've mastered the material, move on to the next part. At the end of your study session, briefly skim through your notes again.

But while review is helpful, cramming last minute is NOT. If at all possible, work ahead so that you won't need to fit all your study into the last day. Cramming overloads your brain with more information than it can process and retain, and your tired mind may struggle to recall even previously learned information when it is overwhelmed with last-minute study. Also, the urgent nature of cramming and the stress placed on your brain contribute to anxiety. You'll be more likely to go to the test feeling unprepared and having trouble thinking clearly.

So don't cram, and don't stay up late before the test, even just to review your notes at a leisurely pace. Your brain needs rest more than it needs to go over the information again. In fact, plan to finish your studies by noon or early afternoon the day before the test. Give your brain the rest of the day to relax or focus on other things, and get a good night's sleep. Then you will be fresh for the test and better able to recall what you've studied.

STEP 6: TAKE A PRACTICE TEST

Many courses offer sample tests, either online or in the study materials. This is an excellent resource to check whether you have mastered the material, as well as to prepare for the test format and environment.

Check the test format ahead of time: the number of questions, the type (multiple choice, free response, etc.), and the time limit. Then create a plan for working through them. For example, if you have 30 minutes to take a 60-question test, your limit is 30 seconds per question. Spend less time on the questions you know well so that you can take more time on the difficult ones.

If you have time to take several practice tests, take the first one open book, with no time limit. Work through the questions at your own pace and make sure you fully understand them. Gradually work up to taking a test under test conditions: sit at a desk with all study materials put away and set a timer. Pace yourself to make sure you finish the test with time to spare and go back to check your answers if you have time.

After each test, check your answers. On the questions you missed, be sure you understand why you missed them. Did you misread the question (tests can use tricky wording)? Did you forget the information? Or was it something you hadn't learned? Go back and study any shaky areas that the practice tests reveal.

Taking these tests not only helps with your grade, but also aids in combating test anxiety. If you're already used to the test conditions, you're less likely to worry about it, and working through tests until you're scoring well gives you a confidence boost. Go through the practice tests until you feel comfortable, and then you can go into the test knowing that you're ready for it.

Test Tips

On test day, you should be confident, knowing that you've prepared well and are ready to answer the questions. But aside from preparation, there are several test day strategies you can employ to maximize your performance.

First, as stated before, get a good night's sleep the night before the test (and for several nights before that, if possible). Go into the test with a fresh, alert mind rather than staying up late to study.

Try not to change too much about your normal routine on the day of the test. It's important to eat a nutritious breakfast, but if you normally don't eat breakfast at all, consider eating just a protein bar. If you're a coffee drinker, go ahead and have your normal coffee. Just make sure you time it so that the caffeine doesn't wear off right in the middle of your test. Avoid sugary beverages, and drink enough water to stay hydrated but not so much that you need a restroom break 10 minutes into the test. If your test isn't first thing in the morning, consider going for a walk or doing a light workout before the test to get your blood flowing.

Allow yourself enough time to get ready, and leave for the test with plenty of time to spare so you won't have the anxiety of scrambling to arrive in time. Another reason to be early is to select a good seat. It's helpful to sit away from doors and windows, which can be distracting. Find a good seat, get out your supplies, and settle your mind before the test begins.

When the test begins, start by going over the instructions carefully, even if you already know what to expect. Make sure you avoid any careless mistakes by following the directions.

Then begin working through the questions, pacing yourself as you've practiced. If you're not sure on an answer, don't spend too much time on it, and don't let it shake your confidence. Either skip it and come back later, or eliminate as many wrong answers as possible and guess among the remaining ones. Don't dwell on these questions as you continue—put them out of your mind and focus on what lies ahead.

Be sure to read all of the answer choices, even if you're sure the first one is the right answer. Sometimes you'll find a better one if you keep reading. But don't second-guess yourself if you do immediately know the answer. Your gut instinct is usually right. Don't let test anxiety rob you of the information you know.

If you have time at the end of the test (and if the test format allows), go back and review your answers. Be cautious about changing any, since your first instinct tends to be correct, but make sure you didn't misread any of the questions or accidentally mark the wrong answer choice. Look over any you skipped and make an educated guess.

At the end, leave the test feeling confident. You've done your best, so don't waste time worrying about your performance or wishing you could change anything. Instead, celebrate the successful completion of this test. And finally, use this test to learn how to deal with anxiety even better next time.

Review Video: Test Anxiety
Visit mometrix.com/academy and enter code: 100340

Important Qualification

Not all anxiety is created equal. If your test anxiety is causing major issues in your life beyond the classroom or testing center, or if you are experiencing troubling physical symptoms related to your anxiety, it may be a sign of a serious physiological or psychological condition. If this sounds like your situation, we strongly encourage you to seek professional help.

Tell Us Your Story

We at Mometrix would like to extend our heartfelt thanks to you for letting us be a part of your journey. It is an honor to serve people from all walks of life, people like you, who are committed to building the best future they can for themselves.

We know that each person's situation is unique. But we also know that, whether you are a young student or a mother of four, you care about working to make your own life and the lives of those around you better.

That's why we want to hear your story.

We want to know why you're taking this test. We want to know about the trials you've gone through to get here. And we want to know about the successes you've experienced after taking and passing your test.

In addition to your story, which can be an inspiration both to us and to others, we value your feedback. We want to know both what you loved about our book and what you think we can improve on.

The team at Mometrix would be absolutely thrilled to hear from you! So please, send us an email at tellusyourstory@mometrix.com or visit us at mometrix.com/tellusyourstory.php and let's stay in touch.

Additional Bonus Material

Due to our efforts to try to keep this book to a manageable length, we've created a link that will give you access to all of your additional bonus material:

mometrix.com/bonus948/ged

Made in United States
Orlando, FL
18 October 2024

52846433R00228